American Presidents

To my children—Ian, Alasdair, and Andrew

American Presidents

*Farewell Messages to the Nation
1796–2001*

Edited by Gleaves Whitney

LEXINGTON BOOKS
Lanham • Boulder • New York • Oxford

LEXINGTON BOOKS

Published in the United States of America
by Lexington Books
An imprint of the Rowman & Littlefield Publishing Group
4720 Boston Way, Lanham, Maryland 20706

12 Hid's Copse Road
Cumnor Hill, Oxford OX2 9JJ, England

British Library Cataloguing in Publication Information Available

Library of Congress Cataloging-in-Publication Data

American presidents : farewell messages to the nation, 1796–2001 /
edited by Gleaves Whitney.
     p. cm.
   Includes bibliographical references and index.
   ISBN 0-7391-0393-8 (cloth : alk. paper)
   1. Presidents—United States—Messages. 2. Political oratory—United
States—History. 3. United States—Politics and government. I.
Whitney, Gleaves.
   J81.4 .A46 2003
   352.23'8'0973—dc21   2002004106

Printed in the United States of America

♾™ The paper used in this publication meets the minimum requirements of
American National Standard for Information Sciences—Permanence of Paper for
Printed Library Materials, ANSI/NISO Z39.48-1992.

Contents

Acknowledgments

Who knows when the seed-idea for a book is planted? In all likelihood this one's origins go back to 1980, when Ronald Reagan challenged Jimmy Carter for the White House. That election year I was an undergraduate at Colorado State University and had the good fortune of taking a class from an outstanding professor of rhetoric, Jim Irvine. Shortly thereafter I took a seminar from his colleague, David Vancil, another outstanding professor of rhetoric. In their different ways, these two champions of the liberal arts and the *trivium* instilled a high regard for the role of political discourse in our constitutional republic. It seems in retrospect only apt that this work should have begun in lively discussions of Plato and Aristotle, Cicero and Quintilian.

Still, the present collection did not come together for some two decades—and then quite suddenly. It arose out of the working needs of a speechwriter and a governor. At about the midpoint of John Engler's third and final term as governor of Michigan, I began to think about what he might say in a farewell address. Researching the speeches of Michigan governors[1] and American presidents, I discovered that no one had published a collection of farewells. A collection of the presidents' inaugural addresses exists, and collections of speeches of individual presidents exist, but there has been no collection of the farewell messages of U.S. presidents.

As I had just worked with Steve Wrinn, a senior editor at Rowman & Littlefield, on another project, I contacted him with this discovery. He was supportive from the outset for he, too, saw the value of gathering the farewell genre into one collection.

Many people helped make this book possible. My appreciation goes to Governor John Engler, who is himself a keen student of the presidents and encouraged the undertaking. At the same time, I wish to acknowledge Elaine Harrison and her dedicated team of professionals at the Library of Michigan. They have never disappointed. I hasten to express appreciation to the many librarians, archivists, and curators in presidential collections around the nation who fielded my queries and responded to my ideas. Among these individuals are Blaise Bisaillon, director, Forbes Library, Northampton, Massachusetts; Jim Cooke, historian and Calvin Coolidge character interpreter, Quincy, Massachusetts; William M. Ferraro of the Ulysses S. Grant Association at Southern Illinois University at Carbondale; Gregg L. Lint, senior associate editor of the Adams Papers, Massachusetts Historical Society, Boston, Massachusetts; George Nash, editor of the Herbert Hoover papers; Meg Nowack, curator at Woodrow Wilson House, Washington, D.C.; and Pauline Testerman, audiovisual archivist, Harry S. Truman Library and Museum, Independence, Missouri.

For additional research, many thanks to my resourceful and congenial colleagues, John Nevin and Joshua Nunez, and to interns Katherine Gale (Johns Hopkins University), Chad Groenhout (Michigan State University), Eric Groenendyk (University of Michigan), Anthony Soloman (Michigan State University), and Jessica Strattard (University of Michigan).

No collection of state papers can be published without exacting—no, excruciating—attention to detail. For their convivial assistance in shepherding this book through production, many thanks go to Erin McKindley, production editor at Rowman & Littlefield, and her editorial assistant, Audrey Babkirk.

The case of Lincoln was particularly intriguing, and I wish to thank Adrianne Noe, director of the National Museum of Health and Medicine in Washington, D.C.; Joanna Downer, Johns Hopkins University School of Medicine, Baltimore, Maryland; and William Anderson, director of the Michigan Department of History, Arts, and Libraries, for their leads and suggestions. Also thanks to colleagues John Miller, David Murley, and G. Tracy Mehan for puzzling through Lincoln's Second Inaugural Address with me.

Also for their encouragement, I wish to thank Steve Wrinn and Martin Hayward at Lexington Books, Professor Wilfred McClay at the University of Tennessee, and my wife, Louise, who gracefully forbears the tyranny of deadlines.

For whatever excellence can be found in my work, I am indebted to the above-named people. For whatever error and folly, I needed no outside assistance.

Finally, most of these messages were gathered and the introductions to them written in the aftermath of September 11, 2001. During our season of national crisis, mourning, and resolve, I have found much inspiration in the words of past commanders-in-chief. Their voice is strong, their belief in America great. The presidents speak of our nation's special destiny in the world, of the strong character of our people who can rise to any challenge.

It is my hope that you, too, are inspired by their words.

Note

1. See the resulting collection, *Messages of the Governors of Michigan*, ed. Gleaves Whitney, vols. 5–9 (Mount Pleasant: Clarke Historical Library/Central Michigan University Press, forthcoming 2003).

Introduction

This book is a collection of the farewell messages of U.S. presidents. The farewell message (also known as the valedictory or exaugural address) is a speech and/or written text delivered by a prominent person to his followers or constituency shortly before his departure or death. The aim usually is to offer insight, advice, and encouragement to posterity. Such messages are a well-established genre in the West's heritage. They are encountered in classical Greek and Roman letters, the Hebrew Scriptures and New Testament, medieval and Renaissance literature, and modern discourse.

Americans have kept the farewell genre alive and well. Many people heard *Time* magazine's 2001 "Person of the Year," New York City Mayor Rudi Giuliani, give a splendid farewell address to a courageous people who have earned the admiration of the world.[1] Other farewell addresses resonate in our national memory. There are General Douglas MacArthur's poignant farewells. One was before the Congress ("Old soldiers never die; they just fade away").[2] Another was given at West Point ("duty, honor, country").[3] Many have read or heard of Lou Gehrig's heartwarming farewell in Yankee Stadium ("I consider myself the luckiest man on the face of this earth").[4] My oldest son tells me that even Bart Simpson gave a farewell address.

The farewell messages of American presidents are important markers in the nation's history. If one were seeking to survey America's past, one could hardly do better than to do so through the eyes of some three-dozen shapers of that past. Presidential farewells bundle together the concerns of past generations of Americans. They offer vivid freeze-frames of key moments in the life of our nation. They are like snapshots of the American temper taken at regular intervals in our history.

In a most interesting way, presidential farewells constitute a great American conversation among the nation's chief executives. Usually much thought has gone into their crafting. Because of their rhetorical excellence, they are literary documents. Because of their contemporary references, they are historical documents. Because of their political context, they are civic documents. Several have transcended the status of period pieces and have become part of our cultural memory. Many Americans are familiar with Washington's warning against a foreign policy involving "entangling alliances."[5] Many are also familiar with Eisenhower's admonitions regarding the "military–industrial complex."

The farewell messages of American presidents assume a variety of forms. Some were written; some were spoken. They may have been intended for a national audience or aimed at a local gathering. They could be formal or informal. Further, they do not have to be called a "farewell address" per se. As this volume will demonstrate, many presidents have chosen not to give a formal farewell address but have seized other opportunities to bid adieu.

1

Whatever the form, whatever the forum, farewell messages tend to stand out. They often pack a moral and rhetorical punch because the president can speak as a statesman. Freed up from reelection concerns, he can be more magnanimous and disinterested than a candidate in the heat of a reelection campaign. As George Washington disarmingly noted at the outset of his farewell message, "These [observations] will be offered to you with the more freedom, as you can only see in them the disinterested warnings of an impartial friend, who can possibly have no personal motive to bias his counsel."

Not all of Washington's successors were so disinterested. Some presidential farewells were self-absorbed; they aimed low at political enemies or engaged in some tit for tat. For the most part, however, a president uses the occasion of the farewell to deal graciously with political opponents. He seeks to transcend partisan politics and speak of the epochal concerns that shaped his times and administration.

For readers who have not encountered these messages before, some wonderful surprises are in store. Many of our less famous presidents, it turns out, were powerfully eloquent. They wrote superb messages that give much instruction and delight.

In many of these messages readers may sense a tension among the past, present, and future. American presidents for the most part were concerned to give a fair rendering of the state of the union; they were not easily tempted to assume the role of prophet. In public life they attended a tough school of experience. They sooner or later learned that "the greater part of wisdom is to look back, even far back, and greet the future with eyes focused by the past." University of Virginia historian Robert Louis Wilken continues: "The gift of discernment must be learned and if our eyes have not been trained to make out where we have been, they will be insentient to what is yet to be."[6]

It is insightful to compare the presidential farewell message with its mirror image, the inaugural address. The pair often provides a presidency with eloquent bookends. Both addresses can be inspiring national testaments because Americans are a hopeful people, and the inaugural and farewell are alike statements of hope—but with this critical difference: Whereas first-term inaugurals are visionary statements untested by Oval Office experience, farewells show how the vision was tested by experience.[7]

John F. Kennedy once put the drama, the unpredictable nature of the presidency this way:

> it is impossible to foretell the precise nature of the problems that will confront you or the specific skills and capacities which those problems will demand. It is an office which called upon a man of peace, Lincoln, to become a great leader in a bloody war; which required a profound believer in limiting the scope of federal government, Jefferson, to expand dramatically the power and range of that government; which challenged a man dedicated to domestic social reform, Franklin Roosevelt, to lead this nation into a deep and irrevocable involvement in world affairs.[8]

The dramatic, unpredictable nature of any presidency helps explain why farewells have a different tone from that of inaugurals. Farewells tend to be more sober, more poignant too. There are the disappointments, defeats, and dashed hopes of any leader. The poignancy is especially evident when the audience senses that a president is retiring not just from the Oval Office, but from this life.[9]

"The time has now come when advanced age and a broken frame warn me to retire from public concerns," wrote Andrew Jackson in his valedictory. Because he would "pass beyond the reach of human events and cease to feel the vicissitudes of human affairs," it was time to bid his countrymen "a last and affectionate farewell."

History of the Formal Presidential Farewell Address

Over the course of American history, forty-two men have served as president of the United States.[10] Collecting their farewell messages is not as cut-and-dried an editorial task as one might initially suppose. To some extent one encounters the same problem that is encountered with inaugural addresses. Not every president delivered an inaugural address.[11] Likewise, not every president gave a formal farewell message to the nation. The first and most obvious reason is that eight of our forty-two presidents died in office.

Moreover—and perhaps surprisingly—of the thirty-four who lived to the end of their final term, only nine delivered a formal farewell to the nation: George Washington, Andrew Jackson, Andrew Johnson, Harry Truman, Dwight Eisenhower, Richard Nixon, Jimmy Carter, Ronald Reagan, and Bill Clinton.

Even a passing glance at this list of chief executives reveals a striking pattern. In the first 160 years of the republic, presidents rarely gave a formal farewell address to the nation. Decades could elapse between such messages (in the case of George Washington and Andrew Jackson, some four decades; in the case of Andrew Johnson and Harry Truman, more than eight decades).[12] Put another way, there was only one formal farewell address in the eighteenth century; there were but two in the nineteenth; and yet there have been six in the last half century. Indeed, it was only during the past fifty years that the formal farewell address to the nation became customary. Why has this happened? Conversely, why was the farewell address relatively rare between Washington and Truman?

Any number of reasons might account for the farewell's rarity prior to the 1950s. Perhaps the nation's first thirty-two presidents were chary of treading on, or competing with, Washington's example. Until Truman only two presidents (Andrew Jackson and Andrew Johnson) formally added to the farewell corpus. Washington's Farewell Address has been regarded as one of the sacred texts in the presidential canon. Part of the reason is that our nation's first presidential farewell was really the work of three founding fathers—Madison, Hamilton, and Washington himself—Olympians in our civil religion. Such an oracle was bound to cast a long shadow over American history. One indicator of the first farewell's eminence is the regularity with which it has been anthologized in collections of great American documents. Another indicator is that, from 1862 on, Washington's Farewell Address has been read annually from the floor of the U.S. Senate, a performance that continues to this day and is one of the Senate's hallowed traditions.[13]

The respect with which Washington's farewell has been treated may suggest a second reason for the rarity of such messages between 1869 and 1953. Upon reading Andrew Johnson's farewell in 1869, the people perhaps perceived a decline in the quality of the genre. Not that Johnson's message was poorly written—on the contrary, it was rhetorically masterful. The problem was the desperate tone. Johnson was human. It is understandable that, as the nation's first impeached president, he would try to vindicate himself, that he would use his farewell to attack political opponents and personal enemies. But if the farewell address were just a well-written personal grouse, who needed it? The contrast with Washington's disinterested advice to posterity, or even with Jackson's ruminations on America at the fifty-year mark under the Constitution, put Johnson's address in an unfavorable light. Until memory of that address faded, perhaps future presidents did not want to be associated with the formal farewell at all.

A third reason that may account for the rarity of farewell addresses prior to the 1950s is that they might have seemed redundant at best, self-aggrandizing at worst. Here is why. The U.S. Constitution requires the president to report periodically to the Congress.[14] Our commanders-in-chief developed the tradition of submitting messages to the legislative branch on an annual basis (until the 1930s, usually during the first week of December). The last such message would typically be submitted about three months prior to retiring from office (March 4).[15] Given this brief span of time, most presidents skipped the formal farewell address and chose instead to devote a portion of their final annual message to the Congress to bid adieu.

The time frame between the last annual message and retirement was considerably shortened in the 1930s from two directions: Constitution and custom. When the Twentieth Amendment was adopted, the president was now to retire from office some six weeks earlier (January 20) than had previously been the case (March 4).[16] About the same time the Twentieth Amendment was adopted, Franklin Delano Roosevelt started the practice of delivering the annual message to the Congress in January rather than December. This rendered a separate farewell address even more superfluous.

A final reason that may account for the rarity of the farewell address prior to the 1950s is that our earlier presidents did not do as much public speaking as presidents nowadays. These days we are used to the annual pomp and circumstance of the state of the union speech. But from Thomas Jefferson through William Howard Taft, annual messages were written, not spoken. They were submitted to the Congress as missives and read by a clerk. Even so commonplace an institution as the presidential news conference was not born until the Wilson administration. And a full-time speechwriter did not work in the White House until the Harding administration.[17]

Prior to the middle of the twentieth century, the limits of technology may have reinforced the tendency to do less speechifying. Orations could not be easily delivered to the whole nation until developments in radio in the 1920s and television in the 1940s made broadcasting more practical. The first president to exploit radio waves for speechifying was Warren Harding on June 14, 1922. Still, not until the 1950s would the formal farewell message to the entire people be resurrected. Why?

Two principal reasons might account for the resurrection of the formal farewell address in 1953—some eighty-four years after the previous formal farewell message (by Andrew Johnson). First, there was a dramatically new world order. The United States was the only global power to emerge from World War II stronger than it had been before the conflict. By the 1950s, America's role as the free world's leader was a *fait accompli*. Isolation, though championed in some quarters, was generally rejected. An assertive *Pax Americana* became the ideal. In the new dispensation, President Washington's warning against an assertive foreign policy seemed antiquated, dangerous even. It may have been prudent advice to previous generations, when a vulnerable nation had to build up its strength. But it did not speak to an America that had come of age, conquered fascistic enemies on two fronts, and emerged as the strongest power the world had ever seen. Nor did it speak to a generation confronted with international communism and constantly en garde against a potent enemy that possessed weapons of mass destruction. Americans found themselves in a new kind of war, the Cold War, with responsibility for a global sphere of influence. Truman realized that the new age called for a new farewell address. Our thirty-third president seized the opportunity upon his exit from office in 1953.

Second, the outbreak of the Cold War coincided with the dramatic growth of the television industry. The leader of the United States and of the free world could now broadcast his message as no leader in human history ever had. Again Truman seized a historic opportunity and thereby revolutionized the delivery of the farewell address to the American people. He established the practice of televising the address from the White House.[18] It is also significant—unprecedented, really—that Truman's farewell address was the first to be delivered as a speech to the entire nation. The three previous formal farewell messages—by Washington, Jackson, and Andrew Johnson—were delivered to the nation via newsprint. Truman's speech was groundbreaking.

Thus was born not just a revival but a new era in the presidential farewell address. Truman was the pivotal figure in the resurrection and transformation of the genre. His example was reinforced by the next president, Dwight Eisenhower, who also delivered a farewell address to the nation (1961). This was the first time in American history in which back-to-back presidents gave formal farewell addresses to the nation.[19] Both presidents had their farewell addresses televised; both used the occasion to focus on the challenge of American power in the world; and both proved to be paradigmatic.

Before moving on, it is well to pause and grasp the unprecedented nature of the Truman–Eisenhower innovations in the genre. Because their farewells were *speeches* and because they were *televised* to the nation, they were quite unlike anything before in American history. Prior to the 1950s, only one in ten presidents gave a formal farewell message, and then it was a printed message. Since the 1950s, more than half our presidents have given a spoken farewell. While the farewell address is not a given in our recent history, a pattern is nevertheless emerging: those who made it a priority to master the television medium—Ronald Reagan and Bill Clinton, for instance—delivered a primetime farewell to the nation. Those who had other priorities—Gerald Ford and George H. W. Bush, for example—did not.

Scope of the Collection

The present collection includes three kinds of presidential messages: (1) formal farewell messages to the nation, (2) final annual messages to Congress, and (3) other messages for a significant audience that served as a farewell. It excludes other types of messages for reasons set out below.

First and most obviously, this volume gathers the nine formal farewell messages that U.S. presidents gave to the nation. The last three words of the preceding sentence are important. The collection is confined to farewells that a president intended for the *entire* nation. Space does not permit collecting every farewell sentiment. Excluded are the valedictories that virtually every president-elect gives to friends and supporters upon leaving his hometown for Washington. Hence Lincoln's "affectionate farewell" to the people of Springfield, Illinois (February 11, 1861)[20]—beautifully crafted as it is—is excluded. That apparently extemporaneous speech was intended for, and heard by, perhaps 1,000 people.[21] And Lincoln had not yet taken the oath of office.

Also excluded are the messages that virtually every ex-president gives upon his homecoming. Thus Jefferson's message "To the Inhabitants of Albemarle County, in Virginia" (April 3, 1809)[22]—while sometimes referred to as a farewell to public life—is not included. It was given after the Sage of Monticello left office, and its scope was provincial rather than national.

Although these "little farewells" are excluded from the present volume, other kinds of messages have found their way in. Presidents who did not give a formal farewell address to the nation often wrapped significant farewell content in other major messages. Like Chinese boxes, one can unpack a message within a message. So, for example, presidents frequently used their last annual message to the Congress to say farewell. It was a ceremonial, large-scale forum in which to thank people, praise colleagues, tell their stories, and bid adieu. The presidents who said adieu in their last annual messages to the Congress rather than in a separate farewell address include most nineteenth-century presidents who lived through their last year in office, as well as a good number of twentieth-century presidents.

Readers will be both instructed and delighted as they discover the wisdom expressed in several of our presidents' final annual messages. At times the content revolves around principles of the highest order. Read seriatim from president to president, such passages form a great conversation over how best to govern the republic. It is a wonderfully American conversation—about ordered liberty, self-government under the rule of law, the permanent things, and the nation's destiny in human history. These passages show our presidents self-consciously and unabashedly playing the role of teacher—in some cases, the role of prophet. Readers will find most of our presidents to be congenial guides to the future. Their lessons in history and governing make for insightful and inspiring reading.

In addition to the content, final annual messages tend to be rhetorically powerful. Readers will encounter heartfelt tributes and encomiums, perorations and summations. Students of rhetoric like to refer to such passages as "ceremonial," "panegyrical," or "epideictic," for the language can be highly polished, even poetic.

Annual messages, it must be kept in mind, are state papers. They are a constitutionally required report on the state of the union. Many of them are voluminous—the size of a small book. Jimmy Carter's sets the record at 34,000 words. (By contrast, John Adams's is less than 1,400 words.) In these pages I do not always reproduce the longer messages in their entirety. I have exercised my prerogative as editor to strike out the minutiae and provincial. Deleted also are much tabulated data. Retained are passages that pertain to a farewell or that give insight into the state of the nation.

Some presidents, it should be noted, used more than one occasion to bid adieu: they submitted a formal farewell message to the nation *and* devoted a portion of their last annual message to Congress to say good-bye. Washington set this precedent and was followed by Jackson, Andrew Johnson, Truman, Eisenhower, and Carter.

Finally, several presidents gave neither a formal farewell address nor a State of the Union speech during their last months in office—President George H. W. Bush, for example. Nevertheless, these presidents used other occasions to give what was tantamount to a farewell. In George H. W. Bush's case, the speech to West Point (January 1993) served the purpose. Since it was covered by the national press (and since it even made reference to George Washington's Farewell Address), it is included in this volume.

And then there are the eight presidents who did not live to the end of their terms. Four were assassinated—Abraham Lincoln, James Garfield, William McKinley, and John F. Kennedy—and four perished from other causes—William Henry Harrison, Zachary Taylor, Warren Harding, and Franklin Roosevelt. A tantalizing "what if" is what they would have said to posterity. In most cases we shall never know.

However, I believe it can be argued that Lincoln did write a farewell—admittedly an unlikely one—in his Second Inaugural Address. The speech was delivered on March 4, 1865, about six weeks before his assassination on April 14. The speech treats of final things, permanent things, and God's inscrutable justice. If passages have the feel of a valedictory, perhaps it is because Lincoln had struggled with premonitions that he would die before completing his second term. These premonitions are well documented. Thus the sixteenth president's second inaugural address is included in the present volume.[23]

Besides Lincoln, three other presidents warrant explanations for having their messages in this volume. One of them is John Adams. The second president did not formally say farewell in his last annual message: He did not yet know that he would lose the election of 1800, and the timing of events is crucial to understanding why. Adams delivered the final message on November 22, 1800. The electors were scheduled to assemble in their respective state capitals on December 4—almost two weeks after the speech.[24] Adams knew from reports how a good number of the electors would vote, but not all of them. Adams biographer John Ferling speculates that "Adams must have continued to hope against hope for a victory until the very end."[25] The end, for Adams, would have come late in the first week of December, when the results of the College showed the president running in third place, behind Jefferson and Burr. But on November 22, all of that was in the future. On November 22, it would have been unwise to express formal farewell sentiments. So despite the fact that the fourth annual message was not composed as the final annual message, the speech is included since Adams knew it was possible to lose.[26]

Another president who warrants an explanation is Woodrow Wilson. By December 1920, when the eighth annual message was being prepared, Wilson had been an invalid for more than a year. Strokes had debilitated him physically and mentally. He no longer had the capacity to fulfill the duties of the office.[27] Thus, while the eighth annual message may be Wilsonian, its author was not really Wilson. It was largely a committee effort that involved his second wife, Edith Bolling Galt Wilson, and a clique of dedicated advisors bent on concealing the gravity of the President's illness. Despite the question of authorship, the message is included because it is still the Wilson *administration's* farewell and thus an important part of the historical record.

Richard Nixon also warrants an explanation. His second farewell speech—to White House staff—was seemingly to a very limited audience, which fact alone would ordinarily exclude the remarks from this collection; every president says good-bye to staff. Yet the thirty-seventh president tellingly noted at the beginning of his speech that it would be covered by a wary national press corps. Nixon was self-consciously addressing two quite different audiences—the sympathetic audience before him and the larger world beyond that, in large measure, had already made up its mind as to his guilt or innocence.

Farewell Themes

Farewell messages are historical documents. They provide a unique survey of American history. They open our view onto a large and detailed panorama of the past. They give insight into the pressing concerns and achievements of each generation of Americans. Indeed, a systematic reading of these state papers gives one a sense of continuity and change in our national life. It is both instructive and ennobling to see how each president redefines and reasserts America's national purpose.

Several recurring thoughts or themes mark the farewell genre. Not all of these thoughts and themes have to be present in one message for that message to qualify as a farewell. But readers will encounter certain topics over and over in the great conversation of the presidents.

Many farewell messages include something like the acknowledgments page at the beginning of a book. It is good form to say thank you to the people who have helped an administration and to mention a few of the virtues that make public service a noble calling. Gratitude is expressed to one's family, colleagues in government, citizens, and God. The display of thanksgiving is often accompanied by humility and contrition—virtues becoming to those who have reached the pinnacle of power. Most presidents are well aware that they are servants of the people, flawed ones at that. For any successes they achieve, it is decent to share the credit with Providence; for any failures, it is good to pray that the nation will not be too harmed. As Washington put it: "In reviewing the incidents of my administration, I am unconscious of intentional error. I am nevertheless too sensible of my defects not to think it probable that I may have committed many errors. Whatever they may be, I fervently beseech the Almighty to avert or mitigate the evils to which they may tend."

Another thought encountered in farewell messages is justification for offering the message. It can be the opportune place for the president to announce that he is not running for reelection. Or the aim can be to offer insight and advice to posterity. In his message, Washington twice noted that he offered advice out of "a solicitude for your welfare." Jackson wrote that as a last gesture of public service he wanted to "use the occasion to offer to you the counsels of age and experience."

Presidents also use the farewell message to tell the story of the administration. It is one last official forum to give their "spin" on what has transpired under their watch and thereby influence what future historians will write about them. One specific policy Washington defended was his much-debated stance of neutrality toward France and Britain, even though it had already been officially set forth on April 22, 1793. Benjamin Harrison used his last annual message to give a large and detailed statistical snapshot of the United States in the early 1890s; his aim was to show that the nation was in good shape despite widening economic strains and fears.

Farewells often offer advice on how to proceed into the future. Washington famously advised his countrymen to avoid imprudent alliances with foreign nations. Eisenhower warned Americans against a host of dangers he saw on the horizon: (1) the growth of the military–industrial complex; (2) the overweening influence of the federal government on university research; (3) the danger of public policy becoming "the captive of a scientific-technological elite"; and, in an especially modern sounding passage, (4) environmental plunder and degradation.

A number of final messages devote some space to what might be called "great ideas"—to the articulation of America's national purpose, to the civic virtues that are desirable in a constitutional republic, and to the first principles of public stewardship and governance. This is the opportunity for the president to make his contribution to the "great conversation" of his predecessors. Leaving the tyranny of details and petty politics behind, he can speak here as a statesman. Already in the introduction of his Farewell Address, our first president broached a number of great ideas and achievements: he praised the stronger union under the new Constitution, the prudent use of the blessings of liberty, the wisdom and virtue necessary for governing a republic, and the need to be exemplary for the sake of other nations struggling to achieve the blessings of liberty. Washington's message inaugurated a great conversation among the presidents. Many of his themes would be picked up in later farewell discourse. The Constitution is perhaps the most dominant theme of presidential farewell discourse. But broad principles of political economy can be articulated as well, as Grover Cleveland and Theodore Roosevelt vividly show. Also, many of the presidents praise Americans for being a practical people who appreciate common sense and whose political assessments rely on "the lamp of experience" rather than on abstract theory and ideology.

Presidents have used their farewell to reaffirm a belief in American exceptionalism—the idea that the nation is unique in world history and has a special destiny. As Ronald Reagan used to put it, following John Winthrop, America is "a city upon a hill." Eisenhower believed this unique destiny imposed special burdens on the United States. "America," he wrote, "is today the strongest, the most influential, and most productive nation in the world. Understandably proud of this preeminence, we yet realize that America's leadership and prestige depend, not merely upon our unmatched material progress, riches, and military strength, but on how we use our power in the interests of world peace and human betterment. Throughout America's adventure in free government, such basic purposes have been to keep the peace; to foster progress in human achievement; and to enhance liberty, dignity, and integrity among peoples and among nations. To strive for less would be unworthy of a free and religious people."

Finally, many presidents have used the occasion of the farewell to wish the country well in the future and to allude to or invoke divine protection. Eisenhower, for instance, offered two prayers in his farewell address. Thoughts about the future do not always bubble with optimism but affirm America's national purpose nevertheless. Noteworthy is Jefferson's parting sentiment—the same Jefferson who oversaw the Louisiana Purchase and was an inspiration for our western expansion: "Looking forward with anxiety to their future destinies, I trust that, in their steady character unshaken by difficulties, in their love of liberty, obedience to law, and support of the public authorities, I see a sure guaranty of the permanence of our republic; and retiring from the charge of their affairs, I carry with me the consolation of a firm persuasion that Heaven has in store for our beloved country long ages to come of prosperity and happiness."

Farewell Rhetoric

In addition to being historical documents, farewell messages are rhetorical documents. About the word "rhetoric." In popular discourse "rhetoric" is mostly used nowadays to describe hypocritical, self-serving flummery—the "barren verbiage current among men," as Lord Tennyson once put it. It is synonymous with "verbage," a portmanteau word of recent coinage that cleverly conveys the idea of "verbal garbage." The negative connotation in current usage is unfortunate because, as traditionally understood, rhetoric is necessary to the public good—especially among a self-governing people who must deliberate, in an open forum, over how they will live together.

As traditionally understood, rhetoric is the art of using language effectively and/or persuasively. The operative word is "art." An art is a body of knowledge, a skill that is acquired by observation, study, and practice. So we say that one masters the *art of rhetoric*.

In the main, American presidents and their ghostwriters and speechwriters were skilled in the art of rhetoric—their farewell discourse was artfully made. The messages in this volume offer lessons enough to fill a textbook. The variety of rhetorical styles and techniques on display is remarkable considering the background of some of the presidents. Their early experiences would seem an unlikely laboratory of rhetorical excellence; a surprising number received little or no formal schooling. Yet even a log-cabin president like Abraham Lincoln would emerge from the wilderness to become a great orator. And Andrew Johnson—a tailor's apprentice whose mother was a tavern maid, whose father was a handyman, and whose wife tutored him in reading—would go on to master the rudiments of rhetoric.

Larger forces have also influenced presidential rhetoric. Until recent decades, American political culture was more formal than it is today. The formality is evident in the nation's early farewells. This makes the early messages seem archaic by today's informal standards. While people nowadays may have difficulty reading the older messages, it is well to remember that the language of Washington's Farewell Address was suited to an eighteenth-century newspaper.

Moreover, until the twentieth century, few farewell messages were orally delivered by the president or even meant to be: Washington's Farewell Address was a state paper run in newspapers, and every final annual message to Congress from Jefferson to Taft was a written statement. Today's highly choreographed farewell address, televised live from the Oval Office, is of recent vintage. Practitioners of the art of rhetoric understand that each medium has its own rhetorical logic: discourse that is written is (or should be) composed differently from discourse that is spoken. Diction, syntax, tone, formality, tropes, sentence length, paragraph length—all can change depending on the circumstances of the communication.

Another factor that bears significantly on rhetoric is the intended audience. Is the intended audience the American people as a whole or their representatives in Congress? As has already been pointed out, Washington set one precedent—that of addressing all American citizens in a formal, written farewell address. He soon set another precedent—that of using his last annual message to the Congress as another forum in which to bid adieu. Most succeeding presidents (until Truman) followed the latter course exclusively and said farewell to the American people through the Congress. That was the custom for more than a century and a half, and that custom bore on the rhetoric.

In recent years, much has been written of the Internet revolution. The expanding presence of the Internet makes it difficult for a president to aim his remarks strictly at a small audience or to control their distribution. Yet the difficulty had already been introduced by radio, television, and other modern technologies. When Nixon gave his farewell speech to White House staff, it was nominally for their ears only. But the fact that reporters were covering the speech made the entire world privy to it. Nixon even commented on how the press would likely distort the circumstances of the speech. Thus his remarks were less an intimate good-bye than a highly public farewell (hence their inclusion in this volume).

Students of rhetoric like to point out that human beings communicate to inform, entertain, and/or persuade. Farewell messages, though occasionally entertaining and usually informational, always seek to persuade. The speaker wants to move his audience to accept *his* principles, *his* interpretation of historical events, *his* advice for the future. In the *Rhetoric*,[28] Aristotle famously analyzed the three modes of persuasion—*ethos* (persuading by one's example and character), *pathos* (persuading by emotional appeals), and *logos* (persuading by reasoned argumentation). Throughout this collection are found abundant examples of all three modes of persuasion.

In addition to the three modes of persuasion, there are the three types of persuasive speech. Aristotle, observing the institutions of ancient Greek city-states, analyzed forensic oratory (seen in today's courthouse), political oratory[29] (seen in today's statehouse), and ceremonial oratory[30] (seen at parades, graduations, anniversaries, tributes, and funerals). Farewell messages typically combine political and ceremonial discourse. For example, when a president delivers his final state of the union address in the U.S. House of Representatives, he perforce utters some political speech. But the tributes he offers to the American people and to the American spirit are distinctly ceremonial.

Another rhetorical consideration is length. The length of farewell discourse varies considerably, depending largely on whether it is to be written or spoken. Washington's written address is 6,090 words—an essay that can be read in one sitting. Truman's spoken farewell is considerably shorter, about 3,700 words, Eisenhower's about 1,900 words. The latter two reflect that they were intended for live radio and television audiences whose attention could be held captive for only a limited period.

The notion of length, when applied to spoken discourse, is not just a function of the time that elapses on a clock. It is also a function of perception. There is clock time, and there is psychological time, and there can be a great difference between the two. The difference comes down to how well a speaker engages the audience and keeps the listeners' attention. We have all seen how an unskilled speaker can make a five-minute introduction seem interminable. By contrast, a skilled orator can make an hour-long presentation seem to fly by in minutes.

Before concluding, some mention should be made of the discipline of rhetoric. Traditionally one of the seven liberal arts, rhetoric long held a venerable place in the *trivium*, alongside grammar and logic. Many of the best-educated presidents were aware of rhetoric's preeminence in the liberal arts. They were familiar with some of the "world's great speeches" from antiquity forward. Indeed, a few presidents could actually read Pericles's *Funeral Oration* and Demosthenes's *Philippics* in Greek and Cicero's orations in Latin. Space does not permit an examination of every type of trope and technique they learned and put into practice—such would require a whole new volume. But readers who are keen on closely analyzing the rhetoric of these messages are urged to consult a good overview of the subject.[31]

Because the discipline of rhetoric reaches back some 2,400 years—to the Sophists, Isocrates, Plato, and Aristotle—many of the technical terms used to analyze rhetoric reveal ancient Greek roots. The jargon can admittedly be daunting if not off-putting. And yet, it is worth the effort to master some of the terms and concepts. Increasing one's vocabulary increases one's perception. The more one knows, the more one sees.

A competent guide will help readers delve into the art of rhetoric and thus into the heart of the liberal arts. There readers will delight in the creativity and playfulness with which humans have used language. They will become more attuned not just to the literal meaning of words, but to figures of speech. Figures of speech are all of the ways in which human beings bend and stretch words to heighten meaning or create a desired effect. Figures of speech have been called the flowers of rhetoric. They give oratory much of its beauty and power.

When Abraham Lincoln spoke, for example, of "binding the nation's wounds" in the aftermath of the bloody Civil War, he was using a figure of speech called personification. By personifying the United States, Lincoln could put the image of an injured human patient in the minds of listeners. It was more compelling than saying, "Let's try to return to normal."

Traditionally there are five major categories of figures.[32]

- Figures of resemblance or relationship—simile, metaphor, kenning, conceit, parallelism, personification, metonymy, synecdochy, and euphemism.
- Figures of over- and understatement—hyperbole, litotes, irony, antithesis, climax, bathos, paradox, oxymoron, and the rhetorical question.
- Figures of sound—alliteration, repetition, anaphora, and onomatopoeia.
- Verbal games and gymnastics—puns and anagrams.
- Errors for which one must be on the watch—the malapropism, spoonerism, and periphrasis.

Finally, Cicero and other great students of rhetoric developed a kind of checklist, a systematic way of judging speeches, that readers may find useful. This checklist relies on the traditional canons of rhetoric that have stood the test of time. Certainly the canons pertain to farewell speeches. Included in most such checklists are (1) content—but more than raw content, the intelligence and creativity with which facts, stories, ideas, and data are generated, selected, and developed; (2) the organization of this material; (3) eloquence; (4) memory; and (5) delivery. Many commentators today rely directly or indirectly on these ancient canons of rhetoric to judge speeches.

Note on the Sources Used

For the farewell messages in this volume, I have relied on authoritative and publicly available texts. For eighteenth-, nineteenth-, and early-twentieth-century presidents (through Taft), I used *A Compilation of the Messages and Papers of the Presidents*, edited initially by James D. Richardson (New York: Bureau of National Literature, 1897 [revised serially until 1917]). The original manuscripts are scattered about the nation in presidential collections and libraries, the most notable being the Manuscripts Division of the Library of Congress. The original manuscript of George Washington's Farewell Address is in the Alderman Library, University of Virginia. Facsimiles of the entire thirty-two-page manuscript in Washington's hand are accessible online at www.virginia.edu/gwpapers/. The text of Andrew Johnson's Farewell Address is from the March 4, 1869 edition of *The New York Times*, which graciously granted permission to reproduce the piece in its entirely.

For Woodrow Wilson's and Calvin Coolidge's final annual messages, I consulted the *Congressional Record*. For twentieth-century presidents from Herbert Hoover to H. W. Bush, I used the *Public Papers of the Presidents of the United States* (United States Government Printing Office, Washington D.C.). For Bill Clinton's farewell address, I used the text released by the White House on the evening of the speech.

Those who wish to listen to twentieth-century addresses as they were delivered should contact the Vincent Voice Library of Michigan State University.

Editorial Treatment

There is a good rule to follow when editing messages that were written or delivered long ago: Do not second-guess the dead. Since the messages in this volume are historic documents, I have left them almost wholly undisturbed. Most archaic diction is preserved. Most alternate spellings are retained.

Ambiguity and awkward constructions are kept intact. I have only regularized the format and the font to make for uniform presentation in this volume. Otherwise the messages read the way they did to earlier generations of Americans.

Notes

1. St. Paul's Chapel, New York City, December 27, 2001.
2. April 19, 1951.
3. May 12, 1962.
4. July 4, 1939, billed as "Lou Gehrig Appreciation Day" at Yankee Stadium.
5. A term, by the way, which is not in Washington's Farewell Address. But it has become customary for commentators to use "entangling alliances" as a shorthand way of capturing our first president's advice.
6. Robert Louis Wilken, "Gregory VII and the Politics of the Spirit," in *The Second One Thousand Years: Ten People Who Defined a Millennium*, ed. Richard John Neuhaus (Grand Rapids, MI: Eerdmans, 2001), 1.
7. There are always exceptions to prove the rule. Of all the presidents who have delivered farewells, only Bill Clinton claimed to "leave the presidency more idealistic" than when he began eight years earlier.
8. John F. Kennedy, "How to Prepare for the Presidency," *Parade Magazine*, September 23, 1962.
9. Wayne Fields, *Union of Words: A History of Presidential Eloquence* (New York: Free Press, 1996), 312.
10. Note that while there have been forty-three administrations, only forty-two men have served in the office. That is because Grover Cleveland served two nonconsecutive terms.
11. Five presidents did not deliver an inaugural address: John Tyler, Millard Fillmore, Andrew Johnson, Chester Arthur, and Gerald R. Ford.
12. Speaking of patterns, I discovered a most curious one in the course of researching presidential farewells. During the nation's first century, the three presidents who gave a formal farewell address—Washington, Jackson, and A. Johnson—were precisely the three individuals who had lost their fathers as infants or young children.
13. For more on this tradition, see http://www.senate.gov/learning/min_3hh.html [accessed October 10, 2001]. It is a heroic tradition to uphold, given that Washington did not intend the Farewell Address to be read aloud. At more than 6,000 words, the Farewell Address takes almost an hour to get through.
14. Article II, section 3, of the Constitution states, "He [the president] shall from time to time give to the Congress Information of the State of the Union, and recommend to their Consideration such Measures as he shall judge necessary and expedient."
15. The March 4 retirement date was prescribed in 1789 by a resolution of the Continental Congress.
16. Adopted on February 6, 1933, the Twentieth Amendment, section 1, states: "The terms of the President and Vice President shall end at noon on the 20 day of January."
17. William Safire, *Safire's New Political Dictionary*, 3rd ed. (New York: Random House, 1993), s.v. "speechwriter," 738. The first full-time White House speechwriter, Judson Welliver, was the "literary clerk" for presidents Harding and Coolidge.
18. Author interview with Pauline Testerman, audiovisual archivist, Harry S. Truman Library and Museum, Independence, MO, October 16, 2001. Truman was paradigmatic in other ways, as well. He delivered the first live televised state of the union address on January 6, 1947, and the first live televised inaugural address on January 20, 1949, in addition to the first live televised farewell address on January 15, 1953.
19. Farewell addresses have been given by back-to-back presidents only twice in U.S. history: Truman (1953) and Eisenhower (1961), as well as Carter (1981) and Reagan (1989).
20. Lincoln's address in its entirety reads:

My Friends—No one, not in my situation, can appreciate my feeling of sadness at this parting. To this place, and the kindness of these people, I owe every thing. Here I have lived a quarter of a century, and have passed from a young to an old man. Here my children have been born, and one is buried. I now leave, not knowing when, or whether ever, I may return, with a task before me greater than that which rested upon Washington. Without the assistance of that Divine Being, who ever attended him, I cannot succeed. With that assistance I cannot fail. Trusting in Him, who can go with me, and remain with you and be everywhere for good, let us confidently hope that all will yet be well. To His care commending you, as I hope in your prayers you will commend me, I bid you an affectionate farewell. (Source: Library of Congress)

21. An article in the *Illinois Journal*, February 12, 1861, mentions "hundreds of his friends and fellow-citizens" were present. The marker erected at the site (Monroe and Tenth Street) by the Illinois State Historical Society asserts there were about 1,000 people in attendance.

22. Jefferson's address in its entirety reads:

Returning to the scenes of my birth and early life, to the society of those with whom I was raised, and who have been ever dear to me, I receive, fellow citizens and neighbors, with inexpressible pleasure, the cordial welcome you are so good as to give me. Long absent on duties which the history of a wonderful era made incumbent on those called to them, the pomp, the turmoil, the bustle, and splendor of office, have drawn but deeper sighs for the tranquil and irresponsible occupations of private life, for the enjoyment of an affectionate intercourse with you, my neighbors and friends, and the endearments of family love, which nature has given us all, as the sweetener of every hour. For these I gladly lay down the distressing burthen of power, and seek, with my fellow citizens, repose and safety under the watchful cares, the labors, and perplexities of younger and abler minds. The anxieties you express to administer to my happiness, do, of themselves, confer that happiness; and the measure will be complete, if my endeavors to fulfill my duties in the several public stations to which I have been called, have obtained for me the approbation of my country. The part which I have acted on the theatre of public life, has been before them; and to their sentence I submit it; but the testimony of my native country, of the individuals who have known me in private life, to my conduct in its various duties and relations, is the more grateful, as proceeding from eyewitnesses and observers, from triers of the vicinage. Of you, then, my neighbors, I may ask, in the face of the world, "whose ox have I taken, or whom have I defrauded? Whom have I oppressed, or of whose hand have I received a bribe to blind mine eyes therewith?" On your verdict I rest with conscious security. Your wishes for my happiness are received with just sensibility, and I offer sincere prayers for your own welfare and prosperity. (Source: University of Virginia Library)

23. See the headnote to Lincoln's Second Inaugural Address for further reasons for including the speech in this volume.

24. Elections were held in a somewhat different manner in 1800, and it is important to understand the difference in order to determine what Adams knew and when he knew it. Until 1845, there was no uniform election day observed throughout the United States. Each state could appoint its electors on any day within thirty-four days of the date in December scheduled for convening the electors. (Congress established the present system for determining a national election day in 1845.) Further, only five of the sixteen states chose electors based on a popular vote; in the other eleven states, the state legislature made the choice.

25. John Ferling, *John Adams: A Life* (New York: Henry Holt, 1996), 403.

26. The election of 1800 was so tortuous, so acrimonious, that it would be another two months before the nation knew who the next president was. It was decided in the House of Representatives. The experience was so unpleasant that it inspired the Twelfth Amendment, ratified in 1804, stipulating that electors should vote for president and vice president on separate ballots. A candidate must have a majority of the electoral votes to be elected vice president.

27. Phyllis Lee Levin, *Edith and Woodrow: The Wilson White House* (New York: Scribner, 2001), 330 ff.

28. Aristotle, *Rhetoric*, any edition.

29. Also called "deliberative."

30. Also called "epideictic," derived from Greek words meaning "fit for display." The speaker persuades by displaying and celebrating the best qualities of his subject.

31. See, for example, *Lend Me Your Ears: Great Speeches in History*, revised edition, ed. William Safire (New York: Norton, 1997); and *The Concise Oxford Dictionary of Literary Terms*, ed. Chris Baldick (Oxford: Oxford University Press, 1990).

32. *Merriam-Webster Encyclopedia of Literature* (Springfield, MA: Merriam-Webster, 1995), s.v. "figure of speech," 415.

1

George Washington (1789–1797)

Of all the founders, only George Washington earned the title "Father of Our Country." He is also the only U.S. president elected without the usual hurly-burly of politics; there were as yet no political parties, and he was elected unanimously by the Electoral College—twice. Washington was a statesman from day one.

Because the newly ratified Constitution provided only a general framework for the executive branch, it was up to the nation's first chief executive to fill in many operational details. Washington brought a wealth of experience, leadership, and dignity to the task. He established precedents that would prove extremely important to the new republic and to future presidents. One important precedent he established was as rhetorical as it was philosophical and political: the Father of Our Country was also the father of the presidential farewell address.

Our first president was hardly unfamiliar with farewell discourse. The valedictory was well established in Western letters. Washington loved theater and had heard numerous valedictories on the stage. His favorite play, Joseph Addison's *Cato*, amounted to a doleful farewell to the Roman republic. Moreover, some five years before becoming president, Washington himself had composed a letter announcing his retirement from the army,[1] a dress rehearsal for the more famous farewell he would give in 1796.

Washington's Farewell Address is one of the most magnificent state papers in American history. Justifiably so, for it initiated a great conversation among our presidents. The questions Washington framed would help his successors grapple with the perennial issues of governance: How do a people best resolve the conflicting claims of order and liberty? Can a people without virtue long enjoy self-government? What are the limits in a constitutional republic of dissent and tolerance, party and faction? Where the people are sovereign, what is the most effective foreign policy? What is America's destiny in the world?

Washington's Farewell Address not only initiated a great American conversation; it also provided posterity with a vivid snapshot of the challenges the new republic faced.[2] Chief among the challenges was the need for unity. The gentleman-planter from Mt. Vernon was bent on retiring from public life after just one term but changed his mind when he saw how factions were splitting apart the government. He decided to serve for two terms to keep the factions at bay.[3]

Another challenge concerned foreign policy. When the French Revolution led to a major war between France and England, Washington thought it prudent to keep the United States neutral. His refusal to adopt the stance of either his Secretary of State Thomas Jefferson, who was pro-French, or his Secretary of the Treasury Alexander Hamilton, who was pro-British, seemed the wisest course until the young nation could hold its own in the world.

Yet another challenge concerned what might be called the culture of freedom. For the American liberty tree to sink deep roots, citizens would need to foster character that was consistent with self-government. Washington believed such character was formed in the crucible of civil and domestic society. By education? Certainly. By morality? Indeed. By religion? Absolutely.

The way Washington's Farewell Address came about is a story in its own right and shows how complex the process of drafting a major message can be. Washington began thinking about expressing some farewell sentiments after just three years in office. (That was when he thought he would be a one-term president.) In 1792, he asked James Madison, a fellow Virginian and close ally in the Congress, to draft up some farewell sentiments. But when opposing factions formed around his strong-willed advisors, he put thoughts of retirement aside and agreed to serve a second term. Once again electors voted for him unanimously.

Washington determined that his second term would be his last. Even he had been viciously attacked. In May 1796, less than a year before retiring, he revisited Madison's 1792 draft. He conflated its ideas with some of his own and committed them to paper. This composition is called Washington's first draft. The president vetted the first draft to two former administration members: John Jay, former chief justice of the Supreme Court who had resigned to become New York governor, and Alexander Hamilton, former treasury secretary who had resigned and was practicing law. It is interesting that none of the three advisors Washington solicited for help was then in the administration.

Hamilton made a detailed outline—an Abstract of Points—of Washington's first draft. Then, after an exchange of letters with the president, he set about composing a new address altogether. Hamilton and Washington's subsequent correspondence helped shape the resulting composition, which Hamilton called his "Original Draft: Copy Considerably Amended." Washington was pleased with Hamilton's draft but thought it too long.

Washington next assembled all the drafts—Madison's 1792 draft, his own first draft, Hamilton's last draft, and everything in between—and drew from them all to prepare his final draft. The final manuscript, thirty-two pages long, was written in his own hand. Washington never intended the address for oral delivery. It was to be disseminated in print. As the national capital had not yet moved to the District of Columbia but was still in Philadelphia, the manuscript was delivered to Philadelphia's largest newspaper, the *American Daily Advertiser*, which ran the address on September 19, 1796. The address was later printed in other newspapers and distributed throughout the sixteen states in the union.

Interestingly, Washington's final manuscript nowhere contained the words "Farewell Address." Given its salutation—"Friends and Fellow-Citizens"—the piece read more like an open letter. Only one newspaper of the time, the *Courier* of New Hampshire, titled the submission "Washington's Farewell Address."[4] That headline spoke truly—and it stuck.

Although the Farewell Address as we know it reflects the work of three men—Madison, Hamilton, and Washington himself—there is no question that Washington made its 6,088 words his own. It was the product of four years of reflection and a lifetime of experience—the final testament, the last patriotic gift, he could leave his countrymen. It was a relatively disinterested farewell,[5] for Washington sought no office or emolument; he mostly wanted to return to a long-neglected Mt. Vernon. Most assuredly, the Farewell Address was Washington's greatest state paper. Even newspapers that had been attacking the president praised the farewell as the work of a statesman.[6]

Rhetorically, Washington addressed his audience as "you." He was writing directly to American citizens. This accounts for his salutation, "Friends and Fellow-Citizens." The publisher of the *American Daily Advertiser*, David Claypoole, heightened the effect when he headlined the piece with: "To the PEOPLE of the United States."

Thematically, the first half of the address is primarily given to constitutional and political considerations. The second half treats cultural considerations, fiscal responsibility, and foreign policy. Following, more specifically, are seven of Washington's concerns, many of which will resurface in later documents in this volume, as subsequent presidents contributed to the great American conversation.

Preservation of the Union

The first third of the farewell argued that "the continuance of the Union" should be "a primary object of patriotic desire." As if to echo the first aim of the Preamble of the U.S. Constitution, he wrote that union is "a main prop of your liberty." He elaborated: "The unity of government which constitutes you one people . . . is a main pillar in the edifice of your real independence, the support of your tranquility at home, your peace abroad; of your safety; of your prosperity; of that very liberty which you so highly prize." Washington anticipated sectionalism and trouble ahead. "But as it is easy to foresee that, from different causes and from different quarters, much pains will be taken, many artifices employed to weaken in your minds the conviction of this truth." He soberly advised not to let that happen. Citizens should be "indignantly frowning upon the first dawning of every attempt to alienate any portion of our country from the rest." Above all, "The name of American, which belongs to you in your national capacity, must always exalt the just pride of patriotism more than any appellation derived from local discriminations."

Rule of Law

Washington wanted citizens to prosper and enjoy in perpetuity "good laws under a free government." "The basis of our political systems is the right of the people to make and to alter their constitutions of government. But the Constitution which at any time exists, till changed by an explicit and authentic act of the whole people, is sacredly obligatory upon all. The very idea of the power and the right of the people to establish government presupposes the duty of every individual to obey the established government."

Historical Wisdom

Washington was no ideologue. If the people were thinking of amending the Constitution, Washington admonished them to rely on historical lessons and political experience rather than on political theory and abstractions: "resist with care the spirit of innovation upon [constitutional] principles," he said, adding that citizens should "remember that time and habit are at least as necessary to fix the true character of governments as of other human institutions; that experience is the surest standard by which to test the real tendency of the existing constitution of a country."

Limited Military

As a former commander in chief, Washington tellingly cautions posterity to avoid "overgrown military establishments which, under any form of government, are inauspicious to liberty, and which are to be regarded as particularly hostile to republican liberty." If not kept in check, they could destroy the republic.

Culture of Liberty

Washington reminded citizens of a fundamental characteristic of human nature—"that love of power, and proneness to abuse it, which predominates in the human heart." As a constitutional republic providing "reciprocal checks in the exercise of political power," Americans have strong institutional means to fight the abuse of power. But "the habits of thinking in a free country" should also keep each branch of government within its respective sphere and restrain it from encroaching on the other branches.

Where do such habits come from ultimately? Culture.

At the center of the address—symbolic, perhaps, considering the subject's importance—Washington shifted to the cultural conditions that are necessary to ordered freedom. He veritably sermonized: "Of all the dispositions and habits which lead to political prosperity, religion and morality are indispensable supports." No citizen "should labor to subvert these great pillars of human happiness, these firmest props of the duties of men and citizens." Politicians "ought to respect and to cherish them." Citizens will be safer, and their property more secure, if there is widespread "sense of religious obligation." Justice will be more surely administered where oaths are backed by morality and where morality is backed by religion. Washington warned, "let us with caution indulge the supposition that morality can be maintained without religion. . . . [R]eason and experience both forbid us to expect that national morality can prevail in exclusion of religious principle."

A bit later Washington recurred to the thought, stating that "virtue or morality is a necessary spring of popular government." Indeed, it extends "to every species of free government. Who that is a sincere friend to it can look with indifference upon attempts to shake the foundation of the fabric?" Washington added, "Can it be that Providence has not connected the permanent felicity of a nation with its virtue? The experiment, at least, is recommended by every sentiment which ennobles human nature. Alas! Is it rendered impossible by its vices?"

Washington also observes that "religion and morality" will assist foreign policy by helping American leaders "Observe good faith and justice towards all nations; cultivate peace and harmony with all."

Education is especially important to republican government. To live in freedom, reason must govern passion. The representatives who make public policy, like the citizens who elect them, must act out of reason, not passion. "Promote then, as an object of primary importance, institutions for the general diffusion of knowledge. In proportion as the structure of a government gives force to public opinion, it is essential that public opinion should be enlightened." He counsels that public opinion should be guided by wise maxims so that citizens and representatives alike can foster sound public policy.

Interestingly, the above thoughts—linking religion and morality and education—echo Article III of the Northwest Ordinance (1787): "Religion, morality, and knowledge, being necessary to good government and the happiness of mankind, schools and the means of education shall forever be encouraged."

Fiscal Responsibility

To keep the new nation strong and in good fiscal order, "cherish public credit," Washington advised. In addition, cultivate peace through strength, avoid large public debts, and as a rule do not pass on to "posterity the burden which we ourselves ought to bear." Such a sound policy will keep taxes—"which are . . . inconvenient and unpleasant"—at a just level.

Foreign Policy

The last quarter of the message is famously devoted to foreign affairs. There was a revolutionary and distinctly un-Machiavellian thought in Washington's words: America was to be different in the conduct of its foreign affairs. America could set a good example to all. The new republic could "give to mankind the magnanimous and too novel example of a people always guided by an exalted justice and benevolence." He rejected duplicity, urging Americans to accept the maxim that "honesty is always the best policy."

Washington's even-handedness is striking. The idea of a "most favored nation" was repellent to him. He enjoined: "Observe good faith and justice towards all nations; cultivate peace and harmony with all." What is more, "even our commercial policy should hold an equal and impartial hand; neither seeking nor granting exclusive favors or preferences."

Then Washington confronted a particularly urgent question in his day, which was what U.S. policy toward the great European powers should be. Three and a half years earlier, Washington had defended his stance of neutrality toward France and Britain, officially set forth on April 22, 1793. But, taking a longer view, Washington warned that the undoing of the new republic could result from within—from Americans with passionate and excessive attachments to other nations. (He especially had in mind France or Britain.) Without doubt, his strongest language in the farewell message is reserved for those whose personal agenda would compromise the U.S.'s vital interests. Passionate attachment to a foreign power "gives to ambitious, corrupted, or deluded citizens (who devote themselves to the favorite nation), facility to betray or sacrifice the interests of their own country, without odium, sometimes even with popularity; gilding, with the appearances of a virtuous sense of obligation, a commendable deference for public opinion, or a laudable zeal for public good, the base or foolish compliances of ambition, corruption, or infatuation."

> The great rule of conduct for us in regard to foreign nations is in extending our commercial relations, to have with them as little political connection as possible. So far as we have already formed engagements, let them be fulfilled with perfect good faith. Here let us stop. Europe has a set of primary interests which to us have none; or a very remote relation. Hence she must be engaged in frequent controversies, the causes of which are essentially foreign to our concerns. Hence, therefore, it must be unwise in us to implicate ourselves by artificial ties in the ordinary vicissitudes of her politics, or the ordinary combinations and collisions of her friendships or enmities.

What was the United States to do regarding defense against mortally dangerous enemies? "Taking care always to keep ourselves by suitable establishments on a respectable defensive posture, we may safely trust to temporary alliances for extraordinary emergencies."

For all of the mention of justice and benevolence, there is also practical politics and not just principle at work. Washington explained that, "With me a predominant motive [for neutrality] has been to endeavor to gain time to our country to settle and mature its yet recent institutions, and to progress without interruption to that degree of strength and consistency which is necessary to give it, humanly speaking, the command of its own fortunes."

Finally, the term "entangling alliances" is not in the text—that is a summation almost universally adopted by later writers.

Farewell Address
(published, not delivered orally) First appeared in David C. Claypoole's Philadelphia newspaper, *American Daily Advertiser* September 19, 1796

Friends and Fellow-Citizens:

The period for a new election of a citizen to administer the executive government of the United States being not far distant, and the time actually arrived when your thoughts must be employed in designating the person who is to be clothed with that important trust, it appears to me proper, especially as it may conduce to a more distinct expression of the public voice, that I should now apprise you of the resolution I have formed to decline being considered among the number of those out of whom a choice is to be made.

I beg you, at the same time, to do me the justice to be assured that this resolution has not been taken without a strict regard to all the considerations appertaining to the relation which binds a dutiful citizen to his country; and that in withdrawing the tender of service, which silence in my situation might imply, I am influenced by no diminution of zeal for your future interest, no deficiency of grateful respect for your past kindness, but am supported by a full conviction that the step is compatible with both.

The acceptance of, and continuance hitherto in, the office to which your suffrages have twice called me have been a uniform sacrifice of inclination to the opinion of duty and to a deference for what appeared to be your desire. I constantly hoped that it would have been much earlier in my power, consistently with motives which I was not at liberty to disregard, to return to that retirement from which I had been reluctantly drawn. The strength of my inclination to do this, previous to the last election, had even led to the preparation of an address to declare it to you; but mature reflection on the then perplexed and critical posture of our affairs with foreign nations, and the unanimous advice of persons entitled to my confidence, impelled me to abandon the idea. I rejoice that the state of your concerns, external as well as internal, no longer renders the pursuit of inclination incompatible with the sentiment of duty or propriety, and am persuaded, whatever partiality may be retained for my services, that, in the present circumstances of our country, you will not disapprove my determination to retire.

The impressions with which I first undertook the arduous trust were explained on the proper occasion. In the discharge of this trust, I will only say that I have, with good intentions, contributed towards the organization and administration of the government the best exertions of which a very fallible judgment was capable. Not unconscious in the outset of the inferiority of my qualifications, experience in my own eyes, perhaps still more in the eyes of others, has strengthened the motives to diffidence of myself; and every day the increasing weight of years admonishes me more and more that the shade of retirement is as necessary to me as it will be welcome. Satisfied that if any circumstances have given peculiar value to my services, they were temporary, I have the consolation to believe that, while choice and prudence invite me to quit the political scene, patriotism does not forbid it.

In looking forward to the moment which is intended to terminate the career of my public life, my feelings do not permit me to suspend the deep acknowledgment of that debt of gratitude which I owe to my beloved country for the many honors it has conferred upon me; still more for the steadfast confidence with which it has supported me; and for the opportunities I have thence enjoyed of manifesting my inviolable attachment, by services faithful and persevering, though in usefulness unequal to my zeal. If benefits have resulted to our country from these services, let it always be remembered to your praise and as an instructive example in our annals, that under circumstances in which the passions, agitated in every direction, were liable to mislead, amidst appearances sometimes dubious, vicissitudes of fortune often discouraging, in situations in which not unfrequently want of success has countenanced the spirit of criticism, the constancy of your support was the essential prop of the efforts and a guaranty of the plans by which they were effected. Profoundly penetrated with this idea, I shall carry it with me to my grave as a strong incitement to unceasing vows that heaven may continue to you the choicest tokens of its beneficence; that your union and brotherly affection may be perpetual; that the free Constitution which is the work of your hands may be sacredly maintained; that its administration in every department may be stamped with wisdom and virtue; that, in fine, the happiness of the people of these States, under the auspices of liberty, may be made complete by so careful a preservation and so prudent a use of this blessing as will acquire to them the glory of recommending it to the applause, the affection, and adoption of every nation which is yet a stranger to it.

Here, perhaps, I ought to stop. But a solicitude for your welfare, which cannot end but with my life, and the apprehension of danger natural to that solicitude, urge me on an occasion like the present to offer to your solemn contemplation and to recommend to your frequent review some sentiments which are the result of much reflection, of no inconsiderable observation, and which appear to me all-important to the permanency of your felicity as a people. These will be offered to you with the more freedom, as you can only see in them the disinterested warnings of a parting friend, who can possibly have no personal motive to bias his counsel. Nor can I forget, as an encouragement to it, your indulgent reception of my sentiments on a former and not dissimilar occasion.

Interwoven as is the love of liberty with every ligament of your hearts, no recommendation of mine is necessary to fortify or confirm the attachment.

The unity of government which constitutes you one people is also now dear to you. It is justly so, for it is a main pillar in the edifice of your real independence, the support of your tranquillity at home, your peace abroad, of your safety, of your prosperity, of that very liberty which you so highly prize. But as it is easy to foresee that, from different causes and from different quarters, much pains will be taken, many artifices employed, to weaken in your minds the conviction of this truth, as this is the point in your political fortress against which the batteries of internal and external enemies will be most constantly and actively (though often covertly and insidiously) directed, it is of infinite moment that you should properly estimate the immense value of your national union to your collective and individual happiness; that you should cherish a cordial, habitual, and immovable attachment to it; accustoming yourselves to think and speak of it as of the palladium of your political safety and prosperity; watching for its preservation with jealous anxiety; discountenancing whatever may suggest even a suspicion that it can in any event be abandoned; and indignantly frowning upon the first dawning of every attempt to alienate any portion of our country from the rest, or to enfeeble the sacred ties which now link together the various parts.

For this you have every inducement of sympathy and interest. Citizens by birth or choice of a common country, that country has a right to concentrate your affections. The name of American, which belongs to you in your national capacity, must always exalt the just pride of patriotism more than any appellation derived from local discriminations. With slight shades of difference, you have the same religion, manners, habits, and political principles. You have in a common cause fought and triumphed together. The independence and liberty you possess are the work of joint counsels and joint efforts of common dangers, sufferings, and successes.

But these considerations, however powerfully they address themselves to your sensibility, are greatly outweighed by those which apply more immediately to your interest. Here every portion of our country finds the most commanding motives for carefully guarding and preserving the union of the whole.

The North, in an unrestrained intercourse with the South, protected by the equal laws of a common government, finds in the productions of the latter great additional resources of maritime and commercial enterprise and precious materials of manufacturing industry. The South, in the same intercourse, benefiting by the agency of the North, sees its agriculture grow and its commerce expand. Turning partly into its own channels the seamen of the North, it finds its particular navigation invigorated; and while it contributes in different ways to nourish and increase the general mass of the national navigation, it looks forward to the protection of a maritime strength, to which itself is unequally adapted. The East, in a like intercourse with the West, already finds, and in the progressive improvement of interior communications by land and water, will more and more find, a valuable vent for the commodities which it brings from abroad, or manufactures at home. The West derives from the East supplies requisite to its growth and comfort, and, what is perhaps of still greater consequence, it must of necessity owe the secure enjoyment of indispensable outlets for its own productions to the weight, influence, and the future maritime strength of the Atlantic side of the Union, directed by an indissoluble community of interest as one nation. Any other tenure by which the West can hold this essential advantage, whether derived from its own separate strength, or from an apostate and unnatural connection with any foreign power, must be intrinsically precarious.

While, then, every part of our country thus feels an immediate and particular interest in union, all the parts combined cannot fail to find in the united mass of means and efforts greater strength, greater resource, proportionably greater security from external danger, a less frequent interruption of their peace by foreign nations, and, what is of inestimable value, they must derive from union an exemption from those broils and wars between themselves, which so frequently afflict neighboring countries not tied together by the same governments, which their own rival ships alone would be sufficient to produce, but which opposite foreign alliances, attachments, and intrigues would stimulate and embitter. Hence, likewise, they will avoid the necessity of those overgrown military establishments which, under any form of government, are inauspicious to liberty, and which are to be regarded as particularly hostile to republican liberty. In this sense it is that your union ought to be considered as a main prop of your liberty, and that the love of the one ought to endear to you the preservation of the other.

These considerations speak a persuasive language to every reflecting and virtuous mind, and exhibit the continuance of the Union as a primary object of patriotic desire. Is there a doubt whether a common government can embrace so large a sphere? Let experience solve it. To listen to mere speculation in such a case were criminal. We are authorized to hope that a proper organization of the whole, with the auxiliary agency of governments for the respective subdivisions, will afford a happy issue to the experiment. It is well worth a fair and full experiment. With such powerful and obvious motives to union affecting all parts of our country, while experience shall not have demonstrated its impracticability, there will always be reason to distrust the patriotism of those who in any quarter may endeavor to weaken its bands.

In contemplating the causes which may disturb our Union, it occurs as matter of serious concern that any ground should have been furnished for characterizing parties by geographical discriminations—Northern and Southern, Atlantic and Western—whence designing men may endeavor to excite a belief that there is a real difference of local interests and views. One of the expedients of party to acquire influence within particular districts is to misrepresent the opinions and aims of other districts. You cannot shield yourselves too much against the jealousies and heartburnings which spring from these misrepresentations; they tend to render alien to each other those who ought to be bound together by fraternal affection. The inhabitants of our Western country have lately had a useful lesson on this head. They have seen in the negotiation by the Executive and in the unanimous ratification by the Senate of the treaty with Spain, and in the universal satisfaction at that event throughout the United States, a decisive proof how unfounded were the suspicions propagated among them of a policy in the General Government and in the Atlantic States unfriendly to their interests in regard to the Mississippi. They have been witnesses to the formation of two treaties—that with Great Britain, and that with Spain—which secure to them everything they could desire in respect to our foreign relations toward confirming their prosperity. Will it not be their wisdom to rely for the preservation of these advantages on the Union by which they were procured? Will they not henceforth be deaf to those advisers, if such there are, who would sever them from their brethren and connect them with aliens?

To the efficacy and permanency of your Union a government for the whole is indispensable. No alliance, however strict, between the parts can be an adequate substitute. They must inevitably experience the infractions and interruptions which all alliances in all times have experienced. Sensible of this momentous truth, you have improved upon your first essay by the adoption of a constitution of government better calculated than your former for an intimate union and for the efficacious management of your common concerns. This government, the offspring of our own choice, uninfluenced and unawed, adopted upon full investigation and mature deliberation, completely free in its principles, in the distribution of its powers, uniting security with energy, and containing within itself a provision for its own amendment, has a just claim to your confidence and your support. Respect for its authority, compliance with its laws, acquiescence in its measures, are duties enjoined by the fundamental maxims of true liberty. The basis of our political systems is the right of the people to make and to alter their constitutions of government. But the Constitution which at any time exists till changed by an explicit and authentic act of the whole people is sacredly obligatory upon all. The very idea of the power and the right of the people to establish government presupposes the duty of every individual to obey the established government.

All obstructions to the execution of the laws, all combinations and associations, under whatever plausible character, with the real design to direct, control, counteract, or awe the regular deliberation and action of the constituted authorities, are destructive of this fundamental principle and of fatal tendency. They serve to organize faction; to give it an artificial and extraordinary force; to put in the place of the delegated will of the nation the will of a party, often a small but artful and enterprising minority of the community; and, according to the alternate triumphs of different parties, to make the public administration the mirror of the ill-concerted and incongruous projects of faction rather than the organ of consistent and wholesome plans, digested by common counsels and modified by mutual interests.

However combinations or associations of the above description may now and then answer popular ends, they are likely in the course of time and things to become potent engines by which cunning, ambitious, and unprincipled men will be enabled to subvert the power of the people, and to usurp for themselves the reins of government, destroying afterwards the very engines which have lifted them to unjust dominion.

Toward the preservation of your government and the permanency of your present happy state, it is requisite not only that you steadily discountenance irregular oppositions to its acknowledged authority, but also that you resist with care the spirit of innovation upon its principles, however specious the pretexts. One method of assault may be to effect in the forms of the Constitution alterations which will impair the energy of the system, and thus to undermine what cannot be directly overthrown. In all the changes to which you may be invited, remember that time and habit are at least as necessary to fix the true character of governments as of other human institutions; that experience is the surest standard by which to test the real tendency of the existing constitution of a country; that facility in changes upon the credit of mere hypothesis and opinion exposes to perpetual change, from the endless variety of hypothesis and opinion; and remember especially that for the efficient management of your common interests in a country so extensive as ours, a government of as much vigor as is consistent with the perfect security of liberty is indispensable. Liberty itself will find in such a government, with powers properly distributed and adjusted, its surest guardian. It is, indeed, little else than a name where the government is too feeble to withstand the enterprises of faction, to confine each member of the society within the limits prescribed by the laws, and to maintain all in the secure and tranquil enjoyment of the rights of person and property.

I have already intimated to you the danger of parties in the State, with particular reference to the founding of them on geographical discriminations. Let me now take a more comprehensive view, and warn you in the most solemn manner against the baneful effects of the spirit of party generally.

This spirit, unfortunately, is inseparable from our nature, having its root in the strongest passions of the human mind. It exists under different shapes in all governments, more or less stifled, controlled, or repressed; but in those of the popular form, it is seen in its greatest rankness and is truly their worst enemy.

The alternate domination of one faction over another, sharpened by the spirit of revenge natural to party dissension, which in different ages and countries has perpetrated the most horrid enormities, is itself a frightful despotism. But this leads at length to a more formal and permanent despotism. The disorders and miseries which result gradually incline the minds of men to seek security and repose in the absolute power of an individual, and sooner or later the chief of some prevailing faction, more able or more fortunate than his competitors, turns this disposition to the purposes of his own elevation on the ruins of public liberty.

Without looking forward to an extremity of this kind (which nevertheless ought not to be entirely out of sight), the common and continual mischiefs of the spirit of party are sufficient to make it the interest and duty of a wise people to discourage and restrain it.

It serves always to distract the public councils and enfeeble the public administration. It agitates the community with ill-founded jealousies and false alarms, kindles the animosity of one part against another, foments occasionally riot and insurrection. It opens the door to foreign influence and corruption, which find a facilitated access to the government itself through the channels of party passions. Thus the policy and the will of one country are subjected to the policy and will of another.

There is an opinion that parties in free countries are useful checks upon the administration of the government, and serve to keep alive the spirit of liberty. This within certain limits is probably true; and in governments of a monarchical cast, patriotism may look with indulgence, if not with favor, upon the spirit of party. But in those of the popular character, in governments purely elective, it is a spirit not to be encouraged. From their natural tendency, it is certain there will always be enough of that spirit for every salutary purpose, and there being constant danger of excess, the effort ought to be by force of public opinion to mitigate and assuage it. A fire not to be quenched, it demands a uniform vigilance to prevent its bursting into a flame, lest, instead of warming, it should consume.

It is important, likewise, that the habits of thinking in a free country should inspire caution in those entrusted with its administration to confine themselves within their respective constitutional spheres, avoiding in the exercise of the powers of one department to encroach upon another. The spirit of encroachment tends to consolidate the powers of all the departments in one, and thus to create, whatever the form of government, a real despotism. A just estimate of that love of power and proneness to abuse it which predominates in the human heart is sufficient to satisfy us of the truth of this position. The necessity of reciprocal checks in the exercise of political power, by dividing and distributing it into different depositories, and constituting each the guardian of the public weal against invasions by the others, has been evinced by experiments ancient and modern, some of them in our country and under our own eyes. To preserve them must be as necessary as to institute them. If in the opinion of the people the distribution or modification of the constitutional powers be in any particular wrong, let it be corrected by an amendment in the way which the Constitution designates. But let there be no change by usurpation; for though this in one instance may be the instrument of good, it is the customary weapon by which free governments are destroyed. The precedent must always greatly overbalance in permanent evil any partial or transient benefit which the use can at any time yield.

Of all the dispositions and habits which lead to political prosperity, religion and morality are indispensable supports. In vain would that man claim the tribute of patriotism who should labor to subvert these great pillars of human happiness—these firmest props of the duties of men and citizens. The mere politician, equally with the pious man, ought to respect and to cherish them. A volume could not trace all their connections with private and public felicity. Let it simply be asked: Where is the security for property, for reputation, for life, if the sense of religious obligation desert the oaths which are the instruments of investigation in courts of justice? And let us with caution indulge the supposition that morality can be maintained without religion. Whatever may be conceded to the influence of refined education on minds of peculiar structure, reason and experience both forbid us to expect that national morality can prevail in exclusion of religious principle.

It is substantially true that virtue or morality is a necessary spring of popular government. The rule, indeed, extends with more or less force to every species of free government. Who that is a sincere friend to it can look with indifference upon attempts to shake the foundation of the fabric?

Promote then, as an object of primary importance, institutions for the general diffusion of knowledge. In proportion as the structure of a government gives force to public opinion, it is essential that public opinion should be enlightened.

As a very important source of strength and security, cherish public credit. One method of preserving it is to use it as sparingly as possible, avoiding occasions of expense by cultivating peace, but remembering also that timely disbursements to prepare for danger frequently prevent much greater disbursements to repel it, avoiding likewise the accumulation of debt, not only by shunning occasions of expense, but by vigorous exertion in time of peace to discharge the debts which unavoidable wars have occasioned, not ungenerously throwing upon posterity the burden which we ourselves ought to bear. The execution of these maxims belongs to your representatives, but it is necessary that public opinion should co-operate. To facilitate to them the performance of their duty, it is essential that you should practically bear in mind that toward the payment of debts there must be revenue; that to have revenue there must be taxes; that no taxes can be devised which are not more or less inconvenient and unpleasant; that the intrinsic embarrassment, inseparable from the selection of the proper objects (which is always a choice of difficulties), ought to be a decisive motive for a candid construction of the conduct of the Government in making it, and for a spirit of acquiescence in the measures for obtaining revenue, which the public exigencies may at any time dictate.

Observe good faith and justice toward all nations. Cultivate peace and harmony with all. Religion and morality enjoin this conduct. And can it be that good policy does not equally enjoin it? It will be worthy of a free, enlightened, and at no distant period a great nation to give to mankind the magnanimous and too novel example of a people always guided by an exalted justice and benevolence. Who can doubt that in the course of time and things the fruits of such a plan would richly repay any temporary advantages which might be lost by a steady adherence to it? Can it be that Providence has not connected the permanent felicity of a nation with its virtue? The experiment, at least, is recommended by every sentiment which ennobles human nature. Alas! Is it rendered impossible by its vices?

In the execution of such a plan, nothing is more essential than that permanent, inveterate antipathies against particular nations, and passionate attachments for others, should be excluded; and that, in place of them, just and amicable feelings toward all should be cultivated. The nation which indulges toward another a habitual hatred or a habitual fondness is in some degree a slave. It is a slave to its animosity or to its affection, either of which is sufficient to lead it astray from its duty and its interest. Antipathy in one nation against another disposes each more readily to offer insult and injury, to lay hold of slight causes of umbrage, and to be haughty and intractable when accidental or trifling occasions of dispute occur.

Hence, frequent collisions, obstinate, envenomed, and bloody contests. The nation, prompted by ill-will and resentment, sometimes impels to war the government, contrary to the best calculations of policy. The government sometimes participates in the national propensity, and adopts through passion what reason would reject. At other times it makes the animosity of the nation subservient to projects of hostility instigated by pride, ambition, and other sinister and pernicious motives. The peace often, sometimes perhaps the liberty, of nations has been the victim.

So likewise, a passionate attachment of one nation for another produces a variety of evils. Sympathy for the favorite nation, facilitating the illusion of an imaginary common interest in cases where no real common interest exists, and infusing into one the enmities of the other, betrays the former into a participation in the quarrels and wars of the latter without adequate inducement or justification. It leads also to concessions to the favorite nation of privileges denied to others, which is apt doubly to injure the nation making the concessions by unnecessarily parting with what ought to have been retained, and by exciting jealousy, ill-will, and a disposition to retaliate in the parties from whom equal privileges are withheld. And it gives to ambitious, corrupted, or deluded citizens (who devote themselves to the favorite nation) facility to betray or sacrifice the interests of their own country without odium, sometimes even with popularity, gilding with the appearances of a virtuous sense of obligation, a commendable deference for public opinion, or a laudable zeal for public good, the base or foolish compliances of ambition, corruption, or infatuation.

As avenues to foreign influence in innumerable ways, such attachments are particularly alarming to the truly enlightened and independent patriot. How many opportunities do they afford to tamper with domestic factions, to practice the arts of seduction, to mislead public opinion, to influence or awe the public councils? Such an attachment of a small or weak toward a great and powerful nation dooms the former to be the satellite of the latter.

Against the insidious wiles of foreign influence (I conjure you to believe me, fellow-citizens) the jealousy of a free people ought to be constantly awake, since history and experience prove that foreign influence is one of the most baneful foes of republican government. But that jealousy, to be useful, must be impartial; else it becomes the instrument of the very influence to be avoided, instead of a defense against it. Excessive partiality for one foreign nation and excessive dislike of another cause those whom they actuate to see danger only on one side, and serve to veil and even second the arts of influence on the other. Real patriots who may resist the intrigues of the favorite are liable to become suspected and odious, while its tools and dupes usurp the applause and confidence of the people to surrender their interests.

The great rule of conduct for us in regard to foreign nations is, in extending our commercial relations, to have with them as little political connection as possible. So far as we have already formed engagements, let them be fulfilled with perfect good faith. Here let us stop.

Europe has a set of primary interests which to us have none or a very remote relation. Hence she must be engaged in frequent controversies, the causes of which are essentially foreign to our concerns. Hence, therefore, it must be unwise in us to implicate ourselves by artificial ties in the ordinary vicissitudes of her politics or the ordinary combinations and collisions of her friendships or enmities.

Our detached and distant situation invites and enables us to pursue a different course. If we remain one people under an efficient government, the period is not far off when we may defy material injury from external annoyance; when we may take such an attitude as will cause the neutrality we may at any time resolve upon to be scrupulously respected; when belligerent nations, under the impossibility of making acquisitions upon us, will not lightly hazard giving us provocation; when we may choose peace or war, as our interest, guided by justice, shall counsel.

Why forego the advantages of so peculiar a situation? Why quit our own to stand upon foreign ground? Why, by interweaving our destiny with that of any part of Europe, entangle our peace and prosperity in the toils of European ambition, rivalship, interest, humor, or caprice?

It is our true policy to steer clear of permanent alliances with any portion of the foreign world, so far, I mean, as we are now at liberty to do it; for let me not be understood as capable of patronizing infidelity to existing engagements. I hold the maxim no less applicable to public than to private affairs, that honesty is always the best policy. I repeat, therefore, let those engagements be observed in their genuine sense. But in my opinion it is unnecessary and would be unwise to extend them.

Taking care always to keep ourselves by suitable establishments on a respectable defensive posture, we may safely trust to temporary alliances for extraordinary emergencies.

Harmony, liberal intercourse with all nations, are recommended by policy, humanity, and interest. But even our commercial policy should hold an equal and impartial hand; neither seeking nor granting exclusive favors or preferences; consulting the natural course of things; diffusing and diversifying by gentle means the streams of commerce, but forcing nothing; establishing with powers so disposed, in order to give trade a stable course, to define the rights of our merchants, and to enable the Government to support them, conventional rules of intercourse, the best that present circumstances and mutual opinion will permit, but temporary and liable to be from time to time abandoned or varied as experience and circumstances shall dictate; constantly keeping in view that it is folly in one nation to look for disinterested favors from another; that it must pay with a portion of its independence for whatever it may accept under that character; that by such acceptance it may place itself in the condition of having given equivalents for nominal favors, and yet of being reproached with ingratitude for not giving more. There can be no greater error than to expect or calculate upon real favors from nation to nation. It is an illusion which experience must cure, which a just pride ought to discard.

In offering to you, my countrymen, these counsels of an old and affectionate friend, I dare not hope they will make the strong and lasting impression I could wish—that they will control the usual current of the passions, or prevent our nation from running the course which has hitherto marked the destiny of nations. But if I may even flatter myself that they may be productive of some partial benefit, some occasional good—that they may now and then recur to moderate the fury of party spirit, to warn against the mischiefs of foreign intrigue, to guard against the impostures of pretended patriotism—this hope will be a full recompense for the solicitude for your welfare by which they have been dictated.

How far in the discharge of my official duties I have been guided by the principles which have been delineated, the public records and other evidences of my conduct must witness to you and to the world. To myself, the assurance of my own conscience is that I have at least believed myself to be guided by them.

In relation to the still subsisting war in Europe, my proclamation of the twenty-second of April, 1793, is the index to my plan. Sanctioned by your approving voice, and by that of your representatives in both houses of Congress, the spirit of that measure has continually governed me, uninfluenced by any attempts to deter or divert me from it.

After deliberate examination, with the aid of the best lights I could obtain, I was well satisfied that our country, under all the circumstances of the case, had a right to take, and was bound in duty and interest to take, a neutral position. Having taken it, I determined as far as should depend upon me to maintain it with moderation, perseverance, and firmness.

The considerations which respect the right to hold this conduct it is not necessary on this occasion to detail. I will only observe that, according to my understanding of the matter, that right so far from being denied by any of the belligerent powers has been virtually admitted by all.

The duty of holding a neutral conduct may be inferred, without anything more, from the obligation which justice and humanity impose on every nation, in cases in which it is free to act, to maintain inviolate the relations of peace and amity toward other nations.

The inducements of interest for observing that conduct will best be referred to your own reflections and experience. With me a predominant motive has been to endeavor to gain time to our country to settle and mature its yet recent institutions, and to progress without interruption to that degree of strength and consistency which is necessary to give it, humanly speaking, the command of its own fortunes.

Though in reviewing the incidents of my Administration I am unconscious of intentional error, I am nevertheless too sensible of my defects not to think it probable that I may have committed many errors. Whatever they may be, I fervently beseech the Almighty to avert or mitigate the evils to which they may tend. I shall also carry with me the hope that my country will never cease to view them with indulgence, and that, after forty five years of my life dedicated to its service with an upright zeal, the faults of incompetent abilities will be consigned to oblivion, as myself must soon be to the mansions of rest.

Relying on its kindness in this as in other things, and actuated by that fervent love toward it which is so natural to a man who views in it the native soil of himself and his progenitors for several generations, I anticipate with pleasing expectation that retreat in which I promise myself to realize without alloy the sweet enjoyment of partaking in the midst of my fellow-citizens the benign influence of good laws under a free government—the ever-favorite object of my heart and the happy reward, as I trust, of our mutual cares, labors, and dangers.

GEO. WASHINGTON

Washington set another precedent that would be observed by many of his successors: that of devoting a part of his final annual message to Congress to bid adieu. Less than three months after his Farewell Address had been published, he submitted his eighth annual message to Congress. The speech is not just a report but is chock-full of insights on governing a republic.

A rule of speechwriting (Winston Churchill recommended it) is to introduce important matter at the beginning, when the speaker best has the audience's attention. Washington's first major theme concerns the Indians on the frontier. It is a theme that virtually every final annual message over the next 100 years will recur to. And always the idea is the same: Indians are uncivilized, so the government must deal firmly with the violent among them even as it negotiates treaties with their leaders and, in the meantime, endeavor to teach as many of them as possible to see and accept the superior ways of American civilization.

Rhetorically, note Washington's skillful use of the rhetorical question—it is used to conclude at least a half dozen paragraphs in the middle of the message.

The final paragraph, 115 words in length, is a stand-alone adieu. It recalls the beginnings of the republic under the Constitution of 1787 and congratulates the nation for its successes thus far. Aware of how youthful and tenuous the American experiment was, he concludes by offering "fervent supplications to the Supreme Ruler of the Universe and Sovereign Arbiter of Nations that

His providential care may still be extended to the United States." The sentiment served as a pair of bookends to the speech, for Washington had begun by expressing "gratitude to the Ruler of the Universe."

Eighth Annual Message
(speech to the Congress)
December 7, 1796

Fellow-Citizens of the Senate and House of Representatives:

In recurring to the internal situation of our country since I had last the pleasure to address you, I find ample reason for a renewed expression of that gratitude to the Ruler of the Universe which a continued series of prosperity has so often and so justly called forth.

The acts of the last session which required special arrangements have been as far as circumstances would admit carried into operation.

Measures calculated to insure a continuance of the friendship of the Indians and to preserve peace along the extent of our interior frontier have been digested and adopted. In the framing of these care has been taken to guard on the one hand our advanced settlements from the predatory incursions of those unruly individuals who can not be restrained by their tribes, and on the other hand to protect the rights secured to the Indians by treaty—to draw them nearer to the civilized state and inspire them with correct conceptions of the power as well as justice of the Government.

The meeting of the deputies from the Creek Nation at Colerain, in the State of Georgia, which had for a principal object the purchase of a parcel of their land by that State, broke up without its being accomplished, the nation having previous to their departure instructed them against making any sale. The occasion, however, has been improved to confirm by a new treaty with the Creeks their preexisting engagements with the United States, and to obtain their consent to the establishment of trading houses and military posts within their boundary, by means of which their friendship and the general peace may be more effectually secured.

The period during the late session at which the appropriation was passed for carrying into effect the treaty of amity, commerce, and navigation between the United States and His Britannic Majesty necessarily procrastinated the reception of the posts stipulated to be delivered beyond the date assigned for that event. As soon, however, as the Governor-General of Canada could be addressed with propriety on the subject, arrangements were cordially and promptly concluded for their evacuation, and the United States took possession of the principal of them, comprehending Oswego, Niagara, Detroit, Michilimackinac, and Fort Miami, where such repairs and additions have been ordered to be made as appeared indispensable. The commissioners appointed on the part of the United States and of Great Britain to determine which in the river St. Croix mentioned in the treaty of peace of 1783, agreed in the choice of Egbert Benson, esq., of New York, for the third commissioner. The whole met at St. Andrew's, in Passamaquoddy Bay, in the beginning of October, and directed surveys to be made of the rivers in dispute; but deeming it impracticable to have these surveys completed before the next year, they adjourned to meet at Boston in August, 1797, for the final decision of the question.

Other commissioners appointed on the part of the United States, agreeably to the seventh article of the treaty with Great Britain, relative to captures and condemnation of vessels and other property, met the commissioners of His Britannic Majesty in London in August last, when John Trumbull, esq., was chosen by lot for the fifth commissioner. In October following the board were to proceed to business. As yet there has been no communication of commissioners on the part of Great Britain to unite with those who have been appointed on the part of the United States for carrying into effect the 6th article of the treaty. The treaty with Spain required that the commissioners for running the boundary line between the territory of the United States and His Catholic Majesty's provinces of East and West Florida should meet at the Natchez before the expiration of 6 months after the exchange of the ratifications, which was effected at Aranjuez on the 25th day of April; and the troops of His Catholic Majesty occupying any posts within the limits of the United States were within the same time period to be withdrawn. The commissioner of the United States therefore commenced his journey for the Natchez in September, and troops were ordered to occupy the posts from which the Spanish garrisons should be withdrawn. Information has been recently received of the appointment of a commissioner on the part of His Catholic Majesty for running the boundary line, but none of any appointment for the adjustment of the claims of our citizens whose vessels were captured by the armed vessels of Spain.

In pursuance of the act of Congress passed in the last session for the protection and relief of American sea-men, agents were appointed, one to reside in Great Britain and the other in the West Indies. The effects of the agency in the West Indies are not yet fully ascertained, but those which have been communicated afford grounds to believe the measure will be beneficial. The agent destined to reside in Great Britain declining to accept the appointment, the business has consequently devolved on the minister of the United States in London, and will command his attention until a new agent shall be appointed.

After many delays and disappointments arising out of the European war, the final arrangements for fulfilling the engagements made to the Dey and Regency of Algiers will in all present appearance be crowned with success, but under great, though inevitable, disadvantages in the pecuniary transactions occasioned by that war, which will render further provision necessary. The actual liberation of all our citizens who were prisoners in Algiers, while it gratifies every feeling of heart, is itself an earnest of a satisfactory termination of the whole negotiation. Measures are in operation for effecting treaties with the Regencies of Tunis and Tripoli.

To an active external commerce the protection of a naval force is indispensable. This is manifest with regard to wars in which a State is itself a party. But besides this, it is in our own experience that the most sincere neutrality is not a sufficient guard against the depredations of nations at war. To secure respect to a neutral flag requires a naval force organized and ready to vindicate it from insult or aggression. This may even prevent the necessity of going to war by discouraging belligerent powers from committing such violations of the rights of the neutral party as may, first or last, leave no other option. From the best information I have been able to obtain it would seem as if our trade to the Mediterranean without a protecting force will always be insecure and our citizens exposed to the calamities from which numbers of them have but just been relieved.

These considerations invite the United States to look to the means, and to set about the gradual creation of a navy. The increasing progress of their navigation promises them at no distant period the requisite supply of seamen, and their means in other respects favor the undertaking. It is an encouragement, likewise, that their particular situation will give weight and influence to a moderate naval force in their hands. Will it not, then, be advisable to begin without delay to provide and lay up the materials for the building and equipping of ships of war, and to proceed in the work by degrees, in proportion as our resources shall render it practicable without inconvenience, so that a future war of Europe may not find our commerce in the same unprotected state in which it was found by the present?

Congress have repeatedly, and not without success, directed their attention to the encouragement of manufactures. The object is of too much consequence not to insure a continuance of their efforts in every way which shall appear eligible. As a general rule, manufactures on public account are inexpedient; but where the state of things in a country leaves little hope that certain branches of manufacture will for a great length of time obtain, when these are of a nature essential to the furnishing and equipping of the public force in time of war, are not establishments for procuring them on public account to the extent of the ordinary demand for the public service recommended by strong considerations of national policy as an exception to the general rule?

Ought our country to remain in such cases dependent on foreign supply, precarious because liable to be interrupted? If the necessary article should in this mode cost more in time of peace, will not the security and independence thence arising form an ample compensation?

Establishments of this sort, commensurate only with the calls of the public service in time of peace, will in time of war easily be extended in proportion to the exigencies of the Government, and may even perhaps be made to yield a surplus for the supply of our citizens at large, so as to mitigate the privations from the interruption of their trade. If adopted, the plan ought to exclude all those branches which are already, or likely soon to be, established in the country, in order that they may be no danger of interference with pursuits of individual industry.

It will not be doubted that with reference either to individual or national welfare agriculture is of primary importance. In proportion as nations advance in population and other circumstances of maturity this truth becomes more apparent, and renders the cultivation of the soil more and more an object of public patronage. Institutions for promoting it grow up, supported by the public purse; and to what object can it be dedicated with greater propriety?

Among the means which have been employed to this end, none have been attended with greater success than the establishment of boards (composed of proper characters) charged with collecting and diffusing information, and enabled by premiums and small pecuniary aids to encourage and assist a spirit of discovery and improvement. This species of establishment contributes doubly to the increase of improvement by stimulating to enterprise and experiment, and by drawing to a common center the results everywhere of individual skill and observation, and spreading them thence over the whole nation. Experience accordingly has shewn that they are very cheap instruments of immense national benefits. I have heretofore proposed to the consideration of Congress the expediency of establishing a national university and also a military academy. The desirableness of both these institutions has so constantly increased with every new view I have taken of the subject that I can not omit the opportunity of once for all recalling your attention to them.

The assembly to which I address myself is too enlightened not to be fully sensible how much a flourishing state of the arts and sciences contributes to national prosperity and reputation.

True it is that our country, much to its honor, contains many seminaries of learning highly respectable and useful; but the funds upon which they rest are too narrow to command the ablest professors in the different departments of liberal knowledge for the institution contemplated, though they would be excellent auxiliaries.

Amongst the motives to such an institution, the assimilation of the principles, opinions, and manners of our countrymen by the common education of a portion of our youth from every quarter well deserves attention. The more homogenous our citizens can be made in these particulars the greater will be our prospect of permanent union; and a primary object of such a national institution should be the education of our youth in the science of government. In a republic what species of knowledge can be equally important and what duty more pressing on its legislature than to patronize a plan for communicating it to those who are to be the future guardians of the liberties of the country?

The institution of a military academy is also recommended by cogent reasons. However pacific the general policy of a nation may be, it ought never to be without an adequate stock of military knowledge for emergencies. The first would impair the energy of its character, and both would hazard its safety or expose it to greater evils when war could not be avoided; besides that, war might often not depend upon its own choice. In proportion as the observance of pacific maxims might exempt a nation from the necessity of practicing the rules of the military art ought to be its care in preserving and transmitting, by proper establishments, the knowledge of that art.

Whatever argument may be drawn from particular examples superficially viewed, a thorough examination of the subject will evince that the art of war is at once comprehensive and complicated, that it demands much previous study, and that the possession of it in its most improved and perfect state is always of great moment to the security of a nation. This, therefore, ought to be a serious care of every government, and for this purpose an academy where a regular course of instruction is given is an obvious expedient which different nations have successfully employed.

The compensation to the officers of the United States in various instances, and in none more than in respect to the most important stations, appear to call for legislative revision. The consequences of a defective provision are of serious import to the Government. If private wealth is to supply the defect of public retribution, it will greatly contract the sphere within which the selection of character for office is to be made, and will proportionally diminish the probability of a choice of men able as well as upright. Besides that, it should be repugnant to the vital principles of our Government virtually to exclude from public trusts talents and virtue unless accompanied by wealth.

While in our external relations some serious inconveniences and embarrassments have been overcome and others lessened, it is with much pain and deep regret I mention that circumstances of a very unwelcome nature have lately occurred. Our trade has suffered and is suffering extensive injuries in the West Indies from the cruisers and agents of the French Republic, and communications have been received from its minister here which indicate the danger of a further disturbance of our commerce by its authority, and which are in other respects far from agreeable.

It has been my constant, sincere, and earnest wish, in conformity with that of our nation, to maintain cordial harmony and a perfectly friendly understanding with that Republic. This wish remains unabated, and I shall persevere in the endeavor to fulfill it to the utmost extent of what shall be consistent with a just and indispensable regard to the rights and honor of our country; nor will I easily cease to cherish the expectation that a spirit of justice, candor, and friendship on the part of the Republic will eventually insure success.

In pursuing this course, however, I can not forget what is due to the character of our Government and nation, or to a full and entire confidence in the good sense, patriotism, self-respect, and fortitude of my countrymen.

I reserve for a special message a more particular communication on this interesting subject.

Gentlemen of the House of Representatives:

I have directed an estimate of the appropriations necessary for the service of the ensuing year to be submitted from the proper Department, with a view of the public receipts and expenditures to the latest period to which an account can be prepared.

It is with satisfaction I am able to inform you that the revenues of the United States continue in a state of progressive improvement.

A reenforcement of the existing provisions for discharging our public debt was mentioned in my address at the opening of the last session. Some preliminary steps were taken toward it, the maturing of which will no doubt engage your zealous attention during the present. I will only add that it will afford me a heart-felt satisfaction to concur in such further measures as will ascertain to our country the prospect of a speedy extinguishment of the debt. Posterity may have cause to regret if from any motive intervals of tranquillity are left unimproved for accelerating this valuable end.

Gentlemen of the Senate and of the House of Representatives:

My solicitude to see the militia of the United States placed on an efficient establishment has been so often and so ardently expressed that I shall but barely recall the subject to your view on the present occasion, at the same time that I shall submit to your inquiry whether our harbors are yet sufficiently secured.

The situation in which I now stand for the last time, in the midst of the representatives of the people of the United States, naturally recalls the period when the administration of the present form of government commenced, and I can not omit the occasion to congratulate you and my country on the success of the experiment, nor to repeat my fervent supplications to the Supreme Ruler of the Universe and Sovereign Arbiter of Nations that His providential care may still be extended to the United States, that the virtue and happiness of the people may be preserved, and that the Government which they have instituted for the protection of their liberties may be perpetual.

GEO. WASHINGTON

Notes

1. The full text of Washington's resignation letter follows:
[To the Continental Congress]
[Annapolis, Md. 23 December 1783]
Mr. President

The great events on which my resignation depended having at length taken place, I have now the honor of offering my sincere Congratulations to Congress & of presenting myself before them to surrender into their hands the trust committed to me, and to claim the indulgence of retiring from the Service of my Country.

Happy in the confirmation of our Independence and Sovereignty, and pleased with the oppertunity afforded the United States of becoming a respectable Nation, I resign with satisfaction the Appointment I accepted with diffidence—A diffidence in my abilities to accomplish so arduous a task, which however was superseded by a confidence in the rectitude of our Cause, the support of the Supreme Power of the Union, and the patronage of Heaven.

The Successful termination of the War has verified the more sanguine expectations—and my gratitude for the interposition of Providence, and the assistance I have received from my Countrymen encreases with every review of the momentous Contest.

While I repeat my obligations to the Army in general, I should do injustice to my own feelings not to acknowledge in this place the peculiar Services and distinguished merits of the Gentlemen who have been attached to my person during the War. It was impossible the choice of confidential Officers to compose my family should have been more fortunate. Permit me Sir, to recommend in particular those, who have continued in Service to the present moment, as worthy of the favorable notice & patronage of Congress.

I consider it an indispensable duty to close this last solemn act of my Official life, by commanding the Interests of our dearest Country to the protection of Almighty God, and those Who have the superintendence of them, to his holy keeping.

Having now finished the work assigned me, I retire from the great theatre of Action—and bidding an Affectionate farewell to this August body under whose orders I have so long acted, I here offer my Commission, and take my leave of all the employments of public life. (Source: National Archives, Washington, DC, Papers of the Continental Congress, item 152)

2. Emphasis is on the word "new" because it had been only eight years since the threshold ninth state, New Hampshire, had ratified the U.S. Constitution (June 21, 1788), making the document the basic law of the land.

3. That precedent endured until 1940 and then was constitutionally enshrined when the Twenty-second Amendment was ratified in 1951.

4. Matthew Spalding, "Introduction to Washington's Farewell Address," in *The Founders' Almanac*, ed. Matthew Spalding (Washington, DC: Heritage Foundation, 2001), 289.

5. Washington was not wholly disinterested. He was mindful of how the Farewell Address would impact the election of 1796. Forrest McDonald writes that Washington's Address was "Possibly the most influential piece of propaganda published during the campaign . . . aimed at getting votes" for the Federalist candidate, John Adams. See Forrest McDonald, *The Presidency of George Washington* (Lawrence: University Press of Kansas, 1974), 182.

6. Washington's final manuscript of the Farewell Address, plus drafts by Madison and Hamilton and letters pertaining to the preparation of those drafts, are owned by the New York Public Library. For the story of how the Farewell Address was composed, see Victor Hugo Paltsits, *Washington's Farewell Address: In Facsimile, with Transliterations of all the Drafts of Washington, Madison, & Hamilton, Together with their Correspondence and Other Supporting Documents* (New York: New York Public Library, 1935), preface. Digitized facsimiles of all thirty-two pages of the final Farewell Address manuscript, in Washington's hand, are at http://www.virginia.edu/gwpapers/farewell/facsimile.html [accessed July 11, 2001].

2

John Adams (1797–1801)

In his diary John Adams periodically declared, "Farewell politicks." But the Atlas of Independence stopped short of giving a formal farewell address to the nation. What sufficed for his final presidential speech was the fourth annual message to the Congress, delivered three months before the bitterly and narrowly contested election of 1800 was resolved. The speech has no explicit farewell content. But it is implicit. By November 22, when Adams delivered the speech, he realized his chances were slim even though technically the Electoral College was still too close to call.

As it turned out, Adams learned in early December that he would not have the votes to continue as president. That was some two weeks after giving the November 22 speech. This may explain why there is no explicit farewell content in the annual message. But biographers have written that Adams strongly suspected it was his last major presidential speech.[1] As early as mid-November, Adams got an unofficial report that he had lost South Carolina, making his reelection highly doubtful.[2]

Adams must have decided at some point that a formal farewell would not be needed, that his fourth annual message provided sufficient closure to his years in office. In deciding not to give a formal farewell address, he established a precedent in his own right. The Adams precedent would exercise a hold on most future presidents up to Harry S. Truman. Indeed, twenty-one of the next twenty-three presidents[3] would let their last annual message to the Congress stand as an adieu.

The nation's second president delivered one of the shortest annual messages in American history. It is only 1,372 words—about an eleven-minute speech. But it hardly lacked for content. The "great national exigency" to which Adams referred was the naval war that broke out between the United States and France during his watch. To Adams's mind, the French Revolution, in contrast to the American Revolution, was a travesty of justice, a betrayal of republican principles. France was the source of his most serious trials as president. It played on center stage during the XYZ Affair (1797) and provided the backdrop to the notorious Alien and Sedition Acts (1798), which the Jeffersonian opposition used against him to great advantage in the election of 1800.

The capital had been recently transferred from Philadelphia (where Washington had spent most of his presidency) to the newly laid out town on the Potomac, Washington, D.C. Adams thought it appropriate to use the occasion to pray to "the Supreme Ruler of the Universe." He prayed that Americans would be a virtuous people and that "pure morals and true religion" would flourish for as long as there was an America. As George Washington had died eleven months earlier, Adams invoked his name and expressed the hope that the new nation and new seat of government would embody the first president's "piety and virtue," his "wisdom and magnanimity," his "constancy and self-government." The simple supplication reveals much about Adams's political philosophy. He believed the American experiment could only succeed if citizens leavened their freedom with virtue. Otherwise liberty would devolve into license, and the republic would crumble from within.

In this lofty prayer might also be found a subtle dig at Thomas Jefferson who, in the recent campaign of 1800, had been portrayed by Federalists as an atheist.

Fourth Annual Message
(speech to the Congress)
November 22, 1800

Gentlemen of the Senate and Gentlemen of the House of Representatives:

Immediately after the adjournment of Congress at their last session in Philadelphia I gave directions, in compliance with the laws, for the removal of the public offices, records, and property. These directions have been executed, and the public officers have since resided and conducted the ordinary business of the Government in this place.

I congratulate the people of the United States on the assembling of Congress at the permanent seat of their Government, and I congratulate you, gentlemen, on the prospect of a residence not to be changed. Although there is cause to apprehend that accommodations are not now so complete as might be wished, yet there is great reason to believe that this inconvenience will cease with the present session.

It would be unbecoming the representatives of this nation to assemble for the first time in this solemn temple without looking up to the Supreme Ruler of the Universe and imploring His blessing.

May this territory be the residence of virtue and happiness! In this city may that piety and virtue, that wisdom and magnanimity, that constancy and self-government, which adorned the great character whose name it bears be forever held in veneration! Here and throughout our country may simple manners, pure morals, and true religion flourish forever!

It is with you, gentlemen, to consider whether the local powers over the District of Columbia vested by the Constitution in the Congress of the United States shall be immediately exercised. If in your opinion this important trust ought now to be executed, you can not fail while performing it to take into view the future probable situation of the territory for the happiness of which you are about to provide. You will consider it as the capital of a great nation advancing with unexampled rapidity in arts, in commerce, in wealth, and in population, and possessing within itself those energies and resources which, if not thrown away or lamentably misdirected, will secure to it a long course of prosperity and self-government.

In compliance with a law of the last session of Congress, the officers and soldiers of the temporary army have been discharged. It affords real pleasure to recollect the honorable testimony they gave of the patriotic motives which brought them into the service of their country, by the readiness and regularity with which they returned to the station of private citizens.

It is in every point of view of such primary importance to carry the laws into prompt and faithful execution, and to render that part of the administration of justice which the Constitution and laws devolve on the Federal courts as convenient to the people as may consist with their present circumstances, that I can not omit once more to recommend to your serious consideration the judiciary system of the United States. No subject is more interesting than this to the public happiness, and to none can those improvements which may have been suggested by experience be more beneficially applied.

A treaty of amity and commerce with the King of Prussia has been concluded and ratified. The ratifications have been exchanged, and I have directed the treaty to be promulgated by proclamation.

The difficulties which suspended the execution of the sixth article of our treaty of amity, commerce, and navigation with Great Britain have not yet been removed. The negotiation on this subject is still depending. As it must be fore the interest and honor of both nations to adjust this difference with good faith, I indulge confidently the expectation that the sincere endeavors of the Government of the United States to bring it to an amicable termination will not be disappointed.

The envoys extraordinary and ministers plenipotentiary from the United States to France were received by the First Consul with the respect due to their character, and three persons with equal powers were appointed to treat with them. Although at the date of the last official intelligence the negotiation had not terminated, yet it is to be hoped that our efforts to effect an accommodation will at length meet with a success proportioned to the sincerity with which they have been so often repeated.

While our best endeavors for the preservation of harmony with all nations will continue to be used, the experience of the world and our own experience admonish us of the insecurity of trusting too confidently to their success. We can not, without committing a dangerous imprudence, abandon those measures of self protection which are adapted to our situation and to which, notwithstanding our pacific policy, the violence and injustice of others may again compel us to resort. While our vast extent of sea coast, the commercial and agriculture habits of our people, the great capital they will continue to trust on the ocean, suggest the system of defense which will be most beneficial to ourselves, our distance from Europe and our resources for maritime strength will enable us to employ it with effect. Seasonable and systematic arrangements, so far as our resources will justify, for a navy adapted to defensive war, and which may in case of necessity be quickly brought into use, seem to be as much recommended by a wise and true economy as by a just regard for our future tranquillity, for the safety of our shores, and for the protection of our property committed to the ocean.

The present Navy of the United States, called suddenly into existence by a great national exigency, has raised us in our own esteem, and by the protection afforded to our commerce has effected to the extent of our expectations the objects for which it was created.

In connection with a navy ought to be contemplated the fortification of some of our principal sea ports and harbors. A variety of considerations, which will readily suggest themselves, urge an attention to this measure of precaution. To give security to our principal ports considerable sums have already been expended, but the works remain incomplete. It is for Congress to determine whether additional appropriations shall be made in order to render competent to the intended purposes the fortifications which have been commenced.

The manufacture of arms within the United States still invites the attention of the National Legislature. At a considerable expense to the public this manufacture has been brought to such a state of maturity as, with continued encouragement, will supersede the necessity of future importations from foreign countries.

Gentlemen of the House of Representatives:

I shall direct the estimates of the appropriations necessary for the ensuing year, together with an account of the public revenue and expenditure to a late period, to be laid before you. I observe with much satisfaction that the product of the revenue during the present year has been more considerable than during any former equal period. This result affords conclusive evidence of the great resources of this country and of the wisdom and efficiency of the measures which have been adopted by Congress for the protection of commerce and preservation of public credit.

Gentlemen of the Senate and Gentlemen of the House of Representatives:

As one of the grand community of nations, our attention is irresistibly drawn to the important scenes which surround us. If they have exhibited an uncommon portion of calamity, it is the province of humanity to deplore and of wisdom to avoid the causes which may have produced it. If, turning our eyes homeward, we find reason to rejoice at the prospect which presents itself; if we perceive the interior of our country prosperous, free, and happy; if all enjoy in safety, under the protection of laws emanating only from the general will, the fruits of their own labor, we ought to fortify and cling to those institutions which have been the source of such real felicity and resist with unabating perseverance the progress of those dangerous innovations which may diminish their influence.

To your patriotism, gentlemen, has been confided the honorable duty of guarding the public interests; and while the past is to your country a sure pledge that it will be faithfully discharged, permit me to assure you that your labors to promote the general happiness will receive from me the most zealous cooperation.

JOHN ADAMS

Notes

1. David McCullough, *John Adams* (New York: Simon & Schuster, 2001), 554.
2. John Ferling, *John Adams: A Life* (New York: Henry Holt, 1996), 507.
3. The other seven presidents between John Adams and Truman died in office and so neither submitted a formal farewell address to the nation nor gave their last scheduled annual message to the Congress.

3

Thomas Jefferson (1801–1809)

Like Adams before him, Jefferson decided not to give a formal farewell address to the nation. Like his predecessor, he used the occasion of his last annual message to the Congress to bid adieu. Unlike his predecessor, Jefferson submitted the annual message in writing.

Why in writing? Because Jefferson disliked public speaking. This personal quirk led him to depart from the precedent of Washington and Adams, who had delivered their annual messages as speeches to the Congress. Thus did Jefferson establish a third precedent—that of submitting the annual message to Capitol Hill in writing. A clerk and not the President would read it to legislators. Jefferson's preference for writing the annual message would prove influential. It became the pattern for more than a century, as president after president followed suit.

Jefferson's final annual message is the shortest of the final written messages—2,675 words. The brevity is interesting considering (1) Jefferson's time in office and (2) the Sage of Monticello's penchant for expressing himself on paper.

Note particularly Jefferson's conclusion. One paragraph in length, a mere 215 words, it serves as the epideictic or ceremonial section of the farewell. Jefferson expressed gratitude to "the two Houses of the Legislature" and to "my fellow citizens," adding that their "support has been my great encouragement under all embarrassments."

Eighth Annual Message
(written to the Congress)
November 8, 1808

The Senate and House of Representatives of the United States:

It would have been a source, fellow-citizens, of much gratification if our last communications from Europe had enabled me to inform you that the belligerent nations, whose disregard of neutral rights has been so destructive to our commerce, had become awakened to the duty and true policy of revoking their unrighteous edicts. That no means might be omitted to produce this salutary effect, I lost no time in availing myself of the act authorizing a suspension, in whole or in part, of the several embargo laws. Our ministers at London and Paris were instructed to explain to the respective Governments there our disposition to exercise the authority in such manner as would withdraw the pretext on which the aggressions were originally founded and open the way for a renewal of that commercial intercourse which it was alleged on all sides had been reluctantly obstructed. As each of those Governments had pledged its readiness to concur in renouncing a measure which reached its adversary through the incontestable rights of neutrals only, and as the measure had been assumed by each as a retaliation for an asserted acquiescence in the aggression of the other, it was reasonably expected that the occasion would have been seized by both for evincing the sincerity of their professions, and for restoring to the commerce of the United States its legitimate freedom. The instructions to our ministers with respect to the different belligerents were necessarily modified with a reference to their different circumstances, and to the condition annexed by law to the Executive power of suspension, requiring a decree of security to our commerce which would not result from a repeal of the decrees of France. Instead of a pledge, therefore, of a suspension of the embargo as to her in case of such a repeal, it was presumed that a sufficient inducement might be found in other considerations, and particularly in the change produced by a compliance with our just demands by one belligerent and a refusal by the other in the relations between the other and the United States. To Great Britain, whose power on the ocean is so ascendant, it was deemed not inconsistent with that condition to state explicitly that on her rescinding her orders in relation to the United States their trade would be opened with her, and remain shut to her enemy in case of his failure to rescind his decrees also. From France no answer has been received, nor any indication that the requisite change in her decrees is contemplated. The favorable reception of the proposition to Great Britain was the less to be doubted, as her orders of council had not only been referred for their vindication to an acquiescence on the part of the United States no longer to be pretended, but as the arrangement proposed, whilst it resisted the illegal decrees of France, involved, moreover, substantially the precise advantages professedly aimed at by the British orders. The arrangement has nevertheless been rejected.

This candid and liberal experiment having thus failed, and no other event having occurred on which a suspension of the embargo by the Executive was authorized, it necessarily remains in the extent originally given to it. We have the satisfaction, however, to reflect that in return for the privations imposed by the measure, and which our fellow citizens in general have borne with patriotism, it has had the important effects of saving our mariners and our vast mercantile property, as well as of affording time for prosecuting the defensive and provisional measures called for by the occasion. It has demonstrated to foreign nations the moderation and firmness which govern our councils, and to our citizens the necessity of uniting in support of the laws and the rights of their country, and has thus long frustrated those usurpations and spoliations which, if resisted, involved war; if submitted to, sacrificed a vital principle of our national independence.

Under a continuance of the belligerent measures which, in defiance of laws which consecrate the rights of neutrals, overspread the ocean with danger, it will rest with the wisdom of Congress to decide on the course best adapted to such a state of things; and bringing with them, as they do, from every part of the Union the sentiments of our constituents, my confidence is strengthened that in forming this decision they will, with an unerring regard to the essential rights and interests of the nation, weigh and compare the painful alternatives out of which a choice is to be made. Nor should I do justice to the virtues which on other occasions have marked the character of our fellow citizens if I did not cherish an equal confidence that the alternative chosen, whatever it may be, will be maintained with all the fortitude and patriotism which the crisis ought to inspire.

The documents containing the correspondences on the subject of the foreign edicts against our commerce, with the instructions given to our ministers at London and Paris, are now laid before you.

The communications made to Congress at their last session explained the posture in which the close of the discussions relating to the attack by a British ship of war on the frigate *Chesapeake* left a subject on which the nation had manifested so honorable a sensibility. Every view of what had passed authorized a belief that immediate steps would be taken by the British Government for redressing a wrong which the more it was investigated appeared the more clearly to require what had not been provided for in the special mission. It is found that no steps have been taken for the purpose. On the contrary, it will be seen in the documents laid before you that the inadmissible preliminary which obstructed the adjustment is still adhered to, and, moreover, that it is now brought into connection with the distinct and irrelative case of the orders in council. The instructions which had been given to our minister at London with a view to facilitate, if necessary, the reparation claimed by the United States are included in the documents communicated.

Our relations with the other powers of Europe have undergone no material changes since your last session. The important negotiations with Spain which had been alternately suspended and resumed necessarily experience a pause under the extraordinary and interesting crisis which distinguishes her internal situation.

With the Barbary Powers we continue in harmony, with the exception of an unjustifiable proceeding of the Dey of Algiers toward our consul to that Regency. Its character and circumstances are now laid before you, and will enable you to decide how far it may, either now or hereafter, call for any measures not within the limits of the Executive authority.

With our Indian neighbors the public peace has been steadily maintained. Some instances of individual wrong have, as at other times, taken place, but in no wise implicating the will of the nation. Beyond the Mississippi the Ioways, the Sacs, and the Alabamas have delivered up for trial and punishment individuals from among themselves accused of murdering citizens of the United States. On this side of the Mississippi the Creeks are exerting themselves to arrest offenders of the same kind, and the Choctaws have manifested their readiness and desire for amicable and just arrangements respecting depredations committed by disorderly persons of their tribe. And, generally, from a conviction that we consider them as a part of ourselves, and cherish with sincerity their rights and interests, the attachment of the Indian tribes is gaining strength daily—is extending from the nearer to the more remote, and will amply requite us for the justice and friendship practiced toward them. Husbandry and household manufacture are advancing among them more rapidly with the Southern than Northern tribes, from circumstances of soil and climate, and one of the two great divisions of the Cherokee Nation have now under consideration to solicit the citizenship of the United States, and to be identified with us in laws and government in such progressive manner as we shall think best.

In consequence of the appropriations of the last session of Congress for the security of our sea port towns and harbors, such works of defense have been erected as seemed to be called for by the situation of the several places, their relative importance, and the scale of expense indicated by the amount of the appropriation. These works will chiefly be finished in the course of the present season, except at New York and New Orleans, where most was to be done; and although a great proportion of the last appropriation has been expended on the former place, yet some further views will be submitted to Congress for rendering its security entirely adequate against naval enterprise. A view of what has been done at the several places, and of what is proposed to be done, shall be communicated as soon as the several reports are received.

Of the gunboats authorized by the act of December last, it has been thought necessary to build only 103 in the present year. These, with those before possessed, are sufficient for the harbors and waters most exposed, and the residents will require little time for their construction when it shall be deemed necessary.

Under the act of the last session for raising an additional military force so many officers were immediately appointed as were necessary for carrying on the business of recruiting, and in proportion as it advanced others have been added. We have reason to believe their success has been satisfactory, although such returns have not yet been received as enable me to present you a statement of the numbers engaged.

I have not thought it necessary in the course of the last season to call for any general detachments of militia or of volunteers under the laws passed for that purpose. For the ensuing season, however, they will be required to be in readiness should their service be wanted. Some small and special detachments have been necessary to maintain the laws of embargo on that portion of our northern frontier which offered peculiar facilities for evasion, but these were replaced as soon as it could be done by bodies of new recruits. By the aid of these and of the armed vessels called into service in other quarters the spirit of disobedience and abuse, which manifested itself early and with sensible effect while we were unprepared to meet it, has been considerably repressed.

Considering the extraordinary character of the times in which we live, our attention should unremittingly be fixed on the safety of our country. For a people who are free, and who mean to remain so, a well organized and armed militia is their best security. It is therefore incumbent on us at every meeting to revise the condition of the militia, and to ask ourselves if it is prepared to repel a powerful enemy at every point of our territories exposed to invasion. Some of the States have paid a laudable attention to this object, but every degree of neglect is to be found among others. Congress alone having the power to produce an uniform state of preparation in this great organ of defense, the interests which they so deeply feel in their own and their country's security will present this as among the most important objects of their deliberation.

Under the acts of March 11 and April 23 respecting arms, the difficulty of procuring them from abroad during the present situation and dispositions of Europe induced us to direct our whole efforts to the means of internal supply. The public factories have therefore been enlarged, additional machineries erected, and, in proportion as artificers can be found or formed, their effect, already more than doubled, may be increased so as to keep pace with the yearly increase of the militia. The annual sums appropriated by the latter have been directed to the encouragement of private factories of arms, and contracts have been entered into with individual undertakers to nearly the amount of the first year's appropriation.

The suspension of our foreign commerce, produced by the injustice of the belligerent powers and the consequent losses and sacrifices of our citizens are subjects of just concern. The situation into which we have thus been forced has impelled us to apply a portion of our industry and capital to internal manufactures and improvements. The extent of this conversion is daily increasing, and little doubt remains that the establishments formed and forming will, under the auspices of cheaper materials and subsistence, the freedom of labor from taxation with us, and of protecting duties and prohibitions, become permanent. The commerce with the Indians, too, within our own boundaries is likely to receive abundant aliment from the same internal source, and will secure to them peace and the progress of civilization, undisturbed by practices hostile to both.

The accounts of the receipts and expenditures during the year ending the 30th of September last being not yet made up, a correct statement will hereafter be transmitted from the Treasury. In the meantime it is ascertained that the receipts have amounted to near $18,000,000, which, with the $8,500,000 in the Treasury at the beginning of the year, have enabled us, after meeting the current demands and interest incurred, to pay $2,300,000 of the principal of our funded debt, and left us in the Treasury on that day near $14,000,000. Of these, $5,350,000 will be necessary to pay what will be due on the 1st day of January next, which will complete the reimbursement of the 8 percent stock. These payments, with those made in the 6 years and a half preceding, will have extinguished $33,580,000 of the principal of the funded debt, being the whole which could be paid or purchased within the limits of the law and of our contracts, and the amount of principal thus discharged will have liberated the revenue from about $2,000,000 of interest and added that sum annually to the disposable surplus. The probable accumulation of the surpluses of revenue beyond what can be applied to the payment of the public debt whenever the freedom and safety of our commerce shall be restored merits the consideration of Congress. Shall it lie unproductive in the public vaults? Shall the revenue be reduced? Or shall it not rather be appropriated to the improvements of roads, canals, rivers, education, and other great foundations of prosperity and union under the powers which Congress may already possess or such amendment to the Constitution as may be approved by the States? While uncertain of the course of things, the time may be advantageously employed in obtaining the powers necessary for a system of improvement, should that be thought best.

Availing myself of this the last occasion which will occur of addressing the two Houses of the Legislature at their meeting, I can not omit the expression of my sincere gratitude for the repeated proofs of confidence manifested to me by themselves and their predecessors since my call to the administration and the many indulgences experienced at their hands. The same grateful acknowledgements are due to my fellow-citizens generally, whose support has been my great encouragement under all embarrassments. In the transaction of their business I can not have escaped error. It is incident to our imperfect nature. But I may say with truth my errors have been of the understanding, not of intention, and that the advancement of their rights and interests has been the constant motive for every measure. On these considerations I solicit their indulgence. Looking forward with anxiety to future destinies, I trust that in their steady character, unshaken by difficulties, in their love of liberty, obedience to law, and support of the public authorities I see a sure guaranty of the permanence of our Republic; and, retiring from the charge of their affairs, I carry with me the consolation of a firm persuasion that Heaven has in store for our beloved country long ages to come of prosperity and happiness.

TH. JEFFERSON

4

James Madison (1809–1817)

The Constitution would become a favorite topic of outgoing presidents. Final annual messages in the nineteenth century are filled with explicit references to constitutional governance. Not surprisingly, that precedent can be traced back to the man called the "Father of the Constitution," James Madison. In a relatively brief final annual message, Madison explicitly refers to the Constitution seven times. By contrast, Washington did not explicitly name the Constitution in his final annual message. Adams mentioned it only twice. Jefferson mentioned it only once.

Washington's farewell Address (as distinguished from his final annual message to the Congress) is another matter. It will be recalled that Madison had a hand in writing the Washington farewell. So it should come as no surprise that the Constitution or constitutional governance is explicitly mentioned nine times in that address. It seems that if Madison had any role in shaping a farewell or final message, the Constitution was going to be discussed.

As one of the most influential shapers of that great document, Madison was perhaps justified to wax eloquent when he wrote:

> I can indulge the proud reflection that the American people have reached in safety and success their fortieth year as an independent nation; that for nearly an entire generation they have had experience of their present Constitution, the offspring of their undisturbed deliberations and of their free choice; that they have found it to bear the trials of adverse as well as prosperous circumstances; to contain in its combination of the federate and elective principles a reconcilement of public strength with individual liberty, of national power for the defense of national rights with a security against wars of injustice, of ambition, and vainglory in the fundamental provision which subjects all questions of war to the will of the nation itself, which is to pay its costs and feel its calamities. Nor is it less a peculiar felicity of this Constitution, so dear to us all, that it is found to be capable, without losing its vital energies, of expanding itself over a spacious territory with the increase and expansion of the community for whose benefit it was established.

In this paean to the Constitution, there is little hint of the crisis to come some four decades hence. However, it is worth noting that James Madison, a Southerner, wrote the first major farewell document to deal with the presence of chattel slavery in the United States.

Eighth Annual Message
(written to the Congress)
December 3, 1816

Fellow-Citizens of the Senate and House of Representatives:

In reviewing the present state of our country, our attention can not be withheld from the effect produced by peculiar seasons which have very generally impaired the annual gifts of the earth and threatened scarcity in particular districts. Such, however, is the variety of soils, of climates, and of products within our extensive limits that the aggregate resources for subsistence are more than sufficient for the aggregate wants. And as far as an economy of consumption, more than usual, may be necessary, our thankfulness is due to Providence for what is far more than a compensation, in the remarkable health which has distinguished the present year.

Amidst the advantages which have succeeded the peace of Europe, and that of the United States with Great Britain, in a general invigoration of industry among us and in the extension of our commerce, the value of which is more and more disclosing itself to commercial nations, it is to be regretted that a depression is experienced by particular branches of our manufactures and by a portion of our navigation. As the first proceeds in an essential degree from an excess of imported merchandise, which carries a check in its own tendency, the cause in its present extent can not be very long in duration. The evil will not, however, be viewed by Congress without a recollection that manufacturing establishments, if suffered to sink too low or languish too long, may not revive after the causes shall have ceased, and that in the vicissitudes of human affairs situations may recur in which a dependence on foreign sources for indispensable supplies may be among the most serious embarrassments.

The depressed state of our navigation is to be ascribed in a material degree to its exclusion from the colonial ports of the nation most extensively connected with us in commerce, and from the indirect operation of that exclusion.

Previous to the late convention at London between the United States and Great Britain the relative state of the navigation laws of the two countries, growing out of the treaty of 1794, had given to the British navigation a material advantage over the American in the intercourse between the American ports and British ports in Europe. The convention of London equalized the laws of the two countries relating to those ports, leaving the intercourse between our ports and the ports of the British colonies subject, as before, to the respective regulations of the parties. The British Government enforcing now regulations which prohibit a trade between its colonies and the United States in American vessels, whilst they permit a trade in British vessels, the American navigation loses accordingly, and the loss is augmented by the advantage which is given to the British competition over the American in the navigation between our ports and British ports in Europe by the circuitous voyages enjoyed by the one and not enjoyed by the other.

The reasonableness of the rule of reciprocity applied to one branch of the commercial intercourse has been pressed on our part as equally applicable to both branches; but it is ascertained that the British cabinet declines all negotiation on the subject, with a disavowal, however, of any disposition to view in an unfriendly light whatever countervailing regulations the United States may oppose to the regulations of which they complain. The wisdom of the Legislature will decide on the course which, under these circumstances, is prescribed by a joint regard to the amicable relations between the two nations and to the just interests of the United States.

I have the satisfaction to state, generally, that we remain in amity with foreign powers.

An occurrence has indeed taken place in the Gulf of Mexico which, if sanctioned by the Spanish Government, may make an exception as to that power. According to the report of our naval commander on that station, one of our public armed vessels was attacked by an over-powering force under a Spanish commander, and the American flag, with the officers and crew, insulted in a manner calling for prompt reparation. This has been demanded. In the mean time a frigate and a smaller vessel of war have been ordered into that Gulf for the protection of our commerce. It would be improper to omit that the representative of His Catholic Majesty in the United States lost no time in giving the strongest assurances that no hostile order could have emanated from his Government, and that it will be as ready to do as to expect whatever the nature of the case and the friendly relations of the two countries shall be found to require.

The posture of our affairs with Algiers at the present moment is not known. The Dey, drawing pretexts from circumstances for which the United States were not answerable, addressed a letter to this Government declaring the treaty last concluded with him to have been annulled by our violation of it, and presenting as the alternative war or a renewal of the former treaty, which stipulated, among other things, an annual tribute. The answer, with an explicit declaration that the United States preferred war to tribute, required his recognition and observance of the treaty last made, which abolishes tribute and the slavery of our captured citizens. The result of the answer has not been received. Should he renew his warfare on our commerce, we rely on the protection it will find in our naval force actually in the Mediterranean.

With the other Barbary States our affairs have undergone no change.

The Indian tribes within our limits appear also disposed to remain at peace. From several of them purchases of lands have been made particularly favorable to the wishes and security of our frontier settlements, as well as to the general interests of the nation. In some instances the titles, though not supported by due proof, and clashing those of one tribe with the claims of another, have been extinguished by double purchases, the benevolent policy of the United States preferring the augmented expense to the hazard of doing injustice or to the enforcement of justice against a feeble and untutored people by means involving or threatening an effusion of blood. I am happy to add that the tranquillity which has been restored among the tribes themselves, as well as between them and our own population, will favor the resumption of the work of civilization which had made an encouraging progress among some tribes, and that the facility is increasing for extending that divided and individual ownership, which exists now in movable property only, to the soil itself, and of thus establishing in the culture and improvement of it the true foundation for a transit from the habits of the savage to the arts and comforts of social life.

As a subject of the highest importance to the national welfare, I must again earnestly recommend to the consideration of Congress a reorganization of the militia on a plan which will form it into classes according to the periods of life more or less adapted to military services. An efficient militia is authorized and contemplated by the Constitution and required by the spirit and safety of free government. The present organization of our militia is universally regarded as less efficient than it ought to be made, and no organization can be better calculated to give to it its due force than a classification which will assign the foremost place in the defense of the country to that portion of its citizens whose activity and animation best enable them to rally to its standard. Besides the consideration that a time of peace is the time when the change can be made with most convenience and equity, it will now be aided by the experience of a recent war in which the militia bore so interesting a part.

Congress will call to mind that no adequate provision has yet been made for the uniformity of weights and measures also contemplated by the Constitution. The great utility of a standard fixed in its nature and founded on the easy rule of decimal proportions is sufficiently obvious. It led the Government at an early stage to preparatory steps for introducing it, and a completion of the work will be a just title to the public gratitude.

The importance which I have attached to the establishment of a university within this District on a scale and for objects worthy of the American nation induces me to renew my recommendation of it to the favorable consideration of Congress. And I particularly invite again their attention to the expediency of exercising their existing powers, and, where necessary, of resorting to the prescribed mode of enlarging them, in order to effectuate a comprehensive system of roads and canals, such as will have the effect of drawing more closely together every part of our country by promoting intercourse and improvements and by increasing the share of every part in the common stock of national prosperity.

Occurrences having taken place which shew that the statutory provisions for the dispensation of criminal justice are deficient in relation both to places and to persons under the exclusive cognizance of the national authority, an amendment of the law embracing such cases will merit the earliest attention of the Legislature. It will be a seasonable occasion also for inquiring how far legislative interposition may be further requisite in providing penalties for offenses designated in the Constitution or in the statutes, and to which either no penalties are annexed or none with sufficient certainty. And I submit to the wisdom of Congress whether a more enlarged revisal of the criminal code be not expedient for the purpose of mitigating in certain cases penalties which were adopted into it antecedent to experiment and examples which justify and recommend a more lenient policy.

The United States, having been the first to abolish within the extent of their authority the transportation of the natives of Africa into slavery, by prohibiting the introduction of slaves and by punishing their citizens participating in the traffic, can not but be gratified at the progress made by concurrent efforts of other nations toward a general suppression of so great an evil. They must feel at the same time the greater solicitude to give the fullest efficacy to their own regulations. With that view, the interposition of Congress appears to be required by the violations and evasions which it is suggested are chargeable on unworthy citizens who mingle in the slave trade under foreign flags and with foreign ports, and by collusive importations of slaves into the United States through adjoining ports and territories. I present the subject to Congress with a full assurance of their disposition to apply all the remedy which can be afforded by an amendment of the law. The regulations which were intended to guard against abuses of a kindred character in the trade between the several States ought also to be rendered more effectual for their humane object.

To these recommendations I add, for the consideration of Congress, the expediency of a remodification of the judiciary establishment, and of an additional department in the executive branch of the Government.

The first is called for by the accruing business which necessarily swells the duties of the Federal courts, and by the great and widening space within which justice is to be dispensed by them. The time seems to have arrived which claims for members of the Supreme Court a relief from itinerary fatigues, incompatible as well with the age which a portion of them will always have attained as with the researches and preparations which are due to their stations and to the juridical reputation of their country. And considerations equally cogent require a more convenient organization of the subordinate tribunals, which may be accomplished without an objectionable increase of the number or expense of the judges.

The extent and variety of executive business also accumulating with the progress of our country and its growing population call for an additional department, to be charged with duties now overburdening other departments and with such as have not been annexed to any department.

The course of experience recommends, as another improvement in the executive establishment, that the provision for the station of Attorney-General, whose residence at the seat of Government, official connections with it, and the management of the public business before the judiciary preclude an extensive participation in professional emoluments, be made more adequate to his services and his relinquishments, and that, with a view to his reasonable accommodation and to a proper depository of his official opinions and proceedings, there be included in the provision the usual appurtenances to a public office.

In directing the legislative attention to the state of the finances it is a subject of great gratification to find that even within the short period which has elapsed since the return of peace the revenue has far exceeded all the current demands upon the Treasury, and that under any probable diminution of its future annual products which the vicissitudes of commerce may occasion it will afford an ample fund for the effectual and early extinguishment of the public debt. It has been estimated that during the year 1816 the actual receipts of revenue at the Treasury, including the balance at the commencement of the year, and excluding the proceeds of loans and Treasury notes, will amount to about the sum of $47,000,000; that during the same year the actual payments at the Treasury, including the payment of the arrearages of the War Department as well as the payment of a considerable excess beyond the annual appropriations, will amount to about the sum of $38,000,000, and that consequently at the close of the year there will be a surplus in the Treasury of about the sum of $9,000,000.

The operations of the Treasury continued to be obstructed by difficulties arising from the condition of the national currency, but they have nevertheless been effectual to a beneficial extent in the reduction of the public debt and the establishment of the public credit. The floating debt of Treasury notes and temporary loans will soon be entirely discharged. The aggregate of the funded debt, composed of debts incurred during the wars of 1776 and 1812, has been estimated with reference to the first of January next at a sum not exceeding $110,000,000. The ordinary annual expenses of the Government for the maintenance of all its institutions, civil, military, and naval, have been estimated at a sum less than $20,000,000, and the permanent revenue to be derived from all the existing sources has been estimated at a sum of $25,000,000.

Upon this general view of the subject it is obvious that there is only wanting to the fiscal prosperity of the Government the restoration of an uniform medium of exchange. The resources and the faith of the nation, displayed in the system which Congress has established, insure respect and confidence both at home and abroad. The local accumulations of the revenue have already enabled the Treasury to meet the public engagements in the local currency of most of the States, and it is expected that the same cause will produce the same effect throughout the Union; but for the interests of the community at large, as well as for the purposes of the Treasury, it is essential that the nation should possess a currency of equal value, credit, and use wherever it may circulate. The Constitution has intrusted Congress exclusively with the power of creating and regulating a currency of that description, and the measures which were taken during the last session in execution of the power give every promise of success. The Bank of the United States has been organized under auspices the most favorable, and can not fail to be an important auxiliary to those measures.

For a more enlarged view of the public finances, with a view of the measures pursued by the Treasury Department previous to the resignation of the late Secretary, I transmit an extract from the last report of that officer. Congress will perceive in it ample proofs of the solid foundation on which the financial prosperity of the nation rests, and will do justice to the distinguished ability and successful exertions with which the duties of the Department were executed during a period remarkable for its difficulties and its peculiar perplexities.

The period of my retiring from the public service being at little distance, I shall find no occasion more proper than the present for expressing to my fellow-citizens my deep sense of the continued confidence and kind support which I have received from them. My grateful recollection of these distinguished marks of their favorable regard can never cease, and with the consciousness that, if I have not served my country with greater ability, I have served it with a sincere devotion will accompany me as a source of unfailing gratification.

Happily, I shall carry with me from the public theater other sources, which those who love their country most will best appreciate. I shall behold it blessed with tranquillity and prosperity at home and with peace and respect abroad. I can indulge the proud reflection that the American people have reached in safety and success their fortieth year as an independent nation; that for nearly an entire generation they have had experience of their present Constitution, the offspring of their undisturbed deliberations and of their free choice; that they have found it to bear the trials of adverse as well as prosperous circumstances; to contain in its combination of the federate and elective principles a reconcilement of public strength with individual liberty, of national power for the defense of national rights with a security against wars of injustice, of ambition, and vainglory in the fundamental provision which subjects all questions of war to the will of the nation itself, which is to pay its costs and feel its calamities. Nor is it less a peculiar felicity of this Constitution, so dear to us all, that it is found to be capable, without losing its vital energies, of expanding itself over a spacious territory with the increase and expansion of the community for whose benefit it was established.

And may I not be allowed to add to this gratifying spectacle that I shall read in the character of the American people, in their devotion to true liberty and to the Constitution which is its palladium, sure presages that the destined career of my country will exhibit a Government pursuing the public good as its sole object, and regulating its means by the great principles consecrated in its charter and by those moral principles to which they are so well allied; a Government which watches over the purity of elections, the freedom of speech and of the press, the trial by jury, and the equal interdict against encroachments and compacts between religion and the state; which maintains inviolably the maxims of public faith, the security of persons and property, and encourages in every authorized mode the general diffusion of knowledge which guarantees to public liberty its permanency and to those who possess the blessing the true enjoyment of it; a Government which avoids intrusions on the internal repose of other nations, and repels them from its own; which does justice to all nations with a readiness equal to the firmness with which it requires justice from them; and which, whilst it refines its domestic code from every ingredient not congenial with the precepts of an enlightened age and the sentiments of a virtuous people, seeks by appeals to reason and by its liberal examples to infuse into the law which governs the civilized world a spirit which may diminish the frequency or circumscribe the calamities of war, and meliorate the social and beneficent relations of peace; a Government, in a word, whose conduct within and without may bespeak the most noble of ambitions—that of promoting peace on earth and good will to man.

These contemplations, sweetening the remnant of my days, will animate my prayers for the happiness of my beloved country, and a perpetuity of the institutions under which it is enjoyed.

JAMES MADISON

5

James Monroe (1817–1825)

With James Monroe we see a distinct trend emerge—that of writing considerably longer final annual messages than the first presidents did. Madison's final annual message is 3,360 words, whereas Monroe's is more than twice as long, at 8,400 words.

Monroe sprinkled his message with the first principles of political economy. For example, he explained that "The principles upon which the commercial policy of the United States is founded . . . are essentially connected with those upon which their independence was declared, and owe their origin to the enlightened men who took the lead in our affairs at that important epoch."

There are at least two major historical references in this last annual message that will help readers today understand the strong sentiments of early Americans. Those who look at a map and are curious where all the Fayette, Fayetteville, and Lafayette place-names come from will gain insight from the following passage. "In August last," Monroe wrote, "[the Marquis de Lafayette] arrived at New York, where he was received with the warmth of affection and gratitude to which his very important and disinterested services and sacrifices in our Revolutionary struggle so eminently entitled him. A corresponding sentiment has since been manifested in his favor throughout every portion of our Union, and affectionate invitations have been given him to extend his visits to them. . . . At every designated point of rendezvous the whole population of the neighboring country has been assembled to greet him, among whom it has excited in a peculiar manner the sensibility of all to behold the surviving members of our Revolutionary contest, civil and military, who had shared with him in the toils and dangers of the war, many of them in a decrepit state. A more interesting spectacle, it is believed, was never witnessed, because none could be founded on purer principles, none proceed from higher or more disinterested motives. That the feelings of those who had fought and bled with him in a common cause should have been much excited was natural." This enthusiasm for the French Marquis helps explain why there are at least four Fayettes, seven Fayettevilles, and eight Lafayettes in the United States to this day.

The second major historical reference is to the Greek war of independence against the Ottoman Turks, then in progress (1821–1829). That war was symbolically important to the new republic because of the history of ancient Greece and its identification with self-government. The Greek war helped inspire a revival of Greek architecture in the America of Monroe's day. That accounts for all the white "temple front" houses and public buildings of the period, many of which stand today.

Eighth Annual Message
(written to the Congress)
December 7, 1824

Fellow-Citizens of the Senate and House of Representatives:

The view which I have now to present to you of our affairs, foreign and domestic, realizes the most sanguine anticipations which have been entertained of the public prosperity. If we look to the whole, our growth as a nation continues to be rapid beyond example; if to the States which compose it, the same gratifying spectacle is exhibited. Our expansion over the vast territory within our limits has been great, without indicating any decline in those sections from which the emigration has been most conspicuous. We have daily gained strength by a native population in every quarter—a population devoted to our happy system of government and cherishing the bond of union with internal affection. Experience has already shown that the difference of climate and of industry, proceeding from that cause, inseparable from such vast domains, and which under other systems might have a repulsive tendency, can not fail to produce with us under wise regulations the opposite effect. What one portion wants the other may supply; and this will be most sensibly felt by the parts most distant from each other, forming thereby a domestic market and an active intercourse between the extremes and throughout every portion of our Union. Thus by a happy distribution of power between the National and State Governments, Governments which rest exclusively on the sovereignty of the people and are fully adequate to the great purposes for which they were respectively instituted, causes which might otherwise lead to dismemberment operate powerfully to draw us closer together. In every other circumstance a correct view of the actual state of our Union must be equally gratifying to our constituents. Our relations with foreign powers are of a friendly character, although certain interesting differences remain unsettled with some. Our revenue under the mild system of impost and tonnage continues to be adequate to all the purposes of the Government. Our agriculture, commerce, manufactures, and navigation flourish. Our fortifications are advancing in the degree authorized by existing appropriations to maturity, and due progress is made in the augmentation of the Navy to the limit prescribed for it by law. For these blessings we owe to Almighty God, from whom we derive them, and with profound reverence, our most grateful and unceasing acknowledgments.

In adverting to our relations with foreign powers, which are always an object of the highest importance, I have to remark that of the subjects which have been brought into discussion with them during the present Administration some have been satisfactorily terminated, others have been suspended, to be resumed hereafter under circumstances more favorable to success, and others are still in negotiation, with the hope that they may be adjusted with mutual accommodation to the interests and to the satisfaction of the respective parties. It has been the invariable object of this Government to cherish the most friendly relations with every power, and on principles and conditions which might make them permanent. A systematic effort has been made to place our commerce with each power on a footing of perfect reciprocity, to settle with each in a spirit of candor and liberality all existing differences, and to anticipate and remove so far as it might be practicable all causes of future variance.

It having been stipulated by the seventh article of the convention of navigation and commerce which was concluded on the 24th of June, 1822, between the United States and France, that the said convention should continue in force for two years from the first of October of that year, and for an indefinite term afterwards, unless one of the parties should declare its intention to renounce it, in which event it should cease to operate at the end of 6 months from such declaration, and no such intention having been announced, the convention having been found advantageous to both parties, it has since remained, and still remains, in force. At the time when that convention was concluded many interesting subjects were left unsettled, and particularly our claim to indemnity for spoliations which were committed on our commerce in the late wars. For these interests and claims it was in the contemplation of the parties to make provision at a subsequent day by a more comprehensive and definitive treaty. The object has been duly attended to since by the Executive, but as yet it has not been accomplished. It is hoped that a favorable opportunity will present itself for opening a negotiation which may embrace and arrange all existing differences and every other concern in which they have a common interest upon the accession of the present King of France, an event which has occurred since the close of the last session of Congress.

With Great Britain our commercial intercourse rests on the same footing that it did at the last session. By the convention of 1815, the commerce between the United States and the British dominions in Europe and the East Indies was arranged on a principle of reciprocity. That convention was confirmed and continued in force, with slight exceptions, by a subsequent treaty for the term of ten years from the 20th of October, 1818, the date of the latter. The trade with the British colonies in the West Indies has not as yet been arranged, by treaty or otherwise, to our satisfaction. An approach to that result has been made by legislative acts, whereby many serious impediments which had been raised by the parties in defense of their respective claims were removed. An earnest desire exists, and has been manifested on the part of this Government, to place the commerce with the colonies, likewise, on a footing of reciprocal advantage, and it is hoped that the British Government, seeing the justice of the proposal and its importance to the colonies, will ere long accede to it.

The commissioners who were appointed for the adjustment of the boundary between the territories of the United States and those of Great Britain, specified in the fifth article of the treaty of Ghent, having disagreed in their decision, and both Governments having agreed to establish that boundary by amicable negotiation between them, it is hoped that it may be satisfactorily adjusted in that mode. The boundary specified by the sixth article has been established by the decision of the commissioners. From the progress made in that provided for by the seventh, according to a report recently received, there is good cause to presume that it will be settled in the course of the ensuing year.

It is a cause of serious regret that no arrangement has yet been finally concluded between the two Governments to secure by joint cooperation the suppression of the slave trade. It was the object of the British Government in the early stages of the negotiation to adopt a plan for the suppression which should include the concession of the mutual right of search by the ships of war of each party of the vessels of the other for suspected offenders. This was objected to by this Government on the principle that as the right of search was a right of war of a belligerent toward a neutral power it might have an ill effect to extend it by treaty, to an offense which had been made comparatively mild, to a time of peace. Anxious, however, for the suppression of this trade, it was thought advisable, in compliance with a resolution of the House of Representatives, founded on an act of Congress, to propose to the British Government an expedient which should be free from that objection and more effectual for the object, by making it piratical. In that mode the enormity of the crime would place the offenders out of the protection of their Government, and involve no question of search or other question between the parties touching their respective rights. It was believed, also, that it would completely suppress the trade in the vessels of both parties, and by their respective citizens and subjects in those of other powers, with whom it was hoped that the odium which would thereby be attached to it would produce a corresponding arrangement, and by means thereof its entire extirpation forever. A convention to this effect was concluded and signed in London on the 13th day of March, 1824, by plenipotentiaries duly authorized by both Governments, to the ratification of which certain obstacles have arisen which are not yet entirely removed. The difference between the parties still remaining has been reduced to a point not of sufficient magnitude, as is presumed, to be permitted to defeat an object so near to the heart of both nations and so desirable to the friends of humanity throughout the world. As objections, however, to the principle recommended by the House of Representatives, or at least to the consequences inseparable from it, and which are understood to apply to the law, have been raised, which may deserve a reconsideration of the whole subject, I have thought it proper to suspend the conclusion of a new convention until the definitive sentiments of Congress may be ascertained. The documents relating to the negotiation are with that intent submitted to your consideration.

Our commerce with Sweden has been placed on a footing of perfect reciprocity by treaty, and with Russia, the Netherlands, Prussia, the free Hanseatic cities, the Dukedom of Oldenburg, and Sardinia by internal regulations on each side, founded on mutual agreement between the respective Governments.

The principles upon which the commercial policy of the United States is founded are to be traced to an early period. They are essentially connected with those upon which their independence was declared, and owe their origin to the enlightened men who took the lead in our affairs at that important epoch. They are developed in their first treaty of commerce with France of 6th February, 1778, and by a formal commission which was instituted immediately after the conclusion of their Revolutionary struggle, for the purpose of negotiating treaties of commerce with every European power. The first treaty of the United States with Prussia, which was negotiated by that commission, affords a signal illustration of those principles. The act of Congress of the 3d March, 1815, adopted immediately after the return of a general peace, was a new overture to foreign nations to establish our commercial relations with them on the basis of free and equal reciprocity. That principle has pervaded all the acts of Congress and all the negotiations of the Executive on the subject.

A convention for the settlement of important questions in relation to the North West coast of this continent and its adjoining seas was concluded and signed at St. Petersburg on the 5th day of April last by the minister plenipotentiary of the United States and plenipotentiaries of the Imperial Government of Russia. It will immediately be laid before the Senate for the exercise of the constitutional authority of that body with reference to its ratification. It is proper to add that the manner in which this negotiation was invited and conducted on the part of the Emperor has been very satisfactory.

The great and extraordinary changes which have happened in the Governments of Spain and Portugal within the last two years, without seriously affecting the friendly relations which under all of them have been maintained with those powers by the United States, have been obstacles to the adjustment of the particular subjects of discussion which have arisen with each. A resolution of the Senate adopted at their last session called for information as to the effect produced upon our relations with Spain by the recognition on the part of the United States of the independent South American Governments. The papers containing that information are now communicated to Congress.

A chargé d'affaires has been received from the independent Government of Brazil. That country, heretofore a colonial possession of Portugal, had some years since been proclaimed by the Sovereign of Portugal himself an independent Kingdom. Since his return to Lisbon a revolution in Brazil has established a new Government there with an imperial title, at the head of which is placed a prince, in whom the regency had been vested by the King at the time of his departure. There is reason to expect that by amicable negotiation the independence of Brazil will ere long be recognized by Portugal herself.

With the remaining powers of Europe, with those on the coast of Barbary, and with all the new South American States our relations are of a friendly character. We have ministers plenipotentiary residing with the Republics of Colombia and Chile, and have received ministers of the same rank from Colombia, Guatemala, Buenos Ayres, and Mexico. Our commercial relations with all those States are mutually beneficial and increasing. With the Republic of Colombia a treaty of commerce has been formed, of which a copy is received and the original daily expected. A negotiation for a like treaty would have been commenced with Buenos Ayres had it not been prevented by the indisposition and lamented decease of Mr. Rodney, our minister there, and to whose memory the most respectful attention has been shewn by the Government of that Republic. An advantageous alteration in our treaty with Tunis has been obtained by our consular agent residing there, the official document of which when received will be laid before the Senate.

The attention of the Government has been drawn with great solicitude to other subjects, and particularly to that relating to a state of maritime war, involving the relative rights of neutral and belligerent in such wars. Most of the difficulties which we have experienced and of the losses which we have sustained since the establishment of our independence have proceeded from the unsettled state of those rights and the extent to which the belligerent claim has been carried against the neutral party. It is impossible to look back on the occurrences of the late wars in Europe, and to behold the disregard which was paid to our rights as a neutral power, and the waste which was made of our commerce by the parties to those wars by various acts of their respective Governments, and under the pretext by each that the other had set the example, without great mortification and a fixed purpose never to submit to the like in future. An attempt to remove those causes of possible variance by friendly negotiation and on just principles which should be applicable to all parties could, it was presumed, be viewed by none other than as a proof of an earnest desire to preserve those relations with every power. In the late war between France and Spain a crisis occurred in which it seemed probable that all controvertible principles involved in such wars might be brought into discussion and settled to the satisfaction of all parties. Propositions having this object in view have been made to the Governments of Great Britain, France, Russia, and of other powers, which have been received in a friendly manner by all, but as yet no treaty has been formed with either for its accomplishment. The policy will, it is presumed, be persevered in, and in the hope that it may be successful.

It will always be recollected that with one of the parties to those wars and from whom we received those injuries, we sought redress by war. From the other, by whose then reigning Government our vessels were seized in port as well as at sea and their cargoes confiscated, indemnity has been expected, but has not yet been rendered. It was under the influence of the latter that our vessels were likewise seized by the Governments of Spain, Holland, Denmark, Sweden, and Naples, and from whom indemnity has been claimed and is still expected, with the exception of Spain, by whom it has been rendered. With both parties we had abundant cause of war, but we had no alternative but to resist that which was most powerful at sea and pressed us nearest at home. With this all differences were settled by a treaty, founded on conditions fair and honorable to both, and which has been so far executed with perfect good faith. It has been earnestly hoped that the other would of its own accord, and from a sentiment of justice and conciliation, make to our citizens the indemnity to which they are entitled, and thereby remove from our relations any just cause of discontent on our side.

It is estimated that the receipts into the Treasury during the current year, exclusive of loans, will exceed $18,500,000, which, with the sum remaining in the Treasury at the end of the last year, amounting to $9,463,922.81 will, after discharging the current disbursements of the year, the interest on the public debt, and upward of $11,633,011.52 of the principal, leave a balance of more than $3,000,000 in the Treasury on the 1st day of January next.

A larger amount of the debt contracted during the late war, bearing an interest of 6 percent, becoming redeemable in the course of the ensuing year than could be discharged by the ordinary revenue, the act of the 26th of May authorized a loan of $5,000,000 at 4½ percent to meet the same. By this arrangement an annual saving will accrue to the public of $75,000.

Under the act of the 24th of May last a loan of $5,000,000 was authorized, in order to meet the awards under the Florida treaty, which was negotiated at par with the Bank of the United States at 4½ percent, the limit of interest fixed by the act. By this provision the claims of our citizens who had sustained so great a loss by spoliations, and from whom indemnity had been so long withheld, were promptly paid. For these advances the public will be amply repaid at no distant day by the sale of the lands in Florida. Of the great advantages resulting from the acquisition of the Territory in other respects too high an estimate can not be formed.

It is estimated that the receipts into the Treasury during the year 1825 will be sufficient to meet the disbursements of the year, including the sum of $10,000,000, which is annually appropriated by the act of constituting the sinking fund to the payment of the principal and interest of the public debt.

The whole amount of the public debt on the 1st of January next may be estimated at $86,000,000, inclusive of $2,500,000 of the loan authorized by the act of the 26th of May last. In this estimate is included a stock of $7,000,000, issued for the purchase of that amount of the capital stock of the Bank of the United States, and which, as the stock of the bank still held by the Government will at least be fully equal to its reimbursement, ought not to be considered as constituting a part of the public debt. Estimating, then, the whole amount of the public debt at $79,000,000 and regarding the annual receipts and expenditures of the Government, a well-founded hope may be entertained that, should no unexpected event occur, the whole of the public debt may be discharged in the course of 10 years, and the Government be left at liberty thereafter to apply such portion of the revenue as may not be necessary for current expenses to such other objects as may be most conducive to the public security and welfare. That the sums applicable to these objects will be very considerable may be fairly concluded when it is recollected that a large amount of the public revenue has been applied since the late war to the construction of the public buildings in this city; to the erection of fortifications along the coast and of arsenals in different parts of the Union; to the augmentation of the Navy; to the extinguishment of the Indian title to large tracts of fertile territory; to the acquisition of Florida; to pensions to Revolutionary officers and soldiers, and to invalids of the late war. On many of these objects the expense will annually be diminished and cease at no distant period on most of them. On the 1st of January, 1817, the public debt amounted to $123,491,965.16, and, notwithstanding the large sums which have been applied to these objects, it has been reduced since that period $37,446,961.78. The last portion of the public debt will be redeemable on the 1st of January, 1835, and, while there is the best reason to believe that the resources of the Government will be continually adequate to such portions of it as may become due in the interval, it is recommended to Congress to seize every opportunity which may present itself to reduce the rate of interest on every part thereof. The high state of the public credit and the great abundance of money are at this time very favorable to such a result. It must be very gratifying to our fellow citizens to witness this flourishing state of the public finances when it is recollected that no burthen whatever has been imposed upon them.

The military establishment in all its branches, in the performance of the various duties assigned to each, justifies the favorable view which was presented of the efficiency of its organization at the last session. All the appropriations have been regularly applied to the objects intended by Congress, and so far as the disbursements have been made the accounts have been rendered and settled without loss to the public. The condition of the Army itself, as relates to the officers and men, in science and discipline is highly respectable. The Military Academy, on which the Army essentially rests, and to which it is much indebted for this state of improvement, has attained, in comparison with any other institution of a like kind, a high degree of perfection. Experience, however, has shewn that the dispersed condition of the corps of artillery is unfavorable to the discipline of that important branch of the military establishment. To remedy this inconvenience, eleven companies have been assembled at the fortification erected at Old Point Comfort as a school for artillery instruction, with intention as they shall be perfected in the various duties of that service to order them to other posts, and, to supply their places with other companies for instruction in like manner. In this mode a complete knowledge of the science and duties of this arm will be extended throughout the whole corps of artillery. But to carry this object fully into effect will require the aid of Congress, to obtain which the subject is now submitted to your consideration.

Of the progress which has been made in the construction of fortifications for the permanent defense of our maritime frontier, according to the plan decided on and to the extent of the existing appropriations, the report of the Secretary of War, which is herewith communicated, will give a detailed account. Their final completion can not fail to give great additional security to that frontier, and to diminish proportionably the expense of defending it in the event of war.

The provisions in several acts of Congress of the last session for the improvement of the navigation of the Mississippi and the Ohio, of the harbor of Presqu'isle, on Lake Erie, and the repair of the Plymouth beach are in a course of regular execution; and there is reason to believe that the appropriation in each instance will be adequate to the object. To carry these improvements fully into effect, the superintendence of them has been assigned to officers of the Corps of Engineers.

Under the act of 30th April last, authorizing the President to cause a survey to be made, with the necessary plans and estimates, of such roads and canals as he might deem of national importance in a commercial or military point of view, or for the transportation of the mail, a board has been instituted, consisting of two distinguished officers of the Corps of Engineers and a distinguished civil engineer, with assistants, who have been actively employed in carrying into effect the object of the act. They have carefully examined the route between the Potomac and the Ohio rivers; between the latter and Lake Erie; between the Alleghany and the Susquehannah; and the routes between the Delaware and the Raritan, Barnstable and Buzzards Bay, and between Boston Harbor and Narraganset Bay. Such portion of the Corps of Topographical Engineers as could be spared from the survey of the coast has been employed in surveying the very important route between the Potomac and the Ohio. Considerable progress has been made in it, but the survey can not be completed until the next season. It is gratifying to add, from the view already taken, that there is good cause to believe that this great national object may be fully accomplished.

It is contemplated to commence early in the next season the execution of the other branch of the act—that which relates to roads—and with the survey of a route from this city, through the Southern States, to New Orleans, the importance of which can not be too highly estimated. All the officers of both the Corps of Engineers who could be spared from other services have been employed in exploring and surveying the routes for canals. To digest a plan for both objects for the great purposes specified will require a thorough knowledge of every part of our Union and of the relation of each part to the others and of all to the seat of the General Government. For such a digest it will be necessary that the information be full, minute, and precise. With a view to these important objects, I submit to the consideration of the Congress the propriety of enlarging both the Corps of Engineers—the Military and Topographical. It need scarcely be remarked that the more extensively these corps are engaged in the improvement of their country, in the execution of the powers of Congress, and in aid of the States in such improvements as lie beyond that limit, when such aid is desired, the happier the effect will be in many views of which the subject is perceptible. By profiting of their science the works will always be well executed, and by giving to the officers such employment our Union will derive all the advantage, in peace as well as in war, from their talents and services which they can afford. In this mode, also, the military will be incorporated with the civil, and unfounded and injurious distinctions and prejudices of every kind be done away. To the corps themselves this service can not fail to be equally useful, since by the knowledge they would thus acquire they would be eminently better qualified in the event of war for the great purposes for which they were instituted.

Our relations with the Indian tribes within our limits have not been materially changed during the year. The hostile disposition evinced by certain tribes on the Missouri during the last year still continues, and has extended in some degree to those on the Upper Mississippi and the Upper Lakes. Several parties of our citizens have been plundered and murdered by those tribes. In order to establish relations of friendship with them, Congress at the last session made an appropriation for treaties with them and for the employment of a suitable military escort to accompany and attend the commissioners at the places appointed for the negotiations. This object has not been effected. The season was too far advanced when the appropriation was made and the distance too great to permit it, but measures have been taken, and all the preparations will be completed to accomplish it at an early period in the next season.

Believing that the hostility of the tribes, particularly on the Upper Mississippi and the Lakes, is in no small degree owing to the wars which are carried on between the tribes residing in that quarter, measures have been taken to bring about a general peace among them, which, if successful, will not only tend to the security of our citizens, but be of great advantage to the Indians themselves.

With the exception of the tribes referred to, our relations with all the others are on the same friendly footing, and it affords me great satisfaction to add that they are making steady advances in civilization and the improvement of their condition. Many of the tribes have already made great progress in the arts of civilized life. This desirable result has been brought about by the humane and persevering policy of the Government, and particularly by means of the appropriation for the civilization of the Indians. There have been established under the provisions of this act 32 schools, containing 916 scholars, who are well instructed in several branches of literature, and likewise in agriculture and the ordinary arts of life.

Under the appropriation to authorize treaties with the Creeks and Quaupaw Indians commissioners have been appointed and negotiations are now pending, but the result is not yet known.

For more full information respecting the principle which has been adopted for carrying into effect the act of Congress authorizing surveys, with plans and estimates for canals and roads, and on every other branch of duty incident to the Department of War, I refer you to the report of the Secretary.

The squadron in the Mediterranean has been maintained in the extent which was proposed in the report of the Secretary of the Navy of the last year, and has afforded to our commerce the necessary protection in that sea. Apprehending, however, that the unfriendly relations which have existed between Algiers and some of the powers of Europe might be extended to us, it has been thought expedient to augment the force there, and in consequence the *North Carolina*, a ship of the line, has been prepared, and will sail in a few days to join it.

The force employed in the Gulf of Mexico and in the neighboring seas for the suppression of piracy has likewise been preserved essentially in the state in which it was during the last year. A persevering effort has been made for the accomplishment of that object, and much protection has thereby been afforded to our commerce, but still the practice is far from being suppressed. From every view which has been taken of the subject it is thought that it will be necessary rather to augment than to diminish our force in that quarter. There is reason to believe that the piracies now complained of are committed by bands of robbers who inhabit the land, and who, by preserving good intelligence with the towns and seizing favorable opportunities, rush forth and fall on unprotected merchant vessels, of which they make an easy prey. The pillage thus taken they carry to their lurking places, and dispose of afterwards at prices tending to seduce the neighboring population. This combination is understood to be of great extent, and is the more to be deprecated because the crime of piracy is often attended with the murder of the crews, these robbers knowing if any survived their lurking places would be exposed and they be caught and punished. That this atrocious practice should be carried to such extent is cause of equal surprise and regret. It is presumed that it must be attributed to the relaxed and feeble state of the local governments, since it is not doubted, from the high character of the governor of Cuba, who is well known and much respected here, that if he had the power he would promptly suppress it. Whether those robbers should be pursued on the land, the local authorities be made responsible for these atrocities, or any other measure be resorted to to suppress them, is submitted to the consideration of Congress.

In execution of the laws for the suppression of the slave trade a vessel has been occasionally sent from that squadron to the coast of Africa with orders to return thence by the usual track of the slave ships, and to seize any of our vessels which might be engaged in that trade. None have been found, and it is believed that none are thus employed. It is well known, however, that the trade still exists under other flags.

The health of our squadron while at Thompsons Island has been much better during the present than it was the last season. Some improvements have been made and others are contemplated there which, it is believed, will have a very salutary effect.

On the Pacific, our commerce has much increased, and on that coast, as well as on that sea, the United States have many important interests which require attention and protection. It is thought that all the considerations which suggested the expediency of placing a squadron on that sea operate with augmented force for maintaining it there, at least in equal extent.

For detailed information respecting the state of our maritime force on each sea, the improvement necessary to be made on either in the organization of the naval establishment generally, and of the laws for its better government I refer you to the report of the Secretary of the Navy, which is herewith communicated.

The revenue of the Post-Office Department has received a considerable augmentation in the present year. The current receipts will exceed the expenditures, although the transportation of the mail within the year has been much increased. A report of the Post-Master General, which is transmitted, will furnish in detail the necessary information respecting the administration and present state of this Department.

In conformity with a resolution of Congress of the last session, an invitation was given to General Lafayette to visit the United States, with an assurance that a ship of war should attend at any port of France which he might designate, to receive and convey him across the Atlantic, whenever it might be convenient for him to sail. He declined the offer of the public ship from motives of delicacy, but assured me that he had long intended and would certainly visit our Union in the course of the present year. In August last he arrived at New York, where he was received with the warmth of affection and gratitude to which his very important and disinterested services and sacrifices in our Revolutionary struggle so eminently entitled him. A corresponding sentiment has since been manifested in his favor throughout every portion of our Union, and affectionate invitations have been given him to extend his visits to them. To these he has yielded all the accommodation in his power. At every designated point of rendezvous the whole population of the neighboring country has been assembled to greet him, among whom it has excited in a peculiar manner the sensibility of all to behold the surviving members of our Revolutionary contest, civil and military, who had shared with him in the toils and dangers of the war, many of them in a decrepit state. A more interesting spectacle, it is believed, was never witnessed, because none could be founded on purer principles, none proceed from higher or more disinterested motives. That the feelings of those who had fought and bled with him in a common cause should have been much excited was natural. There are, however, circumstances attending these interviews which pervaded the whole community and touched the breasts of every age, even the youngest among us. There was not an individual present who had not some relative who had not partaken in those scenes, nor an infant who had not heard the relation of them. But the circumstance which was most sensibly felt, and which his presence brought forcibly to the recollection of all, was the great cause in which we were engaged and the blessings which we have derived from our success in it. The struggle was for independence and liberty, public and personal, and in this we succeeded. The meeting with one who had borne so distinguished a part in that great struggle, and from such lofty and disinterested motives, could not fail to affect profoundly every individual and of every age. It is natural that we should all take a deep interest in his future welfare, as we do. His high claims on our Union are felt, and the sentiment universal that they should be met in a generous spirit. Under these impressions I invite your attention to the subject, with a view that, regarding his very important services, losses, and sacrifices, a provision may be made and tendered to him which shall correspond with the sentiments and be worthy the character of the American people.

In turning our attention to the condition of the civilized world, in which the United States have always taken a deep interest, it is gratifying to see how large a portion of it is blessed with peace. The only wars which now exist within that limit are those between Turkey and Greece, in

Europe, and between Spain and the new Governments, our neighbors, in this hemisphere. In both these wars the cause of independence, of liberty and humanity, continues to prevail. The success of Greece, when the relative population of the contending parties is considered, commands our admiration and applause, and that it has had a similar effect with the neighboring powers is obvious. The feeling of the whole civilized world is excited in a high degree in their favor. May we not hope that these sentiments, winning on the hearts of their respective Governments, may lead to a more decisive result; that they may produce an accord among them to replace Greece on the ground which she formerly held, and to which her heroic exertions at this day so eminently entitle her?

With respect to the contest to which our neighbors are a party, it is evident that Spain as a power is scarcely felt in it. These new States had completely achieved their independence before it was acknowledged by the United States, and they have since maintained it with little foreign pressure. The disturbances which have appeared in certain portions of that vast territory have proceeded from internal causes, which had their origin in their former Governments and have not yet been thoroughly removed. It is manifest that these causes are daily losing their effect, and that these new States are settling down under Governments elective and representative in every branch, similar to our own. In this course we ardently wish them to persevere, under a firm conviction that it will promote their happiness. In this, their career, however, we have not interfered, believing that every people have a right to institute for themselves the government which, in their judgment, may suit them best. Our example is before them, of the good effect of which, being our neighbors, they are competent judges, and to their judgment we leave it, in the expectation that other powers will pursue the same policy. The deep interest which we take in their independence, which we have acknowledged, and in their enjoyment of all the rights incident thereto, especially in the very important one of instituting their own Governments, has been declared, and is known to the world. Separated as we are from Europe by the great Atlantic Ocean, we can have no concern in the wars of the European Governments nor in the causes which produce them. The balance of power between them, into whichever scale it may turn in its various vibrations, can not affect us. It is the interest of the United States to preserve the most friendly relations with every power and on conditions fair, equal, and applicable to all. But in regard to our neighbors our situation is different. It is impossible for the European Governments to interfere in their concerns, especially in those alluded to, which are vital, without affecting us; indeed, the motive which might induce such interference in the present state of the war between the parties, if a war it may be called, would appear to be equally applicable to us. It is gratifying to know that some of the powers with whom we enjoy a very friendly intercourse, and to whom these views have been communicated, have appeared to acquiesce in them.

The augmentation of our population with the expansion of our Union and increased number of States have produced effects in certain branches of our system which merit the attention of Congress. Some of our arrangements, and particularly the judiciary establishment, were made with a view to the original thirteen States only. Since then the United States have acquired a vast extent of territory; eleven new States have been admitted into the Union, and Territories have been laid off for three others, which will likewise be admitted at no distant day.

An organization of the Supreme Court which assigns the judges any portion of the duties which belong to the inferior, requiring their passage over so vast a space under any distribution of the States that may now be made, if not impracticable in the execution, must render it impossible for them to discharge the duties of either branch with advantage to the Union. The duties of the Supreme Court would be of great importance if its decisions were confined to the ordinary limits of other tribunals, but when it is considered that this court decides, and in the last resort, on all the great questions which arise under our Constitution, involving those between the United States individually, between the States and the United States, and between the latter and foreign powers, too high an estimate of their importance can not be formed. The great interests of the nation seem to require that the judges of the Supreme Court should be exempted from every other duty than those which are incident to that high trust. The organization of the inferior courts would of course be adapted to circumstances. It is presumed that such an one might be formed as would secure an able and faithful discharge of their duties, and without any material augmentation of expense.

The condition of the aborigines within our limits, and especially those who are within the limits of any of the States, merits likewise particular attention. Experience has shown that unless the tribes be civilized they can never be incorporated into our system in any form whatever. It has likewise shown that in the regular augmentation of our population with the extension of our settlements their situation will become deplorable, if their extinction is not menaced. Some well-digested plan which will rescue them from such calamities is due to their rights, to the rights of humanity, and to the honor of the nation. Their civilization is indispensable to their safety, and this can be accomplished only by degrees. The process must commence with the infant state, through whom some effect may be wrought on the parental. Difficulties of the most serious character present themselves to the attainment of this very desirable result on the territory on which they now reside. To remove them from it by force, even with a view to their own security and happiness, would be revolting to humanity and utterly unjustifiable. Between the limits of our present States and Territories and the Rocky Mountains and Mexico there is a vast territory to which they might be invited with inducements which might be successful. It is thought if that territory should be divided into districts by previous agreement with the tribes now residing there and civil governments be established in each, with schools for every branch of instruction in literature and the arts of civilized life, that all the tribes now within our limits might gradually be drawn there. The execution of this plan would necessarily be attended with expense, and that not inconsiderable, but it is doubted whether any other can be devised which would be less liable to that objection or more likely to succeed.

In looking to the interests which the United States have on the Pacific Ocean and on the western coast of this continent, the propriety of establishing a military post at the mouth of the Columbia River, or at some other point in that quarter within our acknowledged limits, is submitted to the consideration of Congress. Our commerce and fisheries on that sea and along the coast have much increased and are increasing. It is thought that a military post, to which our ships of war might resort, would afford protection to every interest, and have a tendency to conciliate the tribes to the North West, with whom our trade is extensive. It is thought also that by the establishment of such a post the intercourse between our Western States and Territories and the Pacific and our trade with the tribes residing in the interior on each side of the Rocky Mountains would be essentially promoted. To carry this object into effect the appropriation of an adequate sum to authorize the employment of a frigate, with an officer of the Corps of Engineers, to explore the mouth of the Columbia River and the coast contiguous thereto, to enable the Executive to make such establishment at the most suitable point, is recommended to Congress.

It is thought that attention is also due to the improvement of this city. The communication between the public buildings and in various other parts and the grounds around those buildings require it. It is presumed also that the completion of the canal from the Tiber to the Eastern Branch would have a very salutary effect. Great exertions have been made and expenses incurred by the citizens in improvements of various kinds; but those which are suggested belong exclusively to the Government, or are of a nature to require expenditures beyond their resources. The public lots which are still for sale would, it is not doubted, be more than adequate for these purposes.

From the view above presented it is manifest that the situation of the United States is in the highest degree prosperous and happy. There is no object which as a people we can desire which we do not possess or which is not within our reach. Blessed with governments the happiest which the world ever knew, with no distinct orders in society or divided interests in any portion of the vast territory over which their dominion extends, we have every motive to cling together which can animate a virtuous and enlightened people. The great object is to preserve these blessings, and to hand them down to the latest posterity. Our experience ought to satisfy us that our progress under the most correct and provident policy will not be exempt from danger. Our institutions form an important epoch in the history of the civilized world. On their preservation and in their utmost purity everything will depend. Extending as our interests do to every part of the inhabited globe and to every sea to which our citizens are carried by their industry and enterprise, to which they are invited by the wants of others, and have a right to go, we must either protect them in the enjoyment of their rights or abandon them in certain events to waste and desolation.

Our attitude is highly interesting as relates to other powers, and particularly to our southern neighbors. We have duties to perform with respect to all to which we must be faithful. To every kind of danger we should pay the most vigilant and unceasing attention, remove the cause where it may be practicable, and be prepared to meet it when inevitable.

Against foreign danger the policy of the Government seems to be already settled. The events of the late war admonished us to make our maritime frontier impregnable by a well-digested chain of fortifications, and to give efficient protection to our commerce by augmenting our Navy to a certain extent, which has been steadily pursued, and which it is incumbent upon us to complete as soon as circumstances will permit. In the event of war it is on the maritime frontier that we shall be assailed. It is in that quarter, therefore, that we should be prepared to meet the attack. It is there that our whole force will be called into action to prevent the destruction of our towns and the desolation and pillage of the interior. To give full effect to this policy great improvements will be indispensable. Access to those works by every practicable communication should be made easy and in every direction. The intercourse between every part of our Union should also be promoted and facilitated by the exercise of those powers which may comport with a faithful regard to the great principles of our Constitution. With respect to internal causes, those great principles point out with equal certainty the policy to be pursued. Resting on the people as our Governments do, State and National, with well-defined powers, it is of the highest importance that they severally keep within the limits prescribed to them. Fulfilling that sacred duty, it is of equal importance that the movement between them be harmonious, and in case of any disagreement, should any such occur, a calm appeal be made to the people, and that their voice be heard and promptly obeyed. Both Governments being instituted for the common good, we can not fail to prosper while those who made them are attentive to the conduct of their representatives and control their measures. In the pursuit of these great objects let a generous spirit and national views and feelings be indulged, and let every part recollect that by cherishing that spirit and improving the condition of the others in what relates to their welfare the general interest will not only be promoted, but the local advantage be reciprocated by all.

I can not conclude this communication, the last of the kind which I shall have to make, without recollecting with great sensibility and heartfelt gratitude the many instances of the public confidence and the generous support which I have received from my fellow citizens in the various trusts with which I have been honored. Having commenced my service in early youth, and continued it since with few and short intervals, I have witnessed the great difficulties to which our Union has been exposed, and admired the virtue and intelligence with which they have been surmounted. From the present prosperous and happy state I derive a gratification which I can not express. That these blessings may be preserved and perpetuated will be the object of my fervent and unceasing prayers to the Supreme Ruler of the Universe.

JAMES MONROE

6

John Quincy Adams (1825–1829)

John Quincy Adams—the son of the second president, the leader who dedicated seventy years of his life to public service, the rhetorician known as Old Man Eloquent—this Adams was one of the most literate men of his generation. He had the gift to write an outstanding formal farewell address. But he did not do so. It has been said that, since his views on neutrality made their way into President Washington's Farewell Address, that sufficed for him.

John Quincy Adams did write a final annual message to the Congress. Although he had just passed through a tough election (1828), Adams like many leaders perceived a potentially terrible constitutional crisis looming. The conflicting claims between the states and the national government had not been successfully adjudicated. Growing sectional conflicts aggravated the problem. Adams wrote,

> The United States of America and the people of every State of which they are composed are each of them sovereign powers. The legislative authority of the whole is exercised by Congress under authority granted them in the common Constitution. The legislative power of each State is exercised by assemblies deriving their authority from the constitution of the State. Each is sovereign within its own province. The distribution of power between them presupposes that these authorities will move in harmony with each other. The members of the State and General Governments are all under oath to support both, and allegiance is due to the one and to the other. The case of a conflict between these two powers has not been supposed, nor has any provision been made for it in our institutions.

And that was the rub. The Founders—including his father—had not sufficiently provided a constitutional remedy to a looming constitutional crisis. Not surprisingly, John Quincy Adams referenced the U.S. Constitution or constitutional governance nine times in this message.

Fourth Annual Message
(written to the Congress)
December 2, 1828

Fellow-Citizens of the Senate and of the House of Representatives:

If the enjoyment in profusion of the bounties of Providence forms a suitable subject of mutual gratulation and grateful acknowledgment, we are admonished at this return of the season when the representatives of the nation are assembled to deliberate upon their concerns to offer up the tribute of fervent and grateful hearts for the never failing mercies of Him who ruleth over all. He has again favored us with healthful seasons and abundant harvests; He has sustained us in peace with foreign countries and in tranquillity within our borders; He has preserved us in the quiet and undisturbed possession of civil and religious liberty; He has crowned the year with His goodness, imposing on us no other condition than of improving for our own happiness the blessings bestowed by His hands, and, in the fruition of all His favors, of devoting his faculties with which we have been endowed by Him to His glory and to our own temporal and eternal welfare.

In the relations of our Federal Union with our brethren of the human race the changes which have occurred since the close of your last session have generally tended to the preservation of peace and to the cultivation of harmony. Before your last separation a war had unhappily been kindled between the Empire of Russia, one of those with which our intercourse has been no other than a constant exchange of good offices, and that of the Ottoman Porte, a nation from which geographical distance, religious opinions and maxims of government on their part little suited to the formation of those bonds of mutual benevolence which result from the benefits of commerce had kept us in a state, perhaps too much prolonged, of coldness and alienation. The extensive, fertile, and populous dominions of the Sultan belong rather to the Asiatic than the European division of the human family. They enter but partially into the system of Europe, nor have their wars with Russia and Austria, the European States upon which they border, for more than a century past disturbed the pacific relations of those States with the other great powers of Europe. Neither France nor Prussia nor Great Britain has ever taken part in them, nor is it to be expected that they will at this time. The declaration of war by Russia has received the approbation or acquiescence of her allies, and we may indulge the hope that its progress and termination will be signalized by the moderation and forbearance no less than by the energy of the Emperor Nicholas, and that it will afford the opportunity for such collateral agency in behalf of the suffering Greeks as will secure to them ultimately the triumph of humanity and of freedom.

The state of our particular relations with France has scarcely varied in the course of the present year. The commercial intercourse between the two countries has continued to increase for the mutual benefit of both. The claims of indemnity to numbers of our fellow citizens for depredations upon their property, heretofore committed during the revolutionary governments, remain unadjusted, and still form the subject of earnest representation and remonstrance. Recent advices from the minister of the United States at Paris encourage the expectation that the appeal to the justice of the French Government will ere long receive a favorable consideration.

The last friendly expedient has been resorted to for the decision of the controversy with Great Britain relating to the north-eastern boundary of the United States. By an agreement with the British Government, carrying into effect the provisions of the fifth article of the treaty of Ghent, and the convention of 29th September 1827, His Majesty the King of the Netherlands has by common consent been selected as the umpire between the parties. The proposal to him to accept the designation for the performance of this friendly office will be made at an early day, and the United States, relying upon the justice of their cause, will cheerfully commit the arbitrament of it to a prince equally distinguished for the independence of his spirit, his indefatigable assiduity to the duties of his station, and his inflexible personal probity.

Our commercial relations with Great Britain will deserve the serious consideration of Congress and the exercise of a conciliatory and forbearing spirit in the policy of both Governments. The state of them has been materially changed by the act of Congress, passed at their last session, in alteration of several acts imposing duties on imports, and by acts of more recent date of the British Parliament. The effect of the interdiction of direct trade, commenced by Great Britain and reciprocated by the United States, has been, as was to be foreseen, only to substitute different channels for an exchange of commodities indispensable to the colonies and profitable to a numerous class of our fellow citizens. The exports, the revenue, the navigation of the United States have suffered no diminution by our exclusion from direct access to the British colonies. The colonies pay more dearly for the necessaries of life which their Government burdens with the charges of double voyages, freight, insurance, and commission, and the profits of our exports are somewhat impaired and more injuriously transferred from one portion of our citizens to another. The resumption of this old and otherwise exploded system of colonial exclusion has not secured to the shipping interest of Great Britain the relief which, at the expense of the distant colonies and of the United States, it was expected to afford. Other measures have been resorted to more pointedly bearing upon the navigation of the United States, and which, unless modified by the construction given to the recent acts of Parliament, will be manifestly incompatible with the positive stipulations of the commercial convention existing between the two countries. That convention, however, may be terminated with twelve months' notice, at the option of either party.

A treaty of amity, navigation, and commerce between the United States and His Majesty the Emperor of Austria, King of Hungary and Bohemia, has been prepared for signature by the Secretary of State and by the Baron de Lederer, intrusted with full powers of the Austrian Government. Independently of the new and friendly relations which may be thus commenced with one of the most eminent and powerful nations of the earth, the occasion has been taken in it, as in other recent treaties concluded by the United States, to extend those principles of liberal intercourse and of fair reciprocity which intertwine with the exchanges of commerce the principles of justice and the feelings of mutual benevolence. This system, first proclaimed to the world in the first commercial treaty ever concluded by the United States—that of 6th February 1778, with France—has been invariably the cherished policy of our Union. It is by treaties of commerce alone that it can be made ultimately to prevail as the established system of all civilized nations. With this principle our fathers extended the hand of friendship to every nation of the globe, and to this policy our country has ever since adhered. What ever of regulation in our laws has ever been adopted unfavorable to the interest of any foreign nation has been essentially defensive and counteracting to similar regulations of theirs operating against us.

Immediately after the close of the War of Independence commissioners were appointed by the Congress of the Confederation authorized to conclude treaties with every nation of Europe disposed to adopt them. Before the wars of the French Revolution such treaties had been consummated with the United Netherlands, Sweden, and Prussia. During those wars treaties with Great Britain and Spain had been effected, and those with Prussia and France renewed. In all these some concessions to the liberal principles of intercourse proposed by the United States had been obtained; but as in all the negotiations they came occasionally in collision with previous internal regulations or exclusive and excluding compacts of monopoly with which the other parties had been trammeled, the advances made in them toward the freedom of trade were partial and imperfect. Colonial establishments, chartered companies, and ship building influence pervaded and encumbered the legislation of all the great commercial states; and the United States, in offering free trade and equal privilege to all, were compelled to acquiesce in many exceptions with each of the parties to their treaties, accommodated to their existing laws and anterior agreements.

The colonial system by which this whole hemisphere was bound has fallen into ruins, totally abolished by revolutions converting colonies into independent nations throughout the two American continents, excepting a portion of territory chiefly at the northern extremity of our own, and confined to the remnants of dominion retained by Great Britain over the insular archipelago, geographically the appendages of our part of the globe. With all the rest we have free trade, even with the insular colonies of all the European nations, except Great Britain. Her Government also had manifested approaches to the adoption of a free and liberal intercourse between her colonies and other nations, though by a sudden and scarcely explained revulsion the spirit of exclusion has been revived for operation upon the United States alone.

The conclusion of our last treaty of peace with Great Britain was shortly afterwards followed by a commercial convention, placing the direct intercourse between the two countries upon a footing of more equal reciprocity than had ever before been admitted. The same principle has since been much further extended by treaties with France, Sweden, Denmark, the Hanseatic cities, Prussia, in Europe, and with the Republics of Colombia and of Central America, in this hemisphere. The mutual abolition of discriminating duties and charges upon the navigation and commercial intercourse between the parties is the general maxim which characterizes them all. There is reason to expect that it will at no distant period be adopted by other nations, both of Europe and America, and to hope that by its universal prevalence one of the fruitful sources of wars of commercial competition will be extinguished.

Among the nations upon whose Governments many of our fellow-citizens have had long-pending claims of indemnity for depredations upon their property during a period when the rights of neutral commerce were disregarded was that of Denmark. They were soon after the events occurred the subject of a special mission from the United States, at the close of which the assurance was given by His Danish Majesty that at a period of more tranquillity and of less distress they would be considered, examined, and decided upon in a spirit of determined purpose for the dispensation of justice. I have much pleasure in informing Congress that the fulfillment of this honorable promise is now in progress; that a small portion of the claims has already been settled to the satisfaction of the claimants; and that we have reason to hope that the remainder will shortly be placed in a train of equitable adjustment. This result has always been confidently expected, from the character of personal integrity and of benevolence which the Sovereign of the Danish dominions has through every vicissitude of fortune maintained.

The general aspect of the affairs of our neighboring American nations of the south has been rather of approaching than of settled tranquillity. Internal disturbances have been more frequent among them than their common friends would have desired. Our intercourse with all has continued to be that of friendship and of mutual good will. Treaties of commerce and of boundaries with the United Mexican States have been negotiated, but, from various successive obstacles, not yet brought to a final conclusion.

The civil war which unfortunately still prevails in the Republics of Central America has been unpropitious to the cultivation of our commercial relations with them; and the dissensions and revolutionary changes in the Republics of Colombia and of Peru have been seen with cordial regret by us, who would gladly contribute to the happiness of both. It is with great satisfaction, however, that we have witnessed the recent conclusion of a peace between the Governments of Buenos Ayres and of Brazil, and it is equally gratifying to observe that indemnity has been obtained for some of the injuries which our fellow citizens had sustained in the latter of those countries. The rest are in a train of negotiation, which we hope may terminate to mutual satisfaction, and that it may be succeeded by a treaty of commerce and navigation, upon liberal principles, propitious to a great and growing commerce, already important to the interests of our country.

The condition and prospects of the revenue are more favorable than our most sanguine expectations had anticipated. The balance in the Treasury on the 1st of January last, exclusive of the moneys received under the convention of 13th of November, 1826, with Great Britain, was $5,861,972.83. The receipts into the Treasury from the 1st of January to the 30th of September last, so far as they have been ascertained to form the basis of an estimate, amount to $18,633,580.27, which, with the receipts of the present quarter, estimated at $5,461,283.40, form an aggregate of receipts during the year of $24,094,863.67. The expenditures of the year may probably amount to $25,637,111.63, and leave in the Treasury on the first of January next the sum of $5,125,638.14.

The receipts of the present year have amounted to near two millions more than was anticipated at the commencement of the last session of Congress.

The amount of duties secured on importations from the 1st of January to the 30th of September was about $22,997,000, and that of the estimated accruing revenue is $5,000,000, forming an aggregate for the year of near $28,000,000. This is one million more than the estimate last December for the accruing revenue of the present year, which, with allowances for draw-backs and contingent deficiencies, was expected to produce an actual revenue of $22,300,000. Had these only been realized the expenditures of the year would have been also proportionally reduced, for of these $24,000,000 received upward of $9,000,000 have been applied to the extinction of public debt, bearing an interest of 6 per cent a year, and of course reducing the burden of interest annually payable in future by the amount of more than half a million. The payments on account of interest during the current year exceed $3,000,000, presenting an aggregate of more than $12,000,000 applied during the year to the discharge of the public debt, the whole of which remaining due on the 1st of January next will amount only to $58,362,135.78.

That the revenue of the ensuing year will not fall short of that received in the one now expiring there are indications which can scarcely prove deceptive. In our country an uniform experience of forty years has shown that whatever the tariff of duties upon articles imported from abroad has been, the amount of importations has always borne an average value nearly approaching to that of the exports, though occasionally differing in the balance, some times being more and some times less. It is, indeed, a general law of prosperous commerce that the real value of exports should by a small, and only a small, balance exceed that of imports, that balance being a permanent addition to the wealth of the nation. The extent of the prosperous commerce of the nation must be regulated by the amount of its exports, and an important addition to the value of these will draw after it a corresponding increase of importations. It has happened in the vicissitudes of the seasons that the harvests of all Europe have in the late summer and autumn fallen short of their usual average. A relaxation of the interdict upon the importation of grain and flour from abroad has ensued, a propitious market has been opened to the granaries of our country, and a new prospect of reward presented to the labors of the husband-man, which for several years has been denied. This accession to the profits of agriculture in the middle and western portions of our Union is accidental and temporary. It may continue only for a single year. It may be, as has been often experienced in the revolutions of time, but the first of several scanty harvests in succession. We may consider it certain that for the approaching year it has added an item of large amount to the value of our exports and that it will produce a corresponding increase of importations. It may therefore confidently be foreseen that the revenue of 1829 will equal and probably exceed that of 1828, and will afford the means of extinguishing ten millions more of the principal of the public debt.

This new element of prosperity to that part of our agricultural industry which is occupied in producing the first article of human subsistence is of the most cheering character to the feelings of patriotism. Proceeding from a cause which humanity will view with concern, the sufferings of scarcity in distant lands, it yields a consolatory reflection that this scarcity is in no respect attributable to us; that it comes from the dispensation of Him who ordains all in wisdom and goodness, and who permits evil itself only as an instrument of good; that, far from contributing to this scarcity, our agency will be applied only to the alleviation of its severity, and that in pouring forth from the abundance of our own garners the supplies which will partially restore plenty to those who are in need we shall ourselves reduce our stores and add to the price of our own bread, so as in some degree to participate in the wants which it will be the good fortune of our country to relieve.

The great interests of an agricultural, commercial, and manufacturing nation are so linked in union together that no permanent cause of prosperity to one of them can operate without extending its influence to the others. All these interests are alike under the protecting power of the legislative authority, and the duties of the representative bodies are to conciliate them in harmony together.

So far as the object of taxation is to raise a revenue for discharging the debts and defraying the expenses of the community, its operation should be adapted as much as possible to suit the burden with equal hand upon all in proportion with their ability of bearing it without oppression. But the legislation of one nation is some times intentionally made to bear heavily upon the interests of another. That legislation, adapted, as it is meant to be, to the special interests of its own people, will often press most unequally upon the several component interests of its neighbors. Thus the legislation of Great Britain, when, as has recently been avowed, adapted to the depression of a rival nation, will naturally abound with regulations to interdict upon the productions of the soil or industry of the other which come in competition with its own, and will present encouragement, perhaps even bounty, to the raw material of the other State which it can not produce itself, and which is essential for the use of its manufactures, competitors in the markets of the world with those of its commercial rival.

Such is the state of commercial legislation of Great Britain as it bears upon our interests. It excludes with interdicting duties all importation (except in time of approaching famine) of the great staple of production of our Middle and Western States; it proscribes with equal rigor the bulkier lumber and live stock of the same portion and also of the Northern and Eastern part of our Union. It refuses even the rice of the South unless aggravated with a charge of duty upon the Northern carrier who brings it to them. But the cotton, indispensable for their looms, they will receive almost duty free to weave it into a fabric for our own wear, to the destruction of our own manufactures, which they are enabled thus to undersell.

Is the self-protecting energy of this nation so helpless that there exists in the political institutions of our country no power to counteract the bias of this foreign legislation; that the growers of grain must submit to this exclusion from the foreign markets of their produce; that the shippers must dismantle their ships, the trade of the North stagnate at the wharves, and the manufacturers starve at their looms, while the whole people shall pay tribute to foreign industry to be clad in a foreign garb; that the Congress of the Union are impotent to restore the balance in favor of native industry destroyed by the statutes of another realm?

More just and generous sentiments will, I trust, prevail. If the tariff adopted at the last session of Congress shall be found by experience to bear oppressively upon the interests of any one section of the Union, it ought to be, and I can not doubt will be, so modified as to alleviate its burden. To the voice of just complaint from any portion of their constituents the representatives of the States and of the people will never turn away their ears.

But so long as the duty of the foreign shall operate only as a bounty upon the domestic article; while the planter and the merchant and the shepherd and the husbandman shall be found thriving in their occupations under the duties imposed for the protection of domestic manufactures, they will not repine at the prosperity shared with themselves by their fellow citizens of other professions, nor denounce as violations of the Constitution the deliberate acts of Congress to shield from the wrongs of foreigns the native industry of the Union.

While the tariff of the last session of Congress was a subject of legislative deliberation it was foretold by some of its opposers that one of its necessary consequences would be to impair the revenue. It is yet too soon to pronounce with confidence that this prediction was erroneous. The obstruction of one avenue of trade not unfrequently opens an issue to another. The consequence of the tariff will be to increase the exportation and to diminish the importation of some specific articles; but by the general law of trade the increase of exportation of one article will be followed by an increased importation of others, the duties upon which will supply the deficiencies which the diminished importation would otherwise occasion. The effect of taxation upon revenue can seldom be foreseen with certainty. It must abide the test of experience.

As yet no symptoms of diminution are perceptible in the receipts of the Treasury. As yet little addition of cost has even been experienced upon the articles burdened with heavier duties by the last tariff. The domestic manufacturer supplies the same or a kindred article at a diminished price, and the consumer pays the same tribute to the labor of his own countryman which he must otherwise have paid to foreign industry and toil.

The tariff of the last session was in its details not acceptable to the great interests of any portion of the Union, not even to the interest which it was specially intended to subserve. Its object was to balance the burdens upon native industry imposed by the operation of foreign laws, but not to aggravate the burdens of one section of the Union by the relief afforded to another. To the great principle sanctioned by that act—one of those upon which the Constitution itself was formed—I hope and trust the authorities of the Union will adhere. But if any of the duties imposed by the act only relieve the manufacturer by aggravating the burden of the planter, let a careful revisal of its provisions, enlightened by the practical experience of its effects, be directed to retain those which impart protection to native industry and remove or supply the place of those which only alleviate one great national interest by the depression of another.

The United States of America and the people of every State of which they are composed are each of them sovereign powers. The legislative authority of the whole is exercised by Congress under authority granted them in the common Constitution. The legislative power of each State is exercised by assemblies deriving their authority from the constitution of the State. Each is sovereign within its own province. The distribution of power between them presupposes that these authorities will move in harmony with each other. The members of the State and General Governments are all under oath to support both, and allegiance is due to the one and to the other. The case of a conflict between these two powers has not been supposed, nor has any provision been made for it in our institutions; as a virtuous nation of ancient times existed more than five centuries without a law for the punishment of parricide.

More than once, however, in the progress of our history have the people and the legislatures of one or more States, in moments of excitement, been instigated to this conflict; and the means of effecting this impulse have been allegations that the acts of Congress to be resisted were *unconstitutional*. The people of no one State have ever delegated to their legislature the power of pronouncing an act of Congress unconstitutional, but they have delegated to them powers by the exercise of which the execution of the laws of Congress within the State may be resisted. If we suppose the case of such conflicting legislation sustained by the corresponding executive and judicial authorities, patriotism and philanthropy turn their eyes from the condition in which the parties would be placed, and from that of the people of both, which must be its victims.

The reports from the Secretary of War and the various subordinate offices of the resort of that Department present an exposition of the public administration of affairs connected with them through the course of the current year. The present state of the Army and the distribution of the force of which it is composed will be seen from the report of the Major General. Several alterations in the disposal of the troops have been found expedient in the course of the year, and the discipline of the Army, though not entirely free from exception, has been generally good.

The attention of Congress is particularly invited to that part of the report of the Secretary of War which concerns the existing system of our relations with the Indian tribes. At the establishment of the Federal Government under the present Constitution of the United States the principle was adopted of considering them as foreign and independent powers and also as proprietors of lands. They were, moreover, considered as savages, whom it was our policy and our duty to use our influence in converting to Christianity and in bringing within the pale of civilization.

As independent powers, we negotiated with them by treaties; as proprietors, we purchased of them all the lands which we could prevail upon them to sell; as brethren of the human race, rude and ignorant, we endeavored to bring them to the knowledge of religion and letters. The ultimate design was to incorporate in our own institutions that portion of them which could be converted to the state of civilization. In the practice of European States, before our Revolution, they had been considered as children to be governed; as tenants at discretion, to be dispossessed as occasion might require; as hunters to be indemnified by trifling concessions for removal from the grounds from which their game was extirpated. In changing the system it would seem as if a full contemplation of the consequences of the change had not been taken. We have been far more successful in the acquisition of their lands than in imparting to them the principles or inspiring them with the spirit of civilization. But in appropriating to ourselves their hunting grounds we have brought upon ourselves the obligation of providing them with subsistence; and when we have had the rare good fortune of teaching them the arts of civilization and the doctrines of Christianity we have unexpectedly found them forming in the midst of ourselves communities claiming to be independent of ours and rivals of sovereignty within the territories of the members of our Union. This state of things requires that a remedy should be provided—a remedy which, while it shall do justice to those unfortunate children of nature, may secure to the members of our confederation their rights of sovereignty and of soil. As the outline of a project to that effect, the views presented in the report of the Secretary of War are recommended to the consideration of Congress.

The report from the Engineer Department presents a comprehensive view of the progress which has been made in the great systems promotive of the public interest, commenced and organized under authority of Congress, and the effects of which have already contributed to the security, as they will hereafter largely contribute to the honor and dignity, of the nation.

The first of these great systems is that of fortifications, commenced immediately after the close of our last war, under the salutary experience which the events of that war had impressed upon our countrymen of its necessity. Introduced under the auspices of my immediate predecessor, it has been continued with the persevering and liberal encouragement of the Legislature, and, combined with corresponding exertions for the gradual increase and improvement of the Navy, prepares for our extensive country a condition of defense adapted to any critical emergency which the varying course of events may bring forth. Our advances in these concerted systems have for the last ten years been steady and progressive, and in a few years more will be so completed as to leave no cause for apprehension that our sea coast will ever again offer a theater of hostile invasion.

The next of these cardinal measures of policy is the preliminary to great and lasting works of public improvement in the surveys of roads, examination for the course of canals, and labors for the removal of the obstructions of rivers and harbors, first commenced by the act of Congress of 30th of April, 1824.

The report exhibits in one table the funds appropriated at the last and preceding sessions of Congress for all these fortifications, surveys, and works of public improvement, the manner in which these funds have been applied, the amount expended upon the several works under construction, and the further sums which may be necessary to complete them; in a second, the works projected by the Board of Engineers which have not been commenced, and the estimate of their cost; in a third, the report of the annual Board of Visitors at the Military Academy at West Point.

For thirteen fortifications erecting on various points of our Atlantic coast, from Rhode Island to Louisiana, the aggregate expenditure of the year has fallen little short of $1,000,000. For the preparation of 5 additional reports of reconnoissances and surveys since the last session of Congress, for the civil construction upon 37 different public works commenced, 8 others for which specific appropriations have been made by acts of Congress, and 20 other incipient surveys under the authority given by the act of 30th April, 1824, about $1,000,000 more has been drawn from the Treasury.

To these $2,000,000 is to be added the appropriation of $250,000 to commence the erection of a break-water near the mouth of the Delaware River, the subscriptions to the Delaware and Chesapeake, the Louisville and Portland, the Dismal Swamp, and the Chesapeake and Ohio canals, the large donations of lands to the States of Ohio, Indiana, Illinois, and Alabama for objects of improvements within those States, and the sums appropriated for light-houses, buoys, and piers on the coast; and a full view will be taken of the munificence of the nation in the application of its resources to the improvement of its own condition.

Of these great national under-takings the Academy at West Point is among the most important in itself and the most comprehensive in its consequences. In that institution a part of the revenue of the nation is applied to defray the expense of educating a competent portion of her youth chiefly to the knowledge and the duties of military life. It is the living armory of the nation. While the other works of improvement enumerated in the reports now presented to the attention of Congress are destined to ameliorate the face of nature, to multiply the facilities of communication between the different parts of the Union, to assist the labors, increase the comforts, and enhance the enjoyments of individuals, the instruction acquired at West Point enlarges the dominion and expands the capacities of the mind. Its beneficial results are already experienced in the composition of the Army, and their influence is felt in the intellectual progress of society. The institution is susceptible still of great improvement from benefactions proposed by several successive Boards of Visitors, to whose earnest and repeated recommendations I cheerfully add my own.

With the usual annual reports from the Secretary of the Navy and the Board of Commissioners will be exhibited to the view of Congress the execution of the laws relating to that department of the public service. The repression of piracy in the West Indian and in the Grecian seas has been effectually maintained, with scarcely any exception. During the war between the Governments of Buenos Ayres and of Brazil frequent collisions between the belligerent acts of power and the rights of neutral commerce occurred. Licentious blockades, irregularly enlisted or impressed sea men, and the property of honest commerce seized with violence, and even plundered under legal pretenses, are disorders never separable from the conflicts of war upon the ocean. With a portion of them the correspondence of our commanders on the eastern aspect of the South American coast and among the islands of Greece discover how far we have been involved. In these the honor of our country and the rights of our citizens have been asserted and vindicated. The appearance of new squadrons in the Mediterranean and the blockade of the Dardanelles indicate the danger of other obstacles to the freedom of commerce and the necessity of keeping our naval force in those seas. To the suggestions repeated in the report of the Secretary of the Navy, and tending to the permanent improvement of this institution, I invite the favorable consideration of Congress.

A resolution of the House of Representatives requesting that one of our small public vessels should be sent to the Pacific Ocean and South Sea to examine the coasts, islands, harbors, shoals, and reefs in those seas, and to ascertain their true situation and description, has been put in a train of execution. The vessel is nearly ready to depart. The successful accomplishment of the expedition may be greatly facilitated by suitable legislative provisions, and particularly by an appropriation to defray its necessary expense. The addition of a 2nd, and perhaps a 3rd, vessel, with a slight aggravation of the cost, would contribute much to the safety of the citizens embarked on this under-taking, the results of which may be of the deepest interest to our country.

With the report of the Secretary of the Navy will be submitted, in conformity to the act of Congress of 3d March, 1827 for the gradual improvement of the Navy of the United States, statements of the expenditures under that act and of the measures for carrying the same into effect. Every section of that statute contains a distinct provision looking to the great object of the whole—the gradual improvement of the Navy. Under its salutary sanction stores of ship timber have been procured and are in process of seasoning and preservation for the future uses of the Navy. Arrangements have been made for the preservation of the live oak timber growing on the lands of the United States, and for its reproduction, to supply at future and distant days the waste of that most valuable material for ship building by the great consumption of it yearly for the commercial as well as for the military marine of our country. The construction of the two dry docks at Charlestown and at Norfolk is making satisfactory progress toward a durable establishment. The examinations and inquiries to ascertain the practicability and expediency of a marine railway at Pensacola, though not yet accomplished, have been post-poned but to be more effectually made. The navy yards of the United States have been examined, and plans for their improvement and the preservation of the public property therein at Portsmouth, Charlestown, Philadelphia, Washington, and Gosport, and to which two others are to be added, have been prepared and received my sanction; and no other portion of my public duties has been performed with a more intimate conviction of its importance to the future welfare and security of the Union.

With the report from the Postmaster-General is exhibited a comparative view of the gradual increase of that establishment, from five to five years, since 1792 till this time in the number of post offices, which has grown from less than 200 to nearly 8,000; in the revenue yielded by them, which from $67,000 has swollen to upward of $1,500,000, and in the number of miles of post-roads, which from 5,642 have multiplied to 114,536. While in the same period of time the population of the Union has about thrice doubled, the rate of increase of these offices is nearly 40, and of the revenue and of traveled miles from 20 to 25 for 1. The increase of revenue within the last five years has been nearly equal to the whole revenue of the Department in 1812.

The expenditures of the Department during the year which ended on the 1st of July last have exceeded the receipts by a sum of about $25,000. The excess has been occasioned by the increase of mail conveyances and facilities to the extent of near 800,000 miles. It has been supplied by collections from the post masters of the arrearages of preceding years. While the correct principle seems to be that the income levied by the Department should defray all its expenses, it has never been the policy of this Government to raise from this establishment any revenue to be applied to any other purposes. The suggestion of the Postmaster-General that the insurance of the safe transmission of moneys by the mail might be assumed by the Department for a moderate and competent remuneration will deserve the consideration of Congress.

A report from the commissioner of the public buildings in this city exhibits the expenditures upon them in the course of the current year. It will be seen that the humane and benevolent intentions of Congress in providing, by the act of 20th May, 1826, for the erection of a penitentiary in this District have been accomplished. The authority of further legislation is now required for the removal to this tenement of the offenders against the laws sentenced to atone by personal confinement for their crimes, and to provide a code for their employment and government while thus confined.

The commissioners appointed, conformably to the act of 2d March, 1827, to provide for the adjustment of claims of persons entitled to indemnification under the first article of the treaty of Ghent, and for the distribution among such claimants of the sum paid by the Government of Great Britain under the convention of 13th November, 1826, closed their labors on the 30th of August last by awarding to the claimants the sum of $1,197,422.18, leaving a balance of $7,537.82, which was distributed ratably amongst all the claimants to whom awards had been made, according to the directions of the act.

The exhibits appended to the report from the Commissioner of the General Land Office present the actual condition of that common property of the Union. The amount paid into the Treasury from the proceeds of lands during the year 1827 and for the first half of 1828 falls little short of $2,000,000. The propriety of further extending the time for the extinguishment of the debt due to the United States by the purchasers of the public lands, limited by the act of 21st of March last to the 4th of July next, will claim the consideration of Congress, to whose vigilance and careful attention the regulation, disposal, and preservation of this great national inheritance has by the people of the United States been intrusted.

Among the important subjects to which the attention of the present Congress has already been invited, and which may occupy their further and deliberate discussion, will be the provision to be made for taking the fifth census or enumeration of the inhabitants of the United States. The Constitution of the United States requires that this enumeration should be made within every term of ten years, and the date from which the last enumeration commenced was the first Monday of August of the year 1820. The laws under which the former enumerations were taken were enacted at the session of Congress immediately preceding the operation; but considerable inconveniences were experienced from the delay of legislation to so late a period. That law, like those of the preceding enumerations, directed that the census should be taken by the marshals of the several districts and Territories of the Union under instructions from the Secretary of State. The preparation and transmission to the marshals of those instructions required more time than was then allowed between the passage of the law and the day when the enumeration was to commence. The term of six months limited for the returns of the marshals was also found even then too short, and must be more so now, when an additional population of at least 3,000,000 must be presented upon the returns. As they are to be made at the short session of Congress, it would, as well as from other considerations, be more convenient to commence the enumeration from an earlier period of the year than the 1st of August. The most favorable season would be the spring. On a review of the former enumerations it will be found that the plan for taking every census has contained many improvements upon that of its predecessor. The last is still susceptible of much improvement. The Third Census was the first at which any account was taken of the manufactures of the country. It was repeated at the last enumeration, but the returns in both cases were necessarily very imperfect. They must always be so, resting, of course, only upon the communications voluntarily made by individuals interested in some of the manufacturing establishments. Yet they contained much valuable information, and may by some supplementary provision of the law be rendered more effective. The columns of age, commencing from infancy, have hitherto been confined to a few periods, all under the number of 45 years. Important knowledge would be obtained by extending these columns, in intervals of 10 years, to the utmost boundaries of human life. The labor of taking them would be a trifling addition to that already prescribed, and the result would exhibit comparative tables of longevity highly interesting to the country. I deem it my duty further to observe that much of the imperfections in the returns of the last and perhaps of preceding enumerations proceeded from the inadequateness of the compensations allowed to the marshals and their assistants in taking them.

In closing this communication it only remains for me to assure the Legislature of my continued earnest wish for the adoption of measures recommended by me heretofore and yet to be acted on by them, and of the cordial concurrence on my part in every constitutional provision which may receive their sanction during the session tending to the general welfare.

JOHN QUINCY ADAMS

7

Andrew Jackson (1829–1837)

Andrew Jackson was the first president to tread where only Washington had before and deliver a formal farewell address to the nation. Old Hickory asked Chief Justice Roger Taney to help in its composition.[1] The resulting farewell followed Washington's by some forty years and is about a third longer.[2] Jackson justified his farewell address by referencing the historical context of its composition—the coming golden anniversary of the Constitution:

> We have now lived almost fifty years under the Constitution framed by the sages and patriots of the Revolution. We have had our seasons of peace and of war, with all the evils which precede or follow a state of hostility with powerful nations. We encountered these trials with our Constitution yet in its infancy, and under the disadvantages which a new and untried Government must always feel when it is called upon to put forth its whole strength, without the lights of experience to guide it or the weight of precedents to justify its measures. But we have passed triumphantly through all these difficulties. Our Constitution is no longer a doubtful experiment; and, at the end of nearly half a century, we find that it has preserved unimpaired the liberties of the people, secured the rights of property, and that our country has improved and is flourishing beyond any former example in the history of nations.

Taney's involvement with the drafting of the farewell is apt considering the constitutional issues that challenged the young nation. Who better than the chief justice was prepared to address such questions? Now that the basic framework of the Constitution had been ratified by experience, what counsel could Jackson offer his countrymen?

Jackson's farewell message is a summation of the most challenging issues facing the young republic. It can be divided into eight sections: (1) introduction, (2) review of the state of the nation, (3) the need for the spirit of unity to suppress sectionalism, (4) nullification and states' rights, (5) limits of federal power, (6) currency and banking policy, (7) foreign policy and national defense, and (8) conclusion. Some of these topics—especially the call for a spirit of unity—had been stressed by Washington. In a marked departure, however, only one paragraph of Jackson's address was devoted to foreign policy and national defense—less than 5 percent of the address—whereas almost a quarter of Washington's farewell address was devoted to these topics.

Yet Jackson left no doubt about his attitude to the first president's address. He took particular care to reference his predecessor when he argued against sectionalism and urged support of the Union. With the tone of a biblical admonition, he wrote of the "invaluable legacy of Washington to his countrymen [which] should be cherished in the heart of every citizen to the latest generation." Why? Because when we "dwell upon the pages of his parting address, his paternal counsels would seem to be not merely the offspring of wisdom and foresight, but the voice of prophecy foretelling events and warning us of the evil to come." By paying the father of his country his due, Jackson was able to frame his farewell more as a reminder of his predecessor's great wisdom than an attempt to rival it.

In the "Political Testament," Jackson was clearly preoccupied by a gathering storm. The topic that was beginning to receive much attention in the speeches of the day—understandable given the battles fought over nullification and states' rights—was the Constitution whose golden anniversary was soon to be celebrated. In Jackson's Farewell Address, the Constitution or the explicit idea of constitutional governance is mentioned twenty-four times—more often, by far, than any previous presidential farewell to that point in American history.

Farewell Address, also called "A Political Testament"
March 4, 1837

Fellow-Citizens:

Being about to retire finally from public life, I beg leave to offer you my grateful thanks for the many proofs of kindness and confidence which I have received at your hands. It has been my fortune, in the discharge of public duties, civil and military, frequently to have found myself in difficult and trying situations where prompt decision and energetic action were necessary and where the interest of the country required that high responsibilities should be fearlessly encountered; and it is with the deepest emotions of gratitude that I acknowledge the continued and unbroken confidence with which you have sustained me in every trial. My public life has been a long one, and I cannot hope that it has at all times been free from errors. But I have the consolation of knowing that if mistakes have been committed they have not seriously injured the country I so anxiously endeavored to serve; and at the moment when I surrender my last public trust, I leave this great people prosperous and happy, in the full enjoyment of liberty and peace, and honored and respected by every nation of the world.

If my humble efforts have in any degree contributed to preserve to you these blessings, I have been more than rewarded by the honors you have heaped upon me; and, above all, by the generous confidence with which you have supported me in every peril, and with which you have continued to animate and cheer my path to the closing hour of my political life. The time has now come when advanced age and a broken frame warn me to retire from public concerns, but the recollection of the many favors you have bestowed upon me is engraven upon my heart, and I have felt that I could not part from your service without making this public acknowledgment of the gratitude I owe you. And if I use the occasion to offer to you the counsels of age and experience, you will, I trust, receive them with the same indulgent kindness which you have so often extended to me, and will at least see in them an earnest desire to perpetuate in this favored land the blessings of liberty and equal laws.

We have now lived almost fifty years under the Constitution framed by the sages and patriots of the Revolution. The conflicts in which the nations of Europe were engaged during a great part of this period, the spirit in which they waged war against each other, and our intimate commercial connections with every part of the civilized world rendered it a time of much difficulty for the Government of the United States. We have had our seasons of peace and of war, with all the evils which precede or follow a state of hostility with powerful nations. We encountered these trials with our Constitution yet in its infancy, and under the disadvantages which a new and untried Government must always feel when it is called upon to put forth its whole strength without the lights of experience to guide it or the weight of precedents to justify its measures. But we have passed triumphantly through all these difficulties. Our Constitution is no longer a doubtful experiment, and at the end of nearly half a century we find that it has preserved unimpaired the liberties of the people, secured the rights of property, and that our country has improved and is flourishing beyond any former example in the history of nations.

In our domestic concerns there is everything to encourage us, and if you are true to yourselves nothing can impede your march to the highest point of national prosperity. The States which had so long been retarded in their improvement by the Indian tribes residing in the midst of them are at length relieved from the evil, and this unhappy race—the original dwellers in our land—are now placed in a situation where we may well hope that they will share in the blessings of civilization and be saved from that degradation and destruction to which they were rapidly hastening while they remained in the States; and while the safety and comfort of our own citizens have been greatly promoted by their removal, the philanthropist will rejoice that the remnant of that ill-fated race has been at length placed beyond the reach of injury or oppression, and that the paternal care of the General Government will hereafter watch over them and protect them.

If we turn to our relations with foreign powers, we find our condition equally gratifying. Actuated by the sincere desire to do justice to every nation and to preserve the blessings of peace, our intercourse with them has been conducted on the part of this Government in the spirit of frankness; and I take pleasure in saying that it has generally been met in a corresponding temper. Difficulties of old standing have been surmounted by friendly discussion and the mutual desire to be just; and the claims of our citizens, which had been long withheld, have at length been acknowledged and adjusted, and satisfactory arrangements made for their final payment; and with a limited and, I trust, a temporary exception, our relations with every foreign power are now of the most friendly character, our commerce continually expanding, and our flag respected in every quarter of the world.

These cheering and grateful prospects and these multiplied favors we owe, under Providence, to the adoption of the Federal Constitution. It is no longer a question whether this great country can remain happily united and flourish under our present form of government. Experience, the unerring test of all human undertakings, has shown the wisdom and foresight of those who formed it, and has proved that in the union of these States there is a sure foundation for the brightest hopes of freedom and for the happiness of the people. At every hazard and by every sacrifice, this Union must be preserved.

The necessity of watching with jealous anxiety for the preservation of the Union was earnestly pressed upon his fellow-citizens by the Father of his Country in his Farewell Address. He has there told us that "while experience shall not have demonstrated its impracticability, there will always be reason to distrust the patriotism of those who in any quarter may endeavor to weaken its bands"; and he has cautioned us in the strongest terms against the formation of parties on geographical discriminations, as one of the means which might disturb our union and to which designing men would be likely to resort.

The lessons contained in this invaluable legacy of Washington to his countrymen should be cherished in the heart of every citizen to the latest generation; and perhaps at no period of time could they be more usefully remembered than at the present moment. For when we look upon the scenes that are passing around us, and dwell upon the pages of his parting address, his paternal counsels would seem to be not merely the offspring of wisdom and foresight, but the voice of prophecy foretelling events and warning us of the evil to come. Forty years have passed since this imperishable document was given to his countrymen. The Federal Constitution was then regarded by him as an experiment—and he so speaks of it in his Address—but an experiment upon the success of which the best hopes of his country depended; and we all know that he was prepared to lay down his life, if necessary, to secure to it a full and a fair trial. The trial has been made. It has succeeded beyond the proudest hopes of those who framed it. Every quarter of this widely extended nation has felt its blessings and shared in the general prosperity produced by its adoption. But amid this general prosperity and splendid success, the dangers of which he warned us are becoming every day more evident and the signs of evil are sufficiently apparent to awaken the deepest anxiety in the bosom of the patriot. We behold systematic efforts publicly made to sow the seeds of discord between different parts of the United States and to place party divisions directly upon geographical distinctions; to excite the South against the North and the North against the South; and to force into the controversy the most delicate and exciting topics—topics upon which it is impossible that a large portion of the Union can ever speak without strong emotion. Appeals, too, are constantly made to sectional interests in order to influence the election of the Chief Magistrate, as if it were desired that he should favor a particular quarter of the country instead of fulfilling the duties of his station with impartial justice to all; and the possible dissolution of the Union has at length become an ordinary and familiar subject of discussion. Has the warning voice of Washington been forgotten, or have designs already been formed to sever the Union? Let it not be supposed that I impute to all of those who have taken an active part in these unwise and unprofitable discussions a want of patriotism or of public virtue. The honorable feeling of State pride and local attachments find a place in the bosoms of the most enlightened and pure. But while such men are conscious of their own integrity and honesty of purpose, they ought never to forget that the citizens of other States are their political brethren, and that however mistaken they may be in their views, the great body of them are equally honest and upright with themselves. Mutual suspicions and reproaches may in time create mutual hostility, and artful and designing men will always be found who are ready to foment these fatal divisions and to inflame the natural jealousies of different sections of the country. The history of the world is full of such examples, and especially the history of republics.

What have you to gain by division and dissension? Delude not yourselves with the belief that a breach once made may be afterwards repaired. If the Union is once severed, the line of separation will grow wider and wider, and the controversies which are now debated and settled in the halls of legislation will then be tried in fields of battle and determined by the sword. Neither should you deceive yourselves with the hope that the first line of separation would be the permanent one, and that nothing but harmony and concord would be found in the new associations formed upon the dissolution of this Union. Local interests would still be found there, and unchastened ambition. And if the recollection of common dangers in which the people of these United States stood side by side against the common foe; the memory of victories won by their united valor; the prosperity and happiness they have enjoyed under the present Constitution; the proud name they bear as citizens of this great republic—if all these recollections and proofs of common interest are not strong enough to bind us together as one people, what tie will hold united the new divisions of empire, when these bonds have been broken and this Union dissevered? The first line of separation would not last for a single generation; new fragments would be torn off; new leaders would spring up; and this great and glorious republic would soon be broken into a multitude of petty states, without commerce, without credit, jealous of one another, armed for mutual aggression, loaded with taxes to pay armies and leaders, seeking aid against each other from foreign powers, insulted and trampled upon by the nations of Europe, until, harassed with conflicts and humbled and debased in spirit, they would be ready to submit to the absolute dominion of any military adventurer and to surrender their liberty for the sake of repose. It is impossible to look on the consequences that would inevitably follow the destruction of this Government and not feel indignant when we hear cold calculations about the value of the Union and have so constantly before us a line of conduct so well calculated to weaken its ties.

There is too much at stake to allow pride or passion to influence your decision. Never for a moment believe that the great body of the citizens of any State or States can deliberately intend to do wrong. They may, under the influence of temporary excitement or misguided opinions, commit mistakes; they may be misled for a time by the suggestions of self-interest; but in a community so enlightened and patriotic as the people of the United States, argument will soon make them sensible of their errors, and when convinced they will be ready to repair them. If they have no higher or better motives to govern them, they will at least perceive that their own interest requires them to be just to others as they hope to receive justice at their hands.

But in order to maintain the Union unimpaired, it is absolutely necessary that the laws passed by the constituted authorities should be faithfully executed in every part of the country, and that every good citizen should at all times stand ready to put down, with the combined force of the nation, every attempt at unlawful resistance, under whatever pretext it may be made or whatever shape it may assume. Unconstitutional or oppressive laws may no doubt be passed by Congress, either from erroneous views or the want of due consideration; if they are within the reach of judicial authority, the remedy is easy and peaceful; and if, from the character of the law, it is an abuse of power not within the control of the judiciary, then free discussion and calm appeals to reason and to the justice of the people will not fail to redress the wrong. But until the law shall be declared void by the courts or repealed by Congress, no individual or combination of individuals can be justified in forcibly resisting its execution. It is impossible that any Government can continue to exist upon any other principles. It would cease to be a Government and be unworthy of the name if it had not the power to enforce the execution of its own laws within its own sphere of action.

It is true that cases may be imagined disclosing such a settled purpose of usurpation and oppression on the part of the Government as would justify an appeal to arms. These, however, are extreme cases, which we have no reason to apprehend in a Government where the power is in the hands of a patriotic people. And no citizen who loves his country would in any case whatever resort to forcible resistance, unless he clearly saw that the time had come when a freeman should prefer death to submission; for if such a struggle is once begun and the citizens of one section of the country [are] arrayed in arms against those of another in doubtful conflict, let the battle result as it may; there will be an end of the Union and with it an end to the hopes of freedom. The victory of the injured would not secure to them the blessings of liberty; it would avenge their wrongs, but they would themselves share in the common ruin.

But the Constitution can not be maintained nor the Union preserved in opposition to public feeling by the mere exertion of the coercive powers confided to the General Government. The foundations must be laid in the affections of the people; in the security it gives to life, liberty, character, and property, in every quarter of the country; and in the fraternal attachment which the citizens of the several States bear to one another as members of one political family, mutually contributing to promote the happiness of each other. Hence the citizens of every State should studiously avoid everything calculated to wound the sensibility or offend the just pride of the people of other States; and they should frown upon any proceedings within their own borders likely to disturb the tranquillity of their political brethren in other portions of the Union. In a country so extensive as the United States and with pursuits so varied, the internal regulations of the several States must frequently differ from one another in important particulars, and this difference is unavoidably increased by the varying principles upon which the American colonies were originally planted—principles which had taken deep root in their social relations before the Revolution, and therefore of necessity influencing their policy since they became free and independent States. But each State has the unquestionable right to regulate its own internal concerns according to its own pleasure; and while it does not interfere with the rights of the people of other States or the rights of the Union, every State must be the sole judge of the measures proper to secure the safety of its citizens and promote their happiness; and all efforts on the part of people of other States to cast odium upon their institutions, and all measures calculated to disturb their rights of property or to put in jeopardy their peace and internal tranquillity are in direct opposition to the spirit in which the Union was formed, and must endanger its safety. Motives of philanthropy may be assigned for this unwarrantable interference, and weak men may persuade themselves for a moment that they are laboring in the cause of humanity and asserting the rights of the human race; but everyone, upon sober reflection, will see that nothing but mischief can come from these improper assaults upon the feelings and rights of others. Rest assured that the men found busy in this work of discord are not worthy of your confidence and deserve your strongest reprobation.

In the legislation of Congress also, and in every measure of the General Government, justice to every portion of the United States should be faithfully observed. No free Government can stand without virtue in the people, and a lofty spirit of patriotism; and if the sordid feelings of mere selfishness shall usurp the place which ought to be filled by public spirit, the legislation of Congress will soon be converted into a scramble for personal and sectional advantages. Under our free institutions, the citizens of every quarter of our country are capable of attaining a high degree of prosperity and happiness without seeking to profit themselves at the expense of others; and every such attempt must in the end fail to succeed, for the people in every part of the United States are too enlightened not to understand their own rights and interests and to detect and defeat every effort to gain undue advantages over them; and when such designs are discovered, it naturally provokes resentments which cannot always be easily allayed. Justice—full and ample justice—to every portion of the United States should be the ruling principle of every freeman and should guide the deliberations of every public body, whether it be State or national.

It is well known that there have always been those amongst us who wish to enlarge the powers of the General Government; and experience would seem to indicate that there is a tendency on the part of this Government to overstep the boundaries marked out for it by the Constitution. Its legitimate authority is abundantly sufficient for all the purposes for which it was created; and its powers being expressly enumerated, there can be no justification for claiming anything beyond them. Every attempt to exercise power beyond these limits should be promptly and firmly opposed. For one evil example will lead to other measures still more mischievous; and if the principle of constructive powers or supposed advantages or temporary circumstances shall ever be permitted to justify the assumption of a power not given by the Constitution, the General Government will before long absorb all the powers of legislation, and you will have in effect but one consolidated Government. From the extent of our country, its diversified interests, different pursuits, and different habits, it is too obvious for argument that a single consolidated Government would be wholly inadequate to watch over and protect its interests; and every friend of our free institutions should be always prepared to maintain unimpaired and in full vigor the rights and sovereignty of the States and to confine the action of the General Government strictly to the sphere of its appropriate duties.

There is, perhaps, no one of the powers conferred on the Federal Government so liable to abuse as the taxing power. The most productive and convenient sources of revenue were necessarily given to it, that it might be able to perform the important duties imposed upon it; and the taxes which it lays upon commerce being concealed from the real payer in the price of the article, they do not so readily attract the attention of the people as smaller sums demanded from them directly by the tax gatherer. But the tax imposed on goods enhances by so much the price of the commodity to the consumer, and as many of these duties are imposed on articles of necessity which are daily used by the great body of the people, the money raised by these imposts is drawn from their pockets. Congress has no right under the Constitution to take money from the people unless it is required to execute some one of the specific powers intrusted to the Government; and if they raise more than is necessary for such purposes, it is an abuse of the power of taxation, and unjust and oppressive. It may indeed happen that the revenue will sometimes exceed the amount anticipated when the taxes were laid. When, however, this is ascertained, it is easy to reduce them; and in such a case it is unquestionably the duty of the Government to reduce them, for no circumstances can justify it in assuming a power not given to it by the Constitution nor in taking away the money of the people when it is not needed for the legitimate wants of the Government.

Plain as these principles appear to be, you will yet find that there is a constant effort to induce the General Government to go beyond the limits of its taxing power and to impose unnecessary burdens upon the people. Many powerful interests are continually at work to procure heavy duties on commerce and to swell the revenue beyond the real necessities of the public service, and the country has already felt the injurious effects of their combined influence. They succeeded in obtaining a tariff of duties bearing most oppressively on the agricultural and laboring classes of society and producing a revenue that could not be usefully employed within the range of the powers conferred upon Congress; and in order to fasten upon the people this unjust and unequal system of taxation, extravagant schemes of internal improvement were got up in various quarters to squander the money and to purchase support. Thus one unconstitutional measure was intended to be upheld by another, and the abuse of the power of taxation was to be maintained by usurping the power of expending the money in internal improvements. You can not have forgotten the severe and doubtful struggle through which we passed when the executive department of the Government by its veto endeavored to arrest this prodigal scheme of injustice, and to bring back the legislation of Congress to the boundaries prescribed by the Constitution. The good sense and practical judgment of the people, when the subject was brought before them, sustained the course of the Executive; and this plan of unconstitutional expenditure for the purpose of corrupt influence is, I trust, finally overthrown.

The result of this decision has been felt in the rapid extinguishment of the public debt and the large accumulation of a surplus in the Treasury, notwithstanding the tariff was reduced and is now very far below the amount originally contemplated by its advocates. But, rely upon it, the design to collect an extravagant revenue and to burden you with taxes beyond the economical wants of the Government is not yet abandoned. The various interests which have combined together to impose a heavy tariff and to produce an overflowing Treasury are too strong and have too much at stake to surrender the contest. The corporations and wealthy individuals who are engaged in large manufacturing establishments desire a high tariff to increase their gains. Designing politicians will support it to conciliate their favor and to obtain the means of profuse expenditure for the purpose of purchasing influence in other quarters; and since the people have decided that the Federal Government can not be permitted to employ its income in internal improvements, efforts will be made to seduce and mislead the citizens of the several States by holding out to them the deceitful prospect of benefits to be derived from a surplus revenue collected by the General Government and annually divided among the States. And if, encouraged by these fallacious hopes, the States should disregard the principles of economy which ought to characterize every republican Government, and should indulge in lavish expenditures exceeding their resources, they will before long find themselves oppressed with debts which they are unable to pay, and the temptation will become irresistible to support a high tariff in order to obtain a surplus for distribution. Do not allow yourselves, my fellow-citizens, to be misled on this subject. The Federal Government can not collect a surplus for such purposes without violating the principles of the Constitution and assuming powers which have not been granted. It is, moreover, a system of injustice, and if persisted in will inevitably lead to corruption, and must end in ruin. The surplus revenue will be drawn from the pockets of the people—from the farmer, the mechanic, and the laboring classes of society; but who will receive it when distributed among the States, where it is to be disposed of by leading State politicians who have friends to favor and political partisans to gratify? It will certainly not be returned to those who paid it and who have most need of it and are honestly entitled to it. There is but one safe rule, and that is to confine the General Government rigidly within the sphere of its appropriate duties. It has no power to raise a revenue or impose taxes except for the purposes enumerated in the Constitution; and if its income is found to exceed these wants, it should be forthwith reduced, and the burdens of the people so far lightened.

In reviewing the conflicts which have taken place between different interests in the United States and the policy pursued since the adoption of our present form of Government, we find nothing that has produced such deep-seated evil as the course of legislation in relation to the currency. The Constitution of the United States unquestionably intended to secure to the people a circulating medium of gold and silver. But the establishment of a national bank by Congress, with the privilege of issuing paper money receivable in the payment of the public dues, and the unfortunate course of legislation in the several States upon the same subject, drove from general circulation the constitutional currency and substituted one of paper in its place.

It was not easy for men engaged in the ordinary pursuits of business, whose attention had not been particularly drawn to the subject, to foresee all the consequences of a currency exclusively of paper;

and we ought not on that account to be surprised at the facility with which laws were obtained to carry into effect the paper system. Honest and even enlightened men are sometimes misled by the specious and plausible statements of the designing. But experience has now proved the mischiefs and dangers of a paper currency, and it rests with you to determine whether the proper remedy shall be applied.

The paper system being founded on public confidence and having of itself no intrinsic value, it is liable to great and sudden fluctuations, thereby rendering property insecure and the wages of labor unsteady and uncertain. The corporations which create the paper money can not be relied upon to keep the circulating medium uniform in amount. In times of prosperity when confidence is high, they are tempted by the prospect of gain, or by the influence of those who hope to profit by it to extend their issues of paper beyond the bounds of discretion and the reasonable demands of business. And when these issues have been pushed on from day to day until public confidence is at length shaken, then a reaction takes place, and they immediately withdraw the credits they have given, suddenly curtail their issues, and produce an unexpected and ruinous contraction of the circulating medium which is felt by the whole community. The banks by this means save themselves, and the mischievous consequences of their imprudence or cupidity are visited upon the public. Nor does the evil stop here. These ebbs and flows in the currency and these indiscreet extensions of credit naturally engender a spirit of speculation injurious to the habits and character of the people. We have already seen its effects in the wild spirit of speculation in the public lands and various kinds of stock which, within the last year or two, seized upon such a multitude of our citizens and threatened to pervade all classes of society and to withdraw their attention from the sober pursuits of honest industry. It is not by encouraging this spirit that we shall best pre-serve public virtue and promote the true interests of our country. But if your currency continues as exclusively paper as it now is, it will foster this eager desire to amass wealth without labor; it will multiply the number of dependents on bank accommodations and bank favors; the temptation to obtain money at any sacrifice will become stronger and stronger, and inevitably lead to corruption, which will find its way into your public councils and destroy at no distant day the purity of your Government. Some of the evils which arise from this system of paper press with peculiar hardship upon the class of society least able to bear it. A portion of this currency frequently becomes depreciated or worthless, and all of it is easily counterfeited in such a manner as to require peculiar skill and much experience to distinguish the counterfeit from the genuine note. These frauds are most generally perpetrated in the smaller notes, which are used in the daily transactions of ordinary business; and the losses occasioned by them are commonly thrown upon the laboring classes of society whose situation and pursuits put it out of their power to guard themselves from these impositions and whose daily wages are necessary for their subsistence. It is the duty of every Government so to regulate its currency as to protect this numerous class as far as practicable from the impositions of avarice and fraud. It is more especially the duty of the United States where the Government is emphatically the Government of the people, and where this respectable portion of our citizens are so proudly distinguished from the laboring classes of all other nations by their independent spirit, their love of liberty, their intelligence, and their high tone of moral character. Their industry in peace is the source of our wealth, and their bravery in war has covered us with glory, and the Government of the United States will but ill discharge its duties if it leaves them a prey to such dishonest impositions. Yet it is evident that their interests cannot be effectually protected unless silver and gold are restored to circulation.

These views alone of the paper currency are sufficient to call for immediate reform; but there is another consideration which should still more strongly press it upon your attention.

Recent events have proved that the paper money system of this country may be used as an engine to undermine your free institutions, and that those who desire to engross all power in the hands of the few and to govern by corruption or force are aware of its power and prepared to employ it. Your banks now furnish your only circulating medium, and money is plenty or scarce according to the quantity of notes issued by them. While they have capitals not greatly disproportioned to each other, they are competitors in business, and no one of them can exercise dominion over the rest; and although in the present state of the currency these banks may and do operate injuriously upon the habits of business, the pecuniary concerns, and the moral tone of society, yet, from their number and dispersed situation, they cannot combine for the purpose of political influence; and whatever may be the dispositions of some of them, their power of mischief must necessarily be confined to a narrow space and felt only in their immediate neighborhoods.

But when the charter for the Bank of the United States was obtained from Congress, it perfected the schemes of the paper system and gave to its advocates the position they have struggled to obtain from the commencement of the Federal Government down to the present hour. The immense capital and peculiar privileges bestowed upon it enabled it to exercise despotic sway over the other banks in every part of the country. From its superior strength it could seriously injure, if not destroy, the business of any one of them which might incur its resentment; and it openly claimed for itself the power of regulating the currency throughout the United States. In other words, it asserted (and it undoubtedly possessed) the power to make money plenty or scarce, at its pleasure, at any time, and in any quarter of the Union, by controlling the issues of other banks and permitting an expansion or compelling a general contraction of the circulating medium, according to its own will. The other banking institutions were sensible of its strength, and they soon generally became its obedient instruments, ready at all times to execute its mandates; and with the banks necessarily went also that numerous class of persons in our commercial cities who depend altogether on bank credits for their solvency and means of business, and who are therefore obliged for their own safety to propitiate the favor of the money power by distinguished zeal and devotion in its service. The result of the ill-advised legislation which established this great monopoly was to concentrate the whole moneyed power of the Union, with its boundless means of corruption and its numerous dependents, under the direction and command of one acknowledged head, thus organizing this particular interest as one body and securing to it unity and concert of action throughout the United States and enabling it to bring forward, upon any occasion, its entire and undivided strength to support or defeat any measure of the Government. In the hands of this formidable power, thus perfectly organized, was also placed unlimited dominion over the amount of the circulating medium, giving it the power to regulate the value of property and the fruits of labor in every quarter of the Union and to bestow prosperity or bring ruin upon any city or section of the country as might best comport with its own interest or policy.

We are not left to conjecture how the moneyed power, thus organized and with such a weapon in its hands, would be likely to use it. The distress and alarm which pervaded and agitated the whole country when the Bank of the United States waged war upon the people in order to compel them to submit to its demands cannot yet be forgotten. The ruthless and unsparing temper with which whole cities and communities were oppressed, individuals impoverished and ruined, and a scene of cheerful prosperity suddenly changed into one of gloom and despondency ought to be indelibly impressed on the memory of the people of the United States. If such was its power in a time of peace, what would it not have been in a season of war with an enemy at your doors? No nation but the freemen of the United States could have come out victorious from such a contest; yet, if you had not conquered, the Government would have passed from the hands of the many to the hands of the few; and this organized money power, from its secret conclave, would have dictated the choice of your highest officers and compelled you to make peace or war as best suited their own wishes. The forms of your government might for a time have remained, but its living spirit would have departed from it.

The distress and sufferings inflicted on the people by the bank are some of the fruits of that system of policy which is continually striving to enlarge the authority of the Federal Government beyond the limits fixed by the Constitution. The powers enumerated in that instrument do not confer on Congress the right to establish such a corporation as the Bank of the United States; and the evil consequences which followed may warn us of the danger of departing from the true rule of construction and of permitting temporary circumstances or the hope of better promoting the public welfare to influence, in any degree, our decisions upon the extent of the authority of the General Government. Let us abide by the Constitution as it is written, or amend it in the constitutional mode if it is found to be defective.

The severe lessons of experience will, I doubt not, be sufficient to prevent Congress from again chartering such a monopoly, even if the Constitution did not present an insuperable objection to it. But you must remember, my fellow-citizens, that eternal vigilance by the people is the price of liberty, and that you must pay the price if you wish to secure the blessing. It behooves you, therefore, to be watchful in your States as well as in the Federal Government. The power which the moneyed interest can exercise, when concentrated under a single head, and with our present system of currency, was sufficiently demonstrated in the struggle made by the Bank of the United States. Defeated in the General Government, the same class of intriguers and politicians will now resort to the States and endeavor to obtain there the same organization which they failed to perpetuate in the Union; and with specious and deceitful plans of public advantages and State interests and State pride they will endeavor to establish in the different States one moneyed institution with overgrown capital and exclusive privileges sufficient to enable it to control the operations of the other banks. Such an institution will be pregnant with the same evils produced by the Bank of the United States, although its sphere of action is more confined; and in the State in which it is chartered the money power will be able to embody its whole strength and to move together with undivided force to accomplish any object it may wish to attain. You have already had abundant evidence of its power to inflict injury upon the agricultural, mechanical, and laboring classes of society, and over those whose engagements in trade or speculation render them dependent on bank facilities, the dominion of the State monopoly will be absolute and their obedience unlimited. With such a bank and a paper currency, the money power would in a few years govern the State and control its measures; and if a sufficient number of States can be induced to create such establishments, the time will soon come when it will again take the field against the United States and succeed in perfecting and perpetuating its organization by a charter from Congress.

It is one of the serious evils of our present system of banking that it enables one class of society—and that by no means a numerous one—by its control over the currency to act injuriously upon the interests of all the others and to exercise more than its just proportion of influence in political affairs. The agricultural, the mechanical, and the laboring classes have little or no share in the direction of the great moneyed corporations; and from their habits and the nature of their pursuits, they are incapable of forming extensive combinations to act together with united force. Such concert of action may sometimes be produced in a single city or in a small district of country by means of personal communications with each other; but they have no regular or active correspondence with those who are engaged in similar pursuits in distant places; they have but little patronage to give to the press and exercise but a small share of influence over it; they have no crowd of dependents above them who hope to grow rich without labor by their countenance and favor, and who are therefore always ready to exercise their wishes. The planter, the farmer, the mechanic, and the laborer all know that their success depends upon their own industry and economy and that they must not expect to become suddenly rich by the fruits of their toil. Yet these classes of society form the great body of the people of the United States; they are the bone and sinew of the country—men who love liberty and desire nothing but equal rights and equal laws and who, moreover, hold the great mass of our national wealth, although it is distributed in moderate amounts among the millions of freemen who possess it. But with overwhelming numbers and wealth on their side, they are in constant danger of losing their fair influence in the Government, and with difficulty maintain their just rights against the incessant efforts daily made to encroach upon them. The mischief springs from the power which the moneyed interest derives from a paper currency which they are able to control; from the multitude of corporations with exclusive privileges which they have succeeded in obtaining in the different States and which are employed altogether for their benefit; and unless you become more watchful in your States and check this spirit of monopoly and thirst for exclusive privileges, you will in the end find that the most important powers of Government have been given or bartered away, and the control over your dearest interests has passed into the hands of these corporations.

The paper money system and its natural associates—monopoly and exclusive privileges—have already struck their roots too deep in the soil, and it will require all your efforts to check its further growth and to eradicate the evil. The men who profit by the abuses and desire to perpetuate them will continue to besiege the halls of legislation in the General Government as well as in the States, and will seek by every artifice to mislead and deceive the public servants. It is to yourselves that you must look for safety and the means of guarding and perpetuating your free institutions. In your hands is rightfully placed the sovereignty of the country, and to you every one placed in authority is ultimately responsible. It is always in your power to see that the wishes of the people are carried into faithful execution, and their will, when once made known, must sooner or later be obeyed. And while the people remain, as I trust they ever will, uncorrupted and incorruptible, and continue watchful and jealous of their rights, the Government is safe, and the cause of freedom will continue to triumph over all its enemies.

But it will require steady and persevering exertions on your part to rid yourselves of the iniquities and mischiefs of the paper system and to check the spirit of monopoly and other abuses which have sprung up with it, and of which it is the main support. So many interests are united to resist all reform on this subject that you must not hope the conflict will be a short one nor success easy. My humble efforts have not been spared during my administration of the Government to restore the constitutional currency of gold and silver; and something, I trust, has been done towards the accomplishment of this most desirable object. But enough yet remains to require all your energy and perseverance. The power, however, is in your hands, and the remedy must and will be applied if you determine upon it.

While I am thus endeavoring to press upon your attention the principles which I deem of vital importance in the domestic concerns of the country, I ought not to pass over without notice the important considerations which should govern your policy toward foreign powers. It is unquestionably our true interest to cultivate the most friendly understanding with every nation and to avoid by every honorable means the calamities of war; and we shall best attain this object by frankness and sincerity in our foreign intercourse, by prompt and faithful execution of treaties, and by justice and impartiality in our conduct to all. But no nation, however desirous of peace can hope to escape occasional collisions with other powers; and the soundest dictates of policy require that we should place ourselves in a condition to assert our rights if a resort to force should ever become necessary. Our local situation, our long line of seacoast, indented by numerous bays, with deep rivers opening into the interior, as well as our extended and still increasing commerce, point to the Navy as our natural means of defense. It will in the end be found to be the cheapest and most effectual; and now is the time, in a season of peace and with an overflowing revenue, that we can year after year add to its strength without increasing the burdens of the people. It is your true policy. For your Navy will not only protect your rich and flourishing commerce in distant seas, but will enable you to reach and annoy the enemy and will give to defense its greatest efficiency by meeting danger at a distance from home. It is impossible by any line of fortifications to guard every point from attack against a hostile force advancing from the ocean and selecting its object; but they are indispensable to protect cities from bombardment, dockyards and naval arsenals from destruction, to give shelter to merchant vessels in time of war, and to single ships or weaker squadrons when pressed by superior force. Fortifications of this description can not be too soon completed and armed and placed in a condition of the most perfect preparation. The abundant means we now possess can not be applied in any manner more useful to the country; and when this is done and our naval force sufficiently strengthened and our militia armed, we need not fear that any nation will wantonly insult us or needlessly provoke hostilities. We shall more certainly preserve peace when it is well understood that we are prepared for war.

In presenting to you, my fellow-citizens, these parting counsels, I have brought before you the leading principles upon which I endeavored to administer the Government in the high office with which you twice honored me. Knowing that the path of freedom is continually beset by enemies who often assume the disguise of friends, I have devoted the last hours of my public life to warn you of the dangers. The progress of the United States under our free and happy institutions has surpassed the most sanguine hopes of the founders of the Republic. Our growth has been rapid beyond all former example in numbers, in wealth, in knowledge, and all the useful arts which contribute to the comforts and convenience of man; and from the earliest ages of history to the present day, there never have been thirteen millions of people associated in one political body who enjoyed so much freedom and happiness as the people of these United States. You have no longer any cause to fear danger from abroad; your strength and power are well known throughout the civilized world, as well as the high and gallant bearing of your sons. It is from within, among yourselves—from cupidity, from corruption, from disappointed ambition, and inordinate thirst for power—that factions will be formed and liberty endangered. It is against such designs, whatever disguise the actors may assume, that you have especially to guard yourselves. You have the highest of human trust committed to your care. Providence has showered on this favored land blessings without number, and has chosen you as the guardian of freedom to preserve it for the benefit of the human race. May He who holds in his hands the destinies of nations make you worthy of the favors He has bestowed and enable you, with pure hearts and pure hands and sleepless vigilance, to guard and defend to the end of time the great charge He has committed to your keeping.

My own race is nearly run; advanced age and failing health warn me that before long I must pass beyond the reach of human event and cease to feel the vicissitudes of human affairs. I thank God that my life has been spent in a land of liberty and that He has given me a heart to love my country with the affection of a son. And, filled with gratitude for your constant and unwavering kindness, I bid you a last and affectionate farewell.

ANDREW JACKSON

Four months prior to giving his farewell address, or "Political Testament," Jackson delivered his eighth and final message to the Congress. The two-term president also used the occasion to bid adieu, not just to public life but seemingly to life itself. He presented himself as a tired old man who had run his race. And yet, Jackson would live another eight years, exercising considerable influence on national politics.

Near the beginning of the message, Jackson discussed the war between Mexico and the Republic of Texas. The famous siege of the Alamo was still fresh in American memory, having occurred the previous winter. Dozens of Jackson's fellow Tennesseans, Davy Crockett among them, had died defending the Alamo. In fact, among the Tennesseans was the president's namesake—Andrew Jackson Harrison. While Jackson was not at all happy with Mexican conduct during and after the war with Texas, he did not allow his fiery temperament to overrule a policy of caution and moderation.

Jackson was not so moderate, however, when it came to an institution he loathed and thought unconstitutional—the Second Bank of the United States. Jackson had spent much political capital fighting the bank and its supporters. Not exhausted by the fight, he devoted a fair portion of his final annual message to justifying himself. Four years earlier, in 1832, Jackson had vetoed the bill that would have rechartered the bank; he believed it favored eastern manufacturers at the expense of the common people. Later he removed two secretaries of the treasury for failing to comply with his order to withdraw federal deposits from the bank. This assertion of presidential power—combined with the veto—moved the Senate to censure the president.

About the bank Jackson wrote: "The lessons taught by the Bank of the United States can not well be lost upon the American people. They will take care never again to place so tremendous a power in irresponsible hands."

Excerpts of Jackson's last annual message follow.

Eighth Annual Message
(written to the Congress)
December 5, 1836

Fellow Citizens of the Senate and of the House of Representatives:

Addressing to you the last annual message I shall ever present to the Congress of the United States, it is a source of the most heartfelt satisfaction to be able to congratulate you on the high state of prosperity which our beloved country has attained. With no causes at home or abroad to lessen the confidence with which we look to the future for continuing proofs of the capacity of our free institutions to produce all the fruits of good government, the general condition of our affairs may well excite our national pride.

I can not avoid congratulating you, and my country particularly, on the success of the efforts made during my Administration by the Executive and Legislature, in conformity with the sincere, constant, and earnest desire of the people, to maintain peace and establish cordial relations with all foreign powers. Our gratitude is due to the Supreme Ruler of the Universe, and I invite you to unite with me in offering to Him fervent supplications that His providential care may ever be extended to those who follow us, enabling them to avoid the dangers and the horrors of war consistently with a just and indispensable regard to the rights and honor of our country.

* * *

[Regarding the struggle between the newly formed Republic of Texas and Mexico] It is already known to you, by the correspondence between the two Governments communicated at your last session, that our conduct in relation to that struggle is regulated by the same principles that governed us in the dispute between Spain and Mexico herself, and I trust that it will be found on the most severe scrutiny that our acts have strictly corresponded with our professions. That the inhabitants of the United States should feel strong prepossessions for the one party is not surprising. But this circumstance should of itself teach us great caution, lest it lead us into the great error of suffering public policy to be regulated by partiality or prejudice; and there are considerations connected with the possible result of this contest between the two parties of so much delicacy and importance to the United States that our character requires that we should neither anticipate events nor attempt to control them. The known desire of the Texans to become a part of our system, although its gratification depends upon the reconcilement of various and conflicting interests, necessarily a work of time and uncertain in itself, is calculated to expose our conduct to misconstruction in the eyes of the world. There are already those who, indifferent to principle themselves and prone to suspect the want of it in others, charge us with ambitious designs and insidious policy. You will perceive by the accompanying documents that the extraordinary mission from Mexico has been terminated on the sole ground that the obligations of this Government to itself and to Mexico, under treaty stipulations, have compelled me to trust a discretionary authority to a high officer of our Army to advance into territory claimed as part of Texas if necessary to protect our own or the neighboring frontier from Indian depredation. In the opinion of the Mexican functionary who has just left us, the honor of his country will be wounded by American soldiers entering, with the most amicable avowed purposes, upon ground from which the followers of his Government have been expelled, and over which there is at present no certainty of a serious effort on its part to reestablish its dominion. The departure of this minister was the more singular as he was apprised that the sufficiency of the causes assigned for the advance of our troops by the commanding general had been seriously doubted by me, and there was every reason to suppose that the troops of the United States, their commander having had time to ascertain the truth or falsehood of the information upon which they had been marched to Nacogdoches, would be either there in perfect accordance with the principles admitted to be just in his conference with the Secretary of State by the Mexican minister himself, or were already withdrawn in consequence of the impressive warnings their commanding officer had received from the Department of War. It is hoped and believed that his Government will take a more dispassionate and just view of this subject, and not be disposed to construe a measure of justifiable precaution, made necessary by its known inability in execution of the stipulations of our treaty to act upon the frontier, into an encroachment upon its rights or a stain upon its honor.

In the meantime the ancient complaints of injustice made on behalf of our citizens are disregarded, and new causes of dissatisfaction have arisen, some of them of a character requiring prompt remonstrance and ample and immediate redress. I trust, however, by tempering firmness with courtesy and acting with great forbearance upon every incident that has occurred or that may happen, to do and to obtain justice, and thus avoid the necessity of again bringing this subject to the view of Congress.

It is my duty to remind you that no provision has been made to execute our treaty with Mexico for tracing the boundary line between the two countries. What ever may be the prospect of Mexico's being soon able to execute the treaty on its part, it is proper that we should be in anticipation prepared at all times to perform our obligations, without regard to the probable condition of those with whom we have contracted them.

The result of the confidential inquiries made into the condition and prospects of the newly declared Texan Government will be communicated to you in the course of the session.

* * *

You will perceive from the report of the Secretary of the Treasury that the financial means of the country continue to keep pace with its improvement in all other respects. The receipts into the Treasury during the present year will amount to about $47,691,898; those from customs being estimated at $22,523,151, those from lands at about $24,000,000, and the residue from miscellaneous sources. The expenditures for all objects during the year are estimated not to exceed $32,000,000, which will leave a balance in the Treasury for public purposes on the first day of January next of about $41,723,959. This sum, with the exception of $5,000,000, will be transferred to the several States in accordance with the provisions of the act regulating the deposits of the public money.

The unexpended balances of appropriation on the first day of January next are estimated at $14,636,062, exceeding by $9,636,062 the amount which will be left in the deposit banks, subject to the draft of the Treasurer of the United States, after the contemplated transfers to the several States are made. If, therefore, the future receipts should not be sufficient to meet these outstanding and future appropriations, there may be soon a necessity to use a portion of the funds deposited with the States.

The consequences apprehended when the deposit act of the last session received a reluctant approval have been measurably realized. Though an act merely for the deposit of the surplus moneys of the United States in the State treasuries for safe-keeping until they may be wanted for the service of the General Government, it has been extensively spoken of as an act to give the money to the several States, and they have been advised to use it as a gift, without regard to the means of refunding it when called for. Such a suggestion has doubtless been made without a proper attention to the various principles and interests which are affected by it. It is manifest that the law itself can not sanction such a suggestion, and that as it now stands the States have no more authority to receive and use these deposits without intending to return them than any deposit bank or any individual temporarily charged with the safe-keeping or application of the public money would now have for converting the same to their private use without the consent and against the will of the Government. But independently of the violation of public faith and moral obligation which are involved in this suggestion when examined in reference to the terms of the present deposit act, it is believed that the considerations which should govern the future legislation of Congress on this subject will be equally conclusive against the adoption of any measure recognizing the principles on which the suggestion has been made.

Considering the intimate connection of the subject with the financial interests of the country and its great importance in whatever aspect it can be viewed, I have bestowed upon it the most anxious reflection, and feel it to be my duty to state to Congress such thoughts as have occurred to me, to aid their deliberation in treating it in the manner best calculated to conduce to the common good.

The experience of other nations admonished us to hasten the extinguishment of the public debt; but it will be in vain that we have congratulated each other upon the disappearance of this evil if we do not guard against the equally great one of promoting the unnecessary accumulation of public revenue. No political maxim is better established than that which tells us that an improvident expenditure of money is the parent of profligacy, and that no people can hope to perpetuate their liberties who long acquiesce in a policy which taxes them for objects not necessary to the legitimate and real wants of their Government. Flattering as is the condition of our country at the present period, because of its unexampled advance in all the steps of social and political improvement, it can not be disguised that there is a lurking danger already apparent in the neglect of this warning truth, and that the time has arrived when the representatives of the people should be employed in devising some more appropriate remedy than now exists to avert it.

Under our present revenue system there is every probability that there will continue to be a surplus beyond the wants of the Government, and it has become our duty to decide whether such a result be consistent with the true objects of our Government.

Should a surplus be permitted to accumulate beyond the appropriations, it must be retained in the Treasury, as it now is, or distributed among the people or the States.

To retain it in the Treasury unemployed in any way is impracticable; it is, besides, against the genius of our free institutions to lock up in vaults the treasure of the nation. To take from the people the right of bearing arms and put their weapons of defense in the hands of a standing army would be scarcely more dangerous to their liberties than to permit the Government to accumulate immense amounts of treasure beyond the supplies necessary to its legitimate wants. Such a treasure would doubtless be employed at some time, as it has been in other countries, when opportunity tempted ambition.

To collect it merely for distribution to the States would seem to be highly impolitic, if not as dangerous as the proposition to retain it in the Treasury. The shortest reflection must satisfy everyone that to require the people to pay taxes to the Government merely that they may be paid back again is sporting with the substantial interests of the country, and no system which produces such a result can be expected to receive the public countenance. Nothing could be gained by it even if each individual who contributed a portion of the tax could receive back promptly the same portion. But it is apparent that no system of the kind can ever be enforced which will not absorb a considerable portion of the money to be distributed in salaries and commissions to the agents employed in the process and in the various losses and depreciations which arise from other causes, and the practical effect of such an attempt must ever be to burden the people with taxes, not for purposes beneficial to them, but to swell the profits of deposit banks and support a band of useless public officers.

A distribution to the people is impracticable and unjust in other respects. It would be taking one man's property and giving it to another. Such would be the unavoidable result of a rule of equality (and none other is spoken of or would be likely to be adopted), in as much as there is no mode by which the amount of the individual contributions of our citizens to the public revenue can be ascertained. We know that they contribute unequally, and a rule, therefore, that would distribute to them equally would be liable to all the objections which apply to the principle of an equal division of property. To make the General Government the instrument of carrying this odious principle into effect would be at once to destroy the means of its usefulness and change the character designed for it by the framers of the Constitution.

But the more extended and injurious consequences likely to result from a policy which would collect a surplus revenue from the purpose of distributing it may be forcibly illustrated by an examination of the effects already produced by the present deposit act. This act, although certainly designed to secure the safe-keeping of the public revenue, is not entirely free in its tendencies from any of the objections which apply to this principle of distribution. The Government had without necessity received from the people a large surplus, which, instead of being employed as heretofore and returned to them by means of the public expenditure, was deposited with sundry banks. The banks proceeded to make loans upon this surplus, and thus converted it into banking capital, and in this manner it has tended to multiply bank charters and has had a great agency in producing a spirit of wild speculation. The possession and use of the property out of which this surplus was created belonged to the people, but the Government has transferred its possession to incorporated banks, whose interest and effort it is to make large profits out of its use. This process need only be stated to show its injustice and bad policy.

And the same observations apply to the influence which is produced by the steps necessary to collect as well as to distribute such a revenue. About three-fifths of all the duties on imports are paid in the city of New York, but it is obvious that the means to pay those duties are drawn from every quarter of the Union. Every citizen in every State who purchases and consumes an article which has paid a duty at that port contributes to the accumulating mass. The surplus collected there must therefore be made up of moneys or property withdrawn from other points and other States. Thus the wealth and business of every region from which these surplus funds proceed must be to some extent injured, while that of the place where the funds are concentrated and are employed in banking are proportionably extended. But both in making the transfer of the funds which are first necessary to pay the duties and collect the surplus and in making the retransfer which becomes necessary when the time arrives for the distribution of that surplus there is a considerable period when the funds can not be brought into use, and it is manifest that, besides the loss inevitable from such an operation, its tendency is to produce fluctuations in the business of the country, which are always productive of speculation and detrimental to the interests of regular trade. Argument can scarcely be necessary to show that a measure of this character ought not to receive further legislative encouragement.

By examining the practical operation of the ration for distribution adopted in the deposit bill of the last session we shall discover other features that appear equally objectionable. Let it be assumed, for the sake of argument, that the surplus moneys to be deposited with the States have been collected and belong to them in the ration of their federal representative population—an assumption founded upon the fact that any deficiencies in our future revenue from imposts and public lands must be made up by direct taxes collected from the States in that ration. It is proposed to distribute this surplus— say $30,000,000—not according to the ration in which it has been collected and belongs to the people of the States, but in that of their votes in the colleges of electors of President and Vice President. The effect of a distribution upon that ration is shown by the annexed table, marked A.

By an examination of that table it will be perceived that in the distribution of a surplus of $30,000,000 upon that basis there is a great departure from the principle which regards representation as the true measure of taxation, and it will be found that the tendency of that departure will be to increase whatever inequalities have been supposed to attend the operation of our federal system in respect to its bearings upon the different interests of the Union. In making the basis of representation the basis of taxation the framers of the Constitution intended to equalize the burdens which are necessary to support the Government, and the adoption of that ratio, while it accomplished this object, was also the means of adjusting other great topics arising out of the conflicting views respecting the political equality of the various members of the Confederacy. Whatever, therefore, disturbs the liberal spirit of the compromises which established a rule of taxation so just and equitable, and which experience has proved to be so well adapted to the genius and habits of our people, should be received with the greatest caution and distrust.

A bare inspection in the annexed table of the differences produced by the ration used in the deposit act compared with the results of a distribution according to the ration of direct taxation must satisfy every unprejudiced mind that the former ration contravenes the spirit of the Constitution and produces a degree of injustice in the operations of the Federal Government which would be fatal to the hope of perpetuating it. By the ration of direct taxation, for example, the State of Delaware in the collection of $30,000,000 of revenue would pay into the Treasury $188,716, and in a distribution of $30,000,000 she would receive back from the Government, according to the ration of the deposit bill, the sum of $306,122; and similar results would follow the comparison between the small and the large States throughout the Union, thus realizing to the small States an advantage which would be doubtless as unacceptable to them as a motive for incorporating the principle in any system which would produce it as it would be inconsistent with the rights and expectations of the large States. It was certainly the intention of that provision of the Constitution which declares that "all duties, imposts, and excises" shall "be uniform throughout the United States" to make the burdens of taxation fall equally upon the people in whatever State of the Union they may reside. But what would be the value of such a uniform rule if the moneys raised by it could be immediately returned by a different one which will give to the people of some States much more and to those of others much less than their fair proportions? Were the Federal Government to exempt in express terms the imports, products, and manufactures of some portions of the country from all duties while it imposed heavy ones on others, the injustice could not be greater. It would be easy to show how by the operation of such a principle the large States of the Union would not only have to contribute their just share toward the support of the Federal Government, but also have to bear in some degree the taxes necessary to support the governments of their smaller sisters; but it is deemed unnecessary to state the details where the general principle is so obvious.

A system liable to such objections can never be supposed to have been sanctioned by the framers of the Constitution when they conferred on Congress the taxing power, and I feel persuaded that a mature examination of the subject will satisfy everyone that there are insurmountable difficulties in the operation of any plan which can be devised of collecting revenue for the purpose of distributing it. Congress is only authorized to levy taxes "to pay the debts and provide for the common defense and general welfare of the United States." There is no such provision as would authorize Congress to collect together the property of the country, under the name of revenue, for the purpose of dividing it equally or unequally among the States or the people. Indeed, it is not probable that such an idea ever occurred to the States when they adopted the Constitution. But however this may be, the only safe rule for us in interpreting the powers granted to the Federal Government is to regard the absence of express authority to touch a subject so important and delicate as this as equivalent to a prohibition.

Even if our powers were less doubtful in this respect as the Constitution now stands, there are considerations afforded by recent experience which would seem to make it our duty to avoid a resort to such a system.

All will admit that the simplicity and economy of the State governments mainly depend on the fact that money has to be supplied to support them by the same men, or their agents, who vote it away in appropriations. Hence when there are extravagant and wasteful appropriations there must be a corresponding increase of taxes, and the people, becoming awakened, will necessarily scrutinize the character of measures which thus increase their burdens. By the watchful eye of self-interest the agents of the people in the State governments are repressed and kept within the limits of a just economy. But if the necessity of levying the taxes be taken from those who make the appropriations and thrown upon a more distant and less responsible set of public agents, who have power to approach the people by an indirect and stealthy taxation, there is reason to fear that prodigality will soon supersede those characteristics which have thus far made us look with so much pride and confidence to the State governments as the main-stay of our Union and liberties. The State legislatures, instead of studying to restrict their State expenditures to the smallest possible sum, will claim credit for their profusion, and harass the General Government for increased supplies. Practically there would soon be but one taxing power, and that vested in a body of men far removed from the people, in which the farming and mechanic interests would scarcely be represented. The States would gradually lose their purity as well as their independence; they would not dare to murmur at the proceedings of the General Government, lest they should lose their supplies; all would be merged in a practical consolidation, cemented by wide-spread corruption, which could only be eradicated by one of those bloody revolutions which occasionally over-throw the despotic systems of the Old World.

In all the other aspects in which I have been able to look at the effect of such a principle of distribution upon the best interests of the country I can see nothing to compensate for the disadvantages to which I have adverted. If we consider the protective duties, which are in a great degree the source of the surplus revenue, beneficial to one section of the Union and prejudicial to another, there is no corrective for the evil in such a plan of distribution. On the contrary, there is reason to fear that all the complaints which have sprung from this cause would be aggravated. Everyone must be sensible that a distribution of the surplus must beget a disposition to cherish the means which create it, and any system, therefore, into which it enters must have a powerful tendency to increase rather than diminish the tariff. If it were even admitted that the advantages of such a system could be made equal to all the sections of the Union, the reasons already so urgently calling for a reduction of the revenue would never the less lose none of their force, for it will always be improbable that an intelligent and virtuous community can consent to raise a surplus for the mere purpose of dividing it, diminished as it must inevitably be by the expenses of the various machinery necessary to the process.

The safest and simplest mode of obviating all the difficulties which have been mentioned is to collect only revenue enough to meet the wants of the Government, and let the people keep the balance of their property in their own hands, to be used for their own profit. Each State will then support its own government and contribute its due share toward the support of the General Government. There would be no surplus to cramp and lessen the resources of individual wealth and enterprise, and the banks would be left to their ordinary means. Whatever agitations and fluctuations might arise from our unfortunate paper system, they could never be attributed, justly or unjustly, to the action of the Federal Government. There would be some guaranty that the spirit of wild speculation which seeks to convert the surplus revenue into banking capital would be effectually checked, and that the scenes of demoralization which are now so prevalent through the land would disappear.

Without desiring to conceal that the experience and observation of the last two years have operated a partial change in my views upon this interesting subject, it is nevertheless regretted that the suggestions made by me in my annual messages of 1829 and 1830 have been greatly misunderstood. At that time the great struggle was begun against that latitudinarian construction of the Constitution which authorizes the unlimited appropriation of the revenues of the Union to internal improvements within the States, tending to invest in the hands and place under the control of the General Government all the principal roads and canals of the country, in violation of State rights and in derogation of State authority.

At the same time the condition of the manufacturing interest was such as to create an apprehension that the duties on imports could not without extensive mischief be reduced in season to prevent the accumulation of a considerable surplus after the payment of the national debt. In view of the dangers of such a surplus, and in preference to its application to internal improvements in derogation of the rights and powers of the States, the suggestion of an amendment of the Constitution to authorize its distribution was made. It was an alternative for what were deemed greater evils—a temporary resort to relieve an overburdened treasury until the Government could, without a sudden and destructive revulsion in the business of the country, gradually return to the just principle of raising no more revenue from the people in taxes than is necessary for its economical support.

Even that alternative was not spoken of but in connection with an amendment of the Constitution. No temporary inconvenience can justify the exercise of a prohibited power not granted by that instrument, and it was from a conviction that the power to distribute even a temporary surplus of revenue is of that character that it was suggested only in connection with an appeal to the source of all legal power in the General Government, the States which have established it. No such appeal has been taken, and in my opinion a distribution of the surplus revenue by Congress either to the States or the people is to be considered as among the prohibitions of the Constitution.

As already intimated, my views have undergone a change so far as to be convinced that no alteration of the Constitution in this respect is wise or expedient. The influence of an accumulating surplus upon the credit system of the country, producing dangerous extensions and ruinous contractions, fluctuations in the price of property, rash speculation, idleness, extravagance, and a deterioration of morals, have taught us the important lesson that any transient mischief which may attend the reduction of our revenue to the wants of our Government is to be borne in preference to an over-flowing treasury.

I beg leave to call your attention to another subject intimately associated with the preceding one—the currency of the country.

It is apparent from the whole context of the Constitution, as well as the history of the times which gave birth to it, that it was the purpose of the Convention to establish a currency consisting of the precious metals. These, from their peculiar properties which rendered them the standard of value in all other countries, were adopted in this as well to establish its commercial standard in reference to foreign countries by a permanent rule as to exclude the use of a mutable medium of exchange, such as of certain agricultural commodities recognized by the statutes of some States as a tender for debts, or the still more pernicious expedient of a paper currency. The last, from the experience of the evils of the issues of paper during the Revolution, had become so justly obnoxious as not only to suggest the clause in the Constitution forbidding the emission of bills of credit by the States, but also to produce that vote in the Convention which negatived the proposition to grant power to Congress to charter corporations—a proposition well understood at the time as intended to authorize the establishment of a national bank, which was to issue a currency of bank notes on a capital to be created to some extent out of Government stocks. Although this proposition was refused by a direct vote of the Convention, the object was afterwards in effect obtained by its ingenious advocates through a strained construction of the Constitution. The debts of the Revolution were funded at prices which formed no equivalent compared with the nominal amount of the stock, and under circumstances which exposed the motives of some of those who participated in the passage of the act to distrust.

The facts that the value of the stock was greatly enhanced by the creation of the bank, that it was well understood that such would be the case, and that some of the advocates of the measure were largely benefited by it belong to the history of the times, and are well calculated to diminish the respect which might otherwise have been due to the action of the Congress which created the institution.

On the establishment of a national bank it became the interest of its creditors that gold should be superseded by the paper of the bank as a general currency. A value was soon attached to the gold coins which made their exportation to foreign countries as a mercantile commodity more profitable than their retention and use at home as money. It followed as a matter of course, if not designed by those who established the bank, that the bank became in effect a substitute for the Mint of the United States.

Such was the origin of a national-bank currency, and such the beginning of those difficulties which now appear in the excessive issues of the banks incorporated by the various States.

Although it may not be possible by any legislative means within our power to change at once the system which has thus been introduced, and has received the acquiescence of all portions of the country, it is certainly our duty to do all that is consistent with our constitutional obligations in preventing the mischiefs which are threatened by its undue extension. That the efforts of the fathers of our Government to guard against it by a constitutional provision were founded on an intimate knowledge of the subject has been frequently attested by the bitter experience of the country. The same causes which led them to refuse their sanction to a power authorizing the establishment of incorporations for banking purposes now exist in a much stronger degree to urge us to exert the utmost vigilance in calling into action the means necessary to correct the evils resulting from the unfortunate exercise of the power, and it is hoped that the opportunity for effecting this great good will be improved before the country witnesses new scenes of embarrassment and distress.

Variableness must ever be the characteristic of a currency of which the precious metals are not the chief ingredient, or which can be expanded or contracted without regard to the principles that regulate the value of those metals as a standard in the general trade of the world. With us bank issues constitute such a currency, and must ever do so until they are made dependent on those just proportions of gold and silver as a circulating medium which experience has proved to be necessary not only in this but in all other commercial countries. Where those proportions are not infused into the circulation and do not control it, it is manifest that prices must vary according to the tide of bank issues, and the value and stability of property must stand exposed to all the uncertainty which attends the administration of institutions that are constantly liable to the temptation of an interest distinct from that of the community in which they are established.

The progress of an expansion, or rather a depreciation, of the currency by excessive bank issues is always attended by a loss to the laboring classes. This portion of the community have neither time nor opportunity to watch the ebbs and flows of the money market. Engaged from day to day in their useful toils, they do not perceive that although their wages are nominally the same, or even somewhat higher, they are greatly reduced in fact by the rapid increase of a spurious currency, which, as it appears to make money abound, they are at first inclined to consider a blessing. It is not so with the speculator, by whom this operation is better understood, and is made to contribute to his advantage. It is not until the prices of the necessaries of life become so dear that the laboring classes can not supply their wants out of their wages that the wages rise and gradually reach a justly proportioned rate to that of the products of their labor. When thus, by depreciation in consequence of the quantity of paper in circulation, wages as well as prices become exorbitant, it is soon found that the whole effect of the adulteration is a tariff on our home industry for the benefit of the countries where gold and silver circulate and maintain uniformity and moderation in prices. It is then perceived that the enhancement of the price of land and labor produces a corresponding increase in the price of products until these products do not sustain a competition with similar ones in other countries, and thus both manufactured and agricultural productions cease to bear expectation from the country of the spurious currency, because they can not be sold for cost. This is the process by which specie is banished by the paper of the banks. Their vaults are soon exhausted to pay for foreign commodities. The next step is a stoppage of specie payment—a total degradation of paper as a currency—unusual depression of prices, the ruin of debtors, and the accumulation of property in the hands of creditors and cautious capitalists.

It was in view of these evils, together with the dangerous power wielded by the Bank of the United States and its repugnance to our Constitution, that I was induced to exert the power conferred upon me by the American people to prevent the continuance of that institution. But although various dangers to our republican institutions have been obviated by the failure of that bank to extort from the Government a renewal of its charter, it is obvious that little has been accomplished except a salutary change of public opinion toward restoring to the country the sound currency provided for in the Constitution. In the acts of several of the States prohibiting the circulation of small notes and the auxiliary enactments of Congress at the last session forbidding their reception or payment on public account, the true policy of the country has been advanced and a larger portion of the precious metals infused into our circulating medium. These measures will probably be followed up in due time by the enactment of State laws banishing from circulation bank notes of still higher denominations, and the object may be materially promoted by further acts of Congress forbidding the employment as fiscal agents of such banks as continue to issue notes of low denominations and throw impediments in the way of the circulation of gold and silver.

The effects of an extension of bank credits and overissues of bank paper have been strikingly illustrated in the sales of the public lands. From the returns made by the various registers and receivers in the early part of last summer it was perceived that the receipts arising from the sales of the public lands were increasing to an unprecedented amount. In effect, however, these receipts amounted to nothing more than credits in bank. The banks lent out their notes to speculators. They were paid to the receivers and immediately returned to the banks, to be lent out again and again, being mere instruments to transfer to speculators the most valuable public land and pay the Government by a credit on the books of the banks. Those credits on the books of some of the Western banks, usually called deposits, were already greatly beyond their immediate means of payment, and were rapidly increasing. Indeed, each speculation furnished means for another; for no sooner had one individual or company paid in the notes than they were immediately lent to another for a like purpose, and the banks were extending their business and their issues so largely as to alarm considerate men and render it doubtful whether these bank credits, if permitted to accumulate, would ultimately be of the least value to the Government. The spirit of expansion and speculation was not confined to the deposit banks, but pervaded the whole multitude of banks throughout the Union and was giving rise to new institutions to aggravate the evil.

The safety of the public funds and the interest of the people generally required that these operations should be checked; and it became the duty of every branch of the General and State Governments to adopt all legitimate and proper means to produce that salutary effect. Under this view of my duty I directed the issuing of the order which will be laid before you by the Secretary of the Treasury, requiring payment for the public lands sold to be made in specie, with an exception until the 15th of the present month in favor of actual settlers. This measure has produced many salutary consequences. It checked the career of the Western banks and gave them additional strength in anticipation of the pressure which has since pervaded our Eastern as well as the European commercial cities. By preventing the extension of the credit system it measurably cut off the means of speculation and retarded its progress in monopolizing the most valuable of the public lands. It has tended to save the new States from a non-resident proprietorship, one of the greatest obstacles to the advancement of a new country and the prosperity of an old one. It has tended to keep open the public lands for entry by emigrants at Government prices instead of their being compelled to purchase of speculators at double or triple prices. And it is conveying into the interior large sums in silver and gold, there to enter permanently into the currency of the country and place it on a firmer foundation. It is confidently believed that the country will find in the motives which induced that order and the happy consequences which will have ensued much to commend and nothing to condemn.

It remains for Congress if they approve the policy which dictated this order to follow it up in its various bearings. Much good, in my judgment, would be produced by prohibiting sales of the public lands except to actual settlers at a reasonable reduction of price, and to limit the quantity which shall be sold to them. Although it is believed the General Government never ought to receive anything but the constitutional currency in exchange for the public lands, that point would be of less importance if the lands were sold for immediate settlement and cultivation. Indeed, there is scarcely a mischief arising out of our present land system, including the accumulating surplus of revenues, which would not be remedied at once by a restriction on land sales to actual settlers; and it promises other advantages to the country in general and to the new States in particular which can not fail to receive the most profound consideration of Congress.

Experience continues to realize the expectations entertained as to the capacity of the State banks to perform the duties of fiscal agents for the Government at the time of the removal of the deposits. It was alleged by the advocates of the Bank of the United States that the State banks, whatever might be the regulations of the Treasury Department, could not make the transfers required by the Government or negotiate the domestic exchanges of the country. It is now well ascertained that the real domestic exchanges performed through discounts by the United States Bank and its 25 branches were at least one-third less than those of the deposit banks for an equal period of time; and if a comparison be instituted between the amounts of service rendered by these institutions on the broader basis which has been used by the advocates of the United States Bank in estimating what they consider the domestic exchanges transacted by it, the result will be still more favorable to the deposit banks.

The whole amount of public money transferred by the Bank of the United States in 1832 was $16,000,000. The amount transferred and actually paid by the deposit banks in the year ending the first of October last was $39,319,899; the amount transferred and paid between that period and the 6th of November was $5,399,000, and the amount of transfer warrants outstanding on that day was $14,450,000, making an aggregate of $59,168,894. These enormous sums of money first mentioned have been transferred with the greatest promptitude and regularity, and the rates at which the exchanges have been negotiated previously to the passage of the deposit act were generally below those charged by the Bank of the United States. Independently of these services, which are far greater than those rendered by the United States Bank and its 25 branches, a number of the deposit banks have, with a commendable zeal to aid in the improvement of the currency, imported from abroad, at their own expense, large sums of the precious metals for coinage and circulation.

In the same manner have nearly all the predictions turned out in respect to the effect of the removal of the deposits—a step unquestionably necessary to prevent the evils which it was foreseen the bank itself would endeavor to create in a final struggle to procure a renewal of its charter. It may be thus, too, in some degree with the further steps which may be taken to prevent the excessive issue of other bank paper, but it is to be hoped that nothing will now deter the Federal and State authorities from the firm and vigorous performance of their duties to themselves and to the people in this respect.

In reducing the revenue to the wants of the Government your particular attention is invited to those articles which constitute the necessaries of life. The duty on salt was laid as a war tax, and was no doubt continued to assist in providing for the payment of the war debt. There is no article the release of which from taxation would be felt so generally and so beneficially. To this may be added all kinds of fuel and provisions. Justice and benevolence unite in favor of releasing the poor of our cities from burdens which are not necessary to the support of our Government and tend only to increase the wants of the destitute.

It will be seen by the report of the Secretary of the Treasury and the accompanying documents that the Bank of the United States has made no payment on account of the stock held by the Government in that institution, although urged to pay any portion which might suit its convenience, and that it has given no information when payment may be expected. Nor, although repeatedly requested, has it furnished the information in relation to its condition which Congress authorized the Secretary to collect at their last session. Such measures as are within the power of the Executive have been taken to ascertain the value of the stock and procure the payment as early as possible.

The conduct and present condition of that bank and the great amount of capital vested in it by the United States require your careful attention. Its charter expired on the third day of March last, and it has now no power but that given in the twenty-first section, "to use the corporate name, style, and capacity for the purpose of suits for the final settlement and liquidation of the affairs and accounts of the corporation, and for the sale and disposition of their estate—real, personal, and mixed—but not for any other purpose or in any other manner what so ever, nor for a period exceeding two years after the expiration of the said term of incorporation."

Before the expiration of the charter the stock-holders of the bank obtained an act of incorporation from the legislature of Pennsylvania, excluding only the United States. Instead of proceeding to wind up their concerns and pay over to the United States the amount due on account of the stock held by them, the president and directors of the old bank appear to have transferred the books, papers, notes, obligations, and most or all of its property to this new corporation, which entered upon business as a continuation of the old concern. Amongst other acts of questionable validity, the notes of the expired corporation are known to have been used as its own and again put in circulation. That the old bank had no right to issue or re-issue its notes after the expiration of its charter can not be denied, and that it could not confer any such right on its substitute any more than exercise it itself is equally plain. In law and honesty the notes of the bank in circulation at the expiration of its charter should have been called in by public advertisement, paid up as presented, and, together with those on hand, canceled and destroyed. Their re-issue is sanctioned by no law and warranted by no necessity. If the United States be responsible in their stock for the payment of these notes, their reissue by the new corporation for their own profit is a fraud on the Government. If the United States is not responsible, then there is no legal responsibility in any quarter, and it is a fraud on the country. They are the redeemed notes of a dissolved partnership, but, contrary to the wishes of the retiring partner and without his consent, are again re-issued and circulated.

It is the high and peculiar duty of Congress to decide whether any further legislation be necessary for the security of the large amount of public property now held and in use by the new bank, and for vindicating the rights of the Government and compelling a speedy and honest settlement with all the creditors of the old bank, public and private, or whether the subject shall be left to the power now possessed by the Executive and judiciary. It remains to be seen whether the persons who as managers of the old bank undertook to control the Government, retained the public dividends, shut their doors upon a committee of the House of Representatives, and filled the country with panic to accomplish their own sinister objects may now as managers of a new bank continue with impunity to flood the country with a spurious currency, use the $7M of Government stock for their own profit, and refuse to the United States all information as to the present condition of their own property and the prospect of recovering it into their own possession.

The lessons taught by the Bank of the United States can not well be lost upon the American people. They will take care never again to place so tremendous a power in irresponsible hands, and it will be fortunate if they seriously consider the consequences which are likely to result on a smaller scale from the facility with which corporate powers are granted by their State governments.

It is believed that the law of the last session regulating the deposit banks operates onerously and unjustly upon them in many respects, and it is hoped that Congress, on proper representations, will adopt the modifications which are necessary to prevent this consequence.

The report of the Secretary of War ad interim and the accompanying documents, all which are herewith laid before you, will give you a full view of the diversified and important operations of that Department during the past year.

The military movements rendered necessary by the aggressions of the hostile portions of the Seminole and Creek tribes of Indians, and by other circumstances, have required the active employment of nearly our whole regular force, including the Marine Corps, and of large bodies of militia and volunteers. With all these events so far as they were known at the seat of Government before the termination of your last session you are already acquainted, and it is therefore only needful in this place to lay before you a brief summary of what has since occurred.

The war with the Seminoles during the summer was on our part chiefly confined to the protection of our frontier settlements from the incursions of the enemy, and, as a necessary and important means for the accomplishment of that end, to the maintenance of the posts previously established. In the course of this duty several actions took place, in which the bravery and discipline of both officers and men were conspicuously displayed, and which I have deemed it proper to notice in respect to the former by the granting of brevet rank for gallant services in the field. But as the force of the Indians was not so far weakened by these partial successes as to lead them to submit, and as their savage inroads were frequently repeated, early measures were taken for placing at the disposal of Governor Call, who as commander in chief of the Territorial militia had been temporarily invested with the command, an ample force for the purpose of resuming offensive operations in the most efficient manner so soon as the season should permit. Major-General Jesup was also directed, on the conclusion of his duties in the Creek country, to repair to Florida and assume the command.

The result of the first movement made by the forces under the direction of Governor Call in October last, as detailed in the accompanying papers, excited much surprise and disappointment. A full explanation has been required of the causes which led to the failure of that movement, but has not yet been received. In the mean time, as it was feared that the health of Governor Call, who was understood to have suffered much from sickness, might not be adequate to the crisis, and as Major-General Jesup was known to have reached Florida, that officer was directed to assume command, and to prosecute all needful operations with the utmost promptitude and vigor. From the force at his disposal and the dispositions he has made and is instructed to make, and from the very efficient measures which it is since ascertained have been taken by Governor Call, there is reason to hope that they will soon be enabled to reduce the enemy to subjection. In the mean time, as you will perceive from the report of the Secretary, there is urgent necessity for further appropriations to suppress these hostilities.

Happily for the interests of humanity, the hostilities with the Creeks were brought to a close soon after your adjournment, without that effusion of blood which at one time was apprehended as inevitable. The unconditional submission of the hostile party was followed by their speedy removal to the country assigned them west of the Mississippi. The inquiry as to alleged frauds in the purchase of the reservations of these Indians and the causes of their hostilities, requested by the resolution of the House of Representatives of the first of July last to be made by the President, is now going on through the agency of commissioners appointed for that purpose. Their report may be expected during your present session.

The difficulties apprehended in the Cherokee country have been prevented, and the peace and safety of that region and its vicinity effectually secured, by the timely measures taken by the War Department, and still continued.

The discretionary authority given to General Gaines to cross the Sabine and to occupy a position as far west as Nacogdoches, in case he should deem such a step necessary to the protection of the frontier and to the fulfillment of the stipulations contained in our treaty with Mexico, and the movement subsequently made by that officer have been alluded to in a former part of this message. At the date of the latest intelligence from Nacogdoches our troops were yet at that station, but the officer who has succeeded General Gaines has recently been advised that from the facts known at the seat of Government there would seem to be no adequate cause for any longer maintaining that position, and he was accordingly instructed, in case the troops were not already withdrawn under the discretionary powers before possessed by him, to give the requisite orders for that purpose on the receipt of the instructions, unless he shall then have in his possession such information as shall satisfy him that the maintenance of the post is essential to the protection of our frontiers and to the due execution of our treaty stipulations, as previously explained to him.

Whilst the necessities existing during the present year for the service of militia and volunteers have furnished new proofs of the patriotism of our fellow citizens, they have also strongly illustrated the importance of an increase in the rank and file of the Regular Army. The views of this subject submitted by the Secretary of War in his report meet my entire concurrence, and are earnestly commended to the deliberate attention of Congress. In this connection it is also proper to remind you that the defects in our present militia system are every day rendered more apparent. The duty of making further provision by law for organizing, arming, and disciplining this arm of defense has been so repeatedly presented to Congress by myself and my predecessors that I deem it sufficient on this occasion to refer to the last annual message and to former Executive communications in which the subject has been discussed.

It appears from the reports of the officers charged with mustering into service the volunteers called for under the act of Congress of the last session that more presented themselves at the place of rendezvous in Tennessee than were sufficient to meet the requisition which had been made by the Secretary of War upon the governor of that State. This was occasioned by the omission of the governor to apportion the requisition to the different regiments of militia so as to obtain the proper number of troops and no more. It seems but just to the patriotic citizens who repaired to the general rendezvous under circumstances authorizing them to believe that their services were needed and would be accepted that the expenses incurred by them while absent from their homes should be paid by the Government. I accordingly recommend that a law to this effect be passed by Congress, giving them a compensation which will cover their expenses on the march to and from the place of rendezvous and while there; in connection with which it will also be proper to make provision for such other equitable claims growing out of the service of the militia as may not be embraced in the existing laws.

On the unexpected breaking out of hostilities in Florida, Alabama, and Georgia it became necessary in some cases to take the property of individuals for public use. Provision should be made by law for indemnifying the owners; and I would also respectfully suggest whether some provision may not be made, consistently with the principles of our Government, for the relief of the sufferers by Indian depredations or by the operations of our own troops.

No time was lost after the making of the requisite appropriations in resuming the great national work of completing the unfinished fortifications on our sea-board and of placing them in a proper state of defense. In consequence, however, of the very late day at which those bills were passed, but little progress could be made during the season which has just closed. A very large amount of the moneys granted at your last session accordingly remains unexpended; but as the work will be again resumed at the earliest moment in the coming spring, the balance of the existing appropriations, and in several cases which will be laid before you, with the proper estimates, further sums for the like objects, may be usefully expended during the next year.

* * *

The national policy, founded alike in interest and in humanity, so long and so steadily pursued by this Government for the removal of the Indian tribes originally settled on this side of the Mississippi to the west of that river, may be said to have been consummated by the conclusion of the late treaty with the Cherokees. The measures taken in the execution of that treaty and in relation to our Indian affairs generally will fully appear by referring to the accompanying papers. Without dwelling on the numerous and important topics embraced in them, I again invite your attention to the importance of providing a well-digested and comprehensive system for the protection, supervision, and improvement of the various tribes now planted in the Indian country. The suggestions submitted by the Commissioner of Indian Affairs, and enforced by the Secretary, on this subject, and also in regard to the establishment of additional military posts in the Indian country, are entitled to your profound consideration. Both measures are necessary, for the double purpose of protecting the Indians from intestine war, and in other respects complying with our engagements with them, and of securing our western frontier against incursions which otherwise will assuredly be made on it. The best hopes of humanity in regard to the aboriginal race, the welfare of our rapidly extending settlements, and the honor of the United States are all deeply involved in the relations existing between this Government and the emigrating tribes. I trust, therefore, that the various matters submitted in the accompanying documents in respect to those relations will receive your early and mature deliberation, and that it may issue in the adoption of legislative measures adapted to the circumstances and duties of the present crisis.

* * *

All my experience and reflection confirm the conviction I have so often expressed to Congress in favor of an amendment of the Constitution which will prevent in any event the election of the President and Vice President of the United States devolving on the House of Representatives and the Senate, and I therefore beg leave again to solicit your attention to the subject. There were various other suggestions in my last annual message not acted upon, particularly that relating to the want of uniformity in the laws of the District of Columbia, that are deemed worthy of your favorable consideration.

Before concluding this paper I think it due to the various Executive Departments to bear testimony to their prosperous condition and to the ability and integrity with which they have been conducted. It has been my aim to enforce in all of them a vigilant and faithful discharge of the public business, and it is gratifying to me to believe that there is no just cause of complaint from any quarter at the manner in which they have fulfilled the objects of their creation.

Having now finished the observations deemed proper on this the last occasion I shall have of communicating with the two Houses of Congress at their meeting, I can not omit an expression of the gratitude which is due to the great body of my fellow-citizens, in whose partiality and indulgence I have found encouragement and support in the many difficult and trying scenes through which it has been my lot to pass during my public career. Though deeply sensible that my exertions have not been crowned with a success corresponding to the degree of favor bestowed upon me, I am sure that they will be considered as having been directed by an earnest desire to promote the good of my country, and I am consoled by the persuasion that whatever errors have been committed will find a corrective in the intelligence and patriotism of those who will succeed us. All that has occurred during my Administration is calculated to inspire me with increased confidence in the stability of our institutions; and should I be spared to enter upon that retirement which is so suitable to my age and infirm health and so much desired by me in other respects, I shall not cease to invoke that beneficent Being to whose providence we are already so signally indebted for the continuance of His blessings on our beloved country.

ANDREW JACKSON

Notes

1. Robert V. Remini, *The Life of Andrew Jackson* (New York: Harper Collins, 2001), 332–33.
2. Jackson's farewell address is 8,311 words long; Washington's 6,088.

8

Martin Van Buren (1837–1841)

Martin Van Buren was a Democrat and close ally of Andrew Jackson's. He was still settling into the Oval Office when the panic of 1837 broke out. That panic, caused in part by his predecessor's policies, led to the worst depression the young nation had experienced to date. Credit was tight. Banks stopped converting paper money to gold or silver. An unfavorable balance of trade developed with Great Britain. And crop failure exacerbated the misery. As a result, hundreds of banks and businesses failed. Thousands of people lost their lands. Throughout Van Buren's four years in office, the economy struggled.

This was the dark context of the eighth president's final annual message to the Congress. In it Van Buren devoted much space to an exposition of his economic principles and the constitutionally imposed duty to be a good steward of public resources. He justified maintaining the solvency of the national government, but equally disdained "an overflowing treasury." Like Jackson, he opposed not only rechartering the Bank of the United States but also placing any federal funds in state banks. He fought for the establishment of an independent treasury system to handle government transactions. As for federal aid to internal improvements, he cut off expenditures so totally that the government even sold the tools it had used on public works.

Van Buren was from New York; he was a Northerner. Yet at the beginning of his presidency, he adopted a laissez-faire attitude toward slavery. He was determined to allow the states to sort out whether they would be free or slave. During his years in the White House, however, he became increasingly opposed to the expansion of the peculiar institution. He blocked the annexation of Texas because it would add significantly to slave territory and might precipitate war with Mexico.

In his 1840 bid for reelection, Van Buren lost the support of Jackson, his former patron, and was defeated by the Whigs. Eight years later, he was an unsuccessful candidate for president on the Free Soil ticket.

Fourth Annual Message
(written to the Congress)
December 5, 1840

Fellow-Citizens of the Senate and House of Representatives:

Our devout gratitude is due to the Supreme Being for having graciously continued to our beloved country through the vicissitudes of another year the invaluable blessings of health, plenty, and peace. Seldom has this favored land been so generally exempted from the ravages of disease or the labor of the husbandman more amply rewarded, and never before have our relations with other countries been placed on a more favorable basis than that which they so happily occupy at this critical conjuncture in the affairs of the world. A rigid and persevering abstinence from all interference with the domestic and political relations of other States, alike due to the genius and distinctive character of our Government and to the principles by which it is directed; a faithful observance in the management of our foreign relations of the practice of speaking plainly, dealing justly, and requiring truth and justice in return as the best conservatives of the peace of nations; a strict impartiality in our manifestations of friendship in the commercial privileges we concede and those we require from others—these, accompanied by a disposition as prompt to maintain in every emergency our own rights as we are from principle averse to the invasion of those of others, have given to our country and Government a standing in the great family of nations of which we have just cause to be proud and the advantages of which are experienced by our citizens throughout every portion of the earth to which their enterprising and adventurous spirit may carry them. Few, if any, remain insensible to the value of our friendship or ignorant of the terms on which it can be acquired and by which it can alone be preserved.

A series of questions of long standing, difficult in their adjustment and important in their consequences, in which the rights of our citizens and the honor of the country were deeply involved, have in the course of a few years (the most of them during the successful Administration of my immediate predecessor) been brought to a satisfactory conclusion; and the most important of those remaining are, I am happy to believe, in a fair way of being speedily and satisfactorily adjusted.

With all the powers of the world our relations are those of honorable peace. Since your adjournment nothing serious has occurred to interrupt or threaten this desirable harmony. If clouds have lowered above the other hemisphere, they have not cast their portentous shadows upon our happy shores. Bound by no entangling alliances, yet linked by a common nature and interest with the other nations of mankind, our aspirations are for the preservation of peace, in whose solid and civilizing triumphs all may participate with a generous emulation. Yet it behooves us to be prepared for any event and to be always ready to maintain those just and enlightened principles of national intercourse for which this Government has ever contended. In the shock of contending empires it is only by assuming a resolute bearing and clothing themselves with defensive armor that neutral nations can maintain their independent rights.

The excitement which grew out of the territorial controversy between the United States and Great Britain having in a great measure subsided, it is hoped that a favorable period is approaching for its final settlement. . . .

* * *

The present sound condition of their finances and the success with which embarrassments in regard to them, at times apparently insurmountable, have been overcome are matters upon which the people and Government of the United States may well congratulate themselves. An overflowing

Treasury, however it may be regarded as an evidence of public prosperity, is seldom conducive to the permanent welfare of any people, and experience has demonstrated its incompatibility with the salutary action of political institutions like those of the United States. Our safest reliance for financial efficiency and independence has, on the contrary, been found to consist in ample resources unencumbered with debt, and in this respect the Federal Government occupies a singularly fortunate and truly enviable position. . . .

*   *   *

The policy of the Federal Government in extinguishing as rapidly as possible the national debt, and subsequently in resisting every temptation to create a new one, deserves to be regarded in the same favorable light. Among the many objections to a national debt, the certain tendency of public securities to concentrate ultimately in the coffers of foreign stockholders is one which is every day gathering strength. Already have the resources of many of the States and the future industry of their citizens been indefinitely mortgaged to the subjects of European Governments to the amount of twelve millions annually to pay the constantly accruing interest on borrowed money—a sum exceeding half the ordinary revenues of the whole United States. The pretext which this relation affords to foreigners to scrutinize the management of our domestic affairs, if not actually to intermeddle with them, presents a subject for earnest attention, not to say of serious alarm. Fortunately, the Federal Government, with the exception of an obligation entered into in behalf of the District of Columbia, which must soon be discharged, is wholly exempt from any such embarrassment. It is also, as is believed, the only Government which, having fully and faithfully paid all its creditors, has also relieved itself entirely from debt. To maintain a distinction so desirable and so honorable to our national character should be an object of earnest solicitude. Never should a free people, if it be possible to avoid it, expose themselves to the necessity of having to treat of the peace, the honor, or the safety of the Republic with the governments of foreign creditors, who, however well disposed they may be to cultivate with us in general friendly relations, are nevertheless by the law of their own condition made hostile to the success and permanency of political institutions like ours. Most humiliating may be the embarrassments consequent upon such a condition. Another objection, scarcely less formidable, to the commencement of a new debt is its inevitable tendency to increase in magnitude and to foster national extravagance. He has been an unprofitable observer of events who needs at this day to be admonished of the difficulties which a government habitually dependent on loans to sustain its ordinary expenditures has to encounter in resisting the influences constantly exerted in favor of additional loans; by capitalists, who enrich themselves by government securities for amounts much exceeding the money they actually advance—a prolific source of individual aggrandizement in all borrowing countries; by stockholders, who seek their gains in the rise and fall of public stocks; and by the selfish importunities of applicants for appropriations for works avowedly for the accommodation of the public, but the real objects of which are too frequently the advancement of private interests. The known necessity which so many of the States will be under to impose taxes for the payment of the interest on their debts furnishes an additional and very cogent reason why the Federal Governments should refrain from creating a national debt, by which the people would be exposed to double taxation for a similar object. We possess within ourselves ample resources for every emergency, and we may be quite sure that our citizens in no future exigency will be unwilling to supply the Government with all the means asked for the defense of the country. In time of peace there can, at all events, be no justification for the creation of a permanent debt by the Federal Government. Its limited range of constitutional duties may certainly under such circumstances be performed without such a resort. It has, it is seen, been avoided during four years of greater fiscal difficulties than have existed in a similar period since the adoption of the Constitution, and one also remarkable for the occurrence of extraordinary causes of expenditures.

But to accomplish so desirable an object two things are indispensable: First, that the action of the Federal Government be kept within the boundaries prescribed by its founders, and, secondly, that all appropriations for objects admitted to be constitutional, and the expenditure of them also, be subjected to a standard of rigid but well-considered and practical economy. The first depends chiefly on the people themselves—the opinions they form of the true construction of the Constitution and the confidence they repose in the political sentiments of those they select as their representatives in the Federal Legislature; the second rests upon the fidelity with which their more immediate representatives and other public functionaries discharge the trusts committed to them. The duty of economizing the expenses of the public service is admitted on all hands; yet there are few subjects upon which there exists a wider difference of opinion than is constantly manifested in regard to the fidelity with which that duty is discharged. Neither diversity of sentiment nor even mutual recriminations upon a point in respect to which the public mind is so justly sensitive can well be entirely avoided, and least so at periods of great political excitement. An intelligent people, however, seldom fail to arrive in the end at correct conclusions in such a matter. Practical economy in the management of public affairs can have no adverse influence to contend with more powerful than a large surplus revenue. . . .

* * *

I have deemed this brief summary of our fiscal affairs necessary to the due performance of a duty specially enjoined upon me by the Constitution. It will serve also to illustrate more fully the principles by which I have been guided in reference to two contested points in our public policy which were earliest in their development and have been more important in their consequences than any that have arisen under our complicated and difficult, yet admirable, system of government. I allude to a national debt and a national bank. It was in these that the political contests by which the country has been agitated ever since the adoption of the Constitution in a great measure originated, and there is too much reason to apprehend that the conflicting interests and opposing principles thus marshaled will continue as heretofore to produce similar if not aggravated consequences.

Coming into office the declared enemy of both, I have earnestly endeavored to prevent a resort to either.

The consideration that a large public debt affords an apology, and produces in some degree a necessity also, for resorting to a system and extent of taxation which is not only oppressive throughout, but is likewise so apt to lead in the end to the commission of that most odious of all offenses against the principles of republican government, the prostitution of political power, conferred for the general benefit, to the aggrandizement of particular classes and the gratification of individual cupidity, is alone sufficient, independently of the weighty objections which have already been urged, to render its creation and existence the sources of bitter and unappeasable discord. If we add to this its inevitable tendency to produce and foster extravagant expenditures of the public moneys, by which a necessity is created for new loans and new burdens on the people, and, finally, refer to the examples of every government which has existed for proof, how seldom it is that the system, when once adopted and implanted in the policy of a country, has failed to expand itself until public credit was exhausted and the people were no longer able to endure its increasing weight, it seems impossible to resist the conclusion that no benefits resulting from its career, no extent of conquest, no accession of wealth to particular classes, nor any nor all its combined advantages, can counterbalance its ultimate but certain results—a splendid government and an impoverished people.

If a national bank was, as is undeniable, repudiated by the framers of the Constitution as incompatible with the rights of the States and the liberties of the people; if from the beginning it has been regarded by large portions of our citizens as coming in direct collision with that great and vital amendment of the Constitution which declares that all powers not conferred by that instrument on the General Government are reserved to the States and to the people; if it has been viewed by them as the first great step in the march of latitudinous construction, which unchecked would render that sacred instrument of as little value as an unwritten constitution, dependent, as it would alone be, for its meaning on the interested interpretation of a dominant party, and affording no security to the rights of the minority—if such is undeniably the case, what rational grounds could have been conceived for anticipating aught but determined opposition to such an institution at the present day.

Could a different result have been expected when the consequences which have flowed from its creation, and particularly from its struggles to perpetuate its existence, had confirmed in so striking a manner the apprehensions of its earliest opponents; when it had been so clearly demonstrated that a concentrated money power, wielding so vast a capital and combining such incalculable means of influence, may in those peculiar conjunctures to which this Government is unavoidably exposed prove an overmatch for the political power of the people themselves; when the true character of its capacity to regulate according to its will and its interests and the interests of its favorites the value and production of the labor and property of every man in this extended country had been so fully and fearfully developed; when it was notorious that all classes of this great community had, by means of the power and influence it thus possesses, been infected to madness with a spirit of heedless speculation; when it had been seen that, secure in the support of the combination of influences by which it was surrounded, it could violate its charter and set the laws at defiance with impunity; and when, too, it had become most apparent that to believe that such an accumulation of powers can ever be granted without the certainty of being abused was to indulge in a fatal delusion?

To avoid the necessity of a permanent debt and its inevitable consequences I have advocated and endeavored to carry into effect the policy of confining the appropriations for the public service to such objects only as are clearly within the constitutional authority of the Federal Government; of excluding from its expenses those improvident and unauthorized grants of public money for works of internal improvement which were so wisely arrested by the constitutional interposition of my predecessor, and which, if they had not been so checked, would long before this time have involved the finances of the General Government in embarrassments far greater than those which are now experienced by any of the States; of limiting all our expenditures to that simple, unostentatious, and economical administration of public affairs which is alone consistent with the character of our institutions; of collecting annually from the customs, and the sales of public lands a revenue fully adequate to defray all the expenses thus incurred; but under no pretense whatsoever to impose taxes upon the people to a greater amount than was actually necessary to the public service conducted upon the principles I have stated.

In lieu of a national bank or a dependence upon banks of any description for the management of our fiscal affairs, I recommended the adoption of the system which is now in successful operation. That system affords every requisite facility for the transaction of the pecuniary concerns of the Government; will, it is confidently anticipated, produce in other respects many of the benefits which have been from time to time expected from the creation of a national bank, but which have never been realized; avoid the manifold evils inseparable from such an institution; diminish to a greater extent than could be accomplished by any other measure of reform the patronage of the Federal Government—a wise policy in all governments, but more especially so in one like ours, which works well only in proportion as it is made to rely for its support upon the unbiased and unadulterated opinions of its constituents; do away forever all dependence on corporate bodies either in the raising, collecting, safekeeping, or disbursing the public revenues, and place the Government equally above the temptation of fostering a dangerous and unconstitutional institution at home or the necessity of adapting its policy to the views and interests of a still more formidable money power abroad.

It is by adopting and carrying out these principles under circumstances the most arduous and discouraging that the attempt has been made, thus far successfully, to demonstrate to the people of the United States that a national bank at all times, and a national debt except it be incurred at a period when the honor and safety of the nation demand the temporary sacrifice of a policy which should only be abandoned in such exigencies, are not merely unnecessary, but in direct and deadly hostility to the principles of their Government and to their own permanent welfare.

The progress made in the development of these positions appears in the preceding sketch of the past history and present state of the financial concerns of the Federal Government. The facts there stated fully authorize the assertion that all the purposes for which this Government was instituted have been accomplished during four years of greater pecuniary embarrassment than were ever before experienced in time of peace, and in the face of opposition as formidable as any that was ever before arrayed against the policy of an Administration; that this has been done when the ordinary revenues of the Government were generally decreasing as well from the operation of the laws as the condition of the country, without the creation of a permanent public debt or incurring any liability other than such as the ordinary resources of the Government will speedily discharge, and without the agency of a national bank.

If this view of the proceedings of the Government for the period it embraces be warranted by the facts as they are known to exist; if the Army and Navy have been sustained to the full extent authorized by law, and which Congress deemed sufficient for the defense of the country and the protection of its rights and its honor; if its civil and diplomatic service has been equally sustained; if ample provision has been made for the administration of justice and the execution of the laws; if the claims upon public gratitude in behalf of the soldiers of the Revolution have been promptly met and faithfully discharged; if there have been no failures in defraying the very large expenditures growing out of that long-continued and salutary policy of peacefully removing the Indians to regions of comparative safety and prosperity; if the public faith has at all times and everywhere been most scrupulously maintained by a prompt discharge of the numerous, extended, and diversified claims on the Treasury—if all these great and permanent objects, with many others that might be stated, have for a series of years, marked by peculiar obstacles and difficulties, been successfully accomplished without a resort to a permanent debt or the aid of a national bank, have we not a right to expect that a policy the object of which has been to sustain the public service independently of either of these fruitful sources of discord will receive the final sanction of a people whose unbiased and fairly elicited judgment upon public affairs is never ultimately wrong?

That embarrassments in the pecuniary concerns of individuals of unexampled extent and duration have recently existed in this as in other commercial nations is undoubtedly true. To suppose it necessary now to trace these reverses to their sources would be a reflection on the intelligence of my fellow-citizens. Whatever may have been the obscurity in which the subject was involved during the earlier stages of the revulsion, there can not now be many by whom the whole question is not fully understood.

Not deeming it within the constitutional powers of the General Government to repair private losses sustained by reverses in business having no connection with the public service, either by direct appropriations from the Treasury or by special legislation designed to secure exclusive privileges and immunities to individuals or classes in preference to or at the expense of the great majority necessarily debarred from any participation in them, no attempt to do so has been either made, recommended, or encouraged by the present Executive.

It is believed, however, that the great purposes for the attainment of which the Federal Government was instituted have not been lost sight of. Intrusted only with certain limited powers, cautiously enumerated, distinctly specified, and defined with a precision and clearness which would seem to defy misconstruction, it has been my constant aim to confine myself within the limits so clearly marked out and so carefully guarded. Having always been of opinion that the best preservative of the union of the States is to be found in a total abstinence from the exercise of all doubtful powers on the part of the Federal Government rather than in attempts to assume them by a loose construction of the Constitution or an ingenious perversion of its words, I have endeavored to avoid recommending any measure which I had reason to apprehend would, in the opinion even of a considerable minority of my fellow-citizens, be regarded as trenching on the rights of the States or the provisions of the hallowed instrument of our Union. Viewing the aggregate powers of the Federal Government as a voluntary concession of the States, it seemed to me that such only should be exercised as were at the time intended to be given.

I have been strengthened, too, in the propriety of this course by the conviction that all efforts to go beyond this tend only to produce dissatisfaction and distrust, to excite jealousies, and to provoke resistance. Instead of adding strength to the Federal Government, even when successful they must ever prove a source of incurable weakness by alienating a portion of those whose adhesion is indispensable to the great aggregate of united strength and whose voluntary attachment is in my estimation far more essential to the efficiency of a government strong in the best of all possible strength—the confidence and attachment of all those who make up its constituent elements.

Thus believing, it has been my purpose to secure to the whole people and to every member of the Confederacy, by general, salutary, and equal laws alone, the benefit of those republican institutions which it was the end and aim of the Constitution to establish, and the impartial influence of which is in my judgment indispensable to their preservation. I can not bring myself to believe that the lasting happiness of the people, the prosperity of the States, or the permanency of their Union can be maintained by giving preference or priority to any class of citizens in the distribution of benefits or privileges, or by the adoption of measures which enrich one portion of the Union at the expense of another; nor can I see in the interference of the Federal Government with the local legislation and reserved rights of the States a remedy for present or a security against future dangers.

The first, and assuredly not the least, important step toward relieving the country from the condition into which it had been plunged by excesses in trade, banking, and credits of all kinds was to place the business transactions of the Government itself on a solid basis, giving and receiving in all cases value for value, and neither countenancing nor encouraging in others that delusive system of credits from which it has been found so difficult to escape, and which has left nothing behind it but the wrecks that mark its fatal career.

That the financial affairs of the Government are now and have been during the whole period of these wide-spreading difficulties conducted with a strict and invariable regard to this great fundamental principle, and that by the assumption and maintenance of the stand thus taken on the very threshold of the approaching crisis more than by any other cause or causes whatever the community at large has been shielded from the incalculable evils of a general and indefinite suspension of specie payments, and a consequent annihilation for the whole period it might have lasted of a just and invariable standard of value, will, it is believed, at this period scarcely be questioned.

A steady adherence on the part of the Government to the policy which has produced such salutary results, aided by judicious State legislation and, what is not less important, by the industry, enterprise, perseverance, and economy of the American people, can not fail to raise the whole country at an early period to a state of solid and enduring prosperity, not subject to be again overthrown by the suspension of banks or the explosion of a bloated credit system. It is for the people and their representatives to decide whether or not the permanent welfare of the country (which all good citizens equally desire, however widely they may differ as to the means of its accomplishment) shall be in this way secured, or whether the management of the pecuniary concerns of the Government, and by consequence to a great extent those of individuals also, shall be carried back to a condition of things which fostered those contractions and expansions of the currency and those reckless abuses of credit from the baleful effects of which the country has so deeply suffered—a return that can promise in the end no better results than to reproduce the embarrassments the Government has experienced, and to remove from the shoulders of the present to those of fresh victims the bitter fruits of that spirit of speculative enterprise to which our countrymen are so liable and upon which the lessons of experience are so unavailing. The choice is an important one, and I sincerely hope that it may be wisely made.

*   *   *

The policy of the United States in regard to the Indians, of which a succinct account is given in my message of 1838, and of the wisdom and expediency of which I am fully satisfied, has been continued in active operation throughout the whole period of my Administration. Since the spring of 1837 more than 40,000 Indians have been removed to their new homes west of the Mississippi, and I am happy to add that all accounts concur in representing the result of this measure as eminently beneficial to that people.

The emigration of the Seminoles alone has been attended with serious difficulty and occasioned bloodshed, hostilities having been commenced by the Indians in Florida under the apprehension that they would be compelled by force to comply with their treaty stipulations. The execution of the treaty of Paynes Landing, signed in 1832, but not ratified until 1834, was postponed at the solicitation of the Indians until 1836, when they again renewed their agreement to remove peaceably to their new homes in the West. In the face of this solemn and renewed compact they broke their faith and commenced hostilities by the massacre of Major Dade's command, the murder of their agent, General Thompson, and other acts of cruel treachery. When this alarming and unexpected intelligence reached the seat of Government, every effort appears to have been made to reenforce General Clinch, who commanded the troops then in Florida. General Eustis was dispatched with reenforcements from Charleston, troops were called out from Alabama, Tennessee, and Georgia, and General Scott was sent to take the command, with ample powers and ample means. At the first alarm General Gaines organized a force at New Orleans, and without waiting for orders landed in Florida, where he delivered over the troops he had brought with him to General Scott.

Governor Call was subsequently appointed to conduct a summer campaign, and at the close of it was replaced by General Jesup. These events and changes took place under the Administration of my predecessor. Notwithstanding the exertions of the experienced officers who had command there for eighteen months, on entering upon the administration of the Government I found the Territory of Florida a prey to Indian atrocities. A strenuous effort was immediately made to bring those hostilities to a close, and the army under General Jesup was reenforced until it amounted to 10,000 men, and furnished with abundant supplies of every description. In this campaign a great number of the enemy were captured and destroyed, but the character of the contest only was changed. The Indians, having been defeated in every engagement, dispersed in small bands throughout the country and became an enterprising, formidable, and ruthless banditti. General Taylor, who succeeded General Jesup, used his best exertions to subdue them, and was seconded in his efforts by the officers under his command; but he too failed to protect the Territory from their depredations. By an act of signal and cruel treachery they broke the truce made with them by General MacGrab, who was sent from Washington for the purpose of carrying into effect the expressed wishes of Congress, and have continued their devastations ever since. General Armistead, who was in Florida when General Taylor left the army by permission, assumed the command, and after active summer operations was met by propositions for peace, and from the fortunate coincidence of the arrival in Florida at the same period of a delegation from the Seminoles who are happily settled west of the Mississippi and are now anxious to persuade their countrymen to join them there hopes were for some time entertained that the Indians might be induced to leave the Territory without further difficulty. These hopes have proved fallacious and hostilities have been renewed throughout the whole of the Territory. That this contest has endured so long is to be attributed to causes beyond the control of the Government. Experienced generals have had the command of the troops, officers and soldiers have alike distinguished themselves for their activity, patience, and enduring courage, the army has been constantly furnished with supplies of every description, and we must look for the causes which have so long procrastinated the issue of the contest in the vast extent of the theater of hostilities, the almost insurmountable obstacles presented by the nature of the country, the climate, and the wily character of the savages.

* * *

The exploring expedition at the latest date was preparing to leave the Bay of Islands, New Zealand, in further prosecution of objects which have thus far been successfully accomplished. The discovery of a new continent, which was first seen in latitude 66° 2' south, longitude 154° 27' east, and afterwards in latitude 66° 31' south, longitude 153° 40' east, by Lieutenants Wilkes and Hudson, for an extent of 1,800 miles, but on which they were prevented from landing by vast bodies of ice which encompassed it, is one of the honorable results of the enterprise. Lieutenant Wilkes bears testimony to the zeal and good conduct of his officers and men, and it is but justice to that officer to state that he appears to have performed the duties assigned him with an ardor, ability, and perseverance which give every assurance of an honorable issue to the undertaking.

*   *   *

The suppression of the African slave trade has received the continued attention of the Government. The brig *Dolphin* and schooner *Grampus* have been employed during the last season on the coast of Africa for the purpose of preventing such portions of that trade as were said to be prosecuted under the American flag. After cruising off those parts of the coast most usually resorted to by slavers until the commencement of the rainy season, these vessels returned to the United States for supplies, and have since been dispatched on a similar service.

From the reports of the commanding officers it appears that the trade is now principally carried on under Portuguese colors, and they express the opinion that the apprehension of their presence on the slave coast has in a great degree arrested the prostitution of the American flag to this inhuman purpose. It is hoped that by continuing to maintain this force in that quarter and by the exertions of the officers in command much will be done to put a stop to whatever portion of this traffic may have been carried on under the American flag and to prevent its use in a trade which, while it violates the laws, is equally an outrage on the rights of others and the feelings of humanity. The efforts of the several Governments who are anxiously seeking to suppress this traffic must, however, be directed against the facilities afforded by what are now recognized as legitimate commercial pursuits before that object can be fully accomplished.

Supplies of provisions, water casks, merchandise, and articles connected with the prosecution of the slave trade are, it is understood, freely carried by vessels of different nations to the slave factories, and the effects of the factors are transported openly from one slave station to another without interruption or punishment by either of the nations to which they belong engaged in the commerce of that region. I submit to your judgments whether this Government, having been the first to prohibit by adequate penalties the slave trade, the first to declare it piracy, should not be the first also to forbid to its citizens all trade with the slave factories on the coast of Africa, giving an example to all nations in this respect which if fairly followed can not fail to produce the most effective results in breaking up those dens of iniquity.

M. VAN BUREN

9

John Tyler (1841–1845)

Readers who enjoy patriotic speeches will enjoy the opening of Tyler's fourth and final annual message. He succinctly defined America's national purpose: "In view of the vast wilderness yet to be reclaimed, we may well invite the lover of freedom of every land to take up his abode among us and assist us in the great work of advancing the standard of civilization and giving a wider spread to the arts and refinements of cultivated life." He also marveled at the stability of the American system. He called the peaceful transfer of power to the next duly elected president a "great moral spectacle." He explained that it was made possible by the fact that the American mind possesses a "love of order and obedience to the laws."

These sentiments are all the more remarkable considering Tyler's tumultuous years in the White House. With an understatement characteristic of the age, he referred merely to the "exciting scenes through which we have passed." His administration got off to a terrible start. In the first place, Tyler was the first vice president to become president upon the death of the commander-in-chief. President William Henry Harrison had delivered a long inaugural address in a freezing rain. The sixty-eight-year-old caught a cold and died in thirty days. Second, the political circumstances in which Tyler had run for national office were less than ideal. Tyler was a Virginian and Southern Democrat who left his party to run with Harrison on the Whig Party ticket. So the Democrats felt resentful. And the Whigs never considered him one of their own. In fact, after Harrison died, Tyler met with opposition among some Whig leaders who referred to him as merely the "Acting President." Tyler firmly resisted their attempt at constitutional improvisation. Making sure Article II of the Constitution was scrupulously observed, he fully succeeded to the office of the president. In retrospect, this seems especially fitting considering Tyler was the first president born after the adoption of the Constitution.

Soon after occupying the White House, Tyler realized that there was no reconciling Whig programs (calling for a new Bank of the United States and higher tariffs) with his own deeply held beliefs. As a result, Tyler vetoed most of the Whig-inspired legislation that came to his desk. One veto caused such an uproar that an armed mob marched on the White House and hurled rocks through the windows. Tyler armed the White House servants and stood his ground.

As relations between the Whigs and the president spiraled further downward, the Whigs tried to impeach him—it was the first attempted impeachment of a president in American history. The attempt failed by a vote of 127 to 83.

Given the insuperable difficulties he faced in office, Tyler's final annual message to the Congress is remarkable for its grace and composure. The tone can be profitably compared to that of Andrew Johnson's Farewell Address, which reflected an extremely frustrated president who had been impeached in the House and barely avoided conviction in the Senate.

Fourth Annual Message
(written to the Congress)
December 3, 1844

To the Senate and House of Representatives of the United States:

We have continued cause for expressing our gratitude to the Supreme Ruler of the Universe for the benefits and blessings which our country, under His kind providence, has enjoyed during the past year. Notwithstanding the exciting scenes through which we have passed, nothing has occurred to disturb the general peace or to derange the harmony of our political system. The great moral spectacle has been exhibited of a nation approximating in number to 20,000,000 people having performed the high and important function of electing their Chief Magistrate for the term of four years without the commission of any acts of violence or the manifestation of a spirit of insubordination to the laws. The great and inestimable right of suffrage has been exercised by all who were invested with it under the laws of the different States in a spirit dictated alone by a desire, in the selection of the agent, to advance the interests of the country and to place beyond jeopardy the institutions under which it is our happiness to live. That the deepest interest has been manifested by all our countrymen in the result of the election is not less true than highly creditable to them. Vast multitudes have assembled from time to time at various places for the purpose of canvassing the merits and pretensions of those who were presented for their suffrages, but no armed soldiery has been necessary to restrain within proper limits the popular zeal or to prevent violent outbreaks. A principle much more controlling was found in the love of order and obedience to the laws, which, with mere individual exceptions, everywhere possesses the American mind, and controls with an influence far more powerful than hosts of armed men. We can not dwell upon this picture without recognizing in it that deep and devoted attachment on the part of the people to the institutions under which we live which proclaims their perpetuity. The great objection which has always prevailed against the election by the people of their chief executive officer has been the apprehension of tumults and disorders which might involve in ruin the entire Government. A security against this is found not only in the fact before alluded to, but in the additional fact that we live under a Confederacy embracing already twenty-six States, no one of which has power to control the election. The popular vote in each State is taken at the time appointed by the laws, and such vote is announced by the electoral college without reference to the decision of other States. The right of suffrage and the mode of conducting the election are regulated by the laws of each State, and the election is distinctly federative in all its prominent features. Thus it is that, unlike what might be the results under a consolidated system, riotous proceedings, should they prevail, could only affect the elections in single States without disturbing to any dangerous extent the tranquillity of others. The great experiment of a political confederation each member of which is supreme as to all matters appertaining to its local interests and its internal peace and happiness, while by a voluntary compact with others it confides to the united power of all the protection of its citizens in matters not domestic has been so far crowned with complete success. The world has witnessed its rapid growth in wealth and population, and under the guide and direction of a superintending Providence the developments of the past may be regarded but as the shadowing forth of the mighty future. In the bright prospects of that future we shall find, as patriots and philanthropists, the highest inducements to cultivate and cherish a love of union and to frown down every measure or effort which may be made to alienate the States or the people of the States in sentiment and feeling from each other. A rigid and close adherence to the terms of our political compact and, above all, a sacred observance of the guaranties of the Constitution will preserve union on a foundation which can not be shaken, while personal liberty is placed beyond hazard or jeopardy. The guaranty of religious freedom, of the freedom of the press, of the liberty of speech, of the trial by jury, of the habeas corpus, and of the domestic institutions of each of the States, leaving the private citizen in the full exercise of the high and ennobling attributes of his nature and to each State the privilege (which can only be judiciously exerted by itself) of consulting the means best calculated to advance its own happiness—these are the great and important guaranties of the Constitution which the lovers of liberty must cherish and the advocates of union must ever cultivate. Preserving these and avoiding all interpolations by forced construction under the guise of an imagined expediency upon the Constitution, the influence of our political system is destined to be as actively and as beneficially felt on the distant shores of the Pacific as it is now on those of the Atlantic Ocean. The only formidable impediments in the way of its successful expansion (time and space) are so far in the progress of modification by the improvements of the age as to render no longer speculative the ability of representatives from that remote region to come up to the Capitol, so that their constituents shall participate in all the benefits of Federal legislation. Thus it is that in the progress of time the inestimable principles of civil liberty will be enjoyed by millions yet unborn and the great benefits of our system of government be extended to now distant and uninhabited regions. In view of the vast wilderness yet to be reclaimed, we may well invite the lover of freedom of every land to take up his abode among us and assist us in the great work of advancing the standard of civilization and giving a wider spread to the arts and refinements of cultivated life. Our prayers should evermore be offered up to the Father of the Universe for His wisdom to direct us in the path of our duty so as to enable us to consummate these high purposes.

One of the strongest objections which has been urged against confederacies by writers on government is the liability of the members to be tampered with by foreign governments or the people of foreign states, either in their local affairs or in such as affected the peace of others or endangered the safety of the whole confederacy. We can not hope to be entirely exempt from such attempts on our peace and safety. The United States are becoming too important in population and resources not to attract the observation of other nations. It therefore may in the progress of time occur that opinions entirely abstract in the States which they may prevail and in no degree affecting their domestic institutions may be artfully but secretly encouraged with a view to undermine the Union. Such opinions may become the foundation of political parties, until at last the conflict of opinion, producing an alienation of friendly feeling among the people of the different States, may involve in general destruction the happy institutions under which we live. It should ever be borne in mind that what is true in regard to individuals is equally so in regard to states. An interference of one in the affairs of another is the fruitful cause of family dissensions and neighborhood disputes, and the same cause affects the peace, happiness, and prosperity of states. It may be most devoutly hoped that the good sense of the American people will ever be ready to repel all such attempts should they ever be made.

There has been no material change in our foreign relations since my last annual message to Congress. With all the powers of Europe we continue on the most friendly terms. Indeed, it affords me much satisfaction to state that at no former period has the peace of that enlightened and important quarter of the globe ever been, apparently, more firmly established. The conviction that peace is the true policy of nations would seem to be growing and becoming deeper amongst the enlightened everywhere, and there is no people who have a stronger interest in cherishing the sentiments and adopting the means of preserving and giving it permanence than those of the United States. Amongst these, the first and most effective are, no doubt, the strict observance of justice and the honest and punctual fulfillment of all engagements. But it is not to be forgotten that in the present state of the world it is no less necessary to be ready to enforce their observance and fulfillment in reference to ourselves than to observe and fulfill them on our part in regard to others.

Since the close of your last session a negotiation has been formally entered upon between the Secretary of State and Her Britannic Majesty's minister plenipotentiary and envoy extraordinary residing at Washington relative to the rights of their respective nations in and over the Oregon Territory. That negotiation is still pending. Should it during your session be brought to a definitive conclusion, the result will be promptly communicated to Congress. I would, however, again call your attention to the recommendations contained in previous messages designed to protect and facilitate emigration to that Territory. The establishment of military posts at suitable points upon the extended line of land travel would enable our citizens to emigrate in comparative safety to the fertile regions below the Falls of the Columbia, and make the provision of the existing convention for the joint occupation of the territory by subjects of Great Britain and the citizens of the United States more available than heretofore to the latter. These posts would constitute places of rest for the weary emigrant, where he would be sheltered securely against the danger of attack from the Indians and be enabled to recover from the exhaustion of a long line of travel. Legislative enactments should also be made which should spread over him the aegis of our laws, so as to afford protection to his person and property when he shall have reached his distant home. In this latter respect the British Government has been much more careful of the interests of such of her people as are to be found in that country than the United States. She has made necessary provision for their security and protection against the acts of the viciously disposed and lawless, and her emigrant reposes in safety under the panoply of her laws. Whatever may be the result of the pending negotiation, such measures are necessary. It will afford me the greatest pleasure to witness a happy and favorable termination to the existing negotiation upon terms compatible with the public honor, and the best efforts of the Government will continue to be directed to this end.

It would have given me the highest gratification in this my last annual communication to Congress to have been able to announce to you the complete and entire settlement and adjustment of other matters in difference between the United States and the Government of Her Britannic Majesty, which were adverted to in a previous message. It is so obviously the interest of both countries, in respect to the large and valuable commerce which exists between them, that all causes of complaint, however inconsiderable, should be with the greatest promptitude removed that it must be regarded as cause of regret that any unnecessary delays should be permitted to intervene. It is true that in a pecuniary point of view the matters alluded to are altogether insignificant in amount when compared with the ample resources of that great nation, but they nevertheless, more particularly that limited class which arise under seizures and detentions of American ships on the coast of Africa upon the mistaken supposition indulged in at the time the wrong was committed of their being engaged in the slave trade, deeply affect the sensibilities of this Government and people. Great Britain, having recognized her responsibility to repair all such wrongs by her action in other cases, leaves nothing to be regretted upon the subject as to all cases arising prior to the treaty of Washington than the delay in making suitable reparation in such of them as fall plainly within the principle of others which she has long since adjusted. The injury inflicted by delays in the settlement of these claims falls with severity upon the individual claimants and makes a strong appeal to her magnanimity and sense of justice for a speedy settlement. Other matters arising out of the construction of existing treaties also remain unadjusted, and will continue to be urged upon her attention.

The labors of the joint commission appointed by the two Governments to run the dividing line established by the treaty of Washington were, unfortunately, much delayed in the commencement of the season by the failure of Congress at its last session to make a timely appropriation of funds to meet the expenses of the American party, and by other causes. The United States commissioner, however, expresses his expectation that by increased diligence and energy the party will be able to make up for lost time.

We continue to receive assurances of the most friendly feelings on the part of all the other European powers, with each and all of whom it is so obviously our interest to cultivate the most amicable relations; nor can I anticipate the occurrence of any event which would be likely in any degree to disturb those relations. Russia, the great northern power, under the judicious sway of her Emperor, is constantly advancing in the road of science and improvement, while France, guided by the counsels of her wise Sovereign, pursues a course calculated to consolidate the general peace. Spain has obtained a breathing spell of some duration from the internal convulsions which have through so many years marred her prosperity, while Austria, the Netherlands, Prussia, Belgium, and the other powers of Europe reap a rich harvest of blessings from the prevailing peace.

I informed the two Houses of Congress in my message of December last that instructions had been given to Mr. Wheaton, our minister at Berlin, to negotiate a treaty with the Germanic States composing the Zollverein if it could be done, stipulating, as far as it was practicable to accomplish it, for a reduction of the heavy and onerous duties levied on our tobacco and other leading articles of agricultural production, and yielding in return on our part a reduction of duties on such articles the product of their industry as should not come into competition, or but a limited one, with articles the product of our manufacturing industry. The Executive in giving such instructions considered itself as acting in strict conformity with the wishes of Congress as made known through several measures which it had adopted, all directed to the accomplishment of this important result. The treaty was therefore negotiated, by which essential reductions were secured in the duties levied by the Zollverein on tobacco, rice, and lard, accompanied by a stipulation for the admission of raw cotton free of duty; in exchange for which highly important concessions a reduction of duties imposed by the laws of the United States on a variety of articles, most of which were admitted free of all duty under the act of Congress commonly known as the compromise law, and but few of which were produced in the United States, was stipulated for on our part. This treaty was communicated to the Senate at an early day of its last session, but not acted upon until near its close, when, for the want (as I am bound to presume) of full time to consider it, it was laid upon the table. This procedure had the effect of virtually rejecting it, in consequence of a stipulation contained in the treaty that its ratifications should be exchanged on or before a day which has already passed. The Executive, acting upon the fair inference that the Senate did not intend its absolute rejection, gave instructions to our minister at Berlin to reopen the negotiation so far as to obtain an extension of time for the exchange of ratifications. I regret, however, to say that his efforts in this respect have been unsuccessful. I am nevertheless not without hope that the great advantages which were intended to be secured by the treaty may yet be realized.

I am happy to inform you that Belgium has, by an "*arrête royale*" issued in July last, assimilated the flag of the United States to her own, so far as the direct trade between the two countries is concerned. This measure will prove of great service to our shipping interest, the trade having heretofore been carried on chiefly in foreign bottoms. I flatter myself that she will speedily resort to a modification of her system relating to the tobacco trade, which would decidedly benefit the agriculture of the United States and operate to the mutual advantage of both countries.

No definitive intelligence has yet been received from our minister of the conclusion of a treaty with the Chinese Empire, but enough is known to induce the strongest hopes that the mission will be crowned with success.

With Brazil our relations continue on the most friendly footing. The commercial intercourse between that growing Empire and the United States is becoming daily of greater importance to both, and it is to the interest of both that the firmest relations of amity and good will should continue to be cultivated between them.

The Republic of New Granada still withholds, notwithstanding the most persevering efforts have been employed by our chargé d'affaires, Mr. Blackford, to produce a different result, indemnity in the case of the brig *Morris*; and the Congress of Venezuela, although an arrangement has been effected between our *minister* and the minister of foreign affairs of that Government for the payment of $18,000 in discharge of its liabilities in the same case, has altogether neglected to make provision for its payment. It is to be hoped that a sense of justice will soon induce a settlement of these claims.

Our late minister to Chile, Mr. Pendleton, has returned to the United States without having effected an adjustment in the second claim of the *Macedonian*, which is delayed on grounds altogether frivolous and untenable. Mr. Pendleton's successor has been directed to urge the claim in the strongest terms, and, in the event of a failure to obtain a prompt adjustment, to report the fact to the Executive at as early a day as possible, so that the whole matter may be communicated to Congress.

At your last session I submitted to the attention of Congress the convention with the Republic of Peru of the 17th March, 1841, providing for the adjustment of the claims of citizens of the United States against that Republic, but no definitive action was taken upon the subject. I again invite to it your attention and prompt action.

In my last annual message I felt it to be my duty to make known to Congress, in terms both plain and emphatic, my opinion in regard to the war which has so long existed between Mexico and Texas which since the battle of San Jacinto has consisted altogether of predatory incursions, attended by circumstances revolting to humanity. I repeat now what I then said, that after eight years of feeble and ineffectual efforts to reconquer Texas it was time that the war should have ceased. The United States have a direct interest in the question. The contiguity of the two nations to our territory was but too well calculated to involve our peace. Unjust suspicions were engendered in the mind of one or the other of the belligerents against us, and as a necessary consequence American interests were made to suffer and our peace became daily endangered; in addition to which it must have been obvious to all that the exhaustion produced by the war subjected both Mexico and Texas to the interference of other powers, which, without the interposition of this Government, might eventuate in the most serious injury to the United States. This Government from time to time exerted its friendly offices to bring about a termination of hostilities upon terms honorable alike to both the belligerents. Its efforts in this behalf proved unavailing. Mexico seemed almost without an object to persevere in the war, and no other alternative was left the Executive but to take advantage of the well-known dispositions of Texas and to invite her to enter into a treaty for annexing her territory to that of the United States.

Since your last session Mexico has threatened to renew the war, and has either made or proposes to make formidable preparations for invading Texas. She has issued decrees and proclamations, preparatory to the commencement of hostilities, full of threats revolting to humanity, and which if carried into effect would arouse the attention of all Christendom. This new demonstration of feeling, there is too much reason to believe, has been produced in consequence of the negotiation of the late treaty of annexation with Texas. The Executive, therefore, could not be indifferent to such proceedings, and it felt it to be due as well to itself as to the honor of the country that a strong representation should be made to the Mexican Government upon the subject. This was accordingly done, as will be seen by the copy of the accompanying dispatch from the Secretary of State to the United States envoy at Mexico. Mexico has no right to jeopard the peace of the world by urging any longer a useless and fruitless contest. Such a condition of things would not be tolerated on the European continent. Why should it be on this? A war of desolation, such as is now threatened by Mexico, can not be waged without involving our peace and tranquillity. It is idle to believe that such a war could be looked upon with indifference by our own citizens inhabiting adjoining States; and our neutrality would be violated despite all efforts on the part of the Government to prevent it. The country is settled by emigrants from the United States under invitations held out to them by Spain and Mexico. Those emigrants have left behind them friends and relatives, who would not fail to sympathize with them in their difficulties, and who would be led by those sympathies to participate in their struggles, however energetic the action of the Government to prevent it. Nor would the numerous and formidable bands of Indians—the most warlike to be found in any land—which occupy the extensive regions contiguous to the States of Arkansas and Missouri, and who are in possession of large tracts of country within the limits of Texas, be likely to remain passive. The inclinations of those numerous tribes lead them invariably to war whenever pretexts exist.

Mexico had no just ground of displeasure against this Government or people for negotiating the treaty. What interest of hers was affected by the treaty? She was despoiled of nothing, since Texas was forever lost to her. The independence of Texas was recognized by several of the leading powers of the earth. She was free to treat, free to adopt her own line of policy, free to take the course which she believed was best calculated to secure her happiness.

Her Government and people decided on annexation to the United States, and the Executive saw in the acquisition of such a territory the means of advancing their permanent happiness and glory. What principle of good faith, then, was violated? What rule of political morals trampled under foot? So far as Mexico herself was concerned, the measure should have been regarded by her as highly beneficial. Her inability to reconquer Texas had been exhibited, I repeat, by eight (now nine) years of fruitless and ruinous contest. In the meantime Texas has been growing in population and resources. Emigration has flowed into her territory from all parts of the world in a current which continues to increase in strength. Mexico requires a permanent boundary between that young Republic and herself. Texas at no distant day, if she continues separate and detached from the United States, will inevitably seek to consolidate her strength by adding to her domain the contiguous Provinces of Mexico. The spirit of revolt from the control of the central Government has heretofore manifested itself in some of those Provinces, and it is fair to infer that they would be inclined to take the first favorable opportunity to proclaim their independence and to form close alliances with Texas. The war would thus be endless, or if cessations of hostilities should occur they would only endure for a season. The interests of Mexico, therefore, could in nothing be better consulted than in a peace with her neighbors which would result in the establishment of a permanent boundary. Upon the ratification of the treaty the Executive was prepared to treat with her on the most liberal basis. Hence the boundaries of Texas were left undefined by the treaty. The Executive proposed to settle these upon terms that all the world should have pronounced just and reasonable. No negotiation upon that point could have been undertaken between the United States and Mexico in advance of the ratification of the treaty. We should have had no right, no power, no authority, to have conducted such a negotiation, and to have undertaken it would have been an assumption equally revolting to the pride of Mexico and Texas and subjecting us to the charge of arrogance, while to have proposed in advance of annexation to satisfy Mexico for any contingent interest she might have in Texas would have been to have treated Texas not as an independent power, but as a mere dependency of Mexico. This assumption could not have been acted on by the Executive without setting at defiance your own solemn declaration that that Republic was an independent State. Mexico had, it is true, threatened war against the United States in the event the treaty of annexation was ratified. The Executive could not permit itself to be influenced by this threat. It represented in this the spirit of our people, who are ready to sacrifice much for peace, but nothing to intimidation. A war under any circumstances is greatly to be deplored, and the United States is the last nation to desire it; but if, as the condition of peace, it be required of us to forego the unquestionable right of treating with an independent power of our own continent upon matters highly interesting to both, and that upon a naked and unsustained pretension of claim by a third power to control the free will of the power with whom we treat, devoted as we may be to peace and anxious to cultivate friendly relations with the whole world, the Executive does not hesitate to say that the people of the United States would be ready to brave all consequences sooner than submit to such condition. But no apprehension of war was entertained by the Executive, and I must express frankly the opinion that had the treaty been ratified by the Senate it would have been followed by a prompt settlement, to the entire satisfaction of Mexico, of every matter in difference between the two countries. Seeing, then, that new preparations for hostile invasion of Texas were about to be adopted by Mexico, and that these were brought about because Texas had adopted the suggestions of the Executive upon the subject of annexation, it could not passively have folded its arms and permitted a war, threatened to be accompanied by every act that could mark a barbarous age, to be waged against her because she had done so.

Other considerations of a controlling character influenced the course of the Executive. The treaty which had thus been negotiated had failed to receive the ratification of the Senate. One of the chief objections which was urged against it was found to consist in the fact that the question of annexation had not been submitted to the ordeal of public opinion in the United States. However untenable such an objection was esteemed to be, in view of the unquestionable power of the Executive to negotiate the treaty and the great and lasting interests involved in the question, I felt it to be my duty to submit the whole subject to Congress as the best expounders of popular sentiment. No definitive action having been taken on the subject by Congress, the question referred itself directly to the decision of the States and people. The great popular election which has just terminated afforded the best opportunity of ascertaining the will of the States and the people upon it. Pending that issue it became the imperative duty of the Executive to inform Mexico that the question of annexation was still before the American people, and that until their decision was pronounced any serious invasion of Texas would be regarded as an attempt to forestall their judgment and could not be looked upon with indifference. I am most happy to inform you that no such invasion has taken place; and I trust that whatever your action may be upon it Mexico will see the importance of deciding the matter by a resort to peaceful expedients in preference to those of arms. The decision of the people and the States on this great and interesting subject has been decisively manifested. The question of annexation has been presented nakedly to their consideration. By the treaty itself all collateral and incidental issues which were calculated to divide and distract the public councils were carefully avoided. These were left to the wisdom of the future to determine. It presented, I repeat, the isolated question of annexation, and in that form it has been submitted to the ordeal of public sentiment. A controlling majority of the people and a large majority of the States have declared in favor of immediate annexation. Instructions have thus come up to both branches of Congress from their respective constituents in terms the most emphatic. It is the will of both the people and the States that Texas shall be annexed to the Union promptly and immediately. It may be hoped that in carrying into execution the public will thus declared all collateral issues may be avoided. Future Legislatures can best decide as to the number of States which should be formed out of the territory when the time has arrived for deciding that question. So with all others. By the treaty the United States assumed the payment of the debts of Texas to an amount not exceeding $10,000,000, to be paid, with the exception of a sum falling short of $400,000, exclusively out of the proceeds of the sales of her public lands. We could not with honor take the lands without assuming the full payment of all incumbencies upon them.

Nothing has occurred since your last session to induce a doubt that the dispositions of Texas remain unaltered. No intimation of an altered determination on the part of her Government and people has been furnished to the Executive. She still desires to throw herself under the protection of our laws and to partake of the blessings of our federative system, while every American interest would seem to require it. The extension of our coastwise and foreign trade to an amount almost incalculable, the enlargement of the market for our manufactures, a constantly growing market for our agricultural productions, safety to our frontiers, and additional strength and stability to the Union—these are the results which would rapidly develop themselves upon the consummation of the measure of annexation. In such event I will not doubt but that Mexico would find her true interest to consist in meeting the advances of this Government in a spirit of amity. Nor do I apprehend any serious complaint from any other quarter; no sufficient ground exists for such complaint. We should interfere in no respect with the rights of any other nation. There can not be gathered from the act any design on our part to do so with their possessions on this continent. We have interposed no impediments in the way of such acquisitions of territory, large and extensive as many of them are, as the leading powers of Europe have made from time to time in every part of the world. We seek no conquest made by war. No intrigue will have been resorted to or acts of diplomacy essayed to accomplish the annexation of Texas. Free and independent herself, she asks to be received into our Union. It is a question for our own decision whether she shall be received or not.

The two Governments having already agreed through their respective organs on the terms of annexation, I would recommend their adoption by Congress in the form of a joint resolution or act to be perfected and made binding on the two countries when adopted in like manner by the Government of Texas.

In order that the subject may be fully presented in all its bearings, the correspondence which has taken place in reference to it since the adjournment of Congress between the United States, Texas, and Mexico is herewith transmitted.

The amendments proposed by the Senate to the convention concluded between the United States and Mexico on the 20th of November, 1843, have been transmitted through our minister for the concurrence of the Mexican Government, but, although urged thereto, no action has yet been had on the subject, nor has any answer been given which would authorize a favorable conclusion in the future. The decree of September, 1843, in relation to the retail trade, the order for the expulsion of foreigners, and that of a more recent date in regard to passports—all which are considered as in violation of the treaty of amity and commerce between the two countries—have led to a correspondence of considerable length between the minister for foreign relations and our representatives at Mexico, but without any satisfactory result. They remain still unadjusted, and many and serious inconveniences have already resulted to our citizens in consequence of them.

Questions growing out of the act of disarming a body of Texan troops under the command of Major Snively by an officer in the service of the United States, acting under the orders of our Government, and the forcible entry into the custom-house at Bryarlys Landing, on Red River, by certain citizens of the United States, and taking away therefrom the goods seized by the collector of the customs as forfeited under the laws of Texas, have been adjusted so far as the powers of the Executive extend. The correspondence between the two Governments in reference to both subjects will be found amongst the accompanying documents. It contains a full statement of all the facts and circumstances, with the views taken on both sides and the principles on which the questions have been adjusted. It remains for Congress to make the necessary appropriation to carry the arrangement into effect, which I respectfully recommend.

The greatly improved condition of the Treasury affords a subject for general congratulation. The paralysis which had fallen on trade and commerce, and which subjected the Government to the necessity of resorting to loans and the issue of Treasury notes to a large amount, has passed away, and after the payment of upward of $7,000,000 on account of the interest, and in redemption of more than $5,000,000 of the public debt which falls due on the 1st of January next, and setting apart upward of $2,000,000 for the payment of outstanding Treasury notes and meeting an installment of the debts of the corporate cities of the District of Columbia, an estimated surplus of upward of $7,000,000 over and above the existing appropriations will remain in the Treasury at the close of the fiscal year. Should the Treasury notes continue outstanding as heretofore, that surplus will be considerably augmented. Although all interest has ceased upon them and the Government has invited their return to the Treasury, yet they remain outstanding, affording great facilities to commerce, and establishing the fact that under a well-regulated system of finance the Government has resources within itself which render it independent in time of need, not only of private loans, but also of bank facilities.

The only remaining subject of regret is that the remaining stocks of the Government do not fall due at an earlier day, since their redemption would be entirely within its control. As it is, it may be well worthy the consideration of Congress whether the law establishing the sinking fund (under the operation of which the debts of the Revolution and last war with Great Britain were to a great extent extinguished) should not, with proper modifications, so as to prevent an accumulation of surpluses, and limited in amount to a specific sum, be reenacted. Such provision, which would authorize the Government to go into the market for a purchase of its own stock on fair terms, would serve to maintain its credit at the highest point and prevent to a great extent those fluctuations in the price of its securities which might under other circumstances affect its credit. No apprehension of this sort is at this moment entertained, since the stocks of the Government, which but two years ago were offered for sale to capitalists at home and abroad at a depreciation, and could find no purchasers, are now greatly above par in the hands of the holders; but a wise and prudent forecast admonishes us to place beyond the reach of contingency the public credit.

It must also be a matter of unmingled gratification that under the existing financial system (resting upon the act of 1789 and the resolution of 1816) the currency of the country has attained a state of perfect soundness; and the rates of exchange between different parts of the Union, which in 1841 denoted by their enormous amount the great depreciation and, in fact, worthlessness of the currency in most of the States, are now reduced to little more than the mere expense of transporting specie from place to place and the risk incident to the operation. In a new country like that of the United States, where so many inducements are held out for speculation, the depositories of the surplus revenue, consisting of banks of any description, when it reaches any considerable amount, require the closest vigilance on the part of the Government. All banking institutions, under whatever denomination they may pass, are governed by an almost exclusive regard to the interest of the stockholders. That interest consists in the augmentation of profits in the form of dividends, and a large surplus revenue intrusted to their custody is but too apt to lead to excessive loans and to extravagantly large issues of paper. As a necessary consequence prices are nominally increased and the speculative mania very soon seizes upon the public mind. A fictitious state of prosperity for a season exists, and, in the language of the day, money becomes plenty. Contracts are entered into by individuals resting on this unsubstantial state of things, but the delusion speedily passes away and the country is overrun with an indebtedness so weighty as to overwhelm many and to visit every department of industry with great and ruinous embarrassment. The greatest vigilance becomes necessary on the part of Government to guard against this state of things. The depositories must be given distinctly to understand that the favors of the Government will be altogether withdrawn, or substantially diminished, if its revenues shall be regarded as additions to their banking capital or as the foundation of an enlarged circulation.

The Government, through its revenue, has at all times an important part to perform in connection with the currency, and it greatly depends upon its vigilance and care whether the country be involved in embarrassments similar to those which it has had recently to encounter, or, aided by the action of the Treasury, shall be preserved in a sound and healthy condition.

The dangers to be guarded against are greatly augmented by too large a surplus of revenue. When that surplus greatly exceeds in amount what shall be required by a wise and prudent forecast to meet unforeseen contingencies, the Legislature itself may come to be seized with a disposition to indulge in extravagant appropriations to objects many of which may, and most probably would, be found to conflict with the Constitution. A fancied expediency is elevated above constitutional authority, and a reckless and wasteful extravagance but too certainly follows.

The important power of taxation, which when exercised in its most restricted form is a burthen on labor and production, is resorted to under various pretexts for purposes having no affinity to the motives which dictated its grant, and the extravagance of Government stimulates individual extravagance until the spirit of a wild and ill-regulated speculation involves one and all in its unfortunate results. In view of such fatal consequences, it may be laid down as an axiom rounded in moral and political truth that no greater taxes should be imposed than are necessary for an economical administration of the Government, and that whatever exists beyond should be reduced or modified. This doctrine does in no way conflict with the exercise of a sound discrimination in the selection of the articles to be taxed, which a due regard to the public weal would at all times suggest to the legislative mind. It leaves the range of selection undefined; and such selection should always be made with an eye to the great interests of the country. Composed as is the Union of separate and independent States, a patriotic Legislature will not fail in consulting the interests of the parts to adopt such course as will be best calculated to advance the harmony of the whole, and thus insure that permanency in the policy of the Government without which all efforts to advance the public prosperity are vain and fruitless.

This great and vitally important task rests with Congress, and the Executive can do no more than recommend the general principles which should govern in its execution.

I refer you to the report of the Secretary of War for an exhibition of the condition of the Army, and recommend to you as well worthy your best consideration many of the suggestions it contains. The Secretary in no degree exaggerates the great importance of pressing forward without delay in the work of erecting and finishing the fortifications to which he particularly alludes. Much has been done toward placing our cities and roadsteads in a state of security against the hazards of hostile attack within the last four years; but considering the new elements which have been of late years employed in the propelling of ships and the formidable implements of destruction which have been brought into service, we can not be too active or vigilant in preparing and perfecting the means of defense. I refer you also to his report for a full statement of the condition of the Indian tribes within our jurisdiction. The Executive has abated no effort in carrying into effect the well-established policy of the Government which contemplates a removal of all the tribes residing within the limits of the several States beyond those limits, and it is now enabled to congratulate the country at the prospect of an early consummation of this object. Many of the tribes have already made great progress in the arts of civilized life, and through the operation of the schools established among them, aided by the efforts of the pious men of various religious denominations who devote themselves to the task of their improvement, we may fondly hope that the remains of the formidable tribes which were once masters of this country will in their transition from the savage state to a condition of refinement and cultivation add another bright trophy to adorn the labors of a well-directed philanthropy.

The accompanying report of the Secretary of the Navy will explain to you the situation of that branch of the service. The present organization of the Department imparts to its operations great efficiency, but I concur fully in the propriety of a division of the Bureau of Construction, Equipment, Increase, and Repairs into two bureaus. The subjects as now arranged are incongruous, and require to a certain extent information and qualifications altogether dissimilar.

The operations of the squadron on the coast of Africa have been conducted with all due attention to the object which led to its origination, and I am happy to say that the officers and crews have enjoyed the best possible health under the system adopted by the officer in command. It is believed that the United States is the only nation which has by its laws subjected to the punishment of death as pirates those who may be engaged in the slave trade. A similar enactment on the part of other nations would not fail to be attended by beneficial results.

In consequence of the difficulties which have existed in the way of securing titles for the necessary grounds, operations have not yet been commenced toward the establishment of the navy-yard at Memphis. So soon as the title is perfected no further delay will be permitted to intervene. It is well worthy of your consideration whether Congress should not direct the establishment of a ropewalk in connection with the contemplated navy-yard, as a measure not only of economy, but as highly useful and necessary. The only establishment of the sort now connected with the service is located at Boston, and the advantages of a similar establishment convenient to the hemp-growing region must be apparent to all.

The report of the Secretary presents other matters to your consideration of an important character in connection with the service.

In referring you to the accompanying report of the Postmaster-General it affords me continued cause of gratification to be able to advert to the fact that the affairs of the Department for the last four years have been so conducted as from its unaided resources to meet its large expenditures. On my coming into office a debt of nearly $500,000 existed against the Department, which Congress discharged by an appropriation from the Treasury. The Department on the 4th of March next will be found, under the management of its present efficient head, free of debt or embarrassment, which could only have been done by the observance and practice of the greatest vigilance and economy. The laws have contemplated throughout that the Department should be self-sustained, but it may become necessary, with the wisest regard to the public interests, to introduce amendments and alterations in the system.

There is a strong desire manifested in many quarters so to alter the tariff of letter postage as to reduce the amount of tax at present imposed. Should such a measure be carried into effect to the full extent desired, it can not well be doubted but that for the first years of its operation a diminished revenue would be collected, the supply of which would necessarily constitute a charge upon the Treasury. Whether such a result would be desirable it will be for Congress in its wisdom to determine. It may in general be asserted as true that radical alterations in any system should rather be brought about gradually than by sudden changes and by pursuing this prudent policy in the reduction of letter postage the Department might still sustain itself through the revenue which would accrue by the increase of letters. The state and condition of the public Treasury has heretofore been such as to have precluded the recommendation of any material change. The difficulties upon this head have, however, ceased, and a larger discretion is now left to the Government.

I can not too strongly urge the policy of authorizing the establishment of a line of steamships regularly to ply between this country and foreign ports and upon our own waters for the transportation of the mail. The example of the British Government is well worthy of imitation in this respect. The belief is strongly entertained that the emoluments arising from the transportation of mail matter to foreign countries would operate of itself as an inducement to cause individual enterprise to undertake that branch of the task, and the remuneration of the Government would consist in the addition readily made to our steam navy in case of emergency by the ships so employed. Should this suggestion meet your approval, the propriety of placing such ships under the command of experienced officers of the Navy will not escape your observation. The application of steam to the purposes of naval warfare cogently recommends an extensive steam marine as important in estimating the defenses of the country. Fortunately this may be obtained by us to a great extent without incurring any large amount of expenditure. Steam vessels to be engaged in the transportation of the mails on our principal water courses, lakes, and ports of our coast could also be so constructed as to be efficient as war vessels when needed, and would of themselves constitute a formidable force in order to repel attacks from abroad. We can not be blind to the fact that other nations have already added large numbers of steamships to their naval armaments and that this new and powerful agent is destined to revolutionize the condition of the world. It becomes the United States, therefore, looking to their security, to adopt a similar policy, and the plan suggested will enable them to do so at a small comparative cost.

I take the greatest pleasure in bearing testimony to the zeal and untiring industry which has characterized the conduct of the members of the Executive Cabinet. Each in his appropriate sphere has rendered me the most efficient aid in carrying on the Government, and it will not, I trust, appear out of place for me to bear this public testimony. The cardinal objects which should ever be held in view by those intrusted with the administration of public affairs are rigidly, and without favor or affection, so to interpret the national will expressed in the laws as that injustice should be done to none, justice to all. This has been the rule upon which they have acted, and thus it is believed that few cases, if any, exist wherein our fellow-citizens, who from time to time have been drawn to the seat of Government for the settlement of their transactions with the Government, have gone away dissatisfied. Where the testimony has been perfected and was esteemed satisfactory their claims have been promptly audited, and this in the absence of all favoritism or partiality. The Government which is not just to its own people can neither claim their affection nor the respect of the world. At the same time, the Closest attention has been paid to those matters which relate more immediately to the great concerns of the country. Order and efficiency in each branch of the public service have prevailed, accompanied by a system of the most rigid responsibility on the part of the receiving and disbursing agents. The fact, in illustration of the truth of this remark, deserves to be noticed that the revenues of the Government, amounting in the last four years to upward of $120,000,000, have been collected and disbursed through the numerous governmental agents without the loss by default of any amount worthy of serious commentary.

The appropriations made by Congress for the improvement of the rivers of the West and of the harbors on the Lakes are in a course of judicious expenditure under suitable agents, and are destined, it is to be hoped, to realize all the benefits designed to be accomplished by Congress. I can not, however, sufficiently impress upon Congress the great importance of withholding appropriations from improvements which are not ascertained by previous examination and survey to be necessary for the shelter and protection of trade from the dangers of stores and tempests. Without this precaution the expenditures are but too apt to inure to the benefit of individuals, without reference to the only consideration which can render them constitutional—the public interests and the general good.

I can not too earnestly urge upon you the interests of this District, over which by the Constitution Congress has exclusive jurisdiction. It would be deeply to be regretted should there be at any time ground to complain of neglect on the part of a community which, detached as it is from the parental care of the States of Virginia and Maryland, can only expect aid from Congress as its local legislature. Amongst the subjects which claim your attention is the prompt organization of an asylum for the insane who may be found from time to time sojourning within the District. Such course is also demanded by considerations which apply to branches of the public service. For the necessities in this behalf I invite your particular attention to the report of the Secretary of the Navy.

I have thus, gentlemen of the two Houses of Congress, presented you a true and faithful picture of the condition of public affairs, both foreign and domestic. The wants of the public service are made known to you, and matters of no ordinary importance are urged upon your consideration. Shall I not be permitted to congratulate you on the happy auspices under which you have assembled and at the important change in the condition of things which has occurred in the last three years? During that period questions with foreign powers of vital importance to the peace of our country have been settled and adjusted. A desolating and wasting war with savage tribes has been brought to a close. The internal tranquillity of the country, threatened by agitating questions, has been preserved. The credit of the Government, which had experienced a temporary embarrassment, has been thoroughly restored. Its coffers, which for a season were empty, have been replenished. A currency nearly uniform in its value has taken the place of one depreciated and almost worthless. Commerce and manufactures, which had suffered in common with every other interest, have once more revived, and the whole country exhibits an aspect of prosperity and happiness. Trade and barter, no longer governed by a wild and speculative mania, rest upon a solid and substantial footing, and the rapid growth of our cities in every direction bespeaks most strongly the favorable circumstances by which we are surrounded. My happiness in the retirement which shortly awaits me is the ardent hope which I experience that this state of prosperity is neither deceptive nor destined to be short lived, and that measures which have not yet received its sanction, but which I can not but regard as closely connected with the honor, the glory, and still more enlarged prosperity of the country, are destined at an early day to receive the approval of Congress. Under these circumstances and with these anticipations I shall most gladly leave to others more able than myself the noble and pleasing task of sustaining the public prosperity. I shall carry with me into retirement the gratifying reflection that as my sole object throughout has been to advance the public good I may not entirely have failed in accomplishing it; and this gratification is heightened in no small degree by the fact that when under a deep and abiding sense of duty I have found myself constrained to resort to the qualified veto it has neither been followed by disapproval on the part of the people nor weakened in any degree their attachment to that great conservative feature of our Government.

JOHN TYLER

1 0

James K. Polk (1845–1849)

A common theme of presidential farewells is "American exceptionalism," the belief that the United States is a unique country with a unique destiny in world history. In his last annual message, Polk expressed it well: "To our wise and free institutions it is to be attributed that while other nations have achieved glory at the price of the suffering, distress, and impoverishment of their people, we have won our honorable position in the midst of an uninterrupted prosperity and of an increasing individual comfort and happiness."

Polk led the United States into an "inevitable" war with Mexico. As the nation's eleventh president saw it, that war yielded many benefits. It not only settled differences with our southern neighbor, especially over Texas and California, but it also sent a powerful signal to more distant powers that might contemplate threatening the United States. The Mexican War established that the young republic could successfully prosecute a war beyond its borders. With the confidence that comes from decisive victory, Polk reasserted the Monroe Doctrine and even extended it to warn against European interference with intra-American relations anywhere in North America.

The president was especially proud of the soldiers who fought in the recent war. To him they were a manifestation of American exceptionalism. "Our citizen soldiers," Polk wrote, "are unlike those drawn from the population of any other country. They are composed indiscriminately of all professions and pursuits—of farmers, lawyers, physicians, merchants, manufacturers, mechanics, and laborers—and this not only among the officers, but the private soldiers in the ranks. Our citizen soldiers are unlike those of any other country in other respects. They are armed, and have been accustomed from their youth up to handle and use firearms, and a large proportion of them, especially in the Western and more newly settled States, are expert marksmen. They are men who have a reputation to maintain at home by their good conduct in the field. They are intelligent, and there is an individuality of character which is found in the ranks of no other army. In battle each private man, as well as every officer, fights not only for his country, but for glory and distinction among his fellow-citizens when he shall return to civil life."

One of the reasons Polk went to war against Mexico was to secure California for the United States. Once the Mexican army was beaten and the peace treaty signed, the way was opened for American exploration and settlement. It was not long before there was a spectacular gold rush by the "Forty-niners." To Polk this was just the beginning; he compared the acquisition of California to the Louisiana Purchase. He could foresee the day when California would add greatly to the wealth of the nation.

Finally, there is a fascinating speculation in Polk's annual message. He believed that the westward expansion of the American people preserved the delicate balance of power between the national government and the states; that if there had not been new territories and states, there would be a centralizing tendency, and the national government would grow more powerful than the Founders intended it to be. Ironically, "each new State gives strength and an additional guaranty for the preservation of the Union itself."

Fourth Annual Message
(written to the Congress)
December 5, 1848

Fellow-Citizens of the Senate and of the House of Representatives:

Under the benignant providence of Almighty God the representatives of the States and of the people are again brought together to deliberate for the public good. The gratitude of the nation to the Sovereign Arbiter of All Human Events should be commensurate with the boundless blessings which we enjoy.

Peace, plenty, and contentment reign throughout our borders, and our beloved country presents a sublime moral spectacle to the world.

The troubled and unsettled condition of some of the principal European powers has had a necessary tendency to check and embarrass trade and to depress prices throughout all commercial nations, but notwithstanding these causes, the United States, with their abundant products, have felt their effects less severely than any other country, and all our great interests are still prosperous and successful.

In reviewing the great events of the past year and contrasting the agitated and disturbed state of other countries with our own tranquil and happy condition, we may congratulate ourselves that we are the most favored people on the face of the earth. While the people of other countries are struggling to establish free institutions, under which man may govern himself, we are in the actual enjoyment of them—a rich inheritance from our fathers. While enlightened nations of Europe are convulsed and distracted by civil war or intestine strife, we settle all our political controversies by the peaceful exercise of the rights of freemen at the ballot box.

The great republican maxim, so deeply engraven on the hearts of our people, that the will of the majority, constitutionally expressed, shall prevail, is our sure safeguard against force and violence. It is a subject of just pride that our fame and character as a nation continue rapidly to advance in the estimation of the civilized world.

To our wise and free institutions it is to be attributed that while other nations have achieved glory at the price of the suffering, distress, and impoverishment of their people, we have won our honorable position in the midst of an uninterrupted prosperity and of an increasing individual comfort and happiness.

I am happy to inform you that our relations with all nations are friendly and pacific. Advantageous treaties of commerce have been concluded within the last four years with New Granada, Peru, the Two Sicilies, Belgium, Hanover, Oldenburg, and Mecklenburg-Schwerin. Pursuing our example, the restrictive system of Great Britain, our principal foreign customer, has been relaxed, a more liberal commercial policy has been adopted by other enlightened nations, and our trade has been greatly enlarged and extended. Our country stands higher in the respect of the world than at any former period. To continue to occupy this proud position, it is only necessary to preserve peace and faithfully adhere to the great and fundamental principle of our foreign policy of noninterference in the domestic concerns of other nations. We recognize in all nations the right which we enjoy ourselves, to change and reform their political institutions according to their own will and pleasure. Hence we do not look behind existing governments capable of maintaining their own authority. We recognize all such actual governments, not only from the dictates of true policy, but from a sacred regard for the independence of nations. While this is our settled policy, it does not follow that we can ever be indifferent spectators of the progress of liberal principles. The Government and people of the United States hailed with enthusiasm and delight the establishment of the French Republic, as we now hail the efforts in progress to unite the States of Germany in a confederation similar in many respects to our own Federal Union. If the great and enlightened German States, occupying, as they do, a central and commanding position in Europe, shall succeed in establishing such a confederated government, securing at the same time to the citizens of each State local governments adapted to the peculiar condition of each, with unrestricted trade and intercourse with each other, it will be an important era in the history of human events. Whilst it will consolidate and strengthen the power of Germany, it must essentially promote the cause of peace, commerce, civilization, and constitutional liberty throughout the world.

With all the Governments on this continent our relations, it is believed, are now on a more friendly and satisfactory footing than they have ever been at any former period.

Since the exchange of ratifications of the treaty of peace with Mexico our intercourse with the Government of that Republic has been of the most friendly character. The envoy extraordinary and minister plenipotentiary of the United States to Mexico has been received and accredited, and a diplomatic representative from Mexico of similar rank has been received and accredited by this Government. The amicable relations between the two countries, which had been suspended, have been happily restored, and are destined, I trust, to be long preserved. The two Republics, both situated on this continent, and with coterminous territories, have every motive of sympathy and of interest to bind them together in perpetual amity.

This gratifying condition of our foreign relations renders it unnecessary for me to call your attention more specifically to them.

It has been my constant aim and desire to cultivate peace and commerce with all nations. Tranquility at home and peaceful relations abroad constitute the true permanent policy of our country. War, the scourge of nations, sometimes becomes inevitable, but is always to be avoided when it can be done consistently with the rights and honor of a nation.

One of the most important results of the war into which we were recently forced with a neighboring nation is the demonstration it has afforded of the military strength of our country. Before the late war with Mexico European and other foreign powers entertained imperfect and erroneous views of our physical strength as a nation and of our ability to prosecute war, and especially a war waged out of our own country. They saw that our standing Army on the peace establishment did not exceed 10,000 men. Accustomed themselves to maintain in peace large standing armies for the protection of thrones against their own subjects, as well as against foreign enemies, they had not conceived that it was possible for a nation without such an army, well disciplined and of long service, to wage war successfully. They held in low repute our militia, and were far from regarding them as an effective force, unless it might be for temporary defensive operations when invaded on our own soil. The events of the late war with Mexico have not only undeceived them, but have removed erroneous impressions which prevailed to some extent even among a portion of our own countrymen. That war has demonstrated that upon the breaking out of hostilities not anticipated, and for which no previous preparation had been made, a volunteer army of citizen soldiers equal to veteran troops, and in numbers equal to any emergency, can in a short period be brought into the field. Unlike what would have occurred in any other country, we were under no necessity of resorting to drafts or conscriptions. On the contrary, such was the number of volunteers who patriotically tendered their services that the chief difficulty was in making selections and determining who should be disappointed and compelled to remain at home.

Our citizen soldiers are unlike those drawn from the population of any other country. They are composed indiscriminately of all professions and pursuits—of farmers, lawyers, physicians, merchants, manufacturers, mechanics, and laborers—and this not only among the officers, but the private soldiers in the ranks. Our citizen soldiers are unlike those of any other country in other respects. They are armed, and have been accustomed from their youth up to handle and use firearms, and a large proportion of them, especially in the Western and more newly settled States, are expert marksmen. They are men who have a reputation to maintain at home by their good conduct in the field. They are intelligent, and there is an individuality of character which is found in the ranks of no other army. In battle each private man, as well as every officer, fights not only for his country, but for glory and distinction among his fellow-citizens when he shall return to civil life.

The war with Mexico has demonstrated not only the ability of the Government to organize a numerous army upon a sudden call, but also to provide it with all the munitions and necessary supplies with dispatch, convenience, and ease, and to direct its operations with efficiency. The strength of our institutions has not only been displayed in the valor and skill of our troops engaged in active service in the field, but in the organization of those executive branches which were charged with the general direction and conduct of the war. While too great praise can not be bestowed upon the officers and men who fought our battles, it would be unjust to withhold from those officers necessarily stationed at home, who were charged with the duty of furnishing the Army in proper time and at proper places with all the munitions of war and other supplies so necessary to make it efficient, the commendation to which they are entitled. The credit due to this class of our officers is the greater when it is considered that no army in ancient or modern times was even better appointed or provided than our Army in Mexico. Operating in an enemy's country, removed 2,000 miles from the seat of the Federal Government, its different corps spread over a vast extent of territory, hundreds and even thousands of miles apart from each other, nothing short of the untiring vigilance and extraordinary energy of these officers could have enabled them to provide the Army at all points and in proper season with all that was required for the most efficient service.

It is but an act of justice to declare that the officers in charge of the several executive bureaus, all under the immediate eye and supervision of the Secretary of War, performed their respective duties with ability, energy, and efficiency. They have reaped less of the glory of the war, not having been personally exposed to its perils in battle, than their companions in arms; but without their forecast, efficient aid, and cooperation those in the field would not have been provided with the ample means they possessed of achieving for themselves and their country the unfading honors which they have won for both.

When all these facts are considered, it may cease to be a matter of so much amazement abroad how it happened that our noble Army in Mexico, regulars and volunteers, were victorious upon every battlefield, however fearful the odds against them.

The war with Mexico has thus fully developed the capacity of republican governments to prosecute successfully a just and necessary foreign war with all the vigor usually attributed to more arbitrary forms of government. It has been usual for writers on public law to impute to republics a want of that unity, concentration of purpose, and vigor of execution which are generally admitted to belong to the monarchical and aristocratic forms; and this feature of popular government has been supposed to display itself more particularly in the conduct of a war carried on in an enemy's territory. The war with Great Britain in 1812 was to a great extent confined within our own limits, and shed but little light on this subject; but the war which we have just closed by an honorable peace evinces beyond all doubt that a popular representative government is equal to any emergency which is likely to arise in the affairs of a nation.

The war with Mexico has developed most strikingly and conspicuously another feature in our institutions. It is that without cost to the Government or danger to our liberties we have in the bosom of our society of freemen, available in a just and necessary war, virtually a standing army of 2,000,000 armed citizen soldiers, such as fought the battles of Mexico. But our military strength does not consist alone in our capacity for extended and successful operations on land. The Navy is an important arm of the national defense. If the services of the Navy were not so brilliant as those of the Army in the late war with Mexico, it was because they had no enemy to meet on their own element. While the Army had opportunity of performing more conspicuous service, the Navy largely participated in the conduct of the war. Both branches of the service performed their whole duty to the country. For the able and gallant services of the officers and men of the Navy, acting independently as well as in cooperation with our troops, in the conquest of the Californias, the capture of Vera Cruz, and the seizure and occupation of other important positions on the Gulf and Pacific coasts, the highest praise is due. Their vigilance, energy, and skill rendered the most effective service in excluding munitions of war and other supplies from the enemy, while they secured a safe entrance for abundant supplies for our own Army. Our extended commerce was nowhere interrupted, and for this immunity from the evils of war the country is indebted to the Navy.

High praise is due to the officers of the several executive bureaus, navy-yards, and stations connected with the service, all under the immediate direction of the Secretary of the Navy, for the industry, foresight, and energy with which everything was directed and furnished to give efficiency to that branch of the service. The same vigilance existed in directing the operations of the Navy as of the Army. There was concert of action and of purpose between the heads of the two arms of the service. By the orders which were from time to time issued, our vessels of war on the Pacific and the Gulf of Mexico were stationed in proper time and in proper positions to cooperate efficiently with the Army. By this means their combined power was brought to bear successfully on the enemy.

The great results which have been developed and brought to light by this war will be of immeasurable importance in the future progress of our country. They will tend powerfully to preserve us from foreign collisions, and to enable us to pursue uninterruptedly our cherished policy of "peace with all nations, entangling alliances with none."

Occupying, as we do, a more commanding position among nations than at any former period, our duties and our responsibilities to ourselves and to posterity are correspondingly increased. This will be the more obvious when we consider the vast additions which have been recently made to our territorial possessions and their great importance and value.

Within less than four years the annexation of Texas to the Union has been consummated; all conflicting title to the Oregon Territory south of the forty-ninth degree of north latitude, being all that was insisted on by any of my predecessors, has been adjusted, and New Mexico and Upper California have been acquired by treaty. The area of these several Territories, according to a report carefully prepared by the Commissioner of the General Land Office from the most authentic information in his possession, and which is herewith transmitted, contains 1,193,061 square miles, or 763,559,040 acres; while the area of the remaining twenty-nine States and the territory not yet organized into States east of the Rocky Mountains contains 2,059,513 square miles, or 1,318,126,058 acres. These estimates show that the territories recently acquired, and over which our exclusive jurisdiction and dominion have been extended, constitute a country more than half as large as all that which was held by the United States before their acquisition. If Oregon be excluded from the estimate, there will still remain within the limits of Texas, New Mexico, and California 851,598 square miles, or 545,012,720 acres, being an addition equal to more than one-third of all the territory owned by the United States before their acquisition, and, including Oregon, nearly as great an extent of territory as the whole of Europe, Russia only excepted. The Mississippi, so lately the frontier of our country, is now only its center. With the addition of the late acquisitions, the United States are now estimated to be nearly as large as the whole of Europe. It is estimated by the Superintendent of the Coast Survey in the accompanying report that the extent of the seacoast of Texas on the Gulf of Mexico is upward of 400 miles; of the coast of Upper California on the Pacific, of 970 miles, and of Oregon, including the Straits of Fuca, of 650 miles, making the whole extent of seacoast on the Pacific 1,620 miles and the whole extent on both the Pacific and the Gulf of Mexico 2,020 miles. The length of the coast on the Atlantic from the northern limits of the United States around the capes of Florida to the Sabine, on the eastern boundary of Texas, is estimated to be 3,100 miles; so that the addition of seacoast, including Oregon, is very nearly two-thirds as great as all we possessed before, and, excluding Oregon, is an addition of 1,370 miles, being nearly equal to one-half of the extent of coast which we possessed before these acquisitions. We have now three great maritime fronts—on the Atlantic, the Gulf of Mexico, and the Pacific—making in the whole an extent of seacoast exceeding 5,000 miles. This is the extent of the seacoast of the United States, not including bays, sounds, and small irregularities of the main shore and of the sea islands. If these be included, the length of the shore line of coast, as estimated by the Superintendent of the Coast Survey in his report, would be 33,063 miles.

It would be difficult to calculate the value of these immense additions to our territorial possessions. Texas, lying contiguous to the western boundary of Louisiana, embracing within its limits a part of the navigable tributary waters of the Mississippi and an extensive seacoast, could not long have remained in the hands of a foreign power without endangering the peace of our southwestern frontier. Her products in the vicinity of the tributaries of the Mississippi must have sought a market through these streams, running into and through our territory, and the danger of irritation and collision of interests between Texas as a foreign state and ourselves would have been imminent, while the embarrassments in the commercial intercourse between them must have been constant and unavoidable. Had Texas fallen into the hands or under the influence and control of a strong maritime or military foreign power, as she might have done, these dangers would have been still greater. They have been avoided by her voluntary and peaceful annexation to the United States. Texas, from her position, was a natural and almost indispensable part of our territories. Fortunately, she has been restored to our country, and now constitutes one of the States of our Confederacy, "upon an equal footing with the original States." The salubrity of climate, the fertility of soil, peculiarly adapted to the production of some of our most valuable staple commodities, and her commercial advantages must soon make her one of our most populous States.

New Mexico, though situated in the interior and without a seacoast, is known to contain much fertile land, to abound in rich mines of the precious metals, and to be capable of sustaining a large population. From its position it is the intermediate and connecting territory between our settlements and our possessions in Texas and those on the Pacific Coast.

Upper California, irrespective of the vast mineral wealth recently developed there, holds at this day, in point of value and importance, to the rest of the Union the same relation that Louisiana did when that fine territory was acquired from France forty-five years ago. Extending nearly ten degrees of latitude along the Pacific, and embracing the only safe and commodious harbors on that coast for many hundred miles, with a temperate climate and an extensive interior of fertile lands, it is scarcely possible to estimate its wealth until it shall be brought under the government of our laws and its resources fully developed. From its position it must command the rich commerce of China, of Asia, of the islands of the Pacific, of western Mexico, of Central America, the South American States, and of the Russian possessions bordering on that ocean. A great emporium will doubtless speedily arise on the Californian coast which may be destined to rival in importance New Orleans itself. The depot of the vast commerce which must exist on the Pacific will probably be at some point on the Bay of San Francisco, and will occupy the same relation to the whole western coast of that ocean as New Orleans does to the valley of the Mississippi and the Gulf of Mexico. To this depot our numerous whale ships will resort with their cargoes to trade, refit, and obtain supplies. This of itself will largely contribute to build up a city, which would soon become the center of a great and rapidly increasing commerce. Situated on a safe harbor, sufficiently capacious for all the navies as well as the marine of the world, and convenient to excellent timber for shipbuilding, owned by the United States, it must become our great Western naval depot.

It was known that mines of the precious metals existed to a considerable extent in California at the time of its acquisition. Recent discoveries render it probable that these mines are more extensive and valuable than was anticipated. The accounts of the abundance of gold in that territory are of such an extraordinary character as would scarcely command belief were they not corroborated by the authentic reports of officers in the public service who have visited the mineral district and derived the facts which they detail from personal observation. Reluctant to credit the reports in general circulation as to the quantity of gold, the officer commanding our forces in California visited the mineral district in July last for the purpose of obtaining accurate information on the subject. His report to the War Department of the result of his examination and the facts obtained on the spot is herewith laid before Congress. When he visited the country there were about 4,000 persons engaged in collecting gold. There is every reason to believe that the number of persons so employed has since been augmented. The explorations already made warrant the belief that the supply is very large and that gold is found at various places in an extensive district of country.

Information received from officers of the Navy and other sources, though not so full and minute, confirms the accounts of the commander of our military force in California. It appears also from these reports that mines of quicksilver are found in the vicinity of the gold region. One of them is now being worked, and is believed to be among the most productive in the world.

The effects produced by the discovery of these rich mineral deposits and the success which has attended the labors of those who have resorted to them have produced a surprising change in the state of affairs in California. Labor commands a most exorbitant price, and all other pursuits but that of searching for the precious metals are abandoned. Nearly the whole of the male population of the country have gone to the gold districts. Ships arriving on the coast are deserted by their crews and their voyages suspended for want of sailors. Our commanding officer there entertains apprehensions that soldiers can not be kept in the public service without a large increase of pay. Desertions in his command have become frequent, and he recommends that those who shall withstand the strong temptation and remain faithful should be rewarded.

This abundance of gold and the all-engrossing pursuit of it have already caused in California an unprecedented rise in the price of all the necessaries of life.

That we may the more speedily and fully avail ourselves of the undeveloped wealth of these mines, it is deemed of vast importance that a branch of the Mint of the United States be authorized to be established at your present session in California. Among other signal advantages which would result from such an establishment would be that of raising the gold to its par value in that territory. A branch mint of the United States at the great commercial depot on the west coast would convert into our own coin not only the gold derived from our own rich mines, but also the bullion and specie which our commerce may bring from the whole west coast of Central and South America. The west coast of America and the adjacent interior embrace the richest and best mines of Mexico, New Granada, Central America, Chile, and Peru. The bullion and specie drawn from these countries, and especially from those of western Mexico and Peru, to an amount in value of many millions of dollars, are now annually diverted and carried by the ships of Great Britain to her own ports, to be recoined or used to sustain her national bank, and thus contribute to increase her ability to command so much of the commerce of the world. If a branch mint be established at the great commercial point upon that coast, a vast amount of bullion and specie would flow thither to be recoined, and pass thence to New Orleans, New York, and other Atlantic cities. The amount of our constitutional currency at home would be greatly increased, while its circulation abroad would be promoted. It is well known to our merchants trading to China and the west coast of America that great inconvenience and loss are experienced from the fact that our coins are not current at their par value in those countries.

The powers of Europe, far removed from the west coast of America by the Atlantic Ocean, which intervenes, and by a tedious and dangerous navigation around the southern cape of the continent of America, can never successfully compete with the United States in the rich and extensive commerce which is opened to us at so much less cost by the acquisition of California.

The vast importance and commercial advantages of California have heretofore remained undeveloped by the Government of the country of which it constituted a part. Now that this fine province is a part of our country, all the States of the Union, some more immediately and directly than others, are deeply interested in the speedy development of its wealth and resources. No section of our country is more interested or will be more benefited than the commercial, navigating, and manufacturing interests of the Eastern States. Our planting and farming interests in every part of the Union will be greatly benefited by it. As our commerce and navigation are enlarged and extended, our exports of agricultural products and of manufactures will be increased, and in the new markets thus opened they can not fail to command remunerating and profitable prices.

The acquisition of California and New Mexico, the settlement of the Oregon boundary, and the annexation of Texas, extending to the Rio Grande, are results which, combined, are of greater consequence and will add more to the strength and wealth of the nation than any which have preceded them since the adoption of the Constitution.

But to effect these great results not only California, but New Mexico, must be brought under the control of regularly organized governments. The existing condition of California and of that part of New Mexico lying west of the Rio Grande and without the limits of Texas imperiously demands that Congress should at its present session organize Territorial governments over them.

Upon the exchange of ratifications of the treaty of peace with Mexico, on the 30th of May last, the temporary governments which had been established over New Mexico and California by our military and naval commanders by virtue of the rights of war ceased to derive any obligatory force from that source of authority, and having been ceded to the United States, all government and control over them under the authority of Mexico had ceased to exist. Impressed with the necessity of establishing Territorial governments over them, I recommended the subject to the favorable consideration of Congress in my message communicating the ratified treaty of peace, on the 6th of July last, and invoked their action at that session. Congress adjourned without making any provision for their government. The inhabitants by the transfer of their country had become entitled to the benefit of our laws and Constitution, and yet were left without any regularly organized government. Since that time the very limited power possessed by the Executive has been exercised to preserve and protect them from the inevitable consequences of a state of anarchy. The only government which remained was that established by the military authority during the war. Regarding this to be a de facto government, and that by the presumed consent of the inhabitants it might be continued temporarily, they were advised to conform and submit to it for the short intervening period before Congress would again assemble and could legislate on the subject. The views entertained by the Executive on this point are contained in a communication of the Secretary of State dated the 7th of October last, which was forwarded for publication to California and New Mexico, a copy of which is herewith transmitted. The small military force of the Regular Army which was serving within the limits of the acquired territories at the close of the war was retained in them, and additional forces have been ordered there for the protection of the inhabitants and to preserve and secure the rights and interests of the United States.

No revenue has been or could be collected at the ports in California, because Congress failed to authorize the establishment of custom-houses or the appointment of officers for that purpose.

The Secretary of the Treasury, by a circular letter addressed to collectors of the customs on the 7th day of October last, a copy of which is herewith transmitted, exercised all the power with which he was invested by law.

In pursuance of the act of the 14th of August last, extending the benefit of our post-office laws to the people of California, the Postmaster-General has appointed two agents, who have proceeded, the one to California and the other to Oregon, with authority to make the necessary arrangements for carrying its provisions into effect.

The monthly line of mail steamers from Panama to Astoria has been required to "stop and deliver and take mails at San Diego, Monterey, and San Francisco." These mail steamers, connected by the Isthmus of Panama with the line of mail steamers on the Atlantic between New York and Chagres, will establish a regular mail communication with California.

It is our solemn duty to provide with the least practicable delay for New Mexico and California regularly organized Territorial governments. The causes of the failure to do this at the last session of Congress are well known and deeply to be regretted. With the opening prospects of increased prosperity and national greatness which the acquisition of these rich and extensive territorial possessions affords, how irrational it would be to forego or to reject these advantages by the agitation of a domestic question which is coeval with the existence of our Government itself, and to endanger by internal strifes, geographical divisions, and heated contests for political power, or for any other cause, the harmony of the glorious Union of our confederated States—that Union which binds us together as one people, and which for sixty years has been our shield and protection against every danger. In the eyes of the world and of posterity how trivial and insignificant will be all our internal divisions and struggles compared with the preservation of this Union of the States in all its vigor and with all its countless blessings! No patriot would foment and excite geographical and sectional divisions. No lover of his country would deliberately calculate the value of the Union. Future generations would look in amazement upon the folly of such a course. Other nations at the present day would look upon it with astonishment, and such of them as desire to maintain and perpetuate thrones and monarchical or aristocratical principles will view it with exultation and delight, because in it they will see the elements of faction, which they hope must ultimately overturn our system. Ours is the great example of a prosperous and free self-governed republic, commanding the admiration and the imitation of all the lovers of freedom throughout the world. How solemn, therefore, is the duty, how impressive the call upon us and upon all parts of our country, to cultivate a patriotic spirit of harmony, of good-fellowship, of compromise and mutual concession, in the administration of the incomparable system of government formed by our fathers in the midst of almost insuperable difficulties, and transmitted to us with the injunction that we should enjoy its blessings and hand it down unimpaired to those who may come after us.

In view of the high and responsible duties which we owe to ourselves and to mankind, I trust you may be able at your present session to approach the adjustment of the only domestic question which seriously threatens, or probably ever can threaten, to disturb the harmony and successful operations of our system.

The immensely valuable possessions of New Mexico and California are already inhabited by a considerable population. Attracted by their great fertility, their mineral wealth, their commercial advantages, and the salubrity of the climate, emigrants from the older States in great numbers are already preparing to seek new homes in these inviting regions. Shall the dissimilarity of the domestic institutions in the different States prevent us from providing for them suitable governments? These institutions existed at the adoption of the Constitution, but the obstacles which they interposed were overcome by that spirit of compromise which is now invoked. In a conflict of opinions or of interests, real or imaginary, between different sections of our country, neither can justly demand all which it might desire to obtain. Each, in the true spirit of our institutions, should concede something to the other.

Our gallant forces in the Mexican war, by whose patriotism and unparalleled deeds of arms we obtained these possessions as an indemnity for our just demands against Mexico, were composed of citizens who belonged to no one State or section of our Union. They were men from slaveholding and nonslaveholding States, from the North and the South, from the East and the West. They were all companions in arms and fellow-citizens of the same common country, engaged in the same common cause. When prosecuting that war they were brethren and friends, and shared alike with each other common toils, dangers, and sufferings. Now, when their work is ended, when peace is restored, and they return again to their homes, put off the habiliments of war, take their places in society, and resume their pursuits in civil life, surely a spirit of harmony and concession and of equal regard for the rights of all and of all sections of the Union ought to prevail in providing governments for the acquired territories—the fruits of their common service. The whole people of the United States, and of every State, contributed to defray the expenses of that war, and it would not be just for any one section to exclude another from all participation in the acquired territory. This would not be in consonance with the just system of government which the framers of the Constitution adopted.

The question is believed to be rather abstract than practical whether slavery ever can or would exist in any portion of the acquired territory even if it were left to the option of the slaveholding States themselves. From the nature of the climate and productions in much the larger portion of it, it is certain it could never exist, and in the remainder the probabilities are it would not. But however this may be, the question, involving, as it does, a principle of equality of rights of the separate and several States as equal copartners in the Confederacy, should not be disregarded.

In organizing governments over these territories no duty imposed on Congress by the Constitution requires that they should legislate on the subject of slavery, while their power to do so is not only seriously questioned, but denied by many of the soundest expounders of that instrument. Whether Congress shall legislate or not, the people of the acquired territories, when assembled in convention to form State constitutions, will possess the sole and exclusive power to determine for themselves whether slavery shall or shall not exist within their limits. If Congress shall abstain from interfering with the question, the people of these territories will be left free to adjust it as they may think proper when they apply for admission as States into the Union. No enactment of Congress could restrain the people of any of the sovereign States of the Union, old or new, North or South, slaveholding or nonslaveholding, from determining the character of their own domestic institutions as they may deem wise and proper. Any and all the States possess this right, and Congress can not deprive them of it. The people of Georgia might if they chose so alter their constitution as to abolish slavery within its limits, and the people of Vermont might so alter their constitution as to admit slavery within its limits. Both States would possess the right, though, as all know, it is not probable that either would exert it.

It is fortunate for the peace and harmony of the Union that this question is in its nature temporary and can only continue for the brief period which will intervene before California and New Mexico may be admitted as States into the Union. From the tide of population now flowing into them it is highly probable that this will soon occur.

Considering the several States and the citizens of the several States as equals and entitled to equal rights under the Constitution, if this were an original question it might well be insisted on that the principle of noninterference is the true doctrine and that Congress could not, in the absence of any express grant of power, interfere with their relative rights. Upon a great emergency, however, and under menacing dangers to the Union, the Missouri compromise line in respect to slavery was adopted. The same line was extended farther west in the acquisition of Texas. After an acquiescence of nearly thirty years in the principle of compromise recognized and established by these acts, and to avoid the danger to the Union which might follow if it were now disregarded, I have heretofore expressed the opinion that that line of compromise should be extended on the parallel of 36° 30' from the western boundary of Texas, where it now terminates, to the Pacific Ocean. This is the middle ground of compromise, upon which the different sections of the Union may meet, as they have heretofore met. If this be done, it is confidently believed a large majority of the people of every section of the country, however widely their abstract opinions on the subject of slavery may differ, would cheerfully and patriotically acquiesce in it, and peace and harmony would again fill our borders.

The restriction north of the line was only yielded to in the case of Missouri and Texas upon a principle of compromise, made necessary for the sake of preserving the harmony and possibly the existence of the Union.

It was upon these considerations that at the close of your last session I gave my sanction to the principle of the Missouri compromise line by approving and signing the bill to establish "the Territorial government of Oregon." From a sincere desire to preserve the harmony of the Union, and in deference for the acts of my predecessors, I felt constrained to yield my acquiescence to the extent to which they had gone in compromising this delicate and dangerous question. But if Congress shall now reverse the decision by which the Missouri compromise was effected, and shall propose to extend the restriction over the whole territory, south as well as north of the parallel of 36° 30', it will cease to be a compromise, and must be regarded as an original question.

If Congress, instead of observing the course of noninterference, leaving the adoption of their own domestic institutions to the people who may inhabit these territories, or if, instead of extending the Missouri compromise line to the Pacific, shall prefer to submit the legal and constitutional questions which may arise to the decision of the judicial tribunals, as was proposed in a bill which passed the Senate at your last session, an adjustment may be effected in this mode. If the whole subject be referred to the judiciary, all parts of the Union should cheerfully acquiesce in the final decision of the tribunal created by the Constitution for the settlement of all questions which may arise under the Constitution, treaties, and laws of the United States.

Congress is earnestly invoked, for the sake of the Union, its harmony, and our continued prosperity as a nation, to adjust at its present session this, the only dangerous question which lies in our path, if not in some one of the modes suggested, in some other which may be satisfactory.

In anticipation of the establishment of regular governments over the acquired territories, a joint commission of officers of the Army and Navy has been ordered to proceed to the coast of California and Oregon for the purpose of making reconnaissances and a report as to the proper sites for the erection of fortifications or other defensive works on land and of suitable situations for naval stations. The information which may be expected from a scientific and skillful examination of the whole face of the coast will be eminently useful to Congress when they come to consider the propriety of making appropriations for these great national objects. Proper defenses on land will be necessary for the security and protection of our possessions, and the establishment of navy-yards and a dock for the repair and construction of vessels will be important alike to our Navy and commercial marine. Without such establishments every vessel, whether of the Navy or of the merchant service, requiring repair must at great expense come round Cape Horn to one of our Atlantic yards for that purpose. With such establishments vessels, it is believed, may be built or repaired as cheaply in California as upon the Atlantic coast. They would give employment to many of our enterprising shipbuilders and mechanics and greatly facilitate and enlarge our commerce in the Pacific.

As it is ascertained that mines of gold, silver, copper, and quicksilver exist in New Mexico and California, and that nearly all the lands where they are found belong to the United States, it is deemed important to the public interest that provision be made for a geological and mineralogical examination of these regions. Measures should be adopted to preserve the mineral lands, especially such as contain the precious metals, for the use of the United States, or, if brought into market, to separate them from the farming lands and dispose of them in such manner as to secure a large return of money to the Treasury and at the same time to lead to the development of their wealth by individual proprietors and purchasers. To do this it will be necessary to provide for an immediate survey and location of the lots. If Congress should deem it proper to dispose of the mineral lands, they should be sold in small quantities and at a fixed minimum price.

I recommend that surveyors-general's offices be authorized to be established in New Mexico and California and provision made for surveying and bringing the public lands into market at the earliest practicable period. In disposing of these lands, I recommend that the right of preemption be secured and liberal grants made to the early emigrants who have settled or may settle upon them.

It will be important to extend our revenue laws over these territories, and especially over California, at an early period. There is already a considerable commerce with California, and until ports of entry shall be established and collectors appointed no revenue can be received.

If these and other necessary and proper measures be adopted for the development of the wealth and resources of New Mexico and California and regular Territorial governments be established over them, such will probably be the rapid enlargement of our commerce and navigation and such the addition to the national wealth that the present generation may live to witness the controlling commercial and monetary power of the world transferred from London and other European emporiums to the city of New York.

The apprehensions which were entertained by some of our statesmen in the earlier periods of the Government that our system was incapable of operating with sufficient energy and success over largely extended territorial limits, and that if this were attempted it would fall to pieces by its own weakness, have been dissipated by our experience. By the division of power between the States and Federal Government the latter is found to operate with as much energy in the extremes as in the center. It is as efficient in the remotest of the thirty States which now compose the Union as it was in the thirteen States which formed our Constitution. Indeed, it may well be doubted whether if our present population had been confined within the limits of the original thirteen States the tendencies to centralization and consolidation would not have been such as to have encroached upon the essential reserved rights of the States, and thus to have made the Federal Government a widely different one, practically, from what it is in theory and was intended to be by its framers. So far from entertaining apprehensions of the safety of our system by the extension of our territory, the belief is confidently entertained that each new State gives strength and an additional guaranty for the preservation of the Union itself.

In pursuance of the provisions of the thirteenth article of the treaty of peace, friendship, limits, and settlement with the Republic of Mexico, and of the act of July 29, 1848, claims of our citizens, which had been "already liquidated and decided, against the Mexican Republic" amounting, with the interest thereon, to $2,023,832.51 have been liquidated and paid. There remain to be paid of these claims $74,192.26.

Congress at its last session having made no provision for executing the fifteenth article of the treaty, by which the United States assume to make satisfaction for the "unliquidated claims" of our citizens against Mexico to "an amount not exceeding three and a quarter millions of dollars," the subject is again recommended to your favorable consideration.

The exchange of ratifications of the treaty with Mexico took place on the 30th of May, 1848. Within one year after that time the commissioner and surveyor which each Government stipulates to appoint are required to meet "at the port of San Diego and proceed to run and mark the said boundary in its whole course to the mouth of the Rio Bravo del Norte." It will be seen from this provision that the period within which a commissioner and surveyor of the respective Governments are to meet at San Diego will expire on the 30th of May, 1849. Congress at the close of its last session made an appropriation for "the expenses of running and marking the boundary line" between the two countries, but did not fix the amount of salary which should be paid to the commissioner and surveyor to be appointed on the part of the United States. It is desirable that the amount of compensation which they shall receive should be prescribed by law, and not left, as at present, to Executive discretion.

Measures were adopted at the earliest practicable period to organize the "Territorial government of Oregon," as authorized by the act of the 14th of August last. The governor and marshal of the Territory, accompanied by a small military escort, left the frontier of Missouri in September last, and took the southern route, by the way of Santa Fe and the river Gila, to California, with the intention of proceeding thence in one of our vessels of war to their destination. The governor was fully advised of the great importance of his early arrival in the country, and it is confidently believed he may reach Oregon in the latter part of the present month or early in the next. The other officers for the Territory have proceeded by sea.

In the month of May last I communicated information to Congress that an Indian war had broken out in Oregon, and recommended that authority be given to raise an adequate number of volunteers to proceed without delay to the assistance of our fellow-citizens in that Territory. The authority to raise such a force not having been granted by Congress, as soon as their services could be dispensed with in Mexico orders were issued to the regiment of mounted riflemen to proceed to Jefferson Barracks, in Missouri, and to prepare to march to Oregon as soon as the necessary provision could be made. Shortly before it was ready to march it was arrested by the provision of the act passed by Congress on the last day of the last session, which directed that all the noncommissioned officers, musicians, and privates of that regiment who had been in service in Mexico should, upon their application, be entitled to be discharged. The effect of this provision was to disband the rank and file of the regiment, and before their places could be filled by recruits the season had so far advanced that it was impracticable for it to proceed until the opening of the next spring.

In the month of October last the accompanying communication was received from the governor of the temporary government of Oregon, giving information of the continuance of the Indian disturbances and of the destitution and defenseless condition of the inhabitants. Orders were immediately transmitted to the commander of our squadron in the Pacific to dispatch to their assistance a part of the naval forces on that station, to furnish them with arms and ammunition, and to continue to give them such aid and protection as the Navy could afford until the Army could reach the country.

It is the policy of humanity, and one which has always been pursued by the United States, to cultivate the good will of the aboriginal tribes of this continent and to restrain them from making war and indulging in excesses by mild means rather than by force. That this could have been done with the tribes in Oregon had that Territory been brought under the government of our laws at an earlier period, and had other suitable measures been adopted by Congress, such as now exist in our intercourse with the other Indian tribes within our limits, can not be doubted. Indeed, the immediate and only cause of the existing hostility of the Indians of Oregon is represented to have been the long delay of the United States in making to them some trifling compensation, in such articles as they wanted, for the country now occupied by our emigrants, which the Indians claimed and over which they formerly roamed. This compensation had been promised to them by the temporary government established in Oregon, but its fulfillment had been postponed from time to time for nearly two years, whilst those who made it had been anxiously waiting for Congress to establish a Territorial government over the country. The Indians became at length distrustful of their good faith and sought redress by plunder and massacre, which finally led to the present difficulties. A few thousand dollars in suitable presents, as a compensation for the country which had been taken possession of by our citizens, would have satisfied the Indians and have prevented the war. A small amount properly distributed, it is confidently believed, would soon restore quiet. In this Indian war our fellow-citizens of Oregon have been compelled to take the field in their own defense, have performed valuable military services, and been subjected to expenses which have fallen heavily upon them. Justice demands that provision should be made by Congress to compensate them for their services and to refund to them the necessary expenses which they have incurred.

I repeat the recommendation heretofore made to Congress, that provision be made for the appointment of a suitable number of Indian agents to reside among the tribes of Oregon, and that a small sum be appropriated to enable these agents to cultivate friendly relations with them. If this be done, the presence of a small military force will be all that is necessary to keep them in check and preserve peace. I recommend that similar provisions be made as regards the tribes inhabiting northern Texas, New Mexico, California, and the extensive region lying between our settlements in Missouri and these possessions, as the most effective means of preserving peace upon our borders and within the recently acquired territories.

The Secretary of the Treasury will present in his annual report a highly satisfactory statement of the condition of the finances.

The imports for the fiscal year ending on the 30th of June last were of the value of $154,977,876, of which the amount exported was $21,128,010, leaving $133,849,866 in the country for domestic use. The value of the exports for the same period was $154,032,131, consisting of domestic productions amounting to $132,904,121 and $21,128,010 of foreign articles. The receipts into the Treasury for the same period, exclusive of loans, amounted to $35,436,750.59, of which there was derived from customs $31,757,070.96, from sales of public lands $3,328,642.56, and from miscellaneous and incidental sources $351,037.07.

It will be perceived that the revenue from customs for the last fiscal year exceeded by $757,070.96 the estimate of the Secretary of the Treasury in his last annual report, and that the aggregate receipts during the same period from customs, lands, and miscellaneous sources also exceeded the estimate by the sum of $536,750.59, indicating, however, a very near approach in the estimate to the actual result.

The expenditures during the fiscal year ending on the 30th of June last, including those for the war and exclusive of payments of principal and interest for the public debt, were $42,811,970.03.

It is estimated that the receipts into the Treasury for the fiscal year ending on the 30th of June, 1849, including the balance in the Treasury on the 1st of July last, will amount to the sum of $57,048,969.90, of which $32,000,000, it is estimated, will be derived from customs, $3,000,000 from the sales of the public lands, and $1,200,000 from miscellaneous and incidental sources, including the premium upon the loan, and the amount paid and to be paid into the Treasury on account of military contributions in Mexico, and the sales of arms and vessels and other public property rendered unnecessary for the use of the Government by the termination of the war, and $20,695,435.30 from loans already negotiated, including Treasury notes funded, which, together with the balance in the Treasury on the 1st of July last, make the sum estimated.

The expenditures for the same period, including the necessary payment on account of the principal and interest of the public debt, and the principal and interest of the first installment due to Mexico on the 30th of May next, and other expenditures growing out of the war to be paid during the present year, will amount, including the reimbursement of Treasury notes, to the sum of $54,195,275.06, leaving an estimated balance in the Treasury on the 1st of July, 1849, of $2,853,694.84.

The Secretary of the Treasury will present, as required by law, the estimate of the receipts and expenditures for the next fiscal year. The expenditures as estimated for that year are $33,213,152.73, including $3,799,102.18 for the interest on the public debt and $3,540,000 for the principal and interest due to Mexico on the 30th of May, 1850, leaving the sum of $25,874,050.35, which, it is believed, will be ample for the ordinary peace expenditures.

The operations of the tariff act of 1846 have been such during the past year as fully to meet the public expectation and to confirm the opinion heretofore expressed of the wisdom of the change in our revenue system which was effected by it. The receipts under it into the Treasury for the first fiscal year after its enactment exceeded by the sum of $5,044,403.09 the amount collected during the last fiscal year under the tariff act of 1842, ending the 30th of June, 1846. The total revenue realized from the commencement of its operation, on the 1st of December, 1846, until the close of the last quarter, on the 30th of September last, being twenty-two months, was $56,654,563.79, being a much larger sum than was ever before received from duties during any equal period under the tariff acts of 1824, 1828, 1832, and 1842. Whilst by the repeal of highly protective and prohibitory duties the revenue has been increased, the taxes on the people have been diminished. They have been relieved from the heavy amounts with which they were burthened under former laws in the form of increased prices or bounties paid to favored classes and pursuits.

The predictions which were made that the tariff act of 1846 would reduce the amount of revenue below that collected under the act of 1842, and would prostrate the business and destroy the prosperity of the country, have not been verified. With an increased and increasing revenue, the finances are in a highly flourishing condition. Agriculture, commerce, and navigation are prosperous; the prices of manufactured fabrics and of other products are much less injuriously affected than was to have been anticipated from the unprecedented revulsions which during the last and the present year have overwhelmed the industry and paralyzed the credit and commerce of so many great and enlightened nations of Europe.

Severe commercial revulsions abroad have always heretofore operated to depress and often to affect disastrously almost every branch of American industry. The temporary depression of a portion of our manufacturing interests is the effect of foreign causes, and is far less severe than has prevailed on all former similar occasions.

It is believed that, looking to the great aggregate of all our interests, the whole country was never more prosperous than at the present period, and never more rapidly advancing in wealth and population. Neither the foreign war in which we have been involved, nor the loans which have absorbed so large a portion of our capital, nor the commercial revulsion in Great Britain in 1847, nor the paralysis of credit and commerce throughout Europe in 1848, have affected injuriously to any considerable extent any of the great interests of the country or arrested our onward march to greatness, wealth, and power.

Had the disturbances in Europe not occurred, our commerce would undoubtedly have been still more extended, and would have added still more to the national wealth and public prosperity. But notwithstanding these disturbances, the operations of the revenue system established by the tariff act of 1846 have been so generally beneficial to the Government and the business of the country that no change in its provisions is demanded by a wise public policy, and none is recommended.

The operations of the constitutional treasury established by the act of the 6th of August, 1846, in the receipt, custody, and disbursement of the public money have continued to be successful. Under this system the public finances have been carried through a foreign war, involving the necessity of loans and extraordinary expenditures and requiring distant transfers and disbursements, without embarrassment, and no loss has occurred of any of the public money deposited under its provisions. Whilst it has proved to be safe and useful to the Government, its effects have been most beneficial upon the business of the country. It has tended powerfully to secure an exemption from that inflation and fluctuation of the paper currency so injurious to domestic industry and rendering so uncertain the rewards of labor, and, it is believed, has largely contributed to preserve the whole country from a serious commercial revulsion, such as often occurred under the bank deposit system. In the year 1847 there was a revulsion in the business of Great Britain of great extent and intensity, which was followed by failures in that Kingdom unprecedented in number and amount of losses. This is believed to be the first instance when such disastrous bankruptcies, occurring in a country with which we have such extensive commerce, produced little or no injurious effect upon our trade or currency. We remained but little affected in our money market, and our business and industry were still prosperous and progressive.

During the present year nearly the whole continent of Europe has been convulsed by civil war and revolutions, attended by numerous bankruptcies, by an unprecedented fall in their public securities, and an almost universal paralysis of commerce and industry; and yet, although our trade and the prices of our products must have been somewhat unfavorably affected by these causes, we have escaped a revulsion, our money market is comparatively easy, and public and private credit have advanced and improved.

It is confidently believed that we have been saved from their effect by the salutary operation of the constitutional treasury. It is certain that if the twenty-four millions of specie imported into the country during the fiscal year ending on the 30th of June, 1847, had gone into the banks, as to a great extent it must have done, it would in the absence of this system have been made the basis of augmented bank paper issues, probably to an amount not less than $60,000,000 or $70,000,000, producing, as an inevitable consequence of an inflated currency, extravagant prices for a time and wild speculation, which must have been followed, on the reflux to Europe the succeeding year of so much of that specie, by the prostration of the business of the country, the suspension of the banks, and most extensive bankruptcies. Occurring, as this would have done, at a period when the country was engaged in a foreign war, when considerable loans of specie were required for distant disbursements, and when the banks, the fiscal agents of the Government and the depositories of its money, were suspended, the public credit must have sunk, and many millions of dollars, as was the case during the War of 1812, must have been sacrificed in discounts upon loans and upon the depreciated paper currency which the Government would have been compelled to use.

Under the operations of the constitutional treasury not a dollar has been lost by the depreciation of the currency. The loans required to prosecute the war with Mexico were negotiated by the Secretary of the Treasury above par, realizing a large premium to the Government. The restraining effect of the system upon the tendencies to excessive paper issues by banks has saved the Government from heavy losses and thousands of our business men from bankruptcy and ruin. The wisdom of the system has been tested by the experience of the last two years, and it is the dictate of sound policy that it should remain undisturbed. The modifications in some of the details of this measure, involving none of its essential principles, heretofore recommended, are again presented for your favorable consideration.

In my message of the 6th of July last, transmitting to Congress the ratified treaty of peace with Mexico, I recommended the adoption of measures for the speedy payment of the public debt. In reiterating that recommendation I refer you to the considerations presented in that message in its support. The public debt, including that authorized to be negotiated in pursuance of existing laws, and including Treasury notes, amounted at that time to $65,778,450.41.

Funded stock of the United States amounting to about half a million of dollars has been purchased, as authorized by law, since that period, and the public debt has thus been reduced, the details of which will be presented in the annual report of the Secretary of the Treasury.

The estimates of expenditures for the next fiscal year, submitted by the Secretary of the Treasury, it is believed will be ample for all necessary purposes. If the appropriations made by Congress shall not exceed the amount estimated, the means in the Treasury will be sufficient to defray all the expenses of the Government, to pay off the next installment of $3,000,000 to Mexico, which will fall due on the 30th of May next, and still a considerable surplus will remain, which should be applied to the further purchase of the public stock and reduction of the debt. Should enlarged appropriations be made, the necessary consequence will be to postpone the payment of the debt. Though our debt, as compared with that of most other nations, is small, it is our true policy, and in harmony with the genius of our institutions, that we should present to the world the rare spectacle of a great Republic, possessing vast resources and wealth, wholly exempt from public indebtedness. This would add still more to our strength, and give to us a still more commanding position among the nations of the earth.

The public expenditures should be economical, and be confined to such necessary objects as are clearly within the powers of Congress. All such as are not absolutely demanded should be postponed, and the payment of the public debt at the earliest practicable period should be a cardinal principle of our public policy.

For the reason assigned in my last annual message, I repeat the recommendation that a branch of the Mint of the United States be established at the city of New York. The importance of this measure is greatly increased by the acquisition of the rich mines of the precious metals in New Mexico and California, and especially in the latter.

I repeat the recommendation heretofore made in favor of the graduation and reduction of the price of such of the public lands as have been long offered in the market and have remained unsold, and in favor of extending the rights of preemption to actual settlers on the unsurveyed as well as the surveyed lands. The condition and operations of the Army and the state of other branches of the public service under the supervision of the War Department are satisfactorily presented in the accompanying report of the Secretary of War.

On the return of peace our forces were withdrawn from Mexico, and the volunteers and that portion of the Regular Army engaged for the war were disbanded. Orders have been issued for stationing the forces of our permanent establishment at various positions in our extended country where troops may be required. Owing to the remoteness of some of these positions, the detachments have not yet reached their destination. Notwithstanding the extension of the limits of our country and the forces required in the new territories, it is confidently believed that our present military establishment is sufficient for all exigencies so long as our peaceful relations remain undisturbed.

Of the amount of military contributions collected in Mexico, the sum of $769,650 was applied toward the payment of the first installment due under the treaty with Mexico. The further sum of $346,369.30 has been paid into the Treasury, and unexpended balances still remain in the hands of disbursing officers and those who were engaged in the collection of these moneys. After the proclamation of peace no further disbursements were made of any unexpended moneys arising from this source. The balances on hand were directed to be paid into the Treasury, and individual claims on the fund will remain unadjusted until Congress shall authorize their settlement and payment. These claims are not considerable in number or amount.

I recommend to your favorable consideration the suggestions of the Secretary of War and the Secretary of the Navy in regard to legislation on this subject.

Our Indian relations are presented in a most favorable view in the report from the War Department. The wisdom of our policy in regard to the tribes within our limits is clearly manifested by their improved and rapidly improving condition.

A most important treaty with the Menomonies has been recently negotiated by the Commissioner of Indian Affairs in person, by which all their land in the State of Wisconsin—being about 4,000,000 acres—has been ceded to the United States. This treaty will be submitted to the Senate for ratification at an early period of your present session.

Within the last four years eight important treaties have been negotiated with different Indian tribes, and at a cost of $1,842,000; Indian lands to the amount of more than 18,500,000 acres have been ceded to the United States, and provision has been made for settling in the country west of the Mississippi the tribes which occupied this large extent of the public domain. The title to all the Indian lands within the several States of our Union, with the exception of a few small reservations, is now extinguished, and a vast region opened for settlement and cultivation.

The accompanying report of the Secretary of the Navy gives a satisfactory exhibit of the operations and condition of that branch of the public service.

A number of small vessels, suitable for entering the mouths of rivers, were judiciously purchased during the war, and gave great efficiency to the squadron in the Gulf of Mexico. On the return of peace, when no longer valuable for naval purposes, and liable to constant deterioration, they were sold and the money placed in the Treasury.

The number of men in the naval service authorized by law during the war has been reduced by discharges below the maximum fixed for the peace establishment. Adequate squadrons are maintained in the several quarters of the globe where experience has shown their services may be most usefully employed, and the naval service was never in a condition of higher discipline or greater efficiency.

I invite attention to the recommendation of the Secretary of the Navy on the subject of the Marine Corps. The reduction of the Corps at the end of the war required that four officers of each of the three lower grades should be dropped from the rolls. A board of officers made the selection, and those designated were necessarily dismissed, but without any alleged fault. I concur in opinion with the Secretary that the service would be improved by reducing the number of landsmen and increasing the marines. Such a measure would justify an increase of the number of officers to the extent of the reduction by dismissal, and still the Corps would have fewer officers than a corresponding number of men in the Army.

The contracts for the transportation of the mail in steamships, convertible into war steamers, promise to realize all the benefits to our commerce and to the Navy which were anticipated. The first steamer thus secured to the Government was launched in January, 1847. There are now seven, and in another year there will probably be not less than seventeen afloat. While this great national advantage is secured, our social and commercial intercourse is increased and promoted with Germany, Great Britain, and other parts of Europe, with all the countries on the west coast of our continent, especially with Oregon and California, and between the northern and southern sections of the United States. Considerable revenue may be expected from postages, but the connected line from New York to Chagres, and thence across the Isthmus to Oregon, can not fail to exert a beneficial influence, not now to be estimated, on the interests of the manufactures, commerce, navigation, and currency of the United States. As an important part of the system, I recommend to your favorable consideration the establishment of the proposed line of steamers between New Orleans and Vera Cruz. It promises the most happy results in cementing friendship between the two Republics and extending reciprocal benefits to the trade and manufactures of both.

The report of the Postmaster-General will make known to you the operations of that Department for the past year.

It is gratifying to find the revenues of the Department, under the rates of postage now established by law, so rapidly increasing. The gross amount of postages during the last fiscal year amounted to $4,371,077, exceeding the annual average received for the nine years immediately preceding the passage of the act of the 3d of March, 1845, by the sum of $6,453, and exceeding the amount received for the year ending the 30th of June, 1847, by the sum of $425,184.

The expenditures for the year, excluding the sum of $94,672, allowed by Congress at its last session to individual claimants, and including the sum of $100,500, paid for the services of the line of steamers between Bremen and New York, amounted to $4,198,845, which is less than the annual average for the nine years previous to the act of 1845 by $300,748.

The mail routes on the 30th day of June last were 163,208 miles in extent, being an increase during the last year of 9,390 miles. The mails were transported over them during the same time 41,012,579 miles, making an increase of transportation for the year of 2,124,680 miles, whilst the expense was less than that of the previous year by $4,235.

The increase in the mail transportation within the last three years has been 5,378,310 miles, whilst the expenses were reduced $456,738, making an increase of service at the rate of 15 per cent and a reduction in the expenses of more than 15 per cent.

During the past year there have been employed, under contracts with the Post-Office Department, two ocean steamers in conveying the mails monthly between New York and Bremen, and one, since October last, performing semimonthly service between Charleston and Havana; and a contract has been made for the transportation of the Pacific mails across the Isthmus from Chagres to Panama.

Under the authority given to the Secretary of the Navy, three ocean steamers have been constructed and sent to the Pacific, and are expected to enter upon the mail service between Panama and Oregon and the intermediate ports on the 1st of January next; and a fourth has been engaged by him for the service between Havana and Chagres, so that a regular monthly mail line will be kept up after that time between the United States and our territories on the Pacific.

Notwithstanding this great increase in the mail service, should the revenue continue to increase the present year as it did in the last, there will be received near $450,000 more than the expenditures.

These considerations have satisfied the Postmaster-General that, with certain modifications of the act of 1845, the revenue may be still further increased and a reduction of postages made to a uniform rate of 5 cents, without an interference with the principle, which has been constantly and properly enforced, of making that Department sustain itself.

A well-digested cheap-postage system is the best means of diffusing intelligence among the people, and is of so much importance in a country so extensive as that of the United States that I recommend to your favorable consideration the suggestions of the Postmaster-General for its improvement.

Nothing can retard the onward progress of our country and prevent us from assuming and maintaining the first rank among nations but a disregard of the experience of the past and a recurrence to an unwise public policy. We have just closed a foreign war by an honorable peace—a war rendered necessary and unavoidable in vindication of the national rights and honor. The present condition of the country is similar in some respects to that which existed immediately after the close of the war with Great Britain in 1815, and the occasion is deemed to be a proper one to take a retrospect of the measures of public policy which followed that war. There was at that period of our history a departure from our earlier policy. The enlargement of the powers of the Federal Government by construction, which obtained, was not warranted by any just interpretation of the Constitution. A few years after the close of that war a series of measures was adopted which, united and combined, constituted what was termed by their authors and advocates the "American system."

The introduction of the new policy was for a time favored by the condition of the country, by the heavy debt which had been contracted during the war, by the depression of the public credit, by the deranged state of the finances and the currency, and by the commercial and pecuniary embarrassment which extensively prevailed. These were not the only causes which led to its establishment. The events of the war with Great Britain and the embarrassments which had attended its prosecution had left on the minds of many of our statesmen the impression that our Government was not strong enough, and that to wield its resources successfully in great emergencies, and especially in war, more power should be concentrated in its hands. This increased power they did not seek to obtain by the legitimate and prescribed mode—an amendment of the Constitution—but by construction. They saw Governments in the Old World based upon different orders of society, and so constituted as to throw the whole power of nations into the hands of a few, who taxed and controlled the many without responsibility or restraint. In that arrangement they conceived the strength of nations in war consisted. There was also something fascinating in the ease, luxury, and display of the higher orders, who drew their wealth from the toil of the laboring millions. The authors of the system drew their ideas of political economy from what they had witnessed in Europe, and particularly in Great Britain. They had viewed the enormous wealth concentrated in few hands and had seen the splendor of the overgrown establishments of an aristocracy which was upheld by the restrictive policy. They forgot to look down upon the poorer classes of the English population, upon whose daily and yearly labor the great establishments they so much admired were sustained and supported. They failed to perceive that the scantily fed and half-clad operatives were not only in abject poverty, but were bound in chains of oppressive servitude for the benefit of favored classes, who were the exclusive objects of the care of the Government.

It was not possible to reconstruct society in the United States upon the European plan. Here there was a written Constitution, by which orders and titles were not recognized or tolerated. A system of measures was therefore devised, calculated, if not intended, to withdraw power gradually and silently from the States and the mass of the people, and by construction to approximate our Government to the European models, substituting an aristocracy of wealth for that of orders and titles.

Without reflecting upon the dissimilarity of our institutions and of the condition of our people and those of Europe, they conceived the vain idea of building up in the United States a system similar to that which they admired abroad. Great Britain had a national bank of large capital, in whose hands was concentrated the controlling monetary and financial power of the nation—an institution wielding almost kingly power, and exerting vast influence upon all the operations of trade and upon the policy of the Government itself. Great Britain had an enormous public debt, and it had become a part of her public policy to regard this as a "public blessing." Great Britain had also a restrictive policy, which placed fetters and burdens on trade and trammeled the productive industry of the mass of the nation. By her combined system of policy the landlords and other property holders were protected and enriched by the enormous taxes which were levied upon the labor of the country for their advantage. Imitating this foreign policy, the first step in establishing the new system in the United States was the creation of a national bank. Not foreseeing the dangerous power and countless evils which such an institution might entail on the country, nor perceiving the connection which it was designed to form between the bank and the other branches of the miscalled "American system," but feeling the embarrassments of the Treasury and of the business of the country consequent upon the war, some of our statesmen who had held different and sounder views were induced to yield their scruples and, indeed, settled convictions of its unconstitutionality, and to give it their sanction as an expedient which they vainly hoped might produce relief. It was a most unfortunate error, as the subsequent history and final catastrophe of that dangerous and corrupt institution have abundantly proved. The bank, with its numerous branches ramified into the States, soon brought many of the active political and commercial men in different sections of the country into the relation of debtors to it and dependents upon it for pecuniary favors, thus diffusing throughout the mass of society a great number of individuals of power and influence to give tone to public opinion and to act in concert in cases of emergency. The corrupt power of such a political engine is no longer a matter of speculation, having been displayed in numerous instances, but most signally in the political struggles of 1832, 1833, and 1834 in opposition to the public will represented by a fearless and patriotic President.

But the bank was but one branch of the new system. A public debt of more than $120,000,000 existed, and it is not to be disguised that many of the authors of the new system did not regard its speedy payment as essential to the public prosperity, but looked upon its continuance as no national evil. Whilst the debt existed it furnished aliment to the national bank and rendered increased taxation necessary to the amount of the interest, exceeding $7,000,000 annually.

This operated in harmony with the next branch of the new system, which was a high protective tariff. This was to afford bounties to favored classes and particular pursuits at the expense of all others. A proposition to tax the whole people for the purpose of enriching a few was too monstrous to be openly made. The scheme was therefore veiled under the plausible but delusive pretext of a measure to protect "home industry," and many of our people were for a time led to believe that a tax which in the main fell upon labor was for the benefit of the laborer who paid it. This branch of the system involved a partnership between the Government and the favored classes, the former receiving the proceeds of the tax imposed on articles imported and the latter the increased price of similar articles produced at home, caused by such tax. It is obvious that the portion to be received by the favored classes would, as a general rule, be increased in proportion to the increase of the rates of tax imposed and diminished as those rates were reduced to the revenue standard required by the wants of the Government. The

rates required to produce a sufficient revenue for the ordinary expenditures of Government for necessary purposes were not likely to give to the private partners in this scheme profits sufficient to satisfy
their cupidity, and hence a variety of expedients and pretexts were resorted to for the purpose of enlarging the expenditures and thereby creating a necessity for keeping up a high protective tariff. The
effect of this policy was to interpose artificial restrictions upon the natural course of the business and
trade of the country, and to advance the interests of large capitalists and monopolists at the expense of
the great mass of the people, who were taxed to increase their wealth.

Another branch of this system was a comprehensive scheme of internal improvements, capable of
indefinite enlargement and sufficient to swallow up as many millions annually as could be exacted
from the foreign commerce of the country. This was a convenient and necessary adjunct of the protective tariff. It was to be the great absorbent of any surplus which might at any time accumulate in
the Treasury and of the taxes levied on the people, not for necessary revenue purposes, but for the
avowed object of affording protection to the favored classes.

Auxiliary to the same end, if it was not an essential part of the system itself, was the scheme, which
at a later period obtained, for distributing the proceeds of the sales of the public lands among the
States. Other expedients were devised to take money out of the Treasury and prevent its coming in
from any other source than the protective tariff. The authors and supporters of the system were the
advocates of the largest expenditures, whether for necessary or useful purposes or not, because the
larger the expenditures the greater was the pretext for high taxes in the form of protective duties.

These several measures were sustained by popular names and plausible arguments, by which thousands were deluded. The bank was represented to be an indispensable fiscal agent for the Government; was to equalize exchanges and to regulate and furnish a sound currency, always and everywhere
of uniform value. The protective tariff was to give employment to "American labor" at advanced
prices; was to protect "home industry" and furnish a steady market for the farmer. Internal improvements were to bring trade into every neighborhood and enhance the value of every man's property.
The distribution of the land money was to enrich the States, finish their public works, plant schools
throughout their borders, and relieve them from taxation. But the fact that for every dollar taken out
of the Treasury for these objects a much larger sum was transferred from the pockets of the people to
the favored classes was carefully concealed, as was also the tendency, if not the ultimate design, of the
system to build up an aristocracy of wealth, to control the masses of society, and monopolize the political power of the country.

The several branches of this system were so intimately blended together that in their operation
each sustained and strengthened the others. Their joint operation was to add new burthens of taxation and to encourage a largely increased and wasteful expenditure of public money. It was the interest of the bank that the revenue collected and the disbursements made by the Government should be
large, because, being the depository of the public money, the larger the amount the greater would be
the bank profits by its use. It was the interest of the favored classes, who were enriched by the protective tariff, to have the rates of that protection as high as possible, for the higher those rates the
greater would be their advantage. It was the interest of the people of all those sections and localities
who expected to be benefited by expenditures for internal improvements that the amount collected
should be as large as possible, to the end that the sum disbursed might also be the larger. The States,
being the beneficiaries in the distribution of the land money, had an interest in having the rates of
tax imposed by the protective tariff large enough to yield a sufficient revenue from that source to meet
the wants of the Government without disturbing or taking from them the land fund; so that each of
the branches constituting the system had a common interest in swelling the public expenditures.
They had a direct interest in maintaining the public debt unpaid and increasing its amount, because
this would produce an annual increased drain upon the Treasury to the amount of the interest and
render augmented taxes necessary. The operation and necessary effect of the whole system were to encourage large and extravagant expenditures, and thereby to increase the public patronage, and maintain a rich and splendid government at the expense of a taxed and impoverished people.

It is manifest that this scheme of enlarged taxation and expenditures, had it continued to prevail, must soon have converted the Government of the Union, intended by its framers to be a plain, cheap, and simple confederation of States, united together for common protection and charged with a few specific duties, relating chiefly to our foreign affairs, into a consolidated empire, depriving the States of their reserved rights and the people of their just power and control in the administration of their Government. In this manner the whole form and character of the Government would be changed, not by an amendment of the Constitution, but by resorting to an unwarrantable and unauthorized construction of that instrument.

The indirect mode of levying the taxes by a duty on imports prevents the mass of the people from readily perceiving the amount they pay, and has enabled the few who are thus enriched, and who seek to wield the political power of the country, to deceive and delude them. Were the taxes collected by a direct levy upon the people, as is the case in the States, this could not occur.

The whole system was resisted from its inception by many of our ablest statesmen, some of whom doubted its constitutionality and its expediency, while others believed it was in all its branches a flagrant and dangerous infraction of the Constitution.

That a national bank, a protective tariff—levied not to raise the revenue needed, but for protection merely—internal improvements, and the distribution of the proceeds of the sale of the public lands are measures without the warrant of the Constitution would, upon the maturest consideration, seem to be clear. It is remarkable that no one of these measures, involving such momentous consequences, is authorized by any express grant of power in the Constitution. No one of them is "incident to, as being necessary and proper for the execution of, the specific powers" granted by the Constitution. The authority under which it has been attempted to justify each of them is derived from inferences and constructions of the Constitution which its letter and its whole object and design do not warrant. Is it to be conceived that such immense powers would have been left by the framers of the Constitution to mere inferences and doubtful constructions? Had it been intended to confer them on the Federal Government, it is but reasonable to conclude that it would have been done by plain and unequivocal grants. This was not done; but the whole structure of which the "American system" consisted was reared on no other or better foundation than forced implications and inferences of power, which its authors assumed might be deduced by construction from the Constitution.

But it has been urged that the national bank, which constituted so essential a branch of this combined system of measures, was not a new measure, and that its constitutionality had been previously sanctioned, because a bank had been chartered in 1791 and had received the official signature of President Washington. A few facts will show the just weight to which this precedent should be entitled as bearing upon the question of constitutionality.

Great division of opinion upon the subject existed in Congress. It is well known that President Washington entertained serious doubts both as to the constitutionality and expediency of the measure, and while the bill was before him for his official approval or disapproval so great were these doubts that he required "the opinion in writing" of the members of his Cabinet to aid him in arriving at a decision. His Cabinet gave their opinions and were divided upon the subject, General Hamilton being in favor of and Mr. Jefferson and Mr. Randolph being opposed to the constitutionality and expediency of the bank. It is well known also that President Washington retained the bill from Monday, the 14th, when it was presented to him, until Friday, the 25th of February, being the last moment permitted him by the Constitution to deliberate, when he finally yielded to it his reluctant assent and gave it his signature. It is certain that as late as the 23d of February, being the ninth day after the bill was presented to him, he had arrived at no satisfactory conclusion, for on that day he addressed a note to General Hamilton in which he informs him that "this bill was presented to me by the joint committee of Congress at 12 o'clock on Monday, the 14th instant," and he requested his opinion "to what precise period, by legal interpretation of the Constitution, can the President retain it in his possession before it becomes a law by the lapse of ten days." If the proper construction was that the day on which the bill was presented to the President and the day on which his action was had upon it were both to be counted inclusive, then the time allowed him within which it would be competent for him to re-turn it to the House in which it originated with his objections would expire on Thursday, the 24th of February. General Hamilton on the same day returned an answer, in which he states:

"I give it as my opinion that you have ten days exclusive of that on which the bill was delivered to you and Sundays; hence, in the present case if it is returned on Friday it will be in time."

By this construction, which the President adopted, he gained another day for deliberation, and it was not until the 25th of February that he signed the bill, thus affording conclusive proof that he had at last obtained his own consent to sign it not without great and almost insuperable difficulty. Additional light has been recently shed upon the serious doubts which he had on the subject, amounting at one time to a conviction that it was his duty to withhold his approval from the bill. This is found among the man-uscript papers of Mr. Madison, authorized to be purchased for the use of the Government by an act of the last session of Congress, and now for the first time accessible to the public. From these papers it ap-pears that President Washington, while he yet held the bank bill in his hands, actually requested Mr. Madison, at that time a member of the House of Representatives, to prepare the draft of a veto message for him. Mr. Madison, at his request, did prepare the draft of such a message, and sent it to him on the 21st of February, 1791. A copy of this original draft, in Mr. Madison's own handwriting, was carefully preserved by him, and is among the papers lately purchased by Congress. It is preceded by a note, writ-ten on the same sheet, which is also in Mr. Madison's handwriting, and is as follows:

"February 21, 1791.—Copy of a paper made out and sent to the President, at his request, to be ready in case his judgment should finally decide against the bill for incorporating a national bank, the bill being then before him."

Among the objections assigned in this paper to the bill, and which were submitted for the consid-eration of the President, are the following:

"I object to the bill, because it is an essential principle of the Government that powers not dele-gated by the Constitution can not be rightfully exercised; because the power proposed by the bill to be exercised is not expressly delegated, and because I can not satisfy myself that it results from any ex-press power by fair and safe rules of interpretation."

The weight of the precedent of the bank of 1791 and the sanction of the great name of Washington, which has been so often invoked in its support, are greatly weakened by the development of these facts.

The experiment of that bank satisfied the country that it ought not to be continued, and at the end of twenty years Congress refused to recharter it. It would have been fortunate for the country, and saved thousands from bankruptcy and ruin, had our public men of 1816 resisted the temporary pres-sure of the times upon our financial and pecuniary interests and refused to charter the second bank. Of this the country became abundantly satisfied, and at the close of its twenty years' duration, as in the case of the first bank, it also ceased to exist. Under the repeated blows of President Jackson it reeled and fell, and a subsequent attempt to charter a similar institution was arrested by the veto of President Tyler.

Mr. Madison, in yielding his signature to the charter of 1816, did so upon the ground of the respect due to precedents; and, as he subsequently declared—

"The Bank of the United States, though on the original question held to be unconstitutional, re-ceived the Executive signature."

It is probable that neither the bank of 1791 nor that of 1816 would have been chartered but for the embarrassments of the Government in its finances, the derangement of the currency, and the pe-cuniary pressure which existed, the first the consequence of the War of the Revolution and the sec-ond the consequence of the War of 1812. Both were resorted to in the delusive hope that they would restore public credit and afford relief to the Government and to the business of the country.

Those of our public men who opposed the whole "American system" at its commencement and throughout its progress foresaw and predicted that it was fraught with incalculable mischiefs and must result in serious injury to the best interests of the country. For a series of years their wise counsels were unheeded, and the system was established. It was soon apparent that its practical operation was un-equal and unjust upon different portions of the country and upon the people engaged in different pursuits. All were equally entitled to the favor and protection of the Government. It fostered and elevated the money power and enriched the favored few by taxing labor, and at the expense of the many. Its effect was to "make the rich richer and the poor poorer." Its tendency was to create distinctions in society based on wealth and to give to the favored classes undue control and sway in our Government. It was an organized money power, which resisted the popular will and sought to shape and control the public policy.

Under the pernicious workings of this combined system of measures the country witnessed alternate seasons of temporary apparent prosperity, of sudden and disastrous commercial revulsions, of unprecedented fluctuation of prices and depression of the great interests of agriculture, navigation, and commerce, of general pecuniary suffering, and of final bankruptcy of thousands. After a severe struggle of more than a quarter of a century, the system was overthrown.

The bank has been succeeded by a practical system of finance, conducted and controlled solely by the Government. The constitutional currency has been restored, the public credit maintained unimpaired even in a period of a foreign war, and the whole country has become satisfied that banks, national or State, are not necessary as fiscal agents of the Government. Revenue duties have taken the place of the protective tariff. The distribution of the money derived from the sale of the public lands has been abandoned and the corrupting system of internal improvements, it is hoped, has been effectually checked.

It is not doubted that if this whole train of measures, designed to take wealth from the many and bestow it upon the few, were to prevail the effect would be to change the entire character of the Government. One only danger remains. It is the seductions of that branch of the system which consists in internal improvements, holding out, as it does, inducements to the people of particular sections and localities to embark the Government in them without stopping to calculate the inevitable consequences. This branch of the system is so intimately combined and linked with the others that as surely as an effect is produced by an adequate cause, if it be resuscitated and revived and firmly established it requires no sagacity to foresee that it will necessarily and speedily draw after it the reestablishment of a national bank, the revival of a protective tariff, the distribution of the land money, and not only the postponement to the distant future of the payment of the present national debt, but its annual increase.

I entertain the solemn conviction that if the internal-improvement branch of the "American system" be not firmly resisted at this time the whole series of measures composing it will be speedily reestablished and the country be thrown back from its present high state of prosperity, which the existing policy has produced, and be destined again to witness all the evils, commercial revulsions, depression of prices, and pecuniary embarrassments through which we have passed during the last twenty-five years.

To guard against consequences so ruinous is an object of high national importance, involving, in my judgment, the continued prosperity of the country.

I have felt it to be an imperative obligation to withhold my constitutional sanction from two bills which had passed the two Houses of Congress, involving the principle of the internal improvement branch of the "American system" and conflicting in their provisions with the views here expressed.

This power, conferred upon the President by the Constitution, I have on three occasions during my administration of the executive department of the Government deemed it my duty to exercise, and on this last occasion of making to Congress an annual communication "of the state of the Union" it is not deemed inappropriate to review the principles and considerations which have governed my action. I deem this the more necessary because, after the lapse of nearly sixty years since the adoption of the Constitution, the propriety of the exercise of this undoubted constitutional power by the President has for the first time been drawn seriously in question by a portion of my fellow-citizens.

The Constitution provides that—

"Every bill which shall have passed the House of Representatives and the Senate shall, before it become a law, be presented to the President of the United States. If he approve he *shall* sign it, but if not he *shall* return it with his objections to that House in which it shall have originated, who shall enter the objections at large on their Journal and proceed to reconsider it."

The preservation of the Constitution from infraction is the President's highest duty. He is bound to discharge that duty at whatever hazard of incurring the displeasure of those who may differ with him in opinion. He is bound to discharge it as well by his obligations to the people who have clothed him with his exalted trust as by his oath of office, which he may not disregard. Nor are the obligations of the President in any degree lessened by the prevalence of views different from his own in one or both Houses of Congress. It is not alone hasty and inconsiderate legislation that he is required to check; but if at any time Congress shall, after apparently full deliberation, resolve on measures which he deems subversive of the Constitution or of the vital interests of the country, it is his solemn duty to stand in the breach and resist them. The President is bound to approve or disapprove every bill which passes Congress and is presented to him for his signature. The Constitution makes this his duty, and he can not escape it if he would. He has no election. In deciding upon any bill presented to him he must exercise his own best judgment. If he can not approve, the Constitution commands him to return the bill to the House in which it originated with his objections, and if he fail to do this within ten days (Sundays excepted) it shall become a law without his signature. Right or wrong, he may be overruled by a vote of two-thirds of each House, and in that event the bill becomes a law without his sanction. If his objections be not thus overruled, the subject is only postponed, and is referred to the States and the people for their consideration and decision. The President's power is negative merely, and not affirmative. He can enact no law. The only effect, therefore, of his withholding his approval of a bill passed by Congress is to suffer the existing laws to remain unchanged, and the delay occasioned is only that required to enable the States and the people to consider and act upon the subject in the election of public agents who will carry out their wishes and instructions. Any attempt to coerce the President to yield his sanction to measures which he can not approve would be a violation of the spirit of the Constitution, palpable and flagrant, and if successful would break down the independence of the executive department and make the President, elected by the people and clothed by the Constitution with power to defend their rights, the mere instrument of a majority of Congress. A surrender on his part of the powers with which the Constitution has invested his office would effect a practical alteration of that instrument without resorting to the prescribed process of amendment.

With the motives or considerations which may induce Congress to pass any bill the President can have nothing to do. He must presume them to be as pure as his own, and look only to the practical effect of their measures when compared with the Constitution or the public good.

But it has been urged by those who object to the exercise of this undoubted constitutional power that it assails the representative principle and the capacity of the people to govern themselves; that there is greater safety in a numerous representative body than in the single Executive created by the Constitution, and that the Executive veto is a "one-man power," despotic in its character. To expose the fallacy of this objection it is only necessary to consider the frame and true character of our system. Ours is not a consolidated empire, but a confederated union. The States before the adoption of the Constitution were coordinate, co-equal, and separate independent sovereignties, and by its adoption they did not lose that character. They clothed the Federal Government with certain powers and reserved all others, including their own sovereignty, to themselves. They guarded their own rights as States and the rights of the people by the very limitations which they incorporated into the Federal Constitution, whereby the different departments of the General Government were checks upon each other. That the majority should govern is a general principle controverted by none, but they must govern according to the Constitution, and not according to an undefined and unrestrained discretion, whereby they may oppress the minority.

The people of the United States are not blind to the fact that they may be temporarily misled, and that their representatives, legislative and executive, may be mistaken or influenced in their action by improper motives. They have therefore interposed between themselves and the laws which may be passed by their public agents various representations, such as assemblies, senates, and governors in their several States, a House of Representatives, a Senate, and a President of the United States. The people can by their own direct agency make no law, nor can the House of Representatives, immediately elected by them, nor can the Senate, nor can both together without the concurrence of the President or a vote of two-thirds of both Houses.

Happily for themselves, the people in framing our admirable system of government were conscious of the infirmities of their representatives, and in delegating to them the power of legislation they have fenced them around with checks to guard against the effects of hasty action, of error, of combination, and of possible corruption. Error, selfishness, and faction have often sought to rend asunder this web of checks and subject the Government to the control of fanatic and sinister influences, but these efforts have only satisfied the people of the wisdom of the checks which they have imposed and of the necessity of preserving them unimpaired.

The true theory of our system is not to govern by the acts or decrees of any one set of representatives. The Constitution interposes checks upon all branches of the Government, in order to give time for error to be corrected and delusion to pass away; but if the people settle down into a firm conviction different from that of their representatives they give effect to their opinions by changing their public servants. The checks which the people imposed on their public servants in the adoption of the Constitution are the best evidence of their capacity for self-government. They know that the men whom they elect to public stations are of like infirmities and passions with themselves, and not to be trusted without being restricted by coordinate authorities and constitutional limitations. Who that has witnessed the legislation of Congress for the last thirty years will say that he knows of no instance in which measures not demanded by the public good have been carried? Who will deny that in the State governments, by combinations of individuals and sections, in derogation of the general interest, banks have been chartered, systems of internal improvements adopted, and debts entailed upon the people repressing their growth and impairing their energies for years to come?

After so much experience it can not be said that absolute unchecked power is safe in the hands of any one set of representatives, or that the capacity of the people for self-government, which is admitted in its broadest extent, is a conclusive argument to prove the prudence, wisdom, and integrity of their representatives.

The people, by the Constitution, have commanded the President, as much as they have commanded the legislative branch of the Government, to execute their will. They have said to him in the Constitution, which they require he shall take a solemn oath to support, that if Congress pass any bill which he can not approve "he shall return it to the House in which it originated with his objections." In withholding from it his approval and signature he is executing the will of the people, constitutionally expressed, as much as the Congress that passed it. No bill is presumed to be in accordance with the popular will until it shall have passed through all the branches of the Government required by the Constitution to make it a law. A bill which passes the House of Representatives may be rejected by the Senate, and so a bill passed by the Senate may be rejected by the House. In each case the respective Houses exercise the veto power on the other.

Congress, and each House of Congress, hold under the Constitution a check upon the President, and he, by the power of the qualified veto, a check upon Congress. When the President recommends measures to Congress, he avows in the most solemn form his opinions, gives his voice in their favor, and pledges himself in advance to approve them if passed by Congress. If he acts without due consideration, or has been influenced by improper or corrupt motives, or if from any other cause Congress, or either House of Congress, shall differ with him in opinion, they exercise their veto upon his recommendations and reject them; and there is no appeal from their decision but to the people at the ballot box. These are proper checks upon the Executive, wisely interposed by the Constitution. None will be found to object to them or to wish them removed. It is equally important that the constitutional checks of the Executive upon the legislative branch should be preserved.

If it be said that the Representatives in the popular branch of Congress are chosen directly by the people, it is answered, the people elect the President. If both Houses represent the States and the people, so does the President. The President represents in the executive department the whole people of the United States, as each member of the legislative department represents portions of them.

The doctrine of restriction upon legislative and executive power, while a well-settled public opinion is enabled within a reasonable time to accomplish its ends, has made our country what it is, and has opened to us a career of glory and happiness to which all other nations have been strangers.

In the exercise of the power of the veto the President is responsible not only to an enlightened public opinion, but to the people of the whole Union, who elected him, as the representatives in the legislative branches who differ with him in opinion are responsible to the people of particular States or districts, who compose their respective constituencies. To deny to the President the exercise of this power would be to repeal that provision of the Constitution which confers it upon him. To charge that its exercise unduly controls the legislative will is to complain of the Constitution itself.

If the Presidential veto be objected to upon the ground that it checks and thwarts the popular will, upon the same principle the equality of representation of the States in the Senate should be stricken out of the Constitution. The vote of a Senator from Delaware has equal weight in deciding upon the most important measures with the vote of a Senator from New York, and yet the one represents a State containing, according to the existing apportionment of Representatives in the House of Representatives, but one thirty-fourth part of the population of the other. By the constitutional composition of the Senate a majority of that body from the smaller States represent less than one-fourth of the people of the Union. There are thirty States, and under the existing apportionment of Representatives there are 230 Members in the House of Representatives. Sixteen of the smaller States are represented in that House by but 50 Members, and yet the Senators from these States constitute a majority of the Senate. So that the President may recommend a measure to Congress, and it may receive the sanction and approval of more than three-fourths of the House of Representatives and of all the Senators from the large States, containing more than three-fourths of the whole population of the United States, and yet the measure may be defeated by the votes of the Senators from the smaller States. None, it is presumed, can be found ready to change the organization of the Senate on this account, or to strike that body practically out of existence by requiring that its action shall be conformed to the will of the more numerous branch.

Upon the same principle that the veto of the President should be practically abolished the power of the Vice-President to give the casting vote upon an equal division of the Senate should be abolished also. The Vice-President exercises the veto power as effectually by rejecting a bill by his casting vote as the President does by refusing to approve and sign it. This power has been exercised by the Vice-President in a few instances, the most important of which was the rejection of the bill to recharter the Bank of the United States in 1811. It may happen that a bill may be passed by a large majority of the House of Representatives, and may be supported by the Senators from the larger States, and the Vice-President may reject it by giving his vote with the Senators from the smaller States; and yet none, it is presumed, are prepared to deny to him the exercise of this power under the Constitution.

But it is, in point of fact, untrue that an act passed by Congress is conclusive evidence that it is an emanation of the popular will. A majority of the whole number elected to each House of Congress constitutes a quorum, and a majority of that quorum is competent to pass laws. It might happen that a quorum of the House of Representatives, consisting of a single member more than half of the whole number elected to that House, might pass a bill by a majority of a single vote, and in that case a fraction more than one-fourth of the people of the United States would be represented by those who voted for it. It might happen that the same bill might be passed by a majority of one of a quorum of the Senate, composed of Senators from the fifteen smaller States and a single Senator from a sixteenth State; and if the Senators voting for it happened to be from the eight of the smallest of these States, it would be passed by the votes of Senators from States having but fourteen Representatives in the House of Representatives, and containing less than one-sixteenth of the whole population of the United States. This extreme case is stated to illustrate the fact that the mere passage of a bill by Congress is no conclusive evidence that those who passed it represent the majority of the people of the United States or truly reflect their will. If such an extreme case is not likely to happen, cases that approximate it are of constant occurrence. It is believed that not a single law has been passed since the adoption of the Constitution upon which all the members elected to both Houses have been present and voted. Many of the most important acts which have passed Congress have been carried by a close vote in thin Houses.

Many instances of this might be given. Indeed, our experience proves that many of the most important acts of Congress are postponed to the last days, and often the last hours, of a session, when they are disposed of in haste, and by Houses but little exceeding the number necessary to form a quorum.

Besides, in most of the States the members of the House of Representatives are chosen by pluralities, and not by majorities of all the voters in their respective districts, and it may happen that a majority of that House may be returned by a less aggregate vote of the people than that received by the minority.

If the principle insisted on be sound, then the Constitution should be so changed that no bill shall become a law unless it is voted for by members representing in each House a majority of the whole people of the United States. We must remodel our whole system, strike down and abolish not only the salutary checks lodged in the executive branch, but must strike out and abolish those lodged in the Senate also, and thus practically invest the whole power of the Government in a majority of a single assembly—a majority uncontrolled and absolute, and which may become despotic. To conform to this doctrine of the right of majorities to rule, independent of the checks and limitations of the Constitution, we must revolutionize our whole system; we must destroy the constitutional compact by which the several States agreed to form a Federal Union and rush into consolidation, which must end in monarchy or despotism. No one advocates such a proposition, and yet the doctrine maintained, if carried out, must lead to this result.

One great object of the Constitution in conferring upon the President a qualified negative upon the legislation of Congress was to protect minorities from injustice and oppression by majorities. The equality of their representation in the Senate and the veto power of the President are the constitutional guaranties which the smaller States have that their rights will be respected. Without these guaranties all their interests would be at the mercy of majorities in Congress representing the larger States. To the smaller and weaker States, therefore, the preservation of this power and its exercise upon proper occasions demanding it is of vital importance. They ratified the Constitution and entered into the Union, securing to themselves an equal representation with the larger States in the Senate; and they agreed to be bound by all laws passed by Congress upon the express condition, and none other, that they should be approved by the President or passed, his objections to the contrary notwithstanding, by a vote of two-thirds of both Houses. Upon this condition they have a right to insist as a part of the compact to which they gave their assent.

A bill might be passed by Congress against the will of the whole people of a particular State and against the votes of its Senators and all its Representatives. However prejudicial it might be to the interests of such State, it would be bound by it if the President shall approve it or it shall be passed by a vote of two-thirds of both Houses; but it has a right to demand that the President shall exercise his constitutional power and arrest it if his judgment is against it. If he surrender this power, or fail to exercise it in a case where he can not approve, it would make his formal approval a mere mockery, and would be itself a violation of the Constitution, and the dissenting State would become bound by a law which had not been passed according to the sanctions of the Constitution.

The objection to the exercise of the veto power is founded upon an idea respecting the popular will, which, if carried out, would annihilate State sovereignty and substitute for the present Federal Government a consolidation directed by a supposed numerical majority. A revolution of the Government would be silently effected and the States would be subjected to laws to which they had never given their constitutional consent.

The Supreme Court of the United States is invested with the power to declare, and has declared, acts of Congress passed with the concurrence of the Senate, the House of Representatives, and the approval of the President to be unconstitutional and void, and yet none, it is presumed, can be found who will be disposed to strip this highest judicial tribunal under the Constitution of this acknowledged power—a power necessary alike to its independence and the rights of individuals.

For the same reason that the Executive veto should, according to the doctrine maintained, be rendered nugatory, and be practically expunged from the Constitution, this power of the court should also be rendered nugatory and be expunged, because it restrains the legislative and Executive will, and because the exercise of such a power by the court may be regarded as being in conflict with the capacity of the people to govern themselves. Indeed, there is more reason for striking this power of the court from the Constitution than there is that of the qualified veto of the president, because the decision of the court is final, and can never be reversed even though both Houses of Congress and the President should be unanimous in opposition to it, whereas the veto of the President may be overruled by a vote of two-thirds of both Houses of Congress or by the people at the polls.

It is obvious that to preserve the system established by the Constitution each of the coordinate branches of the Government—the executive, legislative, and judicial—must be left in the exercise of its appropriate powers. If the executive or the judicial branch be deprived of powers conferred upon either as checks on the legislative, the preponderance of the latter will become disproportionate and absorbing and the others impotent for the accomplishment of the great objects for which they were established. Organized, as they are, by the Constitution, they work together harmoniously for the public good. If the Executive and the judiciary shall be deprived of the constitutional powers invested in them, and of their due proportions, the equilibrium of the system must be destroyed, and consolidation, with the most pernicious results, must ensue—a consolidation of unchecked, despotic power, exercised by majorities of the legislative branch.

The executive, legislative, and judicial each constitutes a separate coordinate department of the Government, and each is independent of the others. In the performance of their respective duties under the Constitution neither can in its legitimate action control the others. They each act upon their several responsibilities in their respective spheres. But if the doctrines now maintained be correct, the executive must become practically subordinate to the legislative, and the judiciary must become subordinate to both the legislative and the executive; and thus the whole power of the Government would be merged in a single department. Whenever, if ever, this shall occur, our glorious system of well-regulated self-government will crumble into ruins, to be succeeded, first by anarchy, and finally by monarchy or despotism. I am far from believing that this doctrine is the sentiment of the American people; and during the short period which remains in which it will be my duty to administer the executive department it will be my aim to maintain its independence and discharge its duties without infringing upon the powers or duties of either of the other departments of the Government.

The power of the Executive veto was exercised by the first and most illustrious of my predecessors and by four of his successors who preceded me in the administration of the Government, and it is believed in no instance prejudicially to the public interests. It has never been and there is but little danger that it ever can be abused. No President will ever desire unnecessarily to place his opinion in opposition to that of Congress. He must always exercise the power reluctantly, and only in cases where his convictions make it a matter of stern duty, which he can not escape. Indeed, there is more danger that the President, from the repugnance he must always feel to come in collision with Congress, may fail to exercise it in cases where the preservation of the Constitution from infraction, or the public good, may demand it than that he will ever exercise it unnecessarily or wantonly.

During the period I have administered the executive department of the Government great and important questions of public policy, foreign and domestic, have arisen, upon which it was my duty to act. It may, indeed, be truly said that my Administration has fallen upon eventful times. I have felt most sensibly the weight of the high responsibilities devolved upon me. With no other object than the public good, the enduring fame, and permanent prosperity of my country, I have pursued the convictions of my own best judgment. The impartial arbitrament of enlightened public opinion, present and future, will determine how far the public policy I have maintained and the measures I have from time to time recommended may have tended to advance or retard the public prosperity at home and to elevate or depress the estimate of our national character abroad.

Invoking the blessings of the Almighty upon your deliberations at your present important session, my ardent hope is that in a spirit of harmony and concord you may be guided to wise results, and such as may redound to the happiness, the honor, and the glory of our beloved country.

JAMES K. POLK

11

Millard Fillmore (1850–1853)

"We live in an age of progress, and ours is emphatically a country of progress." Those words summarize the optimism and can-do spirit in Millard Fillmore's final annual message. Fillmore was president only thirty-two months. He was the second man to succeed to the presidency following the death of his predecessor (Zachary Taylor). Fillmore's most important act was to sign the series of bills called the Compromise of 1850, for it pushed back the coming of civil war. That Compromise, however, was itself a battlefield for the last lions of the era—John Calhoun of South Carolina, Henry Clay of Kentucky, and Daniel Webster of Massachusetts. All three senators struggled with and debated the Compromise. Fillmore in fact paid tribute to Webster in the last annual message. His recent death, wrote the thirteenth president, was "lamented throughout the country." And his achievements "earned for him a lasting place in our history."

Embedded in this final annual message is a wonderful tribute to President Washington and the wisdom he expressed in his Farewell Address. Fillmore wrote:

It has been the uniform policy of this Government, from its foundation to the present day, to abstain from all interference in the domestic affairs of other nations. The consequence has been that while the nations of Europe have been engaged in desolating wars our country has pursued its peaceful course to unexampled prosperity and happiness. The wars in which we have been compelled to engage in defense of the rights and honor of the country have been, fortunately, of short duration. During the terrific contest of nation against nation which succeeded the French Revolution we were enabled by the wisdom and firmness of President Washington to maintain our neutrality. While other nations were drawn into this wide-sweeping whirlpool, we sat quiet and unmoved upon our own shores. While the flower of their numerous armies was wasted by disease or perished by hundreds of thousands upon the battlefield, the youth of this favored land were permitted to enjoy the blessings of peace beneath the paternal roof.

Third Annual Message
(written to the Congress)
December 6, 1852

Fellow-Citizens of the Senate and of the House of Representatives:

The brief space which has elapsed since the close of your last session has been marked by no extraordinary political event. The quadrennial election of Chief Magistrate has passed off with less than the usual excitement. However individuals and parties may have been disappointed in the result, it is, nevertheless, a subject of national congratulation that the choice has been effected by the independent suffrages of a free people, undisturbed by those influences which in other countries have too often affected the purity of popular elections.

Our grateful thanks are due to an all-merciful Providence, not only for staying the pestilence which in different forms has desolated some of our cities, but for crowning the labors of the husbandman with an abundant harvest and the nation generally with the blessings of peace and prosperity.

Within a few weeks the public mind has been deeply affected by the death of Daniel Webster, filling at his decease the office of Secretary of State. His associates in the executive government have sincerely sympathized with his family and the public generally on this mournful occasion. His commanding talents, his great political and professional eminence, his well-tried patriotism, and his long and faithful services in the most important public trusts have caused his death to be lamented throughout the country and have earned for him a lasting place in our history.

In the course of the last summer considerable anxiety was caused for a short time by an official intimation from the Government of Great Britain that orders had been given for the protection of the fisheries upon the coasts of the British provinces in North America against the alleged encroachments of the fishing vessels of the United States and France. The shortness of this notice and the season of the year seemed to make it a matter of urgent importance. It was at first apprehended that an increased naval force had been ordered to the fishing grounds to carry into effect the British interpretation of those provisions in the convention of 1818 in reference to the true intent of which the two Governments differ. It was soon discovered that such was not the design of Great Britain, and satisfactory explanations of the real objects of the measure have been given both here and in London.

The unadjusted difference, however, between the two Governments as to the interpretation of the first article of the convention of 1818 is still a matter of importance. American fishing vessels, within nine or ten years, have been excluded from waters to which they had free access for twenty-five years after the negotiation of the treaty. In 1845 this exclusion was relaxed so far as concerns the Bay of Fundy, but the just and liberal intention of the home Government, in compliance with what we think the true construction of the convention, to open all the other outer bays to our fishermen was abandoned in consequence of the opposition of the colonies. Notwithstanding this, the United States have, since the Bay of Fundy was reopened to our fishermen in 1845, pursued the most liberal course toward the colonial fishing interests. By the revenue law of 1846 the duties on colonial fish entering our ports were very greatly reduced, and by the warehousing act it is allowed to be entered in bond without payment of duty. In this way colonial fish has acquired the monopoly of the export trade in our market and is entering to some extent into the home consumption. These facts were among those which increased the sensibility of our fishing interest at the movement in question. These circumstances and the incidents above alluded to have led me to think the moment favorable for a reconsideration of the entire subject of the fisheries on the coasts of the British Provinces, with a view to place them upon a more liberal footing of reciprocal privilege. A willingness to meet us in some arrangement of this kind is understood to exist on the part of Great Britain, with a desire on her part to include in one comprehensive settlement as well this subject as the commercial intercourse between the United States and the British Provinces. I have thought that, whatever arrangements may be made on these two subjects, it is expedient that they should be embraced in separate conventions. The illness and death of the late Secretary of State prevented the commencement of the contemplated negotiation. Pains have been taken to collect the information required for the details of such an arrangement. The subject is attended with considerable difficulty. If it is found practicable to come to an agreement mutually acceptable to the two parties, conventions may be concluded in the course of the present winter. The control of Congress over all the provisions of such an arrangement affecting the revenue will of course be reserved.

The affairs of Cuba formed a prominent topic in my last annual message. They remain in an uneasy condition, and a feeling of alarm and irritation on the part of the Cuban authorities appears to exist. This feeling has interfered with the regular commercial intercourse between the United States and the island and led to some acts of which we have a right to complain. But the Captain-General of Cuba is clothed with no power to treat with foreign governments, nor is he in any degree under the control of the Spanish minister at Washington. Any communication which he may hold with an agent of a foreign power is informal and matter of courtesy. Anxious to put an end to the existing inconveniences (which seemed to rest on a misconception), I directed the newly appointed minister to Mexico to visit Havana on his way to Vera Cruz. He was respectfully received by the Captain-General, who conferred with him freely on the recent occurrences, but no permanent arrangement was effected.

In the meantime the refusal of the Captain-General to allow passengers and the mail to be landed in certain cases, for a reason which does not furnish, in the opinion of this Government, even a good presumptive ground for such prohibition, has been made the subject of a serious remonstrance at Madrid, and I have no reason to doubt that due respect will be paid by the Government of Her Catholic Majesty to the representations which our minister has been instructed to make on the subject.

It is but justice to the Captain-General to add that his conduct toward the steamers employed to carry the mails of the United States to Havana has, with the exceptions above alluded to, been marked with kindness and liberality, and indicates no general purpose of interfering with the commercial correspondence and intercourse between the island and this country.

Early in the present year official notes were received from the ministers of France and England inviting the Government of the United States to become a party with Great Britain and France to a tripartite convention, in virtue of which the three powers should severally and collectively disclaim now and for the future all intention to obtain possession of the island of Cuba, and should bind themselves to discountenance all attempts to that effect on the part of any power or individual whatever. This invitation has been respectfully declined, for reasons which it would occupy too much space in this communication to state in detail, but which led me to think that the proposed measure would be of doubtful constitutionality, impolitic, and unavailing. I have, however, in common with several of my predecessors, directed the ministers of France and England to be assured that the United States entertain no designs against Cuba, but that, on the contrary, I should regard its incorporation into the Union at the present time as fraught with serious peril.

Were this island comparatively destitute of inhabitants or occupied by a kindred race, I should regard it, if voluntarily ceded by Spain, as a most desirable acquisition. But under existing circumstances I should look upon its incorporation into our Union as a very hazardous measure. It would bring into the Confederacy a population of a different national stock, speaking a different language, and not likely to harmonize with the other members. It would probably affect in a prejudicial manner the industrial interests of the South, and it might revive those conflicts of opinion between the different sections of the country which lately shook the Union to its center, and which have been so happily compromised.

The rejection by the Mexican Congress of the convention which had been concluded between that Republic and the United States for the protection of a transit way across the Isthmus of Tehuantepec and of the interests of those citizens of the United States who had become proprietors of the rights which Mexico had conferred on one of her own citizens in regard to that transit has thrown a serious obstacle in the way of the attainment of a very desirable national object. I am still willing to hope that the differences on the subject which exist, or may hereafter arise, between the Governments will be amicably adjusted. This subject, however, has already engaged the attention of the Senate of the United States, and requires no further comment in this communication.

The settlement of the question respecting the port of San Juan de Nicaragua and of the controversy between the Republics of Costa Rica and Nicaragua in regard to their boundaries was considered indispensable to the commencement of the ship canal between the two oceans, which was the subject of the convention between the United States and Great Britain of the 19th of April, 1850. Accordingly, a proposition for the same purposes, addressed to the two Governments in that quarter and to the Mosquito Indians, was agreed to in April last by the Secretary of State and the minister of Her Britannic Majesty. Besides the wish to aid in reconciling the differences of the two Republics, I engaged in the negotiation from a desire to place the great work of a ship canal between the two oceans under one jurisdiction and to establish the important port of San Juan de Nicaragua under the government of a civilized power. The proposition in question was assented to by Costa Rica and the Mosquito Indians. It has not proved equally acceptable to Nicaragua, but it is to be hoped that the further negotiations on the subject which are in train will be carried on in that spirit of conciliation and compromise which ought always to prevail on such occasions, and that they will lead to a satisfactory result.

I have the satisfaction to inform you that the executive government of Venezuela has acknowledged some claims of citizens of the United States which have for many years past been urged by our chargé d'affaires at Caracas. It is hoped that the same sense of justice will actuate the Congress of that Republic in providing the means for their payment.

The recent revolution in Buenos Ayres and the Confederated States having opened the prospect of an improved state of things in that quarter, the Governments of Great Britain and France determined to negotiate with the chief of the new confederacy for the free access of their commerce to the extensive countries watered by the tributaries of the La Plata; and they gave a friendly notice of this purpose to the United States, that we might, if we thought proper, pursue the same course. In compliance with this invitation, our minister at Rio Janeiro and our chargé d'affaires at Buenos Ayres have been fully authorized to conclude treaties with the newly organized confederation or the States composing it. The delays which have taken place in the formation of the new government have as yet prevented the execution of those instructions, but there is every reason to hope that these vast countries will be eventually opened to our commerce.

A treaty of commerce has been concluded between the United States and the Oriental Republic of Uruguay, which will be laid before the Senate. Should this convention go into operation, it will open to the commercial enterprise of our citizens a country of great extent and unsurpassed in natural resources, but from which foreign nations have hitherto been almost wholly excluded.

The correspondence of the late Secretary of State with the Peruvian chargé d'affaires relative to the Lobos Islands was communicated to Congress toward the close of the last session. Since that time, on further investigation of the subject, the doubts which had been entertained of the title of Peru to those islands have been removed, and I have deemed it just that the temporary wrong which had been unintentionally done her from want of information should be repaired by an unreserved acknowledgment of her sovereignty.

I have the satisfaction to inform you that the course pursued by Peru has been creditable to the liberality of her Government. Before it was known by her that her title would be acknowledged at Washington, her minister of foreign affairs had authorized our chargé d'affaires at Lima to announce to the American vessels which had gone to the Lobos for guano that the Peruvian Government was willing to freight them on its own account. This intention has been carried into effect by the Peruvian minister here by an arrangement which is believed to be advantageous to the parties in interest.

Our settlements on the shores of the Pacific have already given a great extension, and in some respects a new direction, to our commerce in that ocean. A direct and rapidly increasing intercourse has sprung up with eastern Asia. The waters of the Northern Pacific, even into the Arctic Sea, have of late years been frequented by our whalemen. The application of steam to the general purposes of navigation is becoming daily more common, and makes it desirable to obtain fuel and other necessary supplies at convenient points on the route between Asia and our Pacific shores. Our unfortunate countrymen who from time to time suffer shipwreck on the coasts of the eastern seas are entitled to protection. Besides these specific objects, the general prosperity of our States on the Pacific requires that an attempt should be made to open the opposite regions of Asia to a mutually beneficial intercourse. It is obvious that this attempt could be made by no power to so great advantage as by the United States, whose constitutional system excludes every idea of distant colonial dependencies. I have accordingly been led to order an appropriate naval force to Japan, under the command of a discreet and intelligent officer of the highest rank known to our service. He is instructed to endeavor to obtain from the Government of that country some relaxation of the inhospitable and antisocial system which it has pursued for about two centuries. He has been directed particularly to remonstrate in the strongest language against the cruel treatment to which our shipwrecked mariners have often been subjected and to insist that they shall be treated with humanity. He is instructed, however, at the same time, to give that Government the amplest assurances that the objects of the United States are such, and such only, as I have indicated, and that the expedition is friendly and peaceful. Notwithstanding the jealousy with which the Governments of eastern Asia regard all overtures from foreigners, I am not without hopes of a beneficial result of the expedition. Should it be crowned with success, the advantages will not be confined to the United States, but, as in the case of China, will be equally enjoyed by all the other maritime powers. I have much satisfaction in stating that in all the steps preparatory to this expedition the Government of the United States has been materially aided by the good offices of the King of the Netherlands, the only European power having any commercial relations with Japan.

In passing from this survey of our foreign relations, I invite the attention of Congress to the condition of that Department of the Government to which this branch of the public business is intrusted. Our intercourse with foreign powers has of late years greatly increased, both in consequence of our own growth and the introduction of many new states into the family of nations. In this way the Department of State has become overburdened. It has by the recent establishment of the Department of the Interior been relieved of some portion of the domestic business. If the residue of the business of that kind—such as the distribution of Congressional documents, the keeping, publishing, and distribution of the laws of the United States, the execution of the copyright law, the subject of reprieves and pardons, and some other subjects relating to interior administration—should be transferred from the Department of State, it would unquestionably be for the benefit of the public service. I would also suggest that the building appropriated to the State Department is not fireproof; that there is reason to think there are defects in its construction, and that the archives of the Government in charge of the Department, with the precious collections of the manuscript papers of Washington, Jefferson, Hamilton, Madison, and Monroe, are exposed to destruction by fire. A similar remark may be made of the buildings appropriated to the War and Navy Departments.

The condition of the Treasury is exhibited in the annual report from that Department. The cash receipts into the Treasury for the fiscal year ending the 30th June last, exclusive of trust funds, were $49,728,386.89, and the expenditures for the same period, likewise exclusive of trust funds, were $46,007,896.20, of which $9,455,815.83 was on account of the principal and interest of the public debt, including the last installment of the indemnity to Mexico under the treaty of Guadalupe Hidalgo, leaving a balance of $14,632,136.37 in the Treasury on the 1st day of July last. Since this latter period further purchases of the principal of the public debt have been made to the extent of

$2,456,547.49, and the surplus in the Treasury will continue to be applied to that object whenever the stock can be procured within the limits as to price authorized by law.

The value of foreign merchandise imported during the last fiscal year was $207,240,101, and the value of domestic productions exported was $149,861,911, besides $17,204,026 of foreign merchandise exported, making the aggregate of the entire exports $167,065,937. Exclusive of the above, there was exported $42,507,285 in specie, and imported from foreign ports $5,262,643.

In my first annual message to Congress I called your attention to what seemed to me some defects in the present tariff, and recommended such modifications as in my judgment were best adapted to remedy its evils and promote the prosperity of the country. Nothing has since occurred to change my views on this important question.

Without repeating the arguments contained in my former message in favor of discriminating protective duties, I deem it my duty to call your attention to one or two other considerations affecting this subject. The first is the effect of large importations of foreign goods upon our currency. Most of the gold of California, as fast as it is coined, finds its way directly to Europe in payment for goods purchased. In the second place, as our manufacturing establishments are broken down by competition with foreigners, the capital invested in them is lost, thousands of honest and industrious citizens are thrown out of employment, and the farmer, to that extent, is deprived of a home market for the sale of his surplus produce. In the third place, the destruction of our manufactures leaves the foreigner without competition in our market, and he consequently raises the price of the article sent here for sale, as is now seen in the increased cost of iron imported from England. The prosperity and wealth of every nation must depend upon its productive industry. The farmer is stimulated to exertion by finding a ready market for his surplus products, and benefited by being able to exchange them without loss of time or expense of transportation for the manufactures which his comfort or convenience requires. This is always done to the best advantage where a portion of the community in which he lives is engaged in other pursuits. But most manufactures require an amount of capital and a practical skill which can not be commanded unless they be protected for a time from ruinous competition from abroad. Hence the necessity of laying those duties upon imported goods which the Constitution authorizes for revenue in such a manner as to protect and encourage the labor of our own citizens. Duties, however, should not be fixed at a rate so high as to exclude the foreign article, but should be so graduated as to enable the domestic manufacturer fairly to compete with the foreigner in our own markets, and by this competition to reduce the price of the manufactured article to the consumer to the lowest rate at which it can be produced. This policy would place the mechanic by the side of the farmer, create a mutual interchange of their respective commodities, and thus stimulate the industry of the whole country and render us independent of foreign nations for the supplies required by the habits or necessities of the people.

Another question, wholly independent of protection, presents itself, and that is, whether the duties levied should be upon the value of the article at the place of shipment, or, where it is practicable, a specific duty, graduated according to quantity, as ascertained by weight or measure. All our duties are at present ad valorem. A certain percentage is levied on the price of the goods at the port of shipment in a foreign country. Most commercial nations have found it indispensable, for the purpose of preventing fraud and perjury, to make the duties specific whenever the article is of such a uniform value in weight or measure as to justify such a duty. Legislation should never encourage dishonesty or crime. It is impossible that the revenue officers at the port where the goods are entered and the duties paid should know with certainty what they cost in the foreign country. Yet the law requires that they should levy the duty according to such cost. They are therefore compelled to resort to very unsatisfactory evidence to ascertain what that cost was. They take the invoice of the importer, attested by his oath, as the best evidence of which the nature of the case admits. But everyone must see that the invoice may be fabricated and the oath by which it is supported false, by reason of which the dishonest importer pays a part only of the duties which are paid by the honest one, and thus indirectly receives from the Treasury of the United States a reward for his fraud and perjury. The reports of the Secretary of the Treasury heretofore made on this subject show conclusively that these frauds have been practiced to a great extent. The tendency is to destroy that high moral character for which our merchants have long been distinguished, to defraud the Government of its revenue, to break down the honest importer by a dishonest competition, and, finally, to transfer the business of importation to foreign and irresponsible agents, to the great detriment of our own citizens. I therefore again most earnestly recommend the adoption of specific duties wherever it is practicable, or a home valuation, to prevent these frauds.

I would also again call your attention to the fact that the present tariff in some cases imposes a higher duty upon the raw material imported than upon the article manufactured from it, the consequence of which is that the duty operates to the encouragement of the foreigner and the discouragement of our own citizens.

For full and detailed information in regard to the general condition of our Indian affairs, I respectfully refer you to the report of the Secretary of the Interior and the accompanying documents.

The Senate not having thought proper to ratify the treaties which have been negotiated with the tribes of Indians in California and Oregon, our relations with them have been left in a very unsatisfactory condition.

In other parts of our territory particular districts of country have been set apart for the exclusive occupation of the Indians, and their right to the lands within those limits has been acknowledged and respected. But in California and Oregon there has been no recognition by the Government of the exclusive right of the Indians to any part of the country. They are therefore mere tenants at sufferance, and liable to be driven from place to place at the pleasure of the whites.

The treaties which have been rejected proposed to remedy this evil by allotting to the different tribes districts of country suitable to their habits of life and sufficient for their support. This provision, more than any other, it is believed, led to their rejection; and as no substitute for it has been adopted by Congress, it has not been deemed advisable to attempt to enter into new treaties of a permanent character, although no effort has been spared by temporary arrangements to preserve friendly relations with them.

If it be the desire of Congress to remove them from the country altogether, or to assign to them particular districts more remote from the settlements of the whites, it will be proper to set apart by law the territory which they are to occupy and to provide the means necessary for removing them to it. Justice alike to our own citizens and to the Indians requires the prompt action of Congress on this subject. The amendments proposed by the Senate to the treaties which were negotiated with the Sioux Indians of Minnesota have been submitted to the tribes who were parties to them, and have received their assent. A large tract of valuable territory has thus been opened for settlement and cultivation, and all danger of collision with these powerful and warlike bands has been happily removed.

The removal of the remnant of the tribe of Seminole Indians from Florida has long been a cherished object of the Government, and it is one to which my attention has been steadily directed. Admonished by past experience of the difficulty and cost of the attempt to remove them by military force, resort has been had to conciliatory measures. By the invitation of the Commissioner of Indian Affairs, several of the principal chiefs recently visited Washington, and whilst here acknowledged in writing the obligation of their tribe to remove with the least possible delay. Late advices from the special agent of the Government represent that they adhere to their promise, and that a council of their people has been called to make their preliminary arrangements. A general emigration may therefore be confidently expected at an early day.

The report from the General Land Office shows increased activity in its operations. The survey of the northern boundary of Iowa has been completed with unexampled dispatch. Within the last year 9,522,953 acres of public land have been surveyed and 8,032,463 acres brought into market.

* * *

Much the larger portion of the labor of arranging and classifying the returns of the last census has been finished, and it will now devolve upon Congress to make the necessary provision for the publication of the results in such form as shall be deemed best. The apportionment of representation on the basis of the new census has been made by the Secretary of the Interior in conformity with the provisions of law relating to that subject, and the recent elections have been made in accordance with it.

I commend to your favorable regard the suggestion contained in the report of the Secretary of the Interior that provision be made by law for the publication and distribution, periodically, of an analytical digest of all the patents which have been or may hereafter be granted for useful inventions and discoveries, with such descriptions and illustrations as may be necessary to present an intelligible view of their nature and operation. The cost of such publication could easily be defrayed out of the patent fund, and I am persuaded that it could be applied to no object more acceptable to inventors and beneficial to the public at large.

An appropriation of $100,000 having been made at the last session for the purchase of a suitable site and for the erection, furnishing, and fitting up of an asylum for the insane of the District of Columbia and of the Army and Navy of the United States, the proper measures have been adopted to carry this beneficent purpose into effect.

By the latest advices from the Mexican boundary commission it appears that the survey of the river Gila from its continence with the Colorado to its supposed intersection with the western line of New Mexico has been completed. The survey of the Rio Grande has also been finished from the point agreed on by the commissioners as "the point where it strikes the southern boundary of New Mexico" to a point 135 miles below Eagle Pass, which is about two-thirds of the distance along the course of the river to its mouth.

The appropriation which was made at the last session of Congress for the continuation of the survey is subject to the following proviso:

"Provided, That no part of this appropriation shall be used or expended until it shall be made satisfactorily to appear to the President of the United States that the southern boundary of New Mexico is not established by the commissioner and surveyor of the United States farther north of the town called 'Paso' than the same is laid down in Disturnell's map, which is added to the treaty."

My attention was drawn to this subject by a report from the Department of the Interior, which reviewed all the facts of the case and submitted for my decision the question whether under existing circumstances any part of the appropriation could be lawfully used or expended for the further prosecution of the work. After a careful consideration of the subject I came to the conclusion that it could not, and so informed the head of that Department. Orders were immediately issued by him to the commissioner and surveyor to make no further requisitions on the Department, as they could not be paid, and to discontinue all operations on the southern line of New Mexico. But as the Department had no exact information as to the amount of provisions and money which remained unexpended in the hands of the commissioner and surveyor, it was left discretionary with them to continue the survey down the Rio Grande as far as the means at their disposal would enable them or at once to disband the commission. A special messenger has since arrived from the officer in charge of the survey on the river with information that the funds subject to his control were exhausted and that the officers and others employed in the service were destitute alike of the means of prosecuting the work and of returning to their homes.

The object of the proviso was doubtless to arrest the survey of the southern and western lines of New Mexico, in regard to which different opinions have been expressed; for it is hardly to be supposed that there could be any objection to that part of the line which extends along the channel of the Rio Grande. But the terms of the law are so broad as to forbid the use of any part of the money for the prosecution of the work, or even for the payment to the officers and agents of the arrearages of pay which are justly due to them.

I earnestly invite your prompt attention to this subject, and recommend a modification of the terms of the proviso, so as to enable the Department to use as much of the appropriation as will be necessary to discharge the existing obligations of the Government and to complete the survey of the Rio Grande to its mouth.

It will also be proper to make further provision by law for the fulfillment of our treaty with Mexico for running and marking the residue of the boundary line between the two countries. Permit me to invite your particular attention to the interests of the District of Columbia, which are confided by the Constitution to your peculiar care.

Among the measures which seem to me of the greatest importance to its prosperity are the introduction of a copious supply of water into the city of Washington and the construction of suitable bridges across the Potomac to replace those which were destroyed by high water in the early part of the present year.

At the last session of Congress an appropriation was made to defray the cost of the surveys necessary for determining the best means of affording an unfailing supply of good and wholesome water. Some progress has been made in the survey, and as soon as it is completed the result will be laid before you.

Further appropriations will also be necessary for grading and paving the streets and avenues and inclosing and embellishing the public grounds within the city of Washington.

I commend all these objects, together with the charitable institutions of the District, to your favorable regard.

Every effort has been made to protect our frontier and that of the adjoining Mexican States from the incursions of the Indian tribes. Of about 11,000 men of which the Army is composed, nearly 8,000 are employed in the defense of the newly acquired territory (including Texas) and of emigrants proceeding thereto. I am gratified to say that these efforts have been unusually successful. With the exception of some partial outbreaks in California and Oregon and occasional depredations on a portion of the Rio Grande, owing, it is believed, to the disturbed state of that border region, the inroads of the Indians have been effectually restrained.

Experience has shown, however, that whenever the two races are brought into contact collisions will inevitably occur. To prevent these collisions the United States have generally set apart portions of their territory for the exclusive occupation of the Indian tribes. A difficulty occurs, however, in the application of this policy to Texas. By the terms of the compact by which that State was admitted into the Union she retained the ownership of all the vacant lands within her limits. The government of that State, it is understood, has assigned no portion of her territory to the Indians, but as fast as her settlements advance lays it off into counties and proceeds to survey and sell it. This policy manifestly tends not only to alarm and irritate the Indians, but to compel them to resort to plunder for subsistence. It also deprives this Government of that influence and control over them without which no durable peace can ever exist between them and the whites. I trust, therefore, that a due regard for her own interests, apart from considerations of humanity and justice, will induce that State to assign a small portion of her vast domain for the provisional occupancy of the small remnants of tribes within her borders, subject, of course, to her ownership and eventual jurisdiction. If she should fail to do this, the fulfillment of our treaty stipulations with Mexico and our duty to the Indians themselves will, it is feared, become a subject of serious embarrassment to the Government. It is hoped, however, that a timely and just provision by Texas may avert this evil.

No appropriations for fortifications were made at the two last sessions of Congress. The cause of this omission is probably to be found in a growing belief that the system of fortifications adopted in 1816, and heretofore acted on, requires revision.

The subject certainly deserves full and careful investigation, but it should not be delayed longer than can be avoided. In the meantime there are certain works which have been commenced, some of them nearly completed, designed to protect our principal seaports from Boston to New Orleans and a few other important points. In regard to the necessity for these works, it is believed that little difference of opinion exists among military men. I therefore recommend that the appropriations necessary to prosecute them be made.

I invite your attention to the remarks on this subject and on others connected with his Department contained in the accompanying report of the Secretary of War.

Measures have been taken to carry into effect the law of the last session making provision for the improvement of certain rivers and harbors, and it is believed that the arrangements made for that purpose will combine efficiency with economy. Owing chiefly to the advanced season when the act was passed, little has yet been done in regard to many of the works beyond making the necessary preparations. With respect to a few of the improvements, the sums already appropriated will suffice to complete them; but most of them will require additional appropriations. I trust that these appropriations will be made, and that this wise and beneficent policy, so auspiciously resumed, will be continued. Great care should be taken, however, to commence no work which is not of sufficient importance to the commerce of the country to be viewed as national in its character. But works which have been commenced should not be discontinued until completed, as otherwise the sums expended will in most cases be lost.

The report from the Navy Department will inform you of the prosperous condition of the branch of the public service committed to its charge. It presents to your consideration many topics and suggestions of which I ask your approval. It exhibits an unusual degree of activity in the operations of the Department during the past year. The preparations for the Japan expedition, to which I have already alluded; the arrangements made for the exploration and survey of the China Seas, the Northern Pacific, and Behrings Straits; the incipient measures taken toward a reconnoissance of the continent of Africa eastward of Liberia; the preparation for an early examination of the tributaries of the river La Plata, which a recent decree of the provisional chief of the Argentine Confederation has opened to navigation—all these enterprises and the means by which they are proposed to be accomplished have commanded my full approbation, and I have no doubt will be productive of most useful results.

Two officers of the Navy were heretofore instructed to explore the whole extent of the Amazon River from the confines of Peru to its mouth. The return of one of them has placed in the possession of the Government an interesting and valuable account of the character and resources of a country abounding in the materials of commerce, and which if opened to the industry of the world will prove an inexhaustible fund of wealth. The report of this exploration will be communicated to you as soon as it is completed.

Among other subjects offered to your notice by the Secretary of the Navy, I select for special commendation, in view of its connection with the interests of the Navy, the plan submitted by him for the establishment of a permanent corps of seamen and the suggestions he has presented for the reorganization of the Naval Academy.

In reference to the first of these, I take occasion to say that I think it will greatly improve the efficiency of the service, and that I regard it as still more entitled to favor for the salutary influence it must exert upon the naval discipline, now greatly disturbed by the increasing spirit of insubordination resulting from our present system. The plan proposed for the organization of the seamen furnishes a judicious substitute for the law of September, 1850, abolishing corporal punishment, and satisfactorily sustains the policy of that act under conditions well adapted to maintain the authority of command and the order and security of our ships. It is believed that any change which proposes permanently to dispense with this mode of punishment should be preceded by a system of enlistment which shall supply the Navy with seamen of the most meritorious class, whose good deportment and pride of character may preclude all occasion for a resort to penalties of a harsh or degrading nature. The safety of a ship and her crew is often dependent upon immediate obedience to a command, and the authority to enforce it must be equally ready. The arrest of a refractory seaman in such moments not only deprives the ship of indispensable aid, but imposes a necessity for double service on others, whose fidelity to their duties may be relied upon in such an emergency. The exposure to this increased and arduous labor since the passage of the act of 1850 has already had, to a most observable and injurious extent, the effect of preventing the enlistment of the best seamen in the Navy. The plan now suggested is designed to promote a condition of service in which this objection will no longer exist. The details of this plan may be established in great part, if not altogether, by the Executive under the authority of existing laws, but I have thought it proper, in accordance with the suggestion of the Secretary of the Navy, to submit it to your approval.

The establishment of a corps of apprentices for the Navy, or boys to be enlisted until they become of age, and to be employed under such regulations as the Navy Department may devise, as proposed in the report, I cordially approve and commend to your consideration; and I also concur in the suggestion that this system for the early training of seamen may be most usefully ingrafted upon the service of our merchant marine. The other proposition of the report to which I have referred—the reorganization of the Naval Academy—I recommend to your attention as a project worthy of your encouragement and support. The valuable services already rendered by this institution entitle it to the continuance of your fostering care.

Your attention is respectfully called to the report of the Postmaster-General for the detailed operation of his Department during the last fiscal year, from which it will be seen that the receipts from postages for that time were less by $1,431,696 than for the preceding fiscal year, being a decrease of about 23 per cent.

This diminution is attributable to the reduction in the rates of postage made by the act of March 3, 1851, which reduction took effect at the commencement of the last fiscal year.

Although in its operation during the last year the act referred to has not fulfilled the predictions of its friends by increasing the correspondence of the country in proportion to the reduction of postage, I should, nevertheless, question the policy of returning to higher rates. Experience warrants the expectation that as the community becomes accustomed to cheap postage correspondence will increase. It is believed that from this cause and from the rapid growth of the country in population and business the receipts of the Department must ultimately exceed its expenses, and that the country may safely rely upon the continuance of the present cheap rate of postage.

In former messages I have, among other things, respectfully recommended to the consideration of Congress the propriety and necessity of further legislation for the protection and punishment of foreign consuls residing in the United States; to revive, with certain modifications, the act of 10th March, 1838, to restrain unlawful military expeditions against the inhabitants of conterminous states or territories; for the preservation and protection from mutilation or theft of the papers, records, and archives of the nation; for authorizing the surplus revenue to be applied to the payment of the public debt in advance of the time when it will become due; for the establishment of land offices for the sale of the public lands in California and the Territory of Oregon; for the construction of a road from the Mississippi Valley to the Pacific Ocean; for the establishment of a bureau of agriculture for the promotion of that interest, perhaps the most important in the country; for the prevention of frauds upon the Government in applications for pensions and bounty lands; for the establishment of a uniform fee bill, prescribing a specific compensation for every service required of clerks, district attorneys, and marshals; for authorizing an additional regiment of mounted men for the defense of our frontiers against the Indians and for fulfilling our treaty stipulations with Mexico to defend her citizens against the Indians "with equal diligence and energy as our own;" for determining the relative rank between the naval and civil officers in our public ships and between the officers of the Army and Navy in the various grades of each; for reorganizing the naval establishment by fixing the number of officers in each grade, and providing for a retired list upon reduced pay of those unfit for active duty; for prescribing and regulating punishments in the Navy; for the appointment of a commission to revise the public statutes of the United States by arranging them in order, supplying deficiencies, correcting incongruities, simplifying their language, and reporting them to Congress for its final action; and for the establishment of a commission to adjudicate and settle private claims against the United States. I am not aware, however, that any of these subjects have been finally acted upon by Congress. Without repeating the reasons for legislation on these subjects which have been assigned in former messages, I respectfully recommend them again to your favorable consideration.

I think it due to the several Executive Departments of this Government to bear testimony to the efficiency and integrity with which they are conducted. With all the careful superintendence which it is possible for the heads of those Departments to exercise, still the due administration and guardianship of the public money must very much depend on the vigilance, intelligence, and fidelity of the subordinate officers and clerks, and especially on those intrusted with the settlement and adjustment of claims and accounts. I am gratified to believe that they have generally performed their duties faithfully and well. They are appointed to guard the approaches to the public Treasury, and they occupy positions that expose them to all the temptations and seductions which the cupidity of peculators and fraudulent claimants can prompt them to employ. It will be but a wise precaution to protect the Government against that source of mischief and corruption, as far as it can be done, by the enactment of all proper legal penalties. The laws in this respect are supposed to be defective, and I therefore deem it my duty to call your attention to the subject and to recommend that provision be made by law for the punishment not only of those who shall accept bribes, but also of those who shall either promise, give, or offer to give to any of those officers or clerks a bribe or reward touching or relating to any matter of their official action or duty.

It has been the uniform policy of this Government, from its foundation to the present day, to abstain from all interference in the domestic affairs of other nations. The consequence has been that while the nations of Europe have been engaged in desolating wars our country has pursued its peaceful course to unexampled prosperity and happiness. The wars in which we have been compelled to engage in defense of the rights and honor of the country have been, fortunately, of short duration. During the terrific contest of nation against nation which succeeded the French Revolution we were enabled by the wisdom and firmness of President Washington to maintain our neutrality. While other nations were drawn into this wide-sweeping whirlpool, we sat quiet and unmoved upon our own shores. While the flower of their numerous armies was wasted by disease or perished by hundreds of thousands upon the battlefield, the youth of this favored land were permitted to enjoy the blessings of peace beneath the paternal roof. While the States of Europe incurred enormous debts, under the burden of which their subjects still groan, and which must absorb no small part of the product of the honest industry of those countries for generations to come, the United States have once been enabled to exhibit the proud spectacle of a nation free from public debt, and if permitted to pursue our prosperous way for a few years longer in peace we may do the same again.

But it is now said by some that this policy must be changed. Europe is no longer separated from us by a voyage of months, but steam navigation has brought her within a few days' sail of our shores. We see more of her movements and take a deeper interest in her controversies. Although no one proposes that we should join the fraternity of potentates who have for ages lavished the blood and treasure of their subjects in maintaining "the balance of power," yet it is said that we ought to interfere between contending sovereigns and their subjects for the purpose of overthrowing the monarchies of Europe and establishing in their place republican institutions. It is alleged that we have heretofore pursued a different course from a sense of our weakness, but that now our conscious strength dictates a change of policy, and that it is consequently our duty to mingle in these contests and aid those who are struggling for liberty.

This is a most seductive but dangerous appeal to the generous sympathies of freemen. Enjoying, as we do, the blessings of a free Government, there is no man who has an American heart that would not rejoice to see these blessings extended to all other nations. We can not witness the struggle between the oppressed and his oppressor anywhere without the deepest sympathy for the former and the most anxious desire for his triumph. Nevertheless, is it prudent or is it wise to involve ourselves in these foreign wars? Is it indeed true that we have heretofore refrained from doing so merely from the degrading motive of a conscious weakness? For the honor of the patriots who have gone before us, I can not admit it. Men of the Revolution, who drew the sword against the oppressions of the mother country and pledged to Heaven "their lives, their fortunes, and their sacred honor" to maintain their freedom, could never have been actuated by so unworthy a motive. They knew no weakness or fear where right or duty pointed the way, and it is a libel upon their fair fame for us, while we enjoy the blessings for which they so nobly fought and bled, to insinuate it. The truth is that the course which they pursued was dictated by a stern sense of international justice, by a statesmanlike prudence and a far-seeing wisdom, looking not merely to the present necessities but to the permanent safety and interest of the country. They knew that the world is governed less by sympathy than by reason and force; that it was not possible for this nation to become a "propagandist" of free principles without arraying against it the combined powers of Europe, and that the result was more likely to be the overthrow of republican liberty here than its establishment there. History has been written in vain for those who can doubt this. France had no sooner established a republican form of government than she manifested a desire to force its blessings on all the world. Her own historian informs us that, hearing of some petty acts of tyranny in a neighboring principality, "the National Convention declared that she would afford succor and fraternity to all nations who wished to recover their liberty, and she gave it in charge to the executive power to give orders to the generals of the French armies to aid all citizens who might have been or should be oppressed in the cause of liberty." Here was the false step which led to her subsequent misfortunes. She soon found herself involved in war with all the rest of Europe. In less than ten years her Government was changed from a republic to an empire, and finally, after shedding rivers of blood, foreign powers restored her exiled dynasty and exhausted Europe sought peace and repose in the unquestioned ascendency of monarchical principles. Let us learn wisdom from her example. Let us remember that revolutions do not always establish freedom. Our own free institutions were not the offspring of our Revolution. They existed before. They were planted in the free charters of self-government under which the English colonies grew up, and our Revolution only freed us from the dominion of a foreign power whose government was at variance with those institutions. But European nations have had no such training for self-government, and every effort to establish it by bloody revolutions has been, and must without that preparation continue to be, a failure. Liberty unregulated by law degenerates into anarchy, which soon becomes the most horrid of all despotisms. Our policy is wisely to govern ourselves, and thereby to set such an example of national justice, prosperity, and true glory as shall teach to all nations the blessings of self-government and the unparalleled enterprise and success of a free people.

We live in an age of progress, and ours is emphatically a country of progress. Within the last half century the number of States in this Union has nearly doubled, the population has almost quadrupled, and our boundaries have been extended from the Mississippi to the Pacific. Our territory is checkered over with railroads and furrowed with canals. The inventive talent of our country is excited to the highest pitch, and the numerous applications for patents for valuable improvements distinguish this age and this people from all others. The genius of one American has enabled our commerce to move against wind and tide and that of another has annihilated distance in the transmission of intelligence. The whole country is full of enterprise. Our common schools are diffusing intelligence among the people and our industry is fast accumulating the comforts and luxuries of life. This is in part owing to our peculiar position, to our fertile soil and comparatively sparse population; but much of it is also owing to the popular institutions under which we live, to the freedom which every man feels to engage in any useful pursuit according to his taste or inclination, and to the entire confidence that his person and property will be protected by the laws. But whatever may be the cause of this unparalleled growth in population, intelligence, and wealth, one thing is clear—that the Government must keep pace with the progress of the people. It must participate in their spirit of enterprise, and while it exacts obedience to the laws and restrains all unauthorized invasions of the rights of neighboring states, it should foster and protect home industry and lend its powerful strength to the improvement of such means of intercommunication as are necessary to promote our internal commerce and strengthen the ties which bind us together as a people.

It is not strange, however much it may be regretted, that such an exuberance of enterprise should cause some individuals to mistake change for progress and the invasion of the rights of others for national prowess and glory. The former are constantly agitating for some change in the organic law, or urging new and untried theories of human rights. The latter are ever ready to engage in any wild crusade against a neighboring people, regardless of the justice of the enterprise and without looking at the fatal consequences to ourselves and to the cause of popular government. Such expeditions, however, are often stimulated by mercenary individuals, who expect to share the plunder or profit of the enterprise without exposing themselves to danger, and are led on by some irresponsible foreigner, who abuses the hospitality of our own Government by seducing the young and ignorant to join in his scheme of personal ambition or revenge under the false and delusive pretense of extending the area of freedom. These reprehensible aggressions but retard the true progress of our nation and tarnish its fair fame. They should therefore receive the indignant frowns of every good citizen who sincerely loves his country and takes a pride in its prosperity and honor.

Our Constitution, though not perfect, is doubtless the best that ever was formed. Therefore let every proposition to change it be well weighed and, if found beneficial, cautiously adopted. Every patriot will rejoice to see its authority so exerted as to advance the prosperity and honor of the nation, whilst he will watch with jealousy any attempt to mutilate this charter of our liberties or pervert its powers to acts of aggression or injustice. Thus shall conservatism and progress blend their harmonious action in preserving the form and spirit of the Constitution and at the same time carry forward the great improvements of the country with a rapidity and energy which freemen only can display.

In closing this my last annual communication, permit me, fellow-citizens, to congratulate you on the prosperous condition of our beloved country. Abroad its relations with all foreign powers are friendly, its rights are respected, and its high place in the family of nations cheerfully recognized. At home we enjoy an amount of happiness, public and private, which has probably never fallen to the lot of any other people. Besides affording to our own citizens a degree of prosperity of which on so large a scale I know of no other instance, our country is annually affording a refuge and a home to multitudes, altogether without example, from the Old World.

We owe these blessings, under Heaven, to the happy Constitution and Government which were bequeathed to us by our fathers, and which it is our sacred duty to transmit in all their integrity to our children. We must all consider it a great distinction and privilege to have been chosen by the people to bear a part in the administration of such a Government. Called by an unexpected dispensation to its highest trust at a season of embarrassment and alarm, I entered upon its arduous duties with extreme diffidence. I claim only to have discharged them to the best of an humble ability, with a single eye to the public good, and it is with devout gratitude in retiring from office that I leave the country in a state of peace and prosperity.

MILLARD FILLMORE

12

Franklin Pierce (1853–1857)

The outbreak of civil war was still more than four years away. Yet in this message we encounter a leader who worried that armed conflict between the North and South was visible on the horizon. Franklin Pierce warned fellow citizens in the North and South against "unreasoning intemperance of thought and language." For "Extremes beget extremes. Violent attack from the North finds its inevitable consequence in the growth of a spirit of angry defiance at the South." Pierce's last annual message is the first to contain a sustained analysis of the dire sectional crises threatening the Union. This was the era of the controversial Kansas–Nebraska Act, which nullified the Compromise of 1850. It was the time of Bleeding Kansas. It was on his watch that debates on the floor of the Congress devolved into fisticuffs.

Pierce was an accomplished orator. He was the first president to memorize his inaugural address and recite it from memory. To put that in perspective, the speech is 3,330 words in length and would have taken almost half an hour to deliver. In his fourth annual message to the Congress, however, Pierce followed the tradition since Jefferson of submitting the address to Capitol Hill in writing.

Fourth Annual Message
(written to the Congress)
December 2, 1856

Fellow-Citizens of the Senate and of the House of Representatives:

The Constitution requires that the President shall from time to time not only recommend to the consideration of Congress such measures as he may judge necessary and expedient, but also that he shall give information to them of the state of the Union. To do this fully involves exposition of all matters in the actual condition of the country, domestic or foreign, which essentially concern the general welfare. While performing his constitutional duty in this respect, the President does not speak merely to express personal convictions, but as the executive minister of the Government, enabled by his position and called upon by his official obligations to scan with an impartial eye the interests of the whole and of every part of the United States.

Of the condition of the domestic interests of the Union—its agriculture, mines, manufactures, navigation, and commerce—it is necessary only to say that the internal prosperity of the country, its continuous and steady advancement in wealth and population and in private as well as public well-being, attest the wisdom of our institutions and the predominant spirit of intelligence and patriotism which, notwithstanding occasional irregularities of opinion or action resulting from popular freedom, has distinguished and characterized the people of America. In the brief interval between the termination of the last and the commencement of the present session of Congress the public mind has been occupied with the care of selecting for another constitutional term the President and Vice-President of the United States.

The determination of the persons who are of right, or contingently, to preside over the administration of the Government is under our system committed to the States and the people. We appeal to them, by their voice pronounced in the forms of law, to call whomsoever they will to the high post of Chief Magistrate.

And thus it is that as the Senators represent the respective States of the Union and the members of the House of Representatives the several constituencies of each State, so the President represents the aggregate population of the United States. Their election of him is the explicit and solemn act of the sole sovereign authority of the Union.

It is impossible to misapprehend the great principles which by their recent political action the people of the United States have sanctioned and announced.

They have asserted the constitutional equality of each and all of the States of the Union as States: they have affirmed the constitutional equality of each and all of the citizens of the United States as citizens, whatever their religion, wherever their birth or their residence; they have maintained the inviolability of the constitutional rights of the different sections of the Union, and they have proclaimed their devoted and unalterable attachment to the Union and to the Constitution, as objects of interest superior to all subjects of local or sectional controversy, as the safeguard of the rights of all, as the spirit and the essence of the liberty, peace, and greatness of the Republic.

In doing this they have at the same time emphatically condemned the idea of organizing in these United States mere geographical parties, of marshaling in hostile array toward each other the different parts of the country, North or South, East or West.

Schemes of this nature, fraught with incalculable mischief, and which the considerate sense of the people has rejected, could have had countenance in no part of the country had they not been disguised by suggestions plausible in appearance, acting upon an excited state of the public mind, induced by causes temporary in their character and, it is to be hoped, transient in their influence.

Perfect liberty of association for political objects and the widest scope of discussion are the received and ordinary conditions of government in our country. Our institutions, framed in the spirit of confidence in the intelligence and integrity of the people, do not forbid citizens, either individually or associated together, to attack by writing, speech, or any other methods short of physical force the Constitution and the very existence of the Union. Under the shelter of this great liberty, and protected by the laws and usages of the Government they assail, associations have been formed in some of the States of individuals who, pretending to seek only to prevent the spread of the institution of slavery into the present or future inchoate States of the Union, are really inflamed with desire to change the domestic institutions of existing States. To accomplish their objects they dedicate themselves to the odious task of depreciating the government organization which stands in their way and of calumniating with indiscriminate invective not only the citizens of particular States with whose laws they find fault, but all others of their fellow citizens throughout the country who do not participate with them in their assaults upon the Constitution, framed and adopted by our fathers, and claiming for the privileges it has secured and the blessings it has conferred the steady support and grateful reverence of their children. They seek an object which they well know to be a revolutionary one. They are perfectly aware that the change in the relative condition of the white and black races in the slavehold-ing States which they would promote is beyond their lawful authority; that to them it is a foreign ob-ject; that it can not be effected by any peaceful instrumentality of theirs; that for them and the States of which they are citizens the only path to its accomplishment is through burning cities, and ravaged fields, and slaughtered populations, and all there is most terrible in foreign complicated with civil and servile war; and that the first step in the attempt is the forcible disruption of a country embracing in its broad bosom a degree of liberty and an amount of individual and public prosperity to which there is no parallel in history, and substituting in its place hostile governments, driven at once and in-evitably into mutual devastation and fratricidal carnage, transforming the now peaceful and felicitous brotherhood into a vast permanent camp of armed men like the rival monarchies of Europe and Asia. Well knowing that such, and such only, are the means and the consequences of their plans and pur-poses, they endeavor to prepare the people of the United States for civil war by doing everything in their power to deprive the Constitution and the laws of moral authority and to undermine the fabric of the Union by appeals to passion and sectional prejudice, by indoctrinating its people with recipro-cal hatred, and by educating them to stand face to face as enemies, rather than shoulder to shoulder as friends.

It is by the agency of such unwarrantable interference, foreign and domestic, that the minds of many otherwise good citizens have been so inflamed into the passionate condemnation of the do-mestic institutions of the Southern States as at length to pass insensibly to almost equally passionate hostility toward their fellow-citizens of those States, and thus finally to fall into temporary fellowship with the avowed and active enemies of the Constitution. Ardently attached to liberty in the abstract, they do not stop to consider practically how the objects they would attain can be accomplished, nor to reflect that, even if the evil were as great as they deem it, they have no remedy to apply, and that it can be only aggravated by their violence and unconstitutional action. A question which is one of the most difficult of all the problems of social institution, political economy, and statesmanship they treat with unreasoning intemperance of thought and language. Extremes beget extremes. Violent at-tack from the North finds its inevitable consequence in the growth of a spirit of angry defiance at the South. Thus in the progress of events we had reached that consummation, which the voice of the peo-ple has now so pointedly rebuked, of the attempt of a portion of the States, by a sectional organiza-tion and movement, to usurp the control of the Government of the United States.

I confidently believe that the great body of those who inconsiderately took this fatal step are sin-cerely attached to the Constitution and the Union. They would upon deliberation shrink with unaf-fected horror from any conscious act of disunion or civil war. But they have entered into a path which leads nowhere unless it be to civil war and disunion, and which has no other possible outlet. They have proceeded thus far in that direction in consequence of the successive stages of their progress hav-ing consisted of a series of secondary issues, each of which professed to be confined within constitu-tional and peaceful limits, but which attempted indirectly what few men were willing to do directly; that is, to act aggressively against the constitutional rights of nearly one-half of the thirty-one States.

In the long series of acts of indirect aggression, the first was the strenuous agitation by citizens of the Northern States, in Congress and out of it, of the question of Negro emancipation in the South-ern States.

The second step in this path of evil consisted of acts of the people of the Northern States, and in several instances of their governments, aimed to facilitate the escape of persons held to service in the Southern States and to prevent their extradition when reclaimed according to law and in virtue of express provisions of the Constitution. To promote this object, legislative enactments and other means were adopted to take away or defeat rights which the Constitution solemnly guaranteed. In or-der to nullify the then existing act of Congress concerning the extradition of fugitives from service, laws were enacted in many States forbidding their officers, under the severest penalties, to participate in the execution of any act of Congress whatever. In this way that system of harmonious cooperation between the authorities of the United States and of the several States, for the maintenance of their common institutions, which existed in the early years of the Republic was destroyed; conflicts of jurisdiction came to be frequent, and Congress found itself compelled, for the support of the Constitution and the vindication of its power, to authorize the appointment of new officers charged with the execution of its acts, as if they and the officers of the States were the ministers, respectively, of foreign governments in a state of mutual hostility rather than fellow-magistrates of a common country peacefully subsisting under the protection of one well-constituted Union. Thus here also aggression was followed by reaction, and the attacks upon the Constitution at this point did but serve to raise up new barriers for its defense and security.

The third stage of this unhappy sectional controversy was in connection with the organization of Territorial governments and the admission of new States into the Union. When it was proposed to admit the State of Maine, by separation of territory from that of Massachusetts, and the State of Missouri, formed of a portion of the territory ceded by France to the United States, representatives in Congress objected to the admission of the latter unless with conditions suited to particular views of public policy. The imposition of such a condition was successfully resisted; but at the same period the question was presented of imposing restrictions upon the residue of the territory ceded by France. That question was for the time disposed of by the adoption of a geographical line of limitation.

In this connection it should not be forgotten that when France, of her own accord, resolved, for considerations of the most farsighted sagacity, to cede Louisiana to the United States, and that accession was accepted by the United States, the latter expressly engaged that "the inhabitants of the ceded territory shall be incorporated in the Union of the United States and admitted as soon as possible, according to the principles of the Federal Constitution, to the enjoyment of all the rights, advantages, and immunities of citizens of the United States; and in the meantime they shall be maintained and protected in the free enjoyment of their liberty, property, and the religion which they profess"; that is to say, while it remains in a Territorial condition its inhabitants are maintained and protected in the free enjoyment of their liberty and property, with a right then to pass into the condition of States on a footing of perfect equality with the original States.

The enactment which established the restrictive geographical line was acquiesced in rather than approved by the States of the Union. It stood on the statute book, however, for a number of years; and the people of the respective States acquiesced in the reenactment of the principle as applied to the State of Texas, and it was proposed to acquiesce in its further application to the territory acquired by the United States from Mexico. But this proposition was successfully resisted by the representatives from the Northern States, who, regardless of the statute line, insisted upon applying restriction to the new territory generally, whether lying north or south of it, thereby repealing it as a legislative compromise, and, on the part of the North, persistently violating the compact, if compact there was.

Thereupon this enactment ceased to have binding virtue in any sense, whether as respects the North or the South, and so in effect it was treated on the occasion of the admission of the State of California and the organization of the Territories of New Mexico, Utah, and Washington.

Such was the state of this question when the time arrived for the organization of the Territories of Kansas and Nebraska. In the progress of constitutional inquiry and reflection it had now at length come to be seen clearly that Congress does not possess constitutional power to impose restrictions of this character upon any present or future State of the Union. In a long series of decisions, on the fullest argument and after the most deliberate consideration, the Supreme Court of the United States had finally determined this point in every form under which the question could arise, whether as affecting public or private rights—in questions of the public domain, of religion, of navigation, and of servitude.

The several States of the Union are by force of the Constitution coequal in domestic legislative power. Congress can not change a law of domestic relation in the State of Maine; no more can it in the State of Missouri. Any statute which proposes to do this is a mere nullity; it takes away no right, it confers none. If it remains on the statute book unrepealed, it remains there only as a monument of error and a beacon of warning to the legislator and the statesman. To repeal it will be only to remove imperfection from the statutes, without affecting, either in the sense of permission, or of prohibition, the action of the States or of their citizens.

Still, when the nominal restriction of this nature, already a dead letter in law, was in terms repealed by the last Congress, in a clause of the act organizing the Territories of Kansas and Nebraska, that repeal was made the occasion of a widespread and dangerous agitation.

It was alleged that the original enactment being a compact of perpetual moral obligation, its repeal constituted an odious breach of faith.

An act of Congress, while it remains unrepealed, more especially if it be constitutionally valid in the judgment of those public functionaries whose duty it is to pronounce on that point, is undoubtedly binding on the conscience of each good citizen of the Republic. But in what sense can it be asserted that the enactment in question was invested with perpetuity and entitled to the respect of a solemn compact? Between whom was the compact? No distinct contending powers of the Government, no separate sections of the Union treating as such, entered into treaty stipulations on the subject. It was a mere clause of an act of Congress, and, like any other controverted matter of legislation, received its final shape and was passed by compromise of the conflicting opinions or sentiments of the members of Congress. But if it had moral authority over men's consciences, to whom did this authority attach? Not to those of the North, who had repeatedly refused to confirm it by extension and who had zealously striven to establish other and incompatible regulations upon the subject. And if, as it thus appears, the supposed compact had no obligatory force as to the North, of course it could not have had any as to the South, for all such compacts must be mutual and of reciprocal obligation.

It has not unfrequently happened that lawgivers, with undue estimation of the value of the law they give or in the view of imparting to it peculiar strength, make it perpetual in terms; but they can not thus bind the conscience, the judgment, and the will of those who may succeed them, invested with similar responsibilities and clothed with equal authority. More careful investigation may prove the law to be unsound in principle. Experience may show it to be imperfect in detail and impracticable in execution. And then both reason and right combine not merely to justify but to require its repeal.

The Constitution, supreme, as it is, over all the departments of the Government—legislative, executive, and judicial—is open to amendment by its very terms; and Congress or the States may, in their discretion, propose amendment to it, solemn compact though it in truth is between the sovereign States of the Union. In the present instance a political enactment which had ceased to have legal power or authority of any kind was repealed. The position assumed that Congress had no moral right to enact such repeal was strange enough, and singularly so in view of the fact that the argument came from those who openly refused obedience to existing laws of the land, having the same popular designation and quality as compromise acts; nay, more, who unequivocally disregarded and condemned the most positive and obligatory injunctions of the Constitution itself, and sought by every means within their reach to deprive a portion of their fellow-citizens of the equal enjoyment of those rights and privileges guaranteed alike to all by the fundamental compact of our Union.

This argument against the repeal of the statute line in question was accompanied by another of congenial character and equally with the former destitute of foundation in reason and truth. It was imputed that the measure originated in the conception of extending the limits of slave labor beyond those previously assigned to it, and that such was its natural as well as intended effect; and these baseless assumptions were made, in the Northern States, the ground of unceasing assault upon constitutional right.

The repeal in terms of a statute, which was already obsolete and also null for unconstitutionality, could have no influence to obstruct or to promote the propagation of conflicting views of political or social institution. When the act organizing the Territories of Kansas and Nebraska was passed, the inherent effect upon that portion of the public domain thus opened to legal settlement was to admit settlers from all the States of the Union alike, each with his convictions of public policy and private interest, there to found, in their discretion, subject to such limitations as the Constitution and acts of Congress might prescribe, new States, hereafter to be admitted into the Union. It was a free field, open alike to all, whether the statute line of assumed restriction were repealed or not. That repeal did not open to free competition of the diverse opinions and domestic institutions a field which without such repeal would have been closed against them; it found that field of competition already opened, in fact and in law. All the repeal did was to relieve the statute book of an objectionable enactment, unconstitutional in effect and injurious in terms to a large portion of the States.

Is it the fact that in all the unsettled regions of the United States, if emigration be left free to act in this respect for itself, without legal prohibitions on either side, slave labor will spontaneously go everywhere in preference to free labor? Is it the fact that the peculiar domestic institutions of the Southern States possess relatively so much of vigor that wheresoever an avenue is freely opened to all the world they will penetrate to the exclusion of those of the Northern States? Is it the fact that the former enjoy, compared with the latter, such irresistibly superior vitality, independent of climate, soil, and all other accidental circumstances, as to be able to produce the supposed result in spite of the assumed moral and natural obstacles to its accomplishment and of the more numerous population of the Northern States?

The argument of those who advocate the enactment of new laws of restriction and condemn the repeal of old ones in effect avers that their particular views of government have no self-extending or self-sustaining power of their own, and will go nowhere unless forced by act of Congress. And if Congress do but pause for a moment in the policy of stern coercion; if it venture to try the experiment of leaving men to judge for themselves what institutions will best suit them; if it be not strained up to perpetual legislative exertion on this point—if Congress proceed thus to act in the very spirit of liberty, it is at once charged with aiming to extend slave labor into all the new Territories of the United States.

Of course these imputations on the intentions of Congress in this respect, conceived, as they were, in prejudice and disseminated in passion, are utterly destitute of any justification in the nature of things and contrary to all the fundamental doctrines and principles of civil liberty and self-government.

While, therefore, in general, the people of the Northern States have never at any time arrogated for the Federal Government the power to interfere directly with the domestic condition of persons in the Southern States, but, on the contrary, have disavowed all such intentions and have shrunk from conspicuous affiliation with those few who pursue their fanatical objects avowedly through the contemplated means of revolutionary change of the Government and with acceptance of the necessary consequences—a civil and servile war—yet many citizens have suffered themselves to be drawn into one evanescent political issue of agitation after another, appertaining to the same set of opinions, and which subsided as rapidly as they arose when it came to be seen, as it uniformly did, that they were incompatible with the compacts of the Constitution and the existence of the Union. Thus when the acts of some of the States to nullify the existing extradition law imposed upon Congress the duty of passing a new one, the country was invited by agitators to enter into party organization for its repeal; but that agitation speedily ceased by reason of the impracticability of its object. So when the statute restriction upon the institutions of new States by a geographical line had been repealed, the country was urged to demand its restoration, and that project also died almost with its birth. Then followed the cry of alarm from the North against imputed Southern encroachmeats, which cry sprang in reality from the spirit of revolutionary attack on the domestic institutions of the South, and, after a troubled existence of a few months, has been rebuked by the voice of a patriotic people.

Of this last agitation, one lamentable feature was that it was carried on at the immediate expense of the peace and happiness of the people of the Territory of Kansas. That was made the battlefield, not so much of opposing factions or interests within itself as of the conflicting passions of the whole people of the United States. Revolutionary disorder in Kansas had its origin in projects of intervention deliberately arranged by certain members of that Congress which enacted the law for the organization of the Territory; and when propagandist colonization of Kansas had thus been undertaken in one section of the Union for the systematic promotion of its peculiar views of policy there ensued as a matter of course a counteraction with opposite views in other sections of the Union.

In consequence of these and other incidents, many acts of disorder, it is undeniable, have been perpetrated in Kansas, to the occasional interruption rather than the permanent suspension of regular government. Aggressive and most reprehensible incursions into the Territory were undertaken both in the North and the South, and entered it on its northern border by the way of Iowa, as well as on the eastern by way of Missouri; and there has existed within it a state of insurrection against the constituted authorities, not without countenance from inconsiderate persons in each of the great sections of the Union. But the difficulties in that Territory have been extravagantly exaggerated for purposes of political agitation elsewhere. The number and gravity of the acts of violence have been magnified partly by statements entirely untrue and partly by reiterated accounts of the same rumors or facts. Thus the Territory has been seemingly filled with extreme violence, when the whole amount of such acts has not been greater than what occasionally passes before us in single cities to the regret of all good citizens, but without being regarded as of general or permanent political consequence.

Imputed irregularities in the elections had in Kansas, like occasional irregularities of the same description in the States, were beyond the sphere of action of the Executive. But incidents of actual violence or of organized obstruction of law, pertinaciously renewed from time to time, have been met as they occurred by such means as were available and as the circumstances required, and nothing of this character now remains to affect the general peace of the Union. The attempt of a part of the inhabitants of the Territory to erect a revolutionary government, though sedulously encouraged and supplied with pecuniary aid from active agents of disorder in some of the States, has completely failed. Bodies of armed men, foreign to the Territory, have been prevented from entering or compelled to leave it; predatory bands, engaged in acts of rapine under cover of the existing political disturbances, have been arrested or dispersed, and every well-disposed person is now enabled once more to devote himself in peace to the pursuits of prosperous industry, for the prosecution of which he undertook to participate in the settlement of the Territory.

It affords me unmingled satisfaction thus to announce the peaceful condition of things in Kansas, especially considering the means to which it was necessary to have recourse for the attainment of the end, namely, the employment of a part of the military force of the United States. The withdrawal of that force from its proper duty of defending the country against foreign foes or the savages of the frontier to employ it for the suppression of domestic insurrection is, when the exigency occurs, a matter of the most earnest solicitude. On this occasion of imperative necessity it has been done with the best results, and my satisfaction in the attainment of such results by such means is greatly enhanced by the consideration that, through the wisdom and energy of the present executive of Kansas and the prudence, firmness, and vigilance of the military officers on duty there tranquillity has been restored without one drop of blood having been shed in its accomplishment by the forces of the United States.

The restoration of comparative tranquillity in that Territory furnishes the means of observing calmly and appreciating at their just value the events which have occurred there and the discussions of which the government of the Territory has been the subject.

We perceive that controversy concerning its future domestic institutions was inevitable; that no human prudence, no form of legislation, no wisdom on the part of Congress, could have prevented it.

It is idle to suppose that the particular provisions of their organic law were the cause of agitation. Those provisions were but the occasion, or the pretext, of an agitation which was inherent in the nature of things. Congress legislated upon the subject in such terms as were most consonant with the principle of popular sovereignty which underlies our Government. It could not have legislated otherwise without doing violence to another great principle of our institutions—the imprescriptible right of equality of the several States.

We perceive also that sectional interests and party passions have been the great impediment to the salutary operation of the organic principles adopted and the chief cause of the successive disturbances in Kansas. The assumption that because in the organization of the Territories of Nebraska and Kansas Congress abstained from imposing restraints upon them to which certain other Territories had been subject, therefore disorders occurred in the latter Territory, is emphatically contradicted by the fact that none have occurred in the former. Those disorders were not the consequence, in Kansas, of the freedom of self-government conceded to that Territory by Congress, but of unjust interference on the part of persons not inhabitants of the Territory. Such interference, wherever it has exhibited itself by acts of insurrectionary character or of obstruction to process of law, has been repelled or suppressed by all the means which the Constitution and the laws place in the hands of the Executive.

In those parts of the United States where, by reason of the inflamed state of the public mind, false rumors and misrepresentations have the greatest currency it has been assumed that it was the duty of the Executive not only to suppress insurrectionary movements in Kansas, but also to see to the regularity of local elections. It needs little argument to show that the President has no such power. All government in the United States rests substantially upon popular election. The freedom of elections is liable to be impaired by the intrusion of unlawful votes or the exclusion of lawful ones, by improper influences, by violence, or by fraud. But the people of the United States are themselves the all sufficient guardians of their own rights, and to suppose that they will not remedy in due season any such incidents of civil freedom is to suppose them to have ceased to be capable of self-government. The President of the United States has not power to interpose in elections, to see to their freedom, to canvass their votes, or to pass upon their legality in the Territories any more than in the States. If he had such power the Government might be republican in form, but it would be a monarchy in fact; and if he had undertaken to exercise it in the case of Kansas he would have been justly subject to the charge of usurpation and of violation of the dearest rights of the people of the United States.

Unwise laws, equally with irregularities at elections, are in periods of great excitement the occasional incidents of even the freest and best political institutions; but all experience demonstrates that in a country like ours, where the right of self-constitution exists in the completest form, the attempt to remedy unwise legislation by resort to revolution is totally out of place, inasmuch as existing legal institutions afford more prompt and efficacious means for the redress of wrong.

I confidently trust that now, when the peaceful condition of Kansas affords opportunity for calm reflection and wise legislation, either the legislative assembly of the Territory or Congress will see that no act shall remain on its statute book violative of the provisions of the Constitution or subversive of the great objects for which that was ordained and established, and will take all other necessary steps to assure to its inhabitants the enjoyment, without obstruction or abridgment, of all the constitutional rights, privileges, and immunities of citizens of the United States, as contemplated by the organic law of the Territory.

Full information in relation to recent events in this Territory will be found in the documents communicated herewith from the Departments of State and War.

I refer you to the report of the Secretary of the Treasury for particular information concerning the financial condition of the Government and the various branches of the public service connected with the Treasury Department.

During the last fiscal year the receipts from customs were for the first time more than $64,000,000, and from all sources $73,918,141, which, with the balance on hand up to the 1st of July, 1855, made the total resources of the year amount to $92,850,117. The expenditures, including $3,000,000 in execution of the treaty with Mexico and excluding sums paid on account of the public debt, amounted to $60,172,401, and including the latter to $72,948,792, the payment on this account having amounted to $12,776,390.

On the 4th of March, 1853, the amount of the public debt was $69,129,937. There was a subsequent increase of $2,750,000 for the debt of Texas, making a total of $71,879,937. Of this the sum of $45,525,319, including premium, has been discharged, reducing the debt to $30,963,909, all which might be paid within a year without embarrassing the public service, but being not yet due and only redeemable at the option of the holder, can not be pressed to payment by the Government.

On examining the expenditures of the last five years it will be seen that the average, deducting payments on account of the public debt and $10,000,000 paid by treaty to Mexico, has been but about

$48,000,000. It is believed that under an economical administration of the Government the average expenditure for the ensuing five years will not exceed that sum, unless extraordinary occasion for its increase should occur. The acts granting bounty lands will soon have been executed, while the extension of our frontier settlements will cause a continued demand for lands and augmented receipts, probably, from that source. These considerations will justify a reduction of the revenue from customs so as not to exceed forty-eight or fifty million dollars. I think the exigency for such reduction is imperative, and again urge it upon the consideration of Congress.

The amount of reduction, as well as the manner of effecting it, are questions of great and general interest, it being essential to industrial enterprise and the public prosperity, as well as the dictate of obvious justice, that the burden of taxation be made to rest as equally as possible upon all classes and all sections and interests of the country.

I have heretofore recommended to your consideration the revision of the revenue laws, prepared under the direction of the Secretary of the Treasury, and also legislation upon some special questions affecting the business of that Department, more especially the enactment of a law to punish the abstraction of official books or papers from the files of the Government and requiring all such books and papers and all other public property to be turned over by the outgoing officer to his successor; of a law requiring disbursing officers to deposit all public money in the vaults of the Treasury or in other legal depositories, where the same are conveniently accessible, and a law to extend existing penal provisions to all persons who may become possessed of public money by deposit or otherwise and who shall refuse or neglect on due demand to pay the same into the Treasury. I invite your attention anew to each of these objects.

The Army during the past year has been so constantly employed against hostile Indians in various quarters that it can scarcely be said, with propriety of language, to have been a peace establishment. Its duties have been satisfactorily performed, and we have reason to expect as a result of the year's operations greater security to the frontier inhabitants than has been hitherto enjoyed. Extensive combinations among the hostile Indians of the Territories of Washington and Oregon at one time threatened the devastation of the newly formed settlements of that remote portion of the country. From recent information we are permitted to hope that the energetic and successful operations conducted there will prevent such combinations in future and secure to those Territories an opportunity to make steady progress in the development of their agricultural and mineral resources.

Legislation has been recommended by me on previous occasions to cure defects in the existing organization and to increase the efficiency of the Army, and further observation has but served to confirm me in the views then expressed and to enforce on my mind the conviction that such measures are not only proper, but necessary.

I have, in addition, to invite the attention of Congress to a change of policy in the distribution of troops and to the necessity of providing a more rapid increase of the military armament. For details of these and other subjects relating to the Army I refer to the report of the Secretary of War.

The condition of the Navy is not merely satisfactory, but exhibits the most gratifying evidences of increased vigor. As it is comparatively small, it is more important that it should be as complete as possible in all the elements of strength; that it should be efficient in the character of its officers, in the zeal and discipline of its men, in the reliability of its ordnance, and in the capacity of its ships. In all these various qualities the Navy has made great progress within the last few years. The execution of the law of Congress of February 28, 1855, "to promote the efficiency of the Navy," has been attended by the most advantageous results. The law for promoting discipline among the men is found convenient and salutary. The system of granting an honorable discharge to faithful seamen on the expiration of the period of their enlistment and permitting them to reenlist after a leave of absence of a few months without cessation of pay is highly beneficial in its influence. The apprentice system recently adopted is evidently destined to incorporate into the service a large number of our countrymen, hitherto so difficult to procure. Several hundred American boys are now on a three years' cruise in our national vessels and will return well-trained seamen. In the Ordnance Department there is a decided and gratifying indication of progress, creditable to it and to the country. The suggestions of the Secretary of the Navy in regard to further improvement in that branch of the service I commend to your favorable action.

The new frigates ordered by Congress are now afloat and two of them in active service. They are superior models of naval architecture, and with their formidable battery add largely to public strength and security. I concur in the views expressed by the Secretary of the Department in favor of a still further increase of our naval force.

The report of the Secretary of the Interior presents facts and views (in relation to internal affairs over which the supervision of his Department extends) of much interest and importance.

The aggregate sales of the public lands during the last fiscal year amount to 9,227,878 acres, for which has been received the sum of $8,821,414. During the same period there have been located with military scrip and land warrants and for other purposes 30,100,230 acres, thus making a total aggregate of 39,328,108 acres. On the 30th of September last surveys had been made of 16,873,699 acres, a large proportion of which is ready for market.

The suggestions in this report in regard to the complication and progressive expansion of the business of the different bureaus of the Department, to the pension system, to the colonization of Indian tribes, and the recommendations in relation to various improvements in the District of Columbia are especially commended to your consideration.

The report of the Postmaster-General presents fully the condition of that Department of the Government. Its expenditures for the last fiscal year were $10,407,868 and its gross receipts $7,620,801, making an excess of expenditure over receipts of $2,787,046. The deficiency of this Department is thus $744,000 greater than for the year ending June 30, 1853. Of this deficiency $330,000 is to be attributed to the additional compensation allowed to postmasters by the act of Congress of June 22, 1854. The mail facilities in every part of the country have been very much increased in that period, and the large addition of railroad service, amounting to 7,908 miles, has added largely to the cost of transportation.

The inconsiderable augmentation of the income of the Post-Office Department under the reduced rates of postage and its increasing expenditures must for the present make it dependent to some extent upon the Treasury for support. The recommendations of the Postmaster-General in relation to the abolition of the franking privilege and his views on the establishment of mail steamship lines deserve the consideration of Congress. I also call the special attention of Congress to the statement of the Postmaster-General respecting the sums now paid for the transportation of mails to the Panama Railroad Company, and commend to their early and favorable consideration the suggestions of that officer in relation to new contracts for mail transportation upon that route, and also upon the Tehuantepec and Nicaragua routes.

The United States continue in the enjoyment of amicable relations with all foreign powers.

When my last annual message was transmitted to Congress two subjects of controversy, one relating to the enlistment of soldiers in this country for foreign service and the other to Central America, threatened to disturb the good understanding between the United States and Great Britain. Of the progress and termination of the former question you were informed at the time, and the other is now in the way of satisfactory adjustment.

The object of the convention between the United States and Great Britain of the 19th of April, 1850, was to secure for the benefit of all nations the neutrality and the common use of any transit way or interoceanic communication across the Isthmus of Panama which might be opened within the limits of Central America. The pretensions subsequently asserted by Great Britain to dominion or control over territories in or near two of the routes, those of Nicaragua and Honduras, were deemed by the United States not merely incompatible with the main object of the treaty, but opposed even to its express stipulations. Occasion of controversy on this point has been removed by an additional treaty, which our minister at London has concluded, and which will be immediately submitted to the Senate for its consideration. Should the proposed supplemental arrangement be concurred in by all the parties to be affected by it, the objects contemplated by the original convention will have been fully attained.

The treaty between the United States and Great Britain of the 5th of June, 1854, which went into effective operation in 1855, put an end to causes of irritation between the two countries, by securing to the United States the right of fishery on the coast of the British North American Provinces, with advantages equal to those enjoyed by British subjects. Besides the signal benefits of this treaty to a large class of our citizens engaged in a pursuit connected to no inconsiderable degree with our national prosperity and strength, it has had a favorable effect upon other interests in the provision it made for reciprocal freedom of trade between the United States and the British Provinces in America.

The exports of domestic articles to those Provinces during the last year amounted to more than $22,000,000, exceeding those of the preceding year by nearly $7,000,000; and the imports therefrom during the same period amounted to more than twenty-one million, an increase of six million upon those of the previous year.

The improved condition of this branch of our commerce is mainly attributable to the above-mentioned treaty.

Provision was made in the first article of that treaty for a commission to designate the mouths of rivers to which the common right of fishery on the coast of the United States and the British Provinces was not to extend. This commission has been employed a part of two seasons, but without much progress in accomplishing the object for which it was instituted, in consequence of a serious difference of opinion between the commissioners, not only as to the precise point where the rivers terminate, but in many instances as to what constitutes a river. These difficulties, however, may be overcome by resort to the umpirage provided for by the treaty.

The efforts perseveringly prosecuted since the commencement of my Administration to relieve our trade to the Baltic from the exaction of Sound dues by Denmark have not yet been attended with success. Other governments have also sought to obtain a like relief to their commerce, and Denmark was thus induced to propose an arrangement to all the European powers interested in the subject, and the manner in which her proposition was received warranting her to believe that a satisfactory arrangement with them could soon be concluded, she made a strong appeal to this Government for temporary suspension of definite action on its part, in consideration of the embarrassment which might result to her European negotiations by an immediate adjustment of the question with the United States. This request has been acceded to upon the condition that the sums collected after the 16th of June last and until the 16th of June next from vessels and cargoes belonging to our merchants are to be considered as paid under protest and subject to future adjustment. There is reason to believe that an arrangement between Denmark and the maritime powers of Europe on the subject will be soon concluded, and that the pending negotiation with the United States may then be resumed and terminated in a satisfactory manner.

With Spain no new difficulties have arisen, nor has much progress been made in the adjustment of pending ones.

Negotiations entered into for the purpose of relieving our commercial intercourse with the island of Cuba of some of its burdens and providing for the more speedy settlement of local disputes growing out of that intercourse have not yet been attended with any results. Soon after the commencement of the late war in Europe this Government submitted to the consideration of all maritime nations two principles for the security of neutral commerce—one that the neutral flag should cover enemies' goods, except articles contraband of war, and the other that neutral property on board merchant vessels of belligerents should be exempt from condemnation, with the exception of contraband articles. These were not presented as new rules of international law, having been generally claimed by neutrals, though not always admitted by belligerents. One of the parties to the war (Russia), as well as several neutral powers, promptly acceded to these propositions, and the two other principal belligerents (Great Britain and France) having consented to observe them for the present occasion, a favorable opportunity seemed to be presented for obtaining a general recognition of them, both in Europe and America. But Great Britain and France, in common with most of the States of Europe, while forbearing to reject, did not affirmatively act upon the overtures of the United States.

While the question was in this position the representatives of Russia, France, Great Britain, Austria, Prussia, Sardinia, and Turkey, assembled at Paris, took into consideration the subject of maritime rights, and put forth a declaration containing the two principles which this Government had submitted nearly two years before to the consideration of maritime powers, and adding thereto the following propositions: "Privateering is and remains abolished," and "Blockades in order to be binding must be effective; that is to say, maintained by a force sufficient really to prevent access to the coast of the enemy"; and to the declaration thus composed of four points, two of which had already been proposed by the United States, this Government has been invited to accede by all the powers represented at Paris except Great Britain and Turkey. To the last of the two additional propositions—that in relation to blockades—there can certainly be no objection. It is merely the definition of what shall constitute the effectual investment of a blockaded place, a definition for which this Government has always contended, claiming indemnity for losses where a practical violation of the rule thus defined has been injurious to our commerce. As to the remaining article of the declaration of the conference of Paris, that "privateering is and remains abolished," I certainly can not ascribe to the powers represented in the conference of Paris any but liberal and philanthropic views in the attempt to change the unquestionable rule of maritime law in regard to privateering. Their proposition was doubtless intended to imply approval of the principle that private property upon the ocean, although it might belong to the citizens of a belligerent state, should be exempted from capture; and had that proposition been so framed as to give full effect to the principle, it would have received my ready assent on behalf of the United States. But the measure proposed is inadequate to that purpose. It is true that if adopted private property upon the ocean would be withdrawn from one mode of plunder, but left exposed meanwhile to another mode, which could be used with increased effectiveness. The aggressive capacity of great naval powers would be thereby augmented, while the defensive ability of others would be reduced. Though the surrender of the means of prosecuting hostilities by employing privateers, as proposed by the conference of Paris, is mutual in terms, yet in practical effect it would be the relinquishment of a right of little value to one class of states, but of essential importance to another and a far larger class. It ought not to have been anticipated that a measure so inadequate to the accomplishment of the proposed object and so unequal in its operation would receive the assent of all maritime powers. Private property would be still left to the depredations of the public armed cruisers.

I have expressed a readiness on the part of this Government to accede to all the principles contained in the declaration of the conference of Paris provided that the one relating to the abandonment of privateering can be so amended as to effect the object for which, as is presumed, it was intended—the immunity of private property on the ocean from hostile capture. To effect this object, it is proposed to add to the declaration that "privateering is and remains abolished" the following amendment:

"And that the private property of subjects and citizens of a belligerent on the high seas shall be exempt from seizure by the public armed vessels of the other belligerent, except it be contraband."

This amendment has been presented not only to the powers which have asked our assent to the declaration to abolish privateering, but to all other maritime states. Thus far it has not been rejected by any, and is favorably entertained by all which have made any communication in reply.

Several of the governments regarding with favor the proposition of the United States have delayed definitive action upon it only for the purpose of consulting with others, parties to the conference of Paris. I have the satisfaction of stating, however, that the Emperor of Russia has entirely and explicitly approved of that modification and will cooperate in endeavoring to obtain the assent of other powers, and that assurances of a similar purport have been received in relation to the disposition of the Emperor of the French. The present aspect of this important subject allows us to cherish the hope that a principle so humane in its character, so just and equal in its operation, so essential to the prosperity of commercial nations, and so consonant to the sentiments of this enlightened period of the world will command the approbation of all maritime powers, and thus be incorporated into the code of international law.

My views on the subject are more fully set forth in the reply of the Secretary of State, a copy of which is herewith transmitted, to the communications on the subject made to this Government, especially to the communication of France.

The Government of the United States has at all times regarded with friendly interest the other States of America, formerly, like this country, European colonies, and now independent members of the great family of nations. But the unsettled condition of some of them, distracted by frequent revolutions, and thus incapable of regular and firm internal administration, has tended to embarrass occasionally our public intercourse by reason of wrongs which our citizens suffer at their hands, and which they are slow to redress.

Unfortunately, it is against the Republic of Mexico, with which it is our special desire to maintain a good understanding, that such complaints are most numerous; and although earnestly urged upon its attention, they have not as yet received the consideration which this Government had a right to expect. While reparation for past injuries has been withheld, others have been added. The political condition of that country, however, has been such as to demand forbearance on the part of the United States. I shall continue my efforts to procure for the wrongs of our citizens that redress which is indispensable to the continued friendly association of the two Republics.

The peculiar condition of affairs in Nicaragua in the early part of the present year rendered it important that this Government should have diplomatic relations with that State. Through its territory had been opened one of the principal thoroughfares across the isthmus connecting North and South America, on which a vast amount of property was transported and to which our citizens resorted in great numbers in passing between the Atlantic and Pacific coasts of the United States. The protection of both required that the existing power in that State should be regarded as a responsible Government, and its minister was accordingly received. But he remained here only a short time. Soon thereafter the political affairs of Nicaragua underwent unfavorable change and became involved in much uncertainty and confusion. Diplomatic representatives from two contending parties have been recently sent to this Government, but with the imperfect information possessed it was not possible to decide which was the Government de facto, and, awaiting further developments, I have refused to receive either.

Questions of the most serious nature are pending between the United States and the Republic of New Granada. The Government of that Republic undertook a year since to impose tonnage duties on foreign vessels in her ports, but the purpose was resisted by this Government as being contrary to existing treaty stipulations with the United States and to rights conferred by charter upon the Panama Railroad Company, and was accordingly refurbished at that time, it being admitted that our vessels were entitled to be exempt from tonnage duty in the free ports of Panama and Aspinwall. But the purpose has been recently revived on the part of New Granada by the enactment of a law to subject vessels visiting her ports to the tonnage duty of 40 cents per ton, and although the law has not been put in force, yet the right to enforce it is still asserted and may at any time be acted on by the Government of that Republic.

The Congress of New Granada has also enacted a law during the last year which levies a tax of more than $3 on every pound of mail matter transported across the Isthmus. The sum thus required to be paid on the mails of the United States would be nearly $2,000,000 annually in addition to the large sum payable by contract to the Panama Railroad Company. If the only objection to this exaction were the exorbitancy of its amount, it could not be submitted to by the United States.

The imposition of it, however, would obviously contravene our treaty with New Granada and infringe the contract of that Republic with the Panama Railroad Company. The law providing for this tax was by its terms to take effect on the 1st of September last, but the local authorities on the Isthmus have been induced to suspend its execution and to await further instructions on the subject from the Government of the Republic. I am not yet advised of the determination of that Government. If a measure so extraordinary in its character and so clearly contrary to treaty stipulations and the contract rights of the Panama Railroad Company, composed mostly of American citizens, should be persisted in, it will be the duty of the United States to resist its execution.

I regret exceedingly that occasion exists to invite your attention to a subject of still graver import in our relations with the Republic of New Granada. On the 15th day of April last a riotous assemblage of the inhabitants of Panama committed a violent and outrageous attack on the premises of the railroad company and the passengers and other persons in or near the same, involving the death of several citizens of the United States, the pillage of many others, and the destruction of a large amount of property belonging to the railroad company. I caused full investigation of that event to be made, and the result shows satisfactorily that complete responsibility for what occurred attaches to the Government of New Granada. I have therefore demanded of that Government that the perpetrators of the wrongs in question should be punished; that provision should be made for the families of citizens of the United States who were killed, with full indemnity for the property pillaged or destroyed.

The present condition of the Isthmus of Panama, in so far as regards the security of persons and property passing over it, requires serious consideration. Recent incidents tend to show that the local authorities can not be relied on to maintain the public peace of Panama, and there is just ground for apprehension that a portion of the inhabitants are meditating further outrages, without adequate measures for the security and protection of persons or property having been taken, either by the State of Panama or by the General Government of New Granada. Under the guaranties of treaty, citizens of the United States have, by the outlay of several million dollars, constructed a railroad across the Isthmus, and it has become the main route between our Atlantic and Pacific possessions, over which multitudes of our citizens and a vast amount of property are constantly passing; to the security and protection of all which and the continuance of the public advantages involved it is impossible for the Government of the United States to be indifferent.

I have deemed the danger of the recurrence of scenes of lawless violence in this quarter so imminent as to make it my duty to station a part of our naval force in the harbors of Panama and Aspinwall, in order to protect the persons and property of the citizens of the United States in those ports and to insure to them safe passage across the Isthmus. And it would, in my judgment, be unwise to withdraw the naval force now in those ports until, by the spontaneous action of the Republic of New Granada or otherwise, some adequate arrangement shall have been made for the protection and security of a line of interoceanic communication, so important at this time not to the United States only, but to all other maritime states, both of Europe and America.

Meanwhile negotiations have been instituted, by means of a special commission, to obtain from New Granada full indemnity for injuries sustained by our citizens on the Isthmus and satisfactory security for the general interests of the United States.

In addressing to you my last annual message the occasion seems to me an appropriate one to express my congratulations, in view of the peace, greatness, and felicity which the United States now possess and enjoy. To point you to the state of the various Departments of the Government and of all the great branches of the public service, civil and military, in order to speak of the intelligence and the integrity which pervades the whole, would be to indicate but imperfectly the administrative condition of the country and the beneficial effects of that on the general welfare. Nor would it suffice to say that the nation is actually at peace at home and abroad; that its industrial interests are prosperous; that the canvas of its mariners whitens every sea, and the plow of its husbandmen is marching steadily onward to the bloodless conquest of the continent; that cities and populous States are springing up, as if by enchantment, from the bosom of our Western wilds, and that the courageous energy of our people is making of these United States the great Republic of the world. These results have not been attained without passing through trials and perils, by experience of which, and thus only, nations can harden into manhood. Our forefathers were trained to the wisdom which conceived and the courage which achieved independence by the circumstances which surrounded them, and they were thus made capable of the creation of the Republic. It devolved on the next generation to consolidate the work of the Revolution, to deliver the country entirely from the influences of conflicting transatlantic partialities or antipathies which attached to our colonial and Revolutionary history, and to organize the practical operation of the constitutional and legal institutions of the Union. To us of this generation remains the not less noble task of maintaining and extending the national power. We have at length reached that stage of our country's career in which the dangers to be encountered and the exertions to be made are the incidents, not of weakness, but of strength. In foreign relations we have to attemper our power to the less happy condition of other Republics in America and to place ourselves in the calmness and conscious dignity of right by the side of the greatest and wealthiest of the Empires of Europe. In domestic relations we have to guard against the shock of the discontents, the ambitions, the interests, and the exuberant, and therefore sometimes irregular, impulses of opinion or of action which are the natural product of the present political elevation, the self-reliance, and the restless spirit of enterprise of the people of the United States.

I shall prepare to surrender the Executive trust to my successor and retire to private life with sentiments of profound gratitude to the good Providence which during the period of my Administration has vouchsafed to carry the country through many difficulties, domestic and foreign, and which enables me to contemplate the spectacle of amicable and respectful relations between ours and all other governments and the establishment of constitutional order and tranquillity throughout the Union.

FRANKLIN PIERCE

13

James Buchanan (1857–1861)

It was James Buchanan's misfortune to inhabit the White House when the nation was rapidly descending to a point of no return: America was spiraling downhill into a hellish war. Decades of sectional controversies provided explosive tinder ready to burst into flame. The North was chagrined by the Supreme Court's Dred Scott decision, decreeing that a slave was not a person but property. John Brown and his band had raided Harper's Ferry. And seven Southern states—Alabama, Florida, Georgia, Louisiana, Mississippi, South Carolina, and Texas—had seceded from the Union. Though open warfare had not yet broken out, the expanding Confederate States of America had successfully declared independence.

Even the economy was troubled. The failure of the Ohio Life Insurance Company of Cincinnati heralded the start of the Panic of 1857 that lasted until the start of the Civil War.

Because of the coming Civil War, Buchanan wondered whether he would be the last president of the United States of America. (Given his worry, it is interesting that our fifteenth president delivered no formal farewell address. But with states seceding, who exactly would the audience have been?) Nevertheless, his last annual message to Congress in some ways serves as a farewell. Its main theme, as with many last annual messages of the era, is the Constitution and constitutional principles. Even Madison is quoted. But in this message the stakes are clearly higher as the nation stands on the brink of war.

Fourth Annual Message
(written to the Congress)
December 3, 1860

Fellow-Citizens of the Senate and House of Representatives:

Throughout the year since our last meeting the country has been eminently prosperous in all its material interests. The general health has been excellent, our harvests have been abundant, and plenty smiles throughout the land. Our commerce and manufactures have been prosecuted with energy and industry, and have yielded fair and ample returns. In short, no nation in the tide of time has ever presented a spectacle of greater material prosperity than we have done until within a very recent period.

Why is it, then, that discontent now so extensively prevails, and the Union of the States, which is the source of all these blessings, is threatened with destruction?

The long-continued and intemperate interference of the Northern people with the question of slavery in the Southern States has at length produced its natural effects. The different sections of the Union are now arrayed against each other, and the time has arrived, so much dreaded by the Father of his Country, when hostile geographical parties have been formed.

I have long foreseen and often forewarned my countrymen of the now impending danger. This does not proceed solely from the claim on the part of Congress or the Territorial legislatures to exclude slavery from the Territories, nor from the efforts of different States to defeat the execution of the fugitive-slave law. All or any of these evils might have been endured by the South without danger to the Union (as others have been) in the hope that time and reflection might apply the remedy. The immediate peril arises not so much from these causes as from the fact that the incessant and violent agitation of the slavery question throughout the North for the last quarter of a century has at length produced its malign influence on the slaves and inspired them with vague notions of freedom. Hence a sense of security no longer exists around the family altar. This feeling of peace at home has given place to apprehensions of servile insurrections. Many a matron throughout the South retires at night in dread of what may befall herself and children before the morning. Should this apprehension of domestic danger, whether real or imaginary, extend and intensify itself until it shall pervade the masses of the Southern people, then disunion will become inevitable. Self-preservation is the first law of nature, and has been implanted in the heart of man by his Creator for the wisest purpose; and no political union, however fraught with blessings and benefits in all other respects, can long continue if the necessary consequence be to render the homes and the firesides of nearly half the parties to it habitually and hopelessly insecure. Sooner or later the bonds of such a union must be severed. It is my conviction that this fatal period has not yet arrived, and my prayer to God is that He would preserve the Constitution and the Union throughout all generations.

But let us take warning in time and remove the cause of danger. It can not be denied that for five and twenty years the agitation at the North against slavery has been incessant. In 1835 pictorial handbills and inflammatory appeals were circulated extensively throughout the South of a character to excite the passions of the slaves, and, in the language of General Jackson, "to stimulate them to insurrection and produce all the horrors of a servile war." This agitation has ever since been continued by the public press, by the proceedings of State and county conventions and by abolition sermons and lectures. The time of Congress has been occupied in violent speeches on this never-ending subject, and appeals, in pamphlet and other forms, indorsed by distinguished names, have been sent forth from this central point and spread broadcast over the Union.

How easy would it be for the American people to settle the slavery question forever and to restore peace and harmony to this distracted country! They, and they alone, can do it. All that is necessary to accomplish the object, and all for which the slave States have ever contended, is to be let alone and permitted to manage their domestic institutions in their own way. As sovereign States, they, and they alone, are responsible before God and the world for the slavery existing among them. For this the people of the North are not more responsible and have no more fight to interfere than with similar institutions in Russia or in Brazil.

Upon their good sense and patriotic forbearance I confess I still greatly rely. Without their aid it is beyond the power of any President, no matter what may be his own political proclivities, to restore peace and harmony among the States. Wisely limited and restrained as is his power under our Constitution and laws, he alone can accomplish but little for good or for evil on such a momentous question.

And this brings me to observe that the election of any one of our fellow-citizens to the office of President does not of itself afford just cause for dissolving the Union. This is more especially true if his election has been effected by a mere plurality, and not a majority of the people, and has resulted from transient and temporary causes, which may probably never again occur. In order to justify a resort to revolutionary resistance, the Federal Government must be guilty of "a deliberate, palpable, and dangerous exercise" of powers not granted by the Constitution. The late Presidential election, however, has been held in strict conformity with its express provisions. How, then, can the result justify a revolution to destroy this very Constitution? Reason, justice, a regard for the Constitution, all require that we shall wait for some overt and dangerous act on the part of the President-elect before resorting to such a remedy. It is said, however, that the antecedents of the President-elect have been sufficient to justify the fears of the South that he will attempt to invade their constitutional rights. But are such apprehensions of contingent danger in the future sufficient to justify the immediate destruction of the noblest system of government ever devised by mortals? From the very nature of his office and its high responsibilities he must necessarily be conservative. The stern duty of administering the vast and complicated concerns of this Government affords in itself a guaranty that he will not attempt any violation of a clear constitutional right.

After all, he is no more than the chief executive officer of the Government. His province is not to make but to execute the laws. And it is a remarkable fact in our history that, notwithstanding the repeated efforts of the antislavery party, no single act has ever passed Congress, unless we may possibly except the Missouri compromise, impairing in the slightest degree the rights of the South to their property in slaves; and it may also be observed, judging from present indications, that no probability exists of the passage of such an act by a majority of both Houses, either in the present or the next Congress. Surely under these circumstances we ought to be restrained from present action by the precept of Him who spake as man never spoke, that "sufficient unto the day is the evil thereof." The day of evil may never come unless we shall rashly bring it upon ourselves.

It is alleged as one cause for immediate secession that the Southern States are denied equal rights with the other States in the common Territories. But by what authority are these denied? Not by Congress, which has never passed, and I believe never will pass, any act to exclude slavery from these Territories; and certainly not by the Supreme Court, which has solemnly decided that slaves are property, and, like all other property, their owners have a right to take them into the common Territories and hold them there under the protection of the Constitution.

So far then, as Congress is concerned, the objection is not to anything they have already done, but to what they may do hereafter. It will surely be admitted that this apprehension of future danger is no good reason for an immediate dissolution of the Union. It is true that the Territorial legislature of Kansas, on the 23d February, 1860, passed in great haste an act over the veto of the governor declaring that slavery "is and shall be forever prohibited in this Territory." Such an act, however, plainly violating the rights of property secured by the Constitution, will surely be declared void by the judiciary whenever it shall be presented in a legal form.

Only three days after my inauguration the Supreme Court of the United States solemnly adjudged that this power did not exist in a Territorial legislature. Yet such has been the factious temper of the times that the correctness of this decision has been extensively impugned before the people, and the question has given rise to angry political conflicts throughout the country. Those who have appealed from this judgment of our highest constitutional tribunal to popular assemblies would, if they could, invest a Territorial legislature with power to annul the sacred rights of property. This power Congress is expressly forbidden by the Federal Constitution to exercise. Every State legislature in the Union is forbidden by its own constitution to exercise it. It can not be exercised in any State except by the people in their highest sovereign capacity, when framing or amending their State constitution. In like manner it can only be exercised by the people of a Territory represented in a convention of delegates for the purpose of framing a constitution preparatory to admission as a State into the Union. Then, and not until then, are they invested with power to decide the question whether slavery shall or shall not exist within their limits. This is an act of sovereign authority, and not of subordinate Territorial legislation. Were it otherwise, then indeed would the equality of the States in the Territories be destroyed, and the rights of property in slaves would depend not upon the guaranties of the Constitution, but upon the shifting majorities of an irresponsible Territorial legislature. Such a doctrine, from its intrinsic unsoundness, can not long influence any considerable portion of our people, much less can it afford a good reason for a dissolution of the Union.

The most palpable violations of constitutional duty which have yet been committed consist in the acts of different State legislatures to defeat the execution of the fugitive-slave law. It ought to be remembered, however, that for these acts neither Congress nor any President can justly be held responsible. Having been passed in violation of the Federal Constitution, they are therefore null and void. All the courts, both State and national, before whom the question has arisen have from the beginning declared the fugitive-slave law to be constitutional. The single exception is that of a State court in Wisconsin, and this has not only been reversed by the proper appellate tribunal, but has met with such universal reprobation that there can be no danger from it as a precedent. The validity of this law has been established over and over again by the Supreme Court of the United States with perfect unanimity. It is rounded upon an express provision of the Constitution, requiring that fugitive slaves who escape from service in one State to another shall be "delivered up" to their masters. Without this provision it is a well-known historical fact that the Constitution itself could never have been adopted by the Convention. In one form or other, under the acts of 1793 and 1850, both being substantially the same, the fugitive-slave law has been the law of the land from the days of Washington until the present moment. Here, then, a clear case is presented in which it will be the duty of the next President, as it has been my own, to act with vigor in executing this supreme law against the conflicting enactments of State legislatures. Should he fail in the performance of this high duty, he will then have manifested a disregard of the Constitution and laws, to the great injury of the people of nearly one-half of the States of the Union. But are we to presume in advance that he will thus violate his duty? This would be at war with every principle of justice and of Christian charity. Let us wait for the overt act. The fugitive-slave law has been carried into execution in every contested case since the commencement of the present Administration, though often, it is to be regretted, with great loss and inconvenience to the master and with considerable expense to the Government. Let us trust that the State legislatures will repeal their unconstitutional and obnoxious enactments. Unless this shall be done without unnecessary delay, it is impossible for any human power to save the Union.

The Southern States, standing on the basis of the Constitution, have a right to demand this act of justice from the States of the North. Should it be refused, then the Constitution, to which all the States are parties, will have been willfully violated by one portion of them in a provision essential to the domestic security and happiness of the remainder. In that event the injured States, after having first used all peaceful and constitutional means to obtain redress, would be justified in revolutionary resistance to the Government of the Union.

I have purposely confined my remarks to revolutionary resistance, because it has been claimed within the last few years that any State, whenever this shall be its sovereign will and pleasure, may secede from the Union in accordance with the Constitution and without any violation of the constitutional rights of the other members of the Confederacy; that as each became parties to the Union by the vote of its own people assembled in convention, so any one of them may retire from the Union in a similar manner by the vote of such a convention.

In order to justify secession as a constitutional remedy, it must be on the principle that the Federal Government is a mere voluntary association of States, to be dissolved at pleasure by any one of the contracting parties. If this be so, the Confederacy is a rope of sand, to be penetrated and dissolved by the first adverse wave of public opinion in any of the States. In this manner our thirty-three States may resolve themselves into as many petty, jarring, and hostile republics, each one retiring from the Union without responsibility whenever any sudden excitement might impel them to such a course. By this process a Union might be entirely broken into fragments in a few weeks which cost our forefathers many years of toil, privation, and blood to establish.

Such a principle is wholly inconsistent with the history as well as the character of the Federal Constitution. After it was framed with the greatest deliberation and care it was submitted to conventions of the people of the several States for ratification. Its provisions were discussed at length in these bodies, composed of the first men of the country. Its opponents contended that it conferred powers upon the Federal Government dangerous to the rights of the States, whilst its advocates maintained that under a fair construction of the instrument there was no foundation for such apprehensions. In that mighty struggle between the first intellects of this or any other country it never occurred to any individual, either among its opponents or advocates, to assert or even to intimate that their efforts were all vain labor, because the moment that any State felt herself aggrieved she might secede from the Union. What a crushing argument would this have proved against those who dreaded that the rights of the States would be endangered by the Constitution! The truth is that it was not until many years after the origin of the Federal Government that such a proposition was first advanced. It was then met and refuted by the conclusive arguments of General Jackson, who in his message of the 16th of January, 1833, transmitting the nullifying ordinance of South Carolina to Congress, employs the following language:

"The right of the people of a single State to absolve themselves at will and without the consent of the other States from their most solemn obligations, and hazard the liberties and happiness of the millions composing this Union, can not be acknowledged. Such authority is believed to be utterly repugnant both to the principles upon which the General Government is constituted and to the objects which it is expressly formed to attain."

It is not pretended that any clause in the Constitution gives countenance to such a theory. It is altogether rounded upon inference; not from any language contained in the instrument itself, but from the sovereign character of the several States by which it was ratified. But is it beyond the power of a State, like an individual, to yield a portion of its sovereign rights to secure the remainder? In the language of Mr. Madison, who has been called the father of the Constitution—

"It was formed by the States; that is, by the people in each of the States acting in their highest sovereign capacity, and formed, consequently, by the same authority which formed the State constitutions. . . . Nor is the Government of the United States, created by the Constitution, less a government, in the strict sense of the term, within the sphere of its powers than the governments created by the constitutions of the States are within their several spheres. It is, like them, organized into legislative, executive, and judiciary departments. It operates, like them directly on persons and things, and, like them, it has at command a physical force for executing the powers committed to it."

It was intended to be perpetual, and not to be annulled at the pleasure of any one of the contracting parties. The old Articles of Confederation were entitled "Articles of Confederation and Perpetual Union between the States," and by the thirteenth article it is expressly declared that "the articles of this Confederation shall be inviolably observed by every State, and the Union shall be perpetual." The preamble to the Constitution of the United States, having express reference to the Articles of Confederation, recites that it was established "in order to form a more perfect union." And yet it is contended that this "more perfect union" does not include the essential attribute of perpetuity.

But that the Union was designed to be perpetual appears conclusively from the nature and extent of the powers conferred by the Constitution on the Federal Government. These powers embrace the very highest attributes of national sovereignty. They place both the sword and the purse under its control. Congress has power to make war and to make peace, to raise and support armies and navies, and to conclude treaties with foreign governments. It is invested with the power to coin money and to regulate the value thereof, and to regulate commerce with foreign nations and among the several States. It is not necessary to enumerate the other high powers which have been conferred upon the Federal Government. In order to carry the enumerated powers into effect, Congress possesses the exclusive right to lay and collect duties on imports, and, in common with the States, to lay and collect all other taxes.

But the Constitution has not only conferred these high powers upon Congress, but it has adopted effectual means to restrain the States from interfering with their exercise. For that purpose it has in strong prohibitory language expressly declared that—

"No State shall enter into any treaty, alliance, or confederation; grant letters of marque and reprisal; coin money; emit bills of credit; make anything but gold and silver coin a tender in payment of debts; pass any bill of attainder, *ex post facto* law, or law impairing the obligation of contracts."

Moreover—

"No State shall without the consent of the Congress lay any imposts or duties on imports or exports, except what may be absolutely necessary for executing its inspection laws."

And if they exceed this amount the excess shall belong, to the United States. And—

"No State shall without the consent of Congress lay any duty of tonnage, keep troops or ships of war in time of peace, enter into any agreement or compact with another State or with a foreign power, or engage in war, unless actually invaded or in such imminent danger as will not admit of delay."

In order still further to secure the uninterrupted exercise of these high powers against State interposition, it is provided that—

"This Constitution and the laws of the United States which shall be made in pursuance thereof, and all treaties made or which shall be made under the authority of the United States, shall be the supreme law of the land, and the judges in every State shall be bound thereby, anything in the constitution or laws of any State to the contrary notwithstanding."

The solemn sanction of religion has been superadded to the obligations of official duty, and all Senators and Representatives of the United States, all members of State legislatures, and all executive and judicial officers, "both of the United States and of the several States, shall be bound by oath or affirmation to support this Constitution."

In order to carry into effect these powers, the Constitution has established a perfect Government in all its forms—legislative, executive, and judicial; and this Government to the extent of its powers acts directly upon the individual citizens of every State, and executes its own decrees by the agency of its own officers. In this respect it differs entirely from the Government under the old Confederation, which was confined to making requisitions on the States in their sovereign character. This left it in the discretion of each whether to obey or to refuse, and they often declined to comply with such requisitions. It thus became necessary for the purpose of removing this barrier and "in order to form a more perfect union" to establish a Government which could act directly upon the people and execute its own laws without the intermediate agency of the States. This has been accomplished by the Constitution of the United States. In short, the Government created by the Constitution, and deriving its authority from the sovereign people of each of the several States, has precisely the same right to exercise its power over the people of all these States in in the enumerated cases that each one of them possesses over subjects not delegated to the United States, but "reserved to the States respectively or to the people."

To the extent of the delegated powers the Constitution of the United States is as much a part of the constitution of each State and is as binding upon its people as though it had been textually inserted therein.

This Government, therefore, is a great and powerful Government, invested with all the attributes of sovereignty over the special subjects to which its authority extends. Its framers never intended to implant in its bosom the seeds of its own destruction, nor were they at its creation guilty of the absurdity of providing for its own dissolution. It was not intended by its framers to be the baseless fabric of a vision, which at the touch of the enchanter would vanish into thin air, but a substantial and mighty fabric, capable of resisting the slow decay of time and of defying the storms of ages. Indeed, well may the jealous patriots of that day have indulged fears that a Government of such high powers might violate the reserved rights of the States, and wisely did they adopt the rule of a strict construction of these powers to prevent the danger. But they did not fear, nor had they any reason to imagine, that the Constitution would ever be so interpreted as to enable any State by her own act, and without the consent of her sister States, to discharge her people from all or any of their federal obligations.

It may be asked, then, Are the people of the States without redress against the tyranny and oppression of the Federal Government? By no means. The right of resistance on the part of the governed against the oppression of their governments can not be denied. It exists independently of all constitutions, and has been exercised at all periods of the world's history. Under it old governments have been destroyed and new ones have taken their place. It is embodied in strong and express language in our own Declaration of Independence. But the distinction must ever be observed that this is revolution against an established government, and not a voluntary secession from it by virtue of an inherent constitutional right. In short, let us look the danger fairly in the face. Secession is neither more nor less than revolution. It may or it may not be a justifiable revolution, but still it is revolution.

What, in the meantime, is the responsibility and true position of the Executive? He is bound by solemn oath, before God and the country, "to take care that the laws be faithfully executed," and from this obligation he can not be absolved by any human power. But what if the performance of this duty, in whole or in part, has been rendered impracticable by events over which he could have exercised no control? Such at the present moment is the case throughout the State of South Carolina so far as the laws of the United States to secure the administration of justice by means of the Federal judiciary are concerned. All the Federal officers within its limits through whose agency alone these laws can be carried into execution have already resigned. We no longer have a district judge, a district attorney, or a marshal in South Carolina. In fact, the whole machinery of the Federal Government necessary for the distribution of remedial justice among the people has been demolished, and it would be difficult, if not impossible, to replace it.

The only acts of Congress on the statute book bearing upon this subject are those of February 28, 1795, and March 3, 1807. These authorize the President, after he shall have ascertained that the marshal, with his *posse comitatus*, is unable to execute civil or criminal process in any particular case, to call forth the militia and employ the Army and Navy to aid him in performing this service, having first by proclamation commanded the insurgents "to disperse and retire peaceably to their respective abodes within a limited time." This duty can not by possibility be performed in a State where no judicial authority exists to issue process, and where there is no marshal to execute it, and where, even if there were such an officer, the entire population would constitute one solid combination to resist him.

The bare enumeration of these provisions proves how inadequate they are without further legislation to overcome a united opposition in a single State, not to speak of other States who may place themselves in a similar attitude. Congress alone has power to decide whether the present laws can or can not be amended so as to carry out more effectually the objects of the Constitution.

The same insuperable obstacles do not lie in the way of executing the laws for the collection of the customs. The revenue still continues to be collected as heretofore at the custom-house in Charleston, and should the collector unfortunately resign a successor may be appointed to perform this duty.

Then, in regard to the property of the United States in South Carolina. This has been purchased for a fair equivalent, "by the consent of the legislature of the State," "for the erection of forts, magazines, arsenals," etc., and over these the authority "to exercise exclusive legislation" has been expressly granted by the Constitution to Congress. It is not believed that any attempt will be made to expel the United States from this property by force; but if in this I should prove to be mistaken, the officer in command of the forts has received orders to act strictly on the defensive. In such a contingency the responsibility for consequences would rightfully rest upon the heads of the assailants.

Apart from the execution of the laws, so far as this may be practicable, the Executive has no authority to decide what shall be the relations between the Federal Government and South Carolina. He has been invested with no such discretion. He possesses no power to change the relations heretofore existing between them, much less to acknowledge the independence of that State. This would be to invest a mere executive officer with the power of recognizing the dissolution of the confederacy among our thirty-three sovereign States. It bears no resemblance to the recognition of a foreign de facto government, involving no such responsibility. Any attempt to do this would, on his part, be a naked act of usurpation. It is therefore my duty to submit to Congress the whole question in all its beatings. The course of events is so rapidly hastening forward that the emergency may soon arise when you may be called upon to decide the momentous question whether you possess the power by force of arms to compel a State to remain in the Union. I should feel myself recreant to my duty were I not to express an opinion on this important subject.

The question fairly stated is, Has the Constitution delegated to Congress the power to coerce a State into submission which is attempting to withdraw or has actually withdrawn from the Confederacy? If answered in the affirmative, it must be on the principle that the power has been conferred upon Congress to declare and to make war against a State. After much serious reflection I have arrived at the conclusion that no such power has been delegated to Congress or to any other department of the Federal Government. It is manifest upon an inspection of the Constitution that this is not among the specific and enumerated powers granted to Congress, and it is equally apparent that its exercise is not "necessary and proper for carrying into execution" any one of these powers. So far from this power having been delegated to Congress, it was expressly refused by the Convention which framed the Constitution.

It appears from the proceedings of that body that on the 31st May, 1787, the clause "authorizing an exertion of the force of the whole against a delinquent State" came up for consideration. Mr. Madison opposed it in a brief but powerful speech, from which I shall extract but a single sentence. He observed:

"The use of force against a State would look more like a declaration of war than an infliction of punishment, and would probably be considered by the party attacked as a dissolution of all previous compacts by which it might be bound."

Upon his motion the clause was unanimously postponed, and was never, I believe, again presented. Soon afterwards, on the 8th June, 1787, when incidentally adverting to the subject, he said: "Any government for the United States formed on the supposed practicability of using force against the unconstitutional proceedings of the States would prove as visionary and fallacious as the government of Congress," evidently meaning the then existing Congress of the old Confederation.

Without descending to particulars, it may be safely asserted that the power to make war against a State is at variance with the whole spirit and intent of the Constitution. Suppose such a war should result in the conquest of a State; how are we to govern it afterwards? Shall we hold it as a province and govern it by despotic power? In the nature of things, we could not by physical force control the will of the people and compel them to elect Senators and Representatives to Congress and to perform all the other duties depending upon their own volition and required from the free citizens of a free State as a constituent member of the Confederacy.

But if we possessed this power, would it be wise to exercise it under existing circumstances? The object would doubtless be to preserve the Union. War would not only present the most effectual means of destroying it, but would vanish all hope of its peaceable reconstruction. Besides, in the fraternal conflict a vast amount of blood and treasure would be expended, rendering future reconciliation between the States impossible. In the meantime, who can foretell what would be the sufferings and privations of the people during its existence?

The fact is that our Union rests upon public opinion, and can never be cemented by the blood of its citizens shed in civil war. If it can not live in the affections of the people, it must one day perish. Congress possesses many means of preserving it by conciliation, but the sword was not placed in their hand to preserve it by force.

But may I be permitted solemnly to invoke my countrymen to pause and deliberate before they determine to destroy this the grandest temple which has ever been dedicated to human freedom since the world began? It has been consecrated by the blood of our fathers, by the glories of the past, and by the hopes of the future. The Union has already made us the most prosperous, and ere long will, if preserved, render us the most powerful, nation on the face of the earth. In every foreign region of the globe the title of American citizen is held in the highest respect, and when pronounced in a foreign land it causes the hearts of our countrymen to swell with honest pride. Surely when we reach the brink of the yawning abyss we shall recoil with horror from the last fatal plunge.

By such a dread catastrophe the hopes of the friends of freedom throughout the world would be destroyed, and a long night of leaden despotism would enshroud the nations. Our example for more than eighty years would not only be lost, but it would be quoted as a conclusive proof that man is unfit for self-government.

It is not every wrong—nay, it is not every grievous wrong—which can justify a resort to such a fearful alternative. This ought to be the last desperate remedy of a despairing people, after every other constitutional means of conciliation had been exhausted. We should reflect that under this free Government there is an incessant ebb and flow in public opinion. The slavery question, like everything human, will have its day. I firmly believe that it has reached and passed the culminating point. But if in the midst of the existing excitement the Union shall perish, the evil may then become irreparable.

Congress can contribute much to avert it by proposing and recommending to the legislatures of the several States the remedy for existing evils which the Constitution has itself provided for its own preservation. This has been tried at different critical periods of our history, and always with eminent success. It is to be found in the fifth article, providing for its own amendment. Under this article amendments have been proposed by two-thirds of both Houses of Congress, and have been "ratified by the legislatures of three-fourths of the several States," and have consequently become parts of the Constitution. To this process the country is indebted for the clause prohibiting Congress from passing any law respecting an establishment of religion or abridging the freedom of speech or of the press or of the right of petition. To this we are also indebted for the bill of rights which secures the people against any abuse of power by the Federal Government. Such were the apprehensions justly entertained by the friends of State rights at that period as to have rendered it extremely doubtful whether the Constitution could have long survived without those amendments.

Again the Constitution was amended by the same process, after the election of President Jefferson by the House of Representatives, in February, 1803. This amendment was rendered necessary to prevent a recurrence of the dangers which had seriously threatened the existence of the Government during the pendency of that election. The article for its own amendment was intended to secure the amicable adjustment of conflicting constitutional questions like the present which might arise between the governments of the States and that of the United States. This appears from contemporaneous history. In this connection I shall merely call attention to a few sentences in Mr. Madison's justly celebrated report, in 1799, to the legislature of Virginia. In this he ably and conclusively defended the resolutions of the preceding legislature against the strictures of several other State legislatures. These were mainly rounded upon the protest of the Virginia legislature against the "alien and sedition acts," as "palpable and alarming infractions of the Constitution." In pointing out the peaceful and constitutional remedies—and he referred to none other—to which the States were authorized to resort on such occasions, he concludes by saying that—

"The legislatures of the States might have made a direct representation to Congress with a view to obtain a rescinding of the two offensive acts, or they might have represented to their respective Senators in Congress their wish that two-thirds thereof would propose an explanatory amendment to the Constitution; or two-thirds of themselves, if such had been their option, might by an application to Congress have obtained a convention for the same object."

This is the very course which I earnestly recommend in order to obtain an "explanatory amendment" of the Constitution on the subject of slavery. This might originate with Congress or the State legislatures, as may be deemed most advisable to attain the object. The explanatory amendment might be confined to the final settlement of the true construction of the Constitution on three special points:

1. An express recognition of the right of property in slaves in the States where it now exists or may hereafter exist.
2. The duty of protecting this right in all the common Territories throughout their Territorial existence, and until they shall be admitted as States into the Union, with or without slavery, as their constitutions may prescribe.

3. A like recognition of the right of the master to have his slave who has escaped from one State to another restored and "delivered up" to him, and of the validity of the fugitive-slave law enacted for this purpose, together with a declaration that all State laws impairing or defeating this right are violations of the Constitution, and are consequently null and void. It may be objected that this construction of the Constitution has already been settled by the Supreme Court of the United States, and what more ought to be required? The answer is that a very large proportion of the people of the United States still contest the correctness of this decision, and never will cease from agitation and admit its binding force until clearly established by the people of the several States in their sovereign character. Such an explanatory amendment would, it is believed, forever terminate the existing dissensions, and restore peace and harmony among the States.

It ought not to be doubted that such an appeal to the arbitrament established by the Constitution itself would be received with favor by all the States of the Confederacy. In any event, it ought to be tried in a spirit of conciliation before any of these States shall separate themselves from the Union.

When I entered upon the duties of the Presidential office, the aspect neither of our foreign nor domestic affairs was at all satisfactory. We were involved in dangerous complications with several nations, and two of our Territories were in a state of revolution against the Government. A restoration of the African slave trade had numerous and powerful advocates. Unlawful military expeditions were countenanced by many of our citizens, and were suffered, in defiance of the efforts of the Government, to escape from our shores for the purpose of making war upon the offending people of neighboring republics with whom we were at peace. In addition to these and other difficulties, we experienced a revulsion in monetary affairs soon after my advent to power of unexampled severity and of ruinous consequences to all the great interests of the country. When we take a retrospect of what was then our condition and contrast this with its material prosperity at the time of the late Presidential election, we have abundant reason to return our grateful thanks to that merciful Providence which has never forsaken us as a nation in all our past trials.

Our relations with Great Britain are of the most friendly character. Since the commencement of my Administration the two dangerous questions arising from the Clayton and Bulwer treaty and from the right of search claimed by the British Government have been amicably and honorably adjusted.

The discordant constructions of the Clayton and Bulwer treaty between the two Governments, which at different periods of the discussion bore a threatening aspect, have resulted in a final settlement entirely satisfactory to this Government. In my last annual message I informed Congress that the British Government had not then "completed treaty arrangements with the Republics of Honduras and Nicaragua in pursuance of the understanding between the two Governments. It is, nevertheless, confidently expected that this good work will ere long be accomplished." This confident expectation has since been fulfilled. Her Britannic Majesty concluded a treaty with Honduras on the 28th November, 1859, and with Nicaragua on the 28th August, 1860, relinquishing the Mosquito protectorate. Besides, by the former the Bay Islands are recognized as a part of the Republic of Honduras. It may be observed that the stipulations of these treaties conform in every "important particular to the amendments adopted by the Senate of the United States to the treaty concluded at London on the 17th October, 1856, between the two Governments. It will be recollected that this treaty was rejected by the British Government because of its objection to the just and important amendment of the Senate to the article relating to Ruatan and the other islands in the Bay of Honduras.

It must be a source of sincere satisfaction to all classes of our fellow-citizens, and especially to those engaged in foreign commerce, that the claim on the part of Great Britain forcibly to visit and search American merchant vessels on the high seas in time of peace has been abandoned. This was by far the most dangerous question to the peace of the two countries which has existed since the War of 1812. Whilst it remained open they might at any moment have been precipitated into a war. This was rendered manifest by the exasperated state of public feeling throughout our entire country produced by the forcible search of American merchant vessels by British cruisers on the coast of Cuba in the spring of 1858. The American people hailed with general acclaim the orders of the Secretary of the Navy to our naval force in the Gulf of Mexico "to protect all vessels of the United States on the high seas from search or detention by the vessels of war of any other nation." These orders might have produced an immediate collision between the naval forces of the two countries. This was most fortunately prevented by an appeal to the justice of Great Britain and to the law of nations as expounded by her own most eminent jurists.

The only question of any importance which still remains open is the disputed title between the two Governments to the island of San Juan, in the vicinity of Washington Territory. As this question is still under negotiation, it is not deemed advisable at the present moment to make any other allusion to the subject.

The recent visit of the Prince of Wales, in a private character, to the people of this country has proved to be a most auspicious event. In its consequences it can not fail to increase the kindred and kindly feelings which I trust may ever actuate the Government and people of both countries in their political and social intercourse with each other.

With France, our ancient and powerful ally, our relations continue to be of the most friendly character. A decision has recently been made by a French judicial tribunal, with the approbation of the Imperial Government, which can not fail to foster the sentiments of mutual regard that have so long existed between the two countries. Under the French law no person can serve in the armies of France unless he be a French citizen. The law of France recognizing the natural right of expatriation, it follows as a necessary consequence that a Frenchman by the fact of having become a citizen of the United States has changed his allegiance and has lost his native character. He can not therefore be compelled to serve in the French armies in case he should return to his native country. These principles were announced in 1852 by the French minister of war and in two late cases have been confirmed by the French judiciary. In these, two natives of France have been discharged from the French army because they had become American citizens. To employ the language of our present minister to France, who has rendered good service on this occasion. "I do not think our French naturalized fellow-citizens will hereafter experience much annoyance on this subject."

* * *

Our relations with Mexico remain in a most unsatisfactory condition. In my last two annual messages I discussed extensively the subject of these relations, and do not now propose to repeat at length the facts and arguments then presented. They proved conclusively that our citizens residing in Mexico and our merchants trading thereto had suffered a series of wrongs and outrages such as we have never patiently borne from any other nation. For these our successive ministers, invoking the faith of treaties, had in the name of their country persistently demanded redress and indemnification, but without the slightest effect. Indeed, so confident had the Mexican authorities become of our patient endurance that they universally believed they might commit these outrages upon American citizens with absolute impunity. Thus wrote our minister in 1856, and expressed the opinion that "nothing but a manifestation of the power of the Government and of its purpose to punish these wrongs will avail."

Afterwards, in 1857, came the adoption of a new constitution for Mexico, the election of a President and Congress under its provisions, and the inauguration of the President. Within one short month, however, this President was expelled from the capital by a rebellion in the army, and the supreme power of the Republic was assigned to General Zuloaga. This usurper was in his turn soon compelled to retire and give place to General Miramon.

Under the constitution which had thus been adopted Señor Juarez, as chief justice of the supreme court, became the lawful President of the Republic, and it was for the maintenance of the constitution and his authority derived from it that the civil war commenced and still continues to be prosecuted.

Throughout the year 1858 the constitutional party grew stronger and stronger. In the previous history of Mexico a successful military revolution at the capital had almost universally been the signal for submission throughout the Republic. Not so on the present occasion. A majority of the citizens persistently sustained the constitutional Government. When this was recognized, in April, 1859, by the Government of the United States, its authority extended over a large majority of the Mexican States and people, including Vera Cruz and all the other important seaports of the Republic. From that period our commerce with Mexico began to revive, and the constitutional Government has afforded it all the protection in its power.

Meanwhile the Government of Miramon still held sway at the capital and over the surrounding country, and continued its outrages against the few American citizens who still had the courage to remain within its power. To cap the climax, after the battle of Tacubaya, in April, 1859, General Marquez ordered three citizens of the United States, two of them physicians, to be seized in the hospital at that place, taken out and shot, without crime and without trial. This was done, notwithstanding our unfortunate countrymen were at the moment engaged in the holy cause of affording relief to the soldiers of both parties who had been wounded in the battle, without making any distinction between them.

The time had arrived, in my opinion, when this Government was bound to exert its power to avenge and redress the wrongs of our citizens and to afford them protection in Mexico. The interposing obstacle was that the portion of the country under the sway of Miramon could not be reached without passing over territory under the jurisdiction of the constitutional Government. Under these circumstances I deemed it my duty to recommend to Congress in my last annual message the employment of a sufficient military force to penetrate into the interior, where the Government of Miramon was to be found, with or, if need be, without the consent of the Juarez Government, though it was not doubted that this consent could be obtained. Never have I had a clearer conviction on any subject than of the justice as well as wisdom of such a policy. No other alternative was left except the entire abandonment of our fellow-citizens who had gone to Mexico under the faith of treaties to the systematic injustice, cruelty, and oppression of Miramon's Government. Besides, it is almost certain that the simple authority to employ this force would of itself have accomplished all our objects without striking a single blow. The constitutional Government would then ere this have been established at the City of Mexico, and would have been ready and willing to the extent of its ability to do us justice.

In addition—and I deem this a most important consideration—European Governments would have been deprived of all pretext to interfere in the territorial and domestic concerns of Mexico. We should thus have been relieved from the obligation of resisting, even by force should this become necessary, any attempt by these Governments to deprive our neighboring Republic of portions of her territory—a duty from which we could not shrink without abandoning the traditional and established policy of the American people. I am happy to observe that, firmly relying upon the justice and good faith of these Governments, there is no present danger that such a contingency will happen.

Having discovered that my recommendations would not be sustained by Congress, the next alternative was to accomplish in some degree, if possible, the same objects by treaty stipulations with the constitutional Government. Such treaties were accordingly concluded by our late able and excellent minister to Mexico, and on the 4th of January last were submitted to the Senate for ratification. As these have not yet received the final action of that body, it would be improper for me to present a detailed statement of their provisions. Still, I may be permitted to express the opinion in advance that they are calculated to promote the agricultural, manufacturing, and commercial interests of the country and to secure our just influence with an adjoining Republic as to whose fortunes and fate we can never feel indifferent, whilst at the same time they provide for the payment of a considerable amount toward the satisfaction of the claims of our injured fellow-citizens.

At the period of my inauguration I was confronted in Kansas by a revolutionary government existing under what is called the "Topeka constitution." Its avowed object was to subdue the Territorial government by force and to inaugurate what was called the "Topeka government" in its stead. To accomplish this object an extensive military organization was formed, and its command intrusted to the most violent revolutionary leaders. Under these circumstances it became my imperative duty to exert the whole constitutional power of the Executive to prevent the flames of civil war from again raging in Kansas, which in the excited state of the public mind, both North and South, might have extended into the neighboring States. The hostile parties in Kansas had been inflamed against each other by emissaries both from the North and the South to a degree of malignity without parallel in our history. To prevent actual collision and to assist the civil magistrates in enforcing the laws, a strong detachment of the Army was stationed in the Territory, ready to aid the marshal and his deputies when lawfully called upon as a posse comitatus in the execution of civil and criminal process. Still, the troubles in Kansas could not have been permanently settled without an election by the people.

The ballot box is the surest arbiter of disputes among freemen. Under this conviction every proper effort was employed to induce the hostile parties to vote at the election of delegates to frame a State constitution, and afterwards at the election to decide whether Kansas should be a slave or free State.

The insurgent party refused to vote at either, lest this might be considered a recognition on their part of the Territorial government established by Congress. A better spirit, however, seemed soon after to prevail, and the two parties met face to face at the third election, held on the first Monday of January, 1858, for members of the legislature and State officers under the Lecompton constitution. The result was the triumph of the antislavery party at the polls. This decision of the ballot box proved clearly that this party were in the majority, and removed the danger of civil war. From that time we have heard little or nothing of the Topeka government, and all serious danger of revolutionary troubles in Kansas was then at an end.

The Lecompton constitution, which had been thus recognized at this State election by the votes of both political parties in Kansas, was transmitted to me with the request that I should present it to Congress. This I could not have refused to do without violating my clearest and strongest convictions of duty. The constitution and all the proceedings which preceded and followed its formation were fair and regular on their face. I then believed, and experience has proved, that the interests of the people of Kansas would have been best consulted by its admission as a State into the Union, especially as the majority within a brief period could have amended the constitution according to their will and pleasure. If fraud existed in all or any of these proceedings, it was not for the President but for Congress to investigate and determine the question of fraud and what ought to be its consequences. If at the first two elections the majority refused to vote, it can not be pretended that this refusal to exercise the elective franchise could invalidate an election fairly held under lawful authority, even if they had not subsequently voted at the third election. It is true that the whole constitution had not been submitted to the people, as I always desired; but the precedents are numerous of the admission of States into the Union without such submission. It would not comport with my present purpose to review the proceedings of Congress upon the Lecompton constitution. It is sufficient to observe that their final action has removed the last vestige of serious revolutionary troubles. The desperate band recently assembled under a notorious outlaw in the southern portion of the Territory to resist the execution of the laws and to plunder peaceful citizens will, I doubt not be speedily subdued and brought to justice.

Had I treated the Lecompton constitution as a nullity and refused to transmit it to Congress, it is not difficult to imagine, whilst recalling the position of the country at that moment, what would have been the disastrous consequences, both in and out of the Territory, from such a dereliction of duty on the part of the Executive.

Peace has also been restored within the Territory of Utah, which at the commencement of my Administration was in a state of open rebellion. This was the more dangerous, as the people, animated by a fanatical spirit and intrenched within their distant mountain fastnesses, might have made a long and formidable resistance. Cost what it might, it was necessary to bring them into subjection to the Constitution and the laws. Sound policy, therefore, as well as humanity, required that this object should if possible be accomplished without the effusion of blood. This could only be effected by sending a military force into the Territory sufficiently strong to convince the people that resistance would be hopeless, and at the same time to offer them a pardon for past offenses on condition of immediate submission to the Government. This policy was pursued with eminent success, and the only cause for regret is the heavy expenditure required to march a large detachment of the Army to that remote region and to furnish it subsistence.

Utah is now comparatively peaceful and quiet, and the military force has been withdrawn, except that portion of it necessary to keep the Indians in check and to protect the emigrant trains on their way to our Pacific possessions.

In my first annual message I promised to employ my best exertions in cooperation with Congress to reduce the expenditures of the Government within the limits of a wise and judicious economy. An overflowing Treasury had produced habits of prodigality and extravagance which could only be gradually corrected. The work required both time and patience. I applied myself diligently to this task from the beginning and was aided by the able and energetic efforts of the heads of the different Executive Departments. The result of our labors in this good cause did not appear in the sum total of our expenditures for the first two years, mainly in consequence of the extraordinary expenditure necessarily incurred in the Utah expedition and the very large amount of the contingent expenses of Congress during this period. These greatly exceeded the pay and mileage of the members.

*   *   *

It has been represented to me from sources which I deem reliable that the inhabitants in several portions of Kansas have been reduced nearly to a state of starvation on account of the almost total failure of their crops, whilst the harvests in every other portion of the country have been abundant. The prospect before them for the approaching winter is well calculated to enlist the sympathies of every heart. The destitution appears to be so general that it can not be relieved by private contributions, and they are in such indigent circumstances as to be unable to purchase the necessaries of life for themselves. I refer the subject to Congress. If any constitutional measure for their relief can be devised, I would recommend its adoption.

I cordially commend to your favorable regard the interests of the people of this District. They are eminently entitled to your consideration, especially since, unlike the people of the States, they can appeal to no government except that of the Union.

JAMES BUCHANAN

1 4

Abraham Lincoln (1861–1865)

Because Abraham Lincoln was murdered just six weeks into his second term—the nation's first assassinated president—the question of a presidential farewell address may seem an odd one. If anyone comments on a Lincoln farewell, it is most likely the president-elect's famous adieu to the people of Springfield, Illinois, on February, 11, 1861. That terse, 150-word statement, delivered on the eve of his fifty-second birthday, is one of the most beautiful farewell addresses in American letters. (See p. 11, note 20, for the full text of the farewell.)

An argument can be made, however, that Lincoln did in fact deliver a presidential farewell—though an unexpected one—in his Second Inaugural Address. This claim is supported by (1) Lincoln's words; (2) medical evidence that the president was gravely ill; (3) a historically corroborated dream-vision that made Lincoln think he would die in office; and (4) textual evidence from the Second Inaugural Address itself.

Lincoln spoke of himself as an "old man" even before he assumed the duties of the presidency.[1] Well before the sixteenth president was scheduled to deliver his second inaugural address, he sensed that he would not live to see the end of his second term.[2] Not that he assumed he would die at the hands of an assassin—he received numerous death threats but generally took them in stride. Rather, Lincoln was worried that he would die of overwork. In 1864, Lincoln conveyed to his friend Owen Lovejoy, "This war is eating my life out; I have a strong impression that I shall not live to see the end."[3] Some months later, at the second inaugural, many spectators observed how gaunt and exhausted the commander-in-chief looked, much older than his fifty-six years.

There is medical evidence that Lincoln was indeed dying. His frequent complaints of fatigue seem to have had an organic cause that was exacerbated by the burdens of the presidency. Based on contemporary accounts, medical doctors have speculated that Lincoln was gravely ill with Marfan syndrome, a connective tissue disorder that can distort a person's growth and lead to fatal heart and lung problems. The disease was identified and named in the late nineteenth century, after Lincoln died. This makes speculation dicey. And yet, the question could be addressed first of all on the basis of contemporary photographs and descriptions of Lincoln, suggesting that he had all the classic physiological markers of the disease. His feet were disproportionately large, and his arms disproportionately long compared to his height. His frame had little body fat. His skin was leathery and sallow. His head was elongated. His face was gaunt. His ears were large and set at a wide angle. The intermittent squint of the left eye suggests that he was hyperoptic. More, Lincoln was also in notoriously bad shape. His complaints of exhaustion worried many around him and suggest to doctors today that his heart was failing. Further circumstantial evidence comes from a man in Lincoln's lineage who was diagnosed with Marfan syndrome in 1960. All these factors provide circumstantial medical evidence that Lincoln was suffering from the disease.[4] The speculation will only end when nondestructive DNA tests can be developed and conducted on samples of Lincoln's tissue.

The claim that the Second Inaugural Address served as a farewell is further supported by one of Lincoln's famous dream-visions, the one in which he saw a double image of himself in the mirror. Circumspection must be brought to the historical analysis of dreams. History and psychotherapy do not readily mix, for the patient cannot be presently examined. And yet, Lincoln told his wife and several close advisors of a dream that clearly disturbed him.[5] As he told it, the dream took place during the campaign year 1860, in his home in Springfield. Feeling exhausted, he lay down on a couch. At some point he looked at the mirror in the room and gazed upon a double image of his face. One image was vivid and full of life; the other image ghostly and gray. Mary Todd Lincoln felt that it was an omen that Lincoln would live through his first term as president, but not complete the second. It apparently troubled Lincoln that he could not later reproduce the optical effect of that double image in the mirror.[6]

In addition to the subjective evidence provided by Lincoln himself (the dreams, complaints of extreme fatigue, and vocalized belief that he would die in office) and the objective evidence provided by medical analysis (the relative with Marfan syndrome and the symptoms of the disease he seemed to manifest), there is textual evidence in the second inaugural address that is suggestive of a farewell. The most remarkable aspect of the speech is the speculation on end things. Lincoln was not just looking forward to a better time for the nation, but also to God's ultimate judgment on the United States of America. Rhetorically the effect is heightened by biblical allusions and words connoting death or the last things—"this second appearing," "the expiration of four years," and "let us judge not, that we be not judged." No president so puzzled in public over God's ways in the affairs of humankind.

Second Inaugural Address
March 4, 1865

Fellow-Countrymen:

At this second appearing to take the oath of the Presidential office there is less occasion for an extended address than there was at the first. Then a statement somewhat in detail of a course to be pursued seemed fitting and proper. Now, at the expiration of four years, during which public declarations have been constantly called forth on every point and phase of the great contest which still absorbs the attention and engrosses the energies of the nation, little that is new could be presented. The progress of our arms, upon which all else chiefly depends, is as well known to the public as to myself, and it is, I trust, reasonably satisfactory and encouraging to all. With high hope for the future, no prediction in regard to it is ventured.

On the occasion corresponding to this four years ago all thoughts were anxiously directed to an impending civil war. All dreaded it, all sought to avert it. While the inaugural address was being delivered from this place, devoted altogether to *saving* the Union without war, insurgent agents were in the city seeking to *destroy* it without war—seeking to dissolve the Union and divide effects by negotiation. Both parties deprecated war, but one of them would *make* war rather than let the nation survive, and the other would *accept* war rather than let it perish, and the war came.

One-eighth of the whole population were colored slaves, not distributed generally over the Union, but localized in the southern part of it. These slaves constituted a peculiar and powerful interest. All knew that this interest was somehow the cause of the war. To strengthen, perpetuate, and extend this interest was the object for which the insurgents would rend the Union even by war, while the Government claimed no right to do more than to restrict the territorial enlargement of it. Neither party expected for the war the magnitude or the duration which it has already attained. Neither anticipated that the *cause* of the conflict might cease with or even before the conflict itself should cease. Each looked for an easier triumph, and a result less fundamental and astounding. Both read the same Bible and pray to the same God, and each invokes His aid against the other. It may seem strange that any men should dare to ask a just God's assistance in wringing their bread from the sweat of other men's faces, but let us judge not, that we be not judged. The prayers of both could not be answered. That of neither has been answered fully. The Almighty has His own purposes. "Woe unto the world because of offenses; for it must needs be that offenses come, but woe to that man by whom the offense cometh." If we shall suppose that American slavery is one of those offenses which, in the providence of God, must needs come, but which, having continued through His appointed time, He now wills to remove, and that He gives to both North and South this terrible war as the woe due to those by whom the offense came, shall we discern therein any departure from those divine attributes which the believers in a living God always ascribe to Him? Fondly do we hope, fervently do we pray, that this mighty scourge of war may speedily pass away. Yet, if God wills that it continue until all the wealth piled by the bondsman's two hundred and fifty years of unrequited toil shall be sunk, and until every drop of blood drawn with the lash shall be paid by another drawn with the sword, as was said three thousand years ago, so still it must be said "the judgments of the Lord are true and righteous altogether."

With malice toward none, with charity for all, with firmness in the right as God gives us to see the right, let us strive on to finish the work we are in, to bind up the nation's wounds, to care for him who shall have borne the battle and for his widow and his orphan, to do all which may achieve and cherish a just and lasting peace among ourselves and with all nations.

MARCH 4, 1865.

Notes

1. In his farewell to the people of Springfield, Illinois, Lincoln stated: "Here I have lived a quarter of a century, and have passed from a young to an old man" (Source: Library of Congress).

2. For Lincoln's obsession with his mortality, see Robert V. Bruce, "The Riddle of Death," in *The Lincoln Enigma: The Changing Faces of an American Icon*, ed. Babor Boritt (Oxford: Oxford University Press, 2001), 130–45, esp. 136–37. See also Dwight Anderson, *Abraham Lincoln: The Quest for Immortality* (New York: Knopf, 1982).

3. Lovejoy quoted in Allen C. Guelzo, *Abraham Lincoln: Redeemer President* (Grand Rapids, MI: Eerdmans, 1999), 428.

4. See, for example, Harold Schwartz, "Abraham Lincoln and the Marfan Syndrome," *Journal of the American Medical Association* 187 (February 15, 1964): 473–79; Harold Schwartz, "Abraham Lincoln and Cardiac Decompensation: A Preliminary Report," *Western Journal of Medicine* 128 (February 1978): 174–77; and V. A. McKusick, "Abraham Lincoln and Marfan Syndrome," *Nature* 352 (July 25, 1991): 280.

5. See, for example, Ward Hill Lamon, *Recollections of Abraham Lincoln*, ed. Dorothy Lamon Teillard (Lincoln: University of Nebraska Press, 1994); Noah Brooks, *Washington in Lincoln's Time* (New York: Rinehart, 1958), 199; *Lincoln Observed: Civil War Dispatches of Noah Brooks*, ed. Michael Burlingame (Baltimore: Johns Hopkins University Press, 1998); and Jean H. Baker, *Mary Todd Lincoln: A Biography* (New York: Norton, 1987), 196–99. See also Roy P. Basler, ed., *Collected Works*, vol. 6 (New Brunswick, NJ: Rutgers University Press, 1953–1955), 256.

6. Carl Sandburg, *Abraham Lincoln* (New York: Harcourt Brace Jovanovich, 1974), 696–97.

1 5

Andrew Johnson (1865–1869)

The United States was still a young nation when Andrew Johnson issued his farewell address—not even a century old. Yet the new republic had been sorely tested by factions, sectionalism, the issue of slavery, foreign wars, civil war, and most recently the assassination of a president. During Johnson's tenure, there may have been an absence of war, but there was hardly peace. The Tennessean's determination to treat the South with leniency was met with resentment and resistance by Radical Republicans in the North.

Moreover, Johnson had been impeached thirteen months prior to composing his farewell address. Up to that point in U.S. history, he was the only president formally charged by a majority of House members with "high crimes and misdemeanors." The vote in the House was 126 to 47 against him. The subsequent trial in the Senate was dramatic; on one of the eleven articles drawn up against him, Johnson dodged conviction and removal from office by a single vote.

It was in these difficult circumstances that the nation's seventeenth president composed a formal farewell address to the nation. The formal farewell was still relatively rare in presidential discourse. Johnson was only the third president in U.S. history, to that point, to issue such an address. The previous farewell address had been issued by Andrew Jackson in 1837, who thought it fitting to offer counsel at the half-century mark under the U.S. Constitution. Previous to that, George Washington issued the first farewell address to help set the new republic on a stable course.

Johnson, too, seized a "constitutional moment" in American history with his farewell address. He meant to revisit certain constitutional principles in the aftermath of a war fought, in part, over interpreting the Constitution. But, given his recent impeachment in the House and trial in the Senate, he wanted even more to vindicate his character. Personal vindication—that is the dominant theme in the address, and it makes Johnson's farewell the least disinterested in the genre. Personal troubles intrude on his address more than on any other presidential farewell with the possible exception of Richard Nixon's. Through it all, Johnson wanted to establish that the Constitution had been his rule and guide. In a remarkable passage he emphasized the restraint he had shown as commander-in-chief: "Let the people whom I am addressing from the Presidential chair during the closing hours of a laborious term, consider how different would have been their present condition had I yielded to the dazzling temptation of foreign conquest, of personal aggrandizement, and the desire to wield additional power."

Johnson's challenges, it must be said, mirrored not just his private world but the larger challenges of the republic. Americans were sorting out how to apply the Constitution to a divided and rapidly changing nation. Because of the Civil War, because of the recent assassination of a president, because of a vindictive "Reconstruction," the nation's confidence in itself had been severely shaken. In this tumultuous atmosphere, it is not surprising that Johnson sought solace in the fundamental law of the land. In the farewell, he referred to the Constitution or constitutional governance forty-two times. By contrast, Washington's Farewell Address contains nine such references; Andrew Jackson's, twenty-one. There is a pattern here.

This pattern—of increasing reference to the Constitution—is all the more apparent when it is realized that Johnson's farewell is the shortest of the three to that point—4,538 words. (Washington's is more than 6,000 words long, and Jackson's is more than 8,000 words long.) Clearly the theme of constitutionality was becoming increasingly dense in farewell discourse with the passage of time.

There is much that posterity might criticize in Johnson's address. The self-absorption, though understandable, is regrettable. Yet it must be granted that he was a skillful writer, in command of powerful rhetorical techniques. It was through rhetorical technique alone that he evoked America's most famous political document, the Declaration of Independence. Here is how. In the latter half of Johnson's farewell—in the paragraph beginning, "Let us turn for a moment to the history"—the president used anaphora to shame his political enemies. Anaphora is the deliberate repetition of a word or phrase at the beginning of successive sentences; it is used to heighten rhetorical effect. Thus Johnson began twelve successive sentences with: "They have. . . ." Anaphora was precisely the technique Thomas Jefferson used in the middle of the Declaration of Independence to declare Americans' grievances against King George III. Jefferson began a succession of eighteen clauses with: "He has. . . . " Even the specific charges leveled against the King bore similarities to those leveled against Johnson's enemies. In case the reader was slow to catch on, Johnson next compared the abuse of the South during Reconstruction with the abuse of the American Colonies on the eve of the Revolution. He then quoted many of the Declaration's clauses verbatim. Through it all, Johnson never mentioned Jefferson or the Declaration by name. Yet the skillful use of rhetorical technique made the references obvious to a literate audience.

In American presidential discourse, Johnson's farewell message stands isolated, like a lone dark mountain over the prairie. It was the last farewell by a president to the nation for some eight decades. There are many possible reasons for this, some of them explored in the introduction. One possibility bears repeating. Perhaps because of Johnson's difficult circumstances, the formal farewell address fell into disfavor. By 1869, it may have seemed that the genre was reduced to a personal grouse. It retained little of the nobility and disinterested wisdom offered in Washington's farewell. Perhaps a generation or two of Americans associated the farewell with a failed presidency, bad news, and the need to settle scores.

But time passes. People forget. The world changes. Harry S. Truman would revive the formal farewell address in 1953.

Farewell Address
(published in the *New York Times* and other newspapers)
Washington, DC
March 4, 1869

TO THE PEOPLE OF THE UNITED STATES:

The robe of office by constitutional limitation this day falls from my shoulders, to be immediately assumed by my successor. For him the forbearance and co-operation of the American people, in all his efforts to administer the Government within the pale of the Federal Constitution, are sincerely invoked. Without ambition to gratify, party ends to subserve, or personal quarrels to avenge, at the sacrifice of the peace and welfare of the country, my earnest desire is to see the Constitution of the Republic again recognized and obeyed as the supreme law of the land, and the whole people—North, South, East, and West—prosperous and happy under its wise provisions.

In surrendering the high office to which I was called four years ago, at a memorable and terrible crisis, it is my privilege, I trust, to say to the people of the United States a few parting words in vindication of an official course so ceaselessly assailed and aspersed by political leaders, to whose plans and wishes my policy to restore the Union has been obnoxious. In a period of difficulty and turmoil almost without precedent in the history of any people, consequent upon the closing scenes of a great rebellion and the assassination of the then President, it was perhaps too much on my part to expect of devoted partisans, who rode on the waves of excitement which at that time swept all before them, that degree of toleration and magnanimity which I sought to recommend and enforce, and which I believe in good time would have advanced us infinitely farther on the road to permanent peace and prosperity than we have thus far attained. Doubtless, had I at the commencement of my term of office unhesitatingly lent its powers, or perverted them to purposes and plans outside of the Constitution, and become an instrument to schemes of confiscation and of general and oppressive disqualifications, I would have been hailed as all that was true, loyal, and discerning—as the reliable head of a party, whatever I might have been as the Executive of the Nation. Unwilling, however, to accede to propositions of extremists, and bound to obey, at every personal hazard my oath to defend the Constitution, I need not perhaps be surprised at having met the fate of others whose only rewards for upholding constitutional rights and laws have been the consciousness of having attempted to do their duty, and the calm judgment of history. At the time a mysterious Providence assigned to me the office of President, I was, by the terms of the Constitution, the Commander-in-Chief of nearly a million of men under arms. One of my first acts was to disband and restore to the vocations of civil life this immense host, and to divest myself so far as I could of the unparalleled powers then incident to the office and the times. Whether or not, in this step I was right, and how far deserving the approbation of all the people, all can now on reflection judge, when reminded of the ruinous condition of public affairs that must have resulted from the continuance in the military service of such a vast number of men.

The close of our domestic conflict found the army eager to distinguish itself in a new field by an effort to punish European intervention in Mexico. By many it was believed and urged that, aside from the assumed justice of the proceeding, a foreign war, in which both sides would cheerfully unite to vindicate the honor of the national flag and further illustrate the national prowess, would be the surest and speediest way of awakening national enthusiasm, reviving devotion to the Union and occupying a force concerning which grave doubts existed as to its willingness, after four years of active campaigning, at once to return to the pursuits of peace. Whether these speculations were true or false, it will be conceded that they existed, and that the predilections of the army were for the time being in the direction indicated. Taking advantage of that feeling, it would have been easy, as the Commander-in-Chief of the Army and Navy, and with all the power and patronage of the Presidential office at my disposal, to turn the concentrated strength of the nation against French interference in Mexico, and to inaugurate a movement which would have been received with favor by the military and a large portion of the people.

It is proper in this connection that I should refer to the almost unlimited additional powers tendered to the Executive by the measures relating to Civil Rights and the Freedmen's Bureau, contrary to most precedents in the experience of public men. The powers thus placed within my grasp were declined as being in violation of the Constitution, dangerous to the liberties of the people, and tending to aggravate rather than lessen the discords naturally resulting from our civil war. With a large army and augmented authority, it would have been no difficult task to direct at pleasure the destinies of the Republic, and to make secure my continuance in the highest office known to our laws. Let the people whom I am addressing from the Presidential chair during the closing hours of a laborious term, consider how different would have been their present condition had I yielded to the dazzling temptation of foreign conquest, of personal aggrandizement, and the desire to wield additional power. Let them with justice consider that if I have not unduly magnified mine office, the public burdens have not been increased by my acts, and other and perhaps thousands or tens of thousands of lives sacrificed to visions of false glory. It cannot, therefore, be charged that my ambition has been of that ordinary or criminal kind which to the detriment of the people's rights and liberties ever seeks to grasp more and unwarranted powers, and to accomplish its purposes, panders too often to popular prejudice and party aims.

What, then, have been the aspirations which guided me in my official acts? Those acts need not at this time an elaborate explanation. They have elsewhere been comprehensively stated and fully discussed, and become a part of the nation's history. By them I am ready to be judged, knowing that, however imperfect, they at least show to the impartial mind that my sole ambition has been to restore the Union of the States, faithfully to execute the office of President, and to the best of my ability to preserve, protect, and defend the Constitution. I cannot be censured if my efforts have been impeded in the interests of party faction, and if a policy, which was intended to reassure and conciliate the people of both sections of the country, was made the occasion of inflaming and dividing still further those who, only recently in arms against each other, yet as individuals and citizens were sincerely desirous, as I shall ever believe, of burying all hostile feelings in the grave of the past. The bitter war was waged on the part of the Government to vindicate the Constitution and save the Union; and if I have erred in trying to bring about a more speedy and lasting peace to extinguish heart burnings and enmities, and to prevent trouble in the South, which, retarding material prosperity in that region, injuriously affected the whole country, I am quite content to rest my case with the more deliberate judgment of the people, and, as I have already intimated, with the distant future.

The war, all must remember, was a stupendous and deplorable mistake. Neither side understood the other, and had this simple fact and its conclusions been kept in view, all that was needed was accomplished by the acknowledgment of the terrible wrong, and the expression of better feeling and earnest endeavor at atonement shown and felt. In the prompt ratification of Constitutional amendments by the Southern States at the close of the war, not accepting the war as a confessed false step on the part of those who inaugurated it, was an error which now only time can cure, and which, even at this late date we should endeavor to palliate, experiencing, moreover, as all have done, the frightful cost of the arbitrament of the sword. Let us in the future cling closer than ever to the Constitution as our only safeguard. It is to be hoped that not until the burdens now pressing upon us with such fearful weight are removed will our people forget the lessons of the war, and that, remembering them from whatever cause, peace between sections and States may be perpetual.

The history of late events in our country, as well as of the greatest Governments of ancient and modern times, teach that we have every thing to fear from a departure from the letter and spirit of the Constitution, and the undue ascendancy of men allowed to assume power in what are considered desperate emergencies. Sylla, on becoming master of Rome, at once adopted measures to crush his enemies and to consolidate the power of his party. He established military colonies throughout Italy, deprived of the full Roman franchise the inhabitants of the Italian towns who had opposed his usurpations, confiscated their lands and gave them to his soldiers, and conferred citizenship upon a great number of slaves belonging to those who had proscribed him, thus creating at Rome a kind of bodyguard for his protection. After having given Rome over to slaughter, and tyrannized beyond all example over those opposed to him and the legions, his terrible instrument of wrong, Sylla could yet feel safe in laying down the ensigns of power so dreadfully abused, and in mingling freely with the families and friends of myriad victims. The fear which he had inspired continued after his voluntary abdication, and even in retirement his will was law to a people who had permitted themselves to be enslaved. What but a subtle knowledge and conviction that the Roman people had become changed, discouraged, and utterly broken in spirit could have induced this daring assumption? What but public indifference to consequences so terrible as to leave Rome open to every calamity, which subsequently befell, her could have justified the conclusions of the Dictator and tyrant in his startling experiment?

We find that in the time which has since elapsed human nature and exigencies in Governments have not greatly changed. Who, a few years ago, in contemplating our future, could have supposed that in a brief period of bitter experience, every thing demanded in the name of military emergency, or dictated by caprice would come to be considered as mere matters of course; that conscription, confiscation, loss of personal liberty, the subjugation of States to military rule, and disfranchisement, with the extension of the right of suffrage merely to accomplish party ends, would receive the passive submission, if not acquiescence, of the people of the Republic?

It has been clearly demonstrated by recent occurrences that encroachments upon the Constitution cannot be prevented by the President, however devoted or determined he may be; that unless the people interpose there is no power under the Constitution to check a dominant majority of two-thirds of the Congress of the United States. An appeal to the nation is attended with too much delay to meet an emergency; while if left free to act, the people would correct in time such evils as might follow legislative usurpation. There is danger that the same power which disregards the Constitution will deprive them of the right to change their rulers except by revolution. We have already seen the jurisdiction of the Judiciary circumscribed when it was apprehended that the Courts would decide against laws having for their sole object the supremacy of party, while the veto power lodged in the Executive by the Constitution for the interest and protection of the people, and exercised by WASHINGTON and his successors, has been rendered nugatory by a partisan majority of two-thirds in each branch of the National Legislature. The Constitution evidently contemplates that when a bill is returned with the President's objections, it will be calmly reconsidered by Congress. Such, however, has not been the practice under present party rule. It has become evident that men who pass a bill under partisan influences are not likely, through patriotic motives, to admit their error, and thereby weaken their own organizations by solemnly confessing it under the official oath. Pride of opinion, if nothing else, has intervened and prevented a calm and dispassionate reconsideration of a bill disapproved by the Executive. Much as I venerate the Constitution, it must be admitted that this condition of affairs has developed a defect which, under the aggressive tendency of the Legislative Department of the Government, may readily work its overthrow. It may, however, be remedied without disturbing the harmony of the instrument. The veto power is generally exercised upon constitutional grounds, and whenever it is so applied, and the bill returned with the Executive's reasons for withholding his signature, it ought to be immediately certified to the Supreme Court of the United States for its decision. If its constitutionality shall be declared by that tribunal, it should then become a law. But if the decision is otherwise, it should fail, without power in Congress to re-enact and make it valid. In cases in which the veto rests upon hasty and inconsiderate legislation, and in which no constitutional question is involved, I would not change the fundamental law; for in such cases no permanent evil can be incorporated into the Federal system. It is obvious that without such an amendment the Government, as it existed under the Constitution prior to the rebellion, may be wholly subverted and overthrown by a two-thirds majority in Congress. It is not therefore difficult to see how easily and how rapidly the people may lose—shall I not say have lost?—their liberties by an unchecked and uncontrollable majority in the law-making power, and when ever deprived of their rights, how powerless they are to regain them.

Let us turn for a moment to the history of the majority in Congress, which has acted in such utter disregard of the Constitution. While public attention has been carefully and constantly turned to the past and expiated sins of the South, the servants of the people, in high places, have boldly betrayed their trust, broken their oaths of obedience to the Constitution, and undermined the very foundations of liberty, justice, and good government. When the rebellion was being suppressed by the volunteered services of patriot soldiers amid the dangers of the battle-field, these men crept, without question, into place and power in the national councils. After all dangers had passed, when no armed foe remained—when a penitent people bowed their heads to the flag and renewed their allegiance to the Government of the United States—then it was that pretended patriots appeared before the nation and began to prate about the thousands of lives and millions of treasure sacrificed in the suppression of the rebellion. They have since persistently sought to inflame the prejudices engendered between the sections, to retard the restoration of peace and harmony, and by every means to keep open and exposed to the poisonous breath of party passion the terrible wounds of a four-years' war. They have prevented the return of peace and the restoration of the Union, in every way rendered delusive the purposes, promises, and pledges by which the army was marshalled, treason rebuked, and rebellion crushed, and made the liberties of the people and the rights and powers of the President objects of constant attack. They have wrested from the President his constitutional power of supreme command of the army and navy. They have destroyed the strength and efficiency of the Executive Department, by making subordinate officers independent of and able to defy their chief. They have attempted to place the President under the power of a bold, defiant, and treacherous Cabinet officer. They have robbed the Executive of the prerogative of pardon, rendered null and void acts of clemency granted to thousands of persons under the provisions of the Constitution, and committed gross usurpation by legislative attempts to exercise this power in favor of party adherents. They have conspired to change the system of our Government by preferring charges against the President in the form of articles of impeachment, and contemplating, before hearing or trial that he should be placed in arrest, held in durance, and when it became their pleasure to pronounce his sentence, driven from place and power in disgrace. They have in time of peace increased the National debt by a reckless expenditure of the public moneys, and thus added to the burdens which already weigh upon the people. They have permitted the nation to suffer the evils of a deranged currency to the enhancement in price of all the necessaries of life. They have maintained a large standing army for the enforcement of their measures of oppression. They have engaged in class legislation and built up and encouraged monopolies, that the few might be enriched at the expense of the many. They have failed to act upon important treaties, thereby endangering our present peaceful relations with foreign Powers.

Their course of usurpation has not been limited to inroads upon the Executive Department. By unconstitutional and Oppressive enactments, the people of ten States of the Union have been reduced to a condition more intolerable than that from which the patriots of the Revolution rebelled. Millions of American citizens can now say of their oppressors, with more truth than our fathers did of British tyrants, that they have "forbidden the Governments to pass laws of immediate and pressing importance, unless suspended until their assent should be obtained"; that they have "refused to pass other laws for the accommodation of large districts of people unless those people would relinquish the right of representation in the Legislature—a right inestimable to them and formidable to tyrants only"; that they have "made judges dependent upon their will alone for the tenure of their offices and the amount and payment of their salaries"; that they have "erected a multitude of new offices, and sent hither swarms of officers to harass our people and eat out their substance"; that they have "affected to render the military independent of and superior to the civil power"; "combined with others to subject us to a jurisdiction foreign to our Constitution and unacknowledged by our laws"; "quartered large bodies of armed troops among us; protected them by a mock trial from punishment for any murders which they should commit on the inhabitants of these States"; imposed "taxes upon us without our consent"; "deprived us in many cases of the benefit of trial by jury"; taken away our charters, excited domestic insurrection amongst us; abolished our most valuable laws; altered fundamentally the forms of our Government; suspended our own Legislatures, and declared themselves invested with power to legislate for us in all cases whatsoever.

This catalogue of crimes, long as it is, is not yet complete. The Constitution vests the Judicial power of the United States "in one Supreme Court," whose jurisdiction "shall extend to all cases arising under this Constitution" and "the laws of the United States." Encouraged by this promise of a refuge from tyranny, a citizen of the United States who, by the order of a military commander, given under the sanction of a cruel and deliberate edict of Congress, had been denied the constitutional rights of liberty of conscience, freedom of the press and of speech, personal freedom from military arrest, of being held to answer for crime only upon presentment and indictment, of trial by jury, of the writ of *habeas corpus*, and the protection of a civil and constitutional Government—a citizen thus deeply wronged appeals to the Supreme Court for the protection guaranteed to him by the organic law of the land. At once a fierce and excited majority, by the ruthless hand of legislature power, stripped the ermine from the Judges, transferred the sword of justice to the General, and remanded the oppressed citizen to a degradation and bondage worse than death.

It will also be recorded as one of the marvels of the times that a party claiming for itself a monopoly of consistency and patriotism, and boasting of its unlimited sway, endeavored, by a costly and deliberate trial, to impeach one who defended the Constitution and the Union, not only throughout the war of the rebellion, but during his whole term of office as Chief Magistrate; but, at the same time, could find no warrant or means at their command to bring to trial even the chief of the rebellion. Indeed, the remarkable failures in this case were so often repeated, that for propriety's sake, if for no other reason, it became at last necessary to extend to him an unconditional pardon. What more plainly than this illustrates the extremity of party management and inconsistency on the one hand, and of faction, vindictiveness, and intolerance on the other? Patriotism will hardly be encouraged when, in such a record, it sees that its instant reward may be the most virulent party abuse and obloquy, if not attempted disgrace. Instead of seeking to make treason odious, it would in truth seem to have been their purpose rather to make the defence of the Constitution and the Union a crime, and to punish fidelity to an oath of office, if counter to party dictation, by all the means at their command.

Happily for the peace of the Country, the war has determined against the assumed power of the States to withdraw at pleasure from the Union. The institution of slavery, also, found its destruction in a rebellion commenced in its interest. It should be borne in mind, however, that the war neither impaired nor destroyed the Constitution, but on the contrary preserved its existence, and made apparent its real power and enduring strength. All the rights granted to the States or reserved to the people are therefore intact. Among those rights is that of the people of each State to declare the qualifications of their own State electors. It is now assumed that Congress can control this vital right, which can never be taken away from the States without impairing the fundamental principles of the Government itself. It is necessary to the existence of the States as well as to the protection of the liberties of the people; for the right to select the elector in whom the political power of the State shall be lodged involves the right of the State to govern itself. When deprived of this prerogative, the State will have no power worth retaining. All will be gone, and they will be subjected to the arbitrary will of Congress. The Government will then be centralized, if not by the passage of laws, then by the adoption, through partisan influence, of an amendment directly in conflict with the original design of the Constitution. This proves how necessary it is [that] the people should require the administration of the three great departments of the Government to be strictly within the limits of the Constitution. Their boundaries have been accurately defined, and neither should be allowed to trespass upon the other; nor, above all, to encroach upon the reserved rights of the people and the States. The troubles of the past four years will prove to the nation blessings if they produce so desirable a result.

Upon those who became young men amid the sound of cannon and the din of arms, and who quietly returned to the farms, the factories, and the schools of the land, will principally devolve the solemn duty of perpetuating the Union of the States, in defence of which hundreds of thousands of their comrades expired, and hundreds of millions of national obligations were incurred. A manly people will not neglect the training necessary to resist aggression, but they should be jealous lest the civil be made subordinate to the military element. We need to encourage in every legitimate way a study of the Constitution for which the war was waged, a knowledge of and reverence for whose wise checks by those so soon to occupy the places filled by their seniors will be the only hope of preserving the Republic. The young men of the nation, not yet under the control of party, must resist the tendency to centralization—an outgrowth of the great rebellion—and be familiar with the fact that the country consists of the "United States," and that when the States surrendered certain great rights for the sake of a more perfect union, they retained rights as valuable and important as those they relinquished for the common weal. This sound old doctrine, far different from the teachings that led to the attempt to secede, and a kindred theory, that States were taken out of the Union by the rash acts of conspirators that happened to dwell within their borders, must be received and advocated with the enthusiasm of early manhood, or the people will be ruled by corrupt combinations of the commercial centers, who, plethoric from wealth, annually migrate to the capital of the nation to purchase special legislation. Until the representatives of the people in Congress more fully exhibit the diverse views and the interests of the whole nation, and laws cease to be made without full discussion at the behest of some party leader, there will never be a proper respect shown by the law-making power either to the Judicial or Executive branch of the Government. The generation just beginning to use the ballot-box, it is believed, only need that their attention should be called to these considerations to indicate by their votes that they wish their representatives to observe all the restraints which the people, in adopting the Constitution, intended to impose upon party excess.

Calmly reviewing my administration of the Government, I feel that (with a sense of accountability to God, having conscientiously endeavored to discharge my whole duty) I have nothing to regret. Events have proved the correctness of the policy set forth in my first and subsequent messages. The woes which have followed the rejection of forbearance, magnanimity, and constitutional rule are known and deplored by the nation. It is a matter of pride and gratification, in retiring from the most exalted position in the gift of a free people, to feel and know that in a long, arduous, and eventful public life my action has never been influenced by desire for gain, and that I can in all sincerity inquire, Whom have I defrauded? Whom have I oppressed? Or whose hand have I received any bribe to blind my eyes therewith? No responsibility for wars that have been waged or blood that has been shed rests upon me. My thoughts have been those of peace, and my effort has ever been to allay contentions among my countrymen.

Forgetting the past, let us return to the first principles of the Government, and unfurling the banner of our country, inscribe upon it in ineffaceable characters, "The Constitution and the Union, one and inseparable."

ANDREW JOHNSON

Three months prior to issuing his farewell address, Johnson wrote out a final annual message in which he made trenchant observations about the Constitution and state of the Union. Excerpts follow.

Fourth Annual Message
(written to the Congress)
December 9, 1868

Fellow-Citizens of the Senate and House of Representatives:

Upon the reassembling of Congress it again becomes my duty to call your attention to the state of the Union and to its continued disorganized condition under the various laws which have been passed upon the subject of reconstruction.

It may be safely assumed as an axiom in the government of states that the greatest wrongs inflicted upon a people are caused by unjust and arbitrary legislation, or by the unrelenting decrees of despotic rulers, and that the timely revocation of injurious and oppressive measures is the greatest good that can be conferred upon a nation. The legislator or ruler who has the wisdom and magnanimity to retrace his steps when convinced of error will sooner or later be rewarded with the respect and gratitude of an intelligent and patriotic people.

Our own history, although embracing a period less than a century, affords abundant proof that most, if not all, of our domestic troubles are directly traceable to violations of the organic law and excessive legislation. The most striking illustrations of this fact are furnished by the enactments of the past three years upon the question of reconstruction. After a fair trial they have substantially failed and proved pernicious in their results, and there seems to be no good reason why they should longer remain upon the statute book. States to which the Constitution guarantees a republican form of government have been reduced to military dependencies in each of which the people have been made subject to the arbitrary will of the commanding general. Although the Constitution requires that each State shall be represented in Congress, Virginia, Mississippi, and Texas are yet excluded from the two Houses, and, contrary to the express provisions of that instrument were denied participation in the recent election for a President and Vice-President of the United States. The attempt to place the white population under the domination of persons of color in the South has impaired, if not destroyed, the kindly relations that had previously existed between them: and mutual distrust has engendered a feeling of animosity which leading in some instances to collision and bloodshed, has prevented that cooperation between the two races so essential to the success of industrial enterprise in the Southern States. Nor have the inhabitants of those States alone suffered from the disturbed condition of affairs growing out of these Congressional enactments. The entire Union has been agitated by grave apprehensions of troubles which might again involve the peace of the nation; its interests have been injuriously affected by the derangement of business and labor, and the consequent want of prosperity throughout that portion of the country.

The Federal Constitution—the *magna charta* of American rights, under whose wise and salutary provisions we have successfully conducted all our domestic and foreign affairs, sustained ourselves in peace and in war, and become a great nation among the powers of the earth—must assuredly be now adequate to the settlement of questions growing out of the civil war, waged alone for its vindication. This great fact is made most manifest by the condition of the country when Congress assembled in the month of December, 1865. Civil strife had ceased, the spirit of rebellion had spent its entire force, in the Southern States the people had warmed into national life, and throughout the whole country a healthy reaction in public sentiment had taken place. By the application of the simple yet effective provisions of the Constitution the executive department, with the voluntary aid of the States, had brought the work of restoration as near completion as was within the scope of its authority, and the nation was encouraged by the prospect of an early and satisfactory adjustment of all its difficulties. Congress, however, intervened, and, refusing to perfect the work so nearly consummated, declined to admit members from the unrepresented States, adopted a series of measures which arrested the progress of restoration, frustrated all that had been so successfully accomplished, and, after three years of agitation and strife, has left the country further from the attainment of union and fraternal feeling than at the inception of the Congressional plan of reconstruction. It needs no argument to show that legislation which has produced such baneful consequences should be abrogated, or else made to conform to the genuine principles of republican government.

Under the influence of party passion and sectional prejudice, other acts have been passed not warranted by the Constitution. . . .

* * *

. . . We should, as far as possible, remove all pretext for violations of the organic law, by remedying such imperfections as time and experience may develop, ever remembering that "the constitution which at any time exists until changed by an explicit and authentic act of the whole people is sacredly obligatory upon all."

In the performance of a duty imposed upon me by the Constitution, I have thus communicated to Congress information of the state of the Union and recommended for their consideration such measures as have seemed to me necessary and expedient. If carried into effect, they will hasten the accomplishment of the great and beneficent purposes for which the Constitution was ordained, and which it comprehensively states were "to form a more perfect Union, establish justice, insure domestic tranquillity, provide for the common defense, promote the general welfare, and secure the blessings of liberty to ourselves and our posterity." In Congress are vested all legislative powers, and upon them devolves the responsibility as well for framing unwise and excessive laws as for neglecting to devise and adopt measures absolutely demanded by the wants of the country. Let us earnestly hope that before the expiration of our respective terms of service, now rapidly drawing to a close, an all-wise Providence will so guide our counsels as to strengthen and preserve the Federal Union, inspire reverence for the Constitution, restore prosperity and happiness to our whole people, and promote "on earth peace, good will toward men."

ANDREW JOHNSON

16

Ulysses S. Grant (1869–1877)

In many ways U. S. Grant's final annual message is typical of the genre. In content and tone, breadth and length, it is in line with other final messages of the period.

And yet, the introduction is unusual for its candor. The opening paragraphs subtly point to the problems that dogged Grant during his eight years in office. The eighteenth president was considered an honorable man, but he managed to surround himself with dishonorable people; more than a whiff of scandal plagued his administration. This no doubt prompted Grant to begin his message with a declaration of his early political naivete. "It was my fortune, or misfortune, to be called to the office of Chief Executive without any previous political training. From the age of 17 I had never even witnessed the excitement attending a Presidential campaign but twice antecedent to my own candidacy, and at but one of them was I eligible as a voter."

By the end of the message, Grant could assure readers that his political naivete never clouded his devotion to the republic: "With the present term of Congress my official life terminates. It is not probable that public affairs will ever again receive attention from me further than as a citizen of the Republic, always taking a deep interest in the honor, integrity, and prosperity of the whole land." An apt closing, considering the scandals that attached to the eighteenth president's administration.

Eighth Annual Message
(written to the Congress)
December 5, 1876

To the Senate and House of Representatives:

In submitting my eighth and last annual message to Congress it seems proper that I should refer to and in some degree recapitulate the events and official acts of the past eight years.

It was my fortune, or misfortune, to be called to the office of Chief Executive without any previous political training. From the age of 17 I had never even witnessed the excitement attending a

Presidential campaign but twice antecedent to my own candidacy, and at but one of them was I eligible as a voter.

Under such circumstances it is but reasonable to suppose that errors of judgment must have occurred. Even had they not, differences of opinion between the Executive, bound by an oath to the strict performance of his duties, and writers and debaters must have arisen. It is not necessarily evidence of blunder on the part of the Executive because there are these differences of views. Mistakes have been made, as all can see and I admit, but it seems to me oftener in the selections made of the assistants appointed to aid in carrying out the various duties of administering the Government—in nearly every case selected without a personal acquaintance with the appointee, but upon recommendations of the representatives chosen directly by the people. It is impossible, where so many trusts are to be allotted, that the right parties should be chosen in every instance. History shows that no Administration from the time of Washington to the present has been free from these mistakes. But I leave comparisons to history, claiming only that I have acted in every instance from a conscientious desire to do what was right, constitutional, within the law, and for the very best interests of the whole people. Failures have been errors of judgment, not of intent.

My civil career commenced, too, at a most critical and difficult time. Less than four years before, the country had emerged from a conflict such as no other nation had ever survived. Nearly one-half of the States had revolted against the Government, and of those remaining faithful to the Union a large percentage of the population sympathized with the rebellion and made an "enemy in the rear" almost as dangerous as the more honorable enemy in the front. The latter committed errors of judgment, but they maintained them openly and courageously; the former received the protection of the Government they would see destroyed, and reaped all the pecuniary advantage to be gained out of the then existing state of affairs, many of them by obtaining contracts and by swindling the Government in the delivery of their goods.

Immediately on the cessation of hostilities the then noble President, who had carried the country so far through its perils, fell a martyr to his patriotism at the hands of an assassin.

The intervening time to my first inauguration was filled up with wranglings between Congress and the new Executive as to the best mode of "reconstruction," or, to speak plainly, as to whether the control of the Government should be thrown immediately into the hands of those who had so recently and persistently tried to destroy it, or whether the victors should continue to have an equal voice with them in this control. Reconstruction, as finally agreed upon, means this and only this, except that the late slave was enfranchised, giving an increase, as was supposed, to the Union-loving and Union-supporting votes. If free in the full sense of the word, they would not disappoint this expectation. Hence at the beginning of my first Administration the work of reconstruction, much embarrassed by the long delay, virtually commenced. It was the work of the legislative branch of the Government. My province was wholly in approving their acts, which I did most heartily, urging the legislatures of States that had not yet done so to ratify the fifteenth amendment to the Constitution. The country was laboring under an enormous debt, contracted in the suppression of rebellion, and taxation was so oppressive as to discourage production. Another danger also threatened us—a foreign war. The last difficulty had to be adjusted and was adjusted without a war and in a manner highly honorable to all parties concerned. Taxes have been reduced within the last seven years nearly $300,000,000, and the national debt has been reduced in the same time over $435,000,000. By refunding the 6 per cent bonded debt for bonds bearing 5 and 4½ per cent interest, respectively, the annual interest has been reduced from over $130,000,000 in 1869 to but little over $100,000,000 in 1876. The balance of trade has been changed from over $130,000,000 against the United States in 1869 to more than $120,000,000 in our favor in 1876.

It is confidently believed that the balance of trade in favor of the United States will increase, not diminish, and that the pledge of Congress to resume specie payments in 1879 will be easily accomplished, even in the absence of much-desired further legislation on the subject.

A policy has been adopted toward the Indian tribes inhabiting a large portion of the territory of the United States which has been humane and has substantially ended Indian hostilities in the whole land except in a portion of Nebraska, and Dakota, Wyoming, and Montana Territories—the Black Hills region and approaches thereto. Hostilities there have grown out of the avarice of the white man, who has violated our treaty stipulations in his search for gold. The question might be asked why the Government has not enforced obedience to the terms of the treaty prohibiting the occupation of the Black Hills region by whites. The answer is simple: The first immigrants to the Black Hills were removed by troops, but rumors of rich discoveries of gold took into that region increased numbers. Gold has actually been found in paying quantity, and an effort to remove the miners would only result in the desertion of the bulk of the troops that might be sent there to remove them. All difficulty in this matter has, however, been removed—subject to the approval of Congress—by a treaty ceding the Black Hills and approaches to settlement by citizens. The subject of Indian policy and treatment is so fully set forth by the Secretary of the Interior and the Commissioner of Indian Affairs, and my views so fully expressed therein, that I refer to their reports and recommendations as my own.

The relations of the United States with foreign powers continue on a friendly footing. Questions have arisen from time to time in the foreign relations of the Government, but the United States have been happily free during the past year from the complications and embarrassments which have surrounded some of the foreign powers. The diplomatic correspondence submitted herewith contains information as to certain of the matters which have occupied the Government.

The cordiality which attends our relations with the powers of the earth has been plainly shown by the general participation of foreign nations in the exhibition which has just closed and by the exertions made by distant powers to show their interest in and friendly feelings toward the United States in the commemoration of the centennial of the nation. The Government and people of the United States have not only fully appreciated this exhibition of kindly feeling, but it may be justly and fairly expected that no small benefits will result both to ourselves and other nations from a better acquaintance, and a better appreciation of our mutual advantages and mutual wants.

Congress at its last session saw fit to reduce the amount usually appropriated for foreign intercourse by withholding appropriations for representatives of the United States in certain foreign countries and for certain consular officers, and by reducing the amounts usually appropriated for certain other diplomatic posts, and thus necessitating a change in the grade of the representatives. For these reasons, immediately upon the passage of the bill making appropriations for the diplomatic and consular service for the present fiscal year, instructions were issued to the representatives of the United States at Bolivia, Ecuador, and Colombia, and to the consular officers for whom no appropriation had been made, to close their respective legations and consulates and cease from the performance of their duties; and in like manner steps were immediately taken to substitute chargés d'affaires for ministers resident in Portugal, Denmark, Greece, Switzerland, and Paraguay.

While thoroughly impressed with the wisdom of sound economy in the foreign service, as in other branches of the Government, I can not escape the conclusion that in some instances the withholding of appropriations will prove an expensive economy, and that the small retrenchment secured by a change of grade in certain diplomatic posts is not an adequate consideration for the loss of influence and importance which will attend our foreign representatives under this reduction. I am of the opinion that a reexamination of the subject will cause a change in some instances in the conclusions reached on these subjects at the last session of Congress.

The Court of Commissioners of Alabama Claims, whose functions were continued by an act of the last session of Congress until the 1st day of January, 1877, has carried on its labors with diligence and general satisfaction. By a report from the clerk of the court, transmitted herewith, bearing date November 14, 1876, it appears that within the time now allowed by law the court will have disposed of all the claims presented for adjudication. This report also contains a statement of the general results of the labors of the court to the date thereof. It is a cause of satisfaction that the method adopted for the satisfaction of the classes of claims submitted to the court, which are of long standing and justly entitled to early consideration, should have proved successful and acceptable.

It is with satisfaction that I am enabled to state that the work of the joint commission for determining the boundary line between the United States and British possessions from the northwest angle of the Lake of the Woods to the Rocky Mountains, commenced in 1872, has been completed. The final agreements of the commissioners, with the maps, have been duly signed, and the work of the commission is complete.

The fixing of the boundary upon the Pacific coast by the protocol of March 10, 1873, pursuant to the award of the Emperor of Germany by Article XXXIV of the treaty of Washington, with the termination of the work of this commission, adjusts and fixes the entire boundary between the United States and the British possessions, except as to the portion of territory ceded by Russia to the United States under the treaty of 1867. The work intrusted to the commissioner and the officers of the Army attached to the commission has been well and satisfactorily performed. The original of the final agreement of the commissioners, signed upon the 29th of May, 1876, with the original official "lists of astronomical stations observed," the original official "list of monuments marking the international boundary line," and the maps, records, and general reports relating to the commission, have been deposited in the Department of State. The official report of the commissioner on the part of the United States, with the report of the chief astronomer of the United States, will be submitted to Congress within a short time.

I reserve for a separate communication to Congress a statement of the condition of the questions which lately arose with Great Britain respecting the surrender of fugitive criminals under the treaty of 1842.

The Ottoman Government gave notice, under date of January 15, 1874, of its desire to terminate the treaty of 1862, concerning commerce and navigation, pursuant to the provisions of the twenty-second article thereof. Under this notice the treaty terminated upon the 5th day of June, 1876. That Government has invited negotiations toward the conclusion of a new treaty.

By the act of Congress of March 23, 1874, the President was authorized, when he should receive satisfactory information that the Ottoman Government or that of Egypt had organized new tribunals likely to secure to citizens of the United States the same impartial justice enjoyed under the exercise of judicial functions by diplomatic and consular officers of the United States, to suspend the operation of the act of June 22, 1860, and to accept for citizens of the United States the jurisdiction of the new tribunals. Satisfactory information having been received of the organization of such new tribunals in Egypt, I caused a proclamation to be issued upon the 27th of March last, suspending the operation of the act of June 22, 1860, in Egypt, according to the provisions of the act. A copy of the proclamation accompanies this message. The United States has united with the other powers in the organization of these courts. It is hoped that the jurisdictional questions which have arisen may be readily adjusted, and that this advance in judicial reform may be hindered by no obstacles.

The necessary legislation to carry into effect the convention respecting commercial reciprocity concluded with the Hawaiian Islands in 1875 having been had, the proclamation to carry into effect the convention, as provided by the act approved August 15, 1876, was duly issued upon the 9th day of September last. A copy thereof accompanies this message.

The commotions which have been prevalent in Mexico for some time past, and which, unhappily, seem to be not yet wholly quieted, have led to complaints of citizens of the United States of injuries by persons in authority. It is hoped, however, that these will ultimately be adjusted to the satisfaction of both Governments. The frontier of the United States in that quarter has not been exempt from acts of violence by citizens of one Republic on those of the other. The frequency of these is supposed to be increased and their adjustment made more difficult by the considerable changes in the course of the lower part of the Rio Grande River, which river is a part of the boundary between the two countries. These changes have placed on either side of that river portions of land which by existing conventions belong to the jurisdiction of the Government on the opposite side of the river. The subject of adjustment of this cause of difficulty is under consideration between the two Republics.

The Government of the United States of Colombia has paid the award in the case of the steamer *Montijo*, seized by authorities of that Government some years since, and the amount has been transferred to the claimants.

It is with satisfaction that I am able to announce that the joint commission for the adjustment of claims between the United States and Mexico under the convention of 1868, the duration of which has been several times extended, has brought its labors to a close. From the report of the agent of the United States, which accompanies the papers transmitted herewith, it will be seen that within the time limited by the commission 1,017 claims on the part of citizens of the United States against Mexico were referred to the commission. Of these claims 831 were dismissed or disallowed, and in 186 cases awards were made in favor of the claimants against the Mexican Republic, amounting in the aggregate to $4,125,622.20. Within the same period 998 claims on the part of citizens of the Mexican Republic against the United States were referred to the commission. Of these claims 831 were dismissed or disallowed, and in 167 cases awards were made in favor of the claimants against the United States, amounting in the aggregate to $150,498.41.

By the terms of the convention the amount of these awards is to be deducted from the amount awarded in favor of our citizens against Mexico, and the balance only to be paid by Mexico to the United States, leaving the United States to make provision for this proportion of the awards in favor of its own citizens. I invite your attention to the legislation which will be necessary to provide for the payment.

In this connection I am pleased to be able to express the acknowledgments due to Sir Edward Thornton, the umpire of the commission, who has given to the consideration of the large number of claims submitted to him much time, unwearied patience, and that firmness and intelligence which are well known to belong to the accomplished representative of Great Britain, and which are likewise recognized by the representative in this country of the Republic of Mexico.

Monthly payments of a very small part of the amount due by the Government of Venezuela to citizens of the United States on account of claims of the latter against that Government continue to be made with reasonable punctuality. That Government has proposed to change the system which it has hitherto pursued in this respect by issuing bonds for part of the amount of the several claims. The proposition, however, could not, it is supposed, properly be accepted, at least without the consent of the holders of certificates of the indebtedness of Venezuela. These are so much dispersed that it would be difficult, if not impossible, to ascertain their disposition on the subject.

In former messages I have called the attention of Congress to the necessity of legislation with regard to fraudulent naturalization and to the subject of expatriation and the election of nationality.

The numbers of persons of foreign birth seeking a home in the United States, the ease and facility with which the honest emigrant may, after the lapse of a reasonable time, become possessed of all the privileges of citizenship of the United States, and the frequent occasions which induce such adopted citizens to return to the country of their birth render the subject of naturalization and the safeguards which experience has proved necessary for the protection of the honest naturalized citizen of paramount importance. The very simplicity in the requirements of law on this question affords opportunity for fraud, and the want of uniformity in the proceedings and records of the various courts and in the forms of the certificates of naturalization issued affords a constant source of difficulty.

I suggest no additional requirements to the acquisition of citizenship beyond those now existing, but I invite the earnest attention of Congress to the necessity and wisdom of some provisions regarding uniformity in the records and certificates, and providing against the frauds which frequently take place and for the vacating of a record of naturalization obtained in fraud.

These provisions are needed in aid and for the protection of the honest citizen of foreign birth, and for the want of which he is made to suffer not infrequently. The United States has insisted upon the right of expatriation, and has obtained, after a long struggle, an admission of the principle contended for by acquiescence therein on the part of many foreign powers and by the conclusion of treaties on that subject. It is, however, but justice to the government to which such naturalized citizens have formerly owed allegiance, as well as to the United States, that certain fixed and definite rules should be adopted governing such cases and providing how expatriation may be accomplished.

While emigrants in large numbers become citizens of the United States, it is also true that persons, both native born and naturalized, once citizens of the United States, either by formal acts or as the effect of a series of facts and circumstances, abandon their citizenship and cease to be entitled to the protection of the United States, but continue on convenient occasions to assert a claim to protection in the absence of provisions on these questions.

And in this connection I again invite your attention to the necessity of legislation concerning the marriages of American citizens contracted abroad, and concerning the status of American women who may marry foreigners and of children born of American parents in a foreign country.

The delicate and complicated questions continually occurring with reference to naturalization, expatriation, and the status of such persons as I have above referred to induce me to earnestly direct your attention again to these subjects.

In like manner I repeat my recommendation that some means be provided for the hearing and determination of the just and subsisting claims of aliens upon the Government of the United States within a reasonable limitation, and of such as may hereafter arise. While by existing provisions of law the Court of Claims may in certain cases be resorted to by an alien claimant, the absence of any general provisions governing all such cases and the want of a tribunal skilled in the disposition of such cases upon recognized fixed and settled principles, either provides no remedy in many deserving cases or compels a consideration of such claims by Congress or the executive department of the Government.

It is believed that other governments are in advance of the United States upon this question, and that the practice now adopted is entirely unsatisfactory.

Congress, by an act approved the 3d day of March, 1875, authorized the inhabitants of the Territory of Colorado to form a State government, with the name of the State of Colorado, and therein provided for the admission of said State, when formed, into the Union upon an equal footing with the original States.

A constitution having been adopted and ratified by the people of that State, and the acting governor having certified to me the facts as provided by said act, together with a copy of such constitution and ordinances as provided for in the said act, and the provisions of the said act of Congress having been duly complied with, I issued a proclamation upon the 1st of August, 1876, a copy of which is hereto annexed.

The report of the Secretary of War shows that the Army has been actively employed during the year in subduing, at the request of the Indian Bureau, certain wild bands of the Sioux Indian Nation and in preserving the peace at the South during the election. The commission constituted under the act of July 24, 1876, to consider and report on the "whole subject of the reform and reorganization of the Army" met in August last, and has collected a large mass of statistics and opinions bearing on the subject before it. These are now under consideration, and their report is progressing. I am advised, though, by the president of the commission that it will be impracticable to comply with the clause of the act requiring the report to be presented, through me, to Congress on the first day of this session, as there has not yet been time for that mature deliberation which the importance of the subject demands. Therefore I ask that the time of making the report be extended to the 29th day of January, 1877.

In accordance with the resolution of August 15, 1876, the Army regulations prepared under the act of March 1, 1875, have not been promulgated, but are held until after the report of the above-mentioned commission shall have been received and acted on.

By the act of August 15, 1876, the cavalry force of the Army was increased by 2,500 men, with the proviso that they should be discharged on the expiration of hostilities. Under this authority the cavalry regiments have been strengthened, and a portion of them are now in the field pursuing the remnants of the Indians with whom they have been engaged during the summer.

The estimates of the War Department are made up on the basis of the number of men authorized by law, and their requirements as shown by years of experience, and also with the purpose on the part of the bureau officers to provide for all contingencies that may arise during the time for which the estimates are made. Exclusive of engineer estimates (presented in accordance with acts of Congress calling for surveys and estimates for improvements at various localities), the estimates now presented are about six millions in excess of the appropriations for the years 1874–75 and 1875–76. This increase is asked in order to provide for the increased cavalry force (should their services be necessary), to prosecute economically work upon important public buildings, to provide for armament of fortifications and manufacture of small arms, and to replenish the working stock in the supply departments. The appropriations for these last named have for the past few years been so limited that the accumulations in store will be entirely exhausted during the present year, and it will be necessary to at once begin to replenish them.

I invite your special attention to the following recommendations of the Secretary of War:

First. That the claims under the act of July 4, 1864, for supplies taken by the Army during the war be removed from the offices of the Quartermaster and Commissary Generals and transferred to the Southern Claims Commission. These claims are of precisely similar nature to those now before the Southern Claims Commission, and the War Department bureaus have not the clerical force for their examination nor proper machinery for investigating the loyalty of the claimants.

Second. That Congress sanction the scheme of an annuity fund for the benefit of the families of deceased officers, and that it also provide for the permanent organization of the Signal Service, both of which were recommended in my last annual message.

Third. That the manufacturing operations of the Ordnance Department be concentrated at three arsenals and an armory, and that the remaining arsenals be sold and the proceeds applied to this object by the Ordnance Department.

The appropriations for river and harbor improvements for the current year were $5,015,000. With my approval, the Secretary of War directed that of this amount $2,000,000 should be expended, and no new works should be begun and none prosecuted which were not of national importance. Subsequently this amount was increased to $2,237,600, and the works are now progressing on this basis.

The improvement of the South Pass of the Mississippi River, under James B. Eads and his associates, is progressing favorably. At the present time there is a channel of 20.3 feet in depth between the jetties at the mouth of the pass and 18.5 feet at the head of the pass. Neither channel, however, has the width required before payments can be made by the United States. A commission of engineer officers is now examining these works, and their reports will be presented as soon as received.

The report of the Secretary of the Navy shows that branch of the service to be in condition as effective as it is possible to keep it with the means and authority given the Department. It is, of course, not possible to rival the costly and progressive establishments of great European powers with the old material of our Navy, to which no increase has been authorized since the war, except the eight small cruisers built to supply the place of others which had gone to decay. Yet the most has been done that was possible with the means at command; and by substantially rebuilding some of our old ships with durable material and completely repairing and refitting our monitor fleet the Navy has been gradually so brought up that, though it does not maintain its relative position among the progressive navies of the world, it is now in a condition more powerful and effective than it ever has been in time of peace.

The complete repairs of our five heavy ironclads are only delayed on account of the inadequacy of the appropriations made last year for the working bureaus of the Department, which were actually less in amount than those made before the war, notwithstanding the greatly enhanced price of labor and materials and the increase in the cost of the naval service growing out of the universal use and great expense of steam machinery. The money necessary for these repairs should be provided at once, that they may be completed without further unnecessary delay and expense.

When this is done, all the strength that there is in our Navy will be developed and useful to its full capacity, and it will be powerful for purposes of defense, and also for offensive action, should the necessity for that arise within a reasonable distance from our shores.

The fact that our Navy is not more modern and powerful than it is has been made a cause of complaint against the Secretary of the Navy by persons who at the same time criticize and complain of his endeavors to bring the Navy that we have to its best and most efficient condition; but the good sense of the country will understand that it is really due to his practical action that we have at this time any effective naval force at command.

The report of the Postmaster-General shows the excess of expenditures (excluding expenditures on account of previous years) over receipts for the fiscal year ended June 30, 1876, to be $4,151,988.66. Estimated expenditures for the fiscal year ending June 30, 1878, are $36,723,432.43. Estimated revenue for same period is $30,645,165, leaving estimated excess of expenditure, to be appropriated as a deficiency, of $6,078,267.43.

The Postmaster-General, like his predecessor, is convinced that a change in the basis of adjusting the salaries of postmasters of the fourth class is necessary for the good of the service as well as for the interests of the Government, and urgently recommends that the compensation of the class of postmasters above mentioned be based upon the business of their respective offices, as ascertained from the sworn returns to the Auditor of stamps canceled.

A few postmasters in the Southern States have expressed great apprehension of their personal safety on account of their connection with the postal service, and have specially requested that their reports of apprehended danger should not be made public lest it should result in the loss of their lives. But no positive testimony of interference has been submitted, except in the case of a mail messenger at Spartanburg, in South Carolina, who reported that he had been violently driven away while in charge of the mails on account of his political affiliations. An assistant superintendent of the Railway Mail Service investigated this case and reported that the messenger had disappeared from his post, leaving his work to be performed by a substitute. The Postmaster-General thinks this case is sufficiently suggestive to justify him in recommending that a more severe punishment should be provided for the offense of assaulting any person in charge of the mails or of retarding or otherwise obstructing them by threats of personal injury.

"A very gratifying result is presented in the fact that the deficiency of this Department during the last fiscal year was reduced to $4,081,790.18, as against $6,169,938.88 of the preceding year. The difference can be traced to the large increase in its ordinary receipts (which greatly exceed the estimates therefor) and a slight decrease in its expenditures."

The ordinary receipts of the Post-Office Department for the past seven fiscal years have increased at an average of over 8 per cent per annum, while the increase of expenditures for the same period has been but about 5.50 per cent per annum, and the decrease of deficiency in the revenues has been at the rate of nearly 2 per cent per annum.

The report of the Commissioner of Agriculture accompanying this message will be found one of great interest, marking, as it does, the great progress of the last century in the variety of products of the soil; increased knowledge and skill in the labor of producing, saving, and manipulating the same to prepare them for the use of man; in the improvements in machinery to aid the agriculturist in his labors, and in a knowledge of those scientific subjects necessary to a thorough system of economy in agricultural production, namely, chemistry, botany, entomology, etc. A study of this report by those interested in agriculture and deriving their support from it will find it of value in pointing out those articles which are raised in greater quantity than the needs of the world require, and must sell, therefore, for less than the cost of production, and those which command a profit over cost of production because there is not an overproduction.

I call special attention to the need of the Department for a new gallery for the reception of the exhibits returned from the Centennial Exhibition, including the exhibits donated by very many foreign nations, and to the recommendations of the Commissioner of Agriculture generally.

The reports of the District Commissioners and the board of health are just received—too late to read them and to make recommendations thereon—and are herewith submitted.

The international exhibition held in Philadelphia this year, in commemoration of the one hundredth anniversary of American independence, has proven a great success, and will, no doubt, be of enduring advantage to the country. It has shown the great progress in the arts, sciences, and mechanical skill made in a single century, and demonstrated that we are but little behind older nations in any one branch, while in some we scarcely have a rival. It has served, too, not only to bring peoples and products of skill and labor from all parts of the world together, but in bringing together people from all sections of our own country, which must prove a great benefit in the information imparted and pride of country engendered.

It has been suggested by scientists interested in and connected with the Smithsonian Institution, in a communication herewith, that the Government exhibit be removed to the capital and a suitable building be erected or purchased for its accommodation as a permanent exhibit. I earnestly recommend this; and believing that Congress would second this view, I directed that all Government exhibits at the Centennial Exhibition should remain where they are, except such as might be injured by remaining in a building not intended as a protection in inclement weather, or such as may be wanted by the Department furnishing them, until the question of permanent exhibition is acted on.

Although the moneys appropriated by Congress to enable the participation of the several Executive Departments in the International Exhibition of 1876 were not sufficient to carry out the undertaking to the full extent at first contemplated, it gives me pleasure to refer to the very efficient and creditable manner in which the board appointed from these several Departments to provide an exhibition on the part of the Government have discharged their duties with the funds placed at their command. Without a precedent to guide them in the preparation of such a display, the success of their labors was amply attested by the sustained attention which the contents of the Government building attracted during the period of the exhibition from both foreign and native visitors.

I am strongly impressed with the value of the collection made by the Government for the purposes of the exhibition, illustrating, as it does, the mineral resources of the country, the statistical and practical evidences of our growth as a nation, and the uses of the mechanical arts and the applications of applied science in the administration of the affairs of Government.

Many nations have voluntarily contributed their exhibits to the United States to increase the interest in any permanent exhibition Congress may provide for. For this act of generosity they should receive the thanks of the people, and I respectfully suggest that a resolution of Congress to that effect be adopted.

The attention of Congress can not be too earnestly called to the necessity of throwing some greater safeguard over the method of choosing and declaring the election of a President. Under the present system there seems to be no provided remedy for contesting the election in any one State. The remedy is partially, no doubt, in the enlightenment of electors. The compulsory support of the free school and the disfranchisement of all who can not read and write the English language, after a fixed probation, would meet my hearty approval. I would not make this apply, however, to those already voters, but I would to all becoming so after the expiration of the probation fixed upon. Foreigners coming to this country to become citizens, who are educated in their own language, should acquire the requisite knowledge of ours during the necessary residence to obtain naturalization. If they did not take interest enough in our language to acquire sufficient knowledge of it to enable them to study the institutions and laws of the country intelligently, I would not confer upon them the right to make such laws nor to select those who do.

I append to this message, for convenient reference, a synopsis of administrative events and of all recommendations to Congress made by me during the last seven years. Time may show some of these recommendations not to have been wisely conceived, but I believe the larger part will do no discredit to the Administration. One of these recommendations met with the united opposition of one political party in the Senate and with a strong opposition from the other, namely, the treaty for the annexation of Santo Domingo to the United States, to which I will specially refer, maintaining, as I do, that if my views had been concurred in, the country would be in a more prosperous condition to-day, both politically and financially.

Santo Domingo is fertile, and upon its soil may be grown just those tropical products of which the United States use so much, and which are produced or prepared for market now by slave labor almost exclusively, namely, sugar, coffee, dyewoods, mahogany, tropical fruits, tobacco, etc. About 75 per cent of the exports of Cuba are consumed in the United States. A large percentage of the exports of Brazil also find the same market. These are paid for almost exclusively in coin, legislation, particularly in Cuba, being unfavorable to a mutual exchange of the products of each country. Flour shipped from the Mississippi River to Havana can pass by the very entrance to the city on its way to a port in Spain, there pay a duty fixed upon articles to be reexported, transferred to a Spanish vessel and brought back almost to the point of starting, paying a second duty, and still leave a profit over what would be received by direct shipment. All that is produced in Cuba could be produced in Santo Domingo. Being a part of the United States, commerce between the island and mainland would be free. There would be no export duties on her shipments nor import duties on those coming here. There would be no import duties upon the supplies, machinery, etc., going from the States. The effect that would have been produced upon Cuban commerce, with these advantages to a rival, is observable at a glance. The Cuban question would have been settled long ago in favor of "free Cuba." Hundreds of American vessels would now be advantageously used in transporting the valuable woods and other products of the soil of the island to a market and in carrying supplies and emigrants to it. The island is but sparsely settled, while it has an area sufficient for the profitable employment of several millions of people. The soil would have soon fallen into the hands of United States capitalists. The products are so valuable in commerce that emigration there would have been encouraged; the emancipated race of the South would have found there a congenial home, where their civil rights would not be disputed and where their labor would be so much sought after that the poorest among them could have found the means to go. Thus in cases of great oppression and cruelty, such as has been practiced upon them in many places within the last eleven years, whole communities would have sought refuge in Santo Domingo. I do not suppose the whole race would have gone, nor is it desirable that they should go. Their labor is desirable—indispensable almost—where they now are. But the possession of this territory would have left the negro "master of the situation," by enabling him to demand his rights at home on pain of finding them elsewhere.

I do not present these views now as a recommendation for a renewal of the subject of annexation, but I do refer to it to vindicate my previous action in regard to it.

With the present term of Congress my official life terminates. It is not probable that public affairs will ever again receive attention from me further than as a citizen of the Republic, always taking a deep interest in the honor, integrity, and prosperity of the whole land.

U. S. GRANT

17

Rutherford B. Hayes (1877–1881)

For many readers, Rutherford Hayes's final annual message may sound remarkably current—and controversial. For example, the Republican leader advocated federal funding of public schools at the local and state level. He also noted the tensions between Muslims and Jews in the Middle East. Other problems, which seemed so important in 1880, are scarcely remembered now—for example, the unresolved claims of the United States and Spain over Florida.

For the most part, however, the missive shows how persistent some problems were in the nation's early history. For example, the sectionalism that concerned George Washington was still a major challenge after a century of nation-building. "It is the desire of the good people of the whole country," admonished Hayes, "that sectionalism as a factor in our politics should disappear."

This remark, aimed at the South, was coupled with another persistent challenge, that of paying more than lip service to the equal rights of all citizens. In the Compromise of 1877 Hayes had agreed to withdraw the last federal troops from the former Confederate States of America and thus end Reconstruction. In return, the nineteenth president wanted to see progress in upholding the "equal-rights amendments to the Constitution."

Fourth Annual Message
(written to the Congress)
December 6, 1880

Fellow-Citizens of the Senate and House of Representatives:

I congratulate you on the continued and increasing prosperity of our country. By the favor of Divine Providence we have been blessed during the past year with health, with abundant harvests, with profitable employment for all our people, and with contentment at home, and with peace and friendship with other nations. The occurrence of the twenty-fourth election of Chief Magistrate has afforded another opportunity to the people of the United States to exhibit to the world a significant example of the peaceful and safe transmission of the power and authority of government from the public servants whose terms of office are about to expire to their newly chosen successors. This example can not fail to impress profoundly thoughtful people of other countries with the advantages which republican institutions afford. The immediate, general, and cheerful acquiescence of all good citizens in the result of the election gives gratifying assurance to our country and to its friends throughout the world that a government based on the free consent of an intelligent and patriotic people possesses elements of strength, stability, and permanency not found in any other form of government.

Continued opposition to the full and free enjoyment of the rights of citizenship conferred upon the colored people by the recent amendments to the Constitution still prevails in several of the late slaveholding States. It has, perhaps, not been manifested in the recent election to any large extent in acts of violence or intimidation. It has, however, by fraudulent practices in connection with the ballots, with the regulations as to the places and manner of voting, and with counting, returning, and canvassing the votes cast, been successful in defeating the exercise of the right preservative of all rights—the right of suffrage—which the Constitution expressly confers upon our enfranchised citizens.

It is the desire of the good people of the whole country that sectionalism as a factor in our politics should disappear. They prefer that no section of the country should be united in solid opposition to any other section. The disposition to refuse a prompt and hearty obedience to the equal-rights amendments to the Constitution is all that now stands in the way of a complete obliteration of sectional lines in our political contests. As long as either of these amendments is flagrantly violated or disregarded, it is safe to assume that the people who placed them in the Constitution, as embodying the legitimate results of the war for the Union, and who believe them to be wise and necessary, will continue to act together and to insist that they shall be obeyed. The paramount question still is as to the enjoyment of the fight by every American citizen who has the requisite qualifications to freely cast his vote and to have it honestly counted. With this question rightly settled, the country will be relieved of the contentions of the past; bygones will indeed be bygones, and political and party issues, with respect to economy and efficiency of administration, internal improvements, the tariff, domestic taxation, education, finance, and other important subjects, will then receive their full share of attention; but resistance to and nullification of the results of the war will unite together in resolute purpose for their support all who maintain the authority of the Government and the perpetuity of the Union, and who adequately appreciate the value of the victory achieved. This determination proceeds from no hostile sentiment or feeling to any part of the people of our country or to any of their interests. The inviolability of the amendments rests upon the fundamental principle of our Government. They are the solemn expression of the will of the people of the United States.

The sentiment that the constitutional rights of all our citizens must be maintained does not grow weaker. It will continue to control the Government of the country. Happily, the history of the late election shows that in many parts of the country where opposition to the fifteenth amendment has heretofore prevailed it is diminishing, and is likely to cease altogether if firm and well-considered action is taken by Congress. I trust the House of Representatives and the Senate, which have the right to judge of the elections, returns, and qualifications of their own members, will see to it that every case of violation of the letter or spirit of the fifteenth amendment is thoroughly investigated, and that no benefit from such violation shall accrue to any person or party. It will be the duty of the Executive, with sufficient appropriations for the purpose, to prosecute unsparingly all who have been engaged in depriving citizens of the rights guaranteed to them by the Constitution.

It is not, however, to be forgotten that the best and surest guaranty of the primary rights of citizenship is to be found in that capacity for self-protection which can belong only to a people whose right to universal suffrage is supported by universal education. The means at the command of the local and State authorities are in many cases wholly inadequate to furnish free instruction to all who need it. This is especially true where before emancipation the education of the people was neglected or prevented, in the interest of slavery. Firmly convinced that the subject of popular education deserves the earnest attention of the people of the whole country, with a view to wise and comprehensive action by the Government of the United States, I respectfully recommend that Congress, by suitable legislation and with proper safeguards, supplement the local educational funds in the several States where the grave duties and responsibilities of citizenship have been devolved on uneducated people by devoting to the purpose grants of the public lands and, if necessary, by appropriations from the Treasury of the United States. Whatever Government can fairly do to promote free popular education ought to be done. Wherever general education is found, peace, virtue, and social order prevail and civil and religious liberty are secure.

In my former annual messages I have asked the attention of Congress to the urgent necessity of a reformation of the civil-service system of the Government. My views concerning the dangers of patronage, or appointments for personal or partisan considerations, have been strengthened by my observation and experience in the Executive office, and I believe these dangers threaten the stability of the Government. Abuses so serious in their nature can not be permanently tolerated. They tend to become more alarming with the enlargement of administrative service, as the growth of the country in population increases the number of officers and placemen employed.

The reasons are imperative for the adoption of fixed rules for the regulation of appointments, promotions, and removals, establishing a uniform method having exclusively in view in every instance the attainment of the best qualifications for the position in question. Such a method alone is consistent with the equal rights of all citizens and the most economical and efficient administration of the public business.

Competitive examinations in aid of impartial appointments and promotions have been conducted for some years past in several of the Executive Departments, and by my direction this system has been adopted in the custom-houses and post-offices of the larger cities of the country. In the city of New York over 2,000 positions in the civil service have been subject in their appointments and tenure of place to the operation of published rules for this purpose during the past two years. The results of these practical trials have been very satisfactory, and have confirmed my opinion in favor of this system of selection. All are subjected to the same tests, and the result is free from prejudice by personal favor or partisan influence. It secures for the position applied for the best qualifications attainable among the competing applicants. It is an effectual protection from the pressure of importunity, which under any other course pursued largely exacts the time and attention of appointing officers, to their great detriment in the discharge of other official duties preventing the abuse of the service for the mere furtherance of private or party purposes, and leaving the employee of the Government, freed from the obligations imposed by patronage, to depend solely upon merit for retention and advancement, and with this constant incentive to exertion and improvement.

These invaluable results have been attained in a high degree in the offices where the rules for appointment by competitive examination have been applied.

A method which has so approved itself by experimental tests at points where such tests may be fairly considered conclusive should be extended to all subordinate positions under the Government. I believe that a strong and growing public sentiment demands immediate measures for securing and enforcing the highest possible efficiency in the civil service and its protection from recognized abuses, and that the experience referred to has demonstrated the feasibility of such measures.

The examinations in the custom-houses and post-offices have been held under many embarrassments and without provision for compensation for the extra labor performed by the officers who have conducted them, and whose commendable interest in the improvement of the public service has induced this devotion of time and labor without pecuniary reward. A continuance of these labors gratuitously ought not to be expected, and without an appropriation by Congress for compensation it is not practicable to extend the system of examinations generally throughout the civil service. It is also highly important that all such examinations should be conducted upon a uniform system and under general supervision. Section 1753 of the Revised Statutes authorizes the President to prescribe the regulations for admission to the civil service of the United States, and for this purpose to employ suitable persons to conduct the requisite inquiries with reference to "the fitness of each candidate, in respect to age, health, character, knowledge, and ability for the branch of service into which he seeks to enter"; but the law is practically inoperative for want of the requisite appropriation.

I therefore recommend an appropriation of $25,000 per annum to meet the expenses of a commission, to be appointed by the President in accordance with the terms of this section, whose duty it shall be to devise a just, uniform, and efficient system of competitive examinations and to supervise the application of the same throughout the entire civil service of the Government. I am persuaded that the facilities which such a commission will afford for testing the fitness of those who apply for office will not only be as welcome a relief to members of Congress as it will be to the President and heads of Departments, but that it will also greatly tend to remove the causes of embarrassment which now inevitably and constantly attend the conflicting claims of patronage between the legislative and executive departments. The most effectual check upon the pernicious competition of influence and official favoritism in the bestowal of office will be the substitution of an open competition of merit between the applicants, in which everyone can make his own record with the assurance that his success will depend upon this alone.

I also recommend such legislation as, while leaving every officer as free as any other citizen to express his political opinions and to use his means for their advancement, shall also enable him to feel as safe as any private citizen in refusing all demands upon his salary for political purposes. A law which should thus guarantee true liberty and justice to all who are engaged in the public service, and likewise contain stringent provisions against the use of official authority to coerce the political action of private citizens or of official subordinates, is greatly to be desired.

The most serious obstacle, however, to an improvement of the civil service, and especially to a reform in the method of appointment and removal, has been found to be the practice, under what is known as the spoils system, by which the appointing power has been so largely encroached upon by members of Congress. The first step in the reform of the civil service must be a complete divorce between Congress and the Executive in the matter of appointments. The corrupting doctrine that "to the victors belong the spoils" is inseparable from Congressional patronage as the established rule and practice of parties in power. It comes to be understood by applicants for office and by the people generally that Representatives and Senators are entitled to disburse the patronage of their respective districts and States. It is not necessary to recite at length the evils resulting from this invasion of the Executive functions. The true principles of Government on the subject of appointments to office, as stated in the national conventions of the leading parties of the country, have again and again been approved by the American people, and have not been called in question in any quarter. These authentic expressions of public opinion upon this all-important subject are the statement of principles that belong to the constitutional structure of the Government.

> Under the Constitution the President and heads of Departments are to make nominations for office. The Senate is to advise and consent to appointments, and the House of Representatives is to accuse and prosecute faithless officers. The best interest of the public service demands that these distinctions be respected; that Senators and Representatives, who may be judges and accusers, should not dictate appointments to office.

To this end the cooperation of the legislative department of the Government is required alike by the necessities of the case and by public opinion. Members of Congress will not be relieved from the demands made upon them with reference to appointments to office until by legislative enactment the pernicious practice is condemned and forbidden.

It is therefore recommended that an act be passed defining the relations of members of Congress with respect to appointment to office by the President; and I also recommend that the provisions of section 1767 and of the sections following of the Revised Statutes, comprising the tenure-of-office act of March 2, 1867, be repealed.

Believing that to reform the system and methods of the civil service in our country is one of the highest and most imperative duties of statesmanship, and that it can be permanently done only by the cooperation of the legislative and executive departments of the Government, I again commend the whole subject to your considerate attention.

It is the recognized duty and purpose of the people of the United States to suppress polygamy where it now exists in our Territories and to prevent its extension. Faithful and zealous efforts have been made by the United States authorities in Utah to enforce the laws against it. Experience has shown that the legislation upon this subject, to be effective, requires extensive modification and amendment. The longer action is delayed the more difficult it will be to accomplish what is desired. Prompt and decided measures are necessary. The Mormon sectarian organization which upholds polygamy has the whole power of making and executing the local legislation of the Territory. By its control of the grand and petit juries it possesses large influence over the administration of justice. Exercising, as the heads of this sect do, the local political power of the Territory, they are able to make effective their hostility to the law of Congress on the subject of polygamy, and, in fact, do prevent its enforcement. Polygamy will not be abolished if the enforcement of the law depends on those who practice and uphold the crime. It can only be suppressed by taking away the political power of the sect which encourages and sustains it.

The power of Congress to enact suitable laws to protect the Territories is ample. It is not a case for halfway measures. The political power of the Mormon sect is increasing. It controls now one of our wealthiest and most populous Territories. It is extending steadily into other Territories. Wherever it goes it establishes polygamy and sectarian political power. The sanctity of marriage and the family relation are the corner stone of our American society and civilization. Religious liberty and the separation of church and state are among the elementary ideas of free institutions. To reestablish the interests and principles which polygamy and Mormonism have imperiled, and to fully reopen to intelligent and virtuous immigrants of all creeds that part of our domain which has been in a great degree closed to general immigration by intolerant and immoral institutions, it is recommended that the government of the Territory of Utah be reorganized.

I recommend that Congress provide for the government of Utah by a governor and judges, or commissioners, appointed by the President and confirmed by the Senate—a government analogous to the provisional government established for the territory northwest of the Ohio by the ordinance of 1787. If, however, it is deemed best to continue the existing form of local government, I recommend that the right to vote, hold office, and sit on juries in the Territory of Utah be confined to those who neither practice nor uphold polygamy. If thorough measures are adopted, it is believed that within a few years the evils which now afflict Utah will be eradicated, and that this Territory will in good time become one of the most prosperous and attractive of the new States of the Union.

Our relations with all foreign countries have been those of undisturbed peace, and have presented no occasion for concern as to their continued maintenance.

My anticipation of an early reply from the British Government to the demand of indemnity to our fishermen for the injuries suffered by that industry at Fortune Bay in January, 1878, which I expressed in my last annual message, was disappointed. This answer was received only in the latter part of April in the present year, and when received exhibited a failure of accord between the two Governments as to the measure of the inshore fishing privilege secured to our fishermen by the treaty of Washington of so serious a character that I made it the subject of a communication to Congress, in which I recommended the adoption of the measures which seemed to me proper to be taken by this Government in maintenance of the rights accorded to our fishermen under the treaty and toward securing an indemnity for the injury these interests had suffered. A bill to carry out these recommendations was under consideration by the House of Representatives at the time of the adjournment of Congress in June last.

Within a few weeks I have received a communication from Her Majesty's Government renewing the consideration of the subject, both of the indemnity for the injuries at Fortune Bay and of the interpretation of the treaty in which the previous correspondence had shown the two Governments to be at variance. Upon both these topics the disposition toward a friendly agreement is manifested by a recognition of our right to an indemnity for the transaction at Fortune Bay, leaving the measure of such indemnity to further conference, and by an assent to the view of this Government, presented in the previous correspondence, that the regulation of conflicting interests of the shore fishery of the provincial seacoasts and the vessel fishery of our fishermen should be made the subject of conference and concurrent arrangement between the two Governments.

I sincerely hope that the basis may be found for a speedy adjustment of the very serious divergence of views in the interpretation of the fishery clauses of the treaty of Washington, which, as the correspondence between the two Governments stood at the close of the last session of Congress, seemed to be irreconcilable.

In the important exhibition of arts and industries which was held last year at Sydney, New South Wales, as well as in that now in progress at Melbourne, the United States have been efficiently and honorably represented. The exhibitors from this country at the former place received a large number of awards in some of the most considerable departments, and the participation of the United States was recognized by a special mark of distinction. In the exhibition at Melbourne the share taken by our country is no less notable, and an equal degree of success is confidently expected.

The state of peace and tranquillity now enjoyed by all the nations of the continent of Europe has its favorable influence upon our diplomatic and commercial relations with them. We have concluded and ratified a convention with the French Republic for the settlement of claims of the citizens of either country against the other. Under this convention a commission, presided over by a distinguished publicist, appointed in pursuance of the request of both nations by His Majesty the Emperor of Brazil, has been organized and has begun its sessions in this city. A congress to consider means for the protection of industrial property has recently been in session in Paris, to which I have appointed the ministers of the United States in France and in Belgium as delegates. The International Commission upon Weights and Measures also continues its work in Paris. I invite your attention to the necessity of an appropriation to be made in time to enable this Government to comply with its obligations under the metrical convention.

Our friendly relations with the German Empire continue without interruption. At the recent International Exhibition of Fish and Fisheries at Berlin the participation of the United States, notwithstanding the haste with which the commission was forced to make its preparations, was extremely successful and meritorious, winning for private exhibitors numerous awards of a high class and for the country at large the principal prize of honor offered by His Majesty the Emperor. The results of this great success can not but be advantageous to this important and growing industry. There have been some questions raised between the two Governments as to the proper effect and interpretation of our treaties of naturalization, but recent dispatches from our minister at Berlin show that favorable progress is making toward an understanding in accordance with the views of this Government, which makes and admits no distinction whatever between the rights of a native and a naturalized citizen of the United States. In practice the complaints of molestation suffered by naturalized citizens abroad have never been fewer than at present.

There is nothing of importance to note in our unbroken friendly relations with the Governments of Austria-Hungary, Russia, Portugal, Sweden and Norway, Switzerland, Turkey, and Greece.

During the last summer several vessels belonging to the merchant marine of this country, sailing in neutral waters of the West Indies, were fired at, boarded, and searched by an armed cruiser of the Spanish Government. The circumstances as reported involve not only a private injury to the persons concerned, but also seemed too little observant of the friendly relations existing for a century between this country and Spain. The wrong was brought to the attention of the Spanish Government in a serious protest and remonstrance, and the matter is undergoing investigation by the royal authorities with a view to such explanation or reparation as may be called for by the facts. The commission sitting in this city for the adjudication of claims of our citizens against the Government of Spain is, I hope, approaching the termination of its labors.

The claims against the United States under the Florida treaty with Spain were submitted to Congress for its action at the late session, and I again invite your attention to this long-standing question, with a view to a final disposition of the matter.

At the invitation of the Spanish Government, a conference has recently been held at the city of Madrid to consider the subject of protection by foreign powers of native Moors in the Empire of Morocco. The minister of the United States in Spain was directed to take part in the deliberations of this conference, the result of which is a convention signed on behalf of all the powers represented. The instrument will be laid before the Senate for its consideration. The Government of the United States has also lost no opportunity to urge upon that of the Emperor of Morocco the necessity, in accordance with the humane and enlightened spirit of the age, of putting an end to the persecutions, which have been so prevalent in that country, of persons of a faith other than the Moslem, and especially of the Hebrew residents of Morocco.

The consular treaty concluded with Belgium has not yet been officially promulgated, owing to the alteration of a word in the text by the Senate of the United States, which occasioned a delay, during which the time allowed for ratification expired. The Senate will be asked to extend the period for ratification.

The attempt to negotiate a treaty of extradition with Denmark failed on account of the objection of the Danish Government to the usual clause providing that each nation should pay the expense of the arrest of the persons whose extradition it asks.

The provision made by Congress at its last session for the expense of the commission which had been appointed to enter upon negotiations with the Imperial Government of China on subjects of great interest to the relations of the two countries enabled the commissioners to proceed at once upon their mission. The Imperial Government was prepared to give prompt and respectful attention to the matters brought under negotiation, and the conferences proceeded with such rapidity and success that on the 17th of November last two treaties were signed at Peking, one relating to the introduction of Chinese into this country and one relating to commerce. Mr. Trescot, one of the commissioners, is now on his way home bringing the treaties, and it is expected that they will be received in season to be laid before the Senate early in January.

Our minister in Japan has negotiated a convention for the reciprocal relief of shipwrecked seamen. I take occasion to urge once more upon Congress the propriety of making provision for the erection of suitable fireproof buildings at the Japanese capital for the use of the American legation and the court-house and jail connected with it. The Japanese Government, with great generosity and courtesy, has offered for this purpose an eligible piece of land.

In my last annual message I invited the attention of Congress to the subject of the indemnity funds received some years ago from China and Japan. I renew the recommendation then made that whatever portions of these funds are due to American citizens should be promptly paid and the residue returned to the nations, respectively, to which they justly and equitably belong.

The extradition treaty with the Kingdom of the Netherlands, which has been for some time in course of negotiation, has during the past year been concluded and duly ratified.

Relations of friendship and amity have been established between the Government of the United States and that of Roumania. We have sent a diplomatic representative to Bucharest, and have received at this capital the special envoy who has been charged by His Royal Highness Prince Charles to announce the independent sovereignty of Roumania. We hope for a speedy development of commercial relations between the two countries.

In my last annual message I expressed the hope that the prevalence of quiet on the border between this country and Mexico would soon become so assured as to justify the modification of the orders then in force to our military commanders in regard to crossing the frontier, without encouraging such disturbances as would endanger the peace of the two countries. Events moved in accordance with these expectations, and the orders were accordingly withdrawn, to the entire satisfaction of our own citizens and the Mexican Government. Subsequently the peace of the border was again disturbed by a savage foray under the command of the Chief Victoria, but by the combined and harmonious action of the military forces of both countries his band has been broken up and substantially destroyed.

There is reason to believe that the obstacles which have so long prevented rapid and convenient communication between the United States and Mexico by railways are on the point of disappearing, and that several important enterprises of this character will soon be set on foot, which can not fail to contribute largely to the prosperity of both countries.

New envoys from Guatemala, Colombia, Bolivia, Venezuela, and Nicaragua have recently arrived at this capital, whose distinction and enlightenment afford the best guaranty of the continuance of friendly relations between ourselves and these sister Republics.

The relations between this Government and that of the United States of Colombia have engaged public attention during the past year, mainly by reason of the project of an interoceanic canal across the Isthmus of Panama, to be built by private capital under a concession from the Colombian Government for that purpose. The treaty obligations subsisting between the United States and Colombia, by which we guarantee the neutrality of the transit and the sovereignty and property of Colombia in the Isthmus, make it necessary that the conditions under which so stupendous a change in the region embraced in this guaranty should be effected—transforming, as it would, this Isthmus from a barrier between the Atlantic and Pacific oceans into a gateway and thoroughfare between them for the navies and the merchant ships of the world—should receive the approval of this Government, as being compatible with the discharge of these obligations on our part and consistent with our interests as the principal commercial power of the Western Hemisphere. The views which I expressed in a special message to Congress in March last in relation to this project I deem it my duty again to press upon your attention. Subsequent consideration has but confirmed the opinion "that it is the right and duty of the United States to assert and maintain such supervision and authority over any interoceanic canal across the isthmus that connects North and South America as will protect our national interest."

The war between the Republic of Chile on the one hand and the allied Republics of Peru and Bolivia on the other still continues. This Government has not felt called upon to interfere in a contest that is within the belligerent rights of the parties as independent states. We have, however, always held ourselves in readiness to aid in accommodating their difference, and have at different times reminded both belligerents of our willingness to render such service.

Our good offices in this direction were recently accepted by all the belligerents, and it was hoped they would prove efficacious; but I regret to announce that the measures which the ministers of the United States at Santiago and Lima were authorized to take with the view to bring about a peace were not successful. In the course of the war some questions have arisen affecting neutral rights. In all of these the ministers of the United States have, under their instructions, acted with promptness and energy in protection of American interests.

The relations of the United States with the Empire of Brazil continue to be most cordial, and their commercial intercourse steadily increases, to their mutual advantage.

The internal disorders with which the Argentine Republic has for some time past been afflicted, and which have more or less influenced its external trade, are understood to have been brought to a close. This happy result may be expected to redound to the benefit of the foreign commerce of that Republic, as well as to the development of its vast interior resources.

In Samoa the Government of King Malietoa, under the support and recognition of the consular representatives of the United States, Great Britain, and Germany, seems to have given peace and tranquillity to the islands. While it does not appear desirable to adopt as a whole the scheme of tripartite local government which has been proposed, the common interests of the three great treaty powers require harmony in their relations to the native frame of government, and this may be best secured by a simple diplomatic agreement between them. It would be well if the consular jurisdiction of our representative at Apia were increased in extent and importance so as to guard American interests in the surrounding and outlying islands of Oceanica.

The obelisk generously presented by the Khedive of Egypt to the city of New York has safely arrived in this country, and will soon be erected in that metropolis. A commission for the liquidation of the Egyptian debt has lately concluded its work, and this Government, at the earnest solicitation of the Khedive, has acceded to the provisions adopted by it, which will be laid before Congress for its information. A commission for the revision of the judicial code of the reform tribunal of Egypt is now in session in Cairo. Mr. Farman, consul-general, and J. M. Batchelder, esq., have been appointed as commissioners to participate in this work. The organization of the reform tribunals will probably be continued for another period of five years.

In pursuance of the act passed at the last session of Congress, invitations have been extended to foreign maritime states to join in a sanitary conference in Washington, beginning the 1st of January. The acceptance of this invitation by many prominent powers gives promise of success in this important measure, designed to establish a system of international notification by which the spread of infectious or epidemic diseases may be more effectively checked or prevented. The attention of Congress is invited to the necessary appropriations for carrying into effect the provisions of the act referred to.

The efforts of the Department of State to enlarge the trade and commerce of the United States, through the active agency of consular officers and through the dissemination of information obtained from them, have been unrelaxed. The interest in these efforts, as developed in our commercial communities, and the value of the information secured by this means to the trade and manufactures of the country were recognized by Congress at its last session, and provision was made for the more frequent publication of consular and other reports by the Department of State. The first issue of this publication has now been prepared, and subsequent issues may regularly be expected. The importance and interest attached to the reports of consular officers are witnessed by the general demand for them by all classes of merchants and manufacturers engaged in our foreign trade. It is believed that the system of such publications is deserving of the approval of Congress, and that the necessary appropriations for its continuance and enlargement will commend itself to your consideration.

The prosperous energies of our domestic industries and their immense production of the subjects of foreign commerce invite, and even require, an active development of the wishes and interests of our people in that direction. Especially important is it that our commercial relations with the Atlantic and Pacific coasts of South America, with the West Indies and the Gulf of Mexico, should be direct, and not through the circuit of European systems, and should be carried on in our own bottoms. The full appreciation of the opportunities which our front on the Pacific Ocean gives to commerce with Japan, China, and the East Indies, with Australia and the island groups which lie along these routes of navigation, should inspire equal efforts to appropriate to our own shipping and to administer by our own capital a due proportion of this trade. Whatever modifications of our regulations of trade and navigation may be necessary or useful to meet and direct these impulses to the enlargement of our exchanges and of our carrying trade I am sure the wisdom of Congress will be ready to supply. One initial measure, however, seems to me so clearly useful and efficient that I venture to press it upon your earnest attention. It seems to be very evident that the provision of regular steam postal communication by aid from government has been the forerunner of the commercial predominance of Great Britain on all these coasts and seas, a greater share in whose trade is now the desire and the intent of our people. It is also manifest that the efforts of other European nations to contend with Great Britain for a share of this commerce have been successful in proportion with their adoption of regular steam postal communication with the markets whose trade they sought. Mexico and the States of South America are anxious to receive such postal communication with this country and to aid in their development. Similar cooperation may be looked for in due time from the Eastern nations and from Australia. It is difficult to see how the lead in this movement can be expected from private interests. In respect of foreign commerce quite as much as in internal trade postal communication seems necessarily a matter of common and public administration, and thus pertaining to Government. I respectfully recommend to your prompt attention such just and efficient measures as may conduce to the development of our foreign commercial exchanges and the building up of our carrying trade.

In this connection I desire also to suggest the very great service which might be expected in enlarging and facilitating our commerce on the Pacific Ocean were a transmarine cable laid from San Francisco to the Sandwich Islands, and thence to Japan at the north and Australia at the south. The great influence of such means of communication on these routes of navigation in developing and securing the due share of our Pacific Coast in the commerce of the world needs no illustration or enforcement. It may be that such an enterprise, useful, and in the end profitable, as it would prove to private investment, may need to be accelerated by prudent legislation by Congress in its aid, and I submit the matter to your careful consideration.

An additional and not unimportant, although secondary, reason for fostering and enlarging the Navy may be found in the unquestionable service to the expansion of our commerce which would be rendered by the frequent circulation of naval ships in the seas and ports of all quarters of the globe. Ships of the proper construction and equipment to be of the greatest efficiency in case of maritime war might be made constant and active agents in time of peace in the advancement and protection of our foreign trade and in the nurture and discipline of young seamen, who would naturally in some numbers mix with and improve the crews of our merchant ships. Our merchants at home and abroad recognize the value to foreign commerce of an active movement of our naval vessels, and the intelligence and patriotic zeal of our naval officers in promoting every interest of their countrymen is a just subject of national pride.

The condition of the financial affairs of the Government, as shown by the report of the Secretary of the Treasury, is very satisfactory. It is believed that the present financial situation of the United States, whether considered with respect to trade, currency, credit, growing wealth, or the extent and variety of our resources, is more favorable than that of any other country of our time, and has never been surpassed by that of any country at any period of its history. All our industries are thriving; the rate of interest is low; new railroads are being constructed; a vast immigration is increasing our population, capital, and labor; new enterprises in great number are in progress, and our commercial relations with other countries are improving.

*   *   *

It is fortunate that this large surplus revenue occurs at a period when it may be directly applied to the payment of the public debt soon to be redeemable. No public duty has been more constantly cherished in the United States than the policy of paying the nation's debt as rapidly as possible.

The debt of the United States, less cash in the Treasury and exclusive of accruing interest, attained its maximum of $2,756,431,571.43 in August, 1865, and has since that time been reduced to $1,886,019,504.65. Of the principal of the debt, $108,758,100 has been paid since March 1, 1877, effecting an annual saving of interest of $6,107,593. The burden of interest has also been diminished by the sale of bonds bearing a low rate of interest and the application of the proceeds to the redemption of bonds bearing a higher rate. The annual saving thus secured since March 1, 1877, is $14,290,453.50. Within a short period over six hundred millions of 5 and 6 per cent bonds will become redeemable. This presents a very favorable opportunity not only to further reduce the principal of the debt, but also to reduce the rate of interest on that which will remain unpaid. I call the attention of Congress to the views expressed on this subject by the Secretary of the Treasury in his annual report, and recommend prompt legislation to enable the Treasury Department to complete the refunding of the debt which is about to mature.

The continuance of specie payments has not been interrupted or endangered since the date of resumption. It has contributed greatly to the revival of business and to our remarkable prosperity. The fears that preceded and accompanied resumption have proved groundless. No considerable amount of United States notes have been presented for redemption, while very large sums of gold bullion, both domestic and imported, are taken to the mints and exchanged for coin or notes. The increase of coin and bullion in the United States since January 1, 1879, is estimated at $227,399,428.

There are still in existence, uncanceled, $346,681,016 of United States legal-tender notes. These notes were authorized as a war measure, made necessary by the exigencies of the conflict in which the United States was then engaged. The preservation of the nation's existence required, in the judgment of Congress, an issue of legal-tender paper money. That it served well the purpose for which it was created is not questioned, but the employment of the notes as paper money indefinitely, after the accomplishment of the object for which they were provided, was not contemplated by the framers of the law under which they were issued. These notes long since became, like any other pecuniary obligation of the Government, a debt to be paid, and when paid to be canceled as mere evidence of an indebtedness no longer existing. I therefore repeat what was said in the annual message of last year, that the retirement from circulation of United States notes with the capacity of legal tender in private contracts is a step to be taken in our progress toward a safe and stable currency which should be accepted as the policy and duty of the Government and the interest and security of the people.

At the time of the passage of the act now in force requiring the coinage of silver dollars, fixing their value, and giving them legal-tender character it was believed by many of the supporters of the measure that the silver dollar which it authorized would speedily become, under the operations of the law, of equivalent value to the gold dollar. There were other supporters of the bill, who, while they doubted as to the probability of this result, nevertheless were willing to give the proposed experiment a fair trial, with a view to stop the coinage if experience should prove that the silver dollar authorized by the bill continued to be of less commercial value than the standard gold dollar.

The coinage of silver dollars under the act referred to began in March, 1878, and has been continued as required by the act. The average rate per month to the present time has been $2,276,492. The total amount coined prior to the 1st of November last was $72,847,750. Of this amount $47,084,450 remain in the Treasury, and only $25,763,291 are in the hands of the people. A constant effort has been made to keep this currency in circulation, and considerable expense has been necessarily incurred for this purpose; but its return to the Treasury is prompt and sure. Contrary to the confident anticipation of the friends of the measure at the time of its adoption, the value of the silver dollar containing 412½ grains of silver has not increased. During the year prior to the passage of the bill authorizing its coinage the market value of the silver which it contained was from 90 to 92 cents as compared with the standard gold dollar. During the last year the average market value of the silver dollar has been 88½ cents.

It is obvious that the legislation of the last Congress in regard to silver, so far as it was based on an anticipated rise in the value of silver as a result of that legislation, has failed to produce the effect then predicted. The longer the law remains in force, requiring, as it does, the coinage of a nominal dollar which in reality is not a dollar, the greater becomes the danger that this country will be forced to accept a single metal as the sole legal standard of value in circulation, and this a standard of less value than it purports to be worth in the recognized money of the world.

The Constitution of the United States, sound financial principles, and our best interests all require that the country should have as its legal-tender money both gold and silver coin of an intrinsic value, as bullion, equivalent to that which upon its face it purports to possess. The Constitution in express terms recognizes both gold and silver as the only true legal-tender money. To banish either of these metals from our currency is to narrow and limit the circulating medium of exchange to the disparagement of important interests. The United States produces more silver than any other country, and is directly interested in maintaining it as one of the two precious metals which furnish the coinage of the world. It will, in my judgment, contribute to this result if Congress will repeal so much of existing legislation as requires the coinage of silver dollars containing only 412½ grains of silver, and in its stead will authorize the Secretary of the Treasury to coin silver dollars of equivalent value, as bullion, with gold dollars. This will defraud no man, and will be in accordance with familiar precedents. Congress on several occasions has altered the ratio of value between gold and silver, in order to establish it more nearly in accordance with the actual ratio of value between the two metals.

In financial legislation every measure in the direction of greater fidelity in the discharge of pecuniary obligations has been found by experience to diminish the rates of interest which debtors are required to pay and to increase the facility with which money can be obtained for every legitimate purpose. Our own recent financial history shows how surely money becomes abundant whenever confidence in the exact performance of moneyed obligations is established.

The Secretary of War reports that, the expenditures of the War Department for the fiscal year ended June 30, 1880, were $39,924,773.03. The appropriations for this Department for the current fiscal year amount to $41,993,630.40.

With respect to the Army, the Secretary invites attention to the fact that its strength is limited by statute (U.S. Revised Statutes, sec. 1115) to not more than 30,000 enlisted men, but that provisos contained in appropriation bills have limited expenditures to the enlistment of but 25,000. It is believed the full legal strength is the least possible force at which the present organization can be maintained, having in view efficiency, discipline, and economy. While the enlistment of this force would add somewhat to the appropriation for pay of the Army, the saving made in other respects would be more than an equivalent for this additional outlay, and the efficiency of the Army would be largely increased.

The rapid extension of the railroad system west of the Mississippi River and the great tide of settlers which has flowed in upon new territory impose on the military an entire change of policy. The maintenance of small posts along wagon and stage routes of travel is no longer necessary. Permanent quarters at points selected, of a more substantial character than those heretofore constructed, will be required. Under existing laws permanent buildings can not be erected without the sanction of Congress, and when sales of military sites and buildings have been authorized the moneys received have reverted to the Treasury and could only become available through a new appropriation. It is recommended that provision be made by a general statute for the sale of such abandoned military posts and buildings as are found to be unnecessary and for the application of the proceeds to the construction of other posts. While many of the present posts are of but slight value for military purposes, owing to the changed condition of the country, their occupation is continued at great expense and inconvenience; because they afford the only available shelter for troops.

The absence of a large number of officers of the line, in active duty, from their regiments is a serious detriment to the maintenance of the service. The constant demand for small detachments, each of which should be commanded by a commissioned officer, and the various details of officers for necessary service away from their commands occasion a scarcity in the number required for company duties. With a view to lessening this drain to some extent, it is recommended that the law authorizing the detail of officers from the active list as professors of tactics and military science at certain colleges and universities be so amended as to provide that all such details be made from the retired list of the Army.

Attention is asked to the necessity of providing by legislation for organizing, arming, and disciplining the active militia of the country, and liberal appropriations are recommended in this behalf. The reports of the Adjutant-General of the Army and the Chief of Ordnance touching this subject fully set forth its importance.

The report of the officer in charge of education in the Army shows that there are 78 schools now in operation in the Army, with an aggregate attendance of 2,305 enlisted men and children. The Secretary recommends the enlistment of 150 schoolmasters, with the rank and pay of commissary-sergeants. An appropriation is needed to supply the judge-advocates of the Army with suitable libraries, and the Secretary recommends that the Corps of Judge-Advocates be placed upon the same footing as to promotion with the other staff corps of the Army. Under existing laws the Bureau of Military Justice consists of one officer (the Judge-Advocate-General), and the Corps of Judge-Advocates of eight officers of equal rank (majors), with a provision that the limit of the corps shall remain at four when reduced by casualty or resignation to that number. The consolidation of the Bureau of Military Justice and the Corps of Judge-Advocates upon the same basis with the other staff corps of the Army would remove an unjust discrimination against deserving officers and subserve the best interests of the service.

Especial attention is asked to the report of the Chief of Engineers upon the condition of our national defenses. From a personal inspection of many of the fortifications referred to, the Secretary is able to emphasize the recommendations made and to state that their incomplete and defenseless condition is discreditable to the country. While other nations have been increasing their means for carrying on offensive warfare and attacking maritime cities, we have been dormant in preparation for defense. Nothing of importance has been done toward strengthening and finishing our casemated works since our late civil war, during which the great guns of modern warfare and the heavy armor of modern fortifications and ships came into use among the nations; and our earthworks, left by a sudden failure of appropriations some years since in all stages of incompletion, are now being rapidly destroyed by the elements.

The two great rivers of the North American continent, the Mississippi and the Columbia, have their navigable waters wholly within the limits of the United States, and are of vast importance to our internal and foreign commerce. The permanency of the important work on the South Pass of the Mississippi River seems now to be assured. There has been no failure whatever in the maintenance of the maximum channel during the six months ended August 9 last. This experiment has opened a broad, deep highway to the ocean, and is an improvement upon the permanent success of which congratulations may be exchanged among people abroad and at home, and especially among the communities of the Mississippi Valley, whose commercial exchanges float in an unobstructed channel safely to and from the sea.

A comprehensive improvement of the Mississippi and its tributaries is a matter of transcendent importance. These great waterways comprise a system of inland transportation spread like network over a large portion of the United States, and navigable to the extent of many thousands of miles. Producers and consumers alike have a common interest in such unequaled facilities for cheap transportation. Geographically, commercially, and politically, they are the strongest tie between the various sections of the country. These channels of communication and interchange are the property of the nation. Its jurisdiction is paramount over their waters, and the plainest principles of public interest require their intelligent and careful supervision, with a view to their protection, improvement, and the enhancement of their usefulness.

The channel of the Columbia River for a distance of about 100 miles from its mouth is obstructed by a succession of bars, which occasion serious delays in navigation and heavy expense for lighterage and towage. A depth of at least 20 feet at low tide should be secured and maintained to meet the requirements of the extensive and growing inland and ocean commerce it subserves. The most urgent need, however, for this great waterway is a permanent improvement of the channel at the mouth of the river.

From Columbia River to San Francisco, a distance of over 600 miles, there is no harbor on our Pacific coast which can be approached during stormy weather. An appropriation of $150,000 was made by the Forty-fifth Congress for the commencement of a breakwater and harbor of refuge, to be located at some point between the Straits of Fuca and San Francisco at which the necessities of commerce, local and general, will be best accommodated. The amount appropriated is thought to be quite inadequate for the purpose intended. The cost of the work, when finished, will be very great, owing to the want of natural advantages for a site at any point on the coast between the designated limits, and it has not been thought to be advisable to undertake the work without a larger appropriation. I commend the matter to the attention of Congress.

The completion of the new building for the War Department is urgently needed, and the estimates for continuing its construction are especially recommended.

The collections of books, specimens, and records constituting the Army Medical Museum and Library are of national importance. The library now contains about 51,500 volumes and 57,000 pamphlets relating to medicine, surgery, and allied topics. The contents of the Army Medical Museum consist of 22,000 specimens, and are unique in the completeness with which both military surgery and the diseases of armies are illustrated. Their destruction would be an irreparable loss, not only to the United States, but to the world. There are filed in the Record and Pension Division over 16,000 bound volumes of hospital records, together with a great quantity of papers, embracing the original records of the hospitals of our armies during the civil war. Aside from their historical value, these records are daily searched for evidence needed in the settlement of large numbers of pension and other claims, for the protection of the Government against attempted frauds, as well as for the benefit of honest claimants. These valuable collections are now in a building which is peculiarly exposed to the danger of destruction by fire. It is therefore earnestly recommended that an appropriation be made for a new fireproof building, adequate for the present needs and reasonable future expansion of these valuable collections. Such a building should be absolutely fireproof; no expenditure for mere architectural display is required. It is believed that a suitable structure can be erected at a cost not to exceed $250,000.

I commend to the attention of Congress the great services of the Commander in Chief of our armies during the war for the Union, whose wise, firm, and patriotic conduct did so much to bring that momentous conflict to a close. The legislation of the United States contains many precedents for the recognition of distinguished military merit, authorizing rank and emoluments to be conferred for eminent services to the country. An act of Congress authorizing the appointment of a Captain-General of the Army, with suitable provisions relating to compensation, retirement, and other details, would, in my judgment, be altogether fitting and proper, and would be warmly approved by the country.

The report of the Secretary of the Navy exhibits the successful and satisfactory management of that Department during the last fiscal year. The total expenditures for the year were $12,916,639.45, leaving unexpended at the close of the year $2,141,682.23 of the amount of available appropriations. The appropriations for the present fiscal year, ending June 30, 1881, are $15,095,061.45, and the total estimates for the next fiscal year, ending June 30, 1882, are $15,953,751.61. The amount drawn by warrant from July 1, 1880, to November 1, 1880, is $5,041,570.45.

The recommendation of the Secretary of the Navy that provision be made for the establishment of some form of civil government for the people of Alaska is approved. At present there is no protection of persons or property in that Territory except such as is afforded by the officers of the United States ship *Jamestown*. This vessel was dispatched to Sitka because of the fear that without the immediate presence of the national authority there was impending danger of anarchy. The steps taken to restore order have been accepted in good faith by both white and Indian inhabitants, and the necessity for this method of restraint does not, in my opinion, now exist. If, however, the *Jamestown* should be withdrawn, leaving the people, as at present, without the ordinary judicial and administrative authority of organized local government, serious consequences might ensue.

The laws provide only for the collection of revenue, the protection of public property, and the transmission of the mails. The problem is to supply a local rule for a population so scattered and so peculiar in its origin and condition. The natives are reported to be teachable and self-supporting, and if properly instructed doubtless would advance rapidly in civilization, and a new factor of prosperity would be added to the national life. I therefore recommend the requisite legislation upon this subject.

The Secretary of the Navy has taken steps toward the establishment of naval coaling stations at the Isthmus of Panama, to meet the requirements of our commercial relations with Central and South America, which are rapidly growing in importance. Locations eminently suitable, both as regards our naval purposes and the uses of commerce, have been selected, one on the east side of the Isthmus, at Chiriqui Lagoon, in the Caribbean Sea, and the other on the Pacific coast, at the Bay of Golfito. The only safe harbors, sufficiently commodious, on the Isthmus are at these points, and the distance between them is less than 100 miles. The report of the Secretary of the Navy concludes with valuable suggestions with respect to the building up of our merchant marine service, which deserve the favorable consideration of Congress.

The report of the Postmaster-General exhibits the continual growth and the high state of efficiency of the postal service. The operations of no Department of the Government, perhaps, represent with greater exactness the increase in the population and the business of the country. In 1860 the postal receipts were $8,518,067.40; in 1880 the receipts were $33,315,479.34. All the inhabitants of the country are directly and personally interested in having proper mail facilities, and naturally watch the Post-Office very closely. This careful oversight on the part of the people has proved a constant stimulus to improvement. During the past year there was an increase of 2,134 post-offices, and the mail routes were extended 27,177 miles, making an additional annual transportation of 10,804,191 miles. The revenues of the postal service for the ensuing year are estimated at $38,845,174.10, and the expenditures at $42,475,932, leaving a deficiency to be appropriated out of the Treasury of $3,630,757.90.

The Universal Postal Union has received the accession of almost all the countries and colonies of the world maintaining organized postal services, and it is confidently expected that all the other countries and colonies now outside the union will soon unite therewith, thus realizing the grand idea and aim of the founders of the union of forming, for purposes of international mail communication, a single postal territory, embracing the world, with complete uniformity of postal charges and conditions of international exchange for all descriptions of correspondence. To enable the United States to do its full share of this great work, additional legislation is asked by the Postmaster-General, to whose recommendations especial attention is called.

The suggestion of the Postmaster-General that it would be wise to encourage, by appropriate legislation, the establishment of American lines of steamers by our own citizens to carry the mails between our own ports and those of Mexico, Central America, South America, and of transpacific countries is commended to the serious consideration of Congress.

The attention of Congress is also invited to the suggestions of the Postmaster-General in regard to postal savings.

The necessity for additional provision to aid in the transaction of the business of the Federal courts becomes each year more apparent. The dockets of the Supreme Court and of the circuit courts in the greater number of the circuits are encumbered with the constant accession of cases. In the former court, and in many instances in the circuit courts, years intervene before it is practicable to bring cases to hearing.

The Attorney-General recommends the establishment of an intermediate court of errors and appeals. It is recommended that the number of judges of the circuit court in each circuit, with the exception of the second circuit, should be increased by the addition of another judge; in the second circuit, that two should be added; and that an intermediate appellate court should be formed in each circuit, to consist of the circuit judges and the circuit justice, and that in the event of the absence of either of these judges the place of the absent judge should be supplied by the judge of one of the district courts in the circuit. Such an appellate court could be safely invested with large jurisdiction, and its decisions would satisfy suitors in many cases where appeals would still be allowed to the Supreme Court. The expense incurred for this intermediate court will require a very moderate increase of the appropriations for the expenses of the Department of Justice. This recommendation is commended to the careful consideration of Congress.

It is evident that a delay of justice, in many instances oppressive and disastrous to suitors, now necessarily occurs in the Federal courts, which will in this way be remedied.

The report of the Secretary of the Interior presents an elaborate account of the operations of that Department during the past year. It gives me great pleasure to say that our Indian affairs appear to be in a more hopeful condition now than ever before. The Indians have made gratifying progress in agriculture, herding, and mechanical pursuits. Many who were a few years ago in hostile conflict with the Government are quietly settling down on farms where they hope to make their permanent homes, building houses and engaging in the occupations of civilized life. The introduction of the freighting business among them has been remarkably fruitful of good results, in giving many of them congenial and remunerative employment and in stimulating their ambition to earn their own support. Their honesty, fidelity, and efficiency as carriers are highly praised. The organization of a police force of Indians has been equally successful in maintaining law and order upon the reservations and in exercising a wholesome moral influence among the Indians themselves. I concur with the Secretary of the Interior in the recommendation that the pay of this force be increased, as an inducement to the best class of young men to enter it.

Much care and attention has been devoted to the enlargement of educational facilities for the Indians. The means available for this important object have been very inadequate. A few additional boarding schools at Indian agencies have been established and the erection of buildings has been begun for several more; but an increase of the appropriations for this interesting undertaking is greatly needed to accommodate the large number of Indian children of school age. The number offered by their parents from all parts of the country for education in the Government schools is much larger than can be accommodated with the means at present available for that purpose. The number of Indian pupils at the normal school at Hampton, Va., under the direction of General Armstrong, has been considerably increased, and their progress is highly encouraging. The Indian school established by the Interior Department in 1879 at Carlisle, Pa., under the direction of Captain Pratt, has been equally successful. It has now nearly 200 pupils of both sexes, representing a great variety of the tribes east of the Rocky Mountains. The pupils in both these institutions receive not only an elementary English education, but are also instructed in housework, agriculture, and useful mechanical pursuits. A similar school was established this year at Forest Grove, Oreg., for the education of Indian youth on the Pacific Coast. In addition to this, thirty-six Indian boys and girls were selected from the Eastern Cherokees and placed in boarding schools in North Carolina, where they are to receive an elementary English education and training in industrial pursuits. The interest shown by Indian parents, even among the so-called wild tribes, in the education of their children is very gratifying, and gives promise that the results accomplished by the efforts now made will be of lasting benefit.

The expenses of Indian education have so far been drawn from the permanent civilization fund at the disposal of the Department of the Interior, but the fund is now so much reduced that the continuance of this beneficial work will in the future depend on specific appropriations by Congress for the purpose; and I venture to express the hope that Congress will not permit institutions so fruitful of good results to perish for want of means for their support. On the contrary, an increase of the number of such schools appears to me highly advisable.

The past year has been unusually free from disturbances among the Indian tribes. An agreement has been made with the Utes by which they surrender their large reservation in Colorado in consideration of an annuity to be paid to them, and agree to settle in severally on certain lands designated for that purpose, as farmers, holding individual title to their land in fee simple, inalienable for a certain period. In this way a costly Indian war has been avoided, which at one time seemed imminent, and for the first time in the history of the country an Indian nation has given up its tribal existence to be settled in severally and to live as individuals under the common protection of the laws of the country.

The conduct of the Indians throughout the country during the past year, with but few noteworthy exceptions, has been orderly and peaceful. The guerrilla warfare carried on for two years by Victoria and his band of Southern Apaches has virtually come to an end by the death of that chief and most of his followers on Mexican soil. The disturbances caused on our northern frontier by Sitting Bull and his men, who had taken refuge in the British dominions, are also likely to cease. A large majority of his followers have surrendered to our military forces, and the remainder are apparently in progress of disintegration.

I concur with the Secretary of the Interior in expressing the earnest hope that Congress will at this session take favorable action on the bill providing for the allotment of lands on the different reservations in severally to the Indians, with patents conferring fee-simple title inalienable for a certain period, and the eventual disposition of the residue of the reservations for general settlement, with the consent and for the benefit of the Indians, placing the latter under the equal protection of the laws of the country. This measure, together with a vigorous prosecution of our educational efforts, will work the most important and effective advance toward the solution of the Indian problem, in preparing for the gradual merging of our Indian population in the great body of American citizenship.

A large increase is reported in the disposal of public lands for settlement during the past year, which marks the prosperous growth of our agricultural industry and a vigorous movement of population toward our unoccupied lands. As this movement proceeds, the codification of our land laws, as well as proper legislation to regulate the disposition of public lands, become of more pressing necessity, and I therefore invite the consideration of Congress to the report and the accompanying draft of a bill made by the Public Lands Commission, which were communicated by me to Congress at the last session. Early action upon this important subject is highly desirable.

The attention of Congress is again asked to the wasteful depredations committed on our public timber lands and the rapid and indiscriminate destruction of our forests. The urgent necessity for legislation to this end is now generally recognized. In view of the lawless character of the depredations committed and the disastrous consequences which will inevitably follow their continuance, legislation has again and again been recommended to arrest the evil and to preserve for the people of our Western States and Territories the timber needed for domestic and other essential uses.

The report of the Director of the Geological Survey is a document of unusual interest. The consolidation of the various geological and geographical surveys and exploring enterprises, each of which has heretofore operated upon an independent plan, without concert, can not fail to be of great benefit to all those industries of the country which depend upon the development of our mineral resources. The labors of the scientific men, of recognized merit, who compose the corps of the Geological Survey, during the first season of their field operations and inquiries, appear to have been very comprehensive, and will soon be communicated to Congress in a number of volumes. The Director of the Survey recommends that the investigations carried on by his bureau, which so far have been confined to the so-called public-land States and Territories, be extended over the entire country, and that the necessary appropriation be made for this purpose. This would be particularly beneficial to the iron, coal, and other mining interests of the Mississippi Valley and of the Eastern and Southern States. The subject is commended to the careful consideration of Congress.

The Secretary of the Interior asks attention to the want of room in the public buildings of the capital, now existing and in progress of construction, for the accommodation of the clerical force employed and of the public records. Necessity has compelled the renting of private buildings in different parts of the city for the location of public offices, for which a large amount of rent is annually paid, while the separation of offices belonging to the same Department impedes the transaction of current business. The Secretary suggests that the blocks surrounding Lafayette Square on the east, north, and west be purchased as the sites for new edifices for the accommodation of the Government offices, leaving the square itself intact, and that if such buildings were constructed upon a harmonious plan of architecture they would add much to the beauty of the national capital, and would, together with the Treasury and the new State, Navy, and War Department building, form one of the most imposing groups of public edifices in the world.

The Commissioner of Agriculture expresses the confident belief that his efforts in behalf of the production of our own sugar and tea have been encouragingly rewarded. The importance of the results attained have attracted marked attention at home and have received the special consideration of foreign nations. The successful cultivation of our own tea and the manufacture of our own sugar would make a difference of many millions of dollars annually in the wealth of the nation.

The report of the Commissioner asks attention particularly to the continued prevalence of an infectious and contagious cattle disease known and dreaded in Europe and Asia as cattle plague, or pleuro-pneumonia. A mild type of this disease in certain sections of our country is the occasion of great loss to our farmers and of serious disturbance to our trade with Great Britain, which furnishes a market for most of our live stock and dressed meats. The value of meat cattle exported from the United States for the eight months ended August 31, 1880, was more than $12,000,000, and nearly double the value for the same period in 1879—an unexampled increase of export trade. Your early attention is solicited to this important matter.

The Commissioner of Education reports a continued increase of public interest in educational affairs, and that the public schools generally throughout the country are well sustained. Industrial training is attracting deserved attention, and colleges for instruction, theoretical and practical, in agriculture and mechanic arts, including the Government schools recently established for the instruction of Indian youth, are gaining steadily in public estimation. The Commissioner asks special attention to the depredations committed on the lands reserved for the future support of public instruction, and to the very great need of help from the nation for schools in the Territories and in the Southern States. The recommendation heretofore made is repeated and urged, that an educational fund be set apart from the net proceeds of the sales of the public lands annually, the income of which and the remainder of the net annual proceeds to be distributed on some satisfactory plan to the States and the Territories and the District of Columbia.

The success of the public schools of the District of Columbia, and the progress made, under the intelligent direction of the board of education and the superintendent, in supplying the educational requirements of the District with thoroughly trained and efficient teachers, is very gratifying. The acts of Congress, from time to time, donating public lands to the several States and Territories in aid of educational interests have proved to be wise measures of public policy, resulting in great and lasting benefit. It would seem to be a matter of simple justice to extend the benefits of this legislation, the wisdom of which has been so fully vindicated by experience, to the District of Columbia.

I again commend the general interests of the District of Columbia to the favorable consideration of Congress. The affairs of the District, as shown by the report of the Commissioners, are in a very satisfactory condition.

In my annual messages heretofore and in my special message of December 19, 1879, I have urged upon the attention of Congress the necessity of reclaiming the marshes of the Potomac adjacent to the capital, and I am constrained by its importance to advert again to the subject. These flats embrace an area of several hundred acres. They are an impediment to the drainage of the city and seriously impair its health. It is believed that with this substantial improvement of its river front the capital would be in all respects one of the most attractive cities in the world. Aside from its permanent population, this city is necessarily the place of residence of persons from every section of the country engaged in the public service. Many others reside here temporarily for the transaction of business with the Government.

It should not be forgotten that the land acquired will probably be worth the cost of reclaiming it and that the navigation of the river will be greatly improved. I therefore again invite the attention of Congress to the importance of prompt provision for this much needed and too long delayed improvement.

The water supply of the city is inadequate. In addition to the ordinary use throughout the city, the consumption by Government is necessarily very great in the navy-yard, arsenal, and the various Departments, and a large quantity is required for the proper preservation of the numerous parks and the cleansing of sewers. I recommend that this subject receive the early attention of Congress, and that in making provision for an increased supply such means be adopted as will have in view the future growth of the city. Temporary expedients for such a purpose can not but be wasteful of money, and therefore unwise. A more ample reservoir, with corresponding facilities for keeping it filled, should, in my judgment, be constructed. I commend again to the attention of Congress the subject of the removal from their present location of the depots of the several railroads entering the city; and I renew the recommendations of my former messages in behalf of the erection of a building for the Congressional Library, the completion of the Washington Monument, and of liberal appropriations in support of the benevolent, reformatory, and penal institutions of the District.

RUTHERFORD B. HAYES

1 8

Chester A. Arthur (1881–1885)

Chester A. Arthur was vice president in the Garfield administration only six months when the commander-in-chief died as a result of complications from an assassin's bullet.

Arthur's presidency tends to be overlooked today, but his final message was more prescient than many realize. He began his final annual message with the usual praise for American citizens: Once again, they were submitting in an orderly manner to the peaceful transition of power to the opposition party. But then Arthur did something unusual. He referred to an earlier presidential election, that of 1876, between Rutherford B. Hayes and Samuel J. Tilden. Early in that contest, Tilden won the popular vote and for a time held a strong lead in the Electoral College. But confusion in three states—South Carolina, Louisiana, and Florida—led to a highly controversial finish, the likes of which would not be seen again until 2000. Arthur, reflecting on that election, was surely wise when he "called the attention of the Congress to the necessity of providing more precise and definite regulations for counting the electoral vote. It is of the gravest importance that this question be solved before conflicting claims to the Presidency shall again distract the country." Arthur's words proved to be a sentiment for the ages.

Stylistically, Arthur's message foreshadowed a distinctly modern development: the short paragraph. Numerous paragraphs are just a sentence or two long. This is noteworthy considering he wrote during the Victorian era, when long passages of purple prose reigned.

Also noteworthy is the conclusion. Arthur's last sentiments are heartfelt thanks to the Congress and to the citizenry. He thus reintroduced a grace note that America's early presidents had usually included in their final annual messages, but that were seldom encountered in the later presidents of the nineteenth century.

Fourth Annual Message
(written to the Congress)
December 1, 1884

To the Congress of the United States:

Since the close of your last session the American people, in the exercise of their highest right of suffrage, have chosen their Chief Magistrate for the four years ensuing.

When it is remembered that at no period in the country's history has the long political contest which customarily precedes the day of the national election been waged with greater fervor and intensity, it is a subject of general congratulation that after the controversy at the polls was over, and while the slight preponderance by which the issue had been determined was as yet unascertained, the public peace suffered no disturbance, but the people everywhere patiently and quietly awaited the result.

Nothing could more strikingly illustrate the temper of the American citizen, his love of order, and his loyalty to law. Nothing could more signally demonstrate the strength and wisdom of our political institutions.

Eight years have passed since a controversy concerning the result of a national election sharply called the attention of the Congress to the necessity of providing more precise and definite regulations for counting the electoral vote.

It is of the gravest importance that this question be solved before conflicting claims to the Presidency shall again distract the country, and I am persuaded that by the people at large any of the measures of relief thus far proposed would be preferred to continued inaction.

Our relations with all foreign powers continue to be amicable.

With Belgium a convention has been signed whereby the scope of present treaties has been so enlarged as to secure to citizens of either country within the jurisdiction of the other equal rights and privileges in the acquisition and alienation of property. A trade-marks treaty has also been concluded.

The war between Chile and Peru is at an end. For the arbitration of the claims of American citizens who during its continuance suffered through the acts of the Chilean authorities a convention will soon be negotiated.

The state of hostilities between France and China continues to be an embarrassing feature of our Eastern relations. The Chinese Government has promptly adjusted and paid the claims of American citizens whose property was destroyed in the recent riots at Canton. I renew the recommendation of my last annual message, that the Canton indemnity fund be returned to China.

The true interpretation of the recent treaty with that country permitting the restriction of Chinese immigration is likely to be again the subject of your deliberations. It may be seriously questioned whether the statute passed at the last session does not violate the treaty rights of certain Chinese who left this country with return certificates valid under the old law, and who now seem to be debarred from relanding for lack of the certificates required by the new.

The recent purchase by citizens of the United States of a large trading fleet heretofore under the Chinese flag has considerably enhanced our commercial importance in the East. In view of the large number of vessels built or purchased by American citizens in other countries and exclusively employed in legitimate traffic between foreign ports under the recognized protection of our flag, it might be well to provide a uniform rule for their registration and documentation, so that the bona fide property rights of our citizens therein shall be duly evidenced and properly guarded.

Pursuant to the advice of the Senate at the last session, I recognized the flag of the International Association of the Kongo as that of a friendly government, avoiding in so doing any prejudgment of conflicting territorial claims in that region. Subsequently, in execution of the expressed wish of the Congress, I appointed a commercial agent for the Kongo basin.

The importance of the rich prospective trade of the Kongo Valley has led to the general conviction that it should be open to all nations upon equal terms. At an international conference for the consideration of this subject called by the Emperor of Germany, and now in session at Berlin, delegates are in attendance on behalf of the United States. Of the results of the conference you will be duly advised.

The Government of Korea has generously aided the efforts of the United States minister to secure suitable premises for the use of the legation. As the conditions of diplomatic intercourse with Eastern nations demand that the legation premises be owned by the represented power, I advise that an appropriation be made for the acquisition of this property by the Government. The United States already possess valuable premises at Tangier as a gift from the Sultan of Morocco. As is stated hereafter, they have lately received a similar gift from the Siamese Government. The Government of Japan stands ready to present to us extensive grounds at Tokyo whereon to erect a suitable building for the legation, court-house, and jail, and similar privileges can probably be secured in China and Persia. The owning of such premises would not only effect a large saving of the present rentals, but would permit of the due assertion of extraterritorial rights in those countries, and would the better serve to maintain the dignity of the United States.

The failure of Congress to make appropriation for our representation at the autonomous court of the Khedive has proved a serious embarrassment in our intercourse with Egypt; and in view of the necessary intimacy of diplomatic relationship due to the participation of this Government as one of the treaty powers in all matters of administration there affecting the rights of foreigners, I advise the restoration of the agency and consulate-general at Cairo on its former basis. I do not conceive it to be the wish of Congress that the United States should withdraw altogether from the honorable position they have hitherto held with respect to the Khedive, or that citizens of this Republic residing or sojourning in Egypt should hereafter be without the aid and protection of a competent representative.

With France the traditional cordial relationship continues. The colossal statue of Liberty Enlightening the World, the generous gift of the people of France, is expected to reach New York in May next. I suggest that Congressional action be taken in recognition of the spirit which has prompted this gift and in aid of the timely completion of the pedestal upon which it is to be placed.

Our relations with Germany, a country which contributes to our own some of the best elements of citizenship, continue to be cordial. The United States have extradition treaties with several of the German States, but by reason of the confederation of those States under the imperial rule the application of such treaties is not as uniform and comprehensive as the interests of the two countries require. I propose, therefore, to open negotiations for a single convention of extradition to embrace all the territory of the Empire.

It affords me pleasure to say that our intercourse with Great Britain continues to be of a most friendly character.

The Government of Hawaii has indicated its willingness to continue for seven years the provisions of the existing reciprocity treaty. Such continuance, in view of the relations of that country to the American system of States, should, in my judgment, be favored.

The revolution in Hayti against the established Government has terminated. While it was in progress it became necessary to enforce our neutrality laws by instituting proceedings against individuals and vessels charged with their infringement. These prosecutions were in all cases successful.

Much anxiety has lately been displayed by various European Governments, and especially by the Government of Italy, for the abolition of our import duties upon works of art. It is well to consider whether the present discrimination in favor of the productions of American artists abroad is not likely to result, as they themselves seem very generally to believe it may, in the practical exclusion of our painters and sculptors from the rich fields for observation, study, and labor which they have hitherto enjoyed.

There is prospect that the long-pending revision of the foreign treaties of Japan may be concluded at a new conference to be held at Tokyo. While this Government fully recognizes the equal and independent station of Japan in the community of nations, it would not oppose the general adoption of such terms of compromise as Japan may be disposed to offer in furtherance of a uniform policy of intercourse with Western nations.

During the past year the increasing good will between our own Government and that of Mexico has been variously manifested. The treaty of commercial reciprocity concluded January 20, 1883, has been ratified and awaits the necessary tariff legislation of Congress to become effective. This legislation will, I doubt not, be among the first measures to claim your attention.

A full treaty of commerce, navigation, and consular rights is much to be desired, and such a treaty I have reason to believe that the Mexican Government stands ready to conclude.

Some embarrassment has been occasioned by the failure of Congress at its last session to provide means for the due execution of the treaty of July 29, 1882, for the resurvey of the Mexican boundary and the relocation of boundary monuments.

With the Republic of Nicaragua a treaty has been concluded which authorizes the construction by the United States of a canal, railway, and telegraph line across the Nicaraguan territory.

By the terms of this treaty 60 miles of the river San Juan, as well as Lake Nicaragua, an inland sea 40 miles in width, are to constitute a part of the projected enterprise.

This leaves for actual canal construction 17 miles on the Pacific side and 36 miles on the Atlantic. To the United States, whose rich territory on the Pacific is for the ordinary purposes of commerce practically cut off from communication by water with the Atlantic ports, the political and commercial advantages of such a project can scarcely be overestimated.

It is believed that when the treaty is laid before you the justice and liberality of its provisions will command universal approval at home and abroad.

The death of our representative at Russia while at his post at St. Petersburg afforded to the Imperial Government a renewed opportunity to testify its sympathy in a manner befitting the intimate friendliness which has ever marked the intercourse of the two countries.

The course of this Government in raising its representation at Bangkok to the diplomatic rank has evoked from Siam evidences of warm friendship and augurs well for our enlarged intercourse. The Siamese Government has presented to the United States a commodious mansion and grounds for the occupancy of the legation, and I suggest that by joint resolution Congress attest its appreciation of this generous gift.

This government has more than once been called upon of late to take action in fulfillment of its international obligations toward Spain. Agitation in the island of Cuba hostile to the Spanish Crown having been fomented by persons abusing the sacred rights of hospitality which our territory affords, the officers of this Government have been instructed to exercise vigilance to prevent infractions of our neutrality laws at Key West and at other points near the Cuban coast. I am happy to say that in the only instance where these precautionary measures were successfully eluded the offenders, when found in our territory, were subsequently tried and convicted.

The growing need of close relationship of intercourse and traffic between the Spanish Antilles and their natural market in the United States led to the adoption in January last of a commercial agreement looking to that end. This agreement has since been superseded by a more carefully framed and comprehensive convention, which I shall submit to the Senate for approval. It has been the aim of this negotiation to open such a favored reciprocal exchange of productions carried under the flag of either country as to make the intercourse between Cuba and Puerto Rico and ourselves scarcely less intimate than the commercial movement between our domestic ports, and to insure a removal of the burdens on shipping in the Spanish Indies, of which in the past our shipowners and shipmasters have so often had cause to complain.

The negotiation of this convention has for a time postponed the prosecution of certain claims of our citizens which were declared to be without the jurisdiction of the late Spanish-American Claims Commission, and which are therefore remitted to diplomatic channels for adjustment. The speedy settlement of these claims will now be urged by this Government.

Negotiations for a treaty of commercial reciprocity with the Dominican Republic have been successfully concluded, and the result will shortly be laid before the Senate.

Certain questions between the United States and the Ottoman Empire still remain unsolved. Complaints on behalf of our citizens are not satisfactorily adjusted. The Porte has sought to withhold from our commerce the right of favored treatment to which we are entitled by existing conventional stipulations, and the revision of the tariffs is unaccomplished.

The final disposition of pending questions with Venezuela has not as yet been reached, but I have good reason to expect an early settlement which will provide the means of reexamining the Caracas awards in conformity with the expressed desire of Congress, and which will recognize the justice of certain claims preferred against Venezuela.

The Central and South American Commission appointed by authority of the act of July 7, 1884, will soon proceed to Mexico. It has been furnished with instructions which will be laid before you. They contain a statement of the general policy of the Government for enlarging its commercial intercourse with American States. The commissioners have been actively preparing for their responsible task by holding conferences in the principal cities with merchants and others interested in Central and South American trade.

The International Meridian Conference lately convened in Washington upon the invitation of the Government of the United States was composed of representatives from twenty-five nations. The conference concluded its labors on the 1st of November, having with substantial unanimity agreed upon the meridian of Greenwich as the starting point whence longitude is to be computed through 180 degrees eastward and westward, and upon the adoption, for all purposes for which it may be found convenient, of a universal day which shall begin at midnight on the initial meridian and whose hours shall be counted from zero up to twenty-four. The formal report of the transactions of this conference will be hereafter transmitted to the Congress.

This Government is in frequent receipt of invitations from foreign states to participate in international exhibitions, often of great interest and importance. Occupying, as we do, an advanced position in the world's production, and aiming to secure a profitable share for our industries in the general competitive markets, it is a matter of serious concern that the want of means for participation in these exhibitions should so often exclude our producers from advantages enjoyed by those of other countries. During the past year the attention of Congress was drawn to the formal invitations in this regard tendered by the Governments of England, Holland, Belgium, Germany, and Austria. The Executive has in some instances appointed honorary commissioners. This is, however, a most unsatisfactory expedient, for without some provision to meet the necessary working expenses of a commission it can effect little or nothing in behalf of exhibitors. An International Inventions Exhibition is to be held in London next May. This will cover a field of special importance, in which our country holds a foremost rank; but the Executive is at present powerless to organize a proper representation of our vast national interests in this direction.

I have in several previous messages referred to this subject. It seems to me that a statute giving to the Executive general discretionary authority to accept such invitations and to appoint honorary commissioners, without salary, and placing at the disposal of the Secretary of State a small fund for defraying their reasonable expenses, would be of great public utility.

This Government has received official notice that the revised international regulations for preventing collisions at sea have been adopted by all the leading maritime powers except the United

States, and came into force on the 1st of September last. For the due protection of our shipping interests the provisions of our statutes should at once be brought into conformity with these regulations.

The question of securing to authors, composers, and artists copyright privileges in this country in return for reciprocal rights abroad is one that may justly challenge your attention. It is true that conventions will be necessary for fully accomplishing this result; but until Congress shall by statute fix the extent to which foreign holders of copyright shall be here privileged it has been deemed inadvisable to negotiate such conventions. For this reason the United States were not represented at the recent conference at Berne.

I recommend that the scope of the neutrality laws of the United States be so enlarged as to cover all patent acts of hostility committed in our territory and aimed against the peace of a friendly nation. Existing statutes prohibit the fitting out of armed expeditions and restrict the shipment of explosives, though the enactments in the latter respect were not framed with regard to international obligations, but simply for the protection of passenger travel. All these statutes were intended to meet special emergencies that had already arisen. Other emergencies have arisen since, and modern ingenuity supplies means for the organization of hostilities without open resort to armed vessels or to filibustering parties.

I see no reason why overt preparations in this country for the commission of criminal acts such as are here under consideration should not be alike punishable whether such acts are intended to be committed in our own country or in a foreign country with which we are at peace. The prompt and thorough treatment of this question is one which intimately concerns the national honor.

Our existing naturalization laws also need revision. Those sections relating to persons residing within the limits of the United States in 1795 and 1798 have now only a historical interest. Section 2172, recognizing the citizenship of the children of naturalized parents, is ambiguous in its terms and partly obsolete. There are special provisions of law favoring the naturalization of those who serve in the Army or in merchant vessels, while no similar privileges are granted those who serve in the Navy or the Marine Corps.

"An uniform rule of naturalization" such as the Constitution contemplates should, among other things, clearly define the status of persons born within the United States subject to a foreign power (section 1992) and of minor children of fathers who have declared their intention to become citizens but have failed to perfect their naturalization. It might be wise to provide for a central bureau of registry, wherein should be filed authenticated transcripts of every record of naturalization in the several Federal and State courts, and to make provision also for the vacation or cancellation of such record in cases where fraud had been practiced upon the court by the applicant himself or where he had renounced or forfeited his acquired citizenship. A just and uniform law in this respect would strengthen the hands of the Government in protecting its citizens abroad and would pave the way for the conclusion of treaties of naturalization with foreign countries.

The legislation of the last session effected in the diplomatic and consular service certain changes and reductions which have been productive of embarrassment. The population and commercial activity of our country are steadily on the increase, and are giving rise to new, varying, and often delicate relationships with other countries. Our foreign establishment now embraces nearly double the area of operations that it occupied twenty years ago. The confinement of such a service within the limits of expenditure then established is not, it seems to me, in accordance with true economy. A community of 60,000,000 people should be adequately represented in its intercourse with foreign nations.

A project for the reorganization of the consular service and for recasting the scheme of extraterritorial jurisdiction is now before you. If the limits of a short session will not allow of its full consideration, I trust that you will not fail to make suitable provision for the present needs of the service.

It has been customary to define in the appropriation acts the rank of each diplomatic office to which a salary is attached. I suggest that this course be abandoned and that it be left to the President, with the advice and consent of the Senate, to fix from time to time the diplomatic grade of the representatives of this Government abroad as may seem advisable, provision being definitely made, however, as now, for the amount of salary attached to the respective stations.

The condition of our finances and the operations of the various branches of the public service which are connected with the Treasury Department are very fully discussed in the report of the Secretary.

* * *

I concur with the Secretary of the Treasury in recommending the immediate suspension of the coinage of silver dollars and of the issuance of silver certificates. This is a matter to which in former communications I have more than once invoked the attention of the National Legislature.

It appears that annually for the past six years there have been coined, in compliance with the requirements of the act of February 28, 1878, more than 27,000,000 silver dollars.

The number now outstanding is reported by the Secretary to be nearly 185,000,000, whereof but little more than 40,000,000, or less than 22 per cent, are in actual circulation. The mere existence of this fact seems to me to furnish of itself a cogent argument for the repeal of the statute which has made such fact possible. But there are other and graver considerations that tend in the same direction.

The Secretary avows his conviction that unless this coinage and the issuance of silver certificates be suspended silver is likely at no distant day to become our sole metallic standard. The commercial disturbance and the impairment of national credit that would be thus occasioned can scarcely be overestimated.

I hope that the Secretary's suggestions respecting the withdrawal from circulation of the $1 and $2 notes will receive your approval. It is likely that a considerable portion of the silver now encumbering the vaults of the Treasury might thus find its way into the currency.

While trade dollars have ceased, for the present at least, to be an element of active disturbance in our currency system, some provision should be made for their surrender to the Government. In view of the circumstances under which they were coined and of the fact that they have never had a legal-tender quality, there should be offered for them only a slight advance over their bullion value.

The Secretary in the course of his report considers the propriety of beautifying the designs of our subsidiary silver coins and of so increasing their weight that they may bear their due ratio of value to the standard dollar. His conclusions in this regard are cordially approved.

In my annual message of 1882 I recommended the abolition of all excise taxes except those relating to distilled spirits. This recommendation is now renewed. In case these taxes shall be abolished the revenues that will still remain to the Government will, in my opinion, not only suffice to meet its reasonable expenditures, but will afford a surplus large enough to permit such tariff reduction as may seem to be advisable when the results of recent revenue laws and commercial treaties shall have shown in what quarters those reductions can be most judiciously effected.

One of the gravest of the problems which appeal to the wisdom of Congress for solution is the ascertainment of the most effective means for increasing our foreign trade and thus relieving the depression under which our industries are now languishing. The Secretary of the Treasury advises that the duty of investigating this subject be intrusted in the first instance to a competent commission. While fully recognizing the considerations that may be urged against this course, I am nevertheless of the opinion that upon the whole no other would be likely to effect speedier or better results.

That portion of the Secretary's report which concerns the condition of our shipping interests can not fail to command your attention. He emphatically recommends that as an incentive to the investment of American capital in American steamships the Government shall, by liberal payments for mail transportation or otherwise, lend its active assistance to individual enterprise, and declares his belief that unless that course be pursued our foreign carrying trade must remain, as it is today, almost exclusively in the hands of foreigners.

One phase of this subject is now especially prominent in view of the repeal by the act of June 26, 1884, of all statutory provisions arbitrarily compelling American vessels to carry the mails to and from the United States. As it is necessary to make provision to compensate the owners of such vessels for performing that service after April, 1885, it is hoped that the whole subject will receive early consideration that will lead to the enactment of such measures for the revival of our merchant marine as the wisdom of Congress may devise.

The 3 per cent bonds of the Government to the amount of more than $100,000,000 have since my last annual message been redeemed by the Treasury. The bonds of that issue still outstanding amount to little over $200,000,000, about one-fourth of which will be retired through the operations of the sinking fund during the coming year. As these bonds still constitute the chief basis for the circulation of the national banks, the question how to avert the contraction of the currency caused by their retirement is one of constantly increasing importance.

It seems to be generally conceded that the law governing this matter exacts from the banks excessive security, and that upon their present bond deposits a larger circulation than is now allowed may be granted with safety. I hope that the bill which passed the Senate at the last session, permitting the issue of notes equal to the face value of the deposited bonds, will commend itself to the approval of the House of Representatives.

In the expenses of the War Department the Secretary reports a decrease of more than $9,000,000. Of this reduction $5,600,000 was effected in the expenditures for rivers and harbors and $2,700,000 in expenditures for the Quartermaster's Department.

Outside of that Department the annual expenses of all the Army bureaus proper (except possibly the Ordnance Bureau) are substantially fixed charges, which can not be materially diminished without a change in the numerical strength of the Army. The expenditures in the Quartermaster's Department can readily be subjected to administrative discretion, and it is reported by the Secretary of War that as a result of exercising such discretion in reducing the number of draft and pack animals in the Army the annual cost of supplying and caring for such animals is now $1,108,085.90 less than it was in 1881.

The reports of military commanders show that the last year has been notable for its entire freedom from Indian outbreaks.

In defiance of the President's proclamation of July 1, 1884, certain intruders sought to make settlements in the Indian Territory. They were promptly removed by a detachment of troops.

During the past session of Congress a bill to provide a suitable fire-proof building for the Army Medical Museum and the library of the Surgeon-General's Office received the approval of the Senate. A similar bill, reported favorably to the House of Representatives by one of its committees, is still pending before that body. It is hoped that during the coming session the measure may become a law, and that thereafter immediate steps may be taken to secure a place of safe deposit for these valuable collections, now in a state of insecurity.

The funds with which the works for the improvement of rivers and harbors were prosecuted during the past year were derived from the appropriations of the act of August 2, 1882, together with such few balances as were on hand from previous appropriations. The balance in the Treasury subject to requisition July 1, 1883, was $10,021,649.55. The amount appropriated during the fiscal year 1884 was $1,319,634.62 and the amount drawn from the Treasury during the fiscal year was $8,228,703.54, leaving a balance of $3,112,580.63 in the Treasury subject to requisition July 1, 1884.

The Secretary of War submits the report of the Chief of Engineers as to the practicability of protecting our important cities on the seaboard by fortifications and other defenses able to repel modern methods of attack. The time has now come when such defenses can be prepared with confidence that they will not prove abortive, and when the possible result of delay in making such preparation is seriously considered, delay seems inexcusable. For the most important cities—those whose destruction or capture would be a national humiliation—adequate defenses, inclusive of guns, may be made by the gradual expenditure of $60,000,000—a sum much less than a victorious enemy could levy as a contribution. An appropriation of about one-tenth of that amount is asked to begin the work, and I concur with the Secretary of War in urging that it be granted.

The War Department is proceeding with the conversion of 10-inch smoothbore guns into 8-inch rifles by lining the former with tubes of forged steel or of coil wrought iron. Fifty guns will be thus converted within the year. This, however, does not obviate the necessity of providing means for the construction of guns of the highest power both for the purposes of coast defense and for the armament of war vessels.

The report of the Gun Foundry Board, appointed April 2, 1883, in pursuance of the act of March 3, 1883, was transmitted to Congress in a special message of February 18, 1884. In my message of March 26, 1884, I called attention to the recommendation of the board that the Government should encourage the production at private steel works of the required material for heavy cannon, and that two Government factories, one for the Army and one for the Navy, should be established for the fabrication of guns from such material. No action having been taken, the board was subsequently reconvened to determine more fully the plans and estimates necessary for carrying out its recommendation. It has received information which indicates that there are responsible steel manufacturers in this country who, although not provided at present with the necessary plant, are willing to construct the same and to make bids for contracts with the Government for the supply of the requisite material for the heaviest guns adapted to modern warfare if a guaranteed order of sufficient magnitude, accompanied by a positive appropriation extending over a series of years, shall be made by Congress. All doubts as to the feasibility of the plan being thus removed, I renew my recommendation that such action be taken by Congress as will enable the Government to construct its own ordnance upon its own territory, and so to provide the armaments demanded by considerations of national safety and honor.

The report of the Secretary of the Navy exhibits the progress which has been made on the new steel cruisers authorized by the acts of August 5, 1882, and March 3, 1883. Of the four vessels under contract, one, the *Chicago*, of 4,500 tons, is more than half finished; the *Atlanta*, of 3,000 tons, has been successfully launched, and her machinery is now fitting; the *Boston*, also of 3,000 tons, is ready for launching, and the *Dolphin*, a dispatch steamer of 1,500 tons, is ready for delivery.

Certain adverse criticisms upon the designs of these cruisers are discussed by the Secretary, who insists that the correctness of the conclusions reached by the Advisory Board and by the Department has been demonstrated by recent developments in shipbuilding abroad.

The machinery of the double-turreted monitors *Puritan*, *Terror*, and *Amphitrite*, contracted for under the act of March 3, 1883, is in process of construction. No work has been done during the past year on their armor for lack of the necessary appropriations. A fourth monitor, the *Monadnock*, still remains unfinished at the navy-yard in California. It is recommended that early steps be taken to complete these vessels and to provide also an armament for the monitor *Miantonomoh*.

The recommendations of the Naval Advisory Board, approved by the Department, comprise the construction of one steel cruiser of 4,500 tons, one cruiser of 3,000 tons, two heavily armed gunboats, one light cruising gunboat, one dispatch vessel armed with Hotchkiss cannon, one armored ram, and three torpedo boats. The general designs, all of which are calculated to meet the existing wants of the service, are now well advanced, and the construction of the vessels can be undertaken as soon as you shall grant the necessary authority.

The act of Congress approved August 7, 1882, authorized the removal to the United States of the bodies of Lieutenant-Commander George W. De Long and his companions of the *Jeannette* expedition. This removal has been successfully accomplished by Lieutenants Harber and Schuetze. The remains were taken from their grave in the Lena Delta in March, 1883, and were retained at Yakutsk until the following winter, the season being too far advanced to admit of their immediate transportation. They arrived at New York February 20, 1884, where they were received with suitable honors.

In pursuance of the joint resolution of Congress approved February 13, 1884, a naval expedition was fitted out for the relief of Lieutenant A. W. Greely, United States Army, and of the party who had been engaged under his command in scientific observations at Lady Franklin Bay. The fleet consisted of the steam sealer *Thetis*, purchased in England; the *Bear*, purchased at St. Johns, Newfoundland; and the *Alert*, which was generously provided by the British Government. Preparations for the expedition were promptly made by the Secretary of the Navy, with the active cooperation of the Secretary of War. Commander George W. Coffin was placed in command of the *Alert* and Lieutenant William H. Emory in command of the *Bear*. The *Thetis* was intrusted to Commander Winfield S. Schley, to whom also was assigned the superintendence of the entire expedition.

Immediately upon its arrival at Upernavik the fleet began the dangerous navigation of Melville Bay, and in spite of every obstacle reached Littleton Island on June 22, a fortnight earlier than any vessel had before attained that point. On the same day it crossed over to Cape Sabine, where Lieutenant Greely and the other survivors of his party were discovered. After taking on board the living and the bodies of the dead, the relief ships sailed for St. Johns, where they arrived on July 17. They were appropriately received at Portsmouth, N.H., on August 1 and at New York on August 8. One of the bodies was landed at the former place. The others were put on shore at Governors Island, and, with the exception of one, which was interred in the national cemetery, were forwarded thence to the destinations indicated by friends. The organization and conduct of this relief expedition reflects great credit upon all who contributed to its success.

In this the last of the stated messages that I shall have the honor to transmit to the Congress of the United States I can not too strongly urge upon its attention the duty of restoring our Navy as rapidly as possible to the high state of efficiency which formerly characterized it. As the long peace that has lulled us into a sense of fancied security may at any time be disturbed, it is plain that the policy of strengthening this arm of the service is dictated by considerations of wise economy, of just regard for our future tranquillity, and of true appreciation of the dignity and honor of the Republic.

The report of the Postmaster-General acquaints you with the present condition and needs of the postal service.

It discloses the gratifying fact that the loss of revenue from the reduction in the rate of letter postage recommended in my message of December 4, 1882, and effected by the act of March 3, 1883, has been much less than was generally anticipated. My recommendation of this reduction was based upon the belief that the actual falling off in receipts from letter postages for the year immediately succeeding the change of rate would be $3,000,000. It has proved to be only $2,275,000.

This is a trustworthy indication that the revenue will soon be restored to its former volume by the natural increase of sealed correspondence.

I confidently repeat, therefore, the recommendation of my last annual message that the single-rate postage upon drop letters be reduced to 1 cent wherever the payment of 2 cents is now required by law. The double rate is only exacted at offices where the carrier system is in operation, and it appears that at those offices the increase in the tax upon local letters defrays the cost not only of its own collection and delivery, but of the collection and delivery of all other mail matter. This is an inequality that ought no longer to exist.

I approve the recommendation of the Postmaster-General that the unit of weight in the rating of first-class matter should be 1 ounce instead of one-half ounce, as it now is. In view of the statistics furnished by the Department, it may well be doubted whether the change would result in any loss of revenue. That it would greatly promote the convenience of the public is beyond dispute.

The free-delivery system has been lately applied to five cities, and the total number of offices in which it is now in operation is 159. Experience shows that its adoption, under proper conditions, is equally an accommodation to the public and an advantage to the postal service. It is more than self-sustaining, and for the reasons urged by the Postmaster-General may properly be extended.

In the opinion of that officer it is important to provide means whereby exceptional dispatch in dealing with letters in free-delivery offices may be secured by payment of extraordinary postage. This scheme might be made effective by employment of a special stamp whose cost should be commensurate with the expense of the extra service.

In some of the large cities private express companies have undertaken to outstrip the Government mail carriers by affording for the prompt transmission of letters better facilities than have hitherto been at the command of the Post-Office.

It has always been the policy of the Government to discourage such enterprises, and in no better mode can that policy be maintained than in supplying the public with the most efficient mail service that, with due regard to its own best interests, can be furnished for its accommodation.

The Attorney-General renews the recommendation contained in his report of last year touching the fees of witnesses and jurors.

He favors radical changes in the fee bill, the adoption of a system by which attorneys and marshals of the United States shall be compensated solely by salaries, and the erection by the Government of a penitentiary for the confinement of offenders against its laws.

Of the varied governmental concerns in charge of the Interior Department the report of its Secretary presents an interesting summary. Among the topics deserving particular attention I refer you to his observations respecting our Indian affairs, the preemption and timber-culture acts, the failure of railroad companies to take title to lands granted by the Government, and the operations of the Pension Office, the Patent Office, the Census Bureau, and the Bureau of Education.

Allusion has been made already to the circumstance that, both as between the different Indian tribes and as between the Indians and the whites, the past year has been one of unbroken peace.

In this circumstance the President is glad to find justification for the policy of the Government in its dealing with the Indian question and confirmation of the views which were fully expressed in his first communication to the Forty-seventh Congress.

The Secretary urges anew the enactment of a statute for the punishment of crimes committed on the Indian reservations, and recommends the passage of the bill now pending in the House of Representatives for the purchase of a tract of 18,000 square miles from the Sioux Reservation. Both these measures are worthy of approval.

I concur with him also in advising the repeal of the preemption law, the enactment of statutes resolving the present legal complications touching lapsed grants to railroad companies, and the funding of the debt of the several Pacific railroads under such guaranty as shall effectually secure its ultimate payment. The report of the Utah Commission will be read with interest.

It discloses the results of recent legislation looking to the prevention and punishment of polygamy in that Territory. I still believe that if that abominable practice can be suppressed by law it can only be by the most radical legislation consistent with the restraints of the Constitution.

I again recommend, therefore, that Congress assume absolute political control of the Territory of Utah and provide for the appointment of commissioners with such governmental powers as in its judgment may justly and wisely be put into their hands.

In the course of this communication reference has more than once been made to the policy of this Government as regards the extension of our foreign trade. It seems proper to declare the general principles that should, in my opinion, underlie our national efforts in this direction. The main conditions of the problem may be thus stated:

We are a people apt in mechanical pursuits and fertile in invention. We cover a vast extent of territory rich in agricultural products and in nearly all the raw materials necessary for successful manufacture. We have a system of productive establishments more than sufficient to supply our own demands. The wages of labor are nowhere else so great. The scale of living of our artisan classes is such as tends to secure their personal comfort and the development of those higher moral and intellectual qualities that go to the making of good citizens. Our system of tax and tariff legislation is yielding a revenue which is in excess of the present needs of the Government.

These are the elements from which it is sought to devise a scheme by which, without unfavorably changing the condition of the workingman, our merchant marine shall be raised from its enfeebled condition and new markets provided for the sale beyond our borders of the manifold fruits of our industrial enterprises. The problem is complex and can be solved by no single measure of innovation or reform.

The countries of the American continent and the adjacent islands are for the United States the natural marts of supply and demand. It is from them that we should obtain what we do not produce or do not produce in sufficiency, and it is to them that the surplus productions of our fields, our mills, and our workshops should flow, under conditions that will equalize or favor them in comparison with foreign competition. Four paths of policy seem to point to this end:

First. A series of reciprocal commercial treaties with the countries of America which shall foster between us and them an unhampered movement of trade. The conditions of these treaties should be the free admission of such merchandise as this country does not produce, in return for the admission free or under a favored scheme of duties of our own products, the benefits of such exchange to apply only to goods carried under the flag of the parties to the contract; the removal on both sides from the vessels so privileged of all tonnage dues and national imposts, so that those vessels may ply unhindered between our ports and those of the other contracting parties, though without infringing on the reserved home coasting trade; the removal or reduction of burdens on the exported products of those countries coming within the benefits of the treaties, and the avoidance of the technical restrictions and penalties by which our intercourse with those countries is at present hampered.

Secondly. The establishment of the consular service of the United States on a salaried footing, thus permitting the relinquishment of consular fees not only as respects vessels under the national flag, but also as respects vessels of the treaty nations carrying goods entitled to the benefits of the treaties.

Thirdly. The enactment of measures to favor the construction and maintenance of a steam carrying marine under the flag of the United States.

Fourthly. The establishment of an uniform currency basis for the countries of America, so that the coined products of our mines may circulate on equal terms throughout the whole system of commonwealths. This would require a monetary union of America, whereby the output of the bullion-producing countries and the circulation of those which yield neither gold nor silver could be adjusted in conformity with the population, wealth, and commercial needs of each. As many of the countries furnish no bullion to the common stock, the surplus production of our mines and mints might thus be utilized and a step taken toward the general remonetization of silver.

To the accomplishment of these ends, so far as they can be attained by separate treaties, the negotiations already concluded and now in progress have been directed; and the favor which this enlarged policy has thus far received warrants the belief that its operations will ere long embrace all, or nearly all, the countries of this hemisphere.

It is by no means desirable, however, that the policy under consideration should be applied to these countries alone. The healthful enlargement of our trade with Europe, Asia, and Africa should be sought by reducing tariff burdens on such of their wares as neither we nor the other American States are fitted to produce, and thus enabling ourselves to obtain in return a better market for our supplies of food, of raw materials, and of the manufactures in which we excel.

It seems to me that many of the embarrassing elements in the great national conflict between protection and free trade may thus be turned to good account; that the revenue may be reduced so as no longer to overtax the people; that protective duties may be retained without becoming burdensome; that our shipping interests may be judiciously encouraged, the currency fixed on firm bases, and, above all, such an unity of interests established among the States of the American system as will be of great and ever-increasing advantage to them all.

All treaties in the line of this policy which have been negotiated or are in process of negotiation contain a provision deemed to be requisite under the clause of the Constitution limiting to the House of Representatives the authority to originate bills for raising revenue.

On the 29th of February last I transmitted to the Congress the first annual report of the Civil Service Commission, together with communications from the heads of the several Executive Departments of the Government respecting the practical workings of the law under which the Commission had been acting. The good results therein foreshadowed have been more than realized.

The system has fully answered the expectations of its friends in securing competent and faithful public servants and in protecting the appointing officers of the Government from the pressure of personal importunity and from the labor of examining the claims and pretensions of rival candidates for public employment.

The law has had the unqualified support of the President and of the heads of the several Departments, and the members of the Commission have performed their duties with zeal and fidelity. Their report will shortly be submitted, and will be accompanied by such recommendations for enlarging the scope of the existing statute as shall commend themselves to the Executive and the Commissioners charged with its administration.

In view of the general and persistent demand throughout the commercial community for a national bankrupt law, I hope that the differences of sentiment which have hitherto prevented its enactment may not outlast the present session.

The pestilence which for the past two years has been raging in the countries of the East recently made its appearance in European ports with which we are in constant communication.

The then Secretary of the Treasury, in pursuance of a proclamation of the President, issued certain regulations restricting and for a time prohibiting the importation of rags and the admission of baggage of immigrants and of travelers arriving from infected quarters. Lest this course may have been without strict warrant of law, I approve the recommendation of the present Secretary that the Congress take action in the premises, and I also recommend the immediate adoption of such measures as will be likely to ward off the dreaded epidemic and to mitigate its severity in case it shall unhappily extend to our shores.

The annual report of the Commissioners of the District of Columbia reviews the operations of the several departments of its municipal government. I ask your careful consideration of its suggestions in respect to legislation, especially commending such as relate to a revision of the civil and criminal code, the performance of labor by persons sentenced to imprisonment in the jail, the construction and occupation of wharves along the river front, and the erection of a suitable building for District offices.

I recommend that in recognition of the eminent services of Ulysses S. Grant, late General of the armies of the United States and twice President of this nation, the Congress confer upon him a suitable pension.

Certain of the measures that seem to me necessary and expedient I have now, in obedience to the Constitution, recommended for your adoption.

As respects others of no less importance I shall content myself with renewing the recommendations already made to the Congress, without restating the grounds upon which such recommendations were based.

The preservation of forests on the public domain, the granting of Government aid for popular education, the amendment of the Federal Constitution so as to make effective the disapproval by the President of particular items in appropriation bills, the enactment of statutes in regard to the filling of vacancies in the Presidential office, and the determining of vexed questions respecting Presidential inability are measures which may justly receive your serious consideration.

As the time draws nigh when I am to retire from the public service, I can not refrain from expressing to the members of the National Legislature with whom I have been brought into personal and official intercourse my sincere appreciation of their unfailing courtesy and of their harmonious cooperation with the Executive in so many measures calculated to promote the best interests of the nation.

And to my fellow-citizens generally I acknowledge a deep sense of obligation for the support which they have accorded me in my administration of the executive department of this Government.

CHESTER A. ARTHUR

19

Grover Cleveland (1885–1889)

Grover Cleveland was president during an important anniversary in American history. He took the occasion of his last annual message to Congress to congratulate the nation that had thrived under the U.S. Constitution. The introduction is a thoughtful meditation on the United States of America at 100 years.

But Cleveland was not just in a celebratory mood. He challenged Americans to think about the founding and apply its lessons to the times. "It is our duty as patriotic citizens," he wrote, "to inquire at the present stage of our progress how the bond of the Government made with the people has been kept and performed." Cleveland found much that was wanting. In this last annual message he waxed philosophic and articulated some of the first principles of political economy as he understood it. Again and again, he stressed the importance of stewardship. In powerful prose, he denounced excessive taxation, onerous regulation, and favoritism in public policy. He heaped scorn on an ideology that was then ascendant—communism, "a hateful thing and a menace to peace and organized government." In summary he enjoined his colleagues: "As public servants we shall do our duty well if we constantly guard the rectitude of our intentions, maintain unsullied our love of country, and with unselfish purpose strive for the public good."

Cleveland, a Democrat, espoused a political philosophy that was in accord with the laissez-faire sentiments expressed by many leaders in his day. The twenty-second president said it far better than most.

Fourth Annual Message
(written to the Congress)
December 3, 1888

To the Congress of the United States:

As you assemble for the discharge of the duties you have assumed as the representatives of a free and generous people, your meeting is marked by an interesting and impressive incident. With the expiration of the present session of the Congress the first century of our constitutional existence as a nation will be completed.

Our survival for one hundred years is not sufficient to assure us that we no longer have dangers to fear in the maintenance, with all its promised blessings, of a government founded upon the freedom of the people. The time rather admonishes us to soberly inquire whether in the past we have always closely kept in the course of safety, and whether we have before us a way plain and clear which leads to happiness and perpetuity.

When the experiment of our Government was undertaken, the chart adopted for our guidance was the Constitution. Departure from the lines there laid down is failure. It is only by a strict adherence to the direction they indicate and by restraint within the limitations they fix that we can furnish proof to the world of the fitness of the American people for self-government.

The equal and exact justice of which we boast as the underlying principle of our institutions should not be confined to the relations of our citizens to each other. The Government itself is under bond to the American people that in the exercise of its functions and powers it will deal with the body of our citizens in a manner scrupulously honest and fair and absolutely just. It has agreed that American citizenship shall be the only credential necessary to justify the claim of equality before the law, and that no condition in life shall give rise to discrimination in the treatment of the people by their Government.

The citizen of our Republic in its early days rigidly insisted upon full compliance with the letter of this bond, and saw stretching out before him a clear field for individual endeavor. His tribute to the support of his Government was measured by the cost of its economical maintenance, and he was secure in the enjoyment of the remaining recompense of his steady and contented toil. In those days the frugality of the people was stamped upon their Government, and was enforced by the free, thoughtful, and intelligent suffrage of the citizen. Combinations, monopolies, and aggregations of capital were either avoided or sternly regulated and restrained. The pomp and glitter of governments less free offered no temptation and presented no delusion to the plain people who, side by side, in friendly competition, wrought for the ennoblement and dignity of man, for the solution of the problem of free government, and for the achievement of the grand destiny awaiting the land which God had given them.

A century has passed. Our cities are the abiding places of wealth and luxury; our manufactories yield fortunes never dreamed of by the fathers of the Republic; our business men are madly striving in the race for riches, and immense aggregations of capital outrun the imagination in the magnitude of their undertakings.

We view with pride and satisfaction this bright picture of our country's growth and prosperity, while only a closer scrutiny develops a somber shading. Upon more careful inspection we find the wealth and luxury of our cities mingled with poverty and wretchedness and unremunerative toil. A crowded and constantly increasing urban population suggests the impoverishment of rural sections and discontent with agricultural pursuits. The farmer's son, not satisfied with his father's simple and laborious life, joins the eager chase for easily acquired wealth.

We discover that the fortunes realized by our manufacturers are no longer solely the reward of sturdy industry and enlightened foresight, but that they result from the discriminating favor of the Government and are largely built upon undue exactions from the masses of our people. The gulf between employers and the employed is constantly widening, and classes are rapidly forming, one comprising the very rich and powerful, while in another are found the toiling poor.

As we view the achievements of aggregated capital, we discover the existence of trusts, combinations, and monopolies, while the citizen is struggling far in the rear or is trampled to death beneath an iron heel. Corporations, which should be the carefully restrained creatures of the law and the servants of the people, are fast becoming the people's masters.

Still congratulating ourselves upon the wealth and prosperity of our country and complacently contemplating every incident of change inseparable from these conditions, it is our duty as patriotic citizens to inquire at the present stage of our progress how the bond of the Government made with the people has been kept and performed.

Instead of limiting the tribute drawn from our citizens to the necessities of its economical administration, the Government persists in exacting from the substance of the people millions which, unapplied and useless, lie dormant in its Treasury. This flagrant injustice and this breach of faith and obligation add to extortion the danger attending the diversion of the currency of the country from the legitimate channels of business.

Under the same laws by which these results are produced the Government permits many millions more to be added to the cost of the living of our people and to be taken from our consumers, which unreasonably swell the profits of a small but powerful minority.

The people must still be taxed for the support of the Government under the operation of tariff laws. But to the extent that the mass of our citizens are inordinately burdened beyond any useful public purpose and for the benefit of a favored few, the Government, under pretext of an exercise of its taxing power, enters gratuitously into partnership with these favorites, to their advantage and to the injury of a vast majority of our people.

This is not equality before the law.

The existing situation is injurious to the health of our entire body politic. It stifles in those for whose benefit it is permitted all patriotic love of country, and substitutes in its place selfish greed and grasping avarice. Devotion to American citizenship for its own sake and for what it should accomplish as a motive to our nation's advancement and the happiness of all our people is displaced by the assumption that the Government, instead of being the embodiment of equality, is but an instrumentality through which especial and individual advantages are to be gained.

The arrogance of this assumption is unconcealed. It appears in the sordid disregard of all but personal interests, in the refusal to abate for the benefit of others one iota of selfish advantage, and in combinations to perpetuate such advantages through efforts to control legislation and improperly influence the suffrages of the people.

The grievances of those not included within the circle of these beneficiaries, when fully realized, will surely arouse irritation and discontent. Our farmers, long suffering and patient, struggling in the race of life with the hardest and most unremitting toil, will not fail to see, in spite of misrepresentations and misleading fallacies, that they are obliged to accept such prices for their products as are fixed in foreign markets where they compete with the farmers of the world; that their lands are declining in value while their debts increase, and that without compensating favor they are forced by the action of the Government to pay for the benefit of others such enhanced prices for the things they need that the scanty returns of their labor fail to furnish their support or leave no margin for accumulation.

Our workingmen, enfranchised from all delusions and no longer frightened by the cry that their wages are endangered by a just revision of our tariff laws, will reasonably demand through such revision steadier employment, cheaper means of living in their homes, freedom for themselves and their children from the doom of perpetual servitude, and an open door to their advancement beyond the limits of a laboring class. Others of our citizens, whose comforts and expenditures are measured by moderate salaries and fixed incomes, will insist upon the fairness and justice of cheapening the cost of necessaries for themselves and their families.

When to the selfishness of the beneficiaries of unjust discrimination under our laws there shall be added the discontent of those who suffer from such discrimination, we will realize the fact that the beneficent purposes of our Government, dependent upon the patriotism and contentment of our people, are endangered.

Communism is a hateful thing and a menace to peace and organized government; but the communism of combined wealth and capital, the outgrowth of overweening cupidity and selfishness, which insidiously undermines the justice and integrity of free institutions, is not less dangerous than the communism of oppressed poverty and toil, which, exasperated by injustice and discontent, attacks with wild disorder the citadel of rule.

He mocks the people who proposes that the Government shall protect the rich and that they in turn will care for the laboring poor. Any intermediary between the people and their Government or the least delegation of the care and protection the Government owes to the humblest citizen in the land makes the boast of free institutions a glittering delusion and the pretended boon of American citizenship a shameless imposition. A just and sensible revision of our tariff laws should be made for the relief of those of our countrymen who suffer under present conditions. Such a revision should receive the support of all who love that justice and equality due to American citizenship; of all who realize that in this justice and equality our Government finds its strength and its power to protect the citizen and his property; of all who believe that the contented competence and comfort of many accord better with the spirit of our institutions than colossal fortunes unfairly gathered in the hands of a few; of all who appreciate that the forbearance and fraternity among our people, which recognize the value of every American interest, are the surest guaranty of our national progress, and of all who desire to see the products of American skill and ingenuity in every market of the world, with a resulting restoration of American commerce.

The necessity of the reduction of our revenues is so apparent as to be generally conceded, but the means by which this end shall be accomplished and the sum of direct benefit which shall result to our citizens present a controversy of the utmost importance. There should be no scheme accepted as satisfactory by which the burdens of the people are only apparently removed. Extravagant appropriations of public money, with all their demoralizing consequences, should not be tolerated, either as a means of relieving the Treasury of its present surplus or as furnishing pretext for resisting a proper reduction in tariff rates. Existing evils and injustice should be honestly recognized, boldly met, and effectively remedied. There should be no cessation of the struggle until a plan is perfected, fair and conservative toward existing industries, but which will reduce the cost to consumers of the necessaries of life, while it provides for our manufacturers the advantage of freer raw materials and permits no injury to the interests of American labor. The cause for which the battle is waged is comprised within lines clearly and distinctly defined. It should never be compromised. It is the people's cause.

It can not be denied that the selfish and private interests which are so persistently heard when efforts are made to deal in a just and comprehensive manner with our tariff laws are related to, if they are not responsible for, the sentiment largely prevailing among the people that the General Government is the fountain of individual and private aid; that it may be expected to relieve with paternal care the distress of citizens and communities, and that from the fullness of its Treasury it should, upon the slightest possible pretext of promoting the general good, apply public funds to the benefit of localities and individuals. Nor can it be denied that there is a growing assumption that, as against the Government and in favor of private claims and interests, the usual rules and limitations of business principles and just dealing should be waived.

These ideas have been unhappily much encouraged by legislative acquiescence. Relief from contracts made with the Government is too easily accorded in favor of the citizen; the failure to support claims against the Government by proof is often supplied by no better consideration than the wealth of the Government and the poverty of the claimant; gratuities in the form of pensions are granted upon no other real ground than the needy condition of the applicant, or for reasons less valid; and large sums are expended for public buildings and other improvements upon representations scarcely claimed to be related to public needs and necessities.

The extent to which the consideration of such matters subordinate and postpone action upon subjects of great public importance, but involving no special private or partisan interest, should arrest attention and lead to reformation.

A few of the numerous illustrations of this condition may be stated.

The crowded condition of the calendar of the Supreme Court, and the delay to suitors and denial of justice resulting therefrom, has been strongly urged upon the attention of the Congress, with a plan for the relief of the situation approved by those well able to judge of its merits. While this subject remains without effective consideration, many laws have been passed providing for the holding of terms of inferior courts at places to suit the convenience of localities, or to lay the foundation of an application for the erection of a new public building.

Repeated recommendations have been submitted for the amendment and change of the laws relating to our public lands so that their spoliation and diversion to other uses than as homes for honest settlers might be prevented. While a measure to meet this conceded necessity of reform remains awaiting the action of the Congress, many claims to the public lands and applications for their donation, in favor of States and individuals, have been allowed.

A plan in aid of Indian management, recommended by those well informed as containing valuable features in furtherance of the solution of the Indian problem, has thus far failed of legislative sanction, while grants of doubtful expediency to railroad corporations, permitting them to pass through Indian reservations, have greatly multiplied.

The propriety and necessity of the erection of one or more prisons for the confinement of United States convicts, and a post-office building in the national capital, are not disputed. But these needs yet remain answered, while scores of public buildings have been erected where their necessity for public purposes is not apparent.

A revision of our pension laws could easily be made which would rest upon just principles and provide for every worthy applicant. But while our general pension laws remain confused and imperfect, hundreds of private pension laws are annually passed, which are the sources of unjust discrimination and popular demoralization.

Appropriation bills for the support of the Government are defaced by items and provisions to meet private ends, and it is freely asserted by responsible and experienced parties that a bill appropriating money for public internal improvement would fail to meet with favor unless it contained items more for local and private advantage than for public benefit.

These statements can be much emphasized by an ascertainment of the proportion of Federal legislation which either bears upon its face its private character or which upon examination develops such a motive power.

And yet the people wait and expect from their chosen representatives such patriotic action as will advance the welfare of the entire country; and this expectation can only be answered by the performance of public duty with unselfish purpose. Our mission among the nations of the earth and our success in accomplishing the work God has given the American people to do require of those intrusted with the making and execution of our laws perfect devotion, above all other things, to the public good.

This devotion will lead us to strongly resist all impatience of constitutional limitations of Federal power and to persistently check the increasing tendency to extend the scope of Federal legislation into the domain of State and local jurisdiction upon the plea of subserving the public welfare. The preservation of the partitions between proper subjects of Federal and local care and regulation is of such importance under the Constitution, which is the law of our very existence, that no consideration of expediency or sentiment should tempt us to enter upon doubtful ground. We have undertaken to discover and proclaim the richest blessings of a free government, with the Constitution as our guide. Let us follow the way it points out; it will not mislead us. And surely no one who has taken upon himself the solemn obligation to support and preserve the Constitution can find justification or solace for disloyalty in the excuse that he wandered and disobeyed in search of a better way to reach the public welfare than the Constitution offers.

What has been said is deemed not inappropriate at a time when, from a century's height, we view the way already trod by the American people and attempt to discover their future path.

The seventh President of the United States—the soldier and statesman and at all times the firm and brave friend of the people—in vindication of his course as the protector of popular rights and the champion of true American citizenship, declared:

> The ambition which leads me on is an anxious desire and a fixed determination to restore to the people unimpaired the sacred trust they have confided to my charge; to heal the wounds of the Constitution and

to preserve it from further violation; to persuade my countrymen, so far as I may, that it is not in a splendid government supported by powerful monopolies and aristocratical establishments that they will find happiness or their liberties protection, but in a plain system, void of pomp, protecting all and granting favors to none, dispensing its blessings like the dews of heaven, unseen and unfelt save in the freshness and beauty they contribute to produce. It is such a government that the genius of our people requires—such an one only under which our States may remain for ages to come united, prosperous, and free.

In pursuance of a constitutional provision requiring the President from time to time to give to the Congress information of the state of the Union, I have the satisfaction to announce that the close of the year finds the United States in the enjoyment of domestic tranquillity and at peace with all the nations. Since my last annual message our foreign relations have been strengthened and improved by performance of international good offices and by new and renewed treaties of amity, commerce, and reciprocal extradition of criminals.

Those international questions which still await settlement are all reasonably within the domain of amicable negotiation, and there is no existing subject of dispute between the United States and any foreign power that is not susceptible of satisfactory adjustment by frank diplomatic treatment.

The questions between Great Britain and the United States relating to the rights of American fishermen, under treaty and international comity, in the territorial waters of Canada and Newfoundland, I regret to say, are not yet satisfactorily adjusted.

These matters were fully treated in my message to the Senate of February 20, 1888, together with which a convention, concluded under my authority with Her Majesty's Government on the 15th of February last, for the removal of all causes of misunderstanding, was submitted by me for the approval of the Senate.

This treaty having been rejected by the Senate, I transmitted a message to the Congress on the 23d of August last reviewing the transactions and submitting for consideration certain recommendations for legislation concerning the important questions involved.

Afterwards, on the 12th of September, in response to a resolution of the Senate, I again communicated fully all the information in my possession as to the action of the government of Canada affecting the commercial relations between the Dominion and the United States, including the treatment of American fishing vessels in the ports and waters of British North America.

These communications have all been published, and therefore opened to the knowledge of both Houses of Congress, although two were addressed to the Senate alone.

Comment upon or repetition of their contents would be superfluous, and I am not aware that anything has since occurred which should be added to the facts therein stated. Therefore I merely repeat, as applicable to the present time, the statement which will be found in my message to the Senate of September 12 last, that—

Since March 3, 1887, no case has been reported to the Department of State wherein complaint was made of unfriendly or unlawful treatment of American fishing vessels on the part of the Canadian authorities in which reparation was not promptly and satisfactorily obtained by the United States consul-general at Halifax.

Having essayed in the discharge of my duty to procure by negotiation the settlement of a longstanding cause of dispute and to remove a constant menace to the good relations of the two countries, and continuing to be of opinion that the treaty of February last, which failed to receive the approval of the Senate, did supply "a satisfactory, practical, and final adjustment, upon a basis honorable and just to both parties, of the difficult and vexed question to which it related," and having subsequently and unavailingly recommended other legislation to Congress which I hoped would suffice to meet the exigency created by the rejection of the treaty, I now again invoke the earnest and immediate attention of the Congress to the condition of this important question as it now stands before them and the country, and for the settlement of which I am deeply solicitous.

Near the close of the month of October last occurrences of a deeply regrettable nature were brought to my knowledge, which made it my painful but imperative duty to obtain with as little delay as possible a new personal channel of diplomatic intercourse in this country with the Government of Great Britain.

The correspondence in relation to this incident will in due course be laid before you, and will disclose the unpardonable conduct of the official referred to in his interference by advice and counsel with the suffrages of American citizens in the very crisis of the Presidential election then near at hand, and also in his subsequent public declarations to justify his action, superadding impugnment of the Executive and Senate of the United States in connection with important questions now pending in controversy between the two Governments.

The offense thus committed was most grave, involving disastrous possibilities to the good relations of the United States and Great Britain, constituting a gross breach of diplomatic privilege and an invasion of the purely domestic affairs and essential sovereignty of the Government to which the envoy was accredited.

Having first fulfilled the just demands of international comity by affording full opportunity for Her Majesty's Government to act in relief of the situation, I considered prolongation of discussion to be unwarranted, and thereupon declined to further recognize the diplomatic character of the person whose continuance in such function would destroy that mutual confidence which is essential to the good understanding of the two Governments and was inconsistent with the welfare and self-respect of the Government of the United States.

The usual interchange of communication has since continued through Her Majesty's legation in this city.

My endeavors to establish by international cooperation measures for the prevention of the extermination of fur seals in Bering Sea have not been relaxed, and I have hopes of being enabled shortly to submit an effective and satisfactory conventional projet with the maritime powers for the approval of the Senate.

The coastal boundary between our Alaskan possessions and British Columbia, I regret to say, has not received the attention demanded by its importance, and which on several occasions heretofore I have had the honor to recommend to the Congress.

The admitted impracticability, if not impossibility, of making an accurate and precise survey and demarcation of the boundary line as it is recited in the treaty with Russia under which Alaska was ceded to the United States renders it absolutely requisite for the prevention of international jurisdictional complications that adequate appropriation for a reconnaissance and survey to obtain proper knowledge of the locality and the geographical features of the boundary should be authorized by Congress with as little delay as possible.

Knowledge to be only thus obtained is an essential prerequisite for negotiation for ascertaining a common boundary, or as preliminary to any other mode of settlement.

It is much to be desired that some agreement should be reached with Her Majesty's Government by which the damages to life and property on the Great Lakes may be alleviated by removing or humanely regulating the obstacles to reciprocal assistance to wrecked or stranded vessels.

The act of June 19, 1878, which offers to Canadian vessels free access to our inland waters in aid of wrecked or disabled vessels, has not yet become effective through concurrent action by Canada. The due protection of our citizens of French origin or descent from claim of military service in the event of their returning to or visiting France has called forth correspondence which was laid before you at the last session.

In the absence of conventional agreement as to naturalization, which is greatly to be desired, this Government sees no occasion to recede from the sound position it has maintained not only with regard to France, but as to all countries with which the United States have not concluded special treaties. Twice within the last year has the imperial household of Germany been visited by death; and I have hastened to express the sorrow of this people, and their appreciation of the lofty character of the late aged Emperor William, and their sympathy with the heroism under suffering of his son the late Emperor Frederick.

I renew my recommendation of two years ago for the passage of a bill for the refunding to certain German steamship lines of the interest upon tonnage dues illegally exacted.

On the 12th [2d] of April last I laid before the House of Representatives full information respecting our interests in Samoa; and in the subsequent correspondence on the same subject, which will be laid before you in due course, the history of events in those islands will be found.

In a message accompanying my approval, on the 1st day of October last, of a bill for the exclusion of Chinese laborers, I laid before Congress full information and all correspondence touching the negotiation of the treaty with China concluded at this capital on the 12th day of March, 1888, and which, having been confirmed by the Senate with certain amendments, was rejected by the Chinese Government. This message contained a recommendation that a sum of money be appropriated as compensation to Chinese subjects who had suffered injuries at the hands of lawless men within our jurisdiction. Such appropriation having been duly made, the fund awaits reception by the Chinese Government.

It is sincerely hoped that by the cessation of the influx of this class of Chinese subjects, in accordance with the expressed wish of both Governments, a cause of unkind feeling has been permanently removed.

On the 9th of August, 1887, notification was given by the Japanese minister at this capital of the adjournment of the conference for the revision of the treaties of Japan with foreign powers, owing to the objection of his Government to the provision in the draft jurisdictional convention which required the submission of the criminal code of the Empire to the powers in advance of its becoming operative. This notification was, however, accompanied with an assurance of Japan's intention to continue the work of revision.

Notwithstanding this temporary interruption of negotiations, it is hoped that improvements may soon be secured in the jurisdictional system as respects foreigners in Japan, and relief afforded to that country from the present undue and oppressive foreign control in matters of commerce.

I earnestly recommend that relief be provided for the injuries accidentally caused to Japanese subjects in the island Ikisima by the target practice of one of our vessels.

A diplomatic mission from Korea has been received, and the formal intercourse between the two countries contemplated by the treaty of 1882 is now established.

Legislative provision is hereby recommended to organize and equip consular courts in Korea.

Persia has established diplomatic representation at this capital, and has evinced very great interest in the enterprise and achievements of our citizens. I am therefore hopeful that beneficial commercial relations between the two countries may be brought about.

I announce with sincere regret that Hayti has again become the theater of insurrection, disorder, and bloodshed. The titular government of president Saloman has been forcibly overthrown and he driven out of the country to France, where he has since died.

The tenure of power has been so unstable amid the war of factions that has ensued since the expulsion of President Saloman that no government constituted by the will of the Haytian people has been recognized as administering responsibly the affairs of that country. Our representative has been instructed to abstain from interference between the warring factions, and a vessel of our Navy has been sent to Haytian waters to sustain our minister and for the protection of the persons and property of American citizens.

Due precautions have been taken to enforce our neutrality laws and prevent our territory from becoming the base of military supplies for either of the warring factions.

Under color of a blockade, of which no reasonable notice had been given, and which does not appear to have been efficiently maintained, a seizure of vessels under the American flag has been reported, and in consequence measures to prevent and redress any molestation of our innocent merchantmen have been adopted.

Proclamation was duly made on the 9th day of November, 1887, of the conventional extensions of the treaty of June 3, 1875, with Hawaii, under which relations of such special and beneficent intercourse have been created.

In the vast field of Oriental commerce now unfolded from our Pacific borders no feature presents stronger recommendations for Congressional action than the establishment of communication by submarine telegraph with Honolulu.

The geographical position of the Hawaiian group in relation to our Pacific States creates a natural interdependency and mutuality of interest which our present treaties were intended to foster, and which make close communication a logical and commercial necessity.

The wisdom of concluding a treaty of commercial reciprocity with Mexico has been heretofore stated in my messages to Congress, and the lapse of time and growth of commerce with that close neighbor and sister Republic confirm the judgment so expressed.

The precise relocation of our boundary line is needful, and adequate appropriation is now recommended.

It is with sincere satisfaction that I am enabled to advert to the spirit of good neighborhood and friendly cooperation and conciliation that has marked the correspondence and action of the Mexican authorities in their share of the task of maintaining law and order about the line of our common boundary.

The long-pending boundary dispute between Costa Rica and Nicaragua was referred to my arbitration, and by an award made on the 22d of March last the question has been finally settled to the expressed satisfaction of both of the parties in interest.

The Empire of Brazil, in abolishing the last vestige of slavery among Christian nations, called forth the earnest congratulations of this Government in expression of the cordial sympathies of our people.

The claims of nearly all other countries against Chile growing out of her late war with Bolivia and Peru have been disposed of, either by arbitration or by a lump settlement. Similar claims of our citizens will continue to be urged upon the Chilean Government, and it is hoped will not be subject to further delays.

A comprehensive treaty of amity and commerce with Peru was proclaimed on November 7 last, and it is expected that under its operation mutual prosperity and good understanding will be promoted.

In pursuance of the policy of arbitration, a treaty to settle the claim of Santos, an American citizen, against Ecuador has been concluded under my authority, and will be duly submitted for the approval of the Senate.

Like disposition of the claim of Carlos Butterfield against Denmark and of Van Bokkelen against Hayti will probably be made, and I trust the principle of such settlements may be extended in practice under the approval of the Senate.

Through unforeseen causes, foreign to the will of both Governments, the ratification of the convention of December 5, 1885, with Venezuela, for the rehearing of claims of citizens of the United States under the treaty of 1866, failed of exchange within the term provided, and a supplementary convention, further extending the time for exchange of ratifications and explanatory of an ambiguous provision of the prior convention, now awaits the advice and consent of the Senate.

Although this matter, in the stage referred to, concerns only the concurrent treaty-making power of one branch of Congress, I advert to it in view of the interest repeatedly and conspicuously shown by you in your legislative capacity in favor of a speedy and equitable adjustment of the questions growing out of the discredited judgments of the previous mixed commission of Caracas. With every desire to do justice to the representations of Venezuela in this regard, the time seems to have come to end this matter, and I trust the prompt confirmation by both parties of the supplementary action referred to will avert the need of legislative or other action to prevent the longer withholding of such rights of actual claimants as may be shown to exist.

As authorized by the Congress, preliminary steps have been taken for the assemblage at this capital during the coming year of the representatives of South and Central American States, together with those of Mexico, Hayti, and San Domingo, to discuss sundry important monetary and commercial topics.

Excepting in those cases where, from reasons of contiguity of territory and the existence of a common border line incapable of being guarded, reciprocal commercial treaties may be found expedient, it is believed that commercial policies inducing freer mutual exchange of products can be most advantageously arranged by independent but cooperative legislation.

In the mode last mentioned the control of our taxation for revenue will be always retained in our own hands unrestricted by conventional agreements with other governments.

In conformity also with Congressional authority, the maritime powers have been invited to confer in Washington in April next upon the practicability of devising uniform rules and measures for the greater security of life and property at sea. A disposition to accept on the part of a number of the powers has already been manifested, and if the cooperation of the nations chiefly interested shall be secured important results may be confidently anticipated.

The act of June 26, 1884, and the acts amendatory thereof, in relation to tonnage duties, have given rise to extended correspondence with foreign nations with whom we have existing treaties of navigation and commerce, and have caused wide and regrettable divergence of opinion in relation to the imposition of the duties referred to. These questions are important, and I shall make them the subject of a special and more detailed communication at the present session.

With the rapid increase of immigration to our shores and the facilities of modern travel, abuses of the generous privileges afforded by our naturalization laws call for their careful revision.

The easy and unguarded manner in which certificates of American citizenship can now be obtained has induced a class, unfortunately large, to avail themselves of the opportunity to become absolved from allegiance to their native land, and yet by a foreign residence to escape any just duty and contribution of service to the country of their proposed adoption. Thus, while evading the duties of citizenship to the United States, they may make prompt claim for its national protection and demand its intervention in their behalf. International complications of a serious nature arise, and the correspondence of the State Department discloses the great number and complexity of the questions which have been raised.

Our laws regulating the issue of passports should be carefully revised, and the institution of a central bureau of registration at the capital is again strongly recommended. By this means full particulars of each case of naturalization in the United States would be secured and properly indexed and recorded, and thus many cases of spurious citizenship would be detected and unjust responsibilities would be avoided.

The reorganization of the consular service is a matter of serious importance to our national interests. The number of existing principal consular offices is believed to be greater than is at all necessary for the conduct of the public business. It need not be our policy to maintain more than a moderate number of principal offices, each supported by a salary sufficient to enable the incumbent to live in comfort, and so distributed as to secure the convenient supervision, through subordinate agencies, of affairs over a considerable district.

I repeat the recommendations heretofore made by me that the appropriations for the maintenance of our diplomatic and consular service should be recast; that the so-called notarial or unofficial fees, which our representatives abroad are now permitted to treat as personal perquisites, should be forbidden; that a system of consular inspection should be instituted, and that a limited number of secretaries of legation at large should be authorized.

Preparations for the centennial celebration, on April 30, 1889, of the inauguration of George Washington as President of the United States, at the city of New York, have been made by a voluntary organization of the citizens of that locality, and believing that an opportunity should be afforded for the expression of the interest felt throughout the country in this event, I respectfully recommend fitting and cooperative action by Congress on behalf of the people of the United States.

The report of the Secretary of the Treasury exhibits in detail the condition of our national finances and the operations of the several branches of the Government related to his Department. The total ordinary revenues of the Government for the fiscal year ended June 30, 1888, amounted to $379,266,074.76. . . .

* * *

I earnestly request that the recommendations contained in the Secretary's report, all of which are, in my opinion, calculated to increase the usefulness and discipline of the Army, may receive the consideration of the Congress. Among these the proposal that there should be provided a plan for the examination of officers to test their fitness for promotion is of the utmost importance. This reform has been before recommended in the reports of the Secretary, and its expediency is so fully demonstrated by the argument he presents in its favor that its adoption should no longer be neglected.

The death of General Sheridan in August last was a national affliction. The Army then lost the grandest of its chiefs. The country lost a brave and experienced soldier, a wise and discreet counselor, and a modest and sensible man. Those who in any manner came within the range of his personal association will never fail to pay deserved and willing homage to his greatness and the glory of his career, but they will cherish with more tender sensibility the loving memory of his simple, generous, and considerate nature.

The Apache Indians, whose removal from their reservation in Arizona followed the capture of those of their number who engaged in a bloody and murderous raid during a part of the years 1885 and 1886, are now held as prisoners of war at Mount Vernon Barracks, in the State of Alabama. They numbered on the 31st day of October, the date of the last report, 83 men, 170 women, 70 boys, and 59 girls; in all, 382 persons. The commanding officer states that they are in good health and contented, and that they are kept employed as fully as is possible in the circumstances. The children, as they arrive at a suitable age, are sent to the Indian schools at Carlisle and Hampton.

Last summer some charitable and kind people asked permission to send two teachers to these Indians for the purpose of instructing the adults as well as such children as should be found there. Such permission was readily granted, accommodations were provided for the teachers, and some portions of the buildings at the barracks were made available for school purposes. The good work contemplated has been commenced, and the teachers engaged are paid by the ladies with whom the plan originated.

I am not at all in sympathy with those benevolent but injudicious people who are constantly insisting that these Indians should be returned to their reservation. Their removal was an absolute necessity if the lives and property of citizens upon the frontier are to be at all regarded by the Government. Their continued restraint at a distance from the scene of their repeated and cruel murders and outrages is still necessary. It is a mistaken philanthropy, every way injurious, which prompts the desire to see these savages returned to their old haunts. They are in their present location as the result of the best judgment of those having official responsibility in the matter, and who are by no means lacking in kind consideration for the Indians. A number of these prisoners have forfeited their lives to outraged law and humanity. Experience has proved that they are dangerous and can not be trusted. This is true not only of those who on the warpath have heretofore actually been guilty of atrocious murder, but of their kindred and friends, who, while they remained upon their reservation, furnished aid and comfort to those absent with bloody intent.

These prisoners should be treated kindly and kept in restraint far from the locality of their former reservation; they should be subjected to efforts calculated to lead to their improvement and the softening of their savage and cruel instincts, but their return to their old home should be persistently resisted.

The Secretary in his report gives a graphic history of these Indians, and recites with painful vividness their bloody deeds and the unhappy failure of the Government to manage them by peaceful means. It will be amazing if a perusal of this history will allow the survival of a desire for the return of these prisoners to their reservation upon sentimental or any other grounds.

The report of the Secretary of the Navy demonstrates very intelligent management in that important Department, and discloses the most satisfactory progress in the work of reconstructing the Navy made during the past year. Of the ships in course of construction five, viz., the *Charleston*, *Baltimore*, *Yorktown*, *Vesuvius*, and the *Petrel*, have in that time been launched and are rapidly approaching completion; and in addition to the above, the *Philadelphia*, the *San Francisco*, the *Newark*, the *Bennington*, the *Concord*, and the *Herreshoff* torpedo boat are all under contract for delivery to the Department during the next year. The progress already made and being made gives good ground for the expectation that these eleven vessels will be incorporated as part of the American Navy within the next twelve months.

The report shows that notwithstanding the large expenditures for new construction and the additional labor they involve the total ordinary or current expenditures of the Department for the three years ending June 30, 1888, are less by more than 20 per cent than such expenditures for the three years ending June 30, 1884.

The various steps which have been taken to improve the business methods of the Department are reviewed by the Secretary. The purchasing of supplies has been consolidated and placed under a responsible bureau head. This has resulted in the curtailment of open purchases, which in the years 1884 and 1885 amounted to over 50 per cent of all the purchases of the Department, to less than 11 per cent; so that at the present time about 90 per cent of the total departmental purchases are made by contract and after competition. As the expenditures on this account exceed an average of $2,000,000 annually, it is evident that an important improvement in the system has been inaugurated and substantial economies introduced. The report of the Postmaster-General shows a marked increase of business in every branch of the postal service.

The number of post-offices on July 1, 1888, was 57,376, an increase of 6,124 in three years and of 2,219 for the last fiscal year.

*   *   *

In the Railway Mail Service there has been an increase in one year of 168 routes, and in the number of miles traveled per annum an increase of 15,795,917.48. The estimated increase of railroad service for the year was 6,000 miles, but the amount of new railroad service actually put on was 12,764.50 miles.

The volume of business in the Money-Order Division, including transactions in postal notes, reached the sum of upward of $143,000,000 for the year.

During the past year parcel-post conventions have been concluded with Barbados, the Bahamas, British Honduras, and Mexico, and are now under negotiation with all the Central and South American States. The increase of correspondence with foreign countries during the past three years is gratifying, and is especially notable and exceptional with the Central and South American States and with Mexico. As the greater part of mail matter exchanged with these countries is commercial in its character, this increase is evidence of the improved business relations with them. The practical operation of the parcel-post conventions, so far as negotiated, has served to fulfill the most favorable predictions as to their benefits. In January last a general postal convention was negotiated with the Dominion of Canada, which went into operation on March 1, and which practically makes one postal territory of the United States and Canada. Under it merchandise parcels may now be transmitted through the mails at fourth-class rates of postage.

It is not possible here to touch even the leading heads of the great postal establishment to illustrate the enormous and rapid growth of its business and the needs for legislative readjustment of much of its machinery that it has outgrown. For these and valuable recommendations of the Postmaster-General attention is earnestly invited to his report.

A Department whose revenues have increased from $19,772,000 in 1870 to $52,700,000 in 1888, despite reductions of postage which have enormously reduced rates of revenue while greatly increasing its business, demands the careful consideration of the Congress as to all matters suggested by those familiar with its operations, and which are calculated to increase its efficiency and usefulness.

A bill proposed by the Postmaster-General was introduced at the last session of the Congress by which a uniform standard in the amount of gross receipts would fix the right of a community to a public building to be erected by the Government for post-office purposes. It was demonstrated that, aside from the public convenience and the promotion of harmony among citizens, invariably disturbed by change of leasings and of site, it was a measure of the highest economy and of sound business judgment. It was found that the Government was paying in rents at the rate of from 7 to 10 per cent per annum on what the cost of such public buildings would be. A very great advantage resulting from such a law would be the prevention of a large number of bills constantly introduced for the erection of public buildings at places, and involving expenditures not justified by public necessity. I trust that this measure will become a law at the present session of Congress.

Of the total number of postmasters 54,874 are of the fourth class. These, of course, receive no allowances whatever for expenses in the service, and their compensation is fixed by percentages on receipts at their respective offices. This rate of compensation may have been, and probably was, at some time just, but the standard has remained unchanged through the several reductions in the rates of postage. Such reductions have necessarily cut down the compensation of these officials, while it undoubtedly increased the business performed by them. Simple justice requires attention to this subject, to the end that fourth-class postmasters may receive at least an equivalent to that which the law itself, fixing the rate, intended for them.

Another class of postal employees whose condition seems to demand legislation is that of clerks in post-offices, and I call especial attention to the repeated recommendations of the Postmaster-General for their classification. Proper legislation of this character for the relief of carriers in the free-delivery service has been frequent. Provision is made for their promotion; for substitutes for them on vacation; for substitutes for holidays; and limiting their hours of labor. Seven million dollars has been appropriated for the current year to provide for them, though the total number of offices where they are employed is but 358 for the past fiscal year, with an estimated increase for the current year of but 40, while the total appropriation for all clerks in offices throughout the United States is $5,950,000.

The legislation affecting the relations of the Government with railroads is in need of revision. While for the most part the railroad companies throughout the country have cordially cooperated with the Post-Office Department in rendering excellent service, yet under the law as it stands, while the compensation to them for carrying the mail is limited and regulated, and although railroads are made post-roads by law, there is no authority reposed anywhere to compel the owner of a railroad to take and carry the United States mails. The only alternative provided by act of Congress in case of refusal is for the Postmaster-General to send mail forward by pony express. This is but an illustration of ill-fitting legislation, reasonable and proper at the time of its enactment, but long since outgrown and requiring readjustment.

It is gratifying to note from the carefully prepared statistics accompanying the Postmaster-General's report that notwithstanding the great expansion of the service the rate of expenditure has been lessened and efficiency has been improved in every branch; that fraud and crime have decreased; that losses from the mails have been reduced; and that the number of complaints of the service made to postmasters and to the Department are far less than ever before.

The transactions of the Department of Justice for the fiscal year ended June 30, 1888, are contained in the report of the Attorney-General, as well as a number of valuable recommendations, the most part of which are repetitions of those previously made, and ought to receive consideration.

It is stated in this report that though judgments in civil suits amounting to $552,021.08 were recovered in favor of the Government during the year, only the sum of $132,934 was collected thereon; and that though fines, penalties, and forfeitures were imposed amounting to $541,808.43, only

$109,648.42 of that sum was paid on account thereof. These facts may furnish an illustration of the sentiment which extensively prevails that a debt due the Government should cause no inconvenience to the citizen.

It also appears from this report that though prior to March, 1885, there had been but 6 convictions in the Territories of Utah and Idaho under the laws of 1862 and 1882, punishing polygamy and unlawful cohabitation as crimes, there have been since that date nearly 600 convictions under these laws and the statutes of 1887; and the opinion is expressed that under such a firm and vigilant execution of these laws and the advance of ideas opposed to the forbidden practices polygamy within the United States is virtually at an end.

Suits instituted by the Government under the provisions of the act of March 3, 1887, for the termination of the corporations known as the Perpetual Emigrating Fund Company and the Church of Jesus Christ of Latter-day Saints have resulted in a decree favorable to the Government, declaring the charters of these corporations forfeited and escheating their property. Such property, amounting in value to more than $800,000, is in the hands of a receiver pending further proceedings, an appeal having been taken to the Supreme Court of the United States.

In the report of the Secretary of the Interior, which will be laid before you, the condition of the various branches of our domestic affairs connected with that Department and its operations during the past year are fully exhibited. But a brief reference to some of the subjects discussed in this able and interesting report can here be made; but I commend the entire report to the attention of the Congress, and trust that the sensible and valuable recommendations it contains will secure careful consideration.

I can not too strenuously insist upon the importance of proper measures to insure a right disposition of our public lands, not only as a matter of present justice, but in forecast of the consequences to future generations. The broad, rich acres of our agricultural plains have been long preserved by nature to become her untrammeled gift to a people civilized and free, upon which should rest in well-distributed ownership the numerous homes of enlightened, equal, and fraternal citizens. They came to national possession with the warning example in our eyes of the entail of iniquities in landed proprietorship which other countries have permitted and still suffer. We have no excuse for the violation of principles cogently taught by reason and example, nor for the allowance of pretexts which have sometimes exposed our lands to colossal greed. Laws which open a door to fraudulent acquisition, or administration which permits favor to rapacious seizure by a favored few of expanded areas that many should enjoy, are accessory to offenses against our national welfare and humanity not to be too severely condemned or punished.

It is gratifying to know that something has been done at last to redress the injuries to our people and check the perilous tendency of the reckless waste of the national domain. That over 80,000,000 acres have been arrested from illegal usurpation, improvident grants, and fraudulent entries and claims, to be taken for the homesteads of honest industry—although less than the greater areas thus unjustly lost—must afford a profound gratification to right-feeling citizens, as it is a recompense for the labors and struggles of the recovery. Our dear experience ought sufficiently to urge the speedy enactment of measures of legislation which will confine the future disposition of our remaining agricultural lands to the uses of actual husbandry and genuine homes.

Nor should our vast tracts of so-called desert lands be yielded up to the monopoly of corporations or grasping individuals, as appears to be much the tendency under the existing statute. These lands require but the supply of water to become fertile and productive. It is a problem of great moment how most wisely for the public good that factor shall be furnished. I can not but think it perilous to suffer either these lands or the sources of their irrigation to fall into the hands of monopolies, which by such means may exercise lordship over the areas dependent on their treatment for productiveness. Already steps have been taken to secure accurate and scientific information of the conditions, which is the prime basis of intelligent action. Until this shall be gained the course of wisdom appears clearly to lie in a suspension of further disposal, which only promises to create rights antagonistic to the common interest. No harm can follow this cautionary conduct. The land will remain, and the public good presents no demand for hasty dispossession of national ownership and control.

I commend also the recommendations that appropriate measures be taken to complete the adjustment of the various grants made to the States for internal improvements and of swamp and overflowed lands, as well as to adjudicate and finally determine the validity and extent of the numerous private land claims. All these are elements of great injustice and peril to the settlers upon the localities affected; and now that their existence can not be avoided, no duty is more pressing than to fix as soon as possible their bounds and terminate the threats of trouble which arise from uncertainty.

The condition of our Indian population continues to improve and the proofs multiply that the transforming change, so much to be desired, which shall substitute for barbarism enlightenment and civilizing education, is in favorable progress. Our relations with these people during the year have been disturbed by no serious disorders, but rather marked by a better realization of their true interests and increasing confidence and good will. These conditions testify to the value of the higher tone of consideration and humanity which has governed the later methods of dealing with them, and commend its continued observance.

Allotments in severalty have been made on some reservations until all those entitled to land thereon have had their shares assigned, and the work is still continued. In directing the execution of this duty I have not aimed so much at rapid dispatch as to secure just and fair arrangements which shall best conduce to the objects of the law by producing satisfaction with the results of the allotments made. No measure of general effect has ever been entered on from which more may be fairly hoped if it shall be discreetly administered. It proffers opportunity and inducement to that independence of spirit and life which the Indian peculiarly needs, while at the same time the inalienability of title affords security against the risks his inexperience of affairs or weakness of character may expose him to in dealing with others. Whenever begun upon any reservation it should be made complete, so that all are brought to the same condition, and as soon as possible community in lands should cease by opening such as remain unallotted to settlement. Contact with the ways of industrious and successful farmers will perhaps add a healthy emulation which will both instruct and stimulate.

But no agency for the amelioration of this people appears to me so promising as the extension, urged by the Secretary, of such complete facilities of education as shall at the earliest possible day embrace all teachable Indian youth, of both sexes, and retain them with a kindly and beneficent hold until their characters are formed and their faculties and dispositions trained to the sure pursuit of some form of useful industry. Capacity of the Indian no longer needs demonstration. It is established. It remains to make the most of it, and when that shall be done the curse will be lifted, the Indian race saved, and the sin of their oppression redeemed. The time of its accomplishment depends upon the spirit and justice with which it shall be prosecuted. It can not be too soon for the Indian nor for the interests and good name of the nation.

The average attendance of Indian pupils on the schools increased by over 900 during the year, and the total enrollment reached 15,212. The cost of maintenance was not materially raised. The number of teachable Indian youth is now estimated at 40,000, or nearly three times the enrollment of the schools. It is believed the obstacles in the way of instructing are all surmountable, and that the necessary expenditure would be a measure of economy.

The Sioux tribes on the great reservation of Dakota refused to assent to the act passed by the Congress at its last session for opening a portion of their lands to settlement, notwithstanding modification of the terms was suggested which met most of their objections. Their demand is for immediate payment of the full price of $1.25 per acre for the entire body of land the occupancy of which they are asked to relinquish.

The manner of submission insured their fair understanding of the law, and their action was undoubtedly as thoroughly intelligent as their capacity admitted. It is at least gratifying that no reproach of overreaching can in any manner lie against the Government, however advisable the favorable completion of the negotiation may have been esteemed.

I concur in the suggestions of the Secretary regarding the Turtle Mountain Indians, the two reservations in California, and the Crees. They should, in my opinion, receive immediate attention.

The number of pensioners added to the rolls during the fiscal year ended June 30, 1888, is 60,252, and increase of pensions was granted in 45,716 cases. The names of 15,730 pensioners were dropped from the rolls during the year from various causes, and at the close of the year the number of persons of all classes receiving pensions was 452,557. Of these there were 806 survivors of the War of 1812, 10,787 widows of those who served in that war, 16,060 soldiers of the Mexican War, and 5,104 widows of said soldiers.

One hundred and two different rates of pensions are paid to these beneficiaries, ranging from $2 to $416.66 per month.

The amount paid for pensions during the fiscal year was $78,775,861.92, being an increase over the preceding year of $5,308,280.22. The expenses attending the maintenance and operation of the Pension Bureau during that period was $3,262,524.67, making the entire expenditures of the Bureau $82,038,386.57, being 21½ per cent of the gross income and nearly 31 per cent of the total expenditures of the Government during the year.

I am thoroughly convinced that our general pension laws should be revised and adjusted to meet as far as possible, in the light of our experience, all meritorious cases. The fact that 102 different rates of pensions are paid can not, in my opinion, be made consistent with justice to the pensioners or to the Government; and the numerous private pension bills that are passed, predicated upon the imperfection of general laws, while they increase in many cases existing inequality and injustice, lend additional force to the recommendation for a revision of the general laws on this subject.

The laxity of ideas prevailing among a large number of our people regarding pensions is becoming every day more marked. The principles upon which they should be granted are in danger of being altogether ignored, and already pensions are often claimed because the applicants are as much entitled as other successful applicants, rather than upon any disability reasonably attributable to military service. If the establishment of vicious precedents be continued, if the granting of pensions be not divorced from partisan and other unworthy and irrelevant considerations, and if the honorable name of veteran unfairly becomes by these means but another term for one who constantly clamors for the aid of the Government, there is danger that injury will be done to the fame and patriotism of many whom our citizens all delight to honor, and that a prejudice will be aroused unjust to meritorious applicants for pensions.

The Department of Agriculture has continued, with a good measure of success, its efforts to develop the processes, enlarge the results, and augment the profits of American husbandry. It has collected and distributed practical information, introduced and tested new plants, checked the spread of contagious diseases of farm animals, resisted the advance of noxious insects and destructive fungous growths, and sought to secure to agricultural labor the highest reward of effort and the fullest immunity from loss. Its records of the year show that the season of 1888 has been one of medium production. A generous supply of the demands of consumption has been assured, and a surplus for exportation, moderate in certain products and bountiful in others, will prove a benefaction alike to buyer and grower.

Four years ago it was found that the great cattle industry of the country was endangered, and those engaged in it were alarmed at the rapid extension of the European lung plague of pleuro-pneumonia. Serious outbreaks existed in Illinois, Missouri, and Kentucky, and in Tennessee animals affected were held in quarantine. Five counties in New York and from one to four counties in each of the States of New Jersey, Pennsylvania, Delaware, and Maryland were almost equally affected.

With this great danger upon us and with the contagion already in the channels of commerce, with the enormous direct and indirect losses already being caused by it, and when only prompt and energetic action could be successful, there were in none of these States any laws authorizing this Department to eradicate the malady or giving the State officials power to cooperate with it for this purpose. The Department even lacked both the requisite appropriation and authority.

By securing State cooperation in connection with authority from Congress the work of eradication has been pressed successfully, and this dreaded disease has been extirpated from the Western States and also from the Eastern States, with the exception of a few restricted areas, which are still under supervision. The danger has thus been removed, and trade and commerce have been freed from the vexatious State restrictions which were deemed necessary for a time.

During the past four years the process of diffusion, as applied to the manufacture of sugar from sorghum and sugar cane, has been introduced into this country and fully perfected by the experiments carried on by the Department of Agriculture. This process is now universally considered to be the most economical one, and it is through it that the sorghum-sugar industry has been established upon a firm basis and the road to its future success opened. The adoption of this diffusion process is also extending in Louisiana and other sugar-producing parts of the country, and will doubtless soon be the only method employed for the extraction of sugar from the cane.

An exhaustive study has also within the same period been undertaken of the subject of food adulteration and the best analytical methods for detecting it. A part of the results of this work has already been published by the Department, which, with the matter in course of preparation, will make the most complete treatise on that subject that has ever been published in any country.

The Department seeks a progressive development. It would combine the discoveries of science with the economics and amelioration of rural practice. A supervision of the endowed experimental-station system recently provided for is a proper function of the Department, and is now in operation. This supervision is very important, and should be wisely and vigilantly directed, to the end that the pecuniary aid of the Government in favor of intelligent agriculture should be so applied as to result in the general good and to the benefit of all our people, thus justifying the appropriations made from the public Treasury.

The adjustment of the relations between the Government and the railroad companies which have received land grants and the guaranty of the public credit in aid of the construction of their roads should receive early attention. The report of a majority of the commissioners appointed to examine the affairs and indebtedness of these roads, in which they favor an extension of the time for the payment of such indebtedness in at least one case where the corporation appears to be able to comply with well-guarded and exact terms of such extension, and the reenforcement of their opinion by gentlemen of undoubted business judgment and experience, appointed to protect the interests of the Government as directors of said corporation, may well lead to the belief that such an extension would be to the advantage of the Government.

The subject should be treated as a business proposition with a view to a final realization of its indebtedness by the Government, rather than as a question to be decided upon prejudice or by way of punishment for previous wrongdoing.

The report of the Commissioners of the District of Columbia, with its accompanying documents, gives in detail the operations of the several departments of the District government, and furnishes evidence that the financial affairs of the District are at present in such satisfactory condition as to justify the Commissioners in submitting to the Congress estimates for desirable and needed improvements.

The Commissioners recommend certain legislation which in their opinion is necessary to advance the interests of the District.

I invite your special attention to their request for such legislation as will enable the Commissioners without delay to collect, digest, and properly arrange the laws by which the District is governed, and which are now embraced in several collections, making them available only with great difficulty and labor. The suggestions they make touching desirable amendments to the laws relating to licenses granted for carrying on the retail traffic in spirituous liquors, to the observance of Sunday, to the proper assessment and collection of taxes, to the speedy punishment of minor offenders, and to the management and control of the reformatory and charitable institutions supported by Congressional appropriations are commended to careful consideration.

I again call attention to the present inconvenience and the danger to life and property attending the operation of steam railroads through and across the public streets and roads of the District. The propriety of such legislation as will properly guard the use of these railroads and better secure the convenience and safety of citizens is manifest.

The consciousness that I have presented but an imperfect statement of the condition of our country and its wants occasions no fear that anything omitted is not known and appreciated by the Congress, upon whom rests the responsibility of intelligent legislation in behalf of a great nation and a confiding people.

As public servants we shall do our duty well if we constantly guard the rectitude of our intentions, maintain unsullied our love of country, and with unselfish purpose strive for the public good.

GROVER CLEVELAND

2 0

Benjamin Harrison (1889–1893)

Benjamin Harrison's last annual message was delivered in an atmosphere of economic unease. Under his watch the surplus in the U.S. Treasury was depleted. The tariffs he supported—the highest in peacetime to that point—had hiked consumer prices to an alarming degree. Voters were restive. In response, Harrison composed an annual message that is a case study in the rhetoric of numbers. The missive is long on data and short on philosophy or even advice to posterity. It neither says farewell nor calls direct attention to the fact that it would be the last annual message the twenty-third president would transmit to the Congress. It is utterly unlike Cleveland's philosophic discourse and meditation on the United States of America at 100.

In its own way, however, the message provides a remarkable statistical snapshot of the United States in 1892. Harrison's aim was to allay fears; he wanted to demonstrate as objectively as possible the underlying health of the nation—not by rhetoric but by reckoning. The message tried to make the case for the dramatic economic growth and expansion the nation was experiencing. Six states had joined the Union during his single term in office. Also significant for the future was the Sherman Anti-Trust Act of 1890, intended to level the economic playing field. It was the first such federal law passed.

Fourth Annual Message
(written to the Congress)
December 6, 1892

To the Senate and House of Representatives:

In submitting my annual message to Congress I have great satisfaction in being able to say that the general conditions affecting the commercial and industrial interests of the United States are in the highest degree favorable. A comparison of the existing conditions with those of the most favored period in the history of the country will, I believe, show that so high a degree of prosperity and so general a diffusion of the comforts of life were never before enjoyed by our people.

The total wealth of the country in 1860 was $16,159,616,068. In 1890 it amounted to $62,610,000,000, an increase of 287 per cent.

The total mileage of railways in the United States in 1860 was 30,626. In 1890 it was 167,741, an increase of 448 per cent; and it is estimated that there will be about 4,000 miles of track added by the close of the year 1892.

The official returns of the Eleventh Census and those of the Tenth Census for seventy-five leading cities furnish the basis for the following comparisons:

In 1880 the capital invested in manufacturing was $1,232,839,670.

In 1890 the capital invested in manufacturing was $2,900,735,884.

In 1880 the number of employees was 1,301,388.

In 1890 the number of employees was 2,251,134.

In 1880 the wages earned were $501,965,778.

In 1890 the wages earned were $1,221,170,454.

In 1880 the value of the product was $2,711,579,899.

In 1890 the value of the product was $4,860,286,837.

I am informed by the Superintendent of the Census that the omission of certain industries in 1880 which were included in 1890 accounts in part for the remarkable increase thus shown, but after making full allowance for differences of method and deducting the returns for all industries not included in the census of 1880 there remain in the reports from these seventy-five cities an increase in the capital employed of $1,522,745,604, in the value of the product of $2,024,236,166, in wages earned of $677,943,929, and in the number of wage earners employed of 856,029. The wage earnings not only show an increased aggregate, but an increase per capita from $386 in 1880 to $547 in 1890, or 41.71 per cent.

The new industrial plants established since October 6, 1890, and up to October 22, 1892, as partially reported in the *American Economist*, number 345, and the extension of existing plants 108; the new capital invested amounts to $40,449,050, and the number of additional employees to 37,285.

The Textile World for July, 1892, states that during the first six months of the present calendar year 135 new factories were built, of which 40 are cotton mills, 48 knitting mills, 26 woolen mills, 15 silk mills, 4 plush mills, and 2 linen mills. Of the 40 cotton mills 21 have been built in the Southern States. Mr. A. B. Shepperson, of the New York Cotton Exchange, estimates the number of working spindles in the United States on September 1, 1892, at 15,200,000, an increase of 660,000 over the year 1891. The consumption of cotton by American mills in 1891 was 2,396,000 bales, and in 1892 2,584,000 bales, an increase of 188,000 bales. From the year 1869 to 1892, inclusive, there has been an increase in the consumption of cotton in Europe of 92 per cent, while during the same period the increased consumption in the United States has been about 150 per cent.

The report of Ira Ayer, special agent of the Treasury Department, shows that at the date of September 30, 1892, there were 32 companies manufacturing tin and terne plate in the United States and 14 companies building new works for such manufacture. The estimated investment in buildings and plants at the close of the fiscal year June 30, 1893, if existing conditions were to be continued, was $5,000,000 and the estimated rate of production 200,000,000 pounds per annum. The actual production for the quarter ending September 30, 1892, was 10,952,725 pounds.

The report of Labor Commissioner Peck, of New York, shows that during the year 1891, in about 6,000 manufacturing establishments in that State embraced within the special inquiry made by him, and representing 67 different industries, there was a net increase over the year 1890 of $30,315,130.68 in the value of the product and of $6,377,925.09 in the amount of wages paid. The report of the commissioner of labor for the State of Massachusetts shows that 3,745 industries in that State paid $129,416,248 in wages during the year 1891, against $126,030,303 in 1890, an increase of $3,335,945, and that there was an increase of $9,932,490 in the amount of capital and of 7,346 in the number of persons employed in the same period.

During the last six months of the year 1891 and the first six months of 1892 the total production of pig iron was 9,710,819 tons, as against 9,202,703 tons in the year 1890, which was the largest annual production ever attained. For the same twelve months of 1891–92 the production of Bessemer ingots was 3,878,581 tons, an increase of 189,710 gross tons over the previously unprecedented yearly production of 3,688,871 gross tons in 1890. The production of Bessemer steel rails for the first six months of 1892 was 772,436 gross tons, as against 702,080 gross tons during the last six months of the year 1891.

The total value of our foreign trade (exports and imports of merchandise) during the last fiscal year was $1,857,680,610, an increase of $128,283,604 over the previous fiscal year. The average annual value of our imports and exports of merchandise for the ten fiscal years prior to 1891 was $1,457,322,019. It will be observed that our foreign trade for 1892 exceeded this annual average value by $400,358,591, an increase of 27.47 per cent. The significance and value of this increase are shown by the fact that the excess in the trade of 1892 over 1891 was wholly in the value of exports, for there was a decrease in the value of imports of $17,513,754.

The value of our exports during the fiscal year 1892 reached the highest figure in the history of the Government, amounting to $1,030,278,148, exceeding by $145,797,338 the exports of 1891 and exceeding the value of the imports by $202,875,686. A comparison of the value of our exports for 1892 with the annual average for the ten years prior to 1891 shows an excess of $265,142,651, or of 34.65 per cent. The value of our imports of merchandise for 1892, which was $829,402,462, also exceeded the annual average value of the ten years prior to 1891 by $135,215,940. During the fiscal year 1892 the value of imports free of duty amounted to $457,999,658, the largest aggregate in the history of our commerce. The value of the imports of merchandise entered free of duty in 1892 was 55.35 per cent of the total value of imports, as compared with 43.35 per cent in 1891 and 33.66 per cent in 1890.

In our coastwise trade a most encouraging development is in progress, there having been in the last four years an increase of 16 per cent. In internal commerce the statistics show that no such period of prosperity has ever before existed. The freight carried in the coastwise trade of the Great Lakes in 1890 aggregated 28,295,959 tons. On the Mississippi, Missouri, and Ohio rivers and tributaries in the same year the traffic aggregated 29,405,046 tons, and the total vessel tonnage passing through the Detroit River during that year was 21,684,000 tons. The vessel tonnage entered and cleared in the foreign trade of London during 1890 amounted to 13,480,767 tons, and of Liverpool 10,941,800 tons, a total for these two great shipping ports of 24,422,568 tons, only slightly in excess of the vessel tonnage passing through the Detroit River. And it should be said that the season for the Detroit River was but 228 days, while of course in London and Liverpool the season was for the entire year. The vessel tonnage passing through the St. Mary's Canal for the fiscal year 1892 amounted to 9,828,874 tons, and the freight tonnage of the Detroit River is estimated for that year at 25,000,000 tons, against 23,209,619 tons in 1891. The aggregate traffic on our railroads for the year 1891 amounted to 704,398,609 tons of freight, compared with 691,344,437 tons in 1890, an increase of 13,054,172 tons.

Another indication of the general prosperity of the country is found in the fact that the number of depositors in savings banks increased from 693,870 in 1860 to 4,258,893 in 1890, an increase of 513 per cent, and the amount of deposits from $149,277,504 in 1860 to $1,524,844,506 in 1890, an increase of 921 per cent. In 1891 the amount of deposits in savings banks was $1,623,079,749. It is estimated that 90 per cent of these deposits represent the savings of wage earners. The bank clearances for nine months ending September 30, 1891, amounted to $41,049,390,08. For the same months in 1892 they amounted to $45,189,601,947, an excess for the nine months of $4,140,211,139.

There never has been a time in our history when work was so abundant or when wages were as high, whether measured by the currency in which they are paid or by their power to supply the necessaries and comforts of life. It is true that the market prices of cotton and wheat have been low. It is one of the unfavorable incidents of agriculture that the farmer can not produce upon orders. He must sow and reap in ignorance of the aggregate production of the year, and is peculiarly subject to the depreciation which follows overproduction. But while the fact I have stated is true as to the crops mentioned, the general average of prices has been such as to give to agriculture a fair participation in the general prosperity. The value of our total farm products has increased from $1,363,646,866 in 1860 to $4,500,000,000 in 1891, as estimated by statisticians, an increase of 230 per cent. The number of hogs January 1, 1891, was 50,625,106 and their value $210,193,925; on January 1, 1892, the number was 52,398,019 and the value $241,031,415. On January 1, 1891, the number of cattle was 36,875,648 and the value $544,127,908; on January 1, 1892, the number was 37,651,239 and the value $570,749,155.

If any are discontented with their state here, if any believe that wages or prices, the returns for honest toil, are inadequate, they should not fail to remember that there is no other country in the world where the conditions that seem to them hard would not be accepted as highly prosperous. The English agriculturist would be glad to exchange the returns of his labor for those of the American farmer and the Manchester workmen their wages for those of their fellows at Fall River. I believe that the protective system, which has now for something more than thirty years continuously prevailed in our legislation, has been a mighty instrument for the development of our national wealth and a most powerful agency in protecting the homes of our workingmen from the invasion of want. I have felt a most solicitous interest to preserve to our working people rates of wages that would not only give daily bread but supply a comfortable margin for those home attractions and family comforts and enjoyments without which life is neither hopeful nor sweet. They are American citizens—a part of the great people for whom our Constitution and Government were framed and instituted—and it can not be a perversion of that Constitution to so legislate as to preserve in their homes the comfort, independence, loyalty, and sense of interest in the Government which are essential to good citizenship in peace, and which will bring this stalwart throng, as in 1861, to the defense of the flag when it is assailed.

It is not my purpose to renew here the argument in favor of a protective tariff. The result of the recent election must be accepted as having introduced a new policy. We must assume that the present tariff, constructed upon the lines of protection, is to be repealed and that there is to be substituted for it a tariff law constructed solely with reference to revenue; that no duty is to be higher because the increase will keep open an American mill or keep up the wages of an American workman, but that in every case such a rate of duty is to be imposed as will bring to the Treasury of the United States the largest returns of revenue. The contention has not been between schedules, but between principles, and it would be offensive to suggest that the prevailing party will not carry into legislation the principles advocated by it and the pledges given to the people. The tariff bills passed by the House of Representatives at the last session were, as I suppose, even in the opinion of their promoters, inadequate, and justified only by the fact that the Senate and House of Representatives were not in accord and that a general revision could not therefore be undertaken.

I recommend that the whole subject of tariff revision be left to the incoming Congress. It is matter of regret that this work must be delayed for at least three months, for the threat of great tariff changes introduces so much uncertainty that an amount, not easily estimated, of business inaction and of diminished production will necessarily result. It is possible also that this uncertainty may result in decreased revenues from customs duties, for our merchants will make cautious orders for foreign goods in view of the prospect of tariff reductions and the uncertainty as to when they will take effect. Those who have advocated a protective tariff can well afford to have their disastrous forecasts of a change of policy disappointed. If a system of customs duties can be framed that will set the idle wheels and looms of Europe in motion and crowd our warehouses with foreign-made goods and at the same time keep our own mills busy; that will give us an increased participation in the "markets of the world" of greater value than the home market we surrender; that will give increased work to foreign workmen upon products to be consumed by our people without diminishing the amount of work to be done here; that will enable the American manufacturer to pay to his workmen from 50 to 100 per cent more in wages than is paid in the foreign mill, and yet to compete in our market and in foreign markets with the foreign producer; that will further reduce the cost of articles of wear and food without reducing the wages of those who produce them; that can be celebrated, after its effects have been realized, as its expectation has been in European as well as in American cities, the authors and promoters of it will be entitled to the highest praise. We have had in our history several experiences of the contrasted effects of a revenue and of a protective tariff, but this generation has not felt them, and the experience of one generation is not highly instructive to the next. The friends of the protective system with undiminished confidence in the principles they have advocated will await the results of the new experiment.

The strained and too often disturbed relations existing between the employees and the employers in our great manufacturing establishments have not been favorable to a calm consideration by the wage earner of the effect upon wages of the protective system. The facts that his wages were the highest paid in like callings in the world and that a maintenance of this rate of wages in the absence of protective duties upon the product of his labor was impossible were obscured by the passion evoked by these contests. He may now be able to review the question in the light of his personal experience under the operation of a tariff for revenue only. If that experience shall demonstrate that present rates of wages are thereby maintained or increased, either absolutely or in their purchasing power, and that the aggregate volume of work to be done in this country is increased or even maintained, so that there are more or as many days' work in a year, at as good or better wages, for the American workmen as has been the case under the protective system, everyone will rejoice. A general process of wage reduction can not be contemplated by any patriotic citizen without the gravest apprehension. It may be, indeed I believe is, possible for the American manufacturer to compete successfully with his foreign rival in many branches of production without the defense of protective duties if the pay rolls are equalized; but the conflict that stands between the producer and that result and the distress of our working people when it is attained are not pleasant to contemplate. The Society of the Unemployed, now holding its frequent and threatening parades in the streets of foreign cities, should not be allowed to acquire an American domicile.

The reports of the heads of the several Executive Departments, which are herewith submitted, have very naturally included a resume of the whole work of the Administration with the transactions of the last fiscal year. The attention not only of Congress but of the country is again invited to the methods of administration which have been pursued and to the results which have been attained. Public revenues amounting to $1,414,079,292.28 have been collected and disbursed without loss from misappropriation, without a single defalcation of such importance as to attract the public attention, and at a diminished per cent of cost for collection. The public business has been transacted not only with fidelity, but progressively and with a view to giving to the people in the fullest possible degree the benefits of a service established and maintained for their protection and comfort.

Our relations with other nations are now undisturbed by any serious controversy. The complicated and threatening differences with Germany and England relating to Samoan affairs, with England in relation to the seal fisheries in the Bering Sea, and with Chile growing out of the *Baltimore* affair have been adjusted.

There have been negotiated and concluded, under section 3 of the tariff law, commercial agreements relating to reciprocal trade with the following countries: Brazil, Dominican Republic, Spain for Cuba and Puerto Rico, Guatemala, Salvador, the German Empire, Great Britain for certain West Indian colonies and British Guiana, Nicaragua, Honduras, and Austria-Hungary.

Of these, those with Guatemala, Salvador, the German Empire, Great Britain, Nicaragua, Honduras, and Austria-Hungary have been concluded since my last annual message. Under these trade arrangements a free or favored admission has been secured in every case for an important list of American products. Especial care has been taken to secure markets for farm products, in order to relieve that great underlying industry of the depression which the lack of an adequate foreign market for our surplus often brings. An opening has also been made for manufactured products that will undoubtedly, if this policy is maintained, greatly augment our export trade. The full benefits of these arrangements can not be realized instantly. New lines of trade are to be opened. The commercial traveler must survey the field. The manufacturer must adapt his goods to the new markets and facilities for exchange must be established. This work has been well begun, our merchants and manufacturers having entered the new fields with courage and enterprise. In the case of food products, and especially with Cuba, the trade did not need to wait, and the immediate results have been most gratifying. If this policy and these trade arrangements can be continued in force and aided by the establishment of American steamship lines, I do not doubt that we shall within a short period secure fully one-third of the total trade of the countries of Central and South America, which now amounts to about $600,000,000 annually. In 1885 we had only 8 per cent of this trade.

The following statistics show the increase in our trade with the countries with which we have reciprocal trade agreements from the date when such agreements went into effect up to September 30, 1892, the increase being in some almost wholly and in others in an important degree the result of these agreements:

The domestic exports to Germany and Austria-Hungary have increased in value from $47,673,756 to $57,993,064, an increase of $10,319,308, or 21.63 per cent. With American countries the value of our exports has increased from $44,160,285 to $54,613,598, an increase of $10,453,313, or 23.67 per cent. The total increase in the value of exports to all the countries with which we have reciprocity agreements has been $20,772,621. This increase is chiefly in wheat, flour, meat, and dairy products and in manufactures of iron and steel and lumber. There has been a large increase in the value of imports from all these countries since the commercial agreements went into effect, amounting to $74,294,525, but it has been entirely in imports from the American countries, consisting mostly of sugar, coffee, india rubber, and crude drugs. The alarmed attention of our European competitors for the South American market has been attracted to this new American policy and to our acquisition and their loss of South American trade.

A treaty providing for the arbitration of the dispute between Great Britain and the United States as to the killing of seals in the Bering Sea was concluded on the 29th of February last. This treaty was accompanied by an agreement prohibiting pelagic sealing pending the arbitration, and a vigorous effort was made during this season to drive out all poaching sealers from the Bering Sea. Six naval vessels, three revenue cutters, and one vessel from the Fish Commission, all under the command of Commander Evans, of the Navy, were sent into the sea, which was systematically patrolled. Some seizures were made, and it is believed that the catch in the Bering Sea by poachers amounted to less than 500 seals. It is true, however, that in the North Pacific, while the seal herds were on their way to the passes between the Aleutian Islands, a very large number, probably 35,000, were taken. The existing statutes of the United States do not restrain our citizens from taking seals in the Pacific Ocean, and perhaps should not unless the prohibition can be extended to the citizens of other nations. I recommend that power be given to the President by proclamation to prohibit the taking of seals in the North Pacific by American vessels in case, either as the result of the findings of the Tribunal of Arbitration or otherwise, the restraints can be applied to the vessels of all countries. The case of the United States for the Tribunal of Arbitration has been prepared with great care and industry by the Hon. John W. Foster, and the counsel who represent this Government express confidence that a result substantially establishing our claims and preserving this great industry for the benefit of all nations will be attained.

During the past year a suggestion was received through the British minister that the Canadian government would like to confer as to the possibility of enlarging upon terms of mutual advantage the commercial exchanges of Canada and of the United States, and a conference was held at Washington, with Mr. Blaine acting for this Government and the British minister at this capital and three members of the Dominion cabinet acting as commissioners on the part of Great Britain. The conference developed the fact that the Canadian government was only prepared to offer to the United States in exchange for the concessions asked the admission of natural products. The statement was frankly made that favored rates could not be given to the United States as against the mother country. This admission, which was foreseen, necessarily terminated the conference upon this question. The benefits of an exchange of natural products would be almost wholly with the people of Canada. Some other topics of interest were considered in the conference, and have resulted in the making of a convention for examining the Alaskan boundary and the waters of Passamaquoddy Bay adjacent to Eastport, Me., and in the initiation of an arrangement for the protection of fish life in the coterminous and neighboring waters of our northern border.

The controversy as to tolls upon the Welland Canal, which was presented to Congress at the last session by special message, having failed of adjustment, I felt constrained to exercise the authority conferred by the act of July 26, 1892, and to proclaim a suspension of the free use of St. Mary's Falls Canal to cargoes in transit to ports in Canada. The Secretary of the Treasury established such tolls as were thought to be equivalent to the exactions unjustly levied upon our commerce in the Canadian canals.

If, as we must suppose, the political relations of Canada and the disposition of the Canadian government are to remain unchanged, a somewhat radical revision of our trade relations should, I think, be made. Our relations must continue to be intimate, and they should be friendly. I regret to say, however, that in many of the controversies, notably those as to the fisheries on the Atlantic, the sealing interests on the Pacific, and the canal tolls, our negotiations with Great Britain have continuously been thwarted or retarded by unreasonable and unfriendly objections and protests from Canada; in the matter of the canal tolls our treaty rights were flagrantly disregarded. It is hardly too much to say that the Canadian Pacific and other railway lines which parallel our northern boundary are sustained by commerce having either its origin or terminus, or both, in the United States. Canadian railroads compete with those of the United States for our traffic, and without the restraints of our interstate-commerce act. Their cars pass almost without detention into and out of our territory.

The Canadian Pacific Railway brought into the United States from China and Japan via British Columbia during the year ended June 30, 1892, 23,239,689 pounds of freight, and it carried from the United States, to be shipped to China and Japan via British Columbia, 24,068,346 pounds of freight. There were also shipped from the United States over this road from Eastern ports of the United States to our Pacific ports during the same year 13,912,073 pounds of freight, and there were received over this road at the United States Eastern ports from ports on the Pacific Coast 13,293,315 pounds of freight. Mr. Joseph Nimmo, Jr., former chief of the Bureau of Statistics, when before the Senate Select Committee on Relations with Canada, April 26, 1890, said that "the value of goods thus transported between different points in the United States across Canadian territory probably amounts to $100,000,000 a year."

There is no disposition on the part of the people or Government of the United States to interfere in the smallest degree with the political relations of Canada. That question is wholly with her own people. It is time for us, however, to consider whether, if the present state of things and trend of things is to continue, our interchanges upon lines of land transportation should not be put upon a different basis and our entire independence of Canadian canals and of the St. Lawrence as an outlet to the sea secured by the construction of an American canal around the Falls of Niagara and the opening of ship communication between the Great Lakes and one of our own seaports. We should not hesitate to avail ourselves of our great natural trade advantages. We should withdraw the support which is given to the railroads and steamship lines of Canada by a traffic that properly belongs to us and no longer furnish the earnings which lighten the otherwise crushing weight of the enormous public subsidies that have been given to them. The subject of the power of the Treasury to deal with this matter without further legislation has been under consideration, but circumstances have postponed a conclusion. It is probable that a consideration of the propriety of a modification or abrogation of the article of the treaty of Washington relating to the transit of goods in bond is involved in any complete solution of the question.

Congress at the last session was kept advised of the progress of the serious and for a time threatening difference between the United States and Chile. It gives me now great gratification to report that the Chilean Government in a most friendly and honorable spirit has tendered and paid as an indemnity to the families of the sailors of the *Baltimore* who were killed and to those who were injured in the outbreak in the city of Valparaiso the sum of $75,000. This has been accepted not only as an indemnity for a wrong done, but as a most gratifying evidence that the Government of Chile rightly appreciates the disposition of this Government to act in a spirit of the most absolute fairness and friendliness in our intercourse with that brave people. A further and conclusive evidence of the mutual respect and confidence now existing is furnished by the fact that a convention submitting to arbitration the mutual claims of the citizens of the respective Governments has been agreed upon. Some of these claims have been pending for many years and have been the occasion of much unsatisfactory diplomatic correspondence.

I have endeavored in every way to assure our sister Republics of Central and South America that the United States Government and its people have only the most friendly disposition toward them all. We do not covet their territory. We have no disposition to be oppressive or exacting in our dealings with any of them, even the weakest. Our interests and our hopes for them all lie in the direction of stable governments by their people and of the largest development of their great commercial resources. The mutual benefits of enlarged commercial exchanges and of a more familiar and friendly intercourse between our peoples we do desire, and in this have sought their friendly cooperation.

I have believed, however, while holding these sentiments in the greatest sincerity, that we must insist upon a just responsibility for any injuries inflicted upon our official representatives or upon our citizens. This insistence, kindly and justly but firmly made, will, I believe, promote peace and mutual respect.

Our relations with Hawaii have been such as to attract an increased interest, and must continue to do so. I deem it of great importance that the projected submarine cable, a survey for which has been made, should be promoted. Both for naval and commercial uses we should have quick communication with Honolulu. We should before this have availed ourselves of the concession made many years ago to this Government for a harbor and naval station at Pearl River. Many evidences of the friendliness of the Hawaiian Government have been given in the past, and it is gratifying to believe that the advantage and necessity of a continuance of very close relations is appreciated.

The friendly act of this Government in expressing to the Government of Italy its reprobation and abhorrence of the lynching of Italian subjects in New Orleans by the payment of 125,000 francs, or $24,330.90, was accepted by the King of Italy with every manifestation of gracious appreciation, and the incident has been highly promotive of mutual respect and good will.

In consequence of the action of the French Government in proclaiming a protectorate over certain tribal districts of the west coast of Africa eastward of the San Pedro River, which has long been regarded as the southeastern boundary of Liberia, I have felt constrained to make protest against this encroachment upon the territory of a Republic which was rounded by citizens of the United States and toward which this country has for many years held the intimate relation of a friendly counselor.

The recent disturbances of the public peace by lawless foreign marauders on the Mexican frontier have afforded this Government an opportunity to testify its good will for Mexico and its earnest purpose to fulfill the obligations of international friendship by pursuing and dispersing the evil doers. The work of relocating the boundary of the treaty of Guadalupe Hidalgo westward from El Paso is progressing favorably.

Our intercourse with Spain continues on a friendly footing. I regret, however, not to be able to report as yet the adjustment of the claims of the American missionaries arising from the disorders at Ponape, in the Caroline Islands, but I anticipate a satisfactory adjustment in view of renewed and urgent representations to the Government at Madrid.

The treatment of the religious and educational establishments of American citizens in Turkey has of late called for a more than usual share of attention. A tendency to curtail the toleration which has so beneficially prevailed is discernible and has called forth the earnest remonstrance of this Government. Harassing regulations in regard to schools and churches have been attempted in certain localities, but not without due protest and the assertion of the inherent and conventional rights of our countrymen. Violations of domicile and search of the persons and effects of citizens of the United

States by apparently irresponsible officials in the Asiatic vilayets have from time to time been reported. An aggravated instance of injury to the property of an American missionary at Bourdour, in the province of Konia, called forth an urgent claim for reparation, which I am pleased to say was promptly heeded by the Government of the Porte. Interference with the trading ventures of our citizens in Asia Minor is also reported, and the lack of consular representation in that region is a serious drawback to instant and effective protection. I can not believe that these incidents represent a settled policy, and shall not cease to urge the adoption of proper remedies.

International copyright has been extended to Italy by proclamation in conformity with the act of March 3, 1891, upon assurance being given that Italian law permits to citizens of the United States the benefit of copyright on substantially the same basis as to subjects of Italy. By a special convention proclaimed January 15, 1892, reciprocal provisions of copyright have been applied between the United States and Germany. Negotiations are in progress with other countries to the same end.

I repeat with great earnestness the recommendation which I have made in several previous messages that prompt and adequate support be given to the American company engaged in the construction of the Nicaragua ship canal. It is impossible to overstate the value from every standpoint of this great enterprise, and I hope that there may be time, even in this Congress, to give to it an impetus that will insure the early completion of the canal and secure to the United States its proper relation to it when completed.

The Congress has been already advised that the invitations of this Government for the assembling of an international monetary conference to consider the question of an enlarged use of silver were accepted by the nations to which they were addressed. The conference assembled at Brussels on the 22d of November, and has entered upon the consideration of this great question. I have not doubted, and have taken occasion to express that belief as well in the invitations issued for this conference as in my public messages, that the free coinage of silver upon an agreed international ratio would greatly promote the interests of our people and equally those of other nations. It is too early to predict what results may be accomplished by the conference. If any temporary check or delay intervenes, I believe that very soon commercial conditions will compel the now reluctant governments to unite with us in this movement to secure the enlargement of the volume of coined money needed for the transaction of the business of the world.

The report of the Secretary of the Treasury will attract especial interest in view of the many misleading statements that have been made as to the state of the public revenues. Three preliminary facts should not only be stated but emphasized before looking into details: First, that the public debt has been reduced since March 4, 1889, $259,074,200, and the annual interest charge $11,684,469; second, that there have been paid out for pensions during this Administration up to November 1, 1892, $432,564,178.70, an excess of $114,466,386.09 over the sum expended during the period from March 1, 1885, to March 1, 1889; and, third, that under the existing tariff up to December 1 about $93,000,000 of revenue which would have been collected upon imported sugars if the duty had been maintained has gone into the pockets of the people, and not into the public Treasury, as before. If there are any who still think that the surplus should have been kept out of circulation by hoarding it in the Treasury, or deposited in favored banks without interest while the Government continued to pay to these very banks interest upon the bonds deposited as security for the deposits, or who think that the extended pension legislation was a public robbery, or that the duties upon sugar should have been maintained, I am content to leave the argument where it now rests while we wait to see whether these criticisms will take the form of legislation.

The revenues for the fiscal year ending June 30, 1892, from all sources were $425,868,260.22, and the expenditures for all purposes were $415,953,806.56, leaving a balance of $9,914,453.66. There were paid during the year upon the public debt $40,570,467.98. The surplus in the Treasury and the bank redemption fund passed by the act of July 14, 1890, to the general fund furnished in large part the cash available and used for the payments made upon the public debt. Compared with the year 1891, our receipts from customs duties fell off $42,069,241.08, while our receipts from internal revenue increased $8,284,823.13, leaving the net loss of revenue from these principal sources $33,784,417.95. The net loss of revenue from all sources was $32,675,972.81.

The revenues, estimated and actual, for the fiscal year ending June 30, 1893, are placed by the Secretary at $463,336,350.44, and the expenditures at $461,336,350.44, showing a surplus of receipts over expenditures of $2,000,000. The cash balance in the Treasury at the end of the fiscal year it is estimated will be $20,992,377.03. So far as these figures are based upon estimates of receipts and expenditures for the remaining months of the current fiscal year, there are not only the usual elements of uncertainty, but some added elements. New revenue legislation, or even the expectation of it, may seriously reduce the public revenues during the period of uncertainty and during the process of business adjustment to the new conditions when they become known. But the Secretary has very wisely refrained from guessing as to the effect of possible changes in our revenue laws, since the scope of those changes and the time of their taking effect can not in any degree be forecast or foretold by him. His estimates must be based upon existing laws and upon a continuance of existing business conditions, except so far as these conditions may be affected by causes other than new legislation.

The estimated receipts for the fiscal year ending June 30, 1894, are $490,121,365.38, and the estimated appropriations $457,261,335.33, leaving an estimated surplus of receipts over expenditures of $32,860,030.05. This does not include any payment to the sinking fund. In the recommendation of the Secretary that the sinking-fund law be repealed I concur. The redemption of bonds since the passage of the law to June 30, 1892, has already exceeded the requirements by the sum of $990,510,681.49. The retirement of bonds in the future before maturity should be a matter of convenience, not of compulsion. We should not collect revenue for that purpose, but only use any casual surplus. To the balance of $32,860,030.05 of receipts over expenditures for the year 1894 should be added the estimated surplus at the beginning of the year, $20,992,377.03, and from this aggregate there must be deducted, as stated by the Secretary, about $44,000,000 of estimated unexpended appropriations.

The public confidence in the purpose and ability of the Government to maintain the parity of all of our money issues, whether coin or paper, must remain unshaken. The demand for gold in Europe and the consequent calls upon us are in a considerable degree the result of the efforts of some of the European Governments to increase their gold reserves, and these efforts should be met by appropriate legislation on our part. The conditions that have created this drain of the Treasury gold are in an important degree political, and not commercial. In view of the fact that a general revision of our revenue laws in the near future seems to be probable, it would be better that any changes should be a part of that revision rather than of a temporary nature.

During the last fiscal year the Secretary purchased under the act of July 14, 1890, 54,355,748 ounces of silver and issued in payment therefor $51,106,608 in notes. The total purchases since the passage of the act have been 120,479,981 ounces and the aggregate of notes issued $116,783,590. The average price paid for silver during the year was 94 cents per ounce, the highest price being $1.02¼ July 1, 1891, and the lowest 83 cents March 21, 1892. In view of the fact that the monetary conference is now sitting and that no conclusion has yet been reached, I withhold any recommendation as to legislation upon this subject.

The report of the Secretary of War brings again to the attention of Congress some important suggestions as to the reorganization of the infantry and artillery arms of the service, which his predecessors have before urgently presented. Our Army is small, but its organization should all the more be put upon the most approved modern basis. The conditions upon what we have called the "frontier" have heretofore required the maintenance of many small posts, but now the policy of concentration is obviously the right one. The new posts should have the proper strategic relations to the only "frontiers" we now have—those of the seacoast and of our northern and part of our southern boundary. I do not think that any question of advantage to localities or to States should determine the location of the new posts. The reorganization and enlargement of the Bureau of Military Information which the Secretary has effected is a work the usefulness of which will become every year more apparent. The work of building heavy guns and the construction of coast defenses has been well begun and should be carried on without check.

The report of the Attorney-General is by law submitted directly to Congress, but I can not refrain from saying that he has conducted the increasing work of the Department of Justice with great professional skill. He has in several directions secured from the courts decisions giving increased protection to the officers of the United States and bringing some classes of crime that escaped local cognizance and punishment into the tribunals of the United States, where they could be tried with impartiality.

The numerous applications for Executive clemency presented in behalf of persons convicted in United States courts and given penitentiary sentences have called my attention to a fact referred to by the Attorney-General in his report, namely, that a time allowance for good behavior for such prisoners is prescribed by the Federal statutes only where the State in which the penitentiary is located has made no such provision. Prisoners are given the benefit of the provisions of the State law regulating the penitentiary to which they may be sent. These are various, some perhaps too liberal and some perhaps too illiberal. The result is that a sentence for five years means one thing if the prisoner is sent to one State for confinement and quite a different thing if he is sent to another. I recommend that a uniform credit for good behavior be prescribed by Congress.

I have before expressed my concurrence in the recommendation of the Attorney-General that degrees of murder should be recognized in the Federal statutes, as they are, I believe, in all the States. These grades are rounded on correct distinctions in crime. The recognition of them would enable the courts to exercise some discretion in apportioning punishment and would greatly relieve the Executive of what is coming to be a very heavy burden—the examination of these cases on application for commutation.

The aggregate of claims pending against the Government in the Court of Claims is enormous. Claims to the amount of nearly $400,000,000 for the taking of or injury to the property of persons claiming to be loyal during the war are now before that court for examination. When to these are added the Indian depredation claims and the French spoliation claims, an aggregate is reached that is indeed startling. In the defense of all these cases the Government is at great disadvantage. The claimants have preserved their evidence, whereas the agents of the Government are sent into the field to rummage for what they can find. This difficulty is peculiarly great where the fact to be established is the disloyalty of the claimant during the war. If this great threat against our revenues is to have no other check, certainly Congress should supply the Department of Justice with appropriations sufficiently liberal to secure the best legal talent in the defense of these claims and to pursue its vague search for evidence effectively.

The report of the Postmaster-General shows a most gratifying increase and a most efficient and progressive management of the great business of that Department. The remarkable increase in revenues, in the number of post-offices, and in the miles of mail carriage furnishes further evidence of the high state of prosperity which our people are enjoying. New offices mean new hamlets and towns, new routes mean the extension of our border settlements, and increased revenues mean an active commerce. The Postmaster-General reviews the whole period of his administration of the office and brings some of his statistics down to the month of November last. The postal revenues have increased during the last year nearly $5,000,000. The deficit for the year ending June 30, 1892, is $848,341 less than the deficiency of the preceding year. The deficiency of the present fiscal year it is estimated will be reduced to $1,552,423, which will not only be extinguished during the next fiscal year but a surplus of nearly $1,000,000 should then be shown. In these calculations the payments to be made under the contracts for ocean mail service have not been included. There have been added 1,590 new mail routes during the year, with a mileage of 8,563 miles, and the total number of new miles of mail trips added during the year is nearly 17,000,000. The number of miles of mail journeys added during the last four years is about 76,000,000, this addition being 21,000,000 miles more than were in operation in the whole country in 1861.

The number of post-offices has been increased by 2,790 during the year, and during the past four years, and up to October 29 last, the total increase in the number of offices has been nearly 9,000. The number of free-delivery offices has been nearly doubled in the last four years, and the number of money-order offices more than doubled within that time.

For the three years ending June 30, 1892, the postal revenue amounted to $197,744,359, which was an increase of $52,263,150 over the revenue for the three years ending June 30, 1888, the increase during the last three years being more than three and a half times as great as the increase during the three years ending June 30, 1888. No such increase as that shown for these three years has ever previously appeared in the revenues of the Department. The Postmaster-General has extended to the post-offices in the larger cities the merit system of promotion introduced by my direction into the Departments here, and it has resulted there, as in the Departments, in a larger volume of work and that better done.

Ever since our merchant marine was driven from the sea by the rebel cruisers during the War of the Rebellion the United States has been paying an enormous annual tribute to foreign countries in the shape of freight and passage moneys. Our grain and meats have been taken at our own docks and our large imports there laid down by foreign shipmasters. An increasing torrent of American travel to Europe has contributed a vast sum annually to the dividends of foreign shipowners. The balance of trade shown by the books of our custom-houses has been very largely reduced and in many years altogether extinguished by this constant drain. In the year 1892 only 12.3 per cent of our imports were brought in American vessels. These great foreign steamships maintained by our traffic are many of them under contracts with their respective Governments by which in time of war they will become a part of their armed naval establishments. Profiting by our commerce in peace, they will become the most formidable destroyers of our commerce in time of war. I have felt, and have before expressed the feeling, that this condition of things was both intolerable and disgraceful. A wholesome change of policy, and one having in it much promise, as it seems to me, was begun by the law of March 3, 1891. Under this law contracts have been made by the Postmaster-General for eleven mail routes. The expenditure involved by these contracts for the next fiscal year approximates $954,123.33. As one of the results already reached sixteen American steamships, of an aggregate tonnage of 57,400 tons, costing $7,400,000, have been built or contracted to be built in American shipyards.

The estimated tonnage of all steamships required under existing contracts is 165,802, and when the full service required by these contracts is established there will be forty-one mail steamers under the American flag, with the probability of further necessary additions in the Brazilian and Argentine service. The contracts recently let for transatlantic service will result in the construction of five ships of 10,000 tons each, costing $9,000,000 to $10,000,000, and will add, with the *City of New York* and *City of Paris*, to which the Treasury Department was authorized by legislation at the last session to give American registry, seven of the swiftest vessels upon the sea to our naval reserve. The contracts made with the lines sailing to Central and South American ports have increased the frequency and shortened the time of the trips, added new ports of call, and sustained some lines that otherwise would almost certainly have been withdrawn. The service to Buenos Ayres is the first to the Argentine Republic under the American flag. The service to Southampton, Boulogne, and Antwerp is also new, and is to be begun with the steamships *City of New York* and *City of Paris* in February next.

I earnestly urge the continuance of the policy inaugurated by this legislation, and that the appropriations required to meet the obligations of the Government under the contracts may be made promptly, so that the lines that have entered into these engagements may not be embarrassed. We have had, by reason of connections with the transcontinental railway lines constructed through our own territory, some advantages in the ocean trade of the Pacific that we did not possess on the Atlantic. The construction of the Canadian Pacific Railway and the establishment under large subventions from Canada and England of fast steamship service from Vancouver with Japan and China seriously threaten our shipping interests in the Pacific. This line of English steamers receives, as is stated by the Commissioner of Navigation, a direct subsidy of $400,000 annually, or $30,767 per trip for thirteen voyages, in addition to some further aid from the Admiralty in connection with contracts under which the vessels may be used for naval purposes. The competing American Pacific mail line under the act of March 3, 1891, receives only $6,389 per round trip.

Efforts have been made within the last year, as I am informed, to establish under similar conditions a line between Vancouver and some Australian port, with a view of seizing there a trade in which we have had a large interest. The Commissioner of Navigation states that a very large per cent of our imports from Asia are now brought to us by English steamships and their connecting railways in Canada. With a view of promoting this trade, especially in tea, Canada has imposed a discriminating duty of 10 per cent upon tea and coffee brought into the Dominion from the United States. If this unequal contest between American lines without subsidy, or with diminished subsidies, and the English Canadian line to which I have referred is to continue, I think we should at least see that the facilities for customs entry and transportation across our territory are not such as to make the Canadian route a favored one, and that the discrimination as to duties to which I have referred is met by a like discrimination as to the importation of these articles from Canada.

No subject, I think, more nearly touches the pride, the power, and the prosperity of our country than this of the development of our merchant marine upon the sea. If we could enter into conference with other competitors and all would agree to withhold government aid, we could perhaps take our chances with the rest; but our great competitors have established and maintained their lines by government subsidies until they now have practically excluded us from participation. In my opinion no choice is left to us but to pursue, moderately at least, the same lines.

The report of the Secretary of the Navy exhibits great progress in the construction of our new Navy. When the present Secretary entered upon his duties, only 3 modern steel vessels were in commission. The vessels since put in commission and to be put in commission during the winter will make a total of 19 during his administration of the Department. During the current year 10 war vessels and 3 navy tugs have been launched, and during the four years 25 vessels will have been launched. Two other large ships and a torpedo boat are under contract and the work upon them well advanced, and the 4 monitors are awaiting only the arrival of their armor, which has been unexpectedly delayed, or they would have been before this in commission.

Contracts have been let during this Administration, under the appropriations for the increase of the Navy, including new vessels and their appurtenances, to the amount of $35,000,000, and there has been expended during the same period for labor at navy-yards upon similar work $8,000,000 without the smallest scandal or charge of fraud or partiality. The enthusiasm and interest of our naval officers, both of the staff and line, have been greatly kindled. They have responded magnificently to the confidence of Congress and have demonstrated to the world an unexcelled capacity in construction, in ordnance, and in everything involved in the building, equipping, and sailing of great war ships.

At the beginning of Secretary Tracy's administration several difficult problems remained to be grappled with and solved before the efficiency in action of our ships could be secured. It is believed that as the result of new processes in the construction of armor plate our later ships will be clothed with defensive plates of higher resisting power than are found on any war vessels afloat. We were without torpedoes. Tests have been made to ascertain the relative efficiency of different constructions, a torpedo has been adopted, and the work of construction is now being carried on successfully. We were without armor-piercing shells and without a shop instructed and equipped for the construction of them. We are now making what is believed to be a projectile superior to any before in use. A smokeless powder has been developed and a slow-burning powder for guns of large caliber. A high explosive capable of use in shells fired from service guns has been found, and the manufacture of gun cotton has been developed so that the question of supply is no longer in doubt.

The development of a naval militia, which has been organized in eight States and brought into cordial and cooperative relations with the Navy, is another important achievement. There are now enlisted in these organizations 1,800 men, and they are likely to be greatly extended. I recommend such legislation and appropriations as will encourage and develop this movement. The recommendations of the Secretary will, I do not doubt, receive the friendly consideration of Congress, for he has enjoyed, as he has deserved, the confidence of all those interested in the development of our Navy, without any division upon partisan lines. I earnestly express the hope that a work which has made such noble progress may not now be stayed. The wholesome influence for peace and the increased sense of security which our citizens domiciled in other lands feel when these magnificent ships under the American flag appear is already most gratefully apparent. The ships from our Navy which will appear in the great naval parade next April in the harbor of New York will be a convincing demonstration to the world that the United States is again a naval power.

The work of the Interior Department, always very burdensome, has been larger than ever before during the administration of Secretary Noble. The disability-pension law, the taking of the Eleventh Census, the opening of vast areas of Indian lands to settlement, the organization of Oklahoma, and the negotiations for the cession of Indian lands furnish some of the particulars of the increased work, and the results achieved testify to the ability, fidelity, and industry of the head of the Department and his efficient assistants.

Several important agreements for the cession of Indian lands negotiated by the commission appointed under the act of March 2, 1889, are awaiting the action of Congress. Perhaps the most important of these is that for the cession of the Cherokee Strip. This region has been the source of great vexation to the executive department and of great friction and unrest between the settlers who desire to occupy it and the Indians who assert title. The agreement which has been made by the commission is perhaps the most satisfactory that could have been reached. It will be noticed that it is conditioned upon its ratification by Congress before March 4, 1893. The Secretary of the Interior, who has given the subject very careful thought, recommends the ratification of the agreement, and I am inclined to follow his recommendation. Certain it is that some action by which this controversy shall be brought to an end and these lands opened to settlement is urgent.

The form of government provided by Congress on May 17, 1884, for Alaska was in its frame and purpose temporary. The increase of population and the development of some important mining and commercial interests make it imperative that the law should be revised and better provision made for the arrest and punishment of criminals.

The report of the Secretary shows a very gratifying state of facts as to the condition of the General Land Office. The work of issuing agricultural patents, which seemed to be hopelessly in arrear when the present Secretary undertook the duties of his office, has been so expedited that the bureau is now upon current business. The relief thus afforded to honest and worthy settlers upon the public lands by giving to them an assured title to their entries has been of incalculable benefit in developing the new States and the Territories.

The Court of Private Land Claims, established by Congress for the promotion of this policy of speedily settling contested land titles, is making satisfactory progress in its work, and when the work is completed a great impetus will be given to the development of those regions where unsettled claims under Mexican grants have so long exercised their repressive influence. When to these results are added the enormous cessions of Indian lands which have been opened to settlement, aggregating during this Administration nearly 26,000,000 acres, and the agreements negotiated and now pending in Congress for ratification by which about 10,000,000 additional acres will be opened to settlement, it will be seen how much has been accomplished.

The work in the Indian Bureau in the execution of the policy of recent legislation has been largely directed to two chief purposes: First, the allotment of lands in severalty to the Indians and the cession to the United States of the surplus lands, and, secondly, to the work of educating the Indian for his own protection in his closer contact with the white man and for the intelligent exercise of his new citizenship. Allotments have been made and patents issued to 5,900 Indians under the present Secretary and Commissioner, and 7,600 additional allotments have been made for which patents are now in process of preparation. The school attendance of Indian children has been increased during that time over 13 per cent, the enrollment for 1892 being nearly 20,000. A uniform system of school text-books and of study has been adopted and the work in these national schools brought as near as may be to the basis of the free common schools of the States. These schools can be transferred and merged into the common-school systems of the States when the Indian has fully assumed his new relation to the organized civil community in which he resides and the new States are able to assume the burden. I have several times been called upon to remove Indian agents appointed by me, and have done so promptly upon every sustained complaint of unfitness or misconduct. I believe, however, that the Indian service at the agencies has been improved and is now administered on the whole with a good degree of efficiency. If any legislation is possible by which the selection of Indian agents can be wholly removed from all partisan suggestions or considerations, I am sure it would be a great relief to the Executive and a great benefit to the service. The appropriation for the subsistence of the Cheyenne and Arapahoe Indians made at the last session of Congress was inadequate. This smaller appropriation was estimated for by the Commissioner upon the theory that the large fund belonging to the tribe in the public Treasury could be and ought to be used for their support. In view, however, of the pending depredation claims against this fund and other considerations, the Secretary of the Interior on the 12th of April last submitted a supplemental estimate for $50,000. This appropriation was not made, as it should have been, and the oversight ought to be remedied at the earliest possible date.

In a special message to this Congress at the last session, I stated the reasons why I had not approved the deed for the release to the United States by the Choctaws and Chickasaws of the lands formerly embraced in the Cheyenne and Arapahoe Reservation and remaining after allotments to that tribe. A resolution of the Senate expressing the opinion of that body that notwithstanding the facts stated in my special message the deed should be approved and the money, $2,991,450, paid over was presented to me May 10, 1892. My special message was intended to call the attention of Congress to the subject, and in view of the fact that it is conceded that the appropriation proceeded upon a false basis as to the amount of lands to be paid for and is by $50,000 in excess of the amount they are entitled to (even if their claim to the land is given full recognition at the rate agreed upon), I have not felt willing to approve the deed, and shall not do so, at least until both Houses of Congress have acted upon the subject. It has been informally proposed by the claimants to release this sum of $50,000, but I have no power to demand or accept such a release, and such an agreement would be without consideration and void.

I desire further to call the attention of Congress to the fact that the recent agreement concluded with the Kiowas and Comanches relates to lands which were a part of the "leased district," and to which the claim of the Choctaws and Chickasaws is precisely that recognized by Congress in the legislation I have referred to. The surplus lands to which this claim would attach in the Kiowa and Comanche Reservation is 2,500,000 acres, and at the same rate the Government will be called upon to pay to the Choctaws and Chickasaws for these lands $3,125,000. This sum will be further augmented, especially if the title of the Indians to the tract now Greer County, Tex., is established. The duty devolved upon me in this connection was simply to pass upon the form of the deed; but as in my opinion the facts mentioned in my special message were not adequately brought to the attention of Congress in connection with the legislation, I have felt that I would not be justified in acting without some new expression of the legislative will.

The report of the Commissioner of Pensions, to which extended notice is given by the Secretary of the Interior in his report, will attract great attention. Judged by the aggregate amount of work done, the last year has been the greatest in the history of the office. I believe that the organization of the office is efficient and that the work has been done with fidelity. The passage of what is known as the disability bill has, as was foreseen, very largely increased the annual disbursements to the disabled veterans of the Civil War. The estimate for this fiscal year was $144,956,000, and that amount was appropriated. A deficiency amounting to $10,508,621 must be provided for at this session. The estimate for pensions for the fiscal year ending June 30, 1894, is $165,000,000. The Commissioner of Pensions believes that if the present legislation and methods are maintained and further additions to the pension laws are not made the maximum expenditure for pensions will be reached June 30, 1894, and will be at the highest point $188,000,000 per annum.

I adhere to the views expressed in previous messages that the care of the disabled soldiers of the War of the Rebellion is a matter of national concern and duty. Perhaps no emotion cools sooner than that of gratitude, but I can not believe that this process has yet reached a point with our people that would sustain the policy of remitting the care of these disabled veterans to the inadequate agencies provided by local laws. The parade on the 20th of September last upon the streets of this capital of 60,000 of the surviving Union veterans of the War of the Rebellion was a most touching and thrilling episode, and the rich and gracious welcome extended to them by the District of Columbia and the applause that greeted their progress from tens of thousands of people from all the States did much to revive the glorious recollections of the Grand Review when these men and many thousand others now in their graves were welcomed with grateful joy as victors in a struggle in which the national unity, honor, and wealth were all at issue.

In my last annual message I called attention to the fact that some legislative action was necessary in order to protect the interests of the Government in its relations with the Union Pacific Railway. The Commissioner of Railroads has submitted a very full report, giving exact information as to the debt, the liens upon the company's property, and its resources. We must deal with the question as we find it and take that course which will under existing conditions best secure the interests of the United States. I recommended in my last annual message that a commission be appointed to deal with this question, and I renew that recommendation and suggest that the commission be given full power.

The report of the Secretary of Agriculture contains not only a most interesting statement of the progressive and valuable work done under the administration of Secretary Rusk, but many suggestions for the enlarged usefulness of this important Department. In the successful efforts to break down the restrictions to the free introduction of our meat products in the countries of Europe the Secretary has been untiring from the first, stimulating and aiding all other Government officers at home and abroad whose official duties enabled them to participate in the work. The total trade in hog products with Europe in May, 1892, amounted to 82,000,000 pounds, against 46,900,000 in the same month of 1891; in June, 1892, the export aggregated 85,700,000 pounds, against 46,500,000 pounds in the same month of the previous year; in July there was an increase of 41 per cent and in August of 55 per cent over the corresponding months of 1891. Over 40,000,000 pounds of inspected pork have been exported since the law was put into operation, and a comparison of the four months of May, June, July, and August, 1892, with the same months of 1891 shows an increase in the number of pounds of our export of pork products of 62 per cent and an increase in value of 66½ per cent. The exports of dressed beef increased from 137,900,000 pounds in 1889 to 220,500,000 pounds in 1892 or about 60 per cent. During the past year there have been exported 394,607 head of live cattle, as against 205,786 exported in 1889. This increased exportation has been largely promoted by the inspection authorized by law and the faithful efforts of the Secretary and his efficient subordinates to make that inspection thorough and to carefully exclude from all cargoes diseased or suspected cattle. The requirement of the English regulations that live cattle arriving from the United States must be slaughtered at the docks had its origin in the claim that pleuro-pneumonia existed among American cattle and that the existence of the disease could only certainly be determined by a post mortem inspection.

The Department of Agriculture has labored with great energy and faithfulness to extirpate this disease, and on the 26th day of September last a public announcement was made by the Secretary that the disease no longer existed anywhere within the United States. He is entirely satisfied after the most searching inquiry that this statement was justified, and that by a continuance of the inspection and quarantine now required of cattle brought into this country the disease can be prevented from again getting any foothold. The value to the cattle industry of the United States of this achievement can hardly be estimated. We can not, perhaps, at once insist that this evidence shall be accepted as satisfactory by other countries; but if the present exemption from the disease is maintained and the inspection of our cattle arriving at foreign ports, in which our own veterinarians participate, confirms it, we may justly expect that the requirement that our cattle shall be slaughtered at the docks will be revoked, as the sanitary restrictions upon our pork products have been. If our cattle can be taken alive to the interior, the trade will be enormously increased.

Agricultural products constituted 78.1 per cent of our unprecedented exports for the fiscal year which closed June 30, 1892, the total exports being $1,030,278,030 and the value of the agricultural products $793,717,676, which exceeds by more than $150,000,000 the shipment of agricultural products in any previous year.

An interesting and a promising work for the benefit of the American farmer has been begun through agents of the Agricultural Department in Europe, and consists in efforts to introduce the various products of Indian corn as articles of human food. The high price of rye offered a favorable opportunity for the experiment in Germany of combining corn meal with rye to produce a cheaper bread. A fair degree of success has been attained, and some mills for grinding corn for food have been introduced. The Secretary is of the opinion that this new use of the products of corn has already stimulated exportations, and that if diligently prosecuted large and important markets can presently be opened for this great American product.

The suggestions of the Secretary for an enlargement of the work of the Department are commended to your favorable consideration. It may, I think, be said without challenge that in no corresponding period has so much been done as during the last four years for the benefit of American agriculture.

The subject of quarantine regulations, inspection, and control was brought suddenly to my attention by the arrival at our ports in August last of vessels infected with cholera. Quarantine regulations should be uniform at all our ports. Under the Constitution they are plainly within the exclusive Federal jurisdiction when and so far as Congress shall legislate. In my opinion the whole subject should be taken into national control and adequate power given to the Executive to protect our people against plague invasions. On the 1st of September last I approved regulations establishing a twenty-day quarantine for all vessels bringing immigrants from foreign ports. This order will be continued in force. Some loss and suffering have resulted to passengers, but a due care for the homes of our people justifies in such cases the utmost precaution. There is danger that with the coming of spring cholera will again appear, and a liberal appropriation should be made at this session to enable our quarantine and port officers to exclude the deadly plague.

But the most careful and stringent quarantine regulations may not be sufficient absolutely to exclude the disease. The progress of medical and sanitary science has been such, however, that if approved precautions are taken at once to put all of our cities and towns in the best sanitary condition, and provision is made for isolating any sporadic cases and for a thorough disinfection, an epidemic can, I am sure, be avoided. This work appertains to the local authorities, and the responsibility and the penalty will be appalling if it is neglected or unduly delayed.

We are peculiarly subject in our great ports to the spread of infectious diseases by reason of the fact that unrestricted immigration brings to us out of European cities, in the overcrowded steerages of great steamships, a large number of persons whose surroundings make them the easy victims of the plague. This consideration, as well as those affecting the political, moral, and industrial interests of our country, leads me to renew the suggestion that admission to our country and to the high privileges of its citizenship should be more restricted and more careful. We have, I think, a right and owe a duty to our own people, and especially to our working people, not only to keep out the vicious, the ignorant, the civil disturber, the pauper, and the contract laborer, but to check the too great flow of immigration now coming by further limitations.

The report of the World's Columbian Exposition has not yet been submitted. That of the board of management of the Government exhibit has been received and is herewith transmitted. The work of construction and of preparation for the opening of the exposition in May next has progressed most satisfactorily and upon a scale of liberality and magnificence that will worthily sustain the honor of the United States.

The District of Columbia is left by a decision of the supreme court of the District without any law regulating the liquor traffic. An old statute of the legislature of the District relating to the licensing of various vocations has hitherto been treated by the Commissioners as giving them power to grant or refuse licenses to sell intoxicating liquors and as subjecting those who sold without licenses to penalties; but in May last the supreme court of the District held against this view of the powers of the Commissioners. It is of urgent importance, therefore, that Congress should supply, either by direct enactment or by conferring discretionary powers upon the Commissioners, proper limitations and restraints upon the liquor traffic in the District. The District has suffered in its reputation by many crimes of violence, a large per cent of them resulting from drunkenness and the liquor traffic. The capital of the nation should be freed from this reproach by the enactment of stringent restrictions and limitations upon the traffic.

In renewing the recommendation which I have made in three preceding annual messages that Congress should legislate for the protection of railroad employees against the dangers incident to the old and inadequate methods of braking and coupling which are still in use upon freight trains, I do so with the hope that this Congress may take action upon the subject. Statistics furnished by the Interstate Commerce Commission show that during the year ending June 30, 1891, there were forty-seven different styles of car couplers reported to be in use, and that during the same period there were 2,660 employees killed and 26,140 injured. Nearly 16 per cent of the deaths occurred in the coupling and uncoupling of cars and over 36 per cent of the injuries had the same origin.

The Civil Service Commission ask for an increased appropriation for needed clerical assistance, which I think should be given. I extended the classified service March 1, 1892, to include physicians, superintendents, assistant superintendents, school-teachers, and matrons in the Indian service, and have had under consideration the subject of some further extensions, but have not as yet fully determined the lines upon which extensions can most properly and usefully be made.

I have in each of the three annual messages which it has been my duty to submit to Congress called attention to the evils and dangers connected with our election methods and practices as they are related to the choice of officers of the National Government. In my last annual message I endeavored to invoke serious attention to the evils of unfair apportionments for Congress. I can not close this message without again calling attention to these grave and threatening evils. I had hoped that it was possible to secure a nonpartisan inquiry by means of a commission into evils the existence of which is known to all, and that out of this might grow legislation from which all thought of partisan advantage should be eliminated and only the higher thought appear of maintaining the freedom and purity of the ballot and the equality of the elector, without the guaranty of which the Government could never have been formed and without the continuance of which it can not continue to exist in peace and prosperity.

It is time that mutual charges of unfairness and fraud between the great parties should cease and that the sincerity of those who profess a desire for pure and honest elections should be brought to the test of their willingness to free our legislation and our election methods from everything that tends to impair the public confidence in the announced result. The necessity for an inquiry and for legislation by Congress upon this subject is emphasized by the fact that the tendency of the legislation in some States in recent years has in some important particulars been away from and not toward free and fair elections and equal apportionments. Is it not time that we should come together upon the high plane of patriotism while we devise methods that shall secure the right of every man qualified by law to cast a free ballot and give to every such ballot an equal value in choosing our public officers and in directing the policy of the Government?

Lawlessness is not less such, but more, where it usurps the functions of the peace officer and of the courts. The frequent lynching of colored people accused of crime is without the excuse, which has sometimes been urged by mobs for a failure to pursue the appointed methods for the punishment of crime, that the accused have an undue influence over courts and juries. Such acts are a reproach to the community where they occur, and so far as they can be made the subject of Federal jurisdiction the strongest repressive legislation is demanded. A public sentiment that will sustain the officers of the law in resisting mobs and in protecting accused persons in their custody should be promoted by every possible means. The officer who gives his life in the brave discharge of this duty is worthy of special honor. No lesson needs to be so urgently impressed upon our people as this, that no worthy end or cause can be promoted by lawlessness.

This exhibit of the work of the Executive Departments is submitted to Congress and to the public in the hope that there will be found in it a due sense of responsibility and an earnest purpose to maintain the national honor and to promote the happiness and prosperity of all our people, and this brief exhibit of the growth and prosperity of the country will give us a level from which to note the increase or decadence that new legislative policies may bring to us. There is no reason why the national influence, power, and prosperity should not observe the same rates of increase that have characterized the past thirty years. We carry the great impulse and increase of these years into the future. There is no reason why in many lines of production we should not surpass all other nations, as we have already done in some. There are no near frontiers to our possible development. Retrogression would be a crime.

BENJ. HARRISON

2 1

Grover Cleveland (1893–1897)

See the first entry on Grover Cleveland, p. 242. Cleveland was the only president who gave two final annual messages to the Congress. The following is the last annual message of his second administration.

Fourth Annual Message
(written to the Congress)
December 7, 1896

To the Congress of the United States:

As representatives of the people in the legislative branch of their Government, you have assembled at a time when the strength and excellence of our free institutions and the fitness of our citizens to enjoy popular rule have been again made manifest. A political contest involving momentous consequences, fraught with feverish apprehension, and creating aggressiveness so intense as to approach bitterness and passion has been waged throughout our land and determined by the decree of free and independent suffrage without disturbance of our tranquillity or the least sign of weakness in our national structure.

When we consider these incidents and contemplate the peaceful obedience and manly submission which have succeeded a heated clash of political opinions, we discover abundant evidence of a determination on the part of our countrymen to abide by every verdict of the popular will and to be controlled at all times by an abiding faith in the agencies established for the direction of the affairs of their Government.

Thus our people exhibit a patriotic disposition which entitles them to demand of those who undertake to make and execute their laws such faithful and unselfish service in their behalf as can only be prompted by a serious appreciation of the trust and confidence which the acceptance of public duty invites.

In obedience to a constitutional requirement I herein submit to the Congress certain information concerning national affairs, with the suggestion of such legislation as in my judgment is necessary and expedient. To secure brevity and avoid tiresome narration I shall omit many details concerning matters within Federal control which, though by no means unimportant, are more profitably discussed in departmental reports. I shall also further curtail this communication by omitting a minute recital of many minor incidents connected with our foreign relations which have heretofore found a place in Executive messages, but are now contained in a report of the Secretary of State, which is herewith submitted.

At the outset of a reference to the more important matters affecting our relations with foreign powers it would afford me satisfaction if I could assure the Congress that the disturbed condition in Asiatic Turkey had during the past year assumed a less hideous and bloody aspect and that, either as a consequence of the awakening of the Turkish Government to the demands of humane civilization or as the result of decisive action on the part of the great nations having the right by treaty to interfere for the protection of those exposed to the rage of mad bigotry and cruel fanaticism, the shocking features of the situation had been mitigated. Instead, however, of welcoming a softened disposition or protective intervention, we have been afflicted by continued and not unfrequent reports of the wanton destruction of homes and the bloody butchery of men, women, and children, made martyrs to their profession of Christian faith.

While none of our citizens in Turkey have thus far been killed or wounded, though often in the midst of dreadful scenes of danger, their safety in the future is by no means assured. Our Government at home and our minister at Constantinople have left nothing undone to protect our missionaries in Ottoman territory, who constitute nearly all the individuals residing there who have a right to claim our protection on the score of American citizenship. Our efforts in this direction will not be relaxed; but the deep feeling and sympathy that have been aroused among our people ought not to so far blind their reason and judgment as to lead them to demand impossible things. The outbreaks of blind fury which lead to murder and pillage in Turkey occur suddenly and without notice, and an attempt on our part to force such a hostile presence there as might be effective for prevention or protection would not only be resisted by the Ottoman Government, but would be regarded as an interruption of their plans by the great nations who assert their exclusive right to intervene in their own time and method for the security of life and property in Turkey.

Several naval vessels are stationed in the Mediterranean as a measure of caution and to furnish all possible relief and refuge in case of emergency.

We have made claims against the Turkish Government for the pillage and destruction of missionary property at Harpoot and Marash during uprisings at those places. Thus far the validity of these demands has not been admitted, though our minister, prior to such outrages and in anticipation of danger, demanded protection for the persons and property of our missionary citizens in the localities mentioned and notwithstanding that strong evidence exists of actual complicity of Turkish soldiers in the work of destruction and robbery.

The facts as they now appear do not permit us to doubt the justice of these claims, and nothing will be omitted to bring about their prompt settlement.

A number of Armenian refugees having arrived at our ports, an order has lately been obtained from the Turkish Government permitting the wives and children of such refugees to join them here. It is hoped that hereafter no obstacle will be interposed to prevent the escape of all those who seek to avoid the perils which threaten them in Turkish dominions.

Our recently appointed consul to Erzerum is at his post and discharging the duties of his office, though for some unaccountable reason his formal exequatur from the Sultan has not been issued.

I do not believe that the present somber prospect in Turkey will be long permitted to offend the sight of Christendom. It so mars the humane and enlightened civilization that belongs to the close of the nineteenth century that it seems hardly possible that the earnest demand of good people throughout the Christian world for its corrective treatment will remain unanswered.

The insurrection in Cuba still continues with all its perplexities. It is difficult to perceive that any progress has thus far been made toward the pacification of the island or that the situation of affairs as depicted in my last annual message has in the least improved. If Spain still holds Havana and the seaports and all the considerable towns, the insurgents still roam at will over at least two-thirds of the inland country. If the determination of Spain to put down the insurrection seems but to strengthen with the lapse of time and is evinced by her unhesitating devotion of largely increased military and naval forces to the task, there is much reason to believe that the insurgents have gained in point of numbers and character and resources and are none the less inflexible in their resolve not to succumb without practically securing the great objects for which they took up arms. If Spain has not yet reestablished her authority, neither have the insurgents yet made good their title to be regarded as an independent state. Indeed, as the contest has gone on the pretense that civil government exists on the island, except so far as Spain is able to maintain it, has been practically abandoned. Spain does keep on foot such a government, more or less imperfectly, in the large towns and their immediate suburbs; but that exception being made, the entire country is either given over to anarchy or is subject to the military occupation of one or the other party. It is reported, indeed, on reliable authority that at the demand of the commander in chief of the insurgent army the putative Cuban government has now given up all attempt to exercise its functions, leaving that government confessedly (what there is the best reason for supposing it always to have been in fact) a government merely on paper.

Were the Spanish armies able to meet their antagonists in the open or in pitched battle, prompt and decisive results might be looked for, and the immense superiority of the Spanish forces in numbers, discipline, and equipment could hardly fail to tell greatly to their advantage. But they are called upon to face a foe that shuns general engagements, that can choose and does choose its own ground, that from the nature of the country is visible or invisible at pleasure, and that fights only from ambuscade and when all the advantages of position and numbers are on its side. In a country where all that is indispensable to life in the way of food, clothing, and shelter is so easily obtainable, especially by those born and bred on the soil, it is obvious that there is hardly a limit to the time during which hostilities of this sort may be prolonged. Meanwhile, as in all cases of protracted civil strife, the passions of the combatants grow more and more inflamed and excesses on both sides become more frequent and more deplorable. They are also participated in by bands of marauders, who, now in the name of one party and now in the name of the other, as may best suit the occasion, carry the country at will and plunder its wretched inhabitants for their own advantage. Such a condition of things would inevitably entail immense destruction of property, even if it were the policy of both parties to prevent it as far as practicable; but while such seemed to be the original policy of the Spanish Government, it has now apparently abandoned it and is acting upon the same theory as the insurgents, namely, that the exigencies of the contest require the wholesale annihilation of property that it may not prove of use and advantage to the enemy.

It is to the same end that, in pursuance of general orders, Spanish garrisons are now being withdrawn from plantations and the rural population required to concentrate itself in the towns. The sure result would seem to be that the industrial value of the island is fast diminishing and that unless there is a speedy and radical change in existing conditions it will soon disappear altogether. That value consists very largely, of course, in its capacity to produce sugar—a capacity already much reduced by the interruptions to tillage which have taken place during the last two years. It is reliably asserted that should these interruptions continue during the current year, and practically extend, as is now threatened, to the entire sugar-producing territory of the island, so much time and so much money will be required to restore the land to its normal productiveness that it is extremely doubtful if capital can be induced to even make the attempt.

The spectacle of the utter ruin of an adjoining country, by nature one of the most fertile and charming on the globe, would engage the serious attention of the Government and people of the United States in any circumstances. In point of fact, they have a concern with it which is by no means of a wholly sentimental or philanthropic character. It lies so near to us as to be hardly separated from our territory. Our actual pecuniary interest in it is second only to that of the people and Government of Spain. It is reasonably estimated that at least from $30,000,000 to $50,000,000 of American capital are invested in plantations and in railroad, mining, and other business enterprises on the island. The volume of trade between the United States and Cuba, which in 1889 amounted to about $64,000,00, rose in 1893 to about $103,000,000, and in 1894, the year before the present insurrection broke out, amounted to nearly $96,000,000. Besides this large pecuniary stake in the fortunes of Cuba, the United States finds itself inextricably involved in the present contest in other ways, both vexatious and costly.

Many Cubans reside in this country, and indirectly promote the insurrection through the press, by public meetings, by the purchase and shipment of arms, by the raising of funds, and by other means which the spirit of our institutions and the tenor of our laws do not permit to be made the subject of criminal prosecutions. Some of them, though Cubans at heart and in all their feelings and interests, have taken out papers as naturalized citizens of the United States—a proceeding resorted to with a view to possible protection by this Government, and not unnaturally regarded with much indignation by the country of their origin. The insurgents are undoubtedly encouraged and supported by the widespread sympathy the people of this country always and instinctively feel for every struggle for better and freer government, and which, in the case of the more adventurous and restless elements of our population, leads in only too many instances to active and personal participation in the contest. The result is that this Government is constantly called upon to protect American citizens, to claim damages for injuries to persons and property, now estimated at many millions of dollars, and to ask explanations and apologies for the acts of Spanish officials whose zeal for the repression of rebellion sometimes blinds them to the immunities belonging to the unoffending citizens of a friendly power. It follows from the same causes that the United States is compelled to actively police a long line of seacoast against unlawful expeditions, the escape of which the utmost vigilance will not always suffice to prevent.

These inevitable entanglements of the United States with the rebellion in Cuba, the large American property interests affected, and considerations of philanthropy and humanity in general have led to a vehement demand in various quarters for some sort of positive intervention on the part of the United States. It was at first proposed that belligerent rights should be accorded to the insurgents—a proposition no longer urged because untimely and in practical operation clearly perilous and injurious to our own interests. It has since been and is now sometimes contended that the independence of the insurgents should be recognized; but imperfect and restricted as the Spanish government of the island may be, no other exists there, unless the will of the military officer in temporary command of a particular district can be dignified as a species of government. It is now also suggested that the United States should buy the island—a suggestion possibly worthy of consideration if there were any evidence of a desire or willingness on the part of Spain to entertain such a proposal. It is urged finally that, all other methods failing, the existing internecine strife in Cuba should be terminated by our intervention, even at the cost of a war between the United States and Spain—a war which its advocates confidently prophesy could neither be large in its proportions nor doubtful in its issue.

The correctness of this forecast need be neither affirmed nor denied. The United States has, nevertheless, a character to maintain as a nation, which plainly dictates that right and not might should be the rule of its conduct. Further, though the United States is not a nation to which peace is a necessity, it is in truth the most pacific of powers and desires nothing so much as to live in amity with all the world. Its own ample and diversified domains satisfy all possible longings for territory, preclude all dreams of conquest, and prevent any casting of covetous eyes upon neighboring regions, however attractive. That our conduct toward Spain and her dominions has constituted no exception to this national disposition is made manifest by the course of our Government, not only thus far during the present insurrection, but during the ten years that followed the rising at Yara in 1868. No other great power, it may safely be said, under circumstances of similar perplexity, would have manifested the same restraint and the same patient endurance. It may also be said that this persistent attitude of the

United States toward Spain in connection with Cuba unquestionably evinces no slight respect and regard for Spain on the part of the American people. They in truth do not forget her connection with the discovery of the Western Hemisphere, nor do they underestimate the great qualities of the Spanish people nor fail to fully recognize their splendid patriotism and their chivalrous devotion to the national honor.

They view with wonder and admiration the cheerful resolution with which vast bodies of men are sent across thousands of miles of ocean and an enormous debt accumulated that the costly possession of the gem of the Antilles may still hold its place in the Spanish crown. And yet neither the Government nor the people of the United States have shut their eyes to the course of events in Cuba or have failed to realize the existence of conceded grievances which have led to the present revolt from the authority of Spain—grievances recognized by the Queen Regent and by the Cortes voiced by the most patriotic enlightened of Spanish statesmen without regard to party, and demonstrated by reforms proposed by the executive and approved by the legislative branch of the Spanish Government. It is in the assumed temper and disposition of the Spanish Government to remedy these grievances, fortified by indications of influential public opinion in Spain, that this Government has hoped to discover the most promising and effective means of composing the present strife with honor and advantage to Spain and with the achievement of all the reasonable objects of the insurrection.

It would seem that if Spain should offer to Cuba genuine autonomy—a measure of home rule which, while preserving the sovereignty of Spain, would satisfy all rational requirements of her Spanish subjects—there should be no just reason why the pacification of the island might not be effected on that basis. Such a result would appear to be in the true interest of all concerned. It would at once stop the conflict which is now consuming the resources of the island and making it worthless for whichever party may ultimately prevail. It would keep intact the possessions of Spain without touching her honor, which will be consulted rather than impugned by the adequate redress of admitted grievances. It would put the prosperity of the island and the fortunes of its inhabitants within their own control without severing the natural and ancient ties which bind them to the mother country, and would yet enable them to test their capacity for self-government under the most favorable conditions. It has been objected on the one side that Spain should not promise autonomy until her insurgent subjects lay down their arms; on the other side, that promised autonomy, however liberal, is insufficient, because without assurance of the promise being fulfilled.

But the reasonableness of a requirement by Spain of unconditional surrender on the part of the insurgent Cubans before their autonomy is conceded is not altogether apparent. It ignores important features of the situation—the stability two years' duration has given to the insurrection; the feasibility of its indefinite prolongation in the nature of things and, as shown by past experience, the utter and imminent ruin of the island unless the present strife is speedily composed; above all the rank abuses which all parties in Spain, all branches of her Government and all her leading public men concede to exist and profess a desire to remove. Facing such circumstances, to withhold the proffer of needed reforms until the parties demanding them put themselves at mercy by throwing down their arms has the appearance of neglecting the gravest of perils and inviting suspicion as to the sincerity of any professed willingness to grant reforms. The objection on behalf of the insurgents that promised reforms can not be relied upon must of course be considered, though we have no right to assume and no reason for assuming that anything Spain undertakes to do for the relief of Cuba will not be done according to both the spirit and the letter of the undertaking.

Nevertheless, realizing that suspicions and precautions on the part of the weaker of two combatants are always natural and not always unjustifiable, being sincerely desirous in the interest of both as well as on its own account that the Cuban problem should be solved with the least possible delay, it was intimated by this Government to the Government of Spain some months ago that if a satisfactory measure of home rule were tendered the Cuban insurgents and would be accepted by them upon a guaranty of its execution the United States would endeavor to find a way not objectionable to Spain of furnishing such guaranty. While no definite response to this intimation has yet been received from the Spanish Government, it is believed to be not altogether unwelcome, while, as already suggested, no reason is perceived why it should not be approved by the insurgents. Neither party can fail to see the importance of early action, and both must realize that to prolong the present state of things for even a short period will add enormously to the time and labor and expenditure necessary to bring about the industrial recuperation of the island. It is therefore fervently hoped on all grounds that earnest efforts for healing the breach between Spain and the insurgent Cubans upon the lines above indicated may be at once inaugurated and pushed to an immediate and successful issue. The friendly offices of the United States, either in the manner above outlined or in any other way consistent with our Constitution and laws, will always be at the disposal of either party.

Whatever circumstances may arise, our policy and our interests would constrain us to object to the acquisition of the island or an interference with its control by any other power.

It should be added that it can not be reasonably assumed that the hitherto expectant attitude of the United States will be indefinitely maintained. While we are anxious to accord all due respect to the sovereignty of Spain, we can not view the pending conflict in all its features and properly apprehend our inevitably close relations to it and its possible results without considering that by the course of events we may be drawn into such an unusual and unprecedented condition as will fix a limit to our patient waiting for Spain to end the contest, either alone and in her own way or with our friendly cooperation.

When the inability of Spain to deal successfully with the insurrection has become manifest and it is demonstrated that her sovereignty is extinct in Cuba for all purposes of its rightful existence, and when a hopeless struggle for its reestablishment has degenerated into a strife which means nothing more than the useless sacrifice of human life and the utter destruction of the very subject-matter of the conflict, a situation will be presented in which our obligations to the sovereignty of Spain will be superseded by higher obligations, which we can hardly hesitate to recognize and discharge. Deferring the choice of ways and methods until the time for action arrives, we should make them depend upon the precise conditions then existing; and they should not be determined upon without giving careful heed to every consideration involving our honor and interest or the international duty we owe to Spain. Until we face the contingencies suggested or the situation is by other incidents imperatively changed we should continue in the line of conduct heretofore pursued, thus in all circumstances exhibiting our obedience to the requirements of public law and our regard for the duty enjoined upon us by the position we occupy in the family of nations.

A contemplation of emergencies that may arise should plainly lead us to avoid their creation, either through a careless disregard of present duty or even an undue stimulation and ill-timed expression of feeling. But I have deemed it not amiss to remind the Congress that a time may arrive when a correct policy and care for our interests, as well as a regard for the interests of other nations and their citizens, joined by considerations of humanity and a desire to see a rich and fertile country intimately related to us saved from complete devastation, will constrain our Government to such action as will subserve the interests thus involved and at the same time promise to Cuba and its inhabitants an opportunity to enjoy the blessings of peace.

The Venezuelan boundary question has ceased to be a matter of difference between Great Britain and the United States, their respective Governments having agreed upon the substantial provisions of a treaty between Great Britain and Venezuela submitting the whole controversy to arbitration. The provisions of the treaty are so eminently just and fair that the assent of Venezuela thereto may confidently be anticipated.

Negotiations for a treaty of general arbitration for all differences between Great Britain and the United States are far advanced and promise to reach a successful consummation at an early date.

The scheme of examining applicants for certain consular positions to test their competency and fitness, adopted under an Executive order issued on the 20th of September, 1895, has fully demonstrated the usefulness of this innovation. In connection with this plan of examination promotions and transfers of deserving incumbents have been quite extensively made, with excellent results.

During the past year 35 appointments have been made in the consular service, 27 of which were made to fill vacancies caused by death or resignation or to supply newly created posts, 2 to succeed incumbents removed for cause, 2 for the purpose of displacing alien consular officials by American citizens, and 4 merely changing the official title of incumbent from commercial agent to consul. Twelve of these appointments were transfers or promotions from other positions under the Department of State, 4 of those appointed had rendered previous service under the Department, 8 were made of persons who passed a satisfactory examination, 7 were appointed to places not included in the order of September 20, 1895, and 4 appointments, as above stated, involved no change of incumbency.

The inspection of consular offices provided for by an appropriation for that purpose at the last session of the Congress has been productive of such wholesome effects that I hope this important work will in the future be continued. I know of nothing that can be done with the same slight expense so improving to the service.

I desire to repeat the recommendation contained in my last annual message in favor of providing at public expense official residences for our ambassadors and ministers at foreign capitals. The reasons supporting this recommendation are strongly stated in the report of the Secretary of State, and the subject seems of such importance that I hope it may receive the early attention of the Congress.

We have during the last year labored faithfully and against unfavorable conditions to secure better preservation of seal life in the Bering Sea. Both the United States and Great Britain have lately dispatched commissioners to these waters to study the habits and condition of the seal herd and the causes of their rapid decrease. Upon the reports of these commissioners, soon to be submitted, and with the exercise of patience and good sense on the part of all interested parties, it is earnestly hoped that hearty cooperation may be secured for the protection against threatened extinction of seal life in the Northern Pacific and Bering Sea.

The Secretary of the Treasury reports that during the fiscal year ended June 30, 1896, the receipts of the Government from all sources amounted to $409,475,408.78. During the same period its expenditures were $434,678,654.48, the excess of expenditures over receipts thus amounting to $25,203,245.70. The ordinary expenditures during the year were $4,015,852.21 less than during the preceding fiscal year. Of the receipts mentioned there was derived from customs the sum of $160,021,751.67 and from internal revenue $146,830,615.66. The receipts from customs show an increase of $7,863,134.22 over those from the same source for the fiscal year ended June 30, 1895, and the receipts from internal revenue an increase of $3,584,537.91.

The value of our imported dutiable merchandise during the last fiscal year was $369,757,470 and the value of free goods imported $409,967,170, being an increase of $6,523,675 in the value of dutiable goods and $41,231,034 in the value of free goods over the preceding year. Our exports of merchandise, foreign and domestic, amounted in value to $882,606,938, being an increase over the preceding year of $75,068,773. The average *ad valorem* duty paid on dutiable goods imported during the year was 39.94 per cent and on free and dutiable goods taken together 20.55 per cent.

The cost of collecting our internal revenue was 2.78 per cent, as against 2.81 per cent for the fiscal year ending June 30, 1895. The total production of distilled spirits, exclusive of fruit brandies, was 86,588,703 taxable gallons, being an increase of 6,639,108 gallons over the preceding year. There was also an increase of 1,443,676 gallons of spirits produced from fruit as compared with the preceding year. The number of barrels of beer produced was 35,859,250, as against 33,589,784 produced in the preceding fiscal year, being an increase of 2,269,466 barrels.

The total amount of gold exported during the last fiscal year was $112,409,947 and of silver $60,541,670, being an increase of $45,941,466 of gold and $13,246,384 of silver over the exportations of the preceding fiscal year. The imports of gold were $33,525,065 and of silver $28,777,186, being $2,859,695 less of gold and $8,566,007 more of silver than during the preceding year.

The total stock of metallic money in the United States at the close of the last fiscal year, ended on the 30th day of June, 1896, was $1,228,326,035, of which $599,597,964, was in gold and $628,728,071 in silver.

On the 1st day of November, 1896, the total stock of money of all kinds in the country was $2,285,410,590, and the amount in circulation, not including that in the Treasury holdings, was $1,627,055,641, being $22.63 per capita upon an estimated population of 71,902,000.

The production of the precious metals in the United States during the calendar year 1895 is estimated to have been 2,254,760 fine ounces of gold, of the value of $46,610,000, and 55,727,000 fine ounces of silver, of the commercial value of $36,445,000 and the coinage value of $72,051,000. The estimated production of these metals throughout the world during the same period was 9,688,821 fine ounces of gold, amounting to $200,285,700 in value, and 169,189,249 fine ounces of silver, of the commercial value of $110,654,000 and of the coinage value of $218,738,100 according to our ratio.

The coinage of these metals in the various countries of the world during the same calendar year amounted to $232,701,438 in gold and $121,996,219 in silver.

The total coinage at the mints of the United States during the fiscal year ended June 30, 1896, amounted to $71,188,468.52, of which $58,878,490 was in gold coins and $12,309,978.52 in standard silver dollars, subsidiary coins, and minor coins.

The number of national banks organized from the time the law authorizing their creation was passed up to October 31, 1896, was 5,051, and of this number 3,679 were at the date last mentioned in active operation, having authorized capital stock of $650,014,895, held by 288,902 shareholders, and circulating notes amounting to $211,412,620.

The total outstanding circulating notes of all national banks on the 31st day of October, 1896, amounted to $234,553,807, including unredeemed but fully secured notes of banks insolvent and in process of liquidation. The increase in national-bank circulation during the year ending on that day was $21,099,429. On October 6, 1896, when the condition of national banks was last reported, the total resources of the 3,679 active institutions were $3,263,685,313.83, which included $1,893,268,839.31 in loans and discounts and $362,165,733.85 in money of all kinds on hand. Of their liabilities $1,597,891,058.03 was due to individual depositors and $209,944,019 consisted of outstanding circulating notes.

There were organized during the year preceding the date last mentioned 28 national banks, located in 15 States, of which 12 were organized in the Eastern States, with a capital of $1,180,000, 6 in the Western States, with a capital of $875,000, and 10 in the Southern States, with a capital of $1,190,000. During the year, however, 37 banks voluntarily abandoned their franchises under the national law, and in the case of 27 others it was found necessary to appoint receivers. Therefore, as compared with the year preceding, there was a decrease of 36 in the number of active banks.

The number of existing banks organized under State laws is 5,708.

The number of immigrants arriving in the United States during the fiscal year was 343,267, of whom 340,468 were permitted to land and 2,799 were debarred on various grounds prescribed by law and returned to the countries whence they came at the expense of the steamship companies by which they were brought in. The increase in immigration over the preceding year amounted to 84,731. It is reported that with some exceptions the immigrants of the past year were of a hardy laboring class, accustomed and able to earn a support for themselves, and it is estimated that the money brought with them amounted to at least $5,000,000, though it was probably much in excess of that sum, since only those having less than $30 are required to disclose the exact amount, and it is known that many brought considerable sums of money to buy land and build homes. Including all the immigrants arriving who were over 14 years of age, 28.63 per cent were illiterate, as against 20.37 per cent of those of that age arriving during the preceding fiscal year. The number of immigrants over 14 years old, the countries from which they came, and the percentage of illiterates among them were as follows: Italy, 57,515, with 54.59 per cent; Ireland, 37,496, with 7 per cent; Russia, 35,188, with 41.14 per cent; Austria-Hungary and provinces, 57,053, with 38.92 per cent; Germany, 25,334, with 2.96 per cent; Sweden, 18,821, with 1.16 per cent; while from Portugal there came 2,067, of whom 77.69 per cent were illiterate. There arrived from Japan during the year only 1,110 immigrants, and it is the opinion of the immigration authorities that the apprehension heretofore existing to some extent of a large immigration from Japan to the United States is without any substantial foundation.

From the Life-Saving Service it is reported that the number of disasters to documented vessels within the limits of its operations during the year was 437. These vessels had on board 4,608 persons, of whom 4,595 were saved and 13 lost. The value of such vessels is estimated at $8,880,140 and of their cargoes $3,846,380, making the total value of property imperiled $12,726,520. Of this amount $11,292,707 was saved and $1,432,750 was lost. Sixty-seven of the vessels were totally wrecked. There were besides 243 casualties to small undocumented craft, on board of which there were 594 persons, of whom 587 were saved and 7 were lost. The value of the property involved in these latter casualties is estimated at $119,265, of which $114,915 was saved and $4,350 was lost. The life-saving crews during the year also rescued or assisted numerous other vessels and warned many from danger by signals, both by day and night. The number of disasters during the year exceeded that of any previous year in the history of the service, but the saving of both life and property was greater than ever before in proportion to the value of the property involved and to the number of persons imperiled.

The operations of the Marine-Hospital Service, the Revenue-Cutter Service, the Steamboat-Inspection Service, the Light-House Service, the Bureau of Navigation, and other branches of public work attached to the Treasury Department, together with various recommendations concerning their support and improvement, are fully stated in the report of the Secretary of the Treasury, to which the attention of the Congress is especially invited.

The report of the Secretary of War exhibits satisfactory conditions in the several branches of the public service intrusted to his charge.

The limit of our military force as fixed by law is constantly and readily maintained. The present discipline and morale of our Army are excellent, and marked progress and efficiency are apparent throughout its entire organization.

With the exception of delicate duties in the suppression of slight Indian disturbances along our southwestern boundary, in which the Mexican troops cooperated, and the compulsory but peaceful return, with the consent of Great Britain, of a band of Cree Indians from Montana to the British possessions, no active operations have been required of the Army during the year past.

Changes in methods of administration, the abandonment of unnecessary posts and consequent concentration of troops, and the exercise of care and vigilance by the various officers charged with the responsibility in the expenditure of the appropriations have resulted in reducing to a minimum the cost of maintenance of our military establishment.

During the past year the work of constructing permanent infantry and cavalry posts has been continued at the places heretofore designated. The Secretary of War repeats his recommendation that appropriations for barracks and quarters should more strictly conform to the needs of the service as judged by the Department rather than respond to the wishes and importunities of localities. It is imperative that much of the money provided for such construction should now be allotted to the erection of necessary quarters for the garrisons assigned to the coast defenses, where many men will be needed to properly care for and operate modern guns. It is essential, too, that early provision be made to supply the necessary force of artillery to meet the demands of this service.

The entire Army has now been equipped with the new magazine arms, and wise policy demands that all available public and private resources should be so employed as to provide within a reasonable time a sufficient number to supply the State militia with these modern weapons and provide an ample reserve for any emergency.

The organized militia numbers 112,879 men. The appropriations for its support by the several States approximate $2,800,000 annually, and $400,000 is contributed by the General Government. Investigation shows these troops to be usually well drilled and inspired with much military interest, but in many instances they are so deficient in proper arms and equipment that a sudden call to active duty would find them inadequately prepared for field service. I therefore recommend that prompt measures be taken to remedy this condition and that every encouragement be given to this deserving body of unpaid and voluntary citizen soldiers, upon whose assistance we must largely rely in time of trouble.

During the past year rapid progress has been made toward the completion of the scheme adopted for the erection and armament of fortifications along our seacoast, while equal progress has been made in providing the material for submarine defense in connection with these works.

It is peculiarly gratifying at this time to note the great advance that has been made in this important undertaking since the date of my annual message to the Fifty-third Congress at the opening of its second session, in December, 1893. At that time I informed the Congress of the approaching completion of nine 12-inch, twenty 10-inch, and thirty-four 8-inch high-power steel guns and seventy-five 12-inch rifled mortars.

This total then seemed insignificant when compared with the great work remaining to be done. Yet it was none the less a source of satisfaction to every citizen when he reflected that it represented the first installment of the new ordnance of American design and American manufacture and demonstrated our ability to supply from our own resources guns of unexcelled power and accuracy.

At that date, however, there were practically no carriages upon which to mount these guns and only thirty-one emplacements for guns and sixty-four for mortars. Nor were all these emplacements in condition to receive their armament. Only one high-power gun was at that time in position for the defense of the entire coast.

Since that time the number of guns actually completed has been increased to a total of twenty-one 12-inch, fifty-six 10-inch, sixty-one 8-inch high-power breech-loading steel guns, ten rapid-fire guns, and eighty-one 16-inch-type guns, fifty 12-inch, fifty-six 10-inch, twenty-seven 8-inch high-power guns, and sixty-six 12-inch rifled mortars; in all, four hundred and twenty-eight guns and mortars.

During the same year, immediately preceding the message referred to, the first modern gun carriage had been completed and eleven more were in process of construction. All but one were of the nondisappearing type. These, however, were not such as to secure necessary cover for the artillery gunners against the intense fire of modern machine rapid-fire and high-power guns.

The inventive genius of ordnance and civilian experts has been taxed in designing carriages that would obviate this fault, resulting, it is believed, in the solution of this difficult problem. Since 1893 the number of gun carriages constructed or building has been raised to a total of 129, of which 90 are on the disappearing principle, and the number of mortar carriages to 152, while the 95 emplacements which were provided for prior to that time have been increased to 280 built and building.

This improved situation is largely due to the recent generous response of Congress to the recommendations of the War Department.

Thus we shall soon have complete about one-fifth of the comprehensive system the first step in which was noted in my message to the Congress of December 4, 1893.

When it is understood that a masonry emplacement not only furnishes a platform for the heavy modern high-power gun, but also in every particular serves the purpose and takes the place of the fort of former days, the importance of the work accomplished is better comprehended.

In the hope that the work will be prosecuted with no less vigor in the future, the Secretary of War has submitted an estimate by which, if allowed, there will be provided and either built or building by the end of the next fiscal year such additional guns, mortars, gun carriages, and emplacements as will represent not far from one-third of the total work to be done under the plan adopted for our coast defenses, thus affording a prospect that the entire work will be substantially completed within six years. In less time than that, however, we shall have attained a marked degree of security.

The experience and results of the past year demonstrate that with a continuation of present careful methods the cost of the remaining work will be much less than the original estimate.

We should always keep in mind that of all forms of military preparation coast defense alone is essentially pacific in its nature. While it gives the sense of security due to a consciousness of strength, it is neither the purpose nor the effect of such permanent fortifications to involve us in foreign complications, but rather to guarantee us against them. They are not temptation to war, but security against it. Thus they are thoroughly in accord with all the traditions of our national diplomacy.

The Attorney-General presents a detailed and interesting statement of the important work done under his supervision during the last fiscal year.

The ownership and management by the Government of penitentiaries for the confinement of those convicted in United States courts of violations of Federal laws, which for many years has been a subject of Executive recommendation, have at last to a slight extent been realized by the utilization of the abandoned military prison at Fort Leavenworth as a United States penitentiary.

This is certainly a movement in the right direction, but it ought to be at once supplemented by the rebuilding or extensive enlargement of this improvised prison and the construction of at least one more, to be located in the Southern States. The capacity of the Leavenworth Penitentiary is so limited that the expense of its maintenance, calculated at a per capita rate upon the number of prisoners it can accommodate, does not make as economical an exhibit as it would if it were large and better adapted to prison purposes; but I am thoroughly convinced that economy, humanity, and a proper sense of responsibility and duty toward those whom we punish for violations of Federal law dictate that the Federal Government should have the entire control and management of the penitentiaries where convicted violators are confined.

It appears that since the transfer of the Fort Leavenworth Military prison to its new uses the work previously done by prisoners confined there, and for which expensive machinery has been provided, has been discontinued. This work consisted of the manufacture of articles for army use, now done elsewhere. On all grounds it is exceedingly desirable that the convicts confined in this penitentiary be allowed to resume work of this description.

It is most gratifying to note the satisfactory results that have followed the inauguration of the new system provided for by the act of May 28, 1896, under which certain Federal officials are compensated by salaries instead of fees. The new plan was put in operation on the 1st day of July, 1896, and already the great economy it enforces, its prevention of abuses, and its tendency to a better enforcement of the laws are strikingly apparent. Detailed evidence of the usefulness of this long-delayed but now happily accomplished reform will be found clearly set forth in the Attorney-General's report.

Our Post-Office Department is in good condition, and the exhibit made of its operations during the fiscal year ended June 30, 1896, if allowance is made for imperfections in the laws applicable to it, is very satisfactory. The total receipts during the year were $82,499,208.40. The total expenditures were $90,626,296.84, exclusive of the $1,559,898.27 which was earned by the Pacific Railroad for transportation and credited on their debt to the Government. There was an increase of receipts over the previous year of $5,516,080.21, or 7.1 per cent, and an increase of expenditures of $3,836,124.02, or 4.42 per cent. The deficit was $1,679,956.19 less than that of the preceding year. The chief expenditures of the postal service are regulated by law and are not in the control of the Postmaster-General. All that he can accomplish by the most watchful administration and economy is to enforce prompt and thorough collection and accounting for public moneys and such minor savings in small expenditures and in letting those contracts, for post-office supplies and star service, which are not regulated by statute.

An effective cooperation between the Auditor's Office and the Post-Office Department and the making and enforcement of orders by the Department requiring immediate notification to their sureties of all delinquencies on the part of postmasters, and compelling such postmasters to make more frequent deposits of postal funds, have resulted in a prompter auditing of their accounts and much less default to the Government than heretofore.

The year's report shows large extensions of both star-route service and railway mail service, with increased postal facilities. Much higher accuracy in handling mails has also been reached, as appears by the decrease of errors in the railway mail service and the reduction of mail matter returned to the Dead-Letter Office.

The deficit for the last year, although much less than that of the last and preceding years, emphasizes the necessity for legislation to correct the growing abuse of second-class rates, to which the deficiency is mainly attributable. The transmission at the rate of 1 cent a pound of serial libraries, advertising sheets, "house organs" (periodicals advertising some particular "house" or institution), sample copies, and the like ought certainly to be discontinued. A glance at the revenues received for the work done last year will show more plainly than any other statement the gross abuse of the postal service and the growing waste of its earnings.

The free matter carried in the mails for the Departments, offices, etc., of the Government and for Congress, in pounds, amounted to 94,480,189.

If this is offset against buildings for post-offices and stations, the rental of which would more than compensate for such free postal service, we have this exhibit:

Weight of mail matter (other than above) transmitted through the mails for the year ending June 30, 1896

Class	Weight Pounds	Revenue
1. Domestic and foreign letters and postal cards, etc. . . .	65,337,343	$60,624,464
2. Newspapers and periodicals, 1 cent per pound	348,988,648	2,996,403
3. Books, seeds, etc., 8 cents a pound	78,701,148	10,324,069
4. Parcels, etc., 15 cents a pound	19,950,187	3,129,321
Total	512,977,326	77,044,257

The remainder of our postal revenue, amounting to something more than $5,000,000 was derived from box rents, registry fees, money-order business, and other similar items.

The entire expenditures of the Department, including pay for transportation credited to the Pacific railroads, were $92,186,195.11, which may be considered as the cost of receiving, carrying, and delivering the above mail matter. It thus appears that though the second-class matter constituted more than two-thirds of the total that was carried, the revenue derived from it was less than one-thirtieth of the total expense.

The average revenue was—

From each pound of first-class matter............. cents	93.0
From each pound of second class*................. mills	8.5
From each pound of third class .... cents	13.1
From each pound of fourth class.................... do	15.6

*Of the second class 52,348 was county-free matter.

The growth in weight of second-class matter has been from 299,000,000 pounds in 1894 to 312,000,000 in 1895 and to almost 349,000,000 in 1896 and it is far outstripping any possible growth of postal revenues.

Our mail service should of course be such as to meet the wants and even the conveniences of our people at a direct charge upon them so light as perhaps to exclude the idea of our Post-Office Department being a Money-making concern; but in the face of a constantly recurring deficiency in its revenues and in view of the fact that we supply the best mail service in the world it seems to me it is quite time to correct the abuses that swell enormously our annual deficit. If we concede the public policy of carrying weekly newspapers free in the county of publication, and even the policy of carrying at less than one-tenth of their cost other *bona fide* newspapers and periodicals, there can be no excuse for subjecting the service to the further immense and increasing loss involved in carrying at the nominal rate of 1 cent a pound the serial libraries, sometimes including trashy and even harmful literature, and other matter which under the loose interpretation of a loose statute have been gradually given second-class rates, thus absorbing all profitable returns derived from first-class matter, which pays three or four times more than its cost, and producing a large annual loss to be paid by general taxation. If such second-class matter paid merely the cost of its handling, our deficit would disappear and a surplus result which might be used to give the people still better mail facilities or cheaper rates of letter postage. I recommend that legislation be at once enacted to correct these abuses and introduce better business ideas in the regulation of our postal rates.

Experience and observation have demonstrated that certain improvements in the organization of the Post-Office Department must be secured before we can gain the full benefit of the immense sums expended in its administration. This involves the following reforms, which I earnestly recommend:

There should be a small addition to the existing inspector service, to be employed in the supervision of the carrier force, which now numbers 13,000 men and performs its service practically without the surveillance exercised over all other branches of the postal or public service. Of course such a lack of supervision and freedom from wholesome disciplinary restraints must inevitably lead to imperfect service. There should also be appointed a few inspectors who could assist the central office in necessary investigation concerning matters of post-office leases, post-office sites, allowances for rent, fuel, and lights, and in organizing and securing the best results from the work of the 14,000 clerks now employed in first and second class offices.

I am convinced that the small expense attending the inauguration of these reforms would actually be a profitable investment.

I especially recommend such a recasting of the appropriations by Congress for the Post-Office Department as will permit the Postmaster-General to proceed with the work of consolidating post-offices. This work has already been entered upon sufficiently to fully demonstrate by experiment and experience that such consolidation is productive of better service, larger revenues, and less expenditures, to say nothing of the further advantage of gradually withdrawing post-offices from the spoils system.

The Universal Postal Union, which now embraces all the civilized world and whose delegates will represent 1,000,000,000 people, will hold its fifth congress in the city of Washington in May, 1897. The United States may be said to have taken the initiative which led to the first meeting of this congress, at Berne in 1874, and the formation of the Universal Postal Union, which brings the postal service of all countries to every man's neighborhood and has wrought marvels in cheapening postal rates and securing absolutely safe mail communication throughout the world. Previous congresses have met in Berne, Paris, Lisbon, and Vienna, and the respective countries in which they have assembled have made generous provision for their accommodation and for the reception and entertainment of the delegates.

In view of the importance of this assemblage and of its deliberations and of the honors and hospitalities accorded to our representatives by other countries on similar occasions, I earnestly hope that such an appropriation will be made for the expenses necessarily attendant upon the coming meeting in our capital city as will be worthy of our national hospitality and indicative of our appreciation of the event.

The work of the Navy Department and its present condition are fully exhibited in the report of the Secretary.

The construction of vessels for our new Navy has been energetically prosecuted by the present Administration upon the general lines previously adopted, the Department having seen no necessity for radical changes in prior methods, and the work was found to be progressing in a manner highly satisfactory. It has been decided, however, to provide in every shipbuilding contract that the builder should pay all trial expenses, and it has also been determined to pay no speed premiums in future contracts. The premiums recently earned and some yet to be decided are features of the contracts made before this conclusion was reached.

On March 4, 1893, there were in commission but two armored vessels—the double-turreted monitors *Miantonomah* and *Monterey*. Since that date, of vessels theretofore authorized, there have been placed in their first commission 3 first-class and 2 second-class battle ships, 2 armored cruisers, 1 harbor-defense ram, and 5 double-turreted monitors, including the *Maine* and the *Puritan*, just completed. Eight new unarmored cruisers and 2 new gunboats have also been commissioned. The *Iowa*, another battle ship, will be completed about March 1, and at least 4 more gunboats will be ready for sea in the early spring.

It is gratifying to state that our ships and their outfits are believed to be equal to the best that can be manufactured elsewhere, and that such, notable reductions have been made in their cost as to justify the statement that quite a number of vessels are now being constructed at rates as low as those that prevail in European shipyards.

Our manufacturing facilities are at this time ample for all possible naval contingencies. Three of our Government navy-yards—those at Mare Island, Cal., Norfolk, Va., and Brooklyn, N. Y.—are equipped for shipbuilding, our ordnance plant in Washington is equal to any in the world, and at the torpedo station we are successfully making the highest grades of smokeless powder. The first-class private shipyards at Newport News, Philadelphia, and San Francisco are building battle ships; eleven contractors, situated in the States of Maine, Rhode Island, Pennsylvania, New Jersey, Maryland, Virginia, and the State of Washington, are constructing gunboats or torpedo boats; two plants are manufacturing large quantities of first-class armor, and American factories are producing automobile torpedoes, powder, projectiles, rapid-fire guns, and everything else necessary for the complete outfit of naval vessels.

There have been authorized by Congress since March, 1893, 5 battle ships, 6 light-draft gunboats, 16 torpedo boats, and 1 submarine torpedo boat. Contracts for the building of all of them have been let. The Secretary expresses the opinion that we have for the present a sufficient supply of cruisers and gunboats, and that hereafter the construction of battle ships and torpedo boats will supply our needs.

Much attention has been given to the methods of carrying on departmental business. Important modifications in the regulations have been made, tending to unify the control of shipbuilding as far as may be under the Bureau of Construction and Repair, and also to improve the mode of purchasing supplies for the Navy by the Bureau of Supplies and Accounts. The establishment under recent acts of Congress of a supply fund with which to purchase these supplies in large quantities and other modifications of methods have tended materially to their cheapening and better quality.

The War College has developed into an institution which it is believed will be of great value to the Navy in teaching the science of war, as well as in stimulating professional zeal in the Navy, and it will be especially useful in the devising of plans for the utilization in case of necessity of all the naval resources of the United States.

The Secretary has persistently adhered to the plan he found in operation for securing labor at navy-yards through boards of labor employment, and has done much to make it more complete and efficient. The naval officers who are familiar with this system and its operation express the decided opinion that its results have been to vastly improve the character of the work done at our yards and greatly reduce its cost.

Discipline among the officers and men of the Navy has been maintained to a high standard and the percentage of American citizens enlisted has been very much increased.

The Secretary is considering and will formulate during the coming winter a plan for laying up ships in reserve, thereby largely reducing the cost of maintaining our vessels afloat. This plan contemplates that battle ships, torpedo boats, and such of the cruisers as are not needed for active service at sea shall be kept in reserve with skeleton crews on board to keep then in condition, cruising only enough to insure the efficiency of the ships and their crews in time of activity.

The economy to result from this system is too obvious to need comment.

The Naval Militia, which was authorized a few years ago as an experiment, has now developed into a body of enterprising young men, active and energetic in the discharge of their duties and promising great usefulness. This establishment has nearly the same relation to our Navy as the National Guard in the different States bears to our Army, and it constitutes a source of supply for our naval forces the importance of which is immediately apparent.

The report of the Secretary of the Interior presents a comprehensive and interesting exhibit of the numerous and important affairs committed to his supervision. It is impossible in this communication to do more than briefly refer to a few of the subjects concerning which the Secretary gives full and instructive information.

The money appropriated on account of this Department and for its disbursement for the fiscal year ended June 30, 1896, amounted to more than $157,000,000, or a greater sum than was appropriated for the entire maintenance of the Government for the two fiscal years ended June 30, 1861.

Our public lands, originally amounting to 1,840,000,000 acres, have been so reduced that only about 600,000,000 acres still remain in Government control, excluding Alaska. The balance, being by far the most valuable portion, has been given away to settlers, to new States, and to railroads or sold at a comparatively nominal sum. The patenting of land in execution of railroad grants has progressed rapidly during the year, and since the 4th day of March, 1893, about 25,000,000 acres have thus been conveyed to these corporations.

I agree with the Secretary that the remainder of our public lands should be more carefully dealt with and their alienation guarded by better economy and greater prudence.

The commission appointed from the membership of the National Academy of Sciences, provided for by an act of Congress, to formulate plans for a national forestry system will, it is hoped, soon be prepared to present the result of thorough and intelligent examination of this important subject.

The total Indian population of the United States is 177,235, according to a census made in 1895, exclusive of those within the State of New York and those comprising the Five Civilized Tribes. Of this number there are approximately 38,000 children of school age. During the year 23,393 of these were enrolled in schools. The progress which has attended recent efforts to extend Indian-school facilities and the anticipation of continued liberal appropriations to that end can not fail to afford the utmost satisfaction to those who believe that the education of Indian children is a prime factor in the accomplishment of Indian civilization.

It may be said in general terms that in every particular the improvement of the Indians under Government care has been most marked and encouraging.

The Secretary, the Commissioner of Indian Affairs, and the agents having charge of Indians to whom allotments have been made strongly urge the passage of a law prohibiting the sale of liquor to allottees who have taken their lands in severalty. I earnestly join in this recommendation and venture to express the hope that the Indian may be speedily protected against this greatest of all obstacles to his well-being and advancement.

The condition of affairs among the Five Civilized Tribes, who occupy large tracts of land in the Indian Territory and who have governments of their own, has assumed such an aspect as to render it almost indispensable that there should be an entire change in the relations of these Indians to the General Government. This seems to be necessary in furtherance of their own interests, as well as for the protection of non-Indian residents in their territory. A commission organized and empowered under several recent laws is now negotiating with these Indians for the relinquishment of their courts and the division of their common lands in severalty and are aiding in the settlement of the troublesome question of tribal membership. The reception of their first proffers of negotiation was not encouraging, but through patience and such conduct on their part as demonstrated that their intentions were friendly and in the interest of the tribes the prospect of success has become more promising. The effort should be to save these Indians from the consequences of their own mistakes and improvidence and to secure to the real Indian his rights as against intruders and professed friends who profit by his retrogression. A change is also needed to protect life and property through the operation of courts conducted according to strict justice and strong enough to enforce their mandates.

As a sincere friend of the Indian, I am exceedingly anxious that these reforms should be accomplished with the consent and aid of the tribes and that no necessity may be presented for radical or drastic legislation. I hope, therefore, that the commission now conducting negotiations will soon be able to report that progress has been made toward a friendly adjustment of existing difficulties.

It appears that a very valuable deposit of gilsonite or asphaltum has been found on the reservation in Utah occupied by the Uncompahgre Ute Indians. Every consideration of care for the public interest and every sensible business reason dictate such management or disposal of this important source of public revenue as will except it from the general rules and incidents attending the ordinary disposition of public lands and secure to the Government a fair share at least of its advantages in place of its transfer for a nominal sum to interested individuals.

I indorse the recommendation made by the present Secretary of the Interior, as well as his predecessor, that a permanent commission, consisting of three members, one of whom shall be an army officer, be created to perform the duties now developing upon the Commissioner and Assistant Commissioner of Indian Affairs. The management of the Bureau involves such numerous and diverse details and the advantages of an uninterrupted policy are so apparent that I hope the change suggested will meet the approval of the Congress.

The diminution of our enormous pension roll and the decrease of pension expenditure, which have been so often confidently foretold, still fail in material realization. The number of pensioners on the rolls at the close of the fiscal year ended June 30, 1896, was 970,678. This is the largest number ever reported. The amount paid exclusively for pensions during the year was $138,214,761.94, a slight decrease from that of the preceding year, while the total expenditures on account of pensions, including the cost of maintaining the Department and expenses attending pension distribution, amounted to $142,206,550.59, or within a very small fraction of one-third of the entire expense of supporting the Government during the same year. The number of new pension certificates issued was 90,640. Of these, 40,374 represent original allowances of claims and 15,878 increases of existing pensions.

The number of persons receiving pensions from the United States, but residing in foreign countries, at the close of the last fiscal year was 3,781, and the amount paid to them during the year was, $582,735.38.

The sum appropriated for the payment of pensions for the current fiscal year, ending June 30, 1897, is $140,000,000, and for the succeeding year it is estimated that the same amount will be necessary.

The Commissioner of Pensions reports that during the last fiscal year 339 indictments were found against violators of the pension laws. Upon these indictments 167 convictions resulted.

In my opinion, based upon such statements as these and much other information and observation, the abuses which have been allowed to creep into our pension system have done incalculable harm in demoralizing our people and undermining good citizenship. I have endeavored within my sphere of official duty to protect our pension roll and make it what it should be, a roll of honor, containing the names of those disabled in their country's service and worthy of their country's affectionate remembrance. When I have seen those who pose as the soldiers' friends active and alert in urging greater laxity and more reckless pension expenditure, while nursing selfish schemes, I have deprecated the approach of a situation when necessary retrenchment and enforced economy may lead to an attack upon pension abuses so determined as to overlook the discrimination due to those who, worthy of a nation's care, ought to live and die under the protection of a nation's gratitude.

The Secretary calls attention to the public interests involved in an adjustment of the obligations of the Pacific railroads to the Government. I deem it to be an important duty to especially present this subject to the consideration of the Congress.

On January 1, 1897, with the amount already matured, more than $13,000,000 of the principal of the subsidy bonds issued by the United States in aid of the construction of the Union Pacific Railway, including its Kansas line, and more than $6,000,000 of like bonds issued in aid of the Central Pacific Railroad, including those issued to the Western Pacific Railroad Company, will have fallen due and been paid or must on that day be paid by the Government. Without any reference to the application of the sinking fund now in the Treasury, this will create such a default on the part of these companies to the Government as will give it the right to at once institute proceedings to foreclose its mortgage lien. In addition to this indebtedness, which will be due January 1, 1897, there will mature between that date and January 1, 1899, the remaining principal of such subsidy bonds, which must also be met by the Government. These amount to more than $20,000,000 on account of the Union Pacific lines and exceed $21,000,000 on account of the Central Pacific lines.

The situation of these roads and the condition of their indebtedness to the Government have been fully set forth in the reports of various committees to the present and prior Congress, and as early as 1887 they were thoroughly examined by a special commission appointed pursuant to an act of Congress. The considerations requiring an adjustment of the Government's relations to the companies have been clearly presented and the conclusion reached with practical uniformity that if these relations are not terminated they should be revised upon a basis securing their safe continuance.

Under section 4 of the act of Congress passed March 3, 1887, the President is charged with the duty, in the event that any mortgage or other incumbrance paramount to the interest of the United States in the property of the Pacific railroads should exist and be lawfully liable to the enforced, to direct the action of the Departments of Treasury and of Justice in the protection of the interest of the United States by redemption or through judicial proceedings, including foreclosures of the Government liens.

In view of the fact that the Congress has for a number of years almost constantly had under consideration various plans for dealing with the conditions existing between these roads and the Government, I have thus far felt justified in withholding action under the statute above mentioned.

In the case of the Union Pacific Company, however, the situation has become especially and immediately urgent. Proceedings have been instituted to foreclose a first mortgage upon those aided parts of the main lines upon which the Government holds a second and subordinate mortgage lien. In consequence of those proceedings and increasing complications, added to the default occurring on the 1st day of January, 1897, a condition will be presented at that date, so far as this company is concerned, that must emphasize the mandate of the act of 1887 and give to Executive duty under its provisions a more imperative aspect. Therefore, unless Congress shall otherwise direct or shall have previously determined upon a different solution the problem, there will hardly appear to exist any reason for delaying beyond the date of the default above mentioned such Executive action as will promise to subserve the public interests and save the Government from the loss threatened by further inaction.

The Department of Agriculture is so intimately related to the welfare of our people and the prosperity of our nation that it should constantly receive the care and encouragement of the Government. From small beginnings it has grown to be the center of agricultural intelligence and the source of aid and encouragement to agricultural efforts. Large sums of money are annually appropriated for the maintenance of this Department, and it must be confessed that the legislation relating to it has not always been directly in the interest of practical farming or properly guarded against waste and extravagance. So far, however, as public money has been appropriated fairly and sensibly to help those who actually till the soil, no expenditure has been more profitably made or more generally approved by the people.

Under the present management of the Department its usefulness has been enhanced in every direction, and at the same time strict economy has been enforced to the utmost extent permitted by Congressional action. From the report of the Secretary it appears that through careful and prudent financial management he has annually saved a large sum from his appropriations, aggregating during his incumbency and up to the close of the present fiscal year nearly one-fifth of the entire amount appropriated. These results have been accomplished by a conscientious study of the real needs of the farmer and such a regard for economy as the genuine farmer ought to appreciate, supplemented by a rigid adherence to civil-service methods in a Department which should be conducted in the interest of agriculture instead of partisan politics.

The Secretary reports that the value of our exports of farm products during the last fiscal year amounted to $570,000,000, an increase of $17,000,000 over those of the year immediately preceding. This statement is not the less welcome because of the fact that, notwithstanding such increase, the proportion of exported agricultural products to our total exports of all descriptions fell off during the year. The benefits of an increase in agricultural exports being assured, the decrease in its proportion to our total exports is the more gratifying when we consider that it is owing to the fact that such total exports for the year increased more than $75,000,000.

The large and increasing exportation of our agricultural products suggests the great usefulness of the organization lately established in the Department for the purpose of giving to those engaged in farming pursuits reliable information concerning the condition, needs, and advantages of different foreign markets. Inasmuch as the success of the farmer depends upon the advantageous sale of his products, and inasmuch as foreign markets must largely be the destination of such products, it is quite apparent that a knowledge of the conditions and wants that affect those markets ought to result in sowing more intelligently and reaping with a better promise of profit. Such information points out the way to a prudent foresight in the selection and cultivation of crops and to a release from the bondage of unreasoning monotony of production, a glutted and depressed market, and constantly recurring unprofitable toil.

In my opinion the gratuitous distribution of seeds by the Department ought to be discontinued. No one can read the statement of the Secretary on this subject and doubt the extravagance and questionable results of this practice. The professed friends of the farmer, and certainly the farmers themselves, are naturally expected to be willing to rid a Department devoted to the promotion of farming interests of a feature which tends so much to its discredit.

The Weather Bureau, now attached to the Department of Agriculture, has continued to extend its sphere of usefulness, and by an uninterrupted improvement in the accuracy of its forecasts has greatly increased it efficiency as an aid and protection to all whose occupations are related to weather conditions.

Omitting further reference to the operations of the Department, I commend the Secretary's report and the suggestions it contains to the careful consideration of the Congress.

The progress made in civil-service reform furnishes a cause for the utmost congratulation. It has survived the doubts of its friends as well as the rancor of its enemies and has gained a permanent place among the agencies destined to cleanse our politics and to improve, economize, and elevate the public service.

There are now in the competitive classified service upward of 84,000 places, more than half of these having been included from time to time since March 4, 1893. A most radical and sweeping extension was made by Executive order dated the 6th day of May, 1896, and if fourth-class postmasterships are not included in the statement it may be said that practically all positions contemplated by the civil-service law are now classified. Abundant reasons exist for including these postmasterships, based upon economy, improved service, and the peace and quiet of neighborhoods. If, however, obstacles prevent such action at present, I earnestly hope that Congress will, without increasing post-office appropriations, so adjust them as to permit in proper cases a consolidation of these post-offices, to the end that through this process the result desired may to a limited extent be accomplished.

The civil-service rules as amended during the last year provide for a sensible and uniform method of promotion, basing eligibility to better positions upon demonstrated efficiency and faithfulness. The absence of fixed rules on this subject has been an infirmity in the system more and more apparent as its other benefits have been better appreciated.

The advantages of civil-service methods in their business aspects are too well understood to require argument. Their application has become a necessity to the executive work of the Government. But those who gain positions through the operation of these methods should be made to understand that the nonpartisan scheme through which they receive their appointment demands from them by way of reciprocity nonpartisan and faithful performance of duty under every Administration and cheerful fidelity to every chief. While they should be encouraged to decently exercise their rights of citizenship and to support through their suffrages the political beliefs they honestly profess, the noisy, pestilent, and partisan employee, who loves political turmoil and contention or who renders lax and grudging service to an Administration not representing his political views, should be promptly and fearlessly dealt with in such a way as to furnish a warning to others who may be likewise disposed.

The annual report of the Commissioners will be duly transmitted, and I commend the important matter they have in charge to the careful consideration of the Congress.

The Interstate Commerce Commission has during the last year supplied abundant evidence of its usefulness and the importance of the work committed to its charge.

Public transportation is a universal necessity, and the question of just and reasonable charges therefor has become of vital importance not only to shippers and carriers, but also to the vast multitude of producers and consumers. The justice and equity of the principles embodied in the existing law passed for the purpose of regulating these charges are everywhere conceded, and there appears to be no question that the policy thus entered upon has a permanent place in our legislation.

As the present statute when enacted was in the nature of the case more or less tentative and experimental, it was hardly expected to supply a complete and adequate system. While its wholesome effects are manifest and have amply justified its enactment, it is evident that all desired reforms in transportation methods have not been fully accomplished. In view of the judicial interpretation which some provisions of this statute have received and the defects disclosed by the efforts made for its enforcement, its revision and amendment appear to be essential, to the end that it may more effectually reach the evils designed to be corrected. I hope the recommendations of the Commission upon this subject will be promptly and favorably considered by the Congress.

I desire to recur to the statements elsewhere made concerning the Government's receipts and expenditures for the purpose of venturing upon some suggestions touching our present tariff law and its operation.

This statute took effect on the 28th day of August, 1894. Whatever may be its shortcomings as a complete measure of tariff reform, it must be conceded that it has opened the way to a freer and greater exchange of commodities between us and other countries, and thus furnished a wider market for our products and manufactures.

The only entire fiscal year during which this law has been in force ended on the 30th day of June, 1896. In that year our imports increased over those of the previous year more than $6,500,000, while the value of the domestic products we exported and which found markets abroad was nearly $70,000,000 more than during the preceding year.

Those who insist that the cost to our people of articles coming to them from abroad for their needful use should only be increased through tariff charges to an extent necessary to meet the expenses of the Government, as well as those who claim that tariff charges may be laid upon such articles beyond the necessities of Government revenue and with the additional purpose of so increasing their price in our markets as to give American manufacturers and producers better and more profitable opportunities, must agree that our tariff laws are only primarily justified as sources of revenue to enable the Government to meet the necessary expenses of its maintenance. Considered as to its efficiency in this aspect, the present law can by no means fall under just condemnation. During the only complete fiscal year of its operation it has yielded nearly $8,000,000 more revenue than was received from tariff duties in the preceding year. There was, nevertheless, a deficit between our receipts and expenditures of a little more than $25,000,000. This, however, was not unexpected.

The situation was such in December last, seven months before the close of the fiscal year, that the Secretary of the Treasury foretold a deficiency of $17,000,000. The great and increasing apprehension and timidity in business circles and the depression in all activities intervening since that time, resulting from causes perfectly well understood and entirely disconnected with our tariff law or its operation, seriously checked the imports we would have otherwise received and readily account for the difference between this estimate of the Secretary and the actual deficiency, as well as for a continued deficit. Indeed, it must be confessed that we could hardly have had a more unfavorable period than the last two years for the collection of tariff revenue. We can not reasonably hope that our recuperation from this business depression will be sudden, but it has already set in with a promise of acceleration and continuance.

I believe our present tariff law, if allowed a fair opportunity, will in the near future yield a revenue which, with reasonably economical expenditures, will overcome all deficiencies. In the meantime no deficit that has occurred or may occur need excite or disturb us. To meet any such deficit we have in the Treasury in addition to a gold reserve of one hundred millions a surplus of more than $128,000,000 applicable to the payment of the expenses of the Government, and which must, unless expended for that purpose, remain a useless hoard, or, if not extravagantly wasted, must in any event be perverted from the purpose of its exaction from our people. The payment, therefore, of any deficiency in the revenue from this fund is nothing more than its proper and legitimate use. The Government thus applying a surplus fortunately in its Treasury to the payment of expenses not met by its current revenues is not at all to be likened to a man living beyond his income and thus incurring debt or encroaching on his principal.

It is not one of the functions of our Government to accumulate and make additions to a fund not needed for immediate expenditure. With individuals it is the chief object of struggle and effort. The application of an accumulated fund by the Government to the payment of its running expenses is a duty. An individual living beyond his income and embarrassing himself with debt or drawing upon his accumulated fund of principal is either unfortunate or improvident. The distinction is between a government charged with the duty of expending for the benefit of the people and for proper purposes all the money it receives from any source, and the individual, who is expected to manifest a natural desire to avoid debt or to accumulate as much as possible and to live within the income derived from such accumulations, to the end that they may be increased or at least remain unimpaired for the future use and enjoyment of himself or the objects of his love and affection who may survive him.

It is immeasurably better to appropriate our surplus to the payment of justifiable expenses than to allow it to become an invitation to reckless appropriations and extravagant expenditures.

I suppose it will not be denied that under the present law our people obtain the necessaries of a comfortable existence at a cheaper rate than formerly. This is a matter of supreme importance, since it is the palpable duty of every just government to make the burdens of taxation as light as possible. The people should not be required to relinquish this privilege of cheaper living except under the stress of their Government's necessity made plainly manifest.

This reference to the condition and prospects of our revenues naturally suggests an allusion to the weakness and vices of our financial methods. They have been frequently pressed upon the attention of Congress in previous Executive communications and the inevitable danger of their continued toleration pointed out. Without now repeating these details, I can not refrain from again earnestly presenting the necessity of the prompt reform of a system opposed to every rule of sound finance and shown by experience to be fraught with the gravest peril and perplexity. The terrible Civil War, which shook the foundations of our Government more than thirty years ago, brought in its train the destruction of property, the wasting of our country's substance, and the estrangement of brethren. These are now past and forgotten. Even the distressing loss of life the conflict entailed is but a sacred memory which fosters patriotic sentiment and keeps alive a tender regard for those who nobly died. And yet there remains with us to-day in full strength and activity, as an incident of that tremendous struggle, a feature of its financial necessities not only unsuited to our present circumstances, but manifestly a disturbing menace to business security and an ever-present agent of monetary distress.

Because we may be enjoying a temporary relief from its depressing influence, this should not lull us into a false security nor lead us to forget the suddenness of past visitations.

I am more convinced than ever that we can have no assured financial peace and safety until the Government currency obligations upon which gold may be demanded from the Treasury are withdrawn from circulation and canceled. This might be done, as has been heretofore recommended, by their exchange for long-term bonds bearing a low rate of interest or by their redemption with the proceeds of such bonds. Even if only the United States notes known as greenbacks were thus retired it is probable that the Treasury notes issued in payment of silver purchases under the act of July 14, 1890, now paid in gold when demanded, would not create much disturbance, as they might from time to time, when received in the Treasury by redemption in gold or otherwise, be gradually and prudently replaced by silver coin.

This plan of issuing bonds for the purpose of redemption certainly appears to be the most effective and direct path to the needed reform. In default of this, however, it would be a step in the right direction if currency obligations redeemable in gold whenever so redeemed should be canceled instead of being reissued. This operation would be a slow remedy, but it would improve present conditions.

National banks should redeem their own notes. They should be allowed to issue circulation to the par value of bonds deposited as security for its redemption and the tax on their circulation should be reduced to one-fourth of 1 per cent.

In considering projects for the retirement of United States notes and Treasury notes issued under the law of 1890, I am of the opinion that we have placed too much stress upon the danger of contracting the currency and have calculated too little upon the gold that would be added to our circulation if invited to us by better and safer financial methods. It is not so much a contraction of our currency that should be avoided as its unequal distribution.

This might be obviated and any fear of harmful contraction at the same time removed by allowing the organization of smaller banks and in less populous communities than are now permitted, and also authorizing existing banks to establish branches in small communities under proper restrictions.

The entire case may be presented by the statement that the day of sensible and sound financial methods will not dawn upon us until our Government abandons the banking business and the accumulation of funds and confines its monetary operations to the receipt of the money contributed by the people for its support and to the expenditure of such money for the people's benefit.

Our business interests and all good citizens long for rest from feverish agitation and the inauguration by the Government of a reformed financial policy which will encourage enterprise and make certain the rewards of labor and industry.

Another topic in which our people rightfully take a deep interest may be here briefly considered. I refer to the existence of trusts and other huge aggregations of capital the object of which is to secure the monopoly of some particular branch of trade, industry, or commerce and to stifle wholesome competition. When these are defended, it is usually on the ground that though they increase profits they also reduce prices, and thus may benefit the public. It must be remembered, however, that a reduction of prices to the people is not one of the real objects of these organizations, nor is their tendency necessarily in that direction. If it occurs in a particular case it is only because it accords with the purposes or interests of those managing the scheme.

Such occasional results fall far short of compensating the palpable evils charged to the account of trusts and monopolies. Their tendency is to crush out individual independence and to hinder or prevent the free use of human faculties and the full development of human character. Through them the farmer, the artisan, and the small trader is in danger of dislodgment from the proud position of being his own master, watchful of all that touches his country's prosperity, in which he has an individual lot, and interested in all that affects the advantages of business of which he is a factor, to be relegated to the level of a mere appurtenance to a great machine, with little hope or opportunity of rising in the scale of responsible and helpful citizenship.

To the instinctive belief that such is the inevitable trend of trusts and monopolies is due the widespread and deep-seated popular aversion in which they are held and the not unreasonable insistence that, whatever may be their incidental economic advantages, their general effect upon personal character, prospects, and usefulness can not be otherwise than injurious.

Though Congress has attempted to deal with this matter by legislation, the laws passed for that purpose thus far have proved ineffective, not because of any lack of disposition or attempt to enforce them, but simply because the laws themselves as interpreted by the courts do not reach the difficulty. If the insufficiencies of existing laws can be remedied by further legislation, it should be done. The fact must be recognized, however, that all Federal legislation on this subject may fall short of its purpose because of inherent obstacles and also because of the complex character of our governmental system, which, while making the Federal authority supreme within its sphere, has carefully limited that sphere by metes and bounds that can not be transgressed. The decision of our highest court on this precise question renders it quite doubtful whether the evils of trusts and monopolies can be adequately treated through Federal action unless they seek directly and purposely to include in their objects transportation or intercourse between States or between the United States and foreign countries.

It does not follow, however, that this is the limit of the remedy that may be applied. Even though it may be found that Federal authority is not broad enough to fully reach the case, there can be no doubt of the power of the several States to act effectively in the premises, and there should be no reason to doubt their willingness to judiciously exercise such power.

In concluding this communication its last words shall be an appeal to the Congress for the most rigid economy in the expenditure of the money it holds in trust for the people. The way to perplexing extravagance is easy, but a return to frugality is difficult. When, however, it is considered that those who bear the burdens of taxation have no guaranty of honest care save in the fidelity of their public servants, the duty of all possible retrenchment is plainly manifest.

When our differences are forgotten and our contests of political opinion are no longer remembered, nothing in the retrospect of our public service will be as fortunate and comforting as the recollection of official duty well performed and the memory of a constant devotion to the interests of our confiding fellow-countrymen.

GROVER CLEVELAND

2 2

Theodore Roosevelt (1901–1909)

Theodore Roosevelt was an accomplished orator. But his last annual message continued a tradition that had begun with Thomas Jefferson—that of giving the annual message in writing rather than in speech. TR was comfortable with that tradition. A prolific writer himself, TR had authored more than a dozen books before becoming president. Remarkable achievements for a forty-two-year-old.

TR had been president for more than seven years when he composed his eighth and final annual message. The missive began in a disarmingly dry manner—with finances. There is nothing to prepare the reader for what is coming. By the fifth paragraph, he embarked on one of the fieriest and most philosophical writings that a U.S. president ever transmitted to Capitol Hill. For sheer energy in debate over the nation's political economy, this final annual message should be read.

It is precisely because of its philosophical content that the message can also be profitably juxtaposed to Grover Cleveland's 1888 final annual message. Cleveland and Roosevelt knew each other from the days when Cleveland was governor of the Empire State and TR was a member of the New York Assembly. Even though one was a Democrat and the other a Republican, they formed a remarkable political alliance. In fact, during their years in Albany together they were nicknamed "The Big One and the Dude"—Cleveland being "The Big One" and TR being "The Dude."[1]

Note especially TR's effort to redefine conservatism away from a Spencerian and toward a Burkean understanding—thus: "A blind and ignorant resistance to every effort for the reform of abuses and for the readjustment of society to modern industrial conditions represents not true conservatism, but an incitement to the wildest radicalism; for wise radicalism and wise conservatism go hand in hand, one bent on progress, the other bent on seeing that no change is made unless in the right direction."

Also:

It is hard to say whether most damage to the country at large would come from entire failure on the part of the public to supervise and control the actions of the great corporations, or from the exercise of the necessary governmental power in a way which would do injustice and wrong to the corporations. Both the preachers of an unrestricted individualism, and the preachers of an oppression which would deny to able men of business the just reward of their initiative and business sagacity, are advocating policies that would be fraught with the gravest harm to the whole country.

And finally this pithy observation: "It is well to keep in mind that exactly as the anarchist is the worst enemy of liberty and the reactionary the worst enemy of order, so the men who defend the rights of property have most to fear from the wrongdoers of great wealth, and the men who are championing popular rights have most to fear from the demagogues who in the name of popular rights would do wrong to and oppress honest business men, honest men of wealth."

TR did much to concentrate power in the office of the president. The eighth annual message reflects all the restless energy for which he became famous. Its arguments also reveal a first-class intellect that was determined to win the arguments of the day.

Eighth Annual Message
(written to the Congress)
December 8, 1908

To the Senate and House of Representatives:

Finances

The financial standing of the Nation at the present time is excellent, and the financial management of the Nation's interests by the Government during the last seven years has shown the most satisfactory results. But our currency system is imperfect, and it is earnestly to be hoped that the Currency Commission will be able to propose a thoroughly good system which will do away with the existing defects.

During the period from July 1, 1901, to September 30, 1908, there was an increase in the amount of money in circulation of $902,991,399. The increase in the per capita during this period was $7.06. Within this time there were several occasions when it was necessary for the Treasury Department to come to the relief of the money market by purchases or redemptions of United States bonds; by increasing deposits in national banks; by stimulating additional issues of national bank notes, and by facilitating importations from abroad of gold. Our imperfect currency system has made these proceedings necessary, and they were effective until the monetary disturbance in the fall of 1907 immensely increased the difficulty of ordinary methods of relief. By the middle of November the available working balance in the Treasury had been reduced to approximately $5,000,000. Clearing house associations throughout the country had been obliged to resort to the expedient of issuing clearing house certificates, to be used as money. In this emergency it was determined to invite subscriptions for $50,000,000 Panama Canal bonds, and $100,000,000 three per cent certificates of indebtedness authorized by the act of June 13, 1898. It was proposed to re-deposit in the national banks the proceeds of these issues, and to permit their use as a basis for additional circulating notes of national banks. The moral effect of this procedure was so great that it was necessary to issue only $24,631,980 of the Panama Canal bonds and $15,436,500 of the certificates of indebtedness.

During the period from July 1, 1901, to September 30, 1908, the balance between the net ordinary receipts and the net ordinary expenses of the Government showed a surplus in the four years 1902, 1903, 1906 and 1907, and a deficit in the years 1904, 1905, 1908 and a fractional part of the fiscal year 1909. The net result was a surplus of $99,283,413.54. The financial operations of the Government during this period, based upon these differences between receipts and expenditures, resulted in a net reduction of the interest-bearing debt of the United States from $987,141,040 to $897,253,990, notwithstanding that there had been two sales of Panama Canal bonds amounting in the aggregate to

$54,631,980, and an issue of three per cent certificates of indebtedness under the act of June 13, 1898, amounting to $15,436,500. Refunding operations of the Treasury Department under the act of March 14, 1900, resulted in the conversion into two per cent consols of 1930 of $200,309,400 bonds bearing higher rates of interest. A decrease of $8,687,956 in the annual interest charge resulted from these operations.

In short, during the seven years and three months there has been a net surplus of nearly one hundred millions of receipts over expenditures, a reduction of the interest-bearing debt by ninety millions, in spite of the extraordinary expense of the Panama Canal, and a saving of nearly nine millions on the annual interest charge. This is an exceedingly satisfactory showing, especially in view of the fact that during this period the Nation has never hesitated to undertake any expenditure that it regarded as necessary. There have been no new taxes and no increase of taxes; on the contrary, some taxes have been taken off; there has been a reduction of taxation.

Corporations

As regards the great corporations engaged in interstate business, and especially the railroad, I can only repeat what I have already again and again said in my messages to the Congress, I believe that under the interstate clause of the Constitution the United States has complete and paramount right to control all agencies of interstate commerce, and I believe that the National Government alone can exercise this right with wisdom and effectiveness so as both to secure justice from, and to do justice to, the great corporations which are the most important factors in modern business. I believe that it is worse than folly to attempt to prohibit all combinations as is done by the Sherman anti-trust law, because such a law can be enforced only imperfectly and unequally, and its enforcement works almost as much hardship as good. I strongly advocate that instead of an unwise effort to prohibit all combinations there shall be substituted a law which shall expressly permit combinations which are in the interest of the public, but shall at the same time give to some agency of the National Government full power of control and supervision over them. One of the chief features of this control should be securing entire publicity in all matters which the public has a right to know, and furthermore, the power, not by judicial but by executive action, to prevent or put a stop to every form of improper favoritism or other wrongdoing.

The railways of the country should be put completely under the Interstate Commerce Commission and removed from the domain of the anti-trust law. The power of the Commission should be made thoroughgoing, so that it could exercise complete supervision and control over the issue of securities as well as over the raising and lowering of rates. As regards rates, at least, this power should be summary. The power to investigate the financial operations and accounts of the railways has been one of the most valuable features in recent legislation. Power to make combinations and traffic agreements should be explicitly conferred upon the railroads, the permission of the Commission being first gained and the combination or agreement being published in all its details. In the interest of the public the representatives of the public should have complete power to see that the railroads do their duty by the public, and as a matter of course this power should also be exercised so as to see that no injustice is done to the railroads. The shareholders, the employees and the shippers all have interests that must be guarded. It is to the interest of all of them that no swindling stock speculation should be allowed, and that there should be no improper issuance of securities. The guiding intelligences necessary for the successful building and successful management of railroads should receive ample remuneration; but no man should be allowed to make money in connection with railroads out of fraudulent overcapitalization and kindred stock-gambling performances; there must be no defrauding of investors, oppression of the farmers and business men who ship freight, or callous disregard of the rights and needs of the employees. In addition to this the interests of the shareholders, of the employees, and of the shippers should all be guarded as against one another. To give any one of them undue and improper consideration is to do injustice to the others. Rates must be made as low as is compatible with giving proper returns to all the employees of the railroad, from the highest to the lowest, and proper returns to the shareholders; but they must not, for instance, be reduced in such fashion as to necessitate a cut in the wages of the employees or the abolition of the proper and legitimate profits of honest share-holders.

Telegraph and telephone companies engaged in interstate business should be put under the juris-diction of the Interstate Commerce Commission.

It is very earnestly to be wished that our people, through their representatives, should act in this matter. It is hard to say whether most damage to the country at large would come from entire failure on the part of the public to supervise and control the actions of the great corporations, or from the exercise of the necessary governmental power in a way which would do injustice and wrong to the corporations. Both the preachers of an unrestricted individualism, and the preachers of an oppres-sion which would deny to able men of business the just reward of their initiative and business sagac-ity, are advocating policies that would be fraught with the gravest harm to the whole country. To per-mit every lawless capitalist, every law-defying corporation, to take any action, no matter how iniquitous, in the effort to secure an improper profit and to build up privilege, would be ruinous to the Republic and would mark the abandonment of the effort to secure in the industrial world the spirit of democratic fair dealing. On the other hand, to attack these wrongs in that spirit of dema-gogy which can see wrong only when committed by the man of wealth, and is dumb and blind in the presence of wrong committed against men of property or by men of no property, is exactly as evil as corruptly to defend the wrongdoing of men of wealth. The war we wage must be waged against mis-conduct, against wrongdoing wherever it is found; and we must stand heartily for the rights of every decent man, whether he be a man of great wealth or a man who earns his livelihood as a wage-worker or a tiller of the soil.

It is to the interest of all of us that there should be a premium put upon individual initiative and in-dividual capacity, and an ample reward for the great directing intelligences alone competent to man-age the great business operations of to-day. It is well to keep in mind that exactly as the anarchist is the worst enemy of liberty and the reactionary the worst enemy of order, so the men who defend the rights of property have most to fear from the wrongdoers of great wealth, and the men who are championing popular rights have most to fear from the demagogues who in the name of popular rights would do wrong to and oppress honest business men, honest men of wealth; for the success of either type of wrongdoer necessarily invites a violent reaction against the cause the wrongdoer nominally upholds. In point of danger to the Nation there is nothing to choose between on the one hand the corruption-ist, the bribe-giver, the bribe-taker, the man who employs his great talent to swindle his fellow-citizens on a large scale, and, on the other hand, the preacher of class hatred, the man who, whether from ig-norance or from willingness to sacrifice his country to his ambition, persuades well-meaning but wrong-headed men to try to destroy the instruments upon which our prosperity mainly rests. Let each group of men beware of and guard against the shortcomings to which that group is itself most liable. Too of-ten we see the business community in a spirit of unhealthy class consciousness deplore the effort to hold to account under the law the wealthy men who in their management of great corporations, whether railroads, street railways, or other industrial enterprises, have behaved in a way that revolts the con-science of the plain, decent people. Such an attitude can not be condemned too severely, for men of property should recognize that they jeopardize the rights of property when they fail heartily to join in the effort to do away with the abuses of wealth. On the other hand, those who advocate proper con-trol on behalf of the public, through the State, of these great corporations, and of the wealth engaged on a giant scale in business operations, must ever keep in mind that unless they do scrupulous justice to the corporation, unless they permit ample profit, and cordially encourage capable men of business so long as they act with honesty, they are striking at the root of our national well-being; for in the long run, under the mere pressure of material distress, the people as a whole would probably go back to the reign of an unrestricted individualism rather than submit to a control by the State so drastic and so foolish, conceived in a spirit of such unreasonable and narrow hostility to wealth, as to prevent business operations from being profitable, and therefore to bring ruin upon the entire business community, and ultimately upon the entire body of citizens.

The opposition to Government control of these great corporations makes its most effective effort in the shape of an appeal to the old doctrine of State's rights. Of course there are many sincere men who now believe in unrestricted individualism in business, just as there were formerly many sincere men who believed in slavery—that is, in the unrestricted right of an individual to own another individual. These men do not by themselves have great weight, however. The effective fight against adequate Government control and supervision of individual, and especially of corporate, wealth engaged in interstate business is chiefly done under cover; and especially under cover of an appeal to State's rights. It is not at all infrequent to read in the same speech a denunciation of predatory wealth fostered by special privilege and defiant of both the public welfare and law of the land, and a denunciation of centralization in the Central Government of the power to deal with this centralized and organized wealth. Of course the policy set forth in such twin denunciations amounts to absolutely nothing, for the first half is nullified by the second half. The chief reason, among the many sound and compelling reasons, that led to the formation of the National Government was the absolute need that the Union, and not the several States, should deal with interstate and foreign commerce; and the power to deal with interstate commerce was granted absolutely and plenarily to the Central Government and was exercised completely as regards the only instruments of interstate commerce known in those days—the waterways, the highroads, as well as the partnerships of individuals who then conducted all of what business there was. Interstate commerce is now chiefly conducted by railroads; and the great corporation has supplanted the mass of small partnerships or individuals. The proposal to make the National Government supreme over, and therefore to give it complete control over, the railroads and other instruments of interstate commerce is merely a proposal to carry out to the letter one of the prime purposes, if not the prime purpose, for which the Constitution was founded. It does not represent centralization. It represents merely the acknowledgment of the patent fact that centralization has already come in business. If this irresponsible outside business power is to be controlled in the interest of the general public it can only be controlled in one way—by giving adequate power of control to the one sovereignty capable of exercising such power—the National Government. Forty or fifty separate state governments can not exercise that power over corporations doing business in most or all of them; first, because they absolutely lack the authority to deal with interstate business in any form; and second, because of the inevitable conflict of authority sure to arise in the effort to enforce different kinds of state regulation, often inconsistent with one another and sometimes oppressive in themselves. Such divided authority can not regulate commerce with wisdom and effect. The Central Government is the only power which, without oppression, can nevertheless thoroughly and adequately control and supervise the large corporations. To abandon the effort for National control means to abandon the effort for all adequate control and yet to render likely continual bursts of action by State legislatures, which can not achieve the purpose sought for, but which can do a great deal of damage to the corporation without conferring any real benefit on the public.

I believe that the more farsighted corporations are themselves coming to recognize the unwisdom of the violent hostility they have displayed during the last few years to regulation and control by the National Government of combinations engaged in interstate business. The truth is that we who believe in this movement of asserting and exercising a genuine control, in the public interest, over these great corporations have to contend against two sets of enemies, who, though nominally opposed to one another, are really allies in preventing a proper solution of the problem. There are, first, the big corporation men, and the extreme individualists among business men, who genuinely believe in utterly unregulated business—that is, in the reign of plutocracy; and, second, the men who, being blind to the economic movements of the day, believe in a movement of repression rather than of regulation of corporations, and who denounce both the power of the railroads and the exercise of the Federal power which alone can really control the railroads. Those who believe in efficient national control, on the other hand, do not in the least object to combinations; do not in the least object to concentration in business administration. On the contrary, they favor both, with the all important proviso that there shall be such publicity about their workings, and such thoroughgoing control over them, as to insure their being in the interest, and not against the interest, of the general public. We do not object to the concentration of wealth and administration; but we do believe in the distribution of the wealth in profits to the real owners, and in securing to the public the full benefit of the concentrated administration. We believe that with concentration in administration there can come both the advantage of a larger ownership and of a more equitable distribution of profits, and at the same time a better service to the commonwealth. We believe that the administration should be for the benefit of the many; and that greed and rascality, practiced on a large scale, should be punished as relentlessly as if practiced on a small scale.

We do not for a moment believe that the problem will be solved by any short and easy method. The solution will come only by pressing various concurrent remedies. Some of these remedies must lie outside the domain of all government. Some must lie outside the domain of the Federal Government. But there is legislation which the Federal Government alone can enact and which is absolutely vital in order to secure the attainment of our purpose. Many laws are needed. There should be regulation by the National Government of the great interstate corporations, including a simple method of account keeping, publicity, supervision of the issue securities, abolition of rebates, and of special privileges. There should be short time franchises for all corporations engaged in public business; including the corporations which get power from water rights. There should be National as well as State guardianship of mines and forests. The labor legislation hereinafter referred to should concurrently be enacted into law.

To accomplish this, means of course a certain increase in the use of—not the creation of—power, by the Central Government. The power already exists; it does not have to be created; the only question is whether it shall be used or left idle—and meanwhile the corporations over which the power ought to be exercised will not remain idle. Let those who object to this increase in the use of the only power available, the national power, be frank, and admit openly that they propose to abandon any effort to control the great business corporations and to exercise supervision over the accumulation and distribution of wealth; for such supervision and control can only come through this particular kind of increase of power. We no more believe in that empiricism which demands absolutely unrestrained individualism than we do in that empiricism which clamors for a deadening socialism which would destroy all individual initiative and would ruin the country with a completeness that not even an unrestrained individualism itself could achieve. The danger to American democracy lies not in the least in the concentration of administrative power in responsible and accountable hands. It lies in having the power insufficiently concentrated, so that no one can be held responsible to the people for its use. Concentrated power is palpable, visible, responsible, easily reached, quickly held to account. Power scattered through many administrators, many legislators, many men who work behind and through legislators and administrators, is impalpable, is unseen, is irresponsible, can not be reached, can not be held to account. Democracy is in peril wherever the administration of political power is scattered among a variety of men who work in secret, whose very names are unknown to the common people. It is not in peril from any man who derives authority from the people, who exercises it in sight of the people, and who is from time to time compelled to give an account of its exercise to the people.

Labor

There are many matters affecting labor and the status of the wage-worker to which I should like to draw your attention, but an exhaustive discussion of the problem in all its aspects is not now necessary. This administration is nearing its end; and, moreover, under our form of government the solution of the problem depends upon the action of the States as much as upon the action of the Nation.

Nevertheless, there are certain considerations which I wish to set before you, because I hope that our people will more and more keep them in mind. A blind and ignorant resistance to every effort for the reform of abuses and for the readjustment of society to modern industrial conditions represents not true conservatism, but an incitement to the wildest radicalism; for wise radicalism and wise conservatism go hand in hand, one bent on progress, the other bent on seeing that no change is made unless in the right direction. I believe in a steady effort, or perhaps it would be more accurate to say in steady efforts in many different directions, to bring about a condition of affairs under which the men who work with hand or with brain, the laborers, the superintendents, the men who produce for the market and the men who find a market for the articles produced, shall own a far greater share than at present of the wealth they produce, and be enabled to invest it in the tools and instruments by which all work is carried on. As far as possible I hope to see a frank recognition of the advantages conferred by machinery, organization, and division of labor, accompanied by an effort to bring about a larger share in the ownership by wage-worker of railway, mill and factory. In farming, this simply means that we wish to see the farmer own his own land; we do not wish to see the farms so large that they become the property of absentee landlords who farm them by tenants, nor yet so small that the farmer becomes like a European peasant. Again, the depositors in our savings banks now number over one-tenth of our entire population. These are all capitalists, who through the savings banks loan their money to the workers—that is, in many cases to themselves—to carry on their various industries. The more we increase their number, the more we introduce the principles of cooperation into our industry. Every increase in the number of small stockholders in corporations is a good thing, for the same reasons; and where the employees are the stockholders the result is particularly good. Very much of this movement must be outside of anything that can be accomplished by legislation; but legislation can do a good deal. Postal savings banks will make it easy for the poorest to keep their savings in absolute safety. The regulation of the national highways must be such that they shall serve all people with equal justice. Corporate finances must be supervised so as to make it far safer than at present for the man of small means to invest his money in stocks. There must be prohibition of child labor, diminution of woman labor, shortening of hours of all mechanical labor; stock watering should be prohibited, and stock gambling so far as is possible discouraged. There should be a progressive inheritance tax on large fortunes. Industrial education should be encouraged. As far as possible we should lighten the burden of taxation on the small man. We should put a premium upon thrift, hard work, and business energy; but these qualities cease to be the main factors in accumulating a fortune long before that fortune reaches a point where it would be seriously affected by any inheritance tax such as I propose. It is eminently right that the Nation should fix the terms upon which the great fortunes are inherited. They rarely do good and they often do harm to those who inherit them in their entirety.

Protection for Wage-Workers

The above is the merest sketch, hardly even a sketch in outline, of the reforms for which we should work. But there is one matter with which the Congress should deal at this session. There should no longer be any paltering with the question of taking care of the wage-workers who, under our present industrial system, become killed, crippled, or worn out as part of the regular incidents of a given business. The majority of wageworkers must have their rights secured for them by State action; but the National Government should legislate in thoroughgoing and far-reaching fashion not only for all employees of the National Government, but for all persons engaged in interstate commerce. The object sought for could be achieved to a measurable degree, as far as those killed or crippled are concerned, by proper employers' liability laws. As far as concerns those who have been worn out, I call your attention to the fact that definite steps toward providing old-age pensions have been taken in many of our private industries. These may be indefinitely extended through voluntary association and contributory schemes, or through the agency of savings banks, as under the recent Massachusetts plan. To strengthen these practical measures should be our immediate duty; it is not at present necessary to consider the larger and more general governmental schemes that most European governments have found themselves obliged to adopt.

Our present system, or rather no system, works dreadful wrong, and is of benefit to only one class of people—the lawyers. When a workman is injured what he needs is not an expensive and doubtful lawsuit, but the certainty of relief through immediate administrative action. The number of accidents which result in the death or crippling of wage-workers, in the Union at large, is simply appalling; in a very few years it runs up a total far in excess of the aggregate of the dead and wounded in any modern war. No academic theory about "freedom of contract" or "constitutional liberty to contract" should be permitted to interfere with this and similar movements. Progress in civilization has everywhere meant a limitation and regulation of contract. I call your especial attention to the bulletin of the Bureau of Labor which gives a statement of the methods of treating the unemployed in European countries, as this is a subject which in Germany, for instance, is treated in connection with making provision for worn-out and crippled workmen.

Pending a thoroughgoing investigation and action there is certain legislation which should be enacted at once. The law, passed at the last session of the Congress, granting compensation to certain classes of employees of the Government, should be extended to include all employees of the Government and should be made more liberal in its terms. There is no good ground for the distinction made in the law between those engaged in hazardous occupations and those not so engaged. If a man is injured or killed in any line of work, it was hazardous in his case. Whether 1 per cent or 10 per cent of those following a given occupation actually suffer injury or death ought not to have any bearing on the question of their receiving compensation. It is a grim logic which says to an injured employee or to the dependents of one killed that he or they are entitled to no compensation because very few people other than he have been injured or killed in that occupation. Perhaps one of the most striking omissions in the law is that it does not embrace peace officers and others whose lives may be sacrificed in enforcing the laws of the United States. The terms of the act providing compensation should be made more liberal than in the present act. A year's compensation is not adequate for a wage-earner's family in the event of his death by accident in the course of his employment. And in the event of death occurring, say, ten or eleven months after the accident, the family would only receive as compensation the equivalent of one or two months' earnings. In this respect the generosity of the United States towards its employees compares most unfavorably with that of every country in Europe—even the poorest.

The terms of the act are also a hardship in prohibiting payment in cases where the accident is in any way due to the negligence of the employee. It is inevitable that daily familiarity with danger will lead men to take chances that can be construed into negligence. So well is this recognized that in practically all countries in the civilized world, except the United States, only a great degree of negligence acts as a bar to securing compensation. Probably in no other respect is our legislation, both State and National, so far behind practically the entire civilized world as in the matter of liability and compensation for accidents in industry. It is humiliating that at European international congresses on accidents the United States should be singled out as the most belated among the nations in respect to employers' liability legislation. This Government is itself a large employer of labor, and in its dealings with its employees it should set a standard in this country which would place it on a par with the most progressive countries in Europe. The laws of the United States in this respect and the laws of European countries have been summarized in a recent Bulletin of the Bureau of Labor, and no American who reads this summary can fail to be struck by the great contrast between our practices and theirs—a contrast not in any sense to our credit.

The Congress should without further delay pass a model employers' liability law for the District of Columbia. The employers' liability act recently declared unconstitutional, on account of apparently including in its provisions employees engaged in intrastate commerce as well as those engaged in interstate commerce, has been held by the local courts to be still in effect so far as its provisions apply to the District of Columbia. There should be no ambiguity on this point. If there is any doubt on the subject, the law should be reenacted with special reference to the District of Columbia. This act, how-ever, applies only to employees of common carriers. In all other occupations the liability law of the District is the old common law. The severity and injustice of the common law in this matter has been in some degree or another modified in the majority of our States, and the only jurisdiction under the exclusive control of the Congress should be ahead and not behind the States of the Union in this re-spect. A comprehensive employers' liability law should be passed for the District of Columbia.

I renew my recommendation made in a previous message that half-holidays be granted during sum-mer to all wageworkers in Government employ.

I also renew my recommendation that the principle of the eight-hour day should as rapidly and as far as practicable be extended to the entire work being carried on by the Government; the present law should be amended to embrace contracts on those public works which the present wording of the act seems to exclude.

The Courts

I most earnestly urge upon the Congress the duty of increasing the totally inadequate salaries now given to our Judges. On the whole there is no body of public servants who do as valuable work, nor whose moneyed reward is so inadequate compared to their work. Beginning with the Supreme Court, the Judges should have their salaries doubled. It is not befitting the dignity of the Nation that its most honored public servants should be paid sums so small compared to what they would earn in private life that the performance of public service by them implies an exceedingly heavy pecuniary sacrifice.

It is earnestly to be desired that some method should be devised for doing away with the long de-lays which now obtain in the administration of justice, and which operate with peculiar severity against persons of small means, and favor only the very criminals whom it is most desirable to punish. These long delays in the final decisions of cases make in the aggregate a crying evil; and a remedy should be devised. Much of this intolerable delay is due to improper regard paid to technicalities which are a mere hindrance to justice. In some noted recent cases this over-regard for technicalities has resulted in a striking denial of justice, and flagrant wrong to the body politic.

At the last election certain leaders of organized labor made a violent and sweeping attack upon the entire judiciary of the country, an attack couched in such terms as to include the most upright, hon-est and broad-minded judges, no less than those of narrower mind and more restricted outlook. It was the kind of attack admirably fitted to prevent any successful attempt to reform abuses of the judiciary, because it gave the champions of the unjust judge their eagerly desired opportunity to shift their ground into a championship of just judges who were unjustly assailed. Last year, before the House Committee on the Judiciary, these same labor leaders formulated their demands, specifying the bill that contained them, refusing all compromise, stating they wished the principle of that bill or noth-ing. They insisted on a provision that in a labor dispute no injunction should issue except to protect a property right, and specifically provided that the right to carry on business should not be construed as a property right; and in a second provision their bill made legal in a labor dispute any act or agree-ment by or between two or more persons that would not have been unlawful if done by a single per-son. In other words, this bill legalized blacklisting and boycotting in every form, legalizing, for in-stance, those forms of the secondary boycott which the anthracite coal strike commission so unreservedly condemned; while the right to carry on a business was explicitly taken out from under that protection which the law throws over property. The demand was made that there should be trial by jury in contempt cases, thereby most seriously impairing the authority of the courts. All this rep-resented a course of policy which, if carried out, would mean the enthronement of class privilege in its crudest and most brutal form, and the destruction of one of the most essential functions of the ju-diciary in all civilized lands.

The violence of the crusade for this legislation, and its complete failure, illustrate two truths which it is essential our people should learn. In the first place, they ought to teach the workingman, the laborer, the wageworker, that by demanding what is improper and impossible he plays into the hands of his foes. Such a crude and vicious attack upon the courts, even if it were temporarily successful, would inevitably in the end cause a violent reaction and would band the great mass of citizens together, forcing them to stand by all the judges, competent and incompetent alike, rather than to see the wheels of justice stopped. A movement of this kind can ultimately result in nothing but damage to those in whose behalf it is nominally undertaken. This is a most healthy truth, which it is wise for all our people to learn. Any movement based on that class hatred which at times assumes the name of "class consciousness" is certain ultimately to fail, and if it temporarily succeeds, to do far-reaching damage. "Class consciousness," where it is merely another name for the odious vice of class selfishness, is equally noxious whether in an employer's association or in a workingman's association. The movement in question was one in which the appeal was made to all workingmen to vote primarily, not as American citizens, but as individuals of a certain class in society. Such an appeal in the first place revolts the more high-minded and far-sighted among the persons to whom it is addressed, and in the second place tends to arouse a strong antagonism among all other classes of citizens, whom it therefore tends to unite against the very organization on whose behalf it is issued. The result is therefore unfortunate from every standpoint. This healthy truth, by the way, will be learned by the socialists if they ever succeed in establishing in this country an important national party based on such class consciousness and selfish class interest.

The wageworkers, the workingmen, the laboring men of the country, by the way in which they repudiated the effort to get them to cast their votes in response to an appeal to class hatred, have emphasized their sound patriotism and Americanism. The whole country has cause to feel pride in this attitude of sturdy independence, in this uncompromising insistence upon acting simply as good citizens, as good Americans, without regard to fancied—and improper—class interests. Such an attitude is an object-lesson in good citizenship to the entire nation.

But the extreme reactionaries, the persons who blind themselves to the wrongs now and then committed by the courts on laboring men, should also think seriously as to what such a movement as this portends. The judges who have shown themselves able and willing effectively to check the dishonest activity of the very rich man who works iniquity by the mismanagement of corporations, who have shown themselves alert to do justice to the wageworker, and sympathetic with the needs of the mass of our people, so that the dweller in the tenement houses, the man who practices a dangerous trade, the man who is crushed by excessive hours of labor, feel that their needs are understood by the courts—these judges are the real bulwark of the courts; these judges, the judges of the stamp of the President-elect, who have been fearless in opposing labor when it has gone wrong, but fearless also in holding to strict account corporations that work iniquity, and far-sighted in seeing that the workingman gets his rights, are the men of all others to whom we owe it that the appeal for such violent and mistaken legislation has fallen on deaf ears, that the agitation for its passage proved to be without substantial basis. The courts are jeopardized primarily by the action of those Federal and State judges who show inability or unwillingness to put a stop to the wrongdoing of very rich men under modern industrial conditions, and inability or unwillingness to give relief to men of small means or wageworkers who are crushed down by these modern industrial conditions; who, in other words, fail to understand and apply the needed remedies for the new wrongs produced by the new and highly complex social and industrial civilization which has grown up in the last half century.

The rapid changes in our social and industrial life which have attended this rapid growth have made it necessary that, in applying to concrete cases the great rule of right laid down in our Constitution, there should be a full understanding and appreciation of the new conditions to which the rules are to be applied. What would have been an infringement upon liberty half a century ago may be the necessary safeguard of liberty to-day. What would have been an injury to property then may be necessary to the enjoyment of property now. Every judicial decision involves two terms—one, as interpretation of the law; the other, the understanding of the facts to which it is to be applied. The great mass of our judicial officers are, I believe, alive to those changes of conditions which so materially affect the performance of their judicial duties. Our judicial system is sound and effective at core, and it remains, and must ever be maintained, as the safeguard of those principles of liberty and justice which stand at the foundation of American institutions; for, as Burke finely said, when liberty and justice are separated, neither is safe. There are, however, some members of the judicial body who have lagged behind in their understanding of these great and vital changes in the body politic, whose minds have never been opened to the new applications of the old principles made necessary by the new conditions. Judges of this stamp do lasting harm by their decisions, because they convince poor men in need of protection that the courts of the land are profoundly ignorant of and out of sympathy with their needs, and profoundly indifferent or hostile to any proposed remedy. To such men it seems a cruel mockery to have any court decide against them on the ground that it desires to preserve "liberty" in a purely technical form, by withholding liberty in any real and constructive sense. It is desirable that the legislative body should possess, and wherever necessary exercise, the power to determine whether in a given case employers and employees are not on an equal footing, so that the necessities of the latter compel them to submit to such exactions as to hours and conditions of labor as unduly to tax their strength; and only mischief can result when such determination is upset on the ground that there must be no "interference with the liberty to contract"—often a merely academic "liberty," the exercise of which is the negation of real liberty.

There are certain decisions by various courts which have been exceedingly detrimental to the rights of wageworkers. This is true of all the decisions that decide that men and women are, by the Constitution, "guaranteed their liberty" to contract to enter a dangerous occupation, or to work an undesirable or improper number of hours, or to work in unhealthy surroundings; and therefore can not recover damages when maimed in that occupation and can not be forbidden to work what the legislature decides is an excessive number of hours, or to carry on the work under conditions which the legislature decides to be unhealthy. The most dangerous occupations are often the poorest paid and those where the hours of work are longest; and in many cases those who go into them are driven by necessity so great that they have practically no alternative. Decisions such as those alluded to above nullify the legislative effort to protect the wage-workers who most need protection from those employers who take advantage of their grinding need. They halt or hamper the movement for securing better and more equitable conditions of labor. The talk about preserving to the misery-hunted beings who make contracts for such service their "liberty" to make them, is either to speak in a spirit of heartless irony or else to show an utter lack of knowledge of the conditions of life among the great masses of our fellow-countrymen, a lack which unfits a judge to do good service just as it would unfit any executive or legislative officer.

There is also, I think, ground for the belief that substantial injustice is often suffered by employees in consequence of the custom of courts issuing temporary injunctions without notice to them, and punishing them for contempt of court in instances where, as a matter of fact, they have no knowledge of any proceedings. Outside of organized labor there is a widespread feeling that this system often works great injustice to wageworkers when their efforts to better their working condition result in industrial disputes. A temporary injunction procured ex parte may as a matter of fact have all the effect of a permanent injunction in causing disaster to the wageworkers' side in such a dispute. Organized labor is chafing under the unjust restraint which comes from repeated resort to this plan of procedure. Its discontent has been unwisely expressed, and often improperly expressed, but there is a sound basis for it, and the orderly and law-abiding people of a community would be in a far stronger position for upholding the courts if the undoubtedly existing abuses could be provided against.

Such proposals as those mentioned above as advocated by the extreme labor leaders contain the vital error of being class legislation of the most offensive kind, and even if enacted into law I believe that the law would rightly be held unconstitutional. Moreover, the labor people are themselves now beginning to invoke the use of the power of injunction. During the last ten years, and within my own knowledge, at least fifty injunctions have been obtained by labor unions in New York City alone, most of them being to protect the union label (a "property right"), but some being obtained for other reasons against employers. The power of injunction is a great equitable remedy, which should on no account be destroyed. But safeguards should be erected against its abuse. I believe that some such provisions as those I advocated a year ago for checking the abuse of the issuance of temporary injunctions should be adopted. In substance, provision should be made that no injunction or temporary restraining order issue otherwise than on notice, except where irreparable injury would otherwise result; and in such case a hearing on the merits of the order should be had within a short fixed period, and, if not then continued after hearing, it should forthwith lapse. Decisions should be rendered immediately, and the chance of delay minimized in every way. Moreover, I believe that the procedure should be sharply defined, and the judge required minutely to state the particulars both of his action and of his reasons therefor, so that the Congress can, if it desires, examine and investigate the same.

The chief lawmakers in our country may be, and often are, the judges, because they are the final seat of authority. Every time they interpret contract, property, vested rights, due process of law, liberty, they necessarily enact into law parts of a system of social philosophy, and as such interpretation is fundamental, they give direction to all law-making. The decisions of the courts on economic and social questions depend upon their economic and social philosophy; and for the peaceful progress of our people during the twentieth century we shall owe most to those judges who hold to a twentieth century economic and social philosophy and not to a long outgrown philosophy, which was itself the product of primitive economic conditions. Of course a judge's views on progressive social philosophy are entirely second in importance to his possession of a high and fine character; which means the possession of such elementary virtues as honesty, courage, and fair-mindedness. The judge who owes his election to pandering to demagogic sentiments or class hatreds and prejudices, and the judge who owes either his election or his appointment to the money or the favor of a great corporation, are alike unworthy to sit on the bench, are alike traitors to the people; and no profundity of legal learning, or correctness of abstract conviction on questions of public policy, can serve as an offset to such shortcomings. But it is also true that judges, like executives and legislators, should hold sound views on the questions of public policy which are of vital interest to the people.

The legislators and executives are chosen to represent the people in enacting and administering the laws. The judges are not chosen to represent the people in this sense. Their function is to interpret the laws. The legislators are responsible for the laws; the judges for the spirit in which they interpret and enforce the laws. We stand aloof from the reckless agitators who would make the judges mere pliant tools of popular prejudice and passion; and we stand aloof from those equally unwise partisans of reaction and privilege who deny the proposition that, inasmuch as judges are chosen to serve the interests of the whole people, they should strive to find out what those interests are, and, so far as they conscientiously can, should strive to give effect to popular conviction when deliberately and duly expressed by the lawmaking body. The courts are to be highly commended and staunchly upheld when they set their faces against wrongdoing or tyranny by a majority; but they are to be blamed when they fail to recognize under a government like ours the deliberate judgment of the majority as to a matter of legitimate policy, when duly expressed by the legislature. Such lawfully expressed and deliberate judgment should be given effect by the courts, save in the extreme and exceptional cases where there has been a clear violation of a constitutional provision. Anything like frivolity or wantonness in upsetting such clearly taken governmental action is a grave offense against the Republic. To protest against tyranny, to protect minorities from oppression, to nullify an act committed in a spasm of popular fury, is to render a service to the Republic. But for the courts to arrogate to themselves functions which properly belong to the legislative bodies is all wrong, and in the end works mischief. The people should not be permitted to pardon evil and slipshod legislation on the theory that the court will set it right; they should be taught that the right way to get rid of a bad law is to have the legislature repeal it, and not to have the courts by ingenious hair-splitting nullify it. A law may be unwise and improper; but it should not for these reasons be declared unconstitutional by a strained interpretation, for the result of such action is to take away from the people at large their sense of responsibility and ultimately to destroy their capacity for orderly self restraint and self government. Under such a popular government as ours, rounded on the theory that in the long run the will of the people is supreme, the ultimate safety of the Nation can only rest in training and guiding the people so that what they will shall be right, and not in devising means to defeat their will by the technicalities of strained construction.

For many of the shortcomings of justice in our country our people as a whole are themselves to blame, and the judges and juries merely bear their share together with the public as a whole. It is discreditable to us as a people that there should be difficulty in convicting murderers, or in bringing to justice men who as public servants have been guilty of corruption, or who have profited by the corruption of public servants. The result is equally unfortunate, whether due to hairsplitting technicalities in the interpretation of law by judges, to sentimentality and class consciousness on the part of juries, or to hysteria and sensationalism in the daily press. For much of this failure of justice no responsibility whatever lies on rich men as such. We who make up the mass of the people can not shift the responsibility from our own shoulders. But there is an important part of the failure which has specially to do with inability to hold to proper account men of wealth who behave badly.

The chief breakdown is in dealing with the new relations that arise from the mutualism, the interdependence of our time. Every new social relation begets a new type of wrongdoing—of sin, to use an old-fashioned word—and many years always elapse before society is able to turn this sin into crime which can be effectively punished at law. During the lifetime of the older men now alive the social relations have changed far more rapidly than in the preceding two centuries. The immense growth of corporations, of business done by associations, and the extreme strain and pressure of modern life, have produced conditions which render the public confused as to who its really dangerous foes are; and among the public servants who have not only shared this confusion, but by some of their acts have increased it, are certain judges. Marked inefficiency has been shown in dealing with corporations and in re-settling the proper attitude to be taken by the public not only towards corporations, but towards labor and towards the social questions arising out of the factory system and the enormous growth of our great cities.

The huge wealth that has been accumulated by a few individuals of recent years, in what has amounted to a social and industrial revolution, has been as regards some of these individuals made possible only by the improper use of the modern corporation. A certain type of modern corporation, with its officers and agents, its many issues of securities, and its constant consolidation with allied undertakings, finally becomes an instrument so complex as to contain a greater number of elements that, under various judicial decisions, lend themselves to fraud and oppression than any device yet evolved in the human brain. Corporations are necessary instruments of modern business. They have been permitted to become a menace largely because the governmental representatives of the people have worked slowly in providing for adequate control over them.

The chief offender in any given case may be an executive, a legislature, or a judge. Every executive head who advises violent, instead of gradual, action, or who advocates ill-considered and sweeping measures of reform (especially if they are tainted with vindictiveness and disregard for the rights of the minority) is particularly blameworthy. The several legislatures are responsible for the fact that our laws are often prepared with slovenly haste and lack of consideration. Moreover, they are often prepared, and still more frequently amended during passage, at the suggestion of the very parties against whom they are afterwards enforced. Our great clusters of corporations, huge trusts and fabulously wealthy multi-millionaires, employ the very best lawyers they can obtain to pick flaws in these statutes after their passage; but they also employ a class of secret agents who seek, under the advice of experts, to render hostile legislation innocuous by making it unconstitutional, often through the insertion of what appear on their face to be drastic and sweeping provisions against the interests of the parties inspiring them; while the demagogues, the corrupt creatures who introduce blackmailing schemes to "strike" corporations, and all who demand extreme, and undesirably radical, measures, show themselves to be the worst enemies of the very public whose loud-mouthed champions they profess to be. A very striking illustration of the consequences of carelessness in the preparation of a statute was the employers' liability law of 1906. In the cases arising under that law, four out of six courts of first instance held it unconstitutional; six out of nine justices of the Supreme Court held that its subject-matter was within the province of congressional action; and four of the nine justices held it valid. It was, however, adjudged unconstitutional by a bare majority of the court—five to four. It was surely a very slovenly piece of work to frame the legislation in such shape as to leave the question open at all.

Real damage has been done by the manifold and conflicting interpretations of the interstate commerce law. Control over the great corporations doing interstate business can be effective only if it is vested with full power in an administrative department, a branch of the Federal executive, carrying out a Federal law; it can never be effective if a divided responsibility is left in both the States and the Nation; it can never be effective if left in the hands of the courts to be decided by lawsuits.

The courts hold a place of peculiar and deserved sanctity under our form of government. Respect for the law is essential to the permanence of our institutions; and respect for the law is largely conditioned upon respect for the courts. It is an offense against the Republic to say anything which can weaken this respect, save for the gravest reason and in the most carefully guarded manner. Our judges should be held in peculiar honor; and the duty of respectful and truthful comment and criticism, which should be binding when we speak of anybody, should be especially binding when we speak of them. On an average they stand above any other servants of the community, and the greatest judges have reached the high level held by those few greatest patriots whom the whole country delights to honor. But we must face the fact that there are wise and unwise judges, just as there are wise and unwise executives and legislators. When a president or a governor behaves improperly or unwisely, the remedy is easy, for his term is short; the same is true with the legislator, although not to the same degree, for he is one of many who belong to some given legislative body, and it is therefore less easy to fix his personal responsibility and hold him accountable therefor. With a judge, who, being human, is also likely to err, but whose tenure is for life, there is no similar way of holding him to responsibility. Under ordinary conditions the only forms of pressure to which he is in any way amenable are public opinion and the action of his fellow judges. It is the last which is most immediately effective, and to which we should look for the reform of abuses. Any remedy applied from without is fraught with risk. It is far better, from every standpoint, that the remedy should come from within. In no other nation in the world do the courts wield such vast and far-reaching power as in the United States. All that is necessary is that the courts as a whole should exercise this power with the farsighted wisdom already shown by those judges who scan the future while they act in the present. Let them exercise this great power not only honestly and bravely, but with wise insight into the needs and fixed purposes of the people, so that they may do justice and work equity, so that they may protect all persons in their rights, and yet break down the barriers of privilege, which is the foe of right.

Forests

If there is any one duty which more than another we owe it to our children and our children's children to perform at once, it is to save the forests of this country, for they constitute the first and most important element in the conservation of the natural resources of the country. There are of course two kinds of natural resources. One is the kind which can only be used as part of a process of exhaustion; this is true of mines, natural oil and gas wells, and the like. The other, and of course ultimately by far the most important, includes the resources which can be improved in the process of wise use; the soil, the rivers, and the forests come under this head. Any really civilized nation will so use all of these three great national assets that the nation will have their benefit in the future. Just as a farmer, after all his life making his living from his farm, will, if he is an expert farmer, leave it as an asset of increased value to his son, so we should leave our national domain to our children, increased in value and not worn out. There are small sections of our own country, in the East and the West, in the Adirondacks, the White Mountains, and the Appalachians, and in the Rocky Mountains, where we can already see for ourselves the damage in the shape of permanent injury to the soil and the river systems which comes from reckless deforestation. It matters not whether this deforestation is due to the actual reckless cutting of timber, to the fires that inevitably follow such reckless cutting of timber, or to reckless and uncontrolled grazing, especially by the great migratory bands of sheep, the unchecked wandering of which over the country means destruction to forests and disaster to the small home makers, the settlers of limited means.

Short-sighted persons, or persons blinded to the future by desire to make money in every way out of the present, sometimes speak as if no great damage would be done by the reckless destruction of our forests. It is difficult to have patience with the arguments of these persons. Thanks to our own recklessness in the use of our splendid forests, we have already crossed the verge of a timber famine in this country, and no measures that we now take can, at least for many years, undo the mischief that has already been done. But we can prevent further mischief being done; and it would be in the highest degree reprehensible to let any consideration of temporary convenience or temporary cost interfere with such action, especially as regards the National Forests which the nation can *now*, at this very moment, control.

All serious students of the question are aware of the great damage that has been done in the Mediterranean countries of Europe, Asia, and Africa by deforestation. The similar damage that has been done in Eastern Asia is less well known. A recent investigation into conditions in North China by Mr. Frank N. Meyer, of the Bureau of Plant Industry of the United States Department of Agriculture, has incidentally furnished in very striking fashion proof of the ruin that comes from reckless deforestation of mountains, and of the further fact that the damage once done may prove practically irreparable. So important are these investigations that I herewith attach as an appendix to my message certain photographs showing present conditions in China. They show in vivid fashion the appalling desolation, taking the shape of barren mountains and gravel- and sand-covered plains, which immediately follows and depends upon the deforestation of the mountains. Not many centuries ago the country of northern China was one of the most fertile and beautiful spots in the entire world, and was heavily forested. We know this not only from the old Chinese records, but from the accounts given by the traveler, Marco Polo. He, for instance, mentions that in visiting the provinces of Shansi and Shensi he observed many plantations of mulberry trees. Now there is hardly a single mulberry tree in either of these provinces, and the culture of the silkworm has moved farther south, to regions of atmospheric moisture. As an illustration of the complete change in the rivers, we may take Polo's statement that a certain river, the Hun Ho, was so large and deep that merchants ascended it from the sea with heavily laden boats; today this river is simply a broad sandy bed, with shallow, rapid currents wandering hither and thither across it, absolutely unnavigable. But we do not have to depend upon written records. The dry wells, and the wells with water far below the former watermark, bear testimony to the good days of the past and the evil days of the present. Wherever the native vegetation has been allowed to remain, as, for instance, here and there around a sacred temple or imperial burying ground, there are still huge trees and tangled jungle, fragments of the glorious ancient forests. The thick, matted forest growth formerly covered the mountains to their summits. All natural factors favored this dense forest growth, and as long as it was permitted to exist the plains at the foot of the mountains were among the most fertile on the globe, and the whole country was a garden. Not the slightest effort was made, however, to prevent the unchecked cutting of the trees, or to secure reforestation. Doubtless for many centuries the tree-cutting by the inhabitants of the mountains worked but slowly in bringing about the changes that have now come to pass; doubtless for generations the inroads were scarcely noticeable. But there came a time when the forest had shrunk sufficiently to make each year's cutting a serious matter, and from that time on the destruction proceeded with appalling rapidity; for of course each year of destruction rendered the forest less able to recuperate, less able to resist next year's inroad. Mr. Meyer describes the ceaseless progress of the destruction even now, when there is so little left to destroy. Every morning men and boys go out armed with mattox or axe, scale the steepest mountain sides, and cut down and grub out, root and branch, the small trees and shrubs still to be found. The big trees disappeared centuries ago, so that now one of these is never seen save in the neighborhood of temples, where they are artificially protected; and even here it takes all the watch and care of the tree-loving priests to prevent their destruction. Each family, each community, where there is no common care exercised in the interest of all of them to prevent deforestation, finds its profit in the immediate use of the fuel which would otherwise be used by some other family or some other community. In the total absence of regulation of the matter in the interest of the whole people, each small group is inevitably pushed into a policy of destruction which can not afford to take thought for the morrow. This is just one of those matters which it is fatal to leave to unsupervised individual control. The forest can only be protected by the State, by the Nation; and the liberty of action of individuals must be conditioned upon what the State or Nation determines to be necessary for the common safety.

The lesson of deforestation in China is a lesson which mankind should have learned many times already from what has occurred in other places. Denudation leaves naked soil; then gullying cuts down to the bare rock; and meanwhile the rock-waste buries the bottomlands. When the soil is gone, men must go; and the process does not take long.

This ruthless destruction of the forests in northern China has brought about, or has aided in bringing about, desolation, just as the destruction of the forests in central Asia aid in bringing ruin to the once rich central Asian cities; just as the destruction of the forest in northern Africa helped towards the ruin of a region that was a fertile granary in Roman days. Shortsighted man, whether barbaric, semi-civilized, or what he mistakenly regards as fully civilized, when he has destroyed the forests, has rendered certain the ultimate destruction of the land itself. In northern China the mountains are now such as are shown by the accompanying photographs, absolutely barren peaks. Not only have the forests been destroyed, but because of their destruction the soil has been washed off the naked rock. The terrible consequence is that it is impossible now to undo the damage that has been done. Many centuries would have to pass before soil would again collect, or could be made to collect, in sufficient quantity once more to support the old-time forest growth. In consequence the Mongol Desert is practically extending eastward over northern China. The climate has changed and is still changing. It has changed even within the last half century, as the work of tree destruction has been consummated. The great masses of arboreal vegetation on the mountains formerly absorbed the heat of the sun and sent up currents of cool air which brought the moisture-laden clouds lower and forced them to precipitate in rain a part of their burden of water. Now that there is no vegetation, the barren mountains, scorched by the sun, send up currents of heated air which drive away instead of attracting the rain clouds, and cause their moisture to be disseminated. In consequence, instead of the regular and plentiful rains which existed in these regions of China when the forests were still in evidence, the unfortunate inhabitants of the deforested lands now see their crops wither for lack of rainfall, while the seasons grow more and more irregular; and as the air becomes dryer certain crops refuse longer to grow at all. That everything dries out faster than formerly is shown by the fact that the level of the wells all over the land has sunk perceptibly, many of them having become totally dry. In addition to the resulting agricultural distress, the watercourses have changed. Formerly they were narrow and deep, with an abundance of clear water the year around; for the roots and humus of the forests caught the rainwater and let it escape by slow, regular seepage. They have now become broad, shallow stream beds, in which muddy water trickles in slender currents during the dry seasons, while when it rains there are freshets, and roaring muddy torrents come tearing down, bringing disaster and destruction everywhere. Moreover, these floods and freshets, which diversify the general dryness, wash away from the mountain sides, and either wash away or cover in the valleys, the rich fertile soil which it took tens of thousands of years for Nature to form; and it is lost forever, and until the forests grow again it can not be replaced. The sand and stones from the mountain sides are washed loose and come rolling down to cover the arable lands, and in consequence, throughout this part of China, many formerly rich districts are now sandy wastes, useless for human cultivation and even for pasture. The cities have been of course seriously affected, for the streams have gradually ceased to be navigable. There is testimony that even within the memory of men now living there has been a serious diminution of the rainfall of northeastern China. The level of the Sungari River in northern Manchuria has been sensibly lowered during the last fifty years, at least partly as the result of the indiscriminate rutting of the forests forming its watershed. Almost all the rivers of northern China have become uncontrollable, and very dangerous to the dwellers along their banks, as a direct result of the destruction of the forests. The journey from Pekin to Jehol shows in melancholy fashion how the soil has been washed away from whole valleys, so that they have been converted into deserts.

In northern China this disastrous process has gone on so long and has proceeded so far that no complete remedy could be applied. There are certain mountains in China from which the soil is gone so utterly that only the slow action of the ages could again restore it; although of course much could be done to prevent the still further eastward extension of the Mongolian Desert if the Chinese Government would act at once. The accompanying cuts from photographs show the inconceivable desolation of the barren mountains in which certain of these rivers rise—mountains, be it remembered, which formerly supported dense forests of larches and firs, now unable to produce any wood, and because of their condition a source of danger to the whole country. The photographs also show the same rivers after they have passed through the mountains, the beds having become broad and sandy because of the deforestation of the mountains. One of the photographs shows a caravan passing through a valley. Formerly, when the mountains were forested, it was thickly peopled by prosperous peasants. Now the floods have carried destruction all over the land and the valley is a stony desert. Another photograph shows a mountain road covered with the stones and rocks that are brought down in the rainy season from the mountains which have already been deforested by human hands. Another shows a pebbly river-bed in southern Manchuria where what was once a great stream has dried up owing to the deforestation in the mountains. Only some scrub wood is left, which will disappear within a half century. Yet another shows the effect of one of the washouts, destroying an arable mountain side, these washouts being due to the removal of all vegetation; yet in this photograph the foreground shows that reforestation is still a possibility in places.

What has thus happened in northern China, what has happened in Central Asia, in Palestine, in North Africa, in parts of the Mediterranean countries of Europe, will surely happen in our country if we do not exercise that wise forethought which should be one of the chief marks of any people calling itself civilized. Nothing should be permitted to stand in the way of the preservation of the forests, and it is criminal to permit individuals to purchase a little gain for themselves through the destruction of forests when this destruction is fatal to the well-being of the whole country in the future.

Inland Waterways

Action should be begun forthwith, during the present session of the Congress, for the improvement of our inland waterways—action which will result in giving us not only navigable but navigated rivers. We have spent hundreds of millions of dollars upon these waterways, yet the traffic on nearly all of them is steadily declining. This condition is the direct result of the absence of any comprehensive and far-seeing plan of waterway improvement. Obviously we can not continue thus to expend the revenues of the Government without return. It is poor business to spend money for inland navigation unless we get it.

Inquiry into the condition of the Mississippi and its principal tributaries reveals very many instances of the utter waste caused by the methods which have hitherto obtained for the so-called "improvement" of navigation. A striking instance is supplied by the "improvement" of the Ohio, which, begun in 1824, was continued under a single plan for half a century. In 1875 a new plan was adopted and followed for a quarter of a century. In 1902 still a different plan was adopted and has since been pursued at a rate which only promises a navigable river in from twenty to one hundred years longer.

Such shortsighted, vacillating, and futile methods are accompanied by decreasing water-borne commerce and increasing traffic congestion on land, by increasing floods, and by the waste of public money. The remedy lies in abandoning the methods which have so signally failed and adopting new ones in keeping with the needs and demands of our people.

In a report on a measure introduced at the first session of the present Congress, the Secretary of War said: "The chief defect in the methods hitherto pursued lies in the absence of executive authority for originating comprehensive plans covering the country or natural divisions thereof." In this opinion I heartily concur. The present methods not only fail to give us inland navigation, but they are injurious to the army as well. What is virtually a permanent detail of the corps of engineers to civilian duty necessarily impairs the efficiency of our military establishment. The military engineers have undoubtedly done efficient work in actual construction, but they are necessarily unsuited by their training and traditions to take the broad view, and to gather and transmit to the Congress the commercial and industrial information and forecasts, upon which waterway improvement must always so largely rest. Furthermore, they have failed to grasp the great underlying fact that every stream is a unit from its source to its mouth, and that all its uses are interdependent. Prominent officers of the Engineer Corps have recently even gone so far as to assert in print that waterways are not dependent upon the conservation of the forests about their headwaters. This position is opposed to all the recent work of the scientific bureaus of the Government and to the general experience of mankind. A physician who disbelieved in vaccination would not be the right man to handle an epidemic of smallpox, nor should we leave a doctor skeptical about the transmission of yellow fever by the Stegomyia mosquito in charge of sanitation at Havana or Panama. So with the improvement of our rivers; it is no longer wise or safe to leave this great work in the hands of men who fail to grasp the essential relations between navigation and general development and to assimilate and use the central facts about our streams.

Until the work of river improvement is undertaken in a modern way it can not have results that will meet the needs of this modern nation. These needs should be met without further dilly-dallying or delay. The plan which promises the best and quickest results is that of a permanent commission authorized to coordinate the work of all the Government departments relating to waterways, and to frame and supervise the execution of a comprehensive plan. Under such a commission the actual work of construction might be entrusted to the reclamation service; or to the military engineers acting with a sufficient number of civilians to continue the work in time of war; or it might be divided between the reclamation service and the corps of engineers. Funds should be provided from current revenues if it is deemed wise—otherwise from the sale of bonds. The essential thing is that the work should go forward under the best possible plan, and with the least possible delay. We should have a new type of work and a new organization for planning and directing it. The time for playing with our waterways is past. The country demands results.

National Parks

I urge that all our National parks adjacent to National forests be placed completely under the control of the forest service of the Agricultural Department, instead of leaving them as they now are, under the Interior Department and policed by the army. The Congress should provide for superintendents with adequate corps of first-class civilian scouts, or rangers, and, further, place the road construction under the superintendent instead of leaving it with the War Department. Such a change in park management would result in economy and avoid the difficulties of administration which now arise from having the responsibility of care and protection divided between different departments. The need for this course is peculiarly great in the Yellowstone Park. This, like the Yosemite, is a great wonderland, and should be kept as a national playground. In both, all wild things should be protected and the scenery kept wholly unmarred.

I am happy to say that I have been able to set aside in various parts of the country small, well-chosen tracts of ground to serve as sanctuaries and nurseries for wild creatures.

Denatured Alcohol

I had occasion in my message of May 4, 1906, to urge the passage of some law putting alcohol, used in the arts, industries, and manufactures, upon the free list—that is, to provide for the withdrawal free of tax of alcohol which is to be denatured for those purposes. The law of June 7, 1906, and its amendment of March 2, 1907, accomplished what was desired in that respect, and the use of denatured alcohol, as intended, is making a fair degree of progress and is entitled to further encouragement and support from the Congress.

Pure Food

The pure food legislation has already worked a benefit difficult to overestimate.

Indian Service

It has been my purpose from the beginning of my administration to take the Indian Service completely out of the atmosphere of political activity, and there has been steady progress toward that end. The last remaining stronghold of politics in that service was the agency system, which had seen its best days and was gradually falling to pieces from natural or purely evolutionary causes, but, like all such survivals, was decaying slowly in its later stages. It seems clear that its extinction had better be made final now, so that the ground can be cleared for larger constructive work on behalf of the Indians, preparatory to their induction into the full measure of responsible citizenship. On November 1 only eighteen agencies were left on the roster; with two exceptions, where some legal questions seemed to stand temporarily in the way, these have been changed to superintendencies, and their heads brought into the classified civil service.

Secret Service

Last year an amendment was incorporated in the measure providing for the Secret Service, which provided that there should be no detail from the Secret Service and no transfer therefrom. It is not too much to say that this amendment has been of benefit only, and could be of benefit only, to the criminal classes. If deliberately introduced for the purpose of diminishing the effectiveness of war against crime it could not have been better devised to this end. It forbade the practices that had been followed to a greater or less extent by the executive heads of various departments for twenty years. To these practices we owe the securing of the evidence which enabled us to drive great lotteries out of business and secure a quarter of a million of dollars in fines from their promoters. These practices have enabled us to get some of the evidence indispensable in order in connection with the theft of government land and government timber by great corporations and by individuals. These practices have enabled us to get some of the evidence indispensable in order to secure the conviction of the wealthiest and most formidable criminals with whom the Government has to deal, both those operating in violation of the anti-trust law and others. The amendment in question was of benefit to no one excepting to these criminals, and it seriously hampers the Government in the detection of crime and the securing of justice. Moreover, it not only affects departments outside of the Treasury, but it tends to hamper the Secretary of the Treasury himself in the effort to utilize the employees of his department so as to best meet the requirements of the public service. It forbids him from preventing frauds upon the customs service, from investigating irregularities in branch mints and assay offices, and has seriously crippled him. It prevents the promotion of employees in the Secret Service, and this further discourages good effort. In its present form the restriction operates only to the advantage of the criminal, of the wrongdoer. The chief argument in favor of the provision was that the Congressmen did not themselves wish to be investigated by Secret Service men. Very little of such investigation has been done in the past; but it is true that the work of the Secret Service agents was partly responsible for the indictment and conviction of a Senator and a Congressman for land frauds in Oregon. I do not believe that it is in the public interest to protect criminally in any branch of the public service, and exactly as we have again and again during the past seven years prosecuted and convicted such criminals who were in the executive branch of the Government, so in my belief we should be given ample means to prosecute them if found in the legislative branch. But if this is not considered desirable a special exception could be made in the law prohibiting the use of the Secret Service force in investigating members of the Congress. It would be far better to do this than to do what actually was done, and strive to prevent or at least to hamper effective action against criminals by the executive branch of the Government.

Postal Savings Banks

I again renew my recommendation for postal savings banks, for depositing savings with the security of the Government behind them. The object is to encourage thrift and economy in the wage-earner and person of moderate means. In 14 States the deposits in savings banks as reported to the Comptroller of the Currency amount to $3,590,245,402, or 98.4 per cent of the entire deposits, while in the remaining 32 States there are only $70,308,543, or 1.6 per cent, showing conclusively that there are many localities in the United States where sufficient opportunity is not given to the people to deposit their savings. The result is that money is kept in hiding and unemployed. It is believed that in the aggregate vast sums of money would be brought into circulation through the instrumentality of the postal savings banks. While there are only 1,453 savings banks reporting to the Comptroller there are more than 61,000 post-offices, 40,000 of which are money order offices. Postal savings banks are now in operation in practically all of the great civilized countries with the exception of the United States.

Parcel Post

In my last annual message I commended the Postmaster-General's recommendation for an extension of the parcel post on the rural routes. The establishment of a local parcel post on rural routes would be to the mutual benefit of the farmer and the country storekeeper, and it is desirable that the routes, serving more than 15,000,000 people, should be utilized to the fullest practicable extent. An amendment was proposed in the Senate at the last session, at the suggestion of the Postmaster-General, providing that, for the purpose of ascertaining the practicability of establishing a special local parcel post system on the rural routes throughout the United States, the Postmaster-General be authorized and directed to experiment and report to the Congress the result of such experiment by establishing a special local parcel post system on rural delivery routes in not to exceed four counties in the United States for packages of fourth-class matter originating on a rural route or at the distributing post office for delivery by rural carriers. It would seem only proper that such an experiment should be tried in order to demonstrate the practicability of the proposition, especially as the Postmaster-General estimates that the revenue derived from the operation of such a system on all the rural routes would amount to many million dollars.

Education

The share that the National Government should take in the broad work of education has not received the attention and the care it rightly deserves. The immediate responsibility for the support and improvement of our educational systems and institutions rests and should always rest with the people of the several States acting through their state and local governments, but the Nation has an opportunity in educational work which must not be lost and a duty which should no longer be neglected.

The National Bureau of Education was established more than forty years ago. Its purpose is to collect and diffuse such information "as shall aid the people of the United States in the establishment and maintenance of efficient school systems and otherwise promote the cause of education throughout the country." This purpose in no way conflicts with the educational work of the States, but may be made of great advantage to the States by giving them the fullest, most accurate, and hence the most helpful information and suggestion regarding the best educational systems. The Nation, through its broader field of activities, its wider opportunity for obtaining information from all the States and from foreign countries, is able to do that which not even the richest States can do, and with the distinct additional advantage that the information thus obtained is used for the immediate benefit of all our people.

With the limited means hitherto provided, the Bureau of Education has rendered efficient service, but the Congress has neglected to adequately supply the bureau with means to meet the educational growth of the country. The appropriations for the general work of the bureau, outside education in Alaska, for the year 1909 are but $87,500—an amount less than they were ten years ago, and some of the important items in these appropriations are less than they were thirty years ago. It is an inexcusable waste of public money to appropriate an amount which is so inadequate as to make it impossible properly to do the work authorized, and it is unfair to the great educational interests of the country to deprive them of the value of the results which can be obtained by proper appropriations.

I earnestly recommend that this unfortunate state of affairs as regards the national educational office be remedied by adequate appropriations. This recommendation is urged by the representatives of our common schools and great state universities and the leading educators, who all unite in requesting favorable consideration and action by the Congress upon this subject.

Census

I strongly urge that the request of the Director of the Census in connection with the decennial work so soon to be begun be complied with and that the appointments to the census force be placed under the civil service law, waiving the geographical requirements as requested by the Director of the Census. The supervisors and enumerators should not be appointed under the civil service law, for the reasons given by the Director. I commend to the Congress the careful consideration of the admirable report of the Director of the Census, and I trust that his recommendations will be adopted and immediate action thereon taken.

Public Health

It is highly advisable that there should be intelligent action on the part of the Nation on the question of preserving the health of the country. Through the practical extermination in San Francisco of disease-bearing rodents our country has thus far escaped the bubonic plague. This is but one of the many achievements of American health officers; and it shows what can be accomplished with a better organization than at present exists. The dangers to public health from food adulteration and from many other sources, such as the menace to the physical, mental and moral development of children from child labor, should be met and overcome. There are numerous diseases, which are now known to be preventable, which are, nevertheless, not prevented. The recent International Congress on Tuberculosis has made us painfully aware of the inadequacy of American public health legislation. This Nation can not afford to lag behind in the world-wide battle now being waged by all civilized people with the microscopic foes of mankind, nor ought we longer to ignore the reproach that this Government takes more pains to protect the lives of hogs and of cattle than of human beings.

Redistribution of Bureaus

The first legislative step to be taken is that for the concentration of the proper bureaus into one of the existing departments. I therefore urgently recommend the passage of a bill which shall authorize a redistribution of the bureaus which shall best accomplish this end.

Government Printing Office

I recommend that legislation be enacted placing under the jurisdiction of the Department of Commerce and Labor the Government Printing Office. At present this office is under the combined control, supervision, and administrative direction of the President and of the Joint Committee on Printing of the two Houses of the Congress. The advantage of having the 4,069 employees in this office and the expenditure of the $5,761,377.57 appropriated therefor supervised by an executive department is obvious, instead of the present combined supervision.

Soldiers' Homes

All Soldiers' Homes should be placed under the complete jurisdiction and control of the War Department.

Independent Bureaus and Commissions

Economy and sound business policy require that all existing independent bureaus and commissions should be placed under the jurisdiction of appropriate executive departments. It is unwise from every standpoint, and results only in mischief, to have any executive work done save by the purely executive bodies, under the control of the President; and each such executive body should be under the immediate supervision of a Cabinet Minister.

Statehood

I advocate the immediate admission of New Mexico and Arizona as States. This should be done at the present session of the Congress. The people of the two Territories have made it evident by their votes that they will not come in as one State. The only alternative is to admit them as two, and I trust that this will be done without delay.

Interstate Fisheries

I call the attention of the Congress to the importance of the problem of the fisheries in the interstate waters. On the Great Lakes we are now, under the very wise treaty of April 11th of this year, endeavoring to come to an international agreement for the preservation and satisfactory use of the fisheries of these waters which can not otherwise be achieved. Lake Erie, for example, has the richest fresh water fisheries in the world; but it is now controlled by the statutes of two Nations, four States, and one Province, and in this Province by different ordinances in different counties. All these political divisions work at cross purposes, and in no case can they achieve protection to the fisheries, on the one hand, and justice to the localities and individuals on the other. The case is similar in Puget Sound.

But the problem is quite as pressing in the interstate waters of the United States. The salmon fisheries of the Columbia River are now but a fraction of what they were twenty-five years ago, and what they would be now if the United States Government had taken complete charge of them by intervening between Oregon and Washington. During these twenty-five years the fishermen of each State have naturally tried to take all they could get, and the two legislatures have never been able to agree on joint action of any kind adequate in degree for the protection of the fisheries. At the moment the fishing on the Oregon side is practically closed, while there is no limit on the Washington side of any kind, and no one can tell what the courts will decide as to the very statutes under which this action and nonaction result. Meanwhile very few salmon reach the spawning grounds, and probably four years hence the fisheries will amount to nothing; and this comes from a struggle between the associated, or gill-net, fishermen on the one hand, and the owners of the fishing wheels up the river. The fisheries of the Mississippi, the Ohio, and the Potomac are also in a bad way. For this there is no remedy except for the United States to control and legislate for the interstate fisheries as part of the business of interstate commerce. In this case the machinery for scientific investigation and for control already exists in the United States Bureau of Fisheries. In this as in similar problems the obvious and simple rule should be followed of having those matters which no particular State can manage taken in hand by the United States; problems which in the seesaw of conflicting State legislatures are absolutely unsolvable are easy enough for Congress to control.

Fisheries and Fur Seals

The federal statute regulating interstate traffic in game should be extended to include fish. New federal fish hatcheries should be established. The administration of the Alaskan fur-seal service should be vested in the Bureau of Fisheries.

Foreign Affairs

This Nation's foreign policy is based on the theory that right must be done between nations precisely as between individuals, and in our actions for the last ten years we have in this matter proven our faith by our deeds. We have behaved, and are behaving, towards other nations as in private life an honorable man would behave towards his fellows.

Latin-American Republics

The commercial and material progress of the twenty Latin-American Republics is worthy of the careful attention of the Congress. No other section of the world has shown a greater proportionate development of its foreign trade during the last ten years and none other has more special claims on the interest of the United States. It offers to-day probably larger opportunities for the legitimate expansion of our commerce than any other group of countries. These countries will want our products in greatly increased quantities, and we shall correspondingly need theirs. The International Bureau of the American Republics is doing a useful work in making these nations and their resources better known to us, and in acquainting them not only with us as a people and with our purposes towards them, but with what we have to exchange for their goods. It is an international institution supported by all the governments of the two Americas.

Panama Canal

The work on the Panama Canal is being done with a speed, efficiency, and entire devotion to duty which make it a model for all work of the kind. No task of such magnitude has ever before been undertaken by any nation; and no task of the kind has ever been better performed. The men on the isthmus, from Colonel Goethals and his fellow commissioners through the entire list of employees who are faithfully doing their duty, have won their right to the ungrudging respect and gratitude of the American people.

Ocean Mail Liners

I again recommend the extension of the ocean mail act of 1891 so that satisfactory American ocean mail lines to South America, Asia, the Philippines, and Australiasia may be established. The creation of such steamship lines should be the natural corollary of the voyage of the battle fleet. It should precede the opening of the Panamal Canal. Even under favorable conditions several years must elapse before such lines can be put into operation. Accordingly I urge that the Congress act promptly where foresight already shows that action sooner or later will be inevitable.

Hawaii

I call particular attention to the Territory of Hawaii. The importance of those islands is apparent, and the need of improving their condition and developing their resources is urgent. In recent years industrial conditions upon the islands have radically changed. The importation of coolie labor has practically ceased, and there is now developing such a diversity in agricultural products as to make possible a change in the land conditions of the Territory, so that an opportunity may be given to the small land owner similar to that on the mainland. To aid these changes, the National Government must provide the necessary harbor improvements on each island, so that the agricultural products can be carried to the markets of the world. The coastwise shipping laws should be amended to meet the special needs of the islands, and the alien contract labor law should be so modified in its application to Hawaii as to enable American and European labor to be brought thither.

We have begun to improve Pearl Harbor for a naval base and to provide the necessary military fortifications for the protection of the islands, but I can not too strongly emphasize the need of appropriations for these purposes of such an amount as will within the shortest possible time make those islands practically impregnable. It is useless to develop the industrial conditions of the islands and establish there bases of supply for our naval and merchant fleets unless we insure, as far as human ingenuity can, their safety from foreign seizure.

One thing to be remembered with all our fortifications is that it is almost useless to make them impregnable from the sea if they are left open to land attack. This is true even of our own coast, but it is doubly true of our insular possessions. In Hawaii, for instance, it is worse than useless to establish a naval station unless we establish it behind fortifications so strong that no landing force can take them save by regular and long-continued siege operations.

The Philippines

Real progress toward self-government is being made in the Philippine Islands. The gathering of a Philippine legislative body and Philippine assembly marks a process absolutely new in Asia, not only as regards Asiatic colonies of European powers but as regards Asiatic possessions of other Asiatic powers; and, indeed, always excepting the striking and wonderful example afforded by the great Empire of Japan, it opens an entirely new departure when compared with anything which has happened among Asiatic powers which are their own masters. Hitherto this Philippine legislature has acted with moderation and self-restraint, and has seemed in practical fashion to realize the eternal truth that there must always be government, and that the only way in which any body of individuals can escape the necessity of being governed by outsiders is to show that they are able to restrain themselves, to keep down wrongdoing and disorder. The Filipino people, through their officials, are therefore making real steps in the direction of self-government. I hope and believe that these steps mark the beginning of a course which will continue till the Filipinos become fit to decide for themselves whether they desire to be an independent nation. But it is well for them (and well also for those Americans who during the past decade have done so much damage to the Filipinos by agitation for an immediate independence for which they were totally unfit) to remember that self-government depends, and must depend, upon the

Filipinos themselves. All we can do is to give them the opportunity to develop the capacity for self-government. If we had followed the advice of the foolish doctrinaires who wished us at any time during the last ten years to turn the Filipino people adrift, we should have shirked the plainest possible duty and have inflicted a lasting wrong upon the Filipino people. We have acted in exactly the opposite spirit. We have given the Filipinos constitutional government—a government based upon justice—and we have shown that we have governed them for their good and not for our aggrandizement. At the present time, as during the past ten years, the inexorable logic of facts shows that this government must be supplied by us and not by them. We must be wise and generous; we must help the Filipinos to master the difficult art of self-control, which is simply another name for self-government. But we can not give them self-government save in the sense of governing them so that gradually they may, if they are able, learn to govern themselves. Under the present system of just laws and sympathetic administration, we have every reason to believe that they are gradually acquiring the character which lies at the basis of self-government, and for which, if it be lacking, no system of laws, no paper constitution, will in any wise serve as a substitute. Our people in the Philippines have achieved what may legitimately be called a marvelous success in giving to them a government which marks on the part of those in authority both the necessary understanding of the people and the necessary purpose to serve them disinterestedly and in good faith. I trust that within a generation the time will arrive when the Philippines can decide for themselves whether it is well for them to become independent, or to continue under the protection of a strong and disinterested power, able to guarantee to the islands order at home and protection from foreign invasion. But no one can prophesy the exact date when it will be wise to consider independence as a fixed and definite policy. It would be worse than folly to try to set down such a date in advance, for it must depend upon the way in which the Philippine people themselves develop the power of self-mastery.

Porto Rico

I again recommend that American citizenship be conferred upon the people of Porto Rico.

Cuba

In Cuba our occupancy will cease in about two months' time, the Cubans have in orderly manner elected their own governmental authorities, and the island will be turned over to them. Our occupation on this occasion has lasted a little over two years, and Cuba has thriven and prospered under it. Our earnest hope and one desire is that the people of the island shall now govern themselves with justice, so that peace and order may be secure. We will gladly help them to this end; but I would solemnly warn them to remember the great truth that the only way a people can permanently avoid being governed from without is to show that they both can and will govern themselves from within.

Japanese Exposition

The Japanese Government has postponed until 1917 the date of the great international exposition, the action being taken so as to insure ample time in which to prepare to make the exposition all that it should be made. The American commissioners have visited Japan and the postponement will merely give ampler opportunity for America to be represented at the exposition. Not since the first international exposition has there been one of greater importance than this will be, marking as it does the fiftieth anniversary of the ascension to the throne of the Emperor of Japan. The extraordinary leap to a foremost place among the nations of the world made by Japan during this half century is something unparalleled in all previous history. This exposition will fitly commemorate and signalize the giant progress that has been achieved. It is the first exposition of its kind that has ever been held in Asia. The United States, because of the ancient friendship between the two peoples, because each of us fronts on the Pacific, and because of the growing commercial relations between this country and Asia, takes a peculiar interest in seeing the exposition made a success in every way.

I take this opportunity publicly to state my appreciation of the way in which in Japan, in Australia, in New Zealand, and in all the States of South America, the battle fleet has been received on its practice voyage around the world. The American Government can not too strongly express its appreciation of the abounding and generous hospitality shown our ships in every port they visited.

The Army

As regards the Army I call attention to the fact that while our junior officers and enlisted men stand very high, the present system of promotion by seniority results in bringing into the higher grades many men of mediocre capacity who have but a short time to serve. No man should regard it as his vested right to rise to the highest rank in the Army any more than in any other profession. It is a curious and by no means creditable fact that there should be so often a failure on the part of the public and its representatives to understand the great need, from the standpoint of the service and the Nation, of refusing to promote respectable, elderly incompetents. The higher places should be given to the most deserving men without regard to seniority; at least seniority should be treated as only one consideration. In the stress of modern industrial competition no business firm could succeed if those responsible for its management were chosen simply on the ground that they were the oldest people in its employment; yet this is the course advocated as regards the Army, and required by law for all grades except those of general officer. As a matter of fact, all of the best officers in the highest ranks of the Army are those who have attained their present position wholly or in part by a process of selection.

The scope of retiring boards should be extended so that they could consider general unfitness to command for any cause, in order to secure a far more rigid enforcement than at present in the elimination of officers for mental, physical or temperamental disabilities. But this plan is recommended only if the Congress does not see fit to provide what in my judgment is far better; that is, for selection in promotion, and for elimination for age. Officers who fail to attain a certain rank by a certain age should be retired—for instance, if a man should not attain field rank by the time he is 45 he should of course be placed on the retired list. General officers should be selected as at present, and one-third of the other promotions should be made by selection, the selection to be made by the President or the Secretary of War from a list of at least two candidates proposed for each vacancy by a board of officers from the arm of the service from which the promotion is to be made. A bill is now before the Congress having for its object to secure the promotion of officers to various grades at reasonable ages through a process of selection, by boards of officers, of the least efficient for retirement with a percentage of their pay depending upon length of service. The bill, although not accomplishing all that should be done, is a long step in the right direction; and I earnestly recommend its passage, or that of a more completely effective measure.

The cavalry arm should be reorganized upon modern lines. This is an arm in which it is peculiarly necessary that the field officers should not be old. The cavalry is much more difficult to form than infantry, and it should be kept up to the maximum both in efficiency and in strength, for it can not be made in a hurry. At present both infantry and artillery are too few in number for our needs. Especial attention should be paid to development of the machine gun. A general service corps should be established. As things are now the average soldier has far too much labor of a nonmilitary character to perform.

National Guard

Now that the organized militia, the National Guard, has been incorporated with the Army as a part of the national forces, it behooves the Government to do every reasonable thing in its power to perfect its efficiency. It should be assisted in its instruction and otherwise aided more liberally than heretofore. The continuous services of many well-trained regular officers will be essential in this connection. Such officers must be specially trained at service schools best to qualify them as instructors of the National Guard. But the detailing of officers for training at the service schools and for duty with the National Guard entails detaching them from their regiments which are already greatly depleted by detachment of officers for assignment to duties prescribed by acts of the Congress.

A bill is now pending before the Congress creating a number of extra officers in the Army, which if passed, as it ought to be, will enable more officers to be trained as instructors of the National Guard and assigned to that duty. In case of war it will be of the utmost importance to have a large number of trained officers to use for turning raw levies into good troops.

There should be legislation to provide a complete plan for organizing the great body of volunteers behind the Regular Army and National Guard when war has come. Congressional assistance should be given those who are endeavoring to promote rifle practice so that our men, in the services or out of them, may know how to use the rifle. While teams representing the United States won the rifle and revolver championships of the world against all comers in England this year, it is unfortunately true that the great body of our citizens shoot less and less as time goes on. To meet this we should encourage rifle practice among schoolboys, and indeed among all classes, as well as in the military services, by every means in our power. Thus, and not otherwise, may we be able to assist in preserving the peace of the world. Fit to hold our own against the strong nations of the earth, our voice for peace will carry to the ends of the earth. Unprepared, and therefore unfit, we must sit dumb and helpless to defend ourselves, protect others, or preserve peace. The first step—in the direction of preparation to avert war if possible, and to be fit for war if it should come—is to teach our men to shoot.

The Navy

I approve the recommendations of the General Board for the increase of the Navy, calling especial attention to the need of additional destroyers and colliers, and above all, of the four battleships. It is desirable to complete as soon as possible a squadron of eight battleships of the best existing type. The *North Dakota*, *Delaware*, *Florida*, and *Utah* will form the first division of this squadron. The four vessels proposed will form the second division. It will be an improvement on the first, the ships being of the heavy, single caliber, all big gun type. All the vessels should have the same tactical qualities—that is, speed and turning circle—and as near as possible these tactical qualities should be the same as in the four vessels before named now being built.

I most earnestly recommend that the General Board be by law turned into a General Staff. There is literally no excuse whatever for continuing the present bureau organization of the Navy. The Navy should be treated as a purely military organization, and everything should be subordinated to the one object of securing military efficiency. Such military efficiency can only be guaranteed in time of war if there is the most thorough previous preparation in time of peace—a preparation, I may add, which will in all probability prevent any need of war. The Secretary must be supreme, and he should have as his official advisers a body of line officers who should themselves have the power to pass upon and coordinate all the work and all the proposals of the several bureaus. A system of promotion by merit, either by selection or by exclusion, or by both processes, should be introduced. It is out of the question, if the present principle of promotion by mere seniority is kept, to expect to get the best results from the higher officers. Our men come too old, and stay for too short a time, in the high command positions.

Two hospital ships should be provided. The actual experience of the hospital ship with the fleet in the Pacific has shown the invaluable work which such a ship does, and has also proved that it is well to have it kept under the command of a medical officer. As was to be expected, all of the anticipations of trouble from such a command have proved completely baseless. It is as absurd to put a hospital ship under a line officer as it would be to put a hospital on shore under such a command. This ought to have been realized before, and there is no excuse for failure to realize it now.

Nothing better for the Navy from every standpoint has ever occurred than the cruise of the battle fleet around the world. The improvement of the ships in every way has been extraordinary, and they have gained far more experience in battle tactics than they would have gained if they had stayed in the Atlantic waters. The American people have cause for profound gratification, both in view of the excellent condition of the fleet as shown by this cruise, and in view of the improvement the cruise has worked in this already high condition. I do not believe that there is any other service in the world in which the average of character and efficiency in the enlisted men is as high as is now the case in our own. I believe that the same statement can be made as to our officers, taken as a whole; but there must be a reservation made in regard to those in the highest ranks—as to which I have already spoken—and in regard to those who have just entered the service; because we do not now get full benefit from our excellent naval school at Annapolis. It is absurd not to graduate the midshipmen as ensigns; to keep them for two years in such an anomalous position as at present the law requires is detrimental to them and to the service. In the academy itself, every first classman should be required in turn to serve as petty officer and officer; his ability to discharge his duties as such should be a prerequisite to his going into the line, and his success in commanding should largely determine his standing at graduation. The Board of Visitors should be appointed in January, and each member should be required to give at least six days' service, only from one to three days' to be performed during June week, which is the least desirable time for the board to be at Annapolis so far as benefiting the Navy by their observations is concerned.

THEODORE ROOSEVELT
THE WHITE HOUSE,
Tuesday, December 8, 1908.

Note

1. See H. Paul Jeffers, *An Honest President: The Life and Presidencies of Grover Cleveland* (New York: William Morrow, 2000), prologue.

23

William Howard Taft (1909–1913)

William Howard Taft's last annual message was so lengthy that it had to be submitted to the Congress in three separate parts. The exhaustive report was hardly unique to him, however. For about a century there had been a tendency to submit longer and longer annual messages. The trend had begun with the nation's fifth president, James Monroe. He was the first to break the 5,000-word barrier in 1821. Andrew Jackson was the first to break the 10,000-word barrier in 1829. He outdid himself by breaking the 15,000-word barrier the very next year. James Polk was the first to break the 20,000-word barrier in 1848, a record that would not be eclipsed for more than a half century. Theodore Roosevelt was the first to break the 25,000-word barrier. The tradition of increasingly verbose annual messages was ably upheld by Taft, whose fourth and final annual message also broke 25,000 words. (Not until Jimmy Carter's final state of the union would the 30,000-word barrier be broken in 1981.)

Taft began his message on the subject of foreign relations. Only in retrospect would this seem eerily apt, given that the West would soon be plunged into a world war.

Fourth Annual Message
(written to the Congress)
December 3, 1912

Part I
On Our Foreign Relations

To the Senate and House of Representatives:

The foreign relations of the United States actually and potentially affect the state of the Union to a degree not widely realized and hardly surpassed by any other factor in the welfare of the whole Nation. The position of the United States in the moral, intellectual, and material relations of the family of nations should be a matter of vital interest to every patriotic citizen. The national prosperity and power impose upon us duties which we can not shirk if we are to be true to our ideals. The tremendous growth of the export trade of the United States has already made that trade a very real factor in the industrial and commercial prosperity of the country. With the development of our industries the foreign commerce of the United States must rapidly become a still more essential factor in its economic welfare. Whether we have a farseeing and wise diplomacy and are not recklessly plunged into unnecessary wars, and whether our foreign policies are based upon an intelligent grasp of present-day world conditions and a clear view of the potentialities of the future, or are governed by a temporary and timid expediency or by narrow views befitting an infant nation, are questions in the alternative consideration of which must convince any thoughtful citizen that no department of national polity offers greater opportunity for promoting the interests of the whole people on the one hand, or greater chance on the other of permanent national injury, than that which deals with the foreign relations of the United States.

The fundamental foreign policies of the United States should be raised high above the conflict of partisanship and wholly dissociated from differences as to domestic policy. In its foreign affairs the United States should present to the world a united front. The intellectual, financial, and industrial interests of the country and the publicist, the wage earner, the farmer, and citizen of whatever occupation must cooperate in a spirit of high patriotism to promote that national solidarity which is indispensable to national efficiency and to the attainment of national ideals.

The relations of the United States with all foreign powers remain upon a sound basis of peace, harmony, and friendship. A greater insistence upon justice to American citizens or interests wherever it may have been denied and a stronger emphasis of the need of mutuality in commercial and other relations have only served to strengthen our friendships with foreign countries by placing those friendships upon a firm foundation of realities as well as aspirations.

Before briefly reviewing the more important events of the last year in our foreign relations, which it is my duty to do as charged with their conduct and because diplomatic affairs are not of a nature to make it appropriate that the Secretary of State make a formal annual report, I desire to touch upon some of the essentials to the safe management of the foreign relations of the United States and to endeavor, also, to define clearly certain concrete policies which are the logical modern corollaries of the undisputed and traditional fundamentals of the foreign policy of the United States.

Reorganization of the State Department

At the beginning of the present administration the United States, having fully entered upon its position as a world power, with the responsibilities thrust upon it by the results of the Spanish-American War, and already engaged in laying the groundwork of a vast foreign trade upon which it should one day become more and more dependent, found itself without the machinery for giving thorough attention to, and taking effective action upon, a mass of intricate business vital to American interests in every country in the world.

The Department of State was an archaic and inadequate machine lacking most of the attributes of the foreign office of any great modern power. With an appropriation made upon my recommendation by the Congress on August 5, 1909, the Department of State was completely reorganized. There were created Divisions of Latin American Affairs and of Far Eastern, Near Eastern, and Western European Affairs. To these divisions were called from the foreign service diplomatic and consular officers possessing experience and knowledge gained by actual service in different parts of the world and thus familiar with political and commercial conditions in the regions concerned. The work was highly specialized. The result is that where previously this Government from time to time would emphasize in its foreign relations one or another policy, now American interests in every quarter of the globe are being cultivated with equal assiduity. This principle of politico-geographical division possesses also the good feature of making possible rotation between the officers of the departmental, the diplomatic, and the consular branches of the foreign service, and thus keeps the whole diplomatic and consular establishments under the Department of State in close touch and equally inspired with the aims and policy of the Government. Through the newly created Division of Information the foreign service is kept fully informed of what transpires from day to day in the international relations of the country, and contemporary foreign comment affecting American interests is promptly brought to the attention of the department. The law offices of the department were greatly strengthened. There were added foreign trade advisers to cooperate with the diplomatic and consular bureaus and the politico-geographical divisions in the innumerable matters where commercial diplomacy or consular work calls for such special knowledge. The same officers, together with the rest of the new organization, are able at all times to give to American citizens accurate information as to conditions in foreign countries with which they have business and likewise to cooperate more effectively with the Congress and also with the other executive departments.

Merit System in Consular and Diplomatic Corps

Expert knowledge and professional training must evidently be the essence of this reorganization. Without a trained foreign service there would not be men available for the work in the reorganized Department of State. President Cleveland had taken the first step toward introducing the merit system in the foreign service. That had been followed by the application of the merit principle, with excellent results, to the entire consular branch. Almost nothing, however, had been done in this direction with regard to the Diplomatic Service. In this age of commercial diplomacy it was evidently of the first importance to train an adequate personnel in that branch of the service. Therefore, on November 26, 1909, by an Executive order I placed the Diplomatic Service up to the grade of secretary of embassy, inclusive, upon exactly the same strict nonpartisan basis of the merit system, rigid examination for appointment and promotion only for efficiency, as had been maintained without exception in the Consular Service.

*   *   *

. . . It is high time that the dignity and power of this great Nation should be fittingly signalized by proper buildings for the occupancy of the Nation's representatives everywhere abroad.

Diplomacy a Hand Maid of Commercial Intercourse and Peace

The diplomacy of the present administration has sought to respond to modern ideas of commercial intercourse. This policy has been characterized as substituting dollars for bullets. It is one that appeals alike to idealistic humanitarian sentiments, to the dictates of sound policy and strategy, and to legitimate commercial aims. It is an effort frankly directed to the increase of American trade upon the axiomatic principle that the Government of the United States shall extend all proper support to every legitimate and beneficial American enterprise abroad. How great have been the results of this diplomacy, coupled with the maximum and minimum provision of the tariff law, will be seen by some consideration of the wonderful increase in the export trade of the United States. Because modern diplomacy is commercial, there has been a disposition in some quarters to attribute to it none but materialistic aims. How strikingly erroneous is such an impression may be seen from a study of the results by which the diplomacy of the United States can be judged.

Successful Efforts in Promotion of Peace

In the field of work toward the ideals of peace this Government negotiated, but to my regret was unable to consummate, two arbitration treaties which set the highest mark of the aspiration of nations toward the substitution of arbitration and reason for war in the settlement of international disputes. Through the efforts of American diplomacy several wars have been prevented or ended. I refer to the successful tripartite mediation of the Argentine Republic, Brazil, and the United States between Peru and Ecuador; the bringing of the boundary dispute between Panama and Costa Rica to peaceful arbitration; the staying of warlike preparations when Haiti and the Dominican Republic were on the verge of hostilities; the stopping of a war in Nicaragua; the halting of internecine strife in Honduras. The Government of the United States was thanked for its influence toward the restoration of amicable relations between the Argentine Republic and Bolivia. The diplomacy of the United States is active in seeking to assuage the remaining ill-feeling between this country and the Republic of Colombia. In the recent civil war in China the United States successfully joined with the other interested powers in urging an early cessation of hostilities. An agreement has been reached between the Governments of Chile and Peru whereby the celebrated Tacna-Arica dispute, which has so long embittered international relations on the west coast of South America, has at last been adjusted. Simultaneously came the news that the boundary dispute between Peru and Ecuador had entered upon a stage of amicable settlement. The position of the United States in reference to the Tacna-Arica dispute between Chile and Peru has been one of nonintervention, but one of friendly influence and pacific counsel throughout the period during which the dispute in question has been the subject of interchange of views between this Government and the two Governments immediately concerned. In the general easing of international tension on the west coast of South America the tripartite mediation, to which I have referred, has been a most potent and beneficent factor.

China

In China the policy of encouraging financial investment to enable that country to help itself has had the result of giving new life and practical application to the open-door policy. The consistent purpose of the present administration has been to encourage the use of American capital in the development of China by the promotion of those essential reforms to which China is pledged by treaties with the United States and other powers. The hypothecation to foreign bankers in connection with certain industrial enterprises, such as the Hukuang railways, of the national revenues upon which these reforms depended, led the Department of State early in the administration to demand for American citizens participation in such enterprises, in order that the United States might have equal rights and an equal voice in all questions pertaining to the disposition of the public revenues concerned. The same policy of promoting international accord among the powers having similar treaty rights as ourselves in the matters of reform, which could not be put into practical effect without the common consent of all, was likewise adopted in the case of the loan desired by China for the reform of its currency. The principle of international cooperation in matters of common interest upon which our policy had already been based in all of the above instances has admittedly been a great factor in that concert of the powers which has been so happily conspicuous during the perilous period of transition through which the great Chinese nation has been passing.

Central America Needs Our Help in Debt Adjustment

In Central America the aim has been to help such countries as Nicaragua and Honduras to help themselves. They are the immediate beneficiaries. The national benefit to the United States is twofold. First, it is obvious that the Monroe doctrine is more vital in the neighborhood of the Panama Canal and the zone of the Caribbean than anywhere else. There, too, the maintenance of that doctrine falls most heavily upon the United States. It is therefore essential that the countries within that sphere shall be removed from the jeopardy involved by heavy foreign debt and chaotic national finances and from the ever-present danger of international complications due to disorder at home. Hence the United States has been glad to encourage and support American bankers who were willing to lend a helping hand to the financial rehabilitation of such countries because this financial rehabilitation and the protection of their customhouses from being the prey of would-be dictators would remove at one stroke the menace of foreign creditors and the menace of revolutionary disorder.

The second advantage of the United States is one affecting chiefly all the southern and Gulf ports and the business and industry of the South. The Republics of Central America and the Caribbean possess great natural wealth. They need only a measure of stability and the means of financial regeneration to enter upon an era of peace and prosperity, bringing profit and happiness to themselves and at the same time creating conditions sure to lead to a flourishing interchange of trade with this country.

I wish to call your especial attention to the recent occurrences in Nicaragua, for I believe the terrible events recorded there during the revolution of the past summer—the useless loss of life, the devastation of property, the bombardment of defenseless cities, the killing and wounding of women and children, the torturing of noncombatants to exact contributions, and the suffering of thousands of human beings—might have been averted had the Department of State, through approval of the loan convention by the Senate, been permitted to carry out its now well-developed policy of encouraging the extending of financial aid to weak Central American States with the primary objects of avoiding just such revolutions by assisting those Republics to rehabilitate their finances, to establish their currency on a stable basis, to remove the customhouses from the danger of revolutions by arranging for their secure administration, and to establish reliable banks.

During this last revolution in Nicaragua, the Government of that Republic having admitted its inability to protect American life and property against acts of sheer lawlessness on the part of the malcontents, and having requested this Government to assume that office, it became necessary to land over 2,000 marines and bluejackets in Nicaragua. Owing to their presence the constituted Government of Nicaragua was free to devote its attention wholly to its internal troubles, and was thus enabled to stamp out the rebellion in a short space of time. When the Red Cross supplies sent to Granada had been exhausted, 8,000 persons having been given food in one day upon the arrival of the American forces, our men supplied other unfortunate, needy Nicaraguans from their own haversacks. I wish to congratulate the officers and men of the United States navy and Marine Corps who took part in reestablishing order in Nicaragua upon their splendid conduct, and to record with sorrow the death of seven American marines and bluejackets. Since the reestablishment of peace and order, elections have been held amid conditions of quiet and tranquillity. Nearly all the American marines have now been withdrawn. The country should soon be on the road to recovery. The only apparent danger now threatening Nicaragua arises from the shortage of funds. Although American bankers have already rendered assistance, they may naturally be loath to advance a loan adequate to set the country upon its feet without the support of some such convention as that of June, 1911, upon which the Senate has not yet acted.

Enforcement of Neutrality Laws

In the general effort to contribute to the enjoyment of peace by those Republics which are near neighbors of the United States, the administration has enforced the so-called neutrality statutes with a new vigor, and those statutes were greatly strengthened in restricting the exportation of arms and munitions by the joint resolution of last March. It is still a regrettable fact that certain American ports are made the rendezvous of professional revolutionists and others engaged in intrigue against the peace of those Republics. It must be admitted that occasionally a revolution in this region is justified as a real popular movement to throw off the shackles of a vicious and tyrannical government. Such was the Nicaraguan revolution against the Zelaya regime. A nation enjoying our liberal institutions can not escape sympathy with a true popular movement, and one so well justified. In very many cases, however, revolutions in the Republics in question have no basis in principle, but are due merely to the machinations of conscienceless and ambitious men, and have no effect but to bring new suffering and fresh burdens to an already oppressed people. The question whether the use of American ports as foci of revolutionary intrigue can be best dealt with by a further amendment to the neutrality statutes or whether it would be safer to deal with special cases by special laws is one worthy of the careful consideration of the Congress.

Visit of Secretary Knox to Central America and the Caribbean

Impressed with the particular importance of the relations between the United States and the Republics of Central America and the Caribbean region, which of necessity must become still more intimate by reason of the mutual advantages which will be presented by the opening of the Panama Canal, I directed the Secretary of State last February to visit these Republics for the purpose of giving evidence of the sincere friendship and good will which the Government and people of the United States bear toward them. Ten Republics were visited. Everywhere he was received with a cordiality of welcome and a generosity of hospitality such as to impress me deeply and to merit our warmest thanks. The appreciation of the Governments and people of the countries visited, which has been appropriately shown in various ways, leaves me no doubt that his visit will conduce to that closer union and better understanding between the United States and those Republics which I have had it much at heart to promote.

Our Mexican Policy

For two years revolution and counter-revolution have distraught the neighboring Republic of Mexico. Brigandage has involved a great deal of depredation upon foreign interests. There have constantly recurred questions of extreme delicacy. On several occasions very difficult situations have arisen on our frontier. Throughout this trying period, the policy of the United States has been one of patient nonintervention, steadfast recognition of constituted authority in the neighboring nation, and the exertion of every effort to care for American interests. I profoundly hope that the Mexican nation may soon resume the path of order, prosperity, and progress. To that nation in its sore troubles, the sympathetic friendship of the United States has been demonstrated to a high degree. There were in Mexico at the beginning of the revolution some thirty or forty thousand American citizens engaged in enterprises contributing greatly to the prosperity of that Republic and also benefiting the important trade between the two countries. The investment of American capital in Mexico has been estimated at $1,000,000,000. The responsibility of endeavoring to safeguard those interests and the dangers inseparable from propinquity to so turbulent a situation have been great, but I am happy to have been able to adhere to the policy above outlined—a policy which I hope may be soon justified by the complete success of the Mexican people in regaining the blessings of peace and good order.

Agricultural Credits

A most important work, accomplished in the past year by the American diplomatic officers in Europe, is the investigation of the agricultural credit system in the European countries. Both as a means to afford relief to the consumers of this country through a more thorough development of agricultural resources and as a means of more sufficiently maintaining the agricultural population, the project to establish credit facilities for the farmers is a concern of vital importance to this Nation. No evidence of prosperity among well-established farmers should blind us to the fact that lack of capital is preventing a development of the Nation's agricultural resources and an adequate increase of the land under cultivation; that agricultural production is fast falling behind the increase in population; and that, in fact, although these well-established farmers are maintained in increasing prosperity because of the natural increase in population, we are not developing the industry of agriculture. We are not breeding in proportionate numbers a race of independent and independence-loving landowners, for a lack of which no growth of cities can compensate. Our farmers have been our mainstay in times of crisis, and in future it must still largely be upon their stability and common sense that this democracy must rely to conserve its principles of self-government.

The need of capital which American farmers feel today had been experienced by the farmers of Europe, with their centuries-old farms, many years ago. The problem had been successfully solved in the Old World and it was evident that the farmers of this country might profit by a study of their systems. I therefore ordered, through the Department of State, an investigation to be made by the diplomatic officers in Europe, and I have laid the results of this investigation before the governors of the various States with the hope that they will be used to advantage in their forthcoming meeting.

Increase of Foreign Trade

In my last annual message I said that the fiscal year ended June 30, 1911, was noteworthy as marking the highest record of exports of American products to foreign countries. The fiscal year 1912 shows that this rate of advance has been maintained, the total domestic exports having a valuation approximately of $2,200,000,000, as compared with a fraction over $2,000,000,000 the previous year. It is also significant that manufactured and partly manufactured articles continue to be the chief commodities forming the volume of our augmented exports, the demands of our own people for consumption requiring that an increasing proportion of our abundant agricultural products be kept at home. In the fiscal year 1911 the exports of articles in the various stages of manufacture, not including foodstuffs partly or wholly manufactured, amounted approximately to $907,500,000. In the fiscal year 1912 the total was nearly $1,022,000,000, a gain of $114,000,000.

Advantage of Maximum and Minimum Tariff Provision

The importance which our manufactures have assumed in the commerce of the world in competition with the manufactures of other countries again draws attention to the duty of this Government to use its utmost endeavors to secure impartial treatment for American products in all markets. Healthy commercial rivalry in international intercourse is best assured by the possession of proper means for protecting and promoting our foreign trade. It is natural that competitive countries should view with some concern this steady expansion of our commerce. If in some instance the measures taken by them to meet it are not entirely equitable, a remedy should be found. In former messages I have described the negotiations of the Department of State with foreign Governments for the adjustment of the maximum and minimum tariff as provided in section 2 of the tariff law of 1909. The advantages secured by the adjustment of our trade relations under this law have continued during the last year, and some additional cases of discriminatory treatment of which we had reason to complain have been removed. The Department of State has for the first time in the history of this country obtained substantial most-favored-nation treatment from all the countries of the world. There are, however, other instances which, while apparently not constituting undue discrimination in the sense of section 2, are nevertheless exceptions to the complete equity of tariff treatment for American products that the Department of State consistently has sought to obtain for American commerce abroad.

Necessity for Supplementary Legislation

These developments confirm the opinion conveyed to you in my annual message of 1911, that while the maximum and minimum provision of the tariff law of 1909 has been fully justified by the success achieved in removing previously existing undue discriminations against American products, yet experience has shown that this feature of the law should be amended in such way as to provide a fully effective means of meeting the varying degrees of discriminatory treatment of American commerce in foreign countries still encountered, as well as to protect against injurious treatment on the part of foreign Governments, through either legislative or administrative measures, the financial interests abroad of American citizens whose enterprises enlarge the market for American commodities.

I can not too strongly recommend to the Congress the passage of some such enabling measure as the bill which was recommended by the Secretary of State in his letter of December 13, 1911. The object of the proposed legislation is, in brief, to enable the Executive to apply, as the case may require, to any or all commodities, whether or not on the free list from a country which discriminates against the United States, a graduated scale of duties tip to the maximum of 25 per cent ad valorem provided in the present law. Flat tariffs are out of date. Nations no longer accord equal tariff treatment to all other nations irrespective of the treatment from them received. Such a flexible power at the command of the Executive would serve to moderate any unfavorable tendencies on the part of those countries from which the importations into the United States are substantially confined to articles on the free list as well as of the countries which find a lucrative market in the United States for their products under existing customs rates. It is very necessary that the American Government should be equipped with weapons of negotiation adapted to modern economic conditions, in order that we may at all times be in a position to gain not only technically just but actually equitable treatment for our trade, and also for American enterprise and vested interests abroad.

Business Secured to Our Country by Direct Official Effort

As illustrating the commercial benefits of the Nation derived from the new diplomacy and its effectiveness upon the material as well as the more ideal side, it may be remarked that through direct official efforts alone there have been obtained in the course of this administration, contracts from foreign Governments involving an expenditure of $50,000,000 in the factories of the United States. Consideration of this fact and some reflection upon the necessary effects of a scientific tariff system and a foreign service alert and equipped to cooperate with the business men of America carry the conviction that the gratifying increase in the export trade of this country is, in substantial amount, due to our improved governmental methods of protecting and stimulating it. It is germane to these observations to remark that in the two years that have elapsed since the successful negotiation of our new treaty with Japan, which at the time seemed to present so many practical difficulties, our export trade to that country has increased at the rate of over $1,000,000 a month. Our exports to Japan for the year ended June 30, 1910, were $21,959,310, while for the year ended June 30, 1912, the exports were $53,478,046, a net increase in the sale of American products of nearly 150 per cent.

Special Claims Arbitration with Great Britain

Under the special agreement entered into between the United States and Great Britain on August 18, 1910, for the arbitration of outstanding pecuniary claims, a schedule of claims and the terms of submission have been agreed upon by the two Governments, and together with the special agreement were approved by the Senate on July 19, 1911, but in accordance with the terms of the agreement they did not go into effect until confirmed by the two Governments by an exchange of notes, which was done on April 26 last. Negotiations are still in progress for a supplemental schedule of claims to be submitted to arbitration under this agreement, and meanwhile the necessary preparations for the arbitration of the claims included in the first schedule have been undertaken and are being carried on under the authority of an appropriation made for that purpose at the last session of Congress. It is anticipated that the two Governments will be prepared to call upon the arbitration tribunal, established under this agreement, to meet at Washington early next year to proceed with this arbitration.

Fur Seal Treaty and Need for Amendment of Our Statute

The act adopted at the last session of Congress to give effect to the fur-seal convention of July 7, 1911, between Great Britain, Japan, Russia, and the United States provided for the suspension of all land killing of seals on the Pribilof Islands for a period of five years, and an objection has now been presented to this provision by the other parties in interest, which raises the issue as to whether or not this prohibition of land killing is inconsistent with the spirit, if not the letter, of the treaty stipulations. The justification of establishing this close season depends, under the terms of the convention, upon how far, if at all, it is necessary for protecting and preserving the American fur-seal herd and for increasing its number. This is a question requiring examination of the present condition of the herd and the treatment which it needs in the light of actual experience and scientific investigation. A careful examination of the subject is now being made, and this Government will soon be in possession of a considerable amount of new information about the American seal herd, which has been secured during the past season and will be of great value in determining this question; and if it should appear that there is any uncertainty as to the real necessity for imposing a close season at this time I shall take an early opportunity to address a special message to Congress on this subject, in the belief that this Government should yield on this point rather than give the slightest ground for the charge that we have been in any way remiss in observing our treaty obligations.

Final Settlement of North Atlantic Fisheries Dispute

On the 20th of July last an agreement was concluded between the United States and Great Britain adopting, with certain modifications, the rules and method of procedure recommended in the award rendered by the North Atlantic Coast Fisheries Arbitration Tribunal on September 7, 1910, for the settlement hereafter, in accordance with the principles laid down in the award, of questions arising with reference to the exercise of the American fishing liberties under Article I of the treaty of October 20, 1818, between the United States and Great Britain. This agreement received the approval of the Senate on August 1 and was formally ratified by the two Governments on November 15 last. The rules and a method of procedure embodied in the award provided for determining by an impartial tribunal the reasonableness of any new fishery regulations on the treaty coasts of Newfoundland and Canada before such regulations could be enforced against American fishermen exercising their treaty liberties on those coasts, and also for determining the delimitation of bays on such coasts more than 10 miles wide, in accordance with the definition adopted by the tribunal of the meaning of the word "bays" as used in the treaty. In the subsequent negotiations between the two Governments, undertaken for the purpose of giving practical effect to these rules and methods of procedure, it was found that certain modifications therein were desirable from the point of view of both Governments, and these negotiations have finally resulted in the agreement above mentioned by which the award recommendations as modified by mutual consent of the two Governments are finally adopted and made effective, thus bringing this century-old controversy to a final conclusion, which is equally beneficial and satisfactory to both Governments.

Imperial Valley and Mexico

In order to make possible the more effective performance of the work necessary for the confinement in their present channel of the waters of the lower Colorado River, and thus to protect the people of the Imperial Valley, as well as in order to reach with the Government of Mexico an understanding regarding the distribution of the waters of the Colorado River, in which both Governments are much interested, negotiations are going forward with a view to the establishment of a preliminary Colorado River commission, which shall have the powers necessary to enable it to do the needful work and with authority to study the question of the equitable distribution of the waters. There is every reason to believe that an understanding upon this point will be reached and that an agreement will be signed in the near future.

Chamizal Dispute

In the interest of the people and city of El Paso this Government has been assiduous in its efforts to bring to an early settlement the long-standing Chamizal dispute with Mexico. Much has been accomplished, and while the final solution of the dispute is not immediate, the favorable attitude lately assumed by the Mexican Government encourages the hope that this troublesome question will be satisfactorily and definitively settled at an early day.

International Commission of Jurists

In pursuance of the convention of August 23, 1906, signed at the Third Pan American Conference, held at Rio de Janeiro, the International Commission of jurists met at that capital during the month of last June. At this meeting 16 American Republics were represented, including the United States, and comprehensive plans for the future work of the commission were adopted. At the next meeting fixed for June, 1914, committees already appointed are instructed to report regarding topics assigned to them.

Opium Conference—Unfortunate Failure of Our Government to Enact Recommended Legislation

In my message on foreign relations communicated to the two Houses of Congress December 7, 1911, I called especial attention to the assembling of the Opium Conference at The Hague, to the fact that that conference was to review all pertinent municipal laws relating to the opium and allied evils, and certainly all international rules regarding these evils, and to the fact that it seemed to me most essential that the Congress should take immediate action on the antinarcotic legislation before the Congress, to which I had previously called attention by a special message.

The international convention adopted by the conference conforms almost entirely to the principles contained in the proposed antinarcotic legislation which has been before the last two Congresses. It was most unfortunate that this Government, having taken the initiative in the international action which eventuated in the important international opium convention, failed to do its share in the great work by neglecting to pass the necessary legislation to correct the deplorable narcotic evils in the United States as well as to redeem international pledges upon which it entered by virtue of the above-mentioned convention. The Congress at its present session should enact into law those bills now before it which have been so carefully drawn up in collaboration between the Department of State and the other executive departments, and which have behind them not only the moral sentiment of the country, but the practical support of all the legitimate trade interests likely to be affected. Since the international convention was signed, adherence to it has been made by several European States not represented at the conference at The Hague and also by seventeen Latin-American Republics.

Europe and the Near East

The war between Italy and Turkey came to a close in October last by the signature of a treaty of peace, subsequently to which the Ottoman Empire renounced sovereignty over Cyrenaica and Tripolitania in favor of Italy. During the past year the Near East has unfortunately been the theater of constant hostilities. Almost simultaneously with the conclusion of peace between Italy and Turkey and their arrival at an adjustment of the complex questions at issue between them, war broke out between

Turkey on the one hand and Bulgaria, Greece, Montenegro, and Servia on the other. The United States has happily been involved neither directly nor indirectly with the causes or questions incident to any of these hostilities and has maintained in regard to them an attitude of absolute neutrality and of complete political disinterestedness. In the second war in which the Ottoman Empire has been engaged the loss of life and the consequent distress on both sides have been appalling, and the United States has found occasion, in the interest of humanity, to carry out the charitable desires of the American people, to extend a measure of relief to the sufferers on either side through the impartial medium of the Red Cross. Beyond this the chief care of the Government of the United States has been to make due provision for the protection of its national residents in belligerent territory. In the exercise of my duty in this matter I have dispatched to Turkish waters a special-service squadron, consisting of two armored cruisers, in order that this Government may if need be bear its part in such measures as it may be necessary for the interested nations to adopt for the safeguarding of foreign lives and property in the Ottoman Empire in the event that a dangerous situation should develop. In the meanwhile the several interested European powers have promised to extend to American citizens the benefit of such precautionary or protective measures as they might adopt, in the same manner in which it has been the practice of this Government to extend its protection to all foreign residents in those countries of the Western Hemisphere in which it has from time to time been the task of the United States to act in the interest of peace and good order. The early appearance of a large fleet of European warships in the Bosphorus apparently assured the protection of foreigners in that quarter, where the presence of the American stationnaire the U.S.S. *Scorpion* sufficed, under the circumstances, to represent the United States. Our cruisers were thus left free to act if need be along the Mediterranean coasts should any unexpected contingency arise affecting the numerous American interests in the neighborhood of Smyrna and Beirut.

Spitzbergen

The great preponderance of American material interests in the subarctic island of Spitzbergen, which has always been regarded politically as "no man's land," impels this Government to a continued and lively interest in the international dispositions to be made for the political governance and administration of that region. The conflict of certain claims of American citizens and others is in a fair way to adjustment, while the settlement of matters of administration, whether by international conference of the interested powers or otherwise, continues to be the subject of exchange of views between the Governments concerned.

Liberia

As a result of the efforts of this Government to place the Government of Liberia in position to pay its outstanding indebtedness and to maintain a stable and efficient government, negotiations for a loan of $1,700,000 have been successfully concluded, and it is anticipated that the payment of the old loan and the issuance of the bonds of the 1912 loan for the rehabilitation of the finances of Liberia will follow at an early date, when the new receivership will go into active operation. The new receivership will consist of a general receiver of customs designated by the Government of the United States and three receivers of customs designated by the Governments of Germany, France, and Great Britain, which countries have commercial interests in the Republic of Liberia.

In carrying out the understanding between the Government of Liberia and that of the United States, and in fulfilling the terms of the agreement between the former Government and the American bankers, three competent ex-army officers are now effectively employed by the Liberian Government in reorganizing the police force of the Republic, not only to keep in order the native tribes in the hinterland but to serve as a necessary police force along the frontier. It is hoped that these measures will assure not only the continued existence but the prosperity and welfare of the Republic of

Liberia. Liberia possesses fertility of soil and natural resources, which should insure to its people a reasonable prosperity. It was the duty of the United States to assist the Republic of Liberia in accordance with our historical interest and moral guardianship of a community founded by American citizens, as it was also the duty of the American Government to attempt to assure permanence to a country of much sentimental and perhaps future real interest to a large body of our citizens.

Morocco

The legation at Tangier is now in charge of our consul general, who is acting as chargé d'affaires, as well as caring for our commercial interests in that country. In view of the fact that many of the foreign powers are now represented by chargés d'affaires it has not been deemed necessary to appoint at the present time a minister to fill a vacancy occurring in that post.

The Far East

The political disturbances in China in the autumn and winter of 1911–12 resulted in the abdication of the Manchu rulers on February 12, followed by the formation of a provisional republican government empowered to conduct the affairs of the nation until a permanent government might be regularly established. The natural sympathy of the American people with the assumption of republican principles by the Chinese people was appropriately expressed in a concurrent resolution of Congress on April 17, 1912. A constituent assembly, composed of representatives duly chosen by the people of China in the elections that are now being held, has been called to meet in January next to adopt a permanent constitution and organize the Government of the nascent Republic. During the formative constitutional stage and pending definite action by the assembly, as expressive of the popular will, and the hoped-for establishment of a stable republican form of government, capable of fulfilling its international obligations, the United States is, according to precedent, maintaining full and friendly de facto relations with the provisional Government.

The new condition of affairs thus created has presented many serious and complicated problems, both of internal rehabilitation and of international relations, whose solution it was realized would necessarily require much time and patience. From the beginning of the upheaval last autumn it was felt by the United States, in common with the other powers having large interests in China, that independent action by the foreign Governments in their own individual interests would add further confusion to a situation already complicated. A policy of international cooperation was accordingly adopted in an understanding, reached early in the disturbances, to act together for the protection of the lives and property of foreigners if menaced, to maintain an attitude of strict impartiality as between the contending factions, and to abstain from any endeavor to influence the Chinese in their organization of a new form of government. In view of the seriousness of the disturbances and their general character, the American minister at Peking was instructed at his discretion to advise our nationals in the affected districts to concentrate at such centers as were easily accessible to foreign troops or men of war. Nineteen of our naval vessels were stationed at various Chinese ports, and other measures were promptly taken for the adequate protection of American interests.

It was further mutually agreed, in the hope of hastening an end to hostilities, that none of the interested powers would approve the making of loans by its nationals to either side. As soon, however, as a united provisional Government of China was assured, the United States joined in a favorable consideration of that Government's request for advances needed for immediate administrative necessities and later for a loan to effect a permanent national reorganization. The interested Governments had already, by common consent, adopted, in respect to the purposes, expenditure, and security of any loans to China made by their nationals, certain conditions which were held to be essential, not only to secure reasonable protection for the foreign investors, but also to safeguard and strengthen China's credit by discouraging indiscriminate borrowing and by insuring the application of the funds toward the establishment of the stable and effective government necessary to China's welfare. In June last representative banking groups of the United States, France, Germany, Great Britain, Japan, and Russia formulated, with the general sanction of their respective Governments, the guaranties that would be expected in relation to the expenditure and security of the large reorganization loan desired by China, which, however, have thus far proved unacceptable to the provisional Government.

Special Mission of Condolence to Japan

In August last I accredited the Secretary of State as special ambassador to Japan, charged with the mission of bearing to the imperial family, the Government, and the people of that Empire the sympathetic message of the American Commonwealth on the sad occasion of the death of His Majesty the Emperor Mutsuhito, whose long and benevolent reign was the greater part of Japan's modern history. The kindly reception everywhere accorded to Secretary Knox showed that his mission was deeply appreciated by the Japanese nation and emphasized strongly the friendly relations that have for so many years existed between the two peoples.

South America

Our relations with the Argentine Republic are most friendly and cordial. So, also, are our relations with Brazil, whose Government has accepted the invitation of the United States to send two army officers to study at the Coast Artillery School at Fort Monroe. The long-standing Alsop claim, which had been the only hindrance to the healthy growth of the most friendly relations between the United States and Chile, having been eliminated through the submission of the question to His Britannic Majesty King George V as "amiable compositeur," it is a cause of much gratification to me that our relations with Chile are now established upon a firm basis of growing friendship. The Chilean Government has placed an officer of the United States Coast Artillery in charge of the Chilean Coast Artillery School, and has shown appreciation of American methods by confiding to an American firm important work for the Chilean coast defenses.

Last year a revolution against the established Government of Ecuador broke out at the principal port of that Republic. Previous to this occurrence the chief American interest in Ecuador, represented by the Guayaquil & Quito Railway Co., incorporated in the United States, had rendered extensive transportation and other services on account to the Ecuadorian Government, the amount of which ran into a sum which was steadily increasing and which the Ecuadorian Government had made no provision to pay, thereby threatening to crush out the very existence of this American enterprise. When tranquillity had been restored to Ecuador as a result of the triumphant progress of the Government forces from Quito, this Government interposed its good offices to the end that the American interests in Ecuador might be saved from complete extinction. As a part of the arrangement which was reached between the parties, and at the request of the Government of Ecuador, I have consented to name an arbitrator, who, acting under the terms of the railroad contract, with an arbitrator named by the Ecuadorian Government, will pass upon the claims that have arisen since the arrangement reached through the action of a similar arbitral tribunal in 1908.

In pursuance of a request made some time ago by the Ecuadorian Government, the Department of State has given much attention to the problem of the proper sanitation of Guayaquil. As a result a detail of officers of the Canal Zone will be sent to Guayaquil to recommend measures that will lead to the complete permanent sanitation of this plague and fever infected region of that Republic, which has for so long constituted a menace to health conditions on the Canal Zone. It is hoped that the report which this mission will furnish will point out a way whereby the modicum of assistance which the United States may properly lend the Ecuadorian Government may be made effective in ridding the west coast of South America of a focus of contagion to the future commercial current passing through the Panama Canal.

In the matter of the claim of John Celestine Landreau against the Government of Peru, which claim arises out of certain contracts and transactions in connection with the discovery and exploitation of guano, and which has been under discussion between the two Governments since 1874, I am glad to report that as the result of prolonged negotiations, which have been characterized by the utmost friendliness and good will on both sides, the Department of State has succeeded in securing the consent of Peru to the arbitration of the claim, and that the negotiations attending the drafting and signature of a protocol submitting the claim to an arbitral tribunal are proceeding with due celerity.

An officer of the American Public Health Service and an American sanitary engineer are now on the way to Iquitos, in the employ of the Peruvian Government, to take charge of the sanitation of that river port. Peru is building a number of submarines in this country, and continues to show every desire to have American capital invested in the Republic.

In July the United States sent undergraduate delegates to the Third International Students Congress held at Lima, American students having been for the first time invited to one of these meetings.

The Republic of Uruguay has shown its appreciation of American agricultural and other methods by sending a large commission to this country and by employing many American experts to assist in building up agricultural and allied industries in Uruguay.

Venezuela is paying off the last of the claims the settlement of which was provided for by the Washington protocols, including those of American citizens. Our relations with Venezuela are most cordial, and the trade of that Republic with the United States is now greater than with any other country.

Central America and the Caribbean

During the past summer the revolution against the administration which followed the assassination of President Caceres a year ago last November brought the Dominican Republic to the verge of administrative chaos, without offering any guaranties of eventual stability in the ultimate success of either party. In pursuance of the treaty relations of the United States with the Dominican Republic, which were threatened by the necessity of suspending the operation under American administration of the customhouses on the Haitian frontier, it was found necessary to dispatch special commissioners to the island to reestablish the customhouses and with a guard sufficient to insure needed protection to the customs administration. The efforts which have been made appear to have resulted in the restoration of normal conditions throughout the Republic. The good offices which the commissioners were able to exercise were instrumental in bringing the contending parties together and in furnishing a basis of adjustment which it is hoped will result in permanent benefit to the Dominican people.

Mindful of its treaty relations, and owing to the position of the Government of the United States as mediator between the Dominican Republic and Haiti in their boundary dispute, and because of the further fact that the revolutionary activities on the Haitian-Dominican frontier had become so active as practically to obliterate the line of demarcation that had been heretofore recognized pending the definitive settlement of the boundary in controversy, it was found necessary to indicate to the two island Governments a provisional de facto boundary line. This was done without prejudice to the rights or obligations of either country in a final settlement to be reached by arbitration. The tentative line chosen was one which, under the circumstances brought to the knowledge of this Government, seemed to conform to the best interests of the disputants. The border patrol which it had been found necessary to reestablish for customs purposes between the two countries was instructed provisionally to observe this line.

The Republic of Cuba last May was in the throes of a lawless uprising that for a time threatened the destruction of a great deal of valuable property—much of it owned by Americans and other foreigners—as well as the existence of the Government itself. The armed forces of Cuba being inadequate to guard property from attack and at the same time properly to operate against the rebels, a force of American marines was dispatched from our naval station at Guantanamo into the Province of Oriente for the protection of American and other foreign life and property. The Cuban Government was thus able to use all its forces in putting down the outbreak, which it succeeded in doing in a period of six weeks. The presence of two American warships in the harbor of Habana during the most critical period of this disturbance contributed in great measure to allay the fears of the inhabitants, including a large foreign colony.

There has been under discussion with the Government of Cuba for some time the question of the release by this Government of its leasehold rights at Bahia Honda, on the northern coast of Cuba, and the enlargement, in exchange therefor, of the naval station which has been established at Guantanamo Bay, on the south. As the result of the negotiations thus carried on, an agreement has been reached between the two Governments providing for the suitable enlargement of the Guantanamo Bay station upon terms which are entirely fair and equitable to all parties concerned.

At the request alike of the Government and both political parties in Panama, an American commission undertook supervision of the recent presidential election in that Republic, where our treaty relations, and, indeed, every geographical consideration, make the maintenance of order and satisfactory conditions of peculiar interest to the Government of the United States. The elections passed without disorder, and the new administration has entered upon its functions.

The Government of Great Britain has asked the support of the United States for the protection of the interests of British holders of the foreign bonded debt of Guatemala. While this Government is hopeful of an arrangement equitable to the British bondholders, it is naturally unable to view the question apart from its relation to the broad subject of financial stability in Central America, in which the policy of the United States does not permit it to escape a vital interest. Through a renewal of negotiations between the Government of Guatemala and American bankers, the aim of which is a loan for the rehabilitation of Guatemalan finances, a way appears to be open by which the Government of Guatemala could promptly satisfy any equitable and just British claims, and at the same time so improve its whole financial position as to contribute greatly to the increased prosperity of the Republic and to redound to the benefit of foreign investments and foreign trade with that country. Failing such an arrangement, it may become impossible for the Government of the United States to escape its obligations in connection with such measures as may become necessary to exact justice to legitimate foreign claims.

In the recent revolution in Nicaragua, which, it was generally admitted, might well have resulted in a general Central American conflict but for the intervention of the United States, the Government of Honduras was especially menaced; but fortunately peaceful conditions were maintained within the borders of that Republic. The financial condition of that country remains unchanged, no means having been found for the final adjustment of pressing outstanding foreign claims. This makes it the more regrettable that the financial convention between the United States and Honduras has thus far failed of ratification. The Government of the United States continues to hold itself ready to cooperate with the Government of Honduras, which it is believed, can not much longer delay the meeting of its foreign obligations, and it is hoped at the proper time American bankers will be willing to cooperate for this purpose.

Necessity for Greater Governmental Effort in Retention and Expansion of Our Foreign Trade

It is not possible to make to the Congress a communication upon the present foreign relations of the United States so detailed as to convey an adequate impression of the enormous increase in the importance and activities of those relations. If this Government is really to preserve to the American people that free opportunity in foreign markets which will soon be indispensable to our prosperity, even greater efforts must be made. Otherwise the American merchant, manufacturer, and exporter will find many a field in which American trade should logically predominate preempted through the more energetic efforts of other governments and other commercial nations.

There are many ways in which through hearty cooperation the legislative and executive branches of this Government can do much. The absolute essential is the spirit of united effort and singleness of purpose. I will allude only to a very few specific examples of action which ought then to result. America can not take its proper place in the most important fields for its commercial activity and enterprise unless we have a merchant marine. American commerce and enterprise can not be effectively fostered in those fields unless we have good American banks in the countries referred to. We need American newspapers in those countries and proper means for public information about them. We need to assure the permanency of a trained foreign service. We need legislation enabling the members of the foreign service to be systematically brought in direct contact with the industrial, manufacturing, and exporting interests of this country in order that American business men may enter the foreign field with a clear perception of the exact conditions to be dealt with and the officers themselves may prosecute their work with a clear idea of what American industrial and manufacturing interests require.

Conclusion

Congress should fully realize the conditions which obtain in the world as we find ourselves at the threshold of our middle age as a Nation. We have emerged full grown as a peer in the great concourse of nations. We have passed through various formative periods. We have been self-centered in the struggle to develop our domestic resources and deal with our domestic questions. The Nation is now too matured to continue in its foreign relations those temporary expedients natural to a people to whom domestic affairs are the sole concern. In the past our diplomacy has often consisted, in normal times, in a mere assertion of the right to international existence. We are now in a larger relation with broader rights of our own and obligations to others than ourselves. A number of great guiding principles were laid down early in the history of this Government. The recent task of our diplomacy has been to adjust those principles to the conditions of to-day, to develop their corollaries, to find practical applications of the old principles expanded to meet new situations. Thus are being evolved bases upon which can rest the superstructure of policies which must grow with the destined progress of this Nation. The successful conduct of our foreign relations demands a broad and a modern view. We can not meet new questions nor build for the future if we confine ourselves to outworn dogmas of the past and to the perspective appropriate at our emergence from colonial times and conditions. The opening of the Panama Canal will mark a new era in our international life and create new and worldwide conditions which, with their vast correlations and consequences, will obtain for hundreds of years to come. We must not wait for events to overtake us unawares. With continuity of purpose we must deal with the problems of our external relations by a diplomacy modern, resourceful, magnanimous, and fittingly expressive of the high ideals of a great nation.

Part II
On Fiscal, Judicial, Military and Insular Affairs
December 6, 1912

To the Senate and House of Representatives:

On the 3d of December I sent a message to the Congress, which was confined to our foreign relations. The Secretary of State makes no report to the President or to Congress, and a review of the history of the transactions of the State Department in one year must therefore be included by the President in his annual message or Congress will not be fully informed of them. A full discussion of all the transactions of the Government, with a view to informing the Congress of the important events of the year and recommending new legislation, requires more space than one message of reasonable length affords. I have therefore adopted the course of sending three or four messages during the first ten days of the session, so as to include reference to the more important matters that should be brought to the attention of the Congress.

Business Conditions

The condition of the country with reference to business could hardly be better. While the four years of the administration now drawing to a close have not developed great speculative expansion or a wide field of new investment, the recovery and progress made from the depressing conditions following the panic of 1907 have been steady and the improvement has been clear and easily traced in the statistics. The business of the country is now on a solid basis. Credits are not unduly extended, and every phase of the situation seems in a state of preparedness for a period of unexampled prosperity. Manufacturing concerns are running at their full capacity and the demand for labor was never so constant and growing. The foreign trade of the country for this year will exceed $4,000,000,000, while the balance in our favor—that of the excess of exports over imports—will exceed $500,000,000. More than half our exports are manufactures or partly manufactured material, while our exports of farm products do not show the same increase because of domestic consumption. It is a year of bumper crops; the total money value of farm products will exceed $9,500,000,000. It is a year when the bushel or unit price of agricultural products has gradually fallen, and yet the total value of the entire crop is greater by over $1,000,000,000 than we have known in our history.

Condition of the Treasury

The condition of the Treasury is very satisfactory. The total interest-bearing debt is $963,777,770, of which $134,631,980 constitute the Panama Canal loan. The noninterest-bearing debt is $378,301,284.90, including $346,681,016 of greenbacks. We have in the Treasury $150,000,000 in gold coin as a reserve against the outstanding greenbacks; and in addition we have a cash balance in the Treasury as a general fund of $167,152,478.99, or an increase of $26,975,552 over the general fund last year.

*   *   *

Our Banking and Currency System

A time when panics seem far removed is the best time for us to prepare our financial system to withstand a storm. The most crying need this country has is a proper banking and currency system. The existing one is inadequate, and everyone who has studied the question admits it.

It is the business of the National Government to provide a medium, automatically contracting and expanding in volume, to meet the needs of trade. Our present system lacks the indispensable quality of elasticity.

The only part of our monetary medium that has elasticity is the bank-note currency. The peculiar provisions of the law requiring national banks to maintain reserves to meet the call of the depositors operates to increase the money stringency when it arises rather than to expand the supply of currency and relieve it. It operates upon each bank and furnishes a motive for the withdrawal of currency from the channels of trade by each bank to save itself, and offers no inducement whatever for the use of the reserve to expand the supply of currency to meet the exceptional demand.

After the panic of 1907 Congress realized that the present system was not adapted to the country's needs and that under it panics were possible that might properly be avoided by legislative provision. Accordingly a monetary commission was appointed which made a report in February, 1912. The system which they recommended involved a National Reserve Association, which was, in certain of its faculties and functions, a bank, and which was given through its governing authorities the power, by issuing circulating notes for approved commercial paper, by fixing discounts, and by other methods of transfer of currency, to expand the supply of the monetary medium where it was most needed to prevent the export or hoarding of gold and generally to exercise such supervision over the supply of money in every part of the country as to prevent a stringency and a panic. The stock in this association was to be distributed to the banks of the whole United States, State and National, in a mixed proportion to bank units and to capital stock paid in. The control of the association was vested in a board of directors to be elected by representatives of the banks, except certain ex-officio directors, three Cabinet officers, and the Comptroller of the Currency. The President was to appoint the governor of the association from three persons to be selected by the directors, while the two deputy governors were to be elected by the board of directors. The details of the plan were worked out with great care and ability, and the plan in general seems to me to furnish the basis for a proper solution of our present difficulties. I feel that the Government might very properly be given a greater voice in the executive committee of the board of directors without danger of injecting politics into its management, but I think the federation system of banks is a good one, provided proper precautions are taken to prevent banks of large capital from absorbing power through ownership of stock in other banks. The objections to a central bank it seems to me are obviated if the ownership of the reserve association is distributed among all the banks of a country in which banking is free. The earnings of the reserve association are limited in percentage to a reasonable and fixed amount, and the profits over and above this are to be turned into the Government Treasury. It is quite probable that still greater security against control by money centers may be worked into the plan.

Certain it is, however, that the objections which were made in the past history of this country to a central bank as furnishing a monopoly of financial power to private individuals, would not apply to an association whose ownership and control is so widely distributed and is divided between all the banks of the country, State and National, on the one hand, and the Chief Executive through three department heads and his Comptroller of the Currency, on the other. The ancient hostility to a national bank, with its branches, in which is concentrated the privilege of doing a banking business and carrying on the financial transactions of the Government, has prevented the establishment of such a bank since it was abolished in the Jackson Administration. Our present national banking law has obviated objections growing out of the same cause by providing a free banking system in which any set of stockholders can establish a national bank if they comply with the conditions of law. It seems to me that the National Reserve Association meets the same objection in a similar way; that is, by giving to each bank, State and National, in accordance with its size, a certain share in the stock of the reserve association, nontransferable and only to be held by the bank while it performs its functions as a partner in the reserve association.

The report of the commission recommends provisions for the imposition of a graduated tax on the expanded currency of such a character as to furnish a motive for reducing the issue of notes whenever their presence in the money market is not required by the exigencies of trade. In other words, the whole system has been worked out with the greatest care. Theoretically it presents a plan that ought to command support. Practically it may require modification in various of its provisions in order to make the security against abuses by combinations among the banks impossible. But in the face of the crying necessity that there is for improvement in our present system, I urgently invite the attention of Congress to the proposed plan and the report of the commission, with the hope that an earnest consideration may suggest amendments and changes within the general plan which will lead to its adoption for the benefit of the country. There is no class in the community more interested in a safe and sane banking and currency system, one which will prevent panics and automatically furnish in each trade center the currency needed in the carrying on of the business at that center, than the wage earner. There is no class in the community whose experience better qualifies them to make suggestions as to the sufficiency of a currency and banking system than the bankers and business men. Ought we, therefore, to ignore their recommendations and reject their financial judgment as to the proper method of reforming our financial system merely because of the suspicion which exists against them in the minds of many of our fellow citizens? Is it not the duty of Congress to take up the plan suggested, examine it from all standpoints, give impartial consideration to the testimony of those whose experience ought to fit them to give the best advice on the subject, and then to adopt some plan which will secure the benefits desired?

A banking and currency system seems far away from the wage earner and the farmer, but the fact is that they are vitally interested in a safe system of currency which shall graduate its volume to the amount needed and which shall prevent times of artificial stringency that frighten capital, stop employment, prevent the meeting of the pay roll, destroy local markets, and produce penury and want.

The Tariff

I have regarded it as my duty in former messages to the Congress to urge the revision of the tariff upon principles of protection. It was my judgment that the customs duties ought to be revised downward, but that the reduction ought not to be below a rate which would represent the difference in the cost of production between the article in question at home and abroad, and for this and other reasons I vetoed several bills which were presented to me in the last session of this Congress. Now that a new Congress has been elected on a platform of a tariff for revenue only rather than a protective tariff, and is to revise the tariff on that basis, it is needless for me to occupy the time of this Congress with arguments or recommendations in favor of a protective tariff.

Before passing from the tariff law, however, known as the Payne tariff law of August 5, 1909, I desire to call attention to section 38 of that act, assessing a special excise tax on corporations. It contains a provision requiring the levy of an additional 50 per cent to the annual tax in cases of neglect to verify the prescribed return or to file it before the time required by law. This additional charge of 50 per cent operates in some cases as a harsh penalty for what may have been a mere inadvertence or unintentional oversight, and the law should be so amended as to mitigate the severity of the charge in such instances. Provision should also be made for the refund of additional taxes heretofore collected because of such infractions in those cases where the penalty imposed has been so disproportionate to the offense as equitably to demand relief.

Budget

The estimates for the next fiscal year have been assembled by the Secretary of the Treasury and by him transmitted to Congress. I purpose at a later day to submit to Congress a form of budget prepared for me and recommended by the President's Commission on Economy and Efficiency, with a view of suggesting the useful and informing character of a properly framed budget.

War Department

The War Department combines within its jurisdiction functions which in other countries usually occupy three departments. It not only has the management of the Army and the coast defenses, but its jurisdiction extends to the government of the Philippines and of Porto Rico and the control of the receivership of the customs revenues of the Dominican Republic; it also includes the recommendation of all plans for the improvement of harbors and waterways and their execution when adopted; and, by virtue of an Executive order, the supervision of the construction of the Panama Canal.

Army Reorganization

Our small Army now consists of 83,809 men, excluding the 5,000 Philippine scouts. Leaving out of consideration the Coast Artillery force, whose position is fixed in our various seacoast defenses, and the present garrisons of our various insular possessions, we have to-day within the continental United States a mobile Army of only about 35,000 men. This little force must be still further drawn upon to supply the new garrisons for the great naval base which is being established at Pearl Harbor, in the Hawaiian Islands, and to protect the locks now rapidly approaching completion at Panama. The forces remaining in the United States are now scattered in nearly 50 Posts, situated for a variety of historical reasons in 24 States. These posts contain only fractions of regiments, averaging less than 700 men each. In time of peace it has been our historical policy to administer these units separately by a geographical organization. In other words, our Army in time of peace has never been a united organization but merely scattered groups of companies, battalions, and regiments, and the first task in time of war has been to create out of these scattered units an Army fit for effective teamwork and cooperation.

To the task of meeting these patent defects, the War Department has been addressing itself during the past year. For many years we had no officer or division whose business it was to study these problems and plan remedies for these defects. With the establishment of the General Staff nine years ago a body was created for this purpose. It has, necessarily, required time to overcome, even in its own personnel, the habits of mind engendered by a century of lack of method, but of late years its work has become systematic and effective, and it has recently been addressing itself vigorously to these problems.

A comprehensive plan of Army reorganization was prepared by the War College Division of the General Staff. This plan was thoroughly discussed last summer at a series of open conferences held by the Secretary of War and attended by representatives from all branches of the Army and from Congress. In printed form it has been distributed to Members of Congress and throughout the Army and the National Guard, and widely through institutions of learning and elsewhere in the United States. In it, for the first time, we have a tentative chart for future progress.

Under the influence of this study definite and effective steps have been taken toward Army reorganization so far as such reorganization lies within the Executive power. Hitherto there has been no difference of policy in the treatment of the organization of our foreign garrisons from those of troops within the United States. The difference of situation is vital, and the foreign garrison should be prepared to defend itself at an instant's notice against a foe who may command the sea. Unlike the troops in the United States, it can not count upon reinforcements or recruitment. It is an outpost upon which will fall the brunt of the first attack in case of war. The historical policy of the United States of carrying its regiments during time of peace at half strength has no application to our foreign garrisons. During the past year this defect has been remedied as to the Philippines garrison. The former garrison of 12 reduced regiments has been replaced by a garrison of 6 regiments at full strength, giving fully the same number of riflemen at an estimated economy in cost of maintenance of over $1,000,000 per year. This garrison is to be permanent. Its regimental units, instead of being transferred periodically back and forth from the United States, will remain in the islands. The officers and men composing these units will, however, serve a regular tropical detail as usual, thus involving no greater hardship upon the personnel and greatly increasing the effectiveness of the garrison. A similar policy is proposed for the Hawaiian and Panama garrisons as fast as the barracks for them are completed. I strongly urge upon Congress that the necessary appropriations for this purpose should be promptly made. It is, in my opinion, of first importance that these national outposts, upon which a successful home defense will, primarily, depend, should be finished and placed in effective condition at the earliest possible day.

The Home Army

Simultaneously with the foregoing steps the War Department has been proceeding with the reorganization of the Army at home. The formerly disassociated units are being united into a tactical organization of three divisions, each consisting of two or three brigades of Infantry and, so far as practicable, a proper proportion of divisional Cavalry and Artillery. Of course, the extent to which this reform can be carried by the Executive is practically limited to a paper organization. The scattered units can be brought under a proper organization, but they will remain physically scattered until Congress supplies the necessary funds for grouping them in more concentrated posts. Until that is done the present difficulty of drilling our scattered groups together, and thus training them for the proper team play, can not be removed. But we shall, at least, have an Army which will know its own organization and will be inspected by its proper commanders, and to which, as a unit, emergency orders can be issued in time of war or other emergency. Moreover, the organization, which in many respects is necessarily a skeleton, will furnish a guide for future development. The separate regiments and companies will know the brigades and divisions to which they belong. They will be maneuvered together whenever maneuvers are established by Congress, and the gaps in their organization will show the pattern into which can be filled new troops as the Nation grows and a larger Army is provided.

Regular Army Reserve

One of the most important reforms accomplished during the past year has been the legislation enacted in the Army appropriation bill of last summer, providing for a Regular Army reserve. Hitherto our national policy has assumed that at the outbreak of war our regiments would be immediately raised to full strength. But our laws have provided no means by which this could be accomplished, or by which the losses of the regiments when once sent to the front could be repaired. In this respect we have neglected the lessons learned by other nations. The new law provides that the soldier, after serving four years with colors, shall pass into a reserve for three years. At his option he may go into the reserve at the end of three years, remaining there for four years. While in the reserve he can be called to active duty only in case of war or other national emergency, and when so called and only in such case will receive a stated amount of pay for all of the period in which he has been a member of the reserve. The legislation is imperfect, in my opinion, in certain particulars, but it is a most important step in the right direction, and I earnestly hope that it will be carefully studied and perfected by Congress.

The National Guard

Under existing law the National Guard constitutes, after the Regular Army, the first line of national defense. Its organization, discipline, training, and equipment, under recent legislation, have been assimilated, as far as possible, to those of the Regular Army, and its practical efficiency, under the effect of this training, has very greatly increased. Our citizen soldiers under present conditions have reached a stage of development beyond which they can not reasonably be asked to go without further direct assistance in the form of pay from the Federal Government. On the other hand, such pay from the National Treasury would not be justified unless it produced a proper equivalent in additional efficiency on the part of the National Guard. The Organized Militia to-day can not be ordered outside of the limits of the United States, and thus can not lawfully be used for general military purposes. The officers and men are ambitious and eager to make themselves thus available and to become an efficient national reserve of citizen soldiery. They are the only force of trained men, other than the Regular Army, upon which we can rely. The so-called militia pay bill, in the form agreed on between the authorities of the War Department and the representatives of the National Guard, in my opinion adequately meets these conditions and offers a proper return for the pay which it is proposed to give to the National Guard. I believe that its enactment into law would be a very long step toward providing this Nation with a first line of citizen soldiery, upon which its main reliance must depend in case of any national emergency. Plans for the organization of the National Guard into tactical divisions, on the same lines as those adopted for the Regular Army, are being formulated by the War College Division of the General Staff.

National Volunteers

The National Guard consists of only about 110,000 men. In any serious war in the past it has always been necessary, and in such a war in the future it doubtless will be necessary, for the Nation to depend, in addition to the Regular Army and the National Guard, upon a large force of volunteers. There is at present no adequate provision of law for the raising of such a force. There is now pending in Congress, however, a bill which makes such provision, and which I believe is admirably adapted to meet the exigencies which would be presented in case of war. The passage of the bill would not entail a dollar's expense upon the Government at this time or in the future until war comes. But if war comes the methods therein directed are in accordance with the best military judgment as to what they ought to be, and the act would prevent the necessity for a discussion of any legislation and the delays incident to its consideration and adoption. I earnestly urge its passage.

Consolidation of the Supply Corps

The Army appropriation act of 1912 also carried legislation for the consolidation of the Quartermaster's Department, the Subsistence Department, and the Pay Corps into a single supply department, to be known as the Quartermaster's Corps. It also provided for the organization of a special force of enlisted men, to be known as the Service Corps, gradually to replace many of the civilian employees engaged in the manual labor necessary in every army. I believe that both of these enactments will improve the administration of our military establishment. The consolidation of the supply corps has already been effected, and the organization of the service corps is being put into effect.

All of the foregoing reforms are in the direction of economy and efficiency. Except for the slight increase necessary to garrison our outposts in Hawaii and Panama, they do not call for a larger Army, but they do tend to produce a much more efficient one. The only substantial new appropriations required are those which, as I have pointed out, are necessary to complete the fortifications and barracks at our naval bases and outposts beyond the sea.

Porto Rico

Porto Rico continues to show notable progress, both commercially and in the spread of education. Its external commerce has increased 17 per cent over the preceding year, bringing the total value up to $92,631,886, or more than five times the value of the commerce of the island in 1901. During the year 160,657 pupils were enrolled in the public schools, as against 145,525 for the preceding year, and as compared with 26,000 for the first year of American administration. Special efforts are under way for the promotion of vocational and industrial training, the need of which is particularly pressing in the island. When the bubonic plague broke out last June, the quick and efficient response of the people of Porto Rico to the demands of modern sanitation was strikingly shown by the thorough campaign which was instituted against the plague and the hearty public opinion which supported the Government's efforts to check its progress and to prevent its recurrence.

The failure thus far to grant American citizenship continues to be the only ground of dissatisfaction. The bill conferring such citizenship has passed the House of Representatives and is now awaiting the action of the Senate. I am heartily in favor of the passage of this bill. I believe that the demand for citizenship is just, and that it is amply earned by sustained loyalty on the part of the inhabitants of the island. But it should be remembered that the demand must be, and in the minds of most Porto Ricans is, entirely disassociated from any thought of statehood. I believe that no substantial approved public opinion in the United States or in Porto Rico contemplates statehood for the island as the ultimate form of relations between us. I believe that the aim to be striven for is the fullest possible allowance of legal and fiscal self-government, with American citizenship as to the bond between us; in other words, a relation analogous to the present relation between Great Britain and such self-governing colonies as Canada and Australia. This would conduce to the fullest and most self-sustaining development of Porto Rico, while at the same time it would grant her the economic and political benefits of being under the American flag.

Philippines

A bill is pending in Congress which revolutionizes the carefully worked out scheme of government under which the Philippine Islands are now governed and which proposes to render them virtually autonomous at once and absolutely independent in eight years. Such a proposal can only be founded on the assumption that we have now discharged our trusteeship to the Filipino people and our responsibility for them to the world, and that they are now prepared for self-government as well as national sovereignty. A thorough and unbiased knowledge of the facts clearly shows that these assumptions are absolutely without justification. As to this, I believe that there is no substantial difference of opinion among any of those who have had the responsibility of facing Philippine problems in the administration of the islands, and I believe that no one to whom the future of this people is a responsible concern can countenance a policy fraught with the direst consequences to those on whose behalf it is ostensibly urged.

In the Philippine Islands we have embarked upon an experiment unprecedented in dealing with dependent people. We are developing there conditions exclusively for their own welfare. We found an archipelago containing 24 tribes and races, speaking a great variety of languages, and with a population over 80 per cent of which could neither read nor write. Through the unifying forces of a common education, of commercial and economic development, and of gradual participation in local self-government we are endeavoring to evolve a homogeneous people fit to determine, when the time arrives, their own destiny. We are seeking to arouse a national spirit and not, as under the older colonial theory, to suppress such a spirit. The character of the work we have been doing is keenly recognized in the Orient, and our success thus far followed with not a little envy by those who, initiating the same policy, find themselves hampered by conditions grown up in earlier days and under different theories of administration. But our work is far from done. Our duty to the Filipinos is far from discharged. Over half a million Filipino students are now in the Philippine schools helping to mold the men of the future into a homogeneous people, but there still remain more than a million Filipino children of school age yet to be reached. Freed from American control the integrating forces of a common education and a common language will cease and the educational system now well started will slip back into inefficiency and disorder.

An enormous increase in the commercial development of the islands has been made since they were virtually granted full access to our markets three years ago, with every prospect of increasing development and diversified industries. Freed from American control such development is bound to decline. Every observer speaks of the great progress in public works for the benefit of the Filipinos, of harbor improvements, of roads and railways, of irrigation and artesian wells, public buildings, and better means of communication. But large parts of the islands are still unreached, still even unexplored, roads and railways are needed in many parts, irrigation systems are still to be installed, and wells to be driven. Whole villages and towns are still without means of communication other than almost impassable roads and trails. Even the great progress in sanitation, which has successfully suppressed smallpox, the bubonic plague, and Asiatic cholera, has found the cause of and a cure for beriberi, has segregated the lepers, has helped to make Manila the most healthful city in the Orient, and to free life throughout the whole archipelago from its former dread diseases, is nevertheless incomplete in many essentials of permanence in sanitary policy. Even more remains to be accomplished. If freed from American control sanitary progress is bound to be arrested and all that has been achieved likely to be lost.

Concurrent with the economic, social, and industrial development of the islands has been the development of the political capacity of the people. By their progressive participation in government the Filipinos are being steadily and hopefully trained for self-government. Under Spanish control they shared in no way in the government. Under American control they have shared largely and increasingly. Within the last dozen years they have gradually been given complete autonomy in the municipalities, the right to elect two-thirds of the provincial governing boards and the lower house of the insular legislature. They have four native members out of nine members of the commission, or upper house. The chief justice and two justices of the supreme court, about one-half of the higher judicial positions, and all of the justices of the peace are natives. In the classified civil service the proportion of Filipinos increased from 51 per cent in 1904 to 67 per cent in 1911. Thus to-day all the municipal employees, over 90 per cent of the provincial employees, and 60 per cent of the officials and employees of the central government are Filipinos. The ideal which has been kept in mind in our political guidance of the islands has been real popular self-government and not mere paper independence. I am happy to say that the Filipinos have done well enough in the places they have filled and in the discharge of the political power with which they have been intrusted to warrant the belief that they can be educated and trained to complete self-government. But the present satisfactory results are due to constant support and supervision at every step by Americans.

If the task we have undertaken is higher than that assumed by other nations, its accomplishment must demand even more patience. We must not forget that we found the Filipinos wholly untrained in government. Up to our advent all other experience sought to repress rather than encourage political power. It takes long time and much experience to ingrain political habits of steadiness and efficiency. Popular self-government ultimately must rest upon common habits of thought and upon a reasonably developed public opinion. No such foundations for self-government, let alone independence are now present in the Philippine Islands. Disregarding even their racial heterogeneity and the lack of ability to think as a nation, it is sufficient to point out that under liberal franchise privileges only about 3 per cent of the Filipinos vote and only 5 per cent of the people are said to read the public press. To confer independence upon the Filipinos now is, therefore, to subject the great mass of their people to the dominance of an oligarchical and, probably, exploiting minority. Such a course will be as cruel to those people as it would be shameful to us.

Our true course is to pursue steadily and courageously the path we have thus far followed; to guide the Filipinos into self-sustaining pursuits; to continue the cultivation of sound political habits through education and political practice; to encourage the diversification of industries, and to realize the advantages of their industrial education by conservatively approved cooperative methods, at once checking the dangers of concentrated wealth and building up a sturdy, independent citizenship. We should do all this with a disinterested endeavor to secure for the Filipinos economic independence and to fit them for complete self-government, with the power to decide eventually, according to their own largest good, whether such self-government shall be accompanied by independence. A present declaration even of future independence would retard progress by the dissension and disorder it would arouse. On our part it would be a disingenuous attempt, under the guise of conferring a benefit on them, to relieve ourselves from the heavy and difficult burden which thus far we have been bravely and consistently sustaining. It would be a disguised policy of scuttle. It would make the helpless Filipino the football of oriental politics, under the protection of a guaranty of their independence, which we would be powerless to enforce.

Regulation of Water Power

There are pending before Congress a large number of bills proposing to grant privileges of erecting dams for the purpose of creating water power in our navigable rivers. The tendency of these bills has brought out an important defect in the existing general dam act. That act does not, in my opinion, grant sufficient power to the Federal Government in dealing with the construction of such dams to exact protective conditions in the interest of navigation. It does not permit the Federal Government, as a condition of its permit, to require that a part of the value thus created shall be applied to the further general improvement and protection of the stream. I believe this to be one of the most important matters of internal improvement now confronting the Government. Most of the navigable rivers of this country are comparatively long and shallow. In order that they may be made fully useful for navigation there has come into vogue a method of improvement known as canalization, or the slack-water method, which consists in building a series of dams and locks, each of which will create a long pool of deep navigable water. At each of these dams there is usually created also water power of commercial value. If the water power thus created can be made available for the further improvement of navigation in the stream, it is manifest that the improvement will be much more quickly effected on the one hand, and, on the other, that the burden on the general taxpayers of the country will be very much reduced. Private interests seeking permits to build water-power dams in navigable streams usually urge that they thus improve navigation, and that if they do not impair navigation they should be allowed to take for themselves the entire profits of the water-power development. Whatever they may do by way of relieving the Government of the expense of improving navigation should be given due consideration, but it must be apparent that there may be a profit beyond a reasonably liberal return upon the private investment which is a potential asset of the Government in carrying out a comprehensive policy of waterway development. It is no objection to the retention and use of such an asset by the Government that a comprehensive waterway policy will include the protection and development of the other public uses of water, which can not and should not be ignored in making and executing plans for the protection and development of navigation. It is also equally clear that inasmuch as the water power thus created is or may be an incident of a general scheme of waterway improvement within the constitutional jurisdiction of the Federal Government, the regulation of such water power lies also within that jurisdiction. In my opinion constructive statesmanship requires that legislation should be enacted which will permit the development of navigation in these great rivers to go hand in hand with the utilization of this by-product of water power, created in the course of the same improvement, and that the general dam act should be so amended as to make this possible. I deem it highly important that the Nation should adopt a consistent and harmonious treatment of these water-power projects, which will preserve for this purpose their value to the Government, whose right it is to grant the permit. Any other policy is equivalent to throwing away a most valuable national asset.

The Panama Canal

During the past year the work of construction upon the canal has progressed most satisfactorily. About 87 per cent of the excavation work has been completed, and more than 93 per cent of the concrete for all the locks is in place. In view of the great interest which has been manifested as to some slides in the Culebra Cut, I am glad to say that the report of Col. Goethals should allay any apprehension on this point. It is gratifying to note that none of the slides which occurred during this year would have interfered with the passage of the ships had the canal, in fact, been in operation, and when the slope pressures will have been finally adjusted and the growth of vegetation will minimize erosion in the banks of the cut, the slide problem will be practically solved and an ample stability assured for the Culebra Cut.

Although the official date of the opening has been set for January 1, 1915, the canal will, in fact, from present indications, be opened for shipping during the latter half of 1913. No fixed date can as yet be set, but shipping interests will be advised as soon as assurances can be given that vessels can pass through without unnecessary delay.

Recognizing the administrative problem in the management of the canal, Congress in the act of August 24, 1912, has made admirable provisions for executive responsibility in the control of the canal and the government of the Canal Zone. The problem of most efficient organization is receiving careful consideration, so that a scheme of organization and control best adapted to the conditions of the canal may be formulated and put in operation as expeditiously as possible.

* * *

Panama Canal Treaty

The proclamation which I have issued in respect to the Panama Canal tolls is in accord with the Panama Canal act passed by this Congress August 24, 1912. We have been advised that the British

Government has prepared a protest against the act and its enforcement in so far as it relieves from the payment of tolls American ships engaged in the American coastwise trade on the ground that it violates British rights under the Hay-Pauncefote treaty concerning the Panama Canal. When the protest is presented, it will be promptly considered and an effort made to reach a satisfactory adjustment of any differences there may be between the two Governments.

Workmen's Compensation Act

The promulgation of an efficient workmen's compensation act, adapted to the particular conditions of the zone, is awaiting adequate appropriation by Congress for the payment of claims arising thereunder. I urge that speedy provision be made in order that we may install upon the zone a system of settling claims for injuries in best accord with modern humane, social, and industrial theories.

* * *

Navy Department

The Navy of the United States is in a greater state of efficiency and is more powerful than it has ever been before, but in the emulation which exists between different countries in respect to the increase of naval and military armaments this condition is not a permanent one. In view of the many improvements and increases by foreign Governments the slightest halt on our part in respect to new construction throws us back and reduces us from a naval power of the first rank and places us among the nations of the second rank. In the past 15 years the Navy has expanded rapidly and yet far less rapidly than our country. From now on reduced expenditures in the Navy means reduced military strength. The world's history has shown the importance of sea power both for adequate defense and for the support of important and definite policies.

I had the pleasure of attending this autumn a mobilization of the Atlantic Fleet, and was glad to observe and note the preparedness of the fleet for instant action. The review brought before the President and the Secretary of the Navy a greater and more powerful collection of vessels than had ever been gathered in American waters. The condition of the fleet and of the officers and enlisted men and of the equipment of the vessels entitled those in authority to the greatest credit.

I again commend to Congress the giving of legislative sanction to the appointment of the naval aids to the Secretary of the Navy. These aids and the council of aids appointed by the Secretary of the Navy to assist him in the conduct of his department have proven to be of the highest utility. They have furnished an executive committee of the most skilled naval experts, who have coordinated the action of the various bureaus in the Navy, and by their advice have enabled the Secretary to give an administration at the same time economical and most efficient. Never before has the United States had a Navy that compared in efficiency with its present one, but never before have the requirements with respect to naval warfare been higher and more exacting than now. A year ago Congress refused to appropriate for more than one battleship. In this I think a great mistake of policy was made, and I urgently recommend that this Congress make up for the mistake of the last session by appropriations authorizing the construction of three battleships, in addition to destroyers, fuel ships, and the other auxiliary vessels as shown in the building program of the general board. We are confronted by a condition in respect to the navies of the world which requires us, if we would maintain our Navy as an insurance of peace, to augment our naval force by at least two battleships a year and by battle cruisers, gunboats, torpedo destroyers, and submarine boats in a proper proportion. We have no desire for war. We would go as far as any nation in the world to avoid war, but we are a world power. Our population, our wealth, our definite policies, our responsibilities in the Pacific and the Atlantic, our defense of the Panama Canal, together with our enormous world trade and our missionary outposts on the frontiers of civilization, require us to recognize our position as one of the foremost in the family of nations, and to clothe ourselves with sufficient naval power to give force to our reasonable demands, and to give weight to our influence in those directions of progress that a powerful Christian nation should advocate.

I observe that the Secretary of the Navy devotes some space to a change in the disciplinary system in vogue in that branch of the service. I think there is nothing quite so unsatisfactory to either the Army or the Navy as the severe punishments necessarily inflicted by court-martial for desertions and purely military offenses, and I am glad to hear that the British have solved this important and difficult matter in a satisfactory way. I commend to the consideration of Congress the details of the new disciplinary system, and recommend that laws be passed putting the same into force both in the Army and the Navy.

I invite the attention of Congress to that part of the report of the Secretary of the Navy in which he recommends the formation of a naval reserve by the organization of the ex-sailors of the Navy.

I repeat my recommendation made last year that proper provision should be made for the rank of the commander in chief of the squadrons and fleets of the Navy. The inconvenience attending the necessary precedence that most foreign admirals have over our own whenever they meet in official functions ought to be avoided. It impairs the prestige of our Navy and is a defect that can be very easily removed.

Department of Justice

This department has been very active in the enforcement of the law. It has been better organized and with a larger force than ever before in the history of the Government. The prosecutions which have been successfully concluded and which are now pending testify to the effectiveness of the departmental work.

The prosecution of trusts under the Sherman antitrust law has gone on without restraint or diminution, and decrees similar to those entered in the Standard Oil and the Tobacco cases have been entered in other suits, like the suits against the Powder Trust and the Bathtub Trust. I am very strongly convinced that a steady, consistent course in this regard, with a continuing of Supreme Court decisions upon new phases of the trust question not already finally decided is going to offer a solution of this much-discussed and troublesome issue in a quiet, calm, and judicial way, without any radical legislation changing the governmental policy in regard to combinations now denounced by the Sherman antitrust law. I have already recommended as an aid in this matter legislation which would declare unlawful certain well-known phases of unfair competition in interstate trade, and I have also advocated voluntary national incorporation for the larger industrial enterprises, with provision for a closer supervision by the Bureau of Corporations, or a board appointed for the purpose, so as to make more certain compliance with the antitrust law on the one hand and to give greater security to the stockholders against possible prosecutions on the other. I believe, however, that the orderly course of litigation in the courts and the regular prosecution of trusts charged with the violation of the antitrust law is producing among business men a clearer and clearer perception of the line of distinction between business that is to be encouraged and business that is to be condemned, and that in this quiet way the question of trusts can be settled and competition retained as an economic force to secure reasonableness in prices and freedom and independence in trade.

Reform of Court Procedure

I am glad to bring to the attention of Congress the fact that the Supreme Court has radically altered the equity rules governing the procedure on the equity side of all Federal courts, and though, as these changes have not been yet put in practice so as to enable us to state from actual results what the reform will accomplish, they are of such a character that we can reasonably prophesy that they will greatly reduce the time and cost of litigation in such courts. The court has adopted many of the shorter methods of the present English procedure, and while it may take a little while for the profession to accustom itself to these methods, it is certain greatly to facilitate litigation. The action of the Supreme Court has been so drastic and so full of appreciation of the necessity for a great reform in court procedure that I have no hesitation in following up this action with a recommendation which I foreshadowed in my message of three years ago, that the sections of the statute governing the procedure in the Federal courts on the common-law side should be so amended as to give to the Supreme Court the same right to make rules of procedure in common law as they have, since the beginning of the court, exercised in equity. I do not doubt that a full consideration of the subject will enable the court while giving effect to the substantial differences in right and remedy between the system of common law and the system of equity so to unite the two procedures into the form of one civil action and to shorten the procedure in such civil action as to furnish a model to all the State courts exercising concurrent jurisdiction with the Federal courts of first instance.

Under the statute now in force the common-law procedure in each Federal court is made to conform to the procedure in the State in which the court is held. In these days, when we should be making progress in court procedure, such a conformity statute makes the Federal method too dependent upon the action of State legislatures. I can but think it a great opportunity for Congress to intrust to the highest tribunal in this country, evidently imbued with a strong spirit in favor of a reform of procedure, the power to frame a model code of procedure, which, while preserving all that is valuable and necessary of the rights and remedies at common law and in equity, shall lessen the burden of the poor litigant to a minimum in the expedition and cheapness with which his cause can be fought or defended through Federal courts to final judgment.

Workman's Compensation Act

The workman's compensation act reported by the special commission appointed by Congress and the Executive, which passed the Senate and is now pending in the House, the passage of which I have in previous messages urged upon Congress, I venture again to call to its attention. The opposition to it which developed in the Senate, but which was overcome by a majority in that body, seemed to me to grow out rather of a misapprehension of its effect than of opposition to its principle. I say again that I think no act can have a better effect directly upon the relations between the employer and employee than this act applying to railroads and common carriers of an interstate character, and I am sure that the passage of the act would greatly relieve the courts of the heaviest burden of litigation that they have, and would enable them to dispatch other business with a speed never before attained in courts of justice in this country.

Part III
Concerning the Work of the Departments of the Post Office, Interior, Agriculture, and Commerce and Labor and District of Columbia
December 19, 1912

To the Senate and House of Representatives:

This is the third of a series of messages in which I have brought to the attention of the Congress the important transactions of the Government in each of its departments during the last year and have discussed needed reforms.

Heads of Departments Should Have Seats on the Floor of Congress

I recommend the adoption of legislation which shall make it the duty of heads of departments—the members of the President's Cabinet—at convenient times to attend the session of the House and the Senate, which shall provide seats for them in each House, and give them the opportunity to take part in all discussions and to answer questions of which they have had due notice. The rigid holding apart of the executive and the legislative branches of this Government has not worked for the great advantage of either. There has been much lost motion in the machinery, due to the lack of cooperation and interchange of views face to face between the representatives of the Executive and the Members of the two legislative branches of the Government. It was never intended that they should be separated in the sense of not being in constant effective touch and relationship to each other. The legislative and the executive each performs its own appropriate function, but these functions must be coordinated. Time and time again debates have arisen in each House upon issues which the information of a particular department head would have enabled him, if present, to end at once by a simple explanation or statement. Time and time again a forceful and earnest presentation of facts and arguments by the representative of the Executive whose duty it is to enforce the law would have brought about a useful reform by amendment, which in the absence of such a statement has failed of passage. I do not think I am mistaken in saying that the presence of the members of the Cabinet on the floor of each House would greatly contribute to the enactment of beneficial legislation. Nor would this in any degree deprive either the legislative or the executive of the independence which separation of the two branches has been intended to promote. It would only facilitate their cooperation in the public interest.

On the other hand, I am sure that the necessity and duty imposed upon department heads of appearing in each House and in answer to searching questions, of rendering upon their feet an account of what they have done, or what has been done by the administration, will spur each member of the Cabinet to closer attention to the details of his department, to greater familiarity with its needs, and to greater care to avoid the just criticism which the answers brought out in questions put and discussions arising between the Members of either House and the members of the Cabinet may properly evoke.

Objection is made that the members of the administration having no vote could exercise no power on the floor of the House, and could not assume that attitude of authority and control which the English parliamentary Government have and which enables them to meet the responsibilities the English system thrusts upon them. I agree that in certain respects it would be more satisfactory if members of the Cabinet could at the same time be Members of both Houses, with voting power, but this is impossible under our system; and while a lack of this feature may detract from the influence of the department chiefs, it will not prevent the good results which I have described above both in the matter of legislation and in the matter of administration. The enactment of such a law would be quite within the power of Congress without constitutional amendment, and it has such possibilities of usefulness that we might well make the experiment, and if we are disappointed the misstep can be easily retraced by a repeal of the enabling legislation.

This is not a new proposition. In the House of Representatives, in the Thirty-eighth Congress, the proposition was referred to a select committee of seven Members. The committee made an extensive report, and urged the adoption of the reform. The report showed that our history had not been without illustration of the necessity and the examples of the practice by pointing out that in early days Secretaries were repeatedly called to the presence of either House for consultation, advice, and information. It also referred to remarks of Mr. Justice Story in his *Commentaries on the Constitution*, in which he urgently presented the wisdom of such a change. This report is to be found in Volume I of the Reports of Committees of the First Session of the Thirty-eighth Congress, April 6, 1864.

Again, on February 4, 1881, a select committee of the Senate recommended the passage of a similar bill, and made a report, in which, while approving the separation of the three branches, the executive, legislative, and judicial, they point out as a reason for the proposed change that, although having a separate existence, the branches are "to cooperate, each with the other, as the different members of the human body must cooperate, with each other in order to form the figure and perform the duties of a perfect man."

The report concluded as follows:

This system will require the selection of the strongest men to be heads of departments and will require them to be well equipped with the knowledge of their offices. It will also require the strongest men to be the leaders of Congress and participate in debate. It will bring these strong men in contact, perhaps into conflict, to advance the public weal, and thus stimulate their abilities and their efforts, and will thus assuredly result to the good of the country.

If it should appear by actual experience that the heads of departments in fact have not time to perform the additional duty imposed on them by this bill, the force in their offices should be increased or the duties devolving on them personally should be diminished. An undersecretary should be appointed to whom could be confided that routine of administration which requires only order and accuracy. The principal officers could then confine their attention to those duties which require wise discretion and intellectual activity. Thus they would have abundance of time for their duties under this bill. Indeed, your committee believes that the public interest would be subserved if the Secretaries were relieved of the harassing cares of distributing clerkships and closely supervising the mere machinery of the departments. Your committee believes that the adoption of this bill and the effective execution of its provisions will be the first step toward a sound civil-service reform which will secure a larger wisdom in the adoption of policies and a better system in their execution.

(Signed) GEO. H. PENDLETON. W. B. ALLISON. D. W. VOORHEES. J. G. BLAINE. M. C. BUTLER. JOHN J. INGALLS. O. H. PLATT. J. T. FARLEY.

It would be difficult to mention the names of higher authority in the practical knowledge of our Government than those which are appended to this report.

Postal Savings Bank System

The Postal Savings Bank System has been extended so that it now includes 4,004 fourth-class post offices, as well as 645 branch offices and stations in the larger cities. There are now 12,812 depositories at which patrons of the system may open accounts. The number of depositors is 300,000 and the amount of their deposits is approximately $28,000,000, not including $1,314,140 which has been with drawn by depositors for the purpose of buying postal savings bonds. Experience demonstrates the value of dispensing with the pass-book and introducing in its place a certificate of deposit. The gross income of the postal savings system for the fiscal year ending June 30, 1913, will amount to $700,000 and the interest payable to depositors to $300,000. The cost of supplies, equipment, and salaries is $700,000. It thus appears that the system lacks $300,000 a year of paying interest and expenses. It is estimated, however, that when the deposits have reached the sum of $50,000,000, which at the present rate they soon will do, the system will be self-sustaining. By law the postal savings funds deposited at each post office are required to be redeposited in local banks. State and national banks to the number of 7,357 have qualified as depositories for these funds. Such deposits are secured by bonds aggregating $54,000,000. Of this amount, $37,000,000 represent municipal bonds.

Parcel Post

In several messages I have favored and recommended the adoption of a system of parcel post. In the postal appropriation act of last year a general system was provided and its installation was directed by the 1st of January. This has entailed upon the Post Office Department a great deal of very heavy labor, but the Postmaster General informs me that on the date selected, to wit, the 1st of January, near at hand, the department will be in readiness to meet successfully the requirements of the public.

Classification of Postmasters

A trial, during the past three years, of the system of classifying fourth-class postmasters in that part of the country lying between the Mississippi River on the west, Canada on the north, the Atlantic Ocean on the east, and Mason and Dixon's line on the south has been sufficiently satisfactory to justify the postal authorities in recommending the extension of the order to include all the fourth-class postmasters in the country. In September, 1912, upon the suggestion of the Postmaster General, I directed him to prepare an order which should put the system in effect, except in Alaska, Guam, Hawaii, Porto Rico, and Samoa. Under date of October 15 I issued such an order which affected 36,000 postmasters. By the order the post offices were divided into groups A and B. Group A includes all postmasters whose compensation is $500 or more, and group B those whose compensation is less than that sum. Different methods are pursued in the selection of the postmasters for group A and group B. Criticism has been made of this order on the ground that the motive for it was political. Nothing could be further from the truth. The order was made before the election and in the interest of efficient public service. I have several times requested Congress to give me authority to put first-, second-, and third-class postmasters, and all other local officers, including internal-revenue officers, customs officers, United States marshals, and the local agents of the other departments under the classification of the civil-service law by taking away the necessity for confirming such appointments by the Senate. I deeply regret the failure of Congress to follow these recommendations. The change would have taken out of politics practically every local officer and would have entirely cured the evils growing out of what under the present law must always remain a remnant of the spoils system.

Compensation to Railways for Carrying Mails

It is expected that the establishment of a parcel post on January 1st will largely increase the amount of mail matter to be transported by the railways, and Congress should be prompt to provide a way by which they may receive the additional compensation to which they will be entitled. The Postmaster General urges that the department's plan for a complete readjustment of the system of paying the railways for carrying the mails be adopted, substituting space for weight as the principal factor in fixing compensation. Under this plan it will be possible to determine without delay what additional payment should be made on account of the parcel post. The Postmaster General's recommendation is based on the results of a far-reaching investigation begun early in the administration with the object of determining what it costs the railways to carry the mails. The statistics obtained during the course of the inquiry show that while many of the railways, and particularly the large systems, were making profits from mail transportations, certain of the lines were actually carrying the mails at a loss. As a result of the investigation the department, after giving the subject careful consideration, decided to urge the abandonment of the present plan of fixing compensation on the basis of the weight of the mails carried, a plan that has proved to be exceedingly expensive and in other respects unsatisfactory. Under the method proposed the railway companies will annually submit to the department reports showing what it costs them to carry the mails, and this cost will be apportioned on the basis of the car space engaged, payment to be allowed at the rate thus determined in amounts that will cover the cost and a reasonable profit. If a railway is not satisfied with the manner in which the department apportions the cost in fixing compensation, it is to have the right, under the new plan, of appealing to the Interstate Commerce Commission. This feature of the proposed law would seem to insure a fair treatment of the railways. It is hoped that Congress will give the matter immediate attention and that the method of compensation recommended by the department or some other suitable plan will be promptly authorized.

Department of the Interior

The Interior Department, in the problems of administration included within its jurisdiction, presents more difficult questions than any other. This has been due perhaps to temporary causes of a political character, but more especially to the inherent difficulty in the performance of some of the functions which are assigned to it. Its chief duty is the guardianship of the public domain and the disposition of that domain to private ownership under homestead, mining, and other laws, by which patents from the Government to the individual are authorized on certain conditions. During the last decade the public seemed to become suddenly aware that a very large part of its domain had passed from its control into private ownership, under laws not well adapted to modern conditions, and also that in the doing of this the provisions of existing law and regulations adopted in accordance with law had not been strictly observed, and that in the transfer of title much fraud had intervened, to the pecuniary benefit of dishonest persons. There arose thereupon a demand for conservation of the public domain, its protection against fraudulent diminution, and the preservation of that part of it from private acquisition which it seemed necessary to keep for future public use. The movement, excellent in the intention which prompted it, and useful in its results, has nevertheless had some bad effects, which the western country has recently been feeling and in respect of which there is danger of a reaction toward older abuses unless we can attain the golden mean, which consists in the prevention of the mere exploitation of the public domain for private purposes while at the same time facilitating its development for the benefit of the local public.

The land laws need complete revision to secure proper conservation on the one hand of land that ought to be kept in public use and, on the other hand, prompt disposition of those lands which ought to be disposed in private ownership or turned over to private use by properly guarded leases. In addition to this there are not enough officials in our Land Department with legal knowledge sufficient promptly to make the decisions which are called for. The whole land-laws system should be reorganized, and not until it is reorganized, will decisions be made as promptly as they ought, or will men who have earned title to public land under the statute receive their patents within a reasonably short period. The present administration has done what it could in this regard, but the necessity for reform and change by a revision of the laws and an increase and reorganization of the force remains, and I submit to Congress the wisdom of a full examination of this subject, in order that a very large and important part of our people in the West may be relieved from a just cause of irritation.

I invite your attention to the discussion by the Secretary of the Interior of the need for legislation with respect to mining claims, leases of coal lands in this country and in Alaska, and for similar disposition of oil, phosphate, and potash lands, and also to his discussion of the proper use to be made of water-power sites held by the Government. Many of these lands are now being withheld from use by the public under the general withdrawal act which was passed by the last Congress. That act was not for the purpose of disposing of the question, but it was for the purpose of preserving the lands until the question could be solved. I earnestly urge that the matter is of the highest importance to our western fellow citizens and ought to command the immediate attention of the legislative branch of the Government.

Another function which the Interior Department has to perform is that of the guardianship of Indians. In spite of everything which has been said in criticism of the policy of our Government toward the Indians, the amount of wealth which is now held by it for these wards per capita shows that the Government has been generous; but the management of so large an estate, with the great variety of circumstances that surround each tribe and each case, calls for the exercise of the highest business discretion, and the machinery provided in the Indian Bureau for the discharge of this function is entirely inadequate. The position of Indian commissioner demands the exercise of business ability of the first order, and it is difficult to secure such talent for the salary provided.

The condition of health of the Indian and the prevalence in the tribes of curable diseases has been exploited recently in the press. In a message to Congress at its last session I brought this subject to its attention and invited a special appropriation, in order that our facilities for overcoming diseases among the Indians might be properly increased, but no action was then taken by Congress on the subject, nor has such appropriation been made since.

The commission appointed by authority of the Congress to report on proper method of securing railroad development in Alaska is formulating its report, and I expect to have an opportunity before the end of this session to submit its recommendations.

Department of Agriculture

The far-reaching utility of the educational system carried on by the Department of Agriculture for the benefit of the farmers of our country calls for no elaboration. Each year there is a growth in the variety of facts which it brings out for the benefit of the farmer, and each year confirms the wisdom of the expenditure of the appropriations made for that department.

Pure-Food Law

The Department of Agriculture is charged with the execution of the pure-food law. The passage of this encountered much opposition from manufacturers and others who feared the effect upon their business of the enforcement of its provisions. The opposition aroused the just indignation of the public, and led to an intense sympathy with the severe and rigid enforcement of the provisions of the new law. It had to deal in many instances with the question whether or not products of large business enterprises, in the form of food preparations, were deleterious to the public health; and while in a great majority of instances this issue was easily determinable, there were not a few cases in which it was hard to draw the line between a useful and a harmful food preparation. In cases like this when a decision involved the destruction of great business enterprises representing the investment of large capital and the expenditure of great energy and ability, the danger of serious injustice was very considerable in the enforcement of a new law under the spur of great public indignation. The public officials charged with executing the law might do injustice in heated controversy through unconscious pride of opinion and obstinacy of conclusion. For this reason President Roosevelt felt justified in creating a board of experts, known as the Remsen Board, to whom in cases of much importance an appeal might be taken and a review had of a decision of the Bureau of Chemistry in the Agricultural Department. I heartily agree that it was wise to create this board in order that injustice might not be done. The questions which arise are not generally those involving palpable injury to health, but they are upon the narrow and doubtful line in respect of which it is better to be in some error not dangerous than to be radically destructive. I think that the time has come for Congress to recognize the necessity for some such tribunal of appeal and to make specific statutory provision for it. While we are struggling to suppress an evil of great proportions like that of impure food, we must provide machinery in the law itself to prevent its becoming an instrument of oppression, and we ought to enable those whose business is threatened with annihilation to have some tribunal and some form of appeal in which they have a complete day in court.

Agricultural Credits

I referred in my first message to the question of improving the system of agricultural credits. The Secretary of Agriculture has made an investigation into the matter of credits in this country, and I commend a consideration of the information which through his agents he has been able to collect. It does not in any way minimize the importance of the proposal, but it gives more accurate information upon some of the phases of the question than we have heretofore had.

Department of Commerce and Labor

I commend to Congress an examination of the report of the Secretary of Commerce and Labor, and especially that part in which he discusses the office of the Bureau of Corporations, the value to commerce of a proposed trade commission, and the steps which he has taken to secure the organization of a national chamber of commerce. I heartily commend his view that the plan of a trade commission which looks to the fixing of prices is altogether impractical and ought not for a moment to be considered as a possible solution of the trust question.

The trust question in the enforcement of the Sherman antitrust law is gradually solving itself, is maintaining the principle and restoring the practice of competition, and if the law is quietly but firmly enforced, business will adjust itself to the statutory requirements, and the unrest in commercial circles provoked by the trust discussion will disappear.

Panama-Pacific International Exposition

In conformity with a joint resolution of Congress, an Executive proclamation was issued last February, inviting the nations of the world to participate in the Panama-Pacific International Exposition to be held at San Francisco to celebrate the construction of the Panama Canal. A sympathetic response was immediately forthcoming, and several nations have already selected the sites for their buildings. In furtherance of my invitation, a special commission visited European countries during the past summer, and received assurance of hearty cooperation in the task of bringing together a universal industrial, military, and naval display on an unprecedented scale. It is evident that the exposition will be an accurate mirror of the world's activities as they appear 400 years after the date of the discovery of the Pacific Ocean.

It is the duty of the United States to make the nations welcome at San Francisco and to facilitate such acquaintance between them and ourselves as will promote the expansion of commerce and familiarize the world with the new trade route through the Panama Canal. The action of the State governments and individuals assures a comprehensive exhibit of the resources of this country and of the progress of the people. This participation by State and individuals should be supplemented by an adequate showing of the varied and unique activities of the National Government. The United States can not with good grace invite foreign governments to erect buildings and make expensive exhibits while itself refusing to participate. Nor would it be wise to forego the opportunity to join with other nations in the inspiring interchange of ideas tending to promote intercourse, friendship, and commerce. It is the duty of the Government to foster and build up commerce through the canal, just as it was the duty of the Government to construct it.

I earnestly recommend the appropriation at this session of such a sum as will enable the United States to construct a suitable building, install a governmental exhibit, and otherwise participate in the Panama-Pacific International Exposition in a manner commensurate with the dignity of a nation whose guests are to be the people of the world. I recommend also such legislation as will facilitate the entry of material intended for exhibition and protect foreign exhibitors against infringement of patents and the unauthorized copying of patterns and designs. All aliens sent to San Francisco to construct and care for foreign buildings and exhibits should be admitted without restraint or embarrassment.

The District of Columbia and the City of Washington

The city of Washington is a beautiful city, with a population of 352,936, of whom 98,667 are colored. The annual municipal budget is about $14,000,000. The presence of the National Capital and other governmental structures constitutes the chief beauty and interest of the city. The public grounds are extensive, and the opportunities for improving the city and making it still more attractive are very great. Under a plan adopted some years ago, one half the cost of running the city is paid by taxation upon the property, real and personal, of the citizens and residents, and the other half is borne by the General Government. The city is expanding at a remarkable rate, and this can only be accounted for by the coming here from other parts of the country of well-to-do people who, having finished their business careers elsewhere, build and make this their permanent place of residence.

On the whole, the city as a municipality is very well governed. It is well lighted, the water supply is good, the streets are well paved, the police force is well disciplined, crime is not flagrant, and while it has purlieus and centers of vice, like other large cities, they are not exploited, they do not exercise any influence or control in the government of the city, and they are suppressed in as far as it has been found practicable. Municipal graft is inconsiderable. There are interior courts in the city that are noisome and centers of disease and the refuge of criminals, but Congress has begun to clean these out, and progress has been made in the case of the most notorious of these, which is known as "Willow Tree Alley." This movement should continue.

The mortality for the past year was at the rate of 17.80 per 1,000 of both races; among the whites it was 14.61 per thousand, and among the blacks 26.12 per thousand. These are the lowest mortality rates ever recorded in the District.

One of the most crying needs in the government of the District is a tribunal or public authority for the purpose of supervising the corporations engaged in the operation of public utilities. Such a bill is pending in Congress and ought to pass. Washington should show itself under the direction of Congress to be a city with a model form of government, but as long as such authority over public utilities is withheld from the municipal government, it must always be defective.

Without undue criticism of the present street railway accommodations, it can be truly said that under the spur of a public utilities commission they might be substantially improved.

While the school system of Washington perhaps might be bettered in the economy of its management and the distribution of its buildings, its usefulness has nevertheless greatly increased in recent years, and it now offers excellent facilities for primary and secondary education.

From time to time there is considerable agitation in Washington in favor of granting the citizens of the city the franchise and constituting an elective government. I am strongly opposed to this change. The history of Washington discloses a number of experiments of this kind, which have always been abandoned as unsatisfactory. The truth is this is a city governed by a popular body, to wit, the Congress of the United States, selected from the people of the United States, who own Washington. The people who come here to live do so with the knowledge of the origin of the city and the restrictions, and therefore voluntarily give up the privilege of living in a municipality governed by popular vote. Washington is so unique in its origin and in its use for housing and localizing the sovereignty of the Nation that the people who live here must regard its peculiar character and must be content to subject themselves to the control of a body selected by all the people of the Nation. I agree that there are certain inconveniences growing out of the government of a city by a national legislature like Congress, and it would perhaps be possible to lessen these by the delegation by Congress to the District Commissioners of greater legislative power for the enactment of local laws than they now possess, especially those of a police character.

Every loyal American has a personal pride in the beauty of Washington and in its development and growth. There is no one with a proper appreciation of our Capital City who would favor a niggardly policy in respect to expenditures from the National Treasury to add to the attractiveness of this city, which belongs to every citizen of the entire country, and which no citizen visits without a sense of pride of ownership. We have had restored by a Commission of Fine Arts, at the instance of a committee of the Senate, the original plan of the French engineer L'Enfant for the city of Washington, and we know with great certainty the course which the improvement of Washington should take. Why should there be delay in making this improvement in so far as it involves the extension of the parking system and the construction of greatly needed public buildings? Appropriate buildings for the State Department, the Department of Justice, and the Department of Commerce and Labor have been projected, plans have been approved, and nothing is wanting but the appropriations for the beginning and completion of the structures. A hall of archives is also badly needed, but nothing has been done toward its construction, although the land for it has long been bought and paid for. Plans have been made for the union of Potomac Park with the valley of Rock Creek and Rock Creek Park, and the necessity for the connection between the Soldiers' Home and Rock Creek Park calls for no comment. I ask again why there should be delay in carrying out these plans? We have the money in the Treasury, the plans are national in their scope, and the improvement should be treated as a national project. The plan will find a hearty approval throughout the country. I am quite sure, from the information which I have, that, at comparatively small expense, from that part of the District of Columbia which was retroceded to Virginia, the portion including the Arlington estate, Fort Myer, and the palisades of the Potomac can be acquired by purchase and the jurisdiction of the State of Virginia over this land ceded to the Nation. This ought to be done.

The construction of the Lincoln Memorial and of a memorial bridge from the base of the Lincoln Monument to Arlington would be an appropriate and symbolic expression of the union of the North and the South at the Capital of the Nation. I urge upon Congress the appointment of a commission to undertake these national improvements, and to submit a plan for their execution; and when the plan has been submitted and approved, and the work carried out, Washington will really become what it ought to be—the most beautiful city in the world.

WILLIAM H. TAFT

Note

For statistical information about annual messages and state of the union addresses, I am indebted to John Wooley and Gerhard Peters, Department of Political Science, University of California, Santa Barbara. See their American Presidency Project, accessible on the Web at www.presidency.ucsb.edu/

24

Woodrow Wilson (1913–1921)

This eighth annual message is problematic for two reasons. First, it is unusual for an annual report to the Congress to be more "a confession of faith" than an assessment of the state of the union or a legislative agenda; the introduction is a paean to democracy and the new "world order" to be based on it. A more serious reason the message is problematic is that, while the sentiments are Wilsonian, the author is not Wilson. Recent scholarship demonstrates that Woodrow Wilson's capacity to fulfill the duties of the presidency ended on the morning of October 2, 1919—more than a year before the eighth annual message was composed. Medical records released in 1990 reveal that the nation's twenty-eighth president suffered coronary thrombosis and a paralyzing stroke. The trauma was so extensive that it precluded anything "more than a minimal state of recovery," according to two attending physicians. Wilson was for the rest of his presidency an invalid, capable only of "mumbled and cryptic" speech.[1] His illness may help explain the relative brevity of the eighth annual message. It is short by the standard of the day—only 2,700 words—half the length of Wilson's 1918 annual message, for example. And among the *written* final annual messages, it is the second shortest in the collection. Only Jefferson wrote a briefer final message.

It is not known who wrote the final draft of the 1920 message—it was likely a committee effort—but the President's second wife, Edith Bolling Galt Wilson, no doubt approved its final formulation before it was transmitted to the Congress. Edith Wilson was extremely jealous of her husband's reputation—so much so that she effectively concealed the gravity of her husband's condition from view. It is not overreaching to say she staged her husband's last months in office. As a result, she has been called everything from a "female regent" to the "first woman president of the United States." Much of the message that follows may reflect more of Edith's sentiments than Woodrow's. Nevertheless, its inclusion is appropriate because it can be regarded as the administration's farewell to the American people.

Eighth Annual Message
(written to the Congress)
December 7, 1920

Gentlemen of the Congress:

When I addressed myself to performing the duty laid upon the President by the Constitution to present to you an annual report on the state of the Union, I found my thought dominated by an immortal sentence of Abraham Lincoln's—"Let us have faith that right makes might, and in that faith let us dare to do our duty as we understand it"—a sentence immortal because it embodies in a form of utter simplicity and purity the essential faith of the nation, the faith in which it was conceived, and the faith in which it has grown to glory and power. With that faith and the birth of a nation founded upon it came the hope into the world that a new order would prevail throughout the affairs of mankind, an order in which reason and right would take precedence over covetousness and force; and I believe that I express the wish and purpose of every thoughtful American when I say that this sentence marks for us in the plainest manner the part we should play alike in the arrangement of our domestic affairs and in our exercise of influence upon the affairs of the world.

By this faith, and by this faith alone, can the world be lifted out of its present confusion and despair. It was this faith which prevailed over the wicked force of Germany. You will remember that the beginning of the end of the war came when the German people found themselves face to face with the conscience of the world and realized that right was everywhere arrayed against the wrong that their government was attempting to perpetrate. I think, therefore, that it is true to say that this was the faith which won the war. Certainly this is the faith with which our gallant men went into the field and out upon the seas to make sure of victory.

This is the mission upon which Democracy came into the world. Democracy is an assertion of the right of the individual to live and to be treated justly as against any attempt on the part of any combination of individuals to make laws which will overburden him or which will destroy his equality among his fellows in the matter of right or privilege; and I think we all realize that the day has come when Democracy is being put upon its final test. The Old World is just now suffering from a wanton rejection of the principle of democracy and a substitution of the principle of autocracy as asserted in the name, but without the authority and sanction, of the multitude. This is the time of all others when Democracy should prove its purity and its spiritual power to prevail. It is surely the manifest destiny of the United States to lead in the attempt to make this spirit prevail.

There are two ways in which the United States can assist to accomplish this great object. First, by offering the example within her own borders of the will and power of Democracy to make and enforce laws which are unquestionably just and which are equal in their administration—laws which secure its full right to labor and yet at the same time safeguard the integrity of property, and particularly of that property which is devoted to the development of industry and the increase of the necessary wealth of the world. Second, by standing for right and justice as toward individual nations. The law of Democracy is for the protection of the weak, and the influence of every democracy in the world should be for the protection of the weak nation, the nation which is struggling toward its right and toward its proper recognition and privilege in the family of nations.

The United States cannot refuse this role of champion without putting the stigma of rejection upon the great and devoted men who brought its government into existence and established it in the face of almost universal opposition and intrigue, even in the face of wanton force, as, for example, against the Orders in Council of Great Britain and the arbitrary Napoleonic decrees which involved us in what we know as the War of 1812.

I urge you to consider that the display of an immediate disposition on the part of the Congress to remedy any injustices or evils that may have shown themselves in our own national life will afford the most effectual offset to the forces of chaos and tyranny which are playing so disastrous a part in the fortunes of the free peoples of more than one part of the world. The United States is of necessity the sample democracy of the world, and the triumph of Democracy depends upon its success.

Recovery from the disturbing and sometimes disastrous effects of the late war has been exceedingly slow on the other side of the water, and has given promise, I venture to say, of early completion only in our own fortunate country; but even with us the recovery halts and is impeded at times, and there are immediately serviceable acts of legislation which it seems to me we ought to attempt, to assist that recovery and prove the indestructible recuperative force of a great government of the people. One of these is to prove that a great democracy can keep house as successfully and in as business-like a fashion as any other government. It seems to me that the first step toward providing this is to supply ourselves with a systematic method of handling our estimates and expenditures and bringing them to the point where they will not be an unnecessary strain upon our income or necessitate unreasonable taxation; in other words, a workable budget system. And I respectfully suggest that two elements are essential to such a system—namely, not only that the proposal of appropriations should be in the hands of a single body, such as a single appropriations committee in each house of the Congress, but also that this body should be brought into such cooperation with the Departments of the Government and with the Treasury of the United States as would enable it to act upon a complete conspectus of the needs of the Government and the resources from which it must draw its income.

I reluctantly vetoed the budget bill passed by the last session of the Congress because of a constitutional objection. The House of Representatives subsequently modified the bill in order to meet this objection. In the revised form, I believe that the bill, coupled with action already taken by the Congress to revise its rules and procedure, furnishes the foundation for an effective national budget system. I earnestly hope, therefore, that one of the first steps to be taken by the present session of the Congress will be to pass the budget bill.

The nation's finances have shown marked improvement during the last year. The total ordinary receipts of $6,694,000,000 for the fiscal year 1920 exceeded those for 1919 by $1,542,000,000, while the total net ordinary expenditures decreased from $18,514,000,000 to $6,403,000,000. The gross public debt, which reached its highest point on August 31, 1919, when it was $26,596,000,000, had dropped on November 30, 1920, to $24,175,000,000.

There has also been a marked decrease in holdings of government war securities by the banking institutions of the country, as well as in the amount of bills held by the Federal Reserve Banks secured by government war obligations. This fortunate result has relieved the banks and left them freer to finance the needs of Agriculture, Industry, and Commerce. It has been due in large part to the reduction of the public debt, especially of the floating debt, but more particularly to the improved distribution of government securities among permanent investors. The cessation of the Government's borrowings, except through short-term certificates of indebtedness, has been a matter of great consequence to the people of the country at large, as well as to the holders of Liberty Bonds and Victory Notes, and has had an important bearing on the matter of effective credit control.

The year has been characterized by the progressive withdrawal of the Treasury from the domestic credit market and from a position of dominant influence in that market. The future course will necessarily depend upon the extent to which economies are practiced and upon the burdens placed upon the Treasury, as well as upon industrial developments and the maintenance of tax receipts at a sufficiently high level. The fundamental fact which at present dominates the Government's financial situation is that seven and a half billions of its war indebtedness mature within the next two and a half years. Of this amount, two and a half billions are floating debt and five billions, Victory Notes and War Savings Certificates. The fiscal program of the Government must be determined with reference to these maturities. Sound policy demands that Government expenditures be reduced to the lowest amount which will permit the various services to operate efficiently and that Government receipts from taxes and salvage be maintained sufficiently high to provide for current requirements, including interest and sinking fund charges on the public debt, and at the same time retire the floating debt and part of the Victory Loan before maturity.

With rigid economy, vigorous salvage operations, and adequate revenues from taxation, a surplus of current receipts over current expenditures can be realized and should be applied to the floating debt. All branches of the Government should cooperate to see that this program is realized. I cannot overemphasize the necessity of economy in Government appropriations and expenditures and the avoidance by the Congress of practices which take money from the Treasury by indefinite or revolving fund appropriations. The estimates for the present year show that over a billion dollars of expenditures were authorized by the last Congress in addition to the amounts shown in the usual compiled statements of appropriations. This strikingly illustrates the importance of making direct and specific appropriations. The relation between the current receipts and current expenditures of the Government during the present fiscal year, as well as during the last half of the last fiscal year, has been disturbed by the extraordinary burdens thrown upon the Treasury by the Transportation Act, in connection with the return of the railroads to private control. Over $600,000,000 has already been paid to the railroads under this act—$350,000,000 during the present fiscal year; and it is estimated that further payments aggregating possibly $650,000,000 must still be made to the railroads during the current year. It is obvious that these large payments have already seriously limited the Government's progress in retiring the floating debt.

Closely connected with this, it seems to me, is the necessity for an immediate consideration of the revision of our tax laws. Simplification of the income and profits taxes has become an immediate necessity. These taxes performed an indispensable service during the war. The need for their simplification, however, is very great, in order to save the taxpayer inconvenience and expense and in order to make his liability more certain and definite. Other and more detailed recommendations with regard to taxes will no doubt be laid before you by the Secretary of the Treasury and the Commissioner of Internal Revenue.

It is my privilege to draw to the attention of Congress for very sympathetic consideration the problem of providing adequate facilities for the care and treatment of former members of the military and naval forces who are sick and disabled as the result of their participation in the war. These heroic men can never be paid in money for the service they patriotically rendered the nation. Their reward will lie rather in realization of the fact that they vindicated the rights of their country and aided in safeguarding civilization. The nation's gratitude must be effectively revealed to them by the most ample provision for their medical care and treatment as well as for their vocational training and placement. The time has come when a more complete program can be formulated and more satisfactorily administered for their treatment and training, and I earnestly urge that the Congress give the matter its early consideration. The Secretary of the Treasury and the Board for Vocational Education will outline in their annual reports proposals covering medical care and rehabilitation which I am sure will engage your earnest study and commend your most generous support.

Permit me to emphasize once more the need for action upon certain matters upon which I dwelt at some length in my message to the second session of the Sixty-sixth Congress. The necessity, for example, of encouraging the manufacture of dyestuffs and related chemicals; the importance of doing everything possible to promote agricultural production along economic lines, to improve agricultural marketing, and to make rural life more attractive and healthful; the need for a law regulating cold storage in such a way as to limit the time during which goods may be kept in storage, prescribing the method of disposing of them if kept beyond the permitted period, and requiring goods released from storage in all cases to bear the date of their receipt. It would also be most serviceable if it were provided that all goods released from cold storage for interstate shipment should have plainly marked upon each package the selling or market price at which they went into storage, in order that the purchaser might be able to learn what profits stood between him and the producer or the wholesale dealer. Indeed, it would be very serviceable to the public if all goods destined for interstate commerce were made to carry upon every packing case whose form made it possible a plain statement of the price at which they left the hands of the producer. I respectfully call your attention also to the recommendations of the message referred to with regard to a federal license for all corporations engaged in interstate commerce.

In brief, the immediate legislative need of the time is the removal of all obstacles to the realization of the best ambitions of our people in their several classes of employment and the strengthening of all instrumentalities by which difficulties are to be met and removed and justice dealt out, whether by law or by some form of mediation and conciliation. I do not feel it to be my privilege at present to suggest the detailed and particular methods by which these objects may be attained, but I have faith that the inquiries of your several committees will discover the way and the method.

In response to what I believe to be the impulse of sympathy and opinion throughout the United States, I earnestly suggest that the Congress authorize the Treasury of the United States to make to the struggling government of Armenia such a loan as was made to several of the Allied governments during the war, and I would also suggest that it would be desirable to provide in the legislation itself that the expenditure of the money thus loaned should be under the supervision of a commission, or at least a commissioner, from the United States in order that revolutionary tendencies within Armenia itself might not be afforded by the loan a further tempting opportunity.

Allow me to call your attention to the fact that the people of the Philippine Islands have succeeded in maintaining a stable government since the last action of the Congress in their behalf, and have thus fulfilled the condition set by the Congress as precedent to a consideration of granting independence to the Islands. I respectfully submit that this condition precedent having been fulfilled, it is now our liberty and our duty to keep our promise to the people of those islands by granting them the independence which they so honorably covet.

I have not so much laid before you a series of recommendations, gentlemen, as sought to utter a confession of faith, of the faith in which I was bred and which it is my solemn purpose to stand by until my last fighting day. I believe this to be the faith of America, the faith of the future, and of all the victories which await national action in the days to come, whether in America or elsewhere.

Note

1. Phyllis Lee Levin, *Edith and Woodrow: The Wilson White House* (New York: Scribner, 2001). Also see the telling account of Wilson's last day in the White House: "A News Report: Wilson's Exit Is Tragic," in *The Papers of Woodrow Wilson*, ed. Arthur S. Link, vol. 67 (Princeton: Princeton University Press, 1992), 205–14.

2 5

Calvin Coolidge (1923–1929)

Recent years have witnessed an effort to look at Calvin Coolidge in a fresh light. It is "important to get beyond the tired cliches, distortions, and inaccuracies which have obscured his record for so many decades,"[1] as one high-level conference put it.

One area in need of having the record set straight is the thirtieth president's rhetoric. Belying the nickname "Silent Cal," Calvin Coolidge was in fact one of the most articulate and eloquent writers ever to occupy the White House. He did not compose a formal farewell address to the nation, but used the final annual message to bid adieu. The tone at the beginning and end of Coolidge's address may remind one of George Washington. Like Washington, Coolidge believed that the American experiment would rise or fall on the character of citizens. The outgoing president praises the fact that the American people "have been able to put trust in each other and trust in their Government."

Sixth Annual Message
(written to the Congress)
December 4, 1928

To the Congress of the United States:

No Congress of the United States ever assembled, on surveying the state of the Union, has met with a more pleasing prospect than that which appears at the present time. In the domestic field there is tranquillity and contentment, harmonious relations between management and wage earner, freedom from industrial strife, and the highest record of years of prosperity. In the foreign field there is peace, the good will which comes from mutual understanding, and the knowledge that the problems which a short time ago appeared so ominous are yielding to the touch of manifest friendship. The great wealth created by our enterprise and industry, and saved by our economy, has had the widest distribution among our own people, and has gone out in a steady stream to serve the charity and the business of the world. The requirements of existence have passed beyond the standard of necessity into the region of luxury. Enlarging production is consumed by an increasing demand at home and an expanding commerce abroad. The country can regard the present with satisfaction and anticipate the future with optimism.

The main source of these unexampled blessings lies in the integrity and character of the American people. They have had great faith, which they have supplemented with mighty works. They have been able to put trust in each other and trust in their Government. Their candor in dealing with foreign governments has commanded respect and confidence. Yet these remarkable powers would have been exerted almost in vain without the constant cooperation and careful administration of the Federal Government.

We have been coming into a period which may be fairly characterized as a conservation of our national resources. Wastefulness in public business and private enterprise has been displaced by constructive economy. This has been accomplished by bringing our domestic and foreign relations more and more under a reign of law. A rule of force has been giving way to a rule of reason. We have substituted for the vicious circle of increasing expenditures, increasing tax rates, and diminishing profits the charmed circle of diminishing expenditures, diminishing tax rates, and increasing profits.

Four times we have made a drastic revision of our internal revenue system, abolishing many taxes and substantially reducing almost all others. Each time the resulting stimulation to business has so increased taxable incomes and profits that a surplus has been reduced. One-third of the national debt has been paid, while much of the other two-thirds has been refunded at lower rates, and these savings of interest and constant economies have enabled us to repeat the satisfying process of more tax reductions. Under this sound and healthful encouragement the national income has increased nearly 50 per cent, until it is estimated to stand well over $90,000,000,000. It has been a method which has performed the seeming miracle of leaving a much greater percentage of earnings in the hands of the taxpayers with scarcely any diminution of the Government revenue. That is constructive economy in the highest degree. It is the corner stone of prosperity. It should not fail to be continued.

This action began by the application of economy to public expenditure. If it is to be permanent, it must be made so by the repeated application of economy. There is no surplus on which to base further tax revision at this time. Last June the estimates showed a threatened deficit for the current fiscal year of $94,000,000. Under my direction the departments began saving all they could out of their present appropriations. The last tax reduction brought an encouraging improvement in business, beginning early in October, which will also increase our revenue. The combination of economy and good times now indicates a surplus of about $37,000,000. This is a margin of less than 1 per cent on our expenditures and makes it obvious that the Treasury is in no condition to undertake increases in expenditures to be made before June 30. It is necessary therefore during the present session to refrain from new appropriations for immediate outlay, or if such are absolutely required to provide for them by new revenue; otherwise, we shall reach the end of the year with the unthinkable result of an unbalanced budget. For the first time during my term of office we face that contingency. I am certain that the Congress would not pass and I should not feel warranted in approving legislation which would involve us in that financial disgrace.

On the whole the finances of the Government are most satisfactory. Last year the national debt was reduced about $906,000,000. The refunding and retirement of the second and third Liberty loans have just been brought to a successful conclusion, which will save about $75,000,000 a year in interest. The unpaid balance has been arranged in maturities convenient for carrying out our permanent debt-paying Program.

The enormous savings made have not been at the expense of any legitimate public need. The Government plant has been kept up and many improvements are under way, while its service is fully manned and the general efficiency of operation has increased. We have been enabled to undertake many new enterprises. Among these are the adjusted compensation of the veterans of the World War, which is costing us $112,000,000 a year; amortizing our liability to the civil service retirement funds, $20,000,000; increase of expenditures for rivers and harbors including flood control,

$43,000,000; public buildings, $47,000,000. In 1928 we spent $50,000,000 in the adjustment of war claims and alien property. These are examples of a large list of items.

Foreign Relations

When we turn from our domestic affairs to our foreign relations, we likewise perceive peace and progress. The Sixth International Conference of American States was held at Habana last winter. It contributed to a better understanding and cooperation among the nations. Eleven important conventions were signed and 71 resolutions passed. Pursuant to the plan then adopted, this Government has invited the other 20 nations of this hemisphere to a conference on conciliation and arbitration, which meets in Washington on December 10. All the nations have accepted and the expectation is justified that important progress will be made in methods for resolving international differences by means of arbitration.

During the year we have signed 11 new arbitration treaties, and 22 more are under negotiation.

Nicaragua

When a destructive and bloody revolution lately broke out in Nicaragua, at the earnest and repeated entreaties of its Government I dispatched our Marine forces there to protect the lives and interests of our citizens. To compose the contending parties, I sent there Col. Henry L. Stimson, former Secretary of War and now Governor General of the Philippine Islands, who secured an agreement that warfare should cease, a national election should be held and peace should be restored. Both parties conscientiously carried out this agreement, with the exception of a few bandits who later mostly surrendered or left the country. President Diaz appointed Brig. Gen. Frank R. McCoy, United States Army, president of the election board, which included also one member of each political party.

A free and fair election has been held and has worked out so successfully that both parties have joined in requesting like cooperation from this country at the election four years hence, to which I have refrained from making any commitments, although our country must be gratified at such an exhibition of success and appreciation. Nicaragua is regaining its prosperity and has taken a long step in the direction of peaceful self-government.

Tacna-Arica

The long-standing differences between Chile and Peru have been sufficiently composed so that diplomatic relations have been resumed by the exchange of ambassadors. Negotiations are hopefully proceeding as this is written for the final adjustment of the differences over their disputed territory.

Mexico

Our relations with Mexico are on a more satisfactory basis than at any time since their revolution. Many misunderstandings have been resolved and the most frank and friendly negotiations promise a final adjustment of all unsettled questions. It is exceedingly gratifying that Ambassador Morrow has been able to bring our two neighboring countries, which have so many interests in common, to a position of confidence in each other and of respect for mutual sovereign rights.

China

The situation in China which a few months ago was so threatening as to call for the dispatch of a large additional force has been much composed. The Nationalist Government has established itself over the country and promulgated a new organic law announcing a program intended to promote the political and economic welfare of the people. We have recognized this Government, encouraged its progress, and have negotiated a treaty restoring to China complete tariff autonomy and guaranteeing our citizens against discriminations. Our trade in that quarter is increasing and our forces are being reduced.

Greek and Austrian Debts

Pending before the Congress is a recommendation for the settlement of the Greek debt and the Austrian debt. Both of these are comparatively small and our country can afford to be generous. The rehabilitation of these countries awaits their settlement. There would also be advantages to our trade. We could scarcely afford to be the only nation that refuses the relief which Austria seeks. The Congress has already granted Austria a long-time moratorium, which it is understood will be waived and immediate payments begun on her debt on the same basis which we have extended to other countries.

Peace Treaty

One of the most important treaties ever laid before the Senate of the United States will be that which the 15 nations recently signed at Paris, and to which 44 other nations have declared their intention to adhere, renouncing war as a national policy and agreeing to resort only to peaceful means for the adjustment of international differences. It is the most solemn declaration against war, the most positive adherence to peace, that it is possible for sovereign nations to make. It does not supersede our inalienable sovereign right and duty of national defense or undertake to commit us before the event to any mode of action which the Congress might decide to be wise if ever the treaty should be broken. But it is a new standard in the world around which can rally the informed and enlightened opinion of nations to prevent their governments from being forced into hostile action by the temporary outbreak of international animosities. The observance of this covenant, so simple and so straightforward, promises more for the peace of the world than any other agreement ever negotiated among the nations.

National Defense

The first duty of our Government to its own citizens and foreigners within its borders is the preservation of order. Unless and until that duty is met a government is not even eligible for recognition among the family of nations. The advancement of world civilization likewise is dependent upon that order among the people of different countries which we term peace. To insure our citizens against the infringement of their legal rights at home and abroad, to preserve order, liberty, and peace by making the law supreme, we have an Army and a Navy.

Both of these are organized for defensive purposes. Our Army could not be much reduced, but does not need to be increased. Such new housing and repairs as are necessary are under way and the 6-year program in aviation is being put into effect in both branches of our service.

Our Navy, according to generally accepted standards, is deficient in cruisers. We have 10 comparatively new vessels, 22 that are old, and 8 to be built. It is evident that renewals and replacements must be provided. This matter was thoroughly canvassed at the last session of the Congress and does not need restatement. The bill before the Senate with the elimination of the time clause should be passed. We have no intention of competing with any other country. This building program is for necessary replacements and to meet our needs for defense.

The cost of national defense is stupendous. It has increased $118,000,000 in the past four years. The estimated expenditure for 1930 is $668,000,000. While this is made up of many items it is, after all, mostly dependent upon numbers. Our defensive needs do not call for any increase in the number of men in the Army or the Navy. We have reached the limit of what we ought to expend for that purpose.

I wish to repeat again for the benefit of the timid and the suspicious that this country is neither militaristic nor imperialistic. Many people at home and abroad, who constantly make this charge, are the same ones who are even more solicitous to have us extend assistance to foreign countries. When such assistance is granted, the inevitable result is that we have foreign interests. For us to refuse the customary support and protection of such interests would be in derogation of the sovereignty of this Nation. Our largest foreign interests are in the British Empire, France, and Italy. Because we are constantly solicitous for those interests, I doubt if anyone would suppose that those countries feel we harbor toward them any militaristic or imperialistic design. As for smaller countries, we certainly do not want any of them. We are more anxious than they are to have their sovereignty respected. Our entire influence is in behalf of their independence. Cuba stands as a witness to our adherence to this principle.

The position of this Government relative to the limitation of armaments, the results already secured, and the developments up to the present time are so well known to the Congress that they do not require any restatement.

Veterans

The magnitude of our present system of veterans' relief is without precedent, and the results have been far-reaching. For years a service pension has been granted to the Grand Army and lately to the survivors of the Spanish-American War. At the time we entered the World War however, Congress departed from the usual pension system followed by our Government. Eleven years have elapsed since our laws were first enacted, initiating a system of compensation, rehabilitation, hospitalization, and insurance for the disabled of the World War and their dependents. The administration of all the laws concerning relief has been a difficult task, but it can safely be stated that these measures have omitted nothing in their desire to deal generously and humanely. We should continue to foster this system and provide all the facilities necessary for adequate care. It is the conception of our Government that the pension roll is an honor roll. It should include all those who are justly entitled to its benefits, but exclude all others.

Annual expenditures for all forms of veterans' relief now approximate $765,000,000, and are increasing from year to year. It is doubtful if the peak of expenditures will be reached even under present legislation for some time yet to come. Further amendments to the existing law will be suggested by the American Legion, the Veterans of Foreign Wars of the United States, the Disabled American Veterans of the World War, and other like organizations, and it may be necessary for administrative purposes, or in order to remove some existing inequalities in the present law, to make further changes. I am sure that such recommendations as may be submitted to the Congress will receive your careful consideration. But because of the vast expenditure now being made, each year, with every assurance that it will increase, and because of the great liberality of the existing law, the proposal of any additional legislation dealing with this subject should receive most searching scrutiny from the Congress.

You are familiar with the suggestion that the various public agencies now dealing with matters of veterans' relief be consolidated in one Government department. Some advantages to this plan seem apparent, especially in the simplification of administration and in the opportunity of bringing about a greater uniformity in the application of veterans' relief. I recommend that a survey be made by the proper committees of Congress dealing with this subject, in order to determine whether legislation to secure this consolidation is desirable.

Agriculture

The past year has been marked by notable though not uniform improvement in agriculture. The general purchasing power of farm products and the volume of production have advanced. This means not only further progress, in overcoming the price disparity into which agriculture was plunged in 1920–21, but also increased efficiency on the part of farmers and a well-grounded confidence in the future of agriculture. The livestock industry has attained the best balance for many years and is prospering conspicuously. Dairymen, beef producers, and poultrymen are receiving substantially larger returns than last year. Cotton, although lower in price than at this time last year, was produced in greater volume and the prospect for cotton incomes is favorable. But progress is never uniform in a vast and highly diversified agriculture or industry. Cash grains, hay, tobacco, and potatoes will bring somewhat smaller returns this year than last. Present indications are, however, that the gross farm income will be somewhat larger than in the crop year 1927–28, when the total was $12,253,000,000. The corresponding figure for 1926–27 was $12,127,000,000, and in 1925–26, $12,670,000,000. Still better results would have been secured this year had there not been an undue increase in the production of certain crops. This is particularly true of potatoes, which have sold at an unremunerative price, or at a loss, as a direct result of overexpansion of acreage.

The present status of agriculture, although greatly improved over that of a few years ago, bespeaks the need of further improvement which calls for determined effort of farmers themselves, encouraged and assisted by wise public policy. The Government has been, and must continue to be, alive to the needs of agriculture.

In the past eight years more constructive legislation of direct benefit to agriculture has been adopted than during any other period. The Department of Agriculture has been broadened and reorganized to insure greater efficiency. The department is laying greater stress on the economic and business phases of agriculture. It is lending every possible assistance to cooperative marketing associations. Regulatory and research work have been segregated in order that each field may be served more effectively.

I can not too strongly commend, in the field of fact finding, the research work of the Department of Agriculture and the State experiment stations. The department now receives annually $4,000,000 more for research than in 1921. In addition, the funds paid to the States for experimentation purposes under the Purnell Act constitute an annual increase in Federal payments to State agricultural experiment stations of $2,400,000 over the amount appropriated in 1921. The program of support for research may wisely be continued and expanded. Since 1921 we have appropriated nearly an additional $2,000,000 for extension work, and this sum is to be increased next year under authorization by the Capper-Ketcham Act.

The Surplus Problem

While these developments in fundamental research, regulation, and dissemination of agricultural information are of distinct help to agriculture, additional effort is needed. The surplus problem demands attention. As emphasized in my last message, the Government should assume no responsibility in normal times for crop surplus clearly due to overextended acreage. The Government should, however, provide reliable information as a guide to private effort; and in this connection fundamental research on prospective supply and demand, as a guide to production and marketing, should be encouraged. Expenditure of public funds to bring in more new land should have most searching scrutiny, so long as our farmers face unsatisfactory prices for crops and livestock produced on land already under cultivation.

Every proper effort should be made to put land to uses for which it is adapted. The reforestation of land best suited for timber production is progressing and should be encouraged, and to this end the forest taxation inquiry was instituted to afford a practical guide for public policy. Improvement has been made in grazing regulation in the forest reserves, not only to protect the ranges, but to preserve the soil from erosion. Similar action is urgently needed to protect other public lands which are now overgrazed and rapidly eroding.

Temporary expedients, though sometimes capable of appeasing the demands of the moment, can not permanently solve the surplus problem and might seriously aggravate it. Hence putting the Government directly into business, subsidies, and price fixing, and the alluring promises of political action as a substitute for private initiative, should be avoided.

The Government should aid in promoting orderly marketing and in handling surpluses clearly due to weather and seasonal conditions. As a beginning there should be created a Federal farm board consisting of able and experienced men empowered to advise producers' associations in establishing central agencies or stabilization corporations to handle surpluses, to seek more economical means of merchandising, and to aid the producer in securing returns according to the quality of his product. A revolving loan fund should be provided for the necessary financing until these agencies shall have developed means of financing their operations through regularly constituted credit institutions. Such a bill should carry authority for raising the money, by loans or otherwise, necessary to meet the expense, as the Treasury has no surplus.

Agriculture has lagged behind industry in achieving that unity of effort which modern economic life demands. The cooperative movement, which is gradually building the needed organization, is in harmony with public interest and therefore merits public encouragement.

The Responsibility of the States

Important phases of public policy related to agriculture lie within the sphere of the States. While successive reductions in Federal taxes have relieved most farmers of direct taxes to the National Government, State and local levies have become a serious burden. This problem needs immediate and thorough study with a view to correction at the earliest possible moment. It will have to be made largely by the States themselves.

Commerce

It is desirable that the Government continue its helpful attitude toward American business. The activities of the Department of Commerce have contributed largely to the present satisfactory position in our international trade, which has reached about $9,000,000,000 annually. There should be no slackening of effort in that direction. It is also important that the department's assistance to domestic commerce be continued. There is probably no way in which the Government can aid sound economic progress more effectively than by cooperation with our business men to reduce wastes in distribution.

Commercial Aeronautics

Continued progress in civil aviation is most gratifying. Demands for airplanes and motors have taxed both the industry and the licensing and inspection service of the Department of Commerce to their capacity. While the compulsory licensing provisions of the air commerce act apply only to equipment and personnel engaged in interstate and foreign commerce, a Federal license may be procured by anyone possessing the necessary qualifications. State legislation, local airport regulations, and insurance requirements make such a license practically indispensable. This results in uniformity of regulation and increased safety in operation, which are essential to aeronautical development. Over 17,000 young men and women have now applied for Federal air pilot's licenses or permits. More than 80 per cent of them applied during the past year.

Our national airway system exceeds 14,000 miles in length and has 7,500 miles lighted for night operations. Provision has been made for lighting 4,000 miles more during the current fiscal year and equipping an equal mileage with radio facilities. Three-quarters of our people are now served by these routes. With the rapid growth of air mail, express, and passenger service, this new transportation medium is daily becoming a more important factor in commerce. It is noteworthy that this development has taken place without governmental subsidies. Commercial passenger flights operating on schedule have reached 13,000 miles per day.

During the next fortnight this Nation will entertain the nations of the world in a celebration of the twenty-fifth anniversary of the first successful airplane flight. The credit for this epoch-making achievement belongs to a citizen of our own country, Orville Wright.

Cuban Parcel Post

I desire to repeat my recommendation of an earlier message, that Congress enact the legislation necessary to make permanent the Parcel Post Convention with Cuba, both as a facility to American commerce and as a measure of equity to Cuba in the one class of goods which that country can send here by parcel post without detriment to our own trade.

Maine Battleship Memorial

When I attended the Pan American Conference at Habana, the President of Cuba showed me a marble statue made from the original memorial that was overturned by a storm after it was erected on the Cuban shore to the memory of the men who perished in the destruction of the battleship *Maine*. As a testimony of friendship and appreciation of the Cuban Government and people he most generously offered to present this to the United States, and I assured him of my pleasure in accepting it. There is no location in the White House for placing so large and heavy a structure, and I therefore urge the Congress to provide by law for some locality where it can be set up.

Railroads

In previous annual messages I have suggested the enactment of laws to promote railroad consolidation with the view of increasing the efficiency of transportation and lessening its cost to the public. While consolidations can and should be made under the present law until it is changed, yet the provisions of the act of 1920 have not been found fully adequate to meet the needs of other methods of consolidation. Amendments designed to remedy these defects have been considered at length by the respective committees of Congress and a bill was reported out late in the last session which I understand has the approval in principle of the Interstate Commerce Commission. It is to be hoped that this legislation may be enacted at an early date.

Experience has shown that the interstate commerce law requires definition and clarification in several other respects, some of which have been pointed out by the Interstate Commerce Commission in its annual reports to the Congress. It will promote the public interest to have the Congress give early consideration to the recommendations there made.

Merchant Marine

The cost of maintaining the United States Government merchant fleet has been steadily reduced. We have established American flag lines in foreign trade where they had never before existed as a means of promoting commerce and as a naval auxiliary. There have been sold to private American capital for operation within the past few years 14 of these lines, which, under the encouragement of the recent legislation passed by the Congress, give promise of continued successful operation. Additional legislation from time to time may be necessary to promote future advancement under private control.

Through the cooperation of the Post Office Department and the Shipping Board long-term contracts are being made with American steamship lines for carrying mail, which already promise the construction of 15 to 20 new vessels and the gradual reestablishment of the American merchant marine as a private enterprise. No action of the National Government has been so beneficial to our shipping. The cost is being absorbed to a considerable extent by the disposal of unprofitable lines operated by the Shipping Board, for which the new law has made a market. Meanwhile it should be our policy to maintain necessary strategic lines under the Government operation until they can be transferred to private capital.

Inter-American Highway

In my message last year I expressed the view that we should lend our encouragement for more good roads to all the principal points on this hemisphere South of the Rio Grande. My view has not changed.

The Pan American Union has recently indorsed it. In some of the countries to the south a great deal of progress is being made in road building. In others, engineering features are often exacting and financing difficult. As those countries enter upon programs for road building we should be ready to contribute from our abundant experience to make their task easier of accomplishment. I prefer not to go into civil life to accomplish this end. We already furnish military and naval advisors, and following this precedent we could draw competent men from these same sources and from the Department of Agriculture.

We should provide our southern neighbors, if they request it, with such engineer advisors for the construction of roads and bridges. Private interests should look with favor upon all reasonable loans sought by these countries to open main lines of travel. Such assistance should be given especially to any project for a highway designed to connect all the countries on this hemisphere and thus facilitate intercourse and closer relations among them.

Air Mail Service

The friendly relations and the extensive, commercial intercourse with the Western Hemisphere to the south of us are being further cemented by the establishment and extension of air mail routes. We shall soon have one from Key West, Fla., over Cuba, Haiti, and Santo Domingo to San Juan, P.R., where it will connect with another route to Trinidad. There will be another route from Key West to the Canal Zone, where connection will be made with a route across the northern coast of South America to Paramaribo. This will give us a circle around the Caribbean under our own control. Additional connections will be made at Colon with a route running down the west coast of South America as far as Conception, Chile, and with the French air mail at Paramaribo running down the eastern coast of South America. The air service already spans our continent, with laterals running to Mexico and Canada, and covering a daily flight of over 28,000 miles, with an average cargo of 15,000 pounds.

Waterways

Our river and harbor improvements are proceeding with vigor. In the past few years we have increased the appropriation for this regular work $28,000,000, besides what is to be expended on flood control. The total appropriation for this year was over $91,000,000. The Ohio River is almost ready for opening; work on the Missouri and other rivers is under way. In accordance with the Mississippi flood law Army engineers are making investigations and surveys on other streams throughout the country with a view to flood control, navigation, water power, and irrigation. Our barge lines are being operated under generous appropriations, and negotiations are developing relative to the St. Lawrence waterway. To Secure the largest benefits from all these waterways joint rates must be established with the railroads, preferably by agreement, but otherwise as a result of congressional action.

We have recently passed several river and harbor bills. The work ordered by the Congress not yet completed, will cost about $243,000,000, besides the hundreds of millions to be spent on the Mississippi flood way. Until we can see our way out of this expense no further river and harbor legislation should be passed, as expenditures to put it into effect would be four or five years away.

Irrigation of Arid Lands

For many years the Federal Government has been committed to the wise policy of reclamation and irrigation. While it has met with some failures due to unwise selection of projects and lack of thorough soil surveys, so that they could not be placed on a sound business basis, on the whole the service has been of such incalculable benefit in so many States that no one would advocate its abandonment. The program to which we are already committed, providing for the construction of new projects authorized by Congress and the completion of old projects, will tax the resources of the reclamation fund over a period of years. The high cost of improving and equipping farms adds to the difficulty of securing settlers for vacant farms on federal projects.

Readjustments authorized by the reclamation relief act of May 25, 1926, have given more favorable terms of repayment to settlers. These new financial arrangements and the general prosperity on irrigation projects have resulted in increased collections by the Department of the Interior of charges due the reclamation fund. Nevertheless, the demand for still smaller yearly payments on some projects continues. These conditions should have consideration in connection with any proposed new projects.

Colorado River

For several years the Congress has considered the erection of a dam on the Colorado River for flood-control, irrigation, and domestic water purposes, all of which may properly be considered as Government functions. There would be an incidental creation of water power which could be used for generating electricity. As private enterprise can very well fill this field, there is no need for the Government to go into it. It is unfortunate that the States interested in this water have been unable to agree among themselves. Nevertheless, any legislation should give every possible safeguard to the present and prospective rights of each of them.

The Congress will have before it, the detailed report of a special board appointed to consider the engineering and economic feasibility of this project. From the short summary which I have seen of it, 11 judge [they consider] the engineering problems can be met at somewhat increased cost over previous estimates. They prefer the Black Canyon site. On the economic features they are not so clear and appear to base their conclusions on many conditions which can not be established with certainty. So far as I can judge, however, from the summary, their conclusions appear sufficiently favorable, so that I feel warranted in recommending a measure which will protect the rights of the States, discharge the necessary Government functions, and leave the electrical field to private enterprise.

Muscle Shoals

The development of other methods of producing nitrates will probably render this plant less important for that purpose than formerly. But we have it, and I am told it still provides a practical method of making nitrates for national defense and farm fertilizers. By dividing the property into its two component parts of power and nitrate plants it would be possible to dispose of the power, reserving the right to any concern that wished to make nitrates to use any power that might be needed for that purpose. Such a disposition of the power plant can be made that will return in rental about $2,000,000 per year. If the Congress would grant the Secretary of War authority to lease the nitrate plant on such terms as would insure the largest production of nitrates, the entire property could begin to function. Such a division, I am aware, has never seemed to appeal to the Congress. I should also gladly approve a bill granting authority to lease the entire property for the production of nitrates.

I wish to avoid building another dam at public expense. Future operators should provide for that themselves. But if they were to be required to repay the cost of such dam with the prevailing commercial rates for interest, this difficulty will be considerably lessened. Nor do I think this property should be made a vehicle for putting the United States Government indiscriminately into the private and retail field of power distribution and nitrate sales.

Conservation

The practical application of economy to the resources of the country calls for conservation. This does not mean that every resource should not be developed to its full degree, but it means that none of them should be wasted. We have a conservation board working on our oil problem. This is of the utmost importance to the future well-being of our people in this age of oil-burning engines and the general application of gasoline to transportation. The Secretary of the Interior should not be compelled to lease oil lands of the Osage Indians when the market is depressed and the future supply is in jeopardy.

While the area of lands remaining in public ownership is small, compared with the vast area in private ownership, the natural resources of those in public ownership are of immense present and future value. This is particularly true as to minerals and water power. The proper bureaus have been classifying these resources to the end that they may be conserved. Appropriate estimates are being submitted, in the Budget, for the further prosecution of this important work.

Immigration

The policy of restrictive immigration should be maintained. Authority should be granted the Secretary of Labor to give immediate preference to learned professions and experts essential to new industries. The reuniting of families should be expedited. Our immigration and naturalization laws might well be codified.

Wage Earner

In its economic life our country has rejected the long accepted law of a limitation of the wage fund, which led to pessimism and despair because it was the doctrine of perpetual poverty, and has substituted for it the American conception that the only limit to profits and wages is production, which is the doctrine of optimism and hope because it leads to prosperity. Here and there the councils of labor are still darkened by the theory that only by limiting individual production can there be any assurance of permanent employment for increasing numbers, but in general, management and wage earner alike have become emancipated from this doom and have entered a new era in industrial thought which has unleashed the productive capacity of the individual worker with an increasing scale of wages and profits, the end of which is not yet. The application of this theory accounts for our widening distribution of wealth. No discovery ever did more to increase the happiness and prosperity of the people.

Since 1922 increasing production has increased wages in general 12.9 per cent, while in certain selected trades they have run as high as 34.9 per cent and 38 per cent. Even in the boot and shoe shops the increase is over 5 per cent and in woolen mills 8.4 per cent, although these industries have not prospered like others. As the rise in living costs in this period is negligible, these figures represent real wage increases.

The cause of constructive economy requires that the Government should cooperate with private interests to eliminate the waste arising from industrial accidents. This item, with all that has been done to reduce it, still reaches enormous proportions with great suffering to the workman and great loss to the country.

Women and Children

The Federal Government should continue its solicitous care for the 8,500,000 women wage earners and its efforts in behalf of public health, which is reducing infant mortality and improving the bodily and mental condition of our citizens.

Civil Service

The most marked change made in the civil service of the Government in the past eight years relates to the increase in salaries. The Board of Actuaries on the retirement act shows by its report, that July 1, 1921 the average salary of the 330,047 employees subject to the act was $1,307, while on June 30, 1927, the average salary of the corresponding, 405,263 was $1,969. This was an increase in six years of nearly 53 per cent. On top of this was the generous increase made at the last session of the Congress generally applicable to Federal employees and another bill increasing the pay in certain branches of the Postal Service beyond the large increase which was made three years ago. This raised the average level from $1,969 to $2,092, making an increase in seven years of over 63 per cent. While it is well known that in the upper brackets the pay in the Federal service is much smaller than in private employment, in the lower brackets, ranging well up over $3,000, it is much higher. It is higher not only in actual money paid, but in privileges granted, a vacation of 30 actual working days, or 5 weeks each year, with additional time running in some departments as high as 30 days for sick leave and the generous provisions of the retirement act. No other body of public servants ever occupied such a fortunate position.

Education

Through the Bureau of Education of the Department of the Interior the Federal Government, acting in an informative and advisory capacity, has rendered valuable service. While this province belongs peculiarly to the States, yet the promotion of education and efficiency in educational methods is a general responsibility of the Federal Government. A survey of negro colleges and universities in the United States has just been completed by the Bureau of Education through funds provided by the institutions themselves and through private sources. The present status of negro higher education was determined and recommendations were made for its advancement. This was one of the numerous cooperative undertakings of the bureau. Following the invitation of the Association of Land Grant Colleges and Universities, the Bureau of Education now has under way the survey of agricultural colleges, authorized by Congress. The purpose of the survey is to ascertain the accomplishments, the status, and the future objectives of this type of educational training. It is now proposed to undertake a survey of secondary schools, which educators insist is timely and essential.

Public Buildings

We, have laid out a public building program for the District of Columbia and the country at large running into hundreds of millions of dollars. Three important structures and one annex are already, under way and one addition has been completed in the City of Washington. In the country sites have been acquired, many buildings are in course of construction, and some are already completed. Plans for all this work are being prepared in order that it may be carried forward as rapidly as possible. This is the greatest building program ever assumed by this Nation. It contemplates structures of utility and of beauty. When it reaches completion the people will be well served and the Federal city will be supplied with the most beautiful and stately public buildings which adorn any capital in the world.

The American Indian

The administration of Indian affairs has been receiving intensive study for several years. The Department of the Interior has been able to provide better supervision of health, education, and industrial advancement of this native race through additional funds provided by the Congress. The present cooperative arrangement existing between the Bureau of Indian Affairs and the Public Health Service should be extended. The Government's responsibility to the American Indian has been acknowledged by annual increases in appropriations to fulfill its obligations to them and to hasten the time when Federal supervision of their affairs may be properly and safely terminated. The movement in Congress and in some of the State legislatures for extending responsibility in Indian affairs to States should be encouraged. A complete participation by the Indian in our economic life is the end to be desired.

The Negro

For 65 years now our Negro population has been under the peculiar care and solicitude of the National Government. The progress which they have made in education and the professions, in wealth and in the arts of civilization, affords one of the most remarkable incidents in this period of world history. They have demonstrated their ability to partake of the advantages of our institutions and to benefit by a free and more and more independent existence. Whatever doubt there may have been of their capacity to assume, the status granted to them by the Constitution of this Union is being rapidly dissipated. Their cooperation in the life of the Nation is constantly enlarging.

Exploiting the Negro problem for political ends is being abandoned and their protection is being increased by those States in which their percentage of population is largest. Every encouragement should be extended for the development of the race. The colored people have been the victims of the crime of lynching, which has in late years somewhat decreased. Some parts of the South already have wholesome laws for its restraint and punishment. Their example might well be followed by other States, and by such immediate remedial legislation as the Federal Government can extend under the Constitution.

Philippine Islands

Under the guidance of Governor General Stimson the economic and political conditions of the Philippine Islands have been raised to a standard never before surpassed. The cooperation between his administration and the people of the islands is complete and harmonious. It would be an advantage if relief from double taxation could be granted by the Congress to our citizens doing business in the islands.

Porto Rico

Due to the terrific storm that swept Porto Rico last September, the people of that island suffered large losses. The Red Cross and the War Department went to their rescue. The property loss is being retrieved. Sugar, tobacco, citrus fruit, and coffee, all suffered damage. The first three can largely look after themselves. The coffee growers will need some assistance, which should be extended strictly on a business basis, and only after most careful investigation. The people of Porto Rico are not asking for charity.

Department of Justice

It is desirable that all the legal activities of the Government be consolidated under the supervision of the Attorney General. In 1870 it was felt necessary to create the Department of Justice for this purpose. During the intervening period, either through legislation creating law officers or departmental action, additional legal positions not under the supervision of the Attorney General have been provided until there are now over 900. Such a condition is as harmful to the interest of the Government now as it was in 1870, and should be corrected by appropriate legislation.

Special Government Counsel

In order to prosecute the oil cases, I suggested and the Congress enacted a law providing for the appointment of two special counsel. They have pursued their work with signal ability, recovering all the leased lands besides nearly $30,000,000 in money, and nearly $17,000,000 in other property. They find themselves hampered by a statute, which the Attorney General construes as applying to them, prohibiting their appearing for private clients before any department. For this reason, one has been compelled to resign. No good result is secured by the application of this rule to these counsel, and as Mr. Roberts has consented to take reappointment if the rule is abrogated I recommend the passage of an amendment to the law creating their office exempting them from the general rule against taking other cases involving the Government.

Prohibition

The country has duly adopted the eighteenth amendment. Those who object to it have the right to advocate its modification or repeal. Meantime, it is binding upon the National and State Governments and all our inhabitants. The Federal enforcement bureau is making every effort to prevent violations, especially through smuggling, manufacture, and transportation, and to prosecute generally all violations for which it can secure evidence. It is bound to continue this policy. Under the terms of the Constitution, however, the obligation is equally on the States to exercise the power which they have through the executive, legislative, judicial, and police branches of their governments in behalf of enforcement. The Federal Government is doing and will continue to do all it can in this direction and is entitled to the active cooperation of the States.

Conclusion

The country is in the midst of an era of prosperity more extensive and of peace more permanent than it has ever before experienced. But, having reached this position, we should not fail to comprehend that it can easily be lost. It needs more effort for its support than the less exalted places of the world. We shall not be permitted to take our ease, but shall continue to be required to spend our days in unremitting toil. The actions of the Government must command the confidence of the country. Without this, our prosperity would be lost. We must extend to other countries the largest measure of generosity, moderation, and patience. In addition to dealing justly, we can well afford to walk humbly.

The end of government is to keep open the opportunity for a more abundant life. Peace and prosperity are not finalities; they are only methods. It is too easy under their influence for a nation to become selfish and degenerate. This test has come to the United States. Our country has been provided with the resources with which it can enlarge its intellectual, moral, and spiritual life. The issue is in the hands of the people. Our faith in man and God is the justification for the belief in our continuing success.

CALVIN COOLIDGE
The White House
December 4, 1928

Note

1. From the brochure "Calvin Coolidge: Examining the Evidence," conference cosponsored by the John F. Kennedy Library and Calvin Coolidge Memorial Foundation, at the Kennedy Library, Boston, MA, July 30–31, 1998.

2 6

Herbert Hoover (1929–1933)

The dark, lengthening shadow that creeps over Hoover's last annual message is the Great Depression. It strongly colored the tone and selection of material. The message confirms the extent to which the Republican Hoover anticipated FDR's enlargement of the federal government to tackle economic and social crises. Hoover maintained that "continued constructive policies promoting the economic recovery of the country must be the paramount duty of the Government." Even more, "With the free development of science and the consequent multitude of inventions, some of which are absolutely revolutionary in our national life, the Government must not only stimulate the social and economic responsibility of individuals and private institutions but it must also give leadership to cooperative action amongst the people which will soften the effect of these revolutions and thus secure social transformations in an orderly manner."

Fourth Annual Message
(written to the Congress)
December 6, 1932

To the Senate and House of Representatives:

In accord with my constitutional duty, I transmit herewith to the Congress information upon the state of the Union together with recommendation of measures for its consideration.

Our country is at peace. Our national defense has been maintained at a high state of effectiveness. All of the executive departments of the Government have been conducted during the year with a high devotion to public interest. There has been a far larger degree of freedom from industrial conflict than hitherto known. Education and science have made further advances. The public health is to-day at its highest known level. While we have recently engaged in the aggressive contest of a national election, its very tranquillity and the acceptance of its results furnish abundant proof of the strength of our institutions.

In the face of widespread hardship our people have demonstrated daily a magnificent sense of humanity, of individual and community responsibility for the welfare of the less fortunate. They have grown in their conceptions and organization for cooperative action for the common welfare.

In the provision against distress during this winter, the great private agencies of the country have been mobilized again; the generosity of our people has again come into evidence to a degree in which all America may take great pride. Likewise the local authorities and the States are engaged everywhere in supplemental measures of relief. The provisions made for loans from the Reconstruction Finance Corporation, to States that have exhausted their own resources, guarantee that there should be no hunger or suffering from cold in the country. The large majority of States are showing a sturdy cooperation in the spirit of the Federal aid.

The Surgeon General, in charge of the Public Health Service, furnishes me with the following information upon the state of public health:

Mortality Rate Per 1,000 of Population on an Annual Basis Representative States

	General	Infant
First 9 months of—		
1928	11.9	67.8
1929	12.0	65.8
1930	11.4	62.0
1931	11.2	60.0
1932	10.6	55.0

The sickness rates from data available show the same trends. These facts indicate the fine endeavor of the agencies which have been mobilized for care of those in distress.

Economic Situation

The unparalleled world-wide economic depression has continued through the year. Due to the European collapse, the situation developed during last fall and winter into a series of most acute crises. The unprecedented emergency measures enacted and policies adopted undoubtedly saved the country from economic disaster. After serving to defend the national security, these measures began in July to show their weight and influence toward improvement of conditions in many parts of the country. The following tables of current business indicators show the general economic movement during the past eleven months.

Monthly Business Indices with Seasonal Variations Eliminated
[Monthly average 1923–1925 = 100]

Year and Month	Industrial Production	Factory Employment	Freight-car Loadings	Department Store Sales, Value	Exports, Value	Imports, Value	Building Contracts, All Types	Industrial Electric Power Consumption
1931								
December	74	69.4	69	81	46	48	38	89.1
1932								
January	72	68.1	64	78	39	42	31	93.9
February	69	67.8	62	78	45	41	27	98.8
March	67	66.4	61	72	41	37	26	88.0
April	63	64.3	59	80	38	36	27	82.2
May	60	62.1	54	73	37	34	26	82.0

continued

Monthly Business Indices with Seasonal Variations Eliminated (*continued*)
[Monthly average 1923–1925 = 100]

Year and Month	Industrial Production	Factory Employment	Freight-car Loadings	Department Store Sales, Value	Exports, Value	Imports, Value	Building Contracts, All Types	Industrial Electric Power Consumption
June	59	60.0	52	71	34	36	27	78.1
July	58	58.3	51	67	32	27	27	79.2
August	60	58.8	51	66	31	29	30	73.5
September	66	60.3	54	70	33	32	30	84.0
October	66	61.1	57	70	33	32	29	84.4

The measures and policies which have procured this turn toward recovery should be continued until the depression is passed, and then the emergency agencies should be promptly liquidated. The expansion of credit facilities by the Federal Reserve System and the Reconstruction Finance Corporation has been of incalculable value. The loans of the latter for reproductive works, and to railways for the creation of employment; its support of the credit structure through loans to banks, insurance companies, railways, building and loan associations, and to agriculture has protected the savings and insurance policies of millions of our citizens and has relieved millions of borrowers from duress; they have enabled industry and business to function and expand. The assistance given to Farm Loan Banks, the establishment of the Home Loan Banks and Agricultural Credit Associations—all in their various ramifications have placed large sums of money at the disposal of the people in protection and aid. Beyond this, the extensive organization of the country in voluntary action has produced profound results.

The following table indicates direct expenditures of the Federal Government in aid to unemployment, agriculture, and financial relief over the past four years. The sums applied to financial relief multiply themselves many fold, being in considerable measure the initial capital supplied to the Reconstruction Finance Corporation, Farm Loan Banks, etc., which will be recovered to the Treasury.

	Public Works[1]	Agricultural Relief and Financial Loans
Fiscal year ending June 30		
1930	$410,420,000	$156,100,000
1931	574,870,000	196,700,000
1932	655,880,000	772,700,000
1933	717,260,000	52,000,000
Total	2,358,430,000	1,177,500,000

[1]Public Building, Highways, Rivers and Harbors and their maintenance, naval and other vessels construction, hospitals, etc.

Continued constructive policies promoting the economic recovery of the country must be the paramount duty of the Government. The result of the agencies we have created and the policies we have pursued has been to buttress our whole domestic financial structure and greatly to restore credit facilities. But progress in recovery requires another element as well—that is fully restored confidence in the future. Institutions and men may have resources and credit but unless they have confidence progress is halting and insecure.

There are three definite directions in which action by the Government at once can contribute to strengthen further the forces of recovery by strengthening of confidence. They are the necessary foundations to any other action, and their accomplishment would at once promote employment and increase prices.

The first of these directions of action is the continuing reduction of all Government expenditures, whether national, State, or local. The difficulties of the country demand undiminished efforts toward economy in government in every direction. Embraced in this problem is the unquestioned balancing of the Federal Budget. That is the first necessity of national stability and is the foundation of further recovery. It must be balanced in an absolutely safe and sure manner if full confidence is to be inspired.

The second direction for action is the complete reorganization at once of our banking system. The shocks to our economic life have undoubtedly been multiplied by the weakness of this system, and until they are remedied recovery will be greatly hampered.

The third direction for immediate action is vigorous and whole souled cooperation with other governments in the economic field. That our major difficulties find their origins in the economic weakness of foreign nations requires no demonstration. The first need to-day is strengthening of commodity prices. That can not be permanently accomplished by artificialities. It must be accomplished by expansion in consumption of goods through the return of stability and confidence in the world at large and that in turn can not be fully accomplished without cooperation with other nations.

Balancing the Budget

I shall in due course present the Executive Budget to the Congress. It will show proposed reductions in appropriations below those enacted by the last session of the Congress by over $830,000,000. In addition I shall present the necessary Executive orders under the recent act authorizing the reorganization of the Federal Government which, if permitted to go into force, will produce still further substantial economies. These sums in reduction of appropriations will, however, be partially offset by an increase of about $250,000,000 in uncontrollable items such as increased debt services, etc. In the Budget there is included only the completion of the Federal public works projects already undertaken or under contract. Speeding up of Federal public works during the past four years as an aid to employment has advanced many types of such improvements to the point where further expansion can not be justified in their usefulness to the Government or the people. As an aid to unemployment we should beyond the normal constructive programs substitute reproductive or so-called self-liquidating works. Loans for such purposes have been provided for through the Reconstruction Finance Corporation. This change in character of projects directly relieves the taxpayer and is capable of expansion into a larger field than the direct Federal works. The reproductive works constitute an addition to national wealth and to future employment, whereas further undue expansion of Federal public works is but a burden upon the future.

The Federal construction program thus limited to commitments and work in progress under the proposed appropriations contemplates expenditures for the next fiscal year, including naval and other vessel construction, as well as other forms of public works and maintenance, of a total of $442,769,000, as compared with $717,262,000 for the present year. The expenditure on such items over the four years ending June 30 next will amount to $2,350,000,000, or an amount of construction work eight times as great as the cost of the Panama Canal and, except for completion of certain long-view projects, places the Nation in many directions well ahead of its requirements for some years to come. A normal program of about $200,000,000 per annum should hereafter provide for the country's necessities and will permit substantial future reduction in Federal expenditures.

I recommend that the furlough system installed last year be continued not only because of the economy produced but because, being tantamount to the "5-day week," it sets an example which should be followed by the country and because it embraces within its workings the "spread work" principle and thus serves to maintain a number of public servants who would otherwise be deprived of all income. I feel, however, in view of the present economic situation and the decrease in the cost of living by over 20 per cent, that some further sacrifice should be made by salaried officials of the Government over and above the 8⅓ per cent reduction under the furlough system. I will recommend that after exempting the first $1,000 of salary there should be a temporary reduction for one year of 11 per cent of that part of all Government salaries in excess of the $1,000 exemption, the result of which, combined with the furlough system, will average about 14.8 per cent reduction in pay to those earning more than $1,000.

I will recommend measures to eliminate certain payments in the veterans' services. I conceive these outlays were entirely beyond the original intentions of Congress in building up veterans' allowances. Many abuses have grown up from ill-considered legislation. They should be eliminated. The Nation should not ask for a reduction in allowances to men and dependents whose disabilities rise out of war service nor to those veterans with substantial service who have become totally disabled from non-war-connected causes and who are at the same time without other support. These latter veterans are a charge on the community at some point, and I feel that in view of their service to the Nation as a whole the responsibility should fall upon the Federal Government.

Many of the economies recommended in the Budget were presented at the last session of the Congress but failed of adoption. If the Economy and Appropriations Committees of the Congress in canvassing these proposed expenditures shall find further reductions which can be made without impairing essential Government services, it will be welcomed both by the country and by myself. But under no circumstances do I feel that the Congress should fail to uphold the total of reductions recommended.

Some of the older revenues and some of the revenues provided under the act passed during the last session of the Congress, particularly those generally referred to as the nuisance taxes, have not been as prolific of income as had been hoped. Further revenue is necessary in addition to the amount of reductions in expenditures recommended. Many of the manufacturers' excise taxes upon selected industries not only failed to produce satisfactory revenue, but they are in many ways unjust and discriminatory. The time has come when, if the Government is to have an adequate basis of revenue to assure a balanced Budget, this system of special manufacturers' excise taxes should be extended to cover practically all manufactures at a uniform rate, except necessary food and possibly some grades of clothing.

At the last session the Congress responded to my request for authority to reorganize the Government departments. The act provides for the grouping and consolidation of executive and administrative agencies according to major purpose, and thereby reducing the number and overlap and duplication of effort. Executive orders issued for these purposes are required to be transmitted to the Congress while in session and do not become effective until after the expiration of 60 calendar days after such transmission, unless the Congress shall sooner approve.

I shall issue such Executive orders within a few days grouping or consolidating over fifty executive and administrative agencies including a large number of commissions and "independent" agencies.

The second step, of course, remains that after these various bureaus and agencies are placed cheek by jowl into such groups, the administrative officers in charge of the groups shall eliminate their overlap and still further consolidate these activities. Therein lie large economies.

The Congress must be warned that a host of interested persons inside and outside the Government whose vision is concentrated on some particular function will at once protest against these proposals. These same sorts of activities have prevented reorganization of the Government for over a quarter of a century. They must be disregarded if the task is to be accomplished.

Banking

The basis of every other and every further effort toward recovery is to reorganize at once our banking system. The shocks to our economic system have undoubtedly multiplied by the weakness of our financial system. I first called attention of the Congress in 1929 to this condition, and I have unceasingly recommended remedy since that time. The subject has been exhaustively investigated both by the committees of the Congress and the officers of the Federal Reserve System. The banking and financial system is presumed to serve in furnishing the essential lubricant to the wheels of industry, agriculture, and commerce, that is, credit. Its diversion from proper use, its improper use, or its insufficiency instantly brings hardship and dislocation in economic life. As a system our banking has failed to meet this great emergency. It can be said without question of doubt that our losses and distress have been greatly augmented by its wholly inadequate organization. Its inability as a system to respond to our needs is today a constant drain upon progress toward recovery. In this statement I am not referring to individual banks or bankers. Thousands of them have shown distinguished courage and ability. On the contrary, I am referring to the system itself, which is so organized, or so lacking in organization, that in an emergency its very mechanism jeopardizes or paralyzes the action of sound banks and its instability is responsible for periodic dangers to our whole economic system.

Bank failures rose in 1931 to 10½ per cent of all the banks as compared to 1½ per cent of the failures of all other types of enterprise. Since January 1, 1930, we have had 4,665 banks suspend, with $3,300,000,000 in deposits. Partly from fears and drains from abroad, partly from these failures themselves (which indeed often caused closing of sound banks), we have witnessed hoarding of currency to an enormous sum, rising during the height of the crisis to over $1,600,000,000. The results from interreaction of cause and effect have expressed themselves in strangulation of credit which at times has almost stifled the Nation's business and agriculture. The losses, suffering, and tragedies of our people are incalculable. Not alone do they lie in the losses of savings to millions of homes, injury by deprival of working capital to thousands of small businesses, but also, in the frantic pressure to recall loans to meet pressures of hoarding and in liquidation of failed banks, millions of other people have suffered in the loss of their homes and farms, businesses have been ruined, unemployment increased, and farmers' prices diminished.

That this failure to function is unnecessary and is the fault of our particular system is plainly indicated by the fact that in Great Britain, where the economic mechanism has suffered far greater shocks than our own, there has not been a single bank failure during the depression. Again in Canada, where the situation has been in large degree identical with our own, there have not been substantial bank failures.

The creation of the Reconstruction Finance Corporation and the amendments to the Federal Reserve Act served to defend the Nation in a great crisis. They are not remedies; they are relief. It is inconceivable that the Reconstruction Corporation, which has extended aid to nearly 6,000 institutions and is manifestly but a temporary device, can go on indefinitely.

It is to-day a matter of satisfaction that the rate of bank failures, of hoarding, and the demands upon the Reconstruction Corporation have greatly lessened. The acute phases of the crisis have obviously passed and the time has now come when this national danger and this failure to respond to national necessities must be ended and the measures to end them can be safely undertaken. Methods of reform have been exhaustively examined. There is no reason now why solution should not be found at the present session of the Congress. Inflation of currency or governmental conduct of banking can have no part in these reforms. The Government must abide within the field of constructive organization, regulation, and the enforcement of safe practices only.

Parallel with reform in the banking laws must be changes in the Federal Farm Loan Banking system and in the Joint Stock Land Banks. Some of these changes should be directed to permanent improvement and some to emergency aid to our people where they wish to fight to save their farms and homes.

I wish again to emphasize this view—that these widespread banking reforms are a national necessity and are the first requisites for further recovery in agriculture and business. They should have immediate consideration as steps greatly needed to further recovery.

Economic Cooperation with Other Nations

Our major difficulties during the past two years find their origins in the shocks from economic collapse abroad which in turn are the aftermath of the Great War. If we are to secure rapid and assured recovery and protection for the future we must cooperate with foreign nations in many measures.

We have actively engaged in a World Disarmament Conference where, with success, we should reduce our own tax burdens and the tax burdens of other major nations. We should increase political stability of the world. We should lessen the danger of war by increasing defensive powers and decreasing offensive powers of nations. We would thus open new vistas of economic expansion for the world.

We are participating in the formulation of a World Economic Conference, successful results from which would contribute much to advance in agricultural prices, employment, and business. Currency depreciation and correlated forces have contributed greatly to decrease in price levels. Moreover, from these origins rise most of the destructive trade barriers now stifling the commerce of the world. We could by successful action increase security and expand trade through stability in international exchange and monetary values. By such action world confidence could be restored. It would bring courage and stability, which will reflect into every home in our land.

The European governments, obligated to us in war debts, have requested that there should be suspension of payments due the United States on December 15 next, to be accompanied by exchange of views upon this debt question. Our Government has informed them that we do not approve of suspension of the December 15 payments. I have stated that I would recommend to the Congress methods to overcome temporary exchange difficulties in connection with this payment from nations where it may be necessary.

In the meantime I wish to reiterate that here are three great fields of international action which must be considered not in part but as a whole. They are of most vital interest to our people. Within them there are not only grave dangers if we fail in right action but there also lie immense opportunities for good if we shall succeed. Within success there lie major remedies for our economic distress and major progress in stability and security to every fireside in our country.

The welfare of our people is dependent upon successful issue of the great causes of world peace, world disarmament, and organized world recovery. Nor is it too much to say that to-day as never before the welfare of mankind and the preservation of civilization depend upon our solution of these questions. Such solutions can not be attained except by honest friendship, by adherence to agreements entered upon until mutually revised and by cooperation amongst nations in a determination to find solutions which will be mutually beneficial.

Other Legislation

I have placed various legislative needs before the Congress in previous messages, and these views require no amplification on this occasion. I have urged the need for reform in our transportation and power regulation, in the antitrust laws as applied to our national resource industries, western range conservation, extension of Federal aid to child health services, membership in the World Court, the ratification of the Great Lakes-St. Lawrence Seaway Treaty, revision of the bankruptcy acts, revision of Federal court procedure, and many other pressing problems.

These and other special subjects I shall where necessary deal with by special communications to the Congress.

The activities of our Government are so great, when combined with the emergency activities which have arisen out of the world crisis, that even the briefest review of them would render the annual message unduly long. I shall therefore avail myself of the fact that every detail of the Government is covered in the reports to the Congress by each of the departments and agencies of the Government.

Conclusion

It seems to me appropriate upon this occasion to make certain general observations upon the principles which must dominate the solution of problems now pressing upon the Nation. Legislation in response to national needs will be effective only if every such act conforms to a complete philosophy of the people's purposes and destiny. Ours is a distinctive government with a unique history and background, consciously dedicated to specific ideals of liberty and to a faith in the inviolable sanctity of the individual human spirit. Furthermore, the continued existence and adequate functioning of our government in preservation of ordered liberty and stimulation of progress depends upon the maintenance of State, local, institutional, and individual sense of responsibility. We have builded a system of individualism peculiarly our own which must not be forgotten in any governmental acts, for from it have grown greater accomplishments than those of any other nation.

On the social and economic sides, the background of our American system and the motivation of progress is essentially that we should allow free play of social and economic forces as far as will not limit equality of opportunity and as will at the same time stimulate the initiative and enterprise of our people. In the maintenance of this balance the Federal Government can permit of no privilege to any person or group. It should act as a regulatory agent and not as a participant in economic and social life. The moment the Government participates, it becomes a competitor with the people. As a competitor it becomes at once a tyranny in whatever direction it may touch. We have around us numerous such experiences, no one of which can be found to have justified itself except in cases where the people as a whole have met forces beyond their control, such as those of the Great War and this great depression, where the full powers of the Federal Government must be exerted to protect the people. But even these must be limited to an emergency sense and must be promptly ended when these dangers are overcome.

With the free development of science and the consequent multitude of inventions, some of which are absolutely revolutionary in our national life, the Government must not only stimulate the social and economic responsibility of individuals and private institutions but it must also give leadership to cooperative action amongst the people which will soften the effect of these revolutions and thus secure social transformations in an orderly manner. The highest form of self-government is the voluntary cooperation within our people for such purposes.

But I would emphasize again that social and economic solutions, as such, will not avail to satisfy the aspirations of the people unless they conform with the traditions of our race deeply grooved in their sentiments through a century and a half of struggle for ideals of life that are rooted in religion and fed from purely spiritual springs.

HERBERT HOOVER
The White House,
December 6, 1932

2 7

Harry S. Truman (1945–1953)

Harry S. Truman was a pivotal figure in the history of presidential farewell addresses. In terms of development of the genre, his formal farewell is second in importance only to Washington's. There are several reasons for his estimable place in the genre. First, Truman revived the farewell address in American presidential discourse. A formal farewell had not been delivered by a U.S. president in more than eighty years—since 1869, in fact, when Andrew Johnson had used the farewell to try to vindicate his character and presidency. Second was the mode of delivery to the nation. America's first three formal farewells had been printed documents. Truman veered from that tradition and gave the first formal farewell speech in American history. Third was the way in which the speech was disseminated. Truman's address was broadcast live over radio and television to the nation and indeed to the world—another first for a formal farewell. Fourth was the fact that Truman used his farewell to depart from Washington's counsel regarding foreign policy. The new era required a new approach. As the Man from Missouri put it a week before delivering the farewell, "There has been no challenge like this in the history of our Republic. We are called upon to rise to the occasion, as no people before us."

Truman was not a popular president when he left office, for a host of reasons domestic and foreign. Besieged by critics, he suffered some of the lowest job-approval ratings in presidential polling history. He must have felt somewhat the same way Andrew Johnson did toward the end of his troubled presidency. Truman wanted the American people better to understand the rationale for and context of his actions. Giving a farewell address amid such popular discontent and controversy was a gamble. Yet Truman delivered. Biographer David McCullough says of the Farewell Address: "It was a speech without rhetorical flourishes or memorable epigrams and it was superb. Truman was at his best. In what it forecast concerning the Cold War, it was more extraordinary than could possibly have been understood at the time."[1]

The theme of Cold War indeed dominates the speech. In unprecedented times, when the threat of atomic war hung over civilization like Damocles's sword, Truman wanted the American people to understand the role and limits of presidential decision-making. Since his farewell was being broadcast live on television, he grasped the full power of the medium. Sitting at his desk, he made TV viewers aware of the office in the West Wing in which he worked, and he famously referred to the proverbial "buck" stopping right at that desk. Truman reached out to the American people to convey that the president is not a marble statue but a man like others. But with this difference: the President must carry the burden of the world's troubles on his shoulders. "I want all of you to realize how big a job, how hard a job, it is." Truman's message—the sum total of his words and images—conveyed the utter loneliness of the president—any president—who must bear final responsibility for the decisions he is called upon to make. War and peace, justice and injustice, liberty and tyranny, prosperity and poverty—all hang in the balance of the president's decisions.

Readers may note the frequent occurrence of the pronoun "I" in these remarks. Truman uttered it 101 times—more by far than any other president in a formal farewell address.

Farewell Address
(broadcast live on radio and television from the White House)
January 15, 1953

My fellow Americans:

I am happy to have this opportunity to talk to you once more before I leave the White House.

Next Tuesday, General Eisenhower will be inaugurated as President of the United States. A short time after the new President takes his oath of office, I will be on the train going back home to Independence, Missouri. I will once again be a plain, private citizen of this great Republic.

That is as it should be. Inauguration Day will be a great demonstration of our democratic process. I am glad to be a part of it—glad to wish General Eisenhower all possible success, as he begins his term—glad the whole world will have a chance to see how simply and how peacefully our American system transfers the vast power of the Presidency from my hands to his. It is a good object lesson in democracy. I am very proud of it. And I know you are, too.

During the last 2 months I have done my best to make this transfer an orderly one. I have talked with my successor on the affairs of the country, both foreign and domestic, and my Cabinet officers have talked with their successors. I want to say that General Eisenhower and his associates have cooperated fully in this effort. Such an orderly transfer from one party to another has never taken place before in our history. I think a real precedent has been set.

In speaking to you tonight, I have no new revelations to make—no political statements—no policy announcements. There are simply a few things in my heart that I want to say to you. I want to say "goodby" and "thanks for your help." And I want to talk to you a little while about what has happened since I became your President.

I am speaking to you from the room where I have worked since April 12, 1945. This is the President's office in the West Wing of the White House. This is the desk where I have signed most of the papers that embodied the decisions I have made as President. It has been the desk of many Presidents, and will be the desk of many more.

Since I became President, I have been to Europe, Mexico, Canada, Brazil, Puerto Rico, and the Virgin Islands, Wake Island, and Hawaii. I have visited almost every State in the Union. I have traveled 135,000 miles by air, 77,000 by rail, and 17,000 by ship. But the mail always followed me, and wherever I happened to be, that's where the office of the President was.

The greatest part of the President's job is to make decisions—big ones and small ones, dozens of them almost every day. The papers may circulate around the Government for a while but they finally reach this desk. And then, there's no place else for them to go. The President—whoever he is—has to decide. He can't pass the buck to anybody. No one else can do the deciding for him. That's his job.

That's what I've been doing here in this room, for almost 8 years. And over in the main part of the White House, there's a study on the second floor—a room much like this one—where I have worked at night and early in the morning on the papers I couldn't get to at the office.

Of course, for more than 3 years Mrs. Truman and I were not living in the White House. We were across the street in the Blair House. That was when the White House almost fell down on us and had to be rebuilt. I had a study over at the Blair House, too, but living in the Blair House was not as convenient as living in the White House. The Secret Service wouldn't let me walk across the street, so I had to get in a car every morning to cross the street to the White House office, again at noon to go to the Blair House for lunch, again to go back to the office after lunch, and finally take an automobile at night to return to the Blair House. Fantastic, isn't it? But necessary, so my guards thought— and they are the bosses on such matters as that.

Now, of course, we're back in the White House. It is in very good condition, and General Eisenhower will be able to take up his residence in the house and work right here. That will be much more convenient for him, and I'm very glad the renovation job was all completed before his term began.

Your new President is taking office in quite different circumstances than when I became President 8 years ago. On April 12, 1945, I had been presiding over the Senate in my capacity as Vice President. When the Senate recessed about 5 o'clock in the afternoon, I walked over to the office of the Speaker of the House, Mr. Rayburn, to discuss pending legislation. As soon as I arrived, I was told that Mr. Early, one of President Roosevelt's secretaries, wanted me to call. I reached Mr. Early, and he told me to come to the White House as quickly as possible, to enter by way of the Pennsylvania Avenue entrance, and to come to Mrs. Roosevelt's study.

When I arrived, Mrs. Roosevelt told me the tragic news, and I felt the shock that all of you felt a little later—when the word came over the radio and appeared in the newspapers. President Roosevelt had died. I offered to do anything I could for Mrs. Roosevelt, and then I asked the Secretary of State to call the Cabinet together.

At 7:09 P.M. I was sworn in as President by Chief Justice Stone in the Cabinet Room.

Things were happening fast in those days. The San Francisco conference to organize the United Nations had been called for April 25th. I was asked if that meeting would go forward. I announced that it would. That was my first decision.

After attending President Roosevelt's funeral, I went to the Hall of the House of Representatives and told a joint session of the Congress that I would carry on President Roosevelt's policies.

On May 7th, Germany surrendered. The announcement was made on May 8th, my 61st birthday.

Mr. Churchill called me shortly after that and wanted a meeting with me and Prime Minister Stalin of Russia. Later on, a meeting was agreed upon, and Churchill, Stalin, and I met at Potsdam in Germany.

Meanwhile, the first atomic explosion took place out in the New Mexico desert.

The war against Japan was still going on. I made the decision that the atomic bomb had to be used to end it. I made that decision in the conviction it would save hundreds of thousands of lives— Japanese as well as American. Japan surrendered, and we were faced with the huge problems of bringing the troops home and reconverting the economy from war to peace.

All these things happened within just a little over 4 months—from April to August 1945. I tell you this to illustrate the tremendous scope of the work your President has to do.

And all these emergencies and all the developments to meet them have required the President to put in long hours—usually 17 hours a day, with no payment for overtime. I sign my name, on the average, 600 times a day, see and talk to hundreds of people every month, shake hands with thousands every year, and still carry on the business of the largest going concern in the whole world. There is no job like it on the face of the earth—in the power which is concentrated here at this desk, and in the responsibility and difficulty of the decisions.

I want all of you to realize how big a job, how hard a job, it is—not for my sake, because I am stepping out of it—but for the sake of my successor. He needs the understanding and the help of every citizen. It is not enough for you to come out once every 4 years and vote for a candidate, and then go back home and say, "Well, I've done my part, now let the new President do the worrying." He can't do the job alone.

Regardless of your politics, whether you are Republican or Democrat, your fate is tied up with what is done here in this room. The President is President of the whole country. We must give him our support as citizens of the United States. He will have mine, and I want you to give him yours.

I suppose that history will remember my term in office as the years when the "cold war" began to overshadow our lives. I have had hardly a day in office that has not been dominated by this all-embracing struggle—this conflict between those who love freedom and those who would lead the world back into slavery and darkness. And always in the background there has been the atomic bomb.

But when history says that my term of office saw the beginning of the cold war, it will also say that in those 8 years we have set the course that can win it. We have succeeded in carving out a new set of policies to attain peace—positive policies, policies of world leadership, policies that express faith in other free people. We have averted world war III up to now, and we may already have succeeded in establishing conditions which can keep that war from happening as far ahead as man can see.

These are great and historic achievements that we can all be proud of. Think of the difference between our course now and our course 30 years ago. After the First World War we withdrew from world affairs—we failed to act in concert with other peoples against aggression—we helped to kill the League of Nations—and we built up tariff barriers that strangled world trade. This time, we avoided those mistakes. We helped to found and sustain the United Nations. We have welded alliances that include the greater part of the free world. And we have gone ahead with other free countries to help build their economies and link us all together in a healthy world trade.

Think back for a moment to the 1930's and you will see the difference. The Japanese moved into Manchuria, and free men did not act. The Fascists moved into Ethiopia, and we did not act. The Nazis marched into the Rhineland, into Austria, into Czechoslovakia, and free men were paralyzed for lack of strength and unity and will.

Think about those years of weakness and indecision, and the World War II which was their evil result. Then think about the speed and courage and decisiveness with which we have moved against the Communist threat since World War II.

The first crisis came in 1945 and 1946, when the Soviet Union refused to honor its agreement to remove its troops from Iran. Members of my Cabinet came to me and asked if we were ready to take the risk that a firm stand involved. I replied that we were. So we took our stand—we made it clear to the Soviet Union that we expected them to honor their agreement—and the Soviet troops were withdrawn from Iran.

Then, in early 1947, the Soviet Union threatened Greece and Turkey. The British sent me a message saying they could no longer keep their forces in that area. Something had to be done at once, or the eastern Mediterranean would be taken over by the Communists. On March 12th, I went before the Congress and stated our determination to help the people of Greece and Turkey maintain their independence. Today, Greece is still free and independent; and Turkey is a bulwark of strength at a strategic corner of the world.

Then came the Marshall plan which saved Europe, the heroic Berlin airlift, and our military aid programs.

We inaugurated the North Atlantic Pact, the Rio Pact binding the Western Hemisphere together, and the defense pacts with countries of the Far Pacific.

Most important of all, we acted in Korea. I was in Independence, Missouri, in June 1950, when Secretary Acheson telephoned me and gave me the news about the invasion of Korea. I told the Secretary to lay the matter at once before the United Nations, and I came on back to Washington.

Flying back over the flatlands of the Middle West and over the Appalachians that summer afternoon, I had a lot of time to think. I turned the problem over in my mind in many ways, but my thoughts kept coming back to the 1930's—to Manchuria, to Ethiopia, the Rhineland, Austria, and finally to Munich.

Here was history repeating itself. Here was another probing action, another testing action. If we let the Republic of Korea go under, some other country would be next, and then another. And all the time, the courage and confidence of the free world would be ebbing away, just as it did in the 1930s. And the United Nations would go the way of the League of Nations.

When I reached Washington, I met immediately with the Secretary of State, the Secretary of Defense, and General Bradley, and the other civilian and military officials who had information and advice to help me decide on what to do. We talked about the problems long and hard. We considered those problems very carefully.

It was not easy to make the decision to send American boys again into battle. I was a soldier in the First World War, and I know what a soldier goes through. I know well the anguish that mothers and fathers and families go through. So I knew what was ahead if we acted in Korea.

But after all this was said, we realized that the issue was whether there would be fighting in a limited area now or on a much larger scale later on—whether there would be some casualties now or many more casualties later.

So a decision was reached—the decision I believe was the most important in my time as President of the United States.

In the days that followed, the most heartening fact was that the American people clearly agreed with the decision.

And in Korea, our men are fighting as valiantly as Americans have ever fought—because they know they are fighting in the same cause of freedom in which Americans have stood ever since the beginning of the Republic.

Where free men had failed the test before, this time we met the test.

We met it firmly. We met it successfully. The aggression has been repelled. The Communists have seen their hopes of easy conquest go down the drain. The determination of free people to defend themselves has been made clear to the Kremlin.

As I have thought about our worldwide struggle with the Communists these past 8 years—day in and day out—I have never once doubted that you, the people of our country, have the will to do what is necessary to win this terrible fight against communism. I know the people of this country have that will and determination, and I have always depended on it. Because I have been sure of that, I have been able to make necessary decisions even though they called for sacrifices by all of us. And I have not been wrong in my judgment of the American people.

That same assurance of our people's determination will be General Eisenhower's greatest source of strength in carrying on this struggle.

Now, once in a while, I get a letter from some impatient person asking, why don't we get it over with? Why don't we issue an ultimatum, make all-out war, drop the atomic bomb?

For most Americans, the answer is quite simple: We are not made that way. We are a moral people. Peace is our goal, with justice and freedom. We cannot, of our own free will, violate the very principles that we are striving to defend. The whole purpose of what we are doing is to prevent world war III. Starting a war is no way to make peace.

But if anyone still thinks that just this once, bad means can bring good ends, then let me remind you of this: We are living in the 8th year of the atomic age. We are not the only nation that is learning to unleash the power of the atom. A third world war might dig the grave not only of our Communist opponents but also of our own society, our world as well as theirs.

Starting an atomic war is totally unthinkable for rational men.

Then, some of you may ask, when and how will the cold war end? I think I can answer that simply. The Communist world has great resources, and it looks strong. But there is a fatal flaw in their society. Theirs is a godless system, a system of slavery; there is no freedom in it, no consent. The Iron

Curtain, the secret police, the constant purges, all these are symptoms of a great basic weakness—the rulers' fear of their own people.

In the long run the strength of our free society, and our ideals, will prevail over a system that has respect for neither God nor man.

Last week, in my State of the Union Message to the Congress—and I hope you will all take the time to read it—I explained how I think we will finally win through.

As the free world grows stronger, more united, more attractive to men on both sides of the Iron Curtain—and as the Soviet hopes for easy expansion are blocked—then there will have to come a time of change in the Soviet world. Nobody can say for sure when that is going to be, or exactly how it will come about, whether by revolution, or trouble in the satellite states, or by a change inside the Kremlin.

Whether the Communist rulers shift their policies of their own free will—or whether the change comes about in some other way—I have not a doubt in the world that a change will occur.

I have a deep and abiding faith in the destiny of free men. With patience and courage, we shall some day move on into a new era—a wonderful golden age—an age when we can use the peaceful tools that science has forged for us to do away with poverty and human misery everywhere on earth.

Think what can be done, once our capital, our skills, our science—most of all atomic energy— can be released from the tasks of defense and turned wholly to peaceful purposes all around the world.

There is no end to what can be done.

I can't help but dream out loud just a little here.

The Tigris and Euphrates Valley can be made to bloom as it did in the times of Babylon and Nineveh. Israel can be made the country of milk and honey as it was in the time of Joshua.

There is a plateau in Ethiopia some 6,000 to 8,000 feet high, that has 65,000 square miles of land just exactly like the corn belt in northern Illinois. Enough food can be raised there to feed a hundred million people.

There are places in South America—places in Colombia and Venezuela and Brazil—just like that plateau in Ethiopia—places where food could be raised for millions of people.

These things can be done, and they are self-liquidating projects. If we can get peace and safety in the world under the United Nations, the developments will come so fast we will not recognize the world in which we now live.

This is our dream of the future—our picture of the world we hope to have when the Communist threat is overcome.

I've talked a lot tonight about the menace of communism—and our fight against it—because that is the overriding issue of our time. But there are some other things we've done that history will record. One of them is that we in America have learned how to attain real prosperity for our people.

We have $62\frac{1}{2}$ million people at work. Businessmen, farmers, laborers, white-collar people, all have better incomes and more of the good things of life than ever before in the history of the world.

There hasn't been a failure of an insured bank in nearly 9 years. No depositor has lost a cent in that period.

And the income of our people has been fairly distributed, perhaps more so than at any other time in recent history.

We have made progress in spreading the blessings of American life to all of our people. There has been a tremendous awakening of the American conscience on the great issues of civil rights—equal economic opportunities, equal rights of citizenship, and equal educational opportunities for all our people, whatever their race or religion or status of birth.

So, as I empty the drawers of this desk, and as Mrs. Truman and I leave the White House, we have no regret. We feel we have done our best in the public service. I hope and believe we have contributed to the welfare of this Nation and to the peace of the world.

When Franklin Roosevelt died, I felt there must be a million men better qualified than I, to take up the Presidential task. But the work was mine to do, and I had to do it. And I have tried to give it everything that was in me.

Through all of it, through all the years that I have worked here in this room, I have been well aware I did not really work alone—that you were working with me.

No President could ever hope to lead our country, or to sustain the burdens of this office, save as the people helped with their support. I have had that help—you have given me that support in all our great essential undertakings to build the free world's strength and keep the peace.

Those are the big things. Those are the things we have done together.

For that I shall be grateful, always.

And now, the time has come for me to say good night—and God bless you all.

A week prior to delivering his farewell address, Truman submitted his 8th State of the Union report to the Congress. It is expressly not a legislative laundry list. Rather it is one of the most remarkable final annual messages in American history, a primer of the postwar world, a history lesson defining the new age in which Americans lived.

Eighth State of the Union Address
(message read aloud by clerks to both houses of the Congress and broadcast to foreign countries)
January 7, 1953

To the Congress of the United States:

I have the honor to report to the Congress on the state of the Union.

This is the eighth such report that, as President, I have been privileged to present to you and to the country. On previous occasions, it has been my custom to set forth proposals for legislative action in the coming year. But that is not my purpose today. The presentation of a legislative program falls properly to my successor, not to me, and I would not infringe upon his responsibility to chart the forward course. Instead, I wish to speak of the course we have been following the past eight years and the position at which we have arrived.

In just two weeks, General Eisenhower will be inaugurated as President of the United States and I will resume—most gladly—my place as a private citizen of this Republic. The Presidency last changed hands eight years ago this coming April. That was a tragic time: a time of grieving for President Roosevelt—the great and gallant human being who had been taken from us; a time of unrelieved anxiety to his successor, thrust so suddenly into the complexities and burdens of the Presidential office.

Not so this time. This time we see the normal transition under our democratic system. One President, at the conclusion of his term, steps back to private life; his successor, chosen by the people, begins his tenure of the office. And the Presidency of the United States continues to function without a moment's break.

Since the election, I have done my best to assure that the transfer from one Administration to another shall be smooth and orderly. From General Eisenhower and his associates, I have had friendly and understanding collaboration in this endeavor. I have not sought to thrust upon him—nor has he sought to take—the responsibility which must be mine until twelve o'clock noon on January twentieth. But together, I hope and believe we have found means whereby the incoming President can obtain the full and detailed information he will need to assume the responsibility the moment he takes the oath of office.

The President-elect is about to take up the greatest burdens, the most compelling responsibilities, given to any man. And I, with you and all Americans, wish for him all possible success in undertaking the tasks that will so soon be his.

What are these tasks? The President is Chief of State, elected representative of all the people, national spokesman for them and to them. He is Commander-in-Chief of our armed forces. He is charged with the conduct of our foreign relations. He is Chief Executive of the Nation's largest civilian organization. He must select and nominate all top officials of the Executive Branch and all Federal judges. And on the legislative side, he has the obligation and the opportunity to recommend, and to approve or veto legislation. Besides all this, it is to him that a great political party turns naturally for leadership, and that, too, he must provide as President.

This bundle of burdens is unique; there is nothing else like it on the face of the earth. Each task could be a full-time job. Together, they would be a tremendous undertaking in the easiest of times.

But our times are not easy; they are hard—as hard and complex, perhaps as any in our history. Now, the President not only has to carry on these tasks in such a way that our democracy may grow and flourish and our people prosper, but he also has to lead the whole free world in overcoming the communist menace—and all this under the shadow of the atomic bomb.

This is a huge challenge to the human being who occupies the Presidential office. But it is not a challenge to him alone, for in reality he cannot meet it alone. The challenge runs not just to him but to his whole Administration, to the Congress, to the country.

Ultimately, no President can master his responsibilities, save as his fellow citizens—indeed, the whole people—comprehend the challenge of our times and move, with him, to meet it.

It has been my privilege to hold the Presidential office for nearly eight years now, and much has been done in which I take great pride. But this is not personal pride. It is pride in the people, in the Nation. It is pride in our political system and our form of government—balky sometimes, mechanically deficient perhaps, in many ways—but enormously alive and vigorous; able through these years to keep the Republic on the right course, rising to the great occasions, accomplishing the essentials, meeting the basic challenge of our times.

There have been misunderstandings and controversies these past eight years, but through it all the President of the United States has had that measure of support and understanding without which no man could sustain the burdens of the Presidential office, or hope to discharge its responsibilities.

For this I am profoundly grateful—grateful to my associates in the Executive Branch—most of them non-partisan civil servants; grateful—despite our disagreements—to the Members of the Congress on both sides of the aisle; grateful especially to the American people, the citizens of this Republic, governors of us all.

We are still so close to recent controversies that some of us may find it hard to understand the accomplishments of these past eight years. But the accomplishments are real and very great, not as the President's, not as the Congress', but as the achievements of our country and all the people in it.

Let me remind you of some of the things we have done since I first assumed my duties as President of the United States.

I took the oath of office on April 12, 1945. In May of that same year, the Nazis surrendered. Then, in July, that great white flash of light, man-made at Alamogordo, heralded swift and final victory in World War II—and opened the doorway to the atomic age.

Consider some of the great questions that were posed for us by sudden, total victory in World War II. Consider also, how well we as a Nation have responded.

Would the American economy collapse, after the war? That was one question. Would there be another depression here—a repetition of 1921 or 1929? The free world feared and dreaded it. The communists hoped for it and built their policies upon that hope.

We answered that question—answered it with a resounding "no."

Our economy has grown tremendously. Free enterprise has flourished as never fore. Sixty-two million people are now gainfully employed, compared with 51 million seven years ago. Private businessmen and farmers have invested more than 200 billion dollars in new plant and equipment since the end of World War II. Prices have risen further than they should have done—but incomes, by and large, have risen even more, so that real living standards are now considerably higher than seven years ago. Aided by sound government policies, our expanding economy has shown the strength and flexibility for swift and almost painless reconversion from war to peace, in 1945 and 1946; for quick reaction and recovery—well before Korea—from the beginnings of recession in 1949. Above all, this live and vital economy of ours has now shown the remarkable capacity to sustain a great mobilization program for defense, a vast outpouring of aid to friends and allies all around the world—and still to produce more goods and services for peaceful use at home than we have ever known before.

This has been our answer, up to now, to those who feared or hoped for a depression in this country. How have we handled our national finances? That was another question arising at war's end. In the administration of the Government, no problem takes more of the President's time, year in and year out, than fashioning the Budget, and the related problem of managing the public debt.

Financing World War II left us with a tremendous public debt, which reached 279 billion dollars at its peak in February, 1946.

Beginning in July, 1946, when war and reconversion financing had ended, we have held quite closely to the sound standard that in times of high employment and high national income, the Federal Budget should be balanced and the debt reduced.

For the four fiscal years from July 1, 1946, to June 30, 1950, we had a net surplus of 4.3 billion dollars. Using this surplus, and the Treasury's excess cash reserves, the debt was reduced substantially, reaching a low point of 251 billion dollars in June, 1949, and ending up at 257 billion dollars on June 30, 1950.

In July of 1950, we began our rapid rearmament, and for two years held very close to a pay-as-we-go policy. But in the current fiscal year and the next, rising expenditures for defense will substantially outrun receipts. This will pose an immediate and serious problem for the new Congress.

Now let me turn to another question we faced at the war's end. Would we take up again, and carry forward, the great projects of social welfare—so badly needed, so long overdue—that the New Deal had introduced into our national life? Would our Government continue to have a heart for the people, or was the progress of the New Deal to be halted in the aftermath of war as decisively as the progress of Woodrow Wilson's New Freedom had been halted after the first world war?

This question, too, we have answered. We have answered it by doubling old age insurance benefits and extending coverage to ten million more people. We have answered it by increasing our minimum wage. We have answered by the three million privately constructed homes that the Federal Government has helped finance since the war—and the 155 thousand units of low rent public housing placed under construction since 1949.

We have answered with the 42 thousand new hospital beds provided since 1946 through the joint efforts of the Federal Government and local communities.

We have answered by helping eight million veterans of World War II to obtain advanced education, 196 thousand to start in business, and 64 thousand to buy farms.

We have answered by continuing to help farmers obtain electric power, until today nearly 90 per cent of our farms have power line electric service.

In these and other ways, we have demonstrated, up to now, that our democracy has not forgotten how to use the powers of the Government to promote the people's welfare and security.

Another of the big post-war questions was this: What we would do with the Nation's natural resources—its soils and water, forests and grasslands. Would we continue the strong conservation movement of the 1930's, or would we, as we did after the First World War, slip back into the practices of monopoly, exploitation, and waste?

The answer is plain. All across our country, the soil conservation movement has spread, aided by Government programs, enriching private and public lands, preserving them from destruction, improving them for future use. In our river basins, we have invested nearly 5 billion dollars of public funds in the last eight years—invested them in projects to control floods, irrigate farmlands, produce low-cost power and get it to the housewives and farmers and businessmen who need it. We have been vigilant in protecting the people's property—lands and forests and oil and minerals.

We have had to fight hard against those who would use our resources for private greed; we have met setbacks; we have had to delay work because of defense priorities, but on the whole we can be proud of our record in protecting our natural heritage, and in using our resources for the public good.

Here is another question we had to face at the war's close: Would we continue, in peace as well as war, to promote equality of opportunity for all our citizens, seeking ways and means to guarantee for all of them the full enjoyment of their civil rights?

During the war we achieved great economic and social gains for millions of our fellow citizens who had been held back by prejudice. Were we prepared, in peacetime, to keep on moving toward full realization of the democratic promise? Or would we let it be submerged, wiped out, in post-war riots and reaction, as after World War I?

We answered these questions in a series of forward steps at every level of government and in many spheres of private life. In our armed forces, our civil service, our universities, our railway trains, the residential districts of our cities—in stores and factories all across the Nation—in the polling booths as well—the barriers are coming down. This is happening, in part, at the mandate of the courts; in part, at the insistence of Federal, State, and local governments; in part, through the enlightened action of private groups and persons in every region and every walk of life.

There has been a great awakening of the American conscience on the issues of civil rights. And all this progress—still far from complete but still continuing—has been our answer, up to now, to those who questioned our intention to live up to the promises of equal freedom for us all.

There was another question posed for us at the war's end, which equally concerned the future course of our democracy: Could the machinery of government and politics in this Republic be changed, improved, adapted rapidly enough to carry through, responsibly and well, the vast, new complicated undertakings called for in our time?

We have answered this question, too, answered it by tackling the most urgent, most specific, problems which the war experience itself had brought into sharp focus. The reorganization of the Congress in 1946; the unification of our armed services, beginning in 1947; the closer integration of foreign and military policy through the National Security Council created that same year; and the Executive reorganizations, before and after the Hoover-Acheson Commission Report in 1949—these are landmarks in our continuing endeavor to make government an effective instrument of service to the people.

I come now to the most vital question of all, the greatest of our concerns: Could there be built in the world a durable structure of security, a lasting peace for all the nations, or would we drift, as after World War I, toward another terrible disaster—a disaster which this time might be the holocaust of atomic war?

That is still the overriding question of our time. We cannot know the answer yet; perhaps we will not know it finally for a long time to come. But day and night, these past eight years, we have been building for peace, searching out the way that leads most surely to security and freedom and justice in the world for us and all mankind.

This, above all else, has been the task of our Republic since the end of World War II, and our accomplishment so far should give real pride to all Americans. At the very least, a total war has been averted, each day up to this hour. And at the most, we may already have succeeded in establishing conditions which can keep that kind of war from happening, for as far ahead as man can see.

The Second World War radically changed the power relationships of the world. Nations once great were left shattered and weak, channels of communication, routes of trade, political and economic ties of many kinds were ripped apart.

And in this changed, disrupted, chaotic situation, the United States and the Soviet Union emerged as the two strongest powers of the world. Each had tremendous human and natural resources, actual or potential, on a scale unmatched by any other nation.

Nothing could make plainer why the world is in its present state—and how that came to pass—than an understanding of the diametrically opposite principles and policies of these two great powers in a war-ruined world. For our part, we in this Republic were—and are—free men, heirs of the American Revolution, dedicated to the truths of our Declaration of Independence: ". . . That all men are created equal, that they are endowed by their Creator with certain unalienable rights . . . That to secure these rights, governments are instituted among men, deriving their just powers from the consent of the governed."

Our post-war objective has been in keeping with this great idea. The United States has sought to use its pre-eminent position of power to help other nations recover from the damage and dislocation of the war. We held out a helping hand to enable them to restore their national lives and to regain their positions as independent, self-supporting members of the great family of nations. This help was given without any attempt on our part to dominate or control any nation. We did not want satellites but partners.

The Soviet Union, however, took exactly the opposite course.

Its rulers saw in the weakened condition of the world not an obligation to assist in the great work of reconstruction, but an opportunity to exploit misery and suffering for the extension of their power. Instead of help, they brought subjugation. They extinguished, blotted out, the national independence of the countries that the military operations of World War II had left within their grasp.

The difference stares at us from the map of Europe today. To the west of the line that tragically divides Europe we see nations continuing to act and live in the light of their own traditions and principles. On the other side, we see the dead uniformity of a tyrannical system imposed by the rulers of the Soviet Union. Nothing could point up more clearly what the global struggle between the free world and the communists is all about.

It is a struggle as old as recorded history; it is freedom versus tyranny.

For the dominant idea of the Soviet regime is the terrible conception that men do not have rights but live at the mercy of the state.

Inevitably this idea of theirs—and all the consequences flowing from it—collided with the efforts of free nations to build a just and peaceful world. The "cold war" between the communists and the free world is nothing more or less than the Soviet attempt to checkmate and defeat our peaceful purposes, in furtherance of their own dread objective.

We did not seek this struggle, God forbid. We did our utmost to avoid it. In World War II, we and the Russians had fought side by side, each in our turn attacked and forced to combat by the aggressors. After the war, we hoped that our wartime collaboration could be maintained, that the frightful experience of Nazi invasion, of devastation in the heart of Russia, had turned the Soviet rulers away from their old proclaimed allegiance to world revolution and communist dominion. But instead, they violated, one by one, the solemn agreements they had made with us in wartime. They sought to use the rights and privileges they had obtained in the United Nations, to frustrate its purposes and cut down its powers as an effective agent of world progress and the keeper of the world's peace.

Despite this outcome, the efforts we made toward peaceful collaboration are a source of our present strength. They demonstrated that we believed what we proclaimed, that we actually sought honest agreements as the way to peace. Our whole moral position, our leadership in the free world today, is fortified by that fact.

The world is divided, not through our fault or failure, but by Soviet design. They, not we, began the cold war. And because the free world saw this happen because men know we made the effort and the Soviet rulers spurned it—the free nations have accepted leadership from our Republic, in meeting and mastering the Soviet offensive.

It seems to me especially important that all of us be clear, in our own thinking, about the nature of the threat we have faced—and will face for a long time to come. The measures we have devised to meet it take shape and pattern only as we understand what we were—and are—up against.

The Soviet Union occupies a territory of 8 million square miles. Beyond its borders, East and West, are the nearly five million square miles of the satellite states—virtually incorporated into the Soviet Union—and of China, now its close partner. This vast land mass contains an enormous store of natural resources sufficient to support an economic development comparable to our own.

That is the Stalinist world. It is a world of great natural diversity in geography and climate, in distribution of resources, in population, language, and living standards, in economic and cultural development. It is a world whose people are not all convinced communists by any means. It is a world where history and national traditions, particularly in its borderlands, tend more toward separation than unification, and run counter to the enforced combination that has been made of these areas today.

But it is also a world of great man-made uniformities, a world that bleeds its population white to build huge military forces; a world in which the police are everywhere and their authority unlimited; a world where terror and slavery are deliberately administered both as instruments of government and as means of production; a world where all effective social power is the state's monopoly—yet the state itself is the creature of the communist tyrants.

The Soviet Union, with its satellites, and China are held in the tight grip of communist party chieftains. The party dominates all social and political institutions. The party regulates and centrally directs the whole economy. In Moscow's sphere, and in Peiping's, all history, philosophy, morality and law are centrally established by rigid dogmas, incessantly drummed into the whole population and subject to interpretation—or to change by none except the party's own inner circle.

And lest their people learn too much of other ways of life, the communists have walled off their world, deliberately and uniformly, from the rest of human society.

That is the communist base of operation in their cold war. In addition, they have at their command hundreds and thousands of dedicated foreign communists, people in nearly every free country who will serve Moscow's ends. Thus the masters of the Kremlin are provided with deluded followers all through the free world whom they can manipulate, cynically and quite ruthlessly, to serve the purposes of the Soviet state.

Given their vast internal base of operations, and their agents in foreign lands, what are the communist rulers trying to do?

Inside their homeland, the communists are trying to maintain and modernize huge military forces. And simultaneously, they are endeavoring to weld their whole vast area and population into a completely self-contained, advanced industrial society. They aim, some day, to equal or better the production levels of Western Europe and North America combined—thus shifting the balance of world economic power, and war potential, to their side.

They have a long way to go and they know it. But they are prepared to levy upon living generations any sacrifice that helps strengthen their armed power, or speed industrial development.

Externally, the communist rulers are trying to expand the boundaries of their world, whenever and wherever they can. This expansion they have pursued steadfastly since the close of World War II, using any means available to them.

Where the Soviet army was present, as in the countries of Eastern Europe, they have gradually squeezed free institutions to death.

Where post-war chaos existed in industrialized nations, as in Western Europe, the local Stalinists tried to gain power through political processes, politically-inspired strikes, and every available means for subverting free institutions to their evil ends.

Where conditions permitted, the Soviet rulers have stimulated and aided armed insurrection by communist-led revolutionary forces, as in Greece, Indo-China, the Philippines, and China, or outright aggression by one of their satellites, as in Korea.

Where the forces of nationalism, independence, and economic change were at work throughout the great sweep of Asia and Africa, the communists tried to identify themselves with the cause of progress, tried to picture themselves as the friends of freedom and advancement—surely one of the most cynical efforts of which history offers record.

Thus, everywhere in the free world, the communists seek to fish in troubled waters, to seize more countries, to enslave more millions of human souls. They were, and are, ready to ally themselves with any group, from the extreme left to the extreme right, that offers them an opportunity to advance their ends.

Geography gives them a central position. They are both a European and an Asian power, with borders touching many of the most sensitive and vital areas in the free world around them. So situated, they can use their armies and their economic power to set up simultaneously a whole series of threats—or inducements—to such widely dispersed places as Western Germany, Iran, and Japan. These pressures and attractions can be sustained at will, or quickly shifted from place to place.

Thus the communist rulers are moving, with implacable will, to create greater strength in their vast empire, and to create weakness and division in the free world, preparing for the time their false creed teaches them must come: the time when the whole world outside their sway will be so torn by strife and contradictions that it will be ripe for the communist plucking.

This is the heart of the distorted Marxist interpretation of history. This is the glass through which Moscow and Peiping look out upon the world, the glass through which they see the rest of us. They seem really to believe that history is on their side. And they are trying to boost "history" along, at every opportunity, in every way they can.

I have set forth here the nature of the communist menace confronting our Republic and the whole free world. This is the measure of the challenge we have faced since World War II—a challenge partly military and partly economic, partly moral and partly intellectual, confronting us at every level of human endeavor and all around the world.

It has been and must be the free world's purpose not only to organize defenses against aggression and subversion, not only to build a structure of resistance and salvation for the community of nations outside the iron curtain, but in addition to give expression and opportunity to the forces of growth and progress in the free world, to so organize and unify the cooperative community of free men that we will not crumble but grow stronger over the years, and the Soviet empire, not the free world, will eventually have to change its ways or fall.

Our whole program of action to carry out this purpose has been directed to meet two requirements. The first of these had to do with security. Like the pioneers who settled this great continent of ours, we have had to carry a musket while we went about our peaceful business. We realized that if we and our allies did not have military strength to meet the growing Soviet military threat, we would never have the opportunity to carry forward our efforts to build a peaceful world of law and order—the only environment in which our free institutions could survive and flourish.

Did this mean we had to drop everything else and concentrate on armies and weapons? Of course it did not: side-by-side with this urgent military requirement, we had to continue to help create conditions of economic and social progress in the world. This work had to be carried forward alongside the first, not only in order to meet the non-military aspects of the communist drive for power, but also because this creative effort toward human progress is essential to bring about the kind of world we as free men want to live in.

These two requirements—military security and human progress—are more closely related in action than we sometimes recognize. Military security depends upon a strong economic underpinning and a stable and hopeful political order; conversely, the confidence that makes for economic and political progress does not thrive in areas that are vulnerable to military conquest.

These requirements are related in another way. Both of them depend upon unity of action among the free nations of the world. This, indeed, has been the foundation of our whole effort, for the drawing together of the free people of the world has become a condition essential not only to their progress, but to their survival as free people. This is the conviction that underlies all the steps we have been taking to strengthen and unify the free nations during the past seven years.

What have these steps been? First of all, how have we gone about meeting the requirement of providing for our security against this world-wide challenge?

Our starting point, as I have said on many occasions, has been and remains the United Nations.

We were prepared, and so were the other nations of the free world, to place our reliance on the machinery of the United Nations to safeguard peace. But before the United Nations could give full expression to the concept of international security embodied in the Charter, it was essential that the five permanent members of the Security Council honor their solemn pledge to cooperate to that end. This the Soviet Union has not done.

I do not need to outline here the dreary record of Soviet obstruction and veto and the unceasing efforts of the Soviet representatives to sabotage the United Nations. It is important, however, to distinguish clearly between the principle of collective security embodied in the Charter and the mechanisms of the United Nations to give that principle effect. We must frankly recognize that the Soviet Union has been able, in certain instances, to stall the machinery of collective security. Yet it has not been able to impair the principle of collective security. The free nations of the world have retained their allegiance to that idea. They have found the means to act despite the Soviet veto, both through the United Nations itself and through the application of this principle in regional and other security arrangements that are fully in harmony with the Charter and give expression to its purposes.

The free world refused to resign itself to collective suicide merely because of the technicality of a Soviet veto.

The principle of collective measures to forestall aggression has found expression in the Treaty of Rio de Janeiro, the North Atlantic Treaty, now extended to include Greece and Turkey, and the several treaties we have concluded to reinforce security in the Pacific area.

But the free nations have not this time fallen prey to the dangerous illusion that treaties alone will stop an aggressor. By a series of vigorous actions, as varied as the nature of the threat, the free nations have successfully thwarted aggression or the threat of aggression in many different parts of the world.

Our country has led or supported these collective measures. The aid we have given to people determined to act in defense of their freedom has often spelled the difference between success and failure.

We all know what we have done, and I shall not review in detail the steps we have taken. Each major step was a milepost in the developing unity, strength and resolute will of the free nations.

The first was the determined and successful effort made through the United Nations to safeguard the integrity and independence of Iran in 1945 and 1946.

Next was our aid and support to embattled Greece, which enabled her to defeat the forces threatening her national independence.

In Turkey, cooperative action resulted in building up a bulwark of military strength for an area vital to the defenses of the entire free world.

In 1949, we began furnishing military aid to our partners in the North Atlantic Community and to a number of other free countries.

The Soviet Union's threats against Germany and Japan, its neighbors to the West and to the East, have been successfully withstood. Free Germany is on its way to becoming a member of the peaceful community of nations, and a partner in the common defense. The Soviet effort to capture Berlin by blockade was thwarted by the courageous Allied airlift. An independent and democratic Japan has been brought back into the community of free nations.

In the Far East, the tactics of communist imperialism have reached heights of violence unmatched elsewhere—and the problem of concerted action by the free nations has been at once more acute and more difficult.

Here, in spite of outside aid and support, the free government of China succumbed to the communist assault. Our aid has enabled the free Chinese to rebuild and strengthen their forces on the island of Formosa. In other areas of the Far East—in Indo-China, Malaya, and the Philippines—our assistance has helped sustain a staunch resistance against communist insurrectionary attacks.

The supreme test, up to this point, of the will and determination of the free nations came in Korea, when communist forces invaded the Republic of Korea, a state that was in a special sense under the protection of the United Nations. The response was immediate and resolute. Under our military leadership, the free nations for the first time took up arms, collectively, to repel aggression.

Aggression was repelled, driven back, punished. Since that time, communist strategy has seen fit to prolong the conflict, in spite of honest efforts by the United Nations to reach an honorable truce. The months of deadlock have demonstrated that the communists cannot achieve by persistence, or by diplomatic trickery, what they failed to achieve by sneak attack. Korea has demonstrated that the free world has the will and the endurance to match the communist effort to overthrow international order through local aggression.

It has been a bitter struggle and it has cost us much in brave lives and human suffering, but it has made it plain that the free nations will fight side by side, that they will not succumb to aggression or intimidation, one by one. This, in the final analysis, is the only way to halt the communist drive to world power. At the heart of the free world's defense is the military strength of the United States.

From 1945 to 1949, the United States was sole possessor of the atomic bomb. That was a great deterrent and protection in itself.

But when the Soviets produced an atomic explosion—as they were bound to do in time—we had to broaden the whole basis of our strength. We had to endeavor to keep our lead in atomic weapons. We had to strengthen our armed forces generally and to enlarge our productive capacity—our mobilization base. Historically, it was the Soviet atomic explosion in the fall of 1949, nine months before the aggression in Korea, which stimulated the planning for our program of defense mobilization.

What we needed was not just a central force that could strike back against aggression. We also needed strength along the outer edges of the free world, defenses for our allies as well as for ourselves, strength to hold the line against attack as well as to retaliate.

We have made great progress on this task of building strong defenses. In the last two and one-half years, we have more than doubled our own defenses, and we have helped to increase the protection of nearly all the other free nations.

All the measures of collective security, resistance to aggression, and the building of defenses constitute the first requirement for the survival and progress of the free world. But, as I have pointed out, they are interwoven with the necessity of taking steps to create and maintain economic and social progress in the free nations. There can be no military strength except where there is economic capacity to back it. There can be no freedom where there is economic chaos or social collapse. For these reasons, our national policy has included a wide range of economic measures.

In Europe, the grand design of the Marshall Plan permitted the people of Britain and France and Italy and a half dozen other countries, with help from the United States, to lift themselves from stagnation and find again the path of rising production, rising incomes, rising standards of living. The situation was changed almost overnight by the Marshall Plan; the people of Europe have a renewed hope and vitality, and they are able to carry a share of the military defense of the free world that would have been impossible a few years ago.

Now the countries of Europe are moving rapidly towards political and economic unity, changing the map of Europe in more hopeful ways than it has been changed for 500 years. Customs unions, European economic institutions like the Schuman Plan, the movement toward European political integration, the European Defense Community—all are signs of practical and effective growth toward greater common strength and unity. The countries of Western Europe, including the free Republic of Germany are working together, and the whole free world is the gainer.

It sometimes happens, in the course of history, that steps taken to meet an immediate necessity serve an ultimate purpose greater than may be apparent at the time. This, I believe, is the meaning of what has been going on in Europe under the threat of aggression. The free nations there, with our help, have been drawing together in defense of their free institutions. In so doing, they have laid the foundations of a unity that will endure as a major creative force beyond the exigencies of this period of history. We may, at this close range, be but dimly aware of the creative surge this movement represents, but I believe it to be of historic importance. I believe its benefits will survive long after communist tyranny is nothing but an unhappy memory.

In Asia and Africa, the economic and social problems are different but no less urgent. There hundreds of millions of people are in ferment, exploding into the twentieth century, thrusting toward equality and independence and improvement in the hard conditions of their lives.

Politically, economically, socially, things cannot and will not stay in their pre-war mold in Africa and Asia. Change must come—is coming—fast. Just in the years I have been President, 12 free nations, with more than 600 million people, have become independent: Burma, Indonesia, the Philippines, Korea, Israel, Libya, India, Pakistan and Ceylon, and the three Associated States of Indo-China, now members of the French Union. These names alone are testimony to the sweep of the great force which is changing the face of half the world.

Working out new relationships among the peoples of the free world would not be easy in the best of times. Even if there were no Communist drive for expansion, there would be hard and complex problems of transition from old social forms, old political arrangements, old economic institutions to the new ones our century demands—problems of guiding change into constructive channels, of helping new nations grow strong and stable. But now, with the Soviet rulers striving to exploit this ferment for their own purposes, the task has become harder and more urgent—terribly urgent.

In this situation, we see the meaning and the importance of the Point IV program, through which we can share our store of know-how and of capital to help these people develop their economies and reshape their societies. As we help Iranians to raise more grain, Indians to reduce the incidence of malaria, Liberians to educate their children better, we are at once helping to answer the desires of the people for advancement, and demonstrating the superiority of freedom over communism. There will be no quick solution for any of the difficulties of the new nations of Asia and Africa—but there may be no solution at all if we do not press forward with full energy to help these countries grow and flourish in freedom and in cooperation with the rest of the free world.

Our measures of economic policy have already had a tremendous effect on the course of events. Eight years ago, the Kremlin thought post-war collapse in Western Europe and Japan—with economic dislocation in America—might give them the signal to advance. We demonstrated they were wrong. Now they wait with hope that the economic recovery of the free world has set the stage for violent and disastrous rivalry among the economically developed nations, struggling for each other's markets and a greater share of trade. Here is another test that we shall have to meet and master in the years immediately ahead. And it will take great ingenuity and effort—and much time—before we prove the Kremlin wrong again. But we can do it. It is true that economic recovery presents its problems, as does economic decline, but they are problems of another order. They are the problems of distributing abundance fairly, and they can be solved by the process of international cooperation that has already brought us so far.

These are the measures we must continue. This is the path we must follow. We must go on, working with our free associates, building an international structure for military defense, and for economic, social, and political progress. We must be prepared for war, because war may be thrust upon us. But the stakes in our search for peace are immensely higher than they have ever been before.

For now we have entered the atomic age, and war has undergone a technological change which makes it a very different thing from what it used to be. War today between the Soviet empire and the free nations might dig the grave not only of our Stalinist opponents, but of our own society, our world as well as theirs.

This transformation has been brought to pass in the seven years from Alamogordo to Eniwetok. It is only seven years, but the new force of atomic energy has turned the world into a very different kind of place.

Science and technology have worked so fast that war's new meaning may not yet be grasped by all the peoples who would be its victims; nor, perhaps, by the rulers in the Kremlin. But I have been President of the United States, these seven years, responsible for the decisions which have brought our science and our engineering to their present place. I know what this development means now. I know something of what it will come to mean in the future.

We in this Government realized, even before the first successful atomic explosion, that this new force spelled terrible danger for all mankind unless it were brought under international control. We promptly advanced proposals in the United Nations to take this new source of energy out of the arena of national rivalries, to make it impossible to use it as a weapon of war. These proposals, so pregnant with benefit for all humanity, were rebuffed by the rulers of the Soviet Union.

The language of science is universal, the movement of science is always forward into the unknown. We could not assume that the Soviet Union would not develop the same weapon, regardless of all our precautions, nor that there were not other and even more terrible means of destruction lying in the unexplored field of atomic energy.

We had no alternative, then, but to press on, to probe the secrets of atomic power to the uttermost of our capacity, to maintain, if we could, our initial superiority in the atomic field. At the same time, we sought persistently for some avenue, some formula, for reaching an agreement with the Soviet rulers that would place this new form of power under effective restraints—that would guarantee no nation would use it in war. I do not have to recount here the proposals we made, the steps taken in the United Nations, striving at least to open a way to ultimate agreement. I hope and believe that we will continue to make these efforts so long as there is the slightest possibility of progress. All civilized nations are agreed on the urgency of the problem, and have shown their willingness to agree on effective measures of control—all save the Soviet Union and its satellites. But they have rejected every reasonable proposal.

Meanwhile, the progress of scientific experiment has outrun our expectations. Atomic science is in the full tide of development; the unfolding of the innermost secrets of matter is uninterrupted and irresistible. Since Alamogordo we have developed atomic weapons with many times the explosive force of the early models, and we have produced them in substantial quantities. And recently, in the thermonuclear tests at Eniwetok, we have entered another stage in the world-shaking development of atomic energy. From now on, man moves into a new era of destructive power, capable of creating explosions of a new order of magnitude, dwarfing the mushroom clouds of Hiroshima and Nagasaki.

We have no reason to think that the stage we have now reached in the release of atomic energy will be the last. Indeed, the speed of our scientific and technical progress over the last seven years shows no signs of abating. We are being hurried forward, in our mastery of the atom, from one discovery to another, toward yet unforeseeable peaks of destructive power.

Inevitably, until we can reach international agreement, this is the path we must follow. And we must realize that no advance we make is unattainable by others, that no advantage in this race can be more than temporary.

The war of the future would be one in which man could extinguish millions of lives at one blow, demolish the great cities of the world, wipe out the cultural achievements of the past, and destroy the very structure of a civilization that has been slowly and painfully built up through hundreds of generations.

Such a war is not a possible policy for rational men. We know this, but we dare not assume that others would not yield to the temptation science is now placing in their hands.

With that in mind, there is something I would say, to Stalin: You claim belief in Lenin's prophecy that one stage in the development of communist society would be war between your world and ours. But Lenin was a pre-atomic man, who viewed society and history with pre-atomic eyes. Something profound has happened since he wrote. War has changed its shape and its dimension. It cannot now be a "stage" in the development of anything save ruin for your regime and your homeland.

I do not know how much time may elapse before the communist rulers bring themselves to recognize this truth. But when they do, they will find us eager to reach understandings that will protect the world from the danger it faces today.

It is no wonder that some people wish that we had never succeeded in splitting the atom. But atomic power, like any other force of nature, is not evil in itself. Properly used, it is an instrumentality for human betterment. As a source of power, as a tool of scientific inquiry, it has untold possibilities. We are already making good progress in the constructive use of atomic power. We could do much more if we were free to concentrate on its peaceful uses exclusively.

Atomic power will be with us all the days of our lives. We cannot legislate it out of existence. We cannot ignore the dangers or the benefits it offers.

I believe that man can harness the forces of the atom to work for the improvement of the lot of human beings everywhere. That is our goal. As a nation, as a people, we must understand this problem, we must handle this new force wisely through our democratic processes. Above all, we must strive, in all earnestness and good faith, to bring it under effective international control. To do this will require much wisdom and patience and firmness. The awe-inspiring responsibility in this field now falls on a new Administration and a new Congress. I will give them my support, as I am sure all our citizens will, in whatever constructive steps they may take to make this newest of man's discoveries a source of good and not of ultimate destruction.

We cannot tell when or whether the attitude of the Soviet rulers may change. We do not know how long it may be before they show a willingness to negotiate effective control of atomic energy and honorable settlements of other world problems. We cannot measure how deep-rooted are the Kremlin's illusions about us. We can be sure, however, that the rulers of the communist world will not change their basic objectives lightly or soon.

The communist rulers have a sense of time about these things wholly unlike our own. We tend to divide our future into short spans, like the two-year life of this Congress, or the four years of the next Presidential term. They seem to think and plan in terms of generations. And there is, therefore, no easy, short-run way to make them see that their plans cannot prevail.

This means there is ahead of us a long hard test of strength and stamina, between the free world and the communist domain—our politics and our economy, our science and technology against the best they can do—our liberty against their slavery—our voluntary concert of free nations against their forced amalgam of "people's republics"—our strategy against their strategy—our nerve against their nerve.

Above all, this is a test of the will and the steadiness of the people of the United States.

There has been no challenge like this in the history of our Republic. We are called upon to rise to the occasion, as no people before us.

What is required of us is not easy. The way we must learn to live, the world we have to live in, cannot be so pleasant, safe or simple as most of us have known before, or confidently hoped to know.

Already we have had to sacrifice a number of accustomed ways of working and of living, much nervous energy, material resources, even human life. Yet if one thing is certain in our future, it is that more sacrifice still lies ahead.

Were we to grow discouraged now, were we to weaken and slack off, the whole structure we have built, these past eight years, would come apart and fall away. Never then, no matter by what stringent means, could our free world regain the ground, the time, the sheer momentum, lost by such a move. There can and should be changes and improvements in our programs, to meet new situations, serve new needs. But to desert the spirit of our basic policies, to step back from them now, would surely start the free world's slide toward the darkness that the communists have prophesied—toward the moment for which they watch and wait.

If we value our freedom and our way of life and want to see them safe, we must meet the challenge and accept its implications, stick to our guns and carry out our policies.

I have set out the basic conditions, as I see them, under which we have been working in the world, and the nature of our basic policies. What, then, of the future? The answer, I believe, is this: As we continue to confound Soviet expectations, as our world grows stronger, more united, more attractive to men on both sides of the iron curtain, then inevitably there will come a time of change within the communist world. We do not know how that change will come about, whether by deliberate decision in the Kremlin, by coup d'etat, by revolution, by defection of satellites, or perhaps by some unforeseen combination of factors such as these.

But if the communist rulers understand they cannot win by war, and if we frustrate their attempts to win by subversion, it is not too much to expect their world to change its character, moderate its aims, become more realistic and less implacable, and recede from the cold war they began.

Do not be deceived by the strong face, the look of monolithic power that the communist dictators wear before the outside world. Remember their power has no basis in consent. Remember they are so afraid of the free world's ideas and ways of life, they do not dare to let their people know about them. Think of the massive effort they put forth to try to stop our Campaign of Truth from reaching their people with its message of freedom.

The masters of the Kremlin live in fear their power and position would collapse were their own people to acquire knowledge, information, comprehension about our free society. Their world has many elements of strength, but this one fatal flaw: the weakness represented by their iron curtain and their police state. Surely, a social order at once so insecure and so fearful, must ultimately lose its competition with our free society.

Provided just one thing—and this I urge you to consider carefully—provided that the free world retains the confidence and the determination to outmatch the best our adversary can accomplish and to demonstrate for uncertain millions on both sides of the iron curtain the superiority of the free way of life.

That is the test upon all the free nations; upon none more than our own Republic.

Our resources are equal to the task. We have the industry, the skills, the basic economic strength. Above all, we have the vigor of free men in a free society. We have our liberties. And while we keep them, while we retain our democratic faith, the ultimate advantage in this hard competition lies with us, not with the communists.

But there are some things that could shift the advantage to their side. One of the things that could defeat us is fear—fear of the task we face, fear of adjusting to it, fear that breeds more fear, sapping our faith, corroding our liberties, turning citizen against citizen, ally against ally. Fear could snatch away the very values we are striving to defend.

Already the danger signals have gone up. Already the corrosive process has begun. And every diminution of our tolerance, each new act of enforced conformity, each idle accusation, each demonstration of hysteria—each new restrictive law—is one more sign that we can lose the battle against fear.

The communists cannot deprive us of our liberties—fear can. The communists cannot stamp out our faith in human dignity—fear can. Fear is an enemy within ourselves, and if we do not root it out, it may destroy the very way of life we are so anxious to protect.

To beat back fear, we must hold fast to our heritage as free men. We must renew our confidence in one another, our tolerance, our sense of being neighbors, fellow citizens. We must take our stand on the Bill of Rights. The inquisition, the star chamber, have no place in a free society.

Our ultimate strength lies, not alone in arms, but in the sense of moral values and moral truths that give meaning and vitality to the purposes of free people. These values are our faith, our inspiration, the source of our strength and our indomitable determination.

We face hard tasks, great dangers. But we are Americans and we have faced hardships and uncertainty before, we have adjusted before to changing circumstances. Our whole history has been a steady training for the work it is now ours to do.

No one can lose heart for the task, none can lose faith in our free ways, who stops to remember where we began, what we have sought, and what accomplished, all together as Americans.

I have lived a long time and seen much happen in our country. And I know out of my own experience, that we can do what must be done.

When I think back to the country I grew up in—and then look at what our country has become—I am quite certain that having done so much, we can do more.

After all, it has been scarcely fifteen years since most Americans rejected out-of-hand the wise counsel that aggressors must be "quarantined." The very concept of collective security, the foundation-stone of all our actions now, was then strange doctrine, shunned and set aside. Talk about adapting; talk about adjusting; talk about responding as a people to the challenge of changed times and circumstances—there has never been a more spectacular example than this great change in America's outlook on the world.

Let all of us pause now, think back, consider carefully the meaning of our national experience. Let us draw comfort from it and faith, and confidence in our future as Americans.

The Nation's business is never finished. The basic questions we have been dealing with, these eight years past, present themselves anew. That is the way of our society. Circumstances change and current questions take on different forms, new complications, year by year. But underneath, the great issues remain the same—prosperity, welfare, human rights, effective democracy, and above all, peace.

Now we turn to the inaugural of our new President. And in the great work he is called upon to do he will have need for the support of a united people, a confident people, with firm faith in one another and in our common cause. I pledge him my support as a citizen of our Republic, and I ask you to give him yours.

To him, to you, to all my fellow citizens, I say, Godspeed.

May God bless our country and our cause.

HARRY S. TRUMAN

Note

1. David McCullough, *Truman* (New York: Simon & Schuster, 1992), 918.

28

Dwight D. Eisenhower (1953–1961)

Dwight Eisenhower was the first Republican president since Hoover. He was also the first president in U.S. history to follow his immediate predecessor, Truman, in delivering a farewell address. (Only one other time in American history have back-to-back presidents given farewell addresses—Carter in 1981, followed by Reagan in 1989.) Surely the burgeoning television industry had much to do with the increasing use of the formal farewell address to mark the end of a presidency. Truman had given the nation's first televised farewell address; Eisenhower, its second. However, unlike Truman, who was unpopular at the end of his presidency, Ike was one of the most beloved heroes of his era. The former supreme commander of western Allied forces during World War II knew how to conduct not just a war, but a public relations campaign.

Ike could be a rousing speechifier when he spoke without a text. He could be dreadful with one. As one historian put it, "Eisenhower's folksy charisma was inhibited by a formal text."[1] So it is perhaps ironic that the most famous speech by which Ike is remembered is his very well prepared and formal farewell address. This is the speech that warned against the "military–industrial complex."

Ike's Farewell Address was composed in a gathering storm. U.S. relations with the Soviet Union were deteriorating. A U-2 spy plane had been shot down by the Soviets on the eve of a summit meeting in Paris. The Kremlin was insisting on American withdrawal from the divided city of Berlin. And the Eisenhower administration had installed an anti-Communist government in South Vietnam. The possibility of U.S. involvement in a "hot" war seemed likely.

The President's health also cast a pall over the farewell address. At that point, Ike was the oldest serving president in U.S. history. He had suffered a major heart attack in 1955 and a stroke two years later.

Eisenhower's message, though more than four decades old, fairly sums up America's challenges in the early 1960s yet stands up well to the test of time. Many of its themes sound remarkably contemporary to later generations. The thrust of the speech was to warn Americans against historically unprecedented developments. In a great rhetorical circle, he warned Americans against: (1) war and the growth of the military–industrial complex; (2) the overweening influence of the federal government on university research, (3) the danger of public policy becoming "the captive of a scientific–technological elite," and, in an especially modern sounding passage, (4) environmental plunder and degradation. Closing the circle, he offered a poignant admonition against the age-old threat of war.

Among the most striking elements in the address are the prayers. Praying in public was not unusual for Ike. This was the president who had his listeners bow their heads to pray during a part of his 1953 inaugural address. Eisenhower was also the president who ordered the phrase, "under God," incorporated into the Pledge of Allegiance.

Ike's Farewell Address, it is important to note, was only the second formal farewell *speech* in American history (Truman's was the first). It is also one of the shortest farewells in the canon—1,917 words—about half the length of Truman's. The pronoun "I" is used rather sparingly, only twenty-two times in the sixteen-minute speech.

Farewell Address
(broadcast by radio and television to the nation)
January 17, 1961

Good evening, my fellow Americans:

First, I should like to express my gratitude to the radio and television networks for the opportunity they have given me over the years to bring reports and messages to our nation. My special thanks go to them for the opportunity of addressing you this evening.

Three days from now, after a half century in the service of our country, I shall lay down the responsibilities of office as, in traditional and solemn ceremony, the authority of the Presidency is vested in my successor.

This evening I come to you with a message of leave-taking and farewell, and to share a few final thoughts with you, my countrymen.

Like every other citizen, I wish the new President, and all who will labor with him, Godspeed. I pray that the coming years will be blessed with peace and prosperity for all.

Our people expect their President and the Congress to find essential agreement on issues of great moment, the wise resolution of which will better shape the future of the nation.

My own relations with the Congress, which began on a remote and tenuous basis when, long ago, a member of the Senate appointed me to West Point, have since ranged to the intimate during the war and immediate post-war period, and finally to the mutually interdependent during these past eight years.

In this final relationship, the Congress and the Administration have, on most vital issues, cooperated well, to serve the national good rather than mere partisanship, and so have assured that the business of the Nation should go forward. So my official relationship with the Congress ends in a feeling, on my part, of gratitude that we have been able to do so much together.

We now stand ten years past the midpoint of a century that has witnessed four major wars among great nations. Three of these involved our own country. Despite these holocausts America is today the strongest, the most influential and most productive nation in the world. Understandably proud of this pre-eminence, we yet realize that America's leadership and prestige depend, not merely upon our unmatched material progress, riches and military strength, but on how we use our power in the interests of world peace and human betterment.

Throughout America's adventure in free government, our basic purposes have been to keep the peace; to foster progress in human achievement; and to enhance liberty, dignity, and integrity among peoples and among nations. To strive for less would be unworthy of a free and religious people. Any failure traceable to arrogance or our lack of comprehension or readiness to sacrifice would inflict upon us a grievous hurt both at home and abroad.

Progress toward these noble goals is persistently threatened by the conflict now engulfing the world. It commands our whole attention, absorbs our very beings. We face a hostile ideology—global in scope, atheistic in character, ruthless in purpose, and insidious in method. Unhappily the danger it poses promises to be of indefinite duration. To meet it successfully, there is called for, not so much the emotional and transitory sacrifices of crisis, but rather those which enable us to carry forward steadily, surely, and without complaint the burdens of a prolonged and complex struggle—with liberty the stake. Only thus shall we remain, despite every provocation, on our charted course toward permanent peace and human betterment.

Crises there will continue to be. In meeting them, whether foreign or domestic, great or small, there is a recurring temptation to feel that some spectacular and costly action could become the miraculous solution to all current difficulties. A huge increase in the newer elements of our defense; development of unrealistic programs to cure every ill in agriculture; a dramatic expansion in basic and applied research—these and many other possibilities, each possibly promising in itself, may be suggested as the only way to the road we wish to travel.

But each proposal must be weighed in light of a broader consideration: the need to maintain balance in and among national programs—balance between the private and the public economy, balance between cost and hoped for advantage—balance between the clearly necessary and the comfortably desirable; balance between our essential requirements as a nation and the duties imposed by the nation upon the individual; balance between actions of the moment and the national welfare of the future. Good judgment seeks balance and progress; lack of it eventually finds imbalance and frustration.

The record of many decades stands as proof that our people and their government have, in the main, understood these truths and have responded to them well in the face of threat and stress.

But threats, new in kind or degree, constantly arise. Of these, I mention two only.

A vital element in keeping the peace is our military establishment. Our arms must be mighty, ready for instant action, so that no potential aggressor may be tempted to risk his own destruction.

Our military organization today bears little relation to that known by any of my predecessors in peacetime, or indeed by the fighting men of World War II or Korea.

Until the latest of our world conflicts, the United States had no armaments industry. American makers of plowshares could, with time and as required, make swords as well. But now we can no longer risk emergency improvisation of national defense; we have been compelled to create a permanent armaments industry of vast proportions. Added to this, three and a half million men and women are directly engaged in the defense establishment. We annually spend on military security more than the net income of all United States corporations.

This conjunction of an immense military establishment and a large arms industry is new in the American experience. The total influence—economic, political, even spiritual—is felt in every city, every State house, every office of the Federal government. We recognize the imperative need for this development. Yet we must not fail to comprehend its grave implications. Our toil, resources and livelihood are all involved; so is the very structure of our society.

In the councils of government, we must guard against the acquisition of unwarranted influence, whether sought or unsought, by the military-industrial complex. The potential for the disastrous rise of misplaced power exists and will persist.

We must never let the weight of this combination endanger our liberties or democratic processes. We should take nothing for granted. Only an alert and knowledgeable citizenry can compel the proper meshing of the huge industrial and military machinery of defense with our peaceful methods and goals, so that security and liberty may prosper together.

Akin to, and largely responsible for the sweeping changes in our industrial-military posture, has been the technological revolution during recent decades.

In this revolution, research has become central; it also becomes more formalized, complex, and costly. A steadily increasing share is conducted for, by, or at the direction of, the Federal government.

Today, the solitary inventor, tinkering in his shop, has been overshadowed by task forces of scientists in laboratories and testing fields. In the same fashion, the free university, historically the fountainhead of free ideas and scientific discovery, has experienced a revolution in the conduct of research. Partly because of the huge costs involved, a government contract becomes virtually a substitute for intellectual curiosity. For every old blackboard there are now hundreds of new electronic computers.

The prospect of domination of the nation's scholars by Federal employment, project allocations, and the power of money is ever present—and is gravely to be regarded.

Yet, in holding scientific research and discovery in respect, as we should, we must also be alert to the equal and opposite danger that public policy could itself become the captive of a scientific-technological elite.

It is the task of statesmanship to mold, to balance, and to integrate these and other forces, new and old, within the principles of our democratic system—ever aiming toward the supreme goals of our free society.

Another factor in maintaining balance involves the element of time. As we peer into society's future, we—you and I, and our government—must avoid the impulse to live only for today, plundering for our own ease and convenience, the precious resources of tomorrow. We cannot mortgage the material assets of our grandchildren without risking the loss also of their political and spiritual heritage. We want democracy to survive for all generations to come, not to become the insolvent phantom of tomorrow.

Down the long lane of the history yet to be written America knows that this world of ours, ever growing smaller, must avoid becoming a community of dreadful fear and hate, and be, instead, a proud confederation of mutual trust and respect.

Such a confederation must be one of equals. The weakest must come to the conference table with the same confidence as do we, protected as we are by our moral, economic, and military strength. That table, though scarred by many past frustrations, cannot be abandoned for the certain agony of the battlefield.

Disarmament, with mutual honor and confidence, is a continuing imperative. Together we must learn how to compose differences, not with arms, but with intellect and decent purpose. Because this need is so sharp and apparent I confess that I lay down my official responsibilities in this field with a definite sense of disappointment. As one who has witnessed the horror and the lingering sadness of war—as one who knows that another war could utterly destroy this civilization which has been so slowly and painfully built over thousands of years—I wish I could say tonight that a lasting peace is in sight.

Happily, I can say that war has been avoided. Steady progress toward our ultimate goal has been made. But, so much remains to be done. As a private citizen, I shall never cease to do what little I can to help the world advance along that road.

So—in this my last good-night to you as your President—I thank you for the many opportunities you have given me for public service in war and peace. I trust that in that service you find some things worthy; as for the rest of it, I know you will find ways to improve performance in the future.

You and I—my fellow citizens—need to be strong in our faith that all nations, under God, will reach the goal of peace with justice. May we be ever unswerving in devotion to principle, confident but humble with power, diligent in pursuit of the Nation's great goals.

To all the peoples of the world, I once more give expression to America's prayerful and continuing aspiration:

We pray that peoples of all faiths, all races, all nations, may have their great human needs satisfied; that those now denied opportunity shall come to enjoy it to the full; that all who yearn for freedom may experience its spiritual blessings; that those who have freedom will understand, also, its heavy responsibilities; that all who are insensitive to the needs of others will learn charity; that the scourges of poverty, disease and ignorance will be made to disappear from the earth; and that, in the goodness of time, all peoples will come to live together in a peace guaranteed by the binding force of mutual respect and love.

Now, on Friday noon, I am to become a private citizen. I am proud to do so. I look forward to it. Thank you, and good night.

Five days prior to delivering his farewell address (a speech), Eisenhower submitted his ninth State of the Union address (in writing) to the Congress. It had never happened before (nor since) for a two-term president to submit that many annual messages to Capitol Hill. The most recent two-term presidents, Ronald Reagan and Bill Clinton, each gave only seven state of the union addresses. Only one president, Franklin Delano Roosevelt, submitted more annual messages than did Ike. Eisenhower noted that, since this was his last opportunity to report on the state of the union, the "function" of this report was different. He wished to extend thanks to all who had assisted him, review the record of his administration, and offer some guidelines for future action. Excerpts of Eisenhower's message follow.

Ninth State of the Union Address
(written to the Congress)
January 12–13, 1961

To the Congress of the United States:

Once again it is my Constitutional duty to assess the state of the Union.

On each such previous occasion during these past eight years I have outlined a forward course designed to achieve our mutual objective—a better America in a world of peace. This time my function is different.

The American people, in free election, have selected new leadership which soon will be entrusted with the management of our government. A new President shortly will lay before you his proposals to shape the future of our great land. To him, every citizen, whatever his political beliefs, prayerfully extends best wishes for good health and for wisdom and success in coping with the problems that confront our Nation.

For my part, I should like, first, to express to you of the Congress, my appreciation of your devotion to the common good and your friendship over these difficult years. I will carry with me pleasant memories of this association in endeavors profoundly significant to all our people.

We have been through a lengthy period in which the control over the executive and legislative branches of government has been divided between our two great political parties. Differences, of course, we have had, particularly in domestic affairs. But in a united determination to keep this Nation strong and free and to utilize our vast resources for the advancement of all mankind, we have carried America to unprecedented heights.

For this cooperative achievement I thank the American people and those in the Congress of both parties who have supported programs in the interest of our country.

I should also like to give special thanks for the devoted service of my associates in the Executive Branch and the hundreds of thousands of career employees who have implemented our diverse government programs.

My second purpose is to review briefly the record of these past eight years in the hope that, out of the sum of these experiences, lessons will emerge that are useful to our Nation. Supporting this review are detailed reports from the several agencies and departments, all of which are now or will shortly be available to the Congress. Throughout the world the years since 1953 have been a period of profound change. The human problems in the world grow more acute hour by hour; yet new gains in science and technology continually extend the promise of a better life. People yearn to be free, to govern themselves; yet a third of the people of the world have no freedom, do not govern themselves. The world recognizes the catastrophic nature of nuclear war; yet it sees the wondrous potential of nuclear peace.

During the period, the United States has forged ahead under a constructive foreign policy. The continuing goal is peace, liberty, and well-being—for others as well as ourselves. The aspirations of all peoples are one—peace with justice in freedom. Peace can only be attained collectively as peoples everywhere unite in their determination that liberty and well-being come to all mankind.

Yet while we have worked to advance national aspirations for freedom, a divisive force has been at work to divert that aspiration into dangerous channels. The Communist movement throughout the world exploits the natural striving of all to be free and attempts to subjugate men rather than free them. These activities have caused and are continuing to cause grave troubles in the world.

Here at home these have been times for careful adjustment of our economy from the artificial impetus of a hot war to constructive growth in a precarious peace. While building a new economic vitality without inflation, we have also increased public expenditures to keep abreast of the needs of a growing population and its attendant new problems, as well as our added international responsibilities. We have worked toward these ends in a context of shared responsibility—conscious of the need for maximum scope to private effort and for State and local, as well as Federal, governmental action.

Success in designing and executing national purposes, domestically and abroad, can only come from a steadfast resolution that integrity in the operation of government and in our relations with each other be fully maintained. Only in this way could our spiritual goals be fully advanced.

*   *   *

In concluding my final message to the Congress, it is fitting to look back to my first—to the aims and ideals I set forth on February 2, 1953: To use America's influence in world affairs to advance the cause of peace and justice, to conduct the affairs of the Executive Branch with integrity and efficiency, to encourage creative initiative in our economy, and to work toward the attainment of the well-being and equality of opportunity of all citizens. Equally, we have honored our commitment to pursue and attain specific objectives. Among them, as stated eight years ago: strengthening of the mutual security program; development of world trade and commerce; ending of hostilities in Korea; creation of a powerful deterrent force; practicing fiscal responsibility; checking the menace of inflation; reducing the tax burden; providing an effective internal security program; developing and conserving our natural resources; reducing governmental interference in the affairs of the farmer; strengthening and improving services by the Department of Labor; and the vigilant guarding of civil and social rights.

I do not close this message implying that all is well—that all problems are solved. For progress implies both new and continuing problems and, unlike Presidential administrations, problems rarely have terminal dates.

Abroad, there is the continuing Communist threat to the freedom of Berlin, an explosive situation in Laos, the problems caused by Communist penetration of Cuba, as well as the many problems connected with the development of the new nations in Africa. These areas, in particular, call for delicate handling and constant review.

At home, several conspicuous problems remain: promoting higher levels of employment, with special emphasis on areas in which heavy unemployment has persisted; continuing to provide for steady economic growth and preserving a sound currency; bringing our balance of payments into more reasonable equilibrium and continuing a high level of confidence in our national and international systems; eliminating heavily excessive surpluses of a few farm commodities; and overcoming deficiencies in our health and educational programs.

Our goal always has been to add to the spiritual, moral, and material strength of our nation. I believe we have done this. But it is a process that must never end. Let us pray that leaders of both the near and distant future will be able to keep the nation strong and at peace, that they will advance the well-being of all our people, that they will lead us on to still higher moral standards, and that, in achieving these goals, they will maintain a reasonable balance between private and governmental responsibility.

DWIGHT D. EISENHOWER

Notes

1. Richard Norton Smith, *Thomas E. Dewey and His Times* (New York: Simon & Schuster, 1982), 586.

2. This written state of the union address was transmitted to the House of Representatives on January 12 and to the Senate on the following day, when it was once again in session.

2 9

Lyndon B. Johnson (1963–1969)

Lyndon Johnson became America's thirty-sixth president on November 22, 1963. He was the only president sworn in on an airplane. Earlier in the day, at 12:30 P.M., John F. Kennedy had been killed by an assassin's bullet as his motorcade snaked its way through downtown Dallas. Johnson took the oath of office en route from his native Texas to Washington, Jacqueline Kennedy at his side.

Despite the tragedy surrounding the start of his presidency, Johnson went on to become an extremely effective chief executive. Much of the reason for his success is that he was able to draw on extensive legislative experience. He had served in the U.S. House since the New Deal era and, at forty-four years of age, had been the youngest minority leader in Senate history. A decade later, in the Oval Office, he used his leadership in Congress to push through what is commonly referred to as the Kennedy tax cut (because JFK had originally proposed it). He also shepherded through one of the most ambitious legislative programs in U.S. history—the Great Society—which he said was "a place where the meaning of man's life matches the marvels of man's labor." Passage of landmark civil rights bills top his list of achievements. All the while he tried to wage a war in Vietnam that would hold back insurgent communists. At first his dual strategy of waging the War on Poverty alongside the war in Vietnam seemed to work. In the election of 1964 (less than one year after the assassination of JFK), LBJ won the presidency with 61 percent of the vote and returned to office with the widest popular margin in American history—more than 15 million votes.

But two intractable difficulties hobbled Johnson's presidency. First, although Great Society programs designed to ameliorate poverty were starting to be implemented, there was widespread rioting in America's inner cities. Second, despite his firm, measured approach to Vietnam, opposition mounted as details of the war bore their way, via television, into America's living rooms. After the enemy's Tet offensive in 1968, many Americans became increasingly frustrated with a war that seemed just to draw the nation deeper and deeper into an abyss. That is the background to LBJ's Renunciation Speech, whose end shocked the nation. He renounced politics, he said, so that he could devote all his remaining energy to helping America achieve a lasting peace.

Renunciation Speech
(broadcast live from the White House)
March 31, 1968

Good evening, my fellow Americans:

Tonight I want to speak to you of peace in Vietnam and Southeast Asia.

No other question so preoccupies our people. No other dream so absorbs the 250 million human beings who live in that part of the world. No other goal motivates American policy in Southeast Asia.

For years, representatives of our Government and others have traveled the world—seeking to find a basis for peace talks.

Since last September, they have carried the offer that I made public at San Antonio.

That offer was this: That the United States would stop its bombardment of North Vietnam when that would lead promptly to productive discussions—and that we would assume that North Vietnam would not take military advantage of our restraint.

Hanoi denounced this offer, both privately and publicly. Even while the search for peace was going on, North Vietnam rushed their preparations for a savage assault on the people, the government, and the allies of South Vietnam.

Their attack—during the Tet holidays—failed to achieve its principal objectives. It did not collapse the elected government of South Vietnam or shatter its army—as the Communists had hoped.

It did not produce a "general uprising" among the people of the cities as they had predicted.

The Communists were unable to maintain control of any of the more than 30 cities that they attacked. And they took very heavy casualties.

But they did compel the South Vietnamese and their allies to move certain forces from the countryside into the cities.

They caused widespread disruption and suffering. Their attacks, and the battles that followed, made refugees of half a million human beings.

The Communists may renew their attack any day.

They are, it appears, trying to make 1968 the year of decision in South Vietnam—the year that brings, if not final victory or defeat, at least a turning point in the struggle.

This much is clear: If they do mount another round of heavy attacks, they will not succeed in destroying the fighting power of South Vietnam and its allies.

But tragically, this is also clear: Many men—on both sides of the struggle—will be lost. A nation that has already suffered 20 years of warfare will suffer once again. Armies on both sides will take new casualties. And the war will go on.

There is no need for this to be so.

There is no need to delay the talks that could bring an end to this long and this bloody war.

Tonight, I renew the offer I made last August—to stop the bombardment of North Vietnam. We ask that talks begin promptly, that they be serious talks on the substance of peace. We assume that during those talks Hanoi will not take advantage of our restraint.

We are prepared to move immediately toward peace through negotiations.

So, tonight, in the hope that this action will lead to early talks, I am taking the first step to deescalate the conflict. We are reducing—substantially reducing—the present level of hostilities.

And we are doing so unilaterally, and at once.

Tonight, I have ordered our aircraft and our naval vessels to make no attacks on North Vietnam, except in the area north of the demilitarized zone where the continuing enemy buildup directly threatens allied forward positions and where the movements of their troops and supplies are clearly related to that threat. The area in which we are stopping our attacks includes almost 90 percent of North Vietnam's population, and most of its territory. Thus there will be no attacks around the principal populated areas, or in the food-producing areas of North Vietnam.

Even this very limited bombing of the North could come to an early end—if our restraint is matched by restraint in Hanoi. But I cannot in good conscience stop all bombing so long as to do so would immediately and directly endanger the lives of our men and our allies. Whether a complete bombing halt becomes possible in the future will be determined by events.

Our purpose in this action is to bring about a reduction in the level of violence that now exists.

It is to save the lives of brave men—and to save the lives of innocent women and children. It is to permit the contending forces to move closer to a political settlement.

And tonight, I call upon the United Kingdom and I call upon the Soviet Union—as cochairmen of the Geneva Conferences, and as permanent members of the United Nations Security Council—to do all they can to move from the unilateral act of deescalation that I have just announced toward genuine peace in Southeast Asia. Now, as in the past, the United States is ready to send its representatives to any forum, at any time, to discuss the means of bringing this ugly war to an end.

I am designating one of our most distinguished Americans, Ambassador Averell Harriman, as my personal representative for such talks. In addition, I have asked Ambassador Llewellyn Thompson, who returned from Moscow for consultation, to be available to join Ambassador Harriman at Geneva or any other suitable place—just as soon as Hanoi agrees to a conference.

I call upon President Ho Chi Minh to respond positively, and favorably, to this new step toward peace.

But if peace does not come now through negotiations, it will come when Hanoi understands that our common resolve is unshakable, and our common strength is invincible.

Tonight, we and the other allied nations are contributing 600,000 fighting men to assist 700,000 South Vietnamese troops in defending their little country.

Our presence there has always rested on this basic belief: The main burden of preserving their freedom must be carried out by them—by the South Vietnamese themselves.

We and our allies can only help to provide a shield behind which the people of South Vietnam can survive and can grow and develop. On their efforts—on their determination and resourcefulness—the outcome will ultimately depend.

That small, beleaguered nation has suffered terrible punishment for more than 20 years.

I pay tribute once again tonight to the great courage and endurance of its people.

South Vietnam supports armed forces tonight of almost 700,000 men—and I call your attention to the fact that this is the equivalent of more than 10 million in our own population. Its people maintain their firm determination to be free of domination by the North.

There has been substantial progress, I think, in building a durable government during these last 3 years. The South Vietnam of 1965 could not have survived the enemy's Tet offensive of 1968. The elected government of South Vietnam survived that attack—and is rapidly repairing the devastation that it wrought.

The South Vietnamese know that further efforts are going to be required:

—to expand their own armed forces,
—to move back into the countryside as quickly as possible,
—to increase their taxes,
—to select the very best men that they have for civil and military responsibility,
—to achieve a new unity within their constitutional government, and

—to include in the national effort all those groups who wish to preserve South Vietnam's control over its own destiny.

Last week President Thieu ordered the mobilization of 135,000 additional South Vietnamese. He plans to reach—as soon as possible—a total military strength of more than 800,000 men.

To achieve this, the Government of South Vietnam started the drafting of 19-year-olds on March 1st. On May 1st, the Government will begin the drafting of 18-year-olds.

Last month, 10,000 men volunteered for military service—that was two and a half times the number of volunteers during the same month last year. Since the middle of January, more than 48,000 South Vietnamese have joined the armed forces—and nearly half of them volunteered to do so.

All men in the South Vietnamese armed forces have had their tours of duty extended for the duration of the war, and reserves are now being called up for immediate active duty.

President Thieu told his people last week:

"We must make greater efforts and accept more sacrifices because, as I have said many times, this is our country. The existence of our nation is at stake, and this is mainly a Vietnamese responsibility."

He warned his people that a major national effort is required to root out corruption and incompetence at all levels of government.

We applaud this evidence of determination on the part of South Vietnam. Our first priority will be to support their effort.

We shall accelerate the reequipment of South Vietnam's armed forces—in order to meet the enemy's increased firepower. This will enable them progressively to undertake a larger share of combat operations against the Communist invaders.

On many occasions I have told the American people that we would send to Vietnam those forces that are required to accomplish our mission there. So, with that as our guide, we have previously authorized a force level of approximately 525,000.

Some weeks ago—to help meet the enemy's new offensive—we sent to Vietnam about 11,000 additional Marine and airborne troops. They were deployed by air in 48 hours, on an emergency basis. But the artillery, tank, aircraft, medical, and other units that were needed to work with and to support these infantry troops in combat could not then accompany them by air on that short notice.

In order that these forces may reach maximum combat effectiveness, the Joint Chiefs of Staff have recommended to me that we should prepare to send—during the next 5 months—support troops totaling approximately 13,500 men.

A portion of these men will be made available from our active forces. The balance will come from reserve component units which will be called up for service.

The actions that we have taken since the beginning of the year

—to reequip the South Vietnamese forces,
—to meet our responsibilities in Korea, as well as our responsibilities in Vietnam,
—to meet price increases and the cost of activating and deploying reserve forces,
—to replace helicopters and provide the other military supplies we need,

all of these actions are going to require additional expenditures.

The tentative estimate of those additional expenditures is $2.5 billion in this fiscal year, and $2.6 billion in the next fiscal year.

These projected increases in expenditures for our national security will bring into sharper focus the Nation's need for immediate action: action to protect the prosperity of the American people and to protect the strength and the stability of our American dollar.

On many occasions I have pointed out that, without a tax bill or decreased expenditures, next year's deficit would again be around $20 billion. I have emphasized the need to set strict priorities in our spending. I have stressed that failure to act and to act promptly and decisively would raise very strong doubts throughout the world about America's willingness to keep its financial house in order.

Yet Congress has not acted. And tonight we face the sharpest financial threat in the postwar era—a threat to the dollar's role as the keystone of international trade and finance in the world.

Last week, at the monetary conference in Stockholm, the major industrial countries decided to take a big step toward creating a new international monetary asset that will strengthen the international monetary system. I am very proud of the very able work done by Secretary Fowler and Chairman Martin of the Federal Reserve Board.

But to make this system work the United States just must bring its balance of payments to—or very close to—equilibrium. We must have a responsible fiscal policy in this country. The passage of a tax bill now, together with expenditure control that the Congress may desire and dictate, is absolutely necessary to protect this Nation's security, to continue our prosperity, and to meet the needs of our people.

What is at stake is 7 years of unparalleled prosperity. In those 7 years, the real income of the average American, after taxes, rose by almost 30 percent—a gain as large as that of the entire preceding 19 years.

So the steps that we must take to convince the world are exactly the steps we must take to sustain our own economic strength here at home. In the past 8 months, prices and interest rates have risen because of our inaction.

We must, therefore, now do everything we can to move from debate to action—from talking to voting. There is, I believe—I hope there is—in both Houses of the Congress—a growing sense of urgency that this situation just must be acted upon and must be corrected.

My budget in January was, we thought, a tight one. It fully reflected our evaluation of most of the demanding needs of this Nation.

But in these budgetary matters, the President does not decide alone. The Congress has the power and the duty to determine appropriations and taxes. The Congress is now considering our proposals and they are considering reductions in the budget that we submitted.

As part of a program of fiscal restraint that includes the tax surcharge, I shall approve appropriate reductions in the January budget when and if Congress so decides that that should be done.

One thing is unmistakably clear, however: Our deficit just must be reduced. Failure to act could bring on conditions that would strike hardest at those people that all of us are trying so hard to help.

These times call for prudence in this land of plenty. I believe that we have the character to provide it, and tonight I plead with the Congress and with the people to act promptly to serve the national interest, and thereby serve all of our people.

Now let me give you my estimate of the chances for peace:

—the peace that will one day stop the bloodshed in South Vietnam,
—that will permit all the Vietnamese people to rebuild and develop their land,
—that will permit us to turn more fully to our own tasks here at home.

I cannot promise that the initiative that I have announced tonight will be completely successful in achieving peace any more than the 30 others that we have undertaken and agreed to in recent years.

But it is our fervent hope that North Vietnam, after years of fighting that have left the issue unresolved, will now cease its efforts to achieve a military victory and will join with us in moving toward the peace table.

And there may come a time when South Vietnamese—on both sides—are able to work out a way to settle their own differences by free political choice rather than by war.

As Hanoi considers its course, it should be in no doubt of our intentions. It must not miscalculate the pressures within our democracy in this election year.

We have no intention of widening this war.

But the United States will never accept a fake solution to this long and arduous struggle and call it peace.

No one can foretell the precise terms of an eventual settlement.

Our objective in South Vietnam has never been the annihilation of the enemy. It has been to bring about a recognition in Hanoi that its objective—taking over the South by force—could not be achieved.

We think that peace can be based on the Geneva Accords of 1954—under political conditions that permit the South Vietnamese—all the South Vietnamese—to chart their course free of any outside domination or interference, from us or from anyone else.

So tonight I reaffirm the pledge that we made at Manila—that we are prepared to withdraw our forces from South Vietnam as the other side withdraws its forces to the north, stops the infiltration, and the level of violence thus subsides.

Our goal of peace and self-determination in Vietnam is directly related to the future of all of Southeast Asia—where much has happened to inspire confidence during the past 10 years. We have done all that we knew how to do to contribute and to help build that confidence.

A number of its nations have shown what can be accomplished under conditions of security. Since 1966, Indonesia, the fifth largest nation in all the world, with a population of more than 100 million people, has had a government that is dedicated to peace with its neighbors and improved conditions for its own people. Political and economic cooperation between nations has grown rapidly.

I think every American can take a great deal of pride in the role that we have played in bringing this about in Southeast Asia. We can rightly judge—as responsible Southeast Asians themselves do—that the progress of the past 3 years would have been far less likely—if not completely impossible—if America's sons and others had not made their stand in Vietnam.

At Johns Hopkins University, about 3 years ago, I announced that the United States would take part in the great work of developing Southeast Asia, including the Mekong Valley, for all the people of that region. Our determination to help build a better land—a better land for men on both sides of the present conflict—has not diminished in the least. Indeed, the ravages of war, I think, have made it more urgent than ever.

So, I repeat on behalf of the United States again tonight what I said at Johns Hopkins—that North Vietnam could take its place in this common effort just as soon as peace comes.

Over time, a wider framework of peace and security in Southeast Asia may become possible. The new cooperation of the nations of the area could be a foundation-stone. Certainly friendship with the nations of such a Southeast Asia is what the United States seeks—and that is all that the United States seeks.

One day, my fellow citizens, there will be peace in Southeast Asia.

It will come because the people of Southeast Asia want it—those whose armies are at war tonight, and those who, though threatened, have thus far been spared. Peace will come because Asians were willing to work for it—and to sacrifice for it—and to die by the thousands for it.

But let it never be forgotten: Peace will come also because America sent her sons to help secure it.

It has not been easy—far from it. During the past $4\frac{1}{2}$ years, it has been my fate and my responsibility to be Commander in Chief. I have lived—daily and nightly—with the cost of this war. I know the pain that it has inflicted. I know, perhaps better than anyone, the misgivings that it has aroused.

Throughout this entire, long period, I have been sustained by a single principle: that what we are doing now, in Vietnam, is vital not only to the security of Southeast Asia, but it is vital to the security of every American.

Surely we have treaties which we must respect. Surely we have commitments that we are going to keep. Resolutions of the Congress testify to the need to resist aggression in the world and in Southeast Asia.

But the heart of our involvement in South Vietnam—under three different Presidents, three separate administrations—has always been America's own security.

And the larger purpose of our involvement has always been to help the nations of Southeast Asia become independent and stand alone, self-sustaining, as members of a great world community—at peace with themselves, and at peace with all others.

With such an Asia, our country—and the world—will be far more secure than it is tonight.

I believe that a peaceful Asia is far nearer to reality because of what America has done in Vietnam. I believe that the men who endure the dangers of battle—fighting there for us tonight—are helping the entire world avoid far greater conflicts, far wider wars, far more destruction, than this one.

The peace that will bring them home someday will come. Tonight I have offered the first in what I hope will be a series of mutual moves toward peace.

I pray that it will not be rejected by the leaders of North Vietnam. I pray that they will accept it as a means by which the sacrifices of their own people may be ended. And I ask your help and your support, my fellow citizens, for this effort to reach across the battlefield toward an early peace.

Finally, my fellow Americans, let me say this: Of those to whom much is given, much is asked. I cannot say and no man could say that no more will be asked of us.

Yet, I believe that now, no less than when the decade began, this generation of Americans is willing to "pay any price, bear any burden, meet any hardship, support any friend, oppose any foe to assure the survival and the success of liberty."

Since those words were spoken by John F. Kennedy, the people of America have kept that compact with mankind's noblest cause.

And we shall continue to keep it.

Yet, I believe that we must always be mindful of this one thing, whatever the trials and the tests ahead. The ultimate strength of our country and our cause will lie not in powerful weapons or infinite resources or boundless wealth, but will lie in the unity of our people.

This I believe very deeply.

Throughout my entire public career I have followed the personal philosophy that I am a free man, an American, a public servant, and a member of my party, in that order always and only.

For 37 years in the service of our Nation, first as a Congressman, as a Senator, and as Vice President, and now as your President, I have put the unity of the people first. I have put it ahead of any divisive partisanship.

And in these times as in times before, it is true that a house divided against itself by the spirit of faction, of party, of region, of religion, of race, is a house that cannot stand.

There is division in the American house now.

There is divisiveness among us all tonight. And holding the trust that is mine, as President of all the people, I cannot disregard the peril to the progress of the American people and the hope and the prospect of peace for all peoples.

So, I would ask all Americans, whatever their personal interests or concern, to guard against divisiveness and all its ugly consequences.

Fifty-two months and 10 days ago, in a moment of tragedy and trauma, the duties of this office fell upon me. I asked then for your help and God's, that we might continue America on its course, binding up our wounds, healing our history, moving forward in new unity, to clear the American agenda and to keep the American commitment for all of our people.

United we have kept that commitment. United we have enlarged that commitment.

Through all time to come, I think America will be a stronger nation, a more just society, and a land of greater opportunity and fulfillment because of what we have all done together in these years of unparalleled achievement.

Our reward will come in the life of freedom, peace, and hope that our children will enjoy through ages ahead.

What we won when all of our people united just must not now be lost in suspicion, distrust, self-ishness, and politics among any of our people.

Believing this as I do, I have concluded that I should not permit the Presidency to become involved in the partisan divisions that are developing in this political year.

With America's sons in the fields far away, with America's future under challenge right here at home, with our hopes and the world's hopes for peace in the balance every day, I do not believe that I should devote an hour or a day of my time to any personal partisan causes or to any duties other than the awesome duties of this office—the Presidency of your country.

Accordingly, I shall not seek, and I will not accept, the nomination of my party for another term as your President.

But let men everywhere know, however, that a strong, a confident, and a vigilant America stands ready tonight to seek an honorable peace—and stands ready tonight to defend an honored cause—whatever the price, whatever the burden, whatever the sacrifice that duty may require.

Thank you for listening.

Good night and God bless all of you.

Johnson expressed reluctance to give the sixth annual message, since it coincided with his departure from office. But he decided to use the occasion to bid adieu to so many friends with whom he had served on Capitol Hill. As he put it,"I rejected and rejected and then finally accepted the congressional leadership's invitation to come here to speak this farewell to you in person tonight." The end is a gracious and touching tribute to American public servants.

Sixth State of the Union Address
(speech to the Congress)
January 14, 1969

Mr. Speaker, Mr. President, Members of the Congress and my fellow Americans:

For the sixth and the last time, I present to the Congress my assessment of the State of the Union.

I shall speak to you tonight about challenge and opportunity—and about the commitments that all of us have made together that will, if we carry them out, give America our best chance to achieve the kind of great society that we all want.

Every President lives, not only with what is, but with what has been and what could be.

Most of the great events in his Presidency are part of a larger sequence extending back through several years and extending back through several other administrations.

Urban unrest, poverty, pressures on welfare, education of our people, law enforcement and law and order, the continuing crisis in the Middle East, the conflict in Vietnam, the dangers of nuclear war, the great difficulties of dealing with the Communist powers, all have this much in common: They and their causes—the causes that gave rise to them—all of these have existed with us for many years. Several Presidents have already sought to try to deal with them. One or more Presidents will try to resolve them or try to contain them in the years that are ahead of us.

But if the Nation's problems are continuing, so are this great Nation's assets:

—our economy,
—the democratic system,

—our sense of exploration, symbolized most recently by the wonderful flight of the Apollo 8, in
which all Americans took great pride,
—the good commonsense and sound judgment of the American people, and
—their essential love of justice.

We must not ignore our problems. But neither should we ignore our strengths. Those strengths
are available to sustain a President of either party—to support his progressive efforts both at home and
overseas.

Unfortunately, the departure of an administration does not mean the end of the problems that
this administration has faced. The effort to meet the problems must go on, year after year, if the momentum that we have all mounted together in these past years is not to be lost.

Although the struggle for progressive change is continuous, there are times when a watershed is
reached—when there is—if not really a break with the past—at least the fulfillment of many of its
oldest hopes, and a stepping forth into a new environment, to seek new goals.

I think the past 5 years have been such a time.

We have finished a major part of the old agenda.

Some of the laws that we wrote have already, in front of our eyes, taken on the flesh of achievement.

Medicare that we were unable to pass for so many years is now a part of American life.

Voting rights and the voting booth that we debated so long back in the fifties, and the doors to
public service, are open at last to all Americans regardless of their color.

Schools and school children all over America tonight are receiving Federal assistance to go to
good schools.

Preschool education—Head Start—is already here to stay and, I think, so are the Federal programs that tonight are keeping more than a million and a half of the cream of our young people in
the colleges and the universities of this country.

Part of the American earth—not only in description on a map, but in the reality of our shores,
our hills, our parks, our forests, and our mountains—has been permanently set aside for the American public and for their benefit. And there is more that will be set aside before this administration
ends.

Five million Americans have been trained for jobs in new Federal programs.

I think it is most important that we all realize tonight that this Nation is close to full employment—with less unemployment than we have had at any time in almost 20 years. That is not in theory; that is in fact. Tonight, the unemployment rate is down to 3.3 percent. The number of jobs has
grown more than $8\frac{1}{2}$ million in the last 5 years. That is more than in all the preceding 12 years.

These achievements completed the full cycle, from idea to enactment and, finally, to a place in
the lives of citizens all across this country.

I wish it were possible to say that everything that this Congress and the administration achieved
during this period had already completed that cycle. But a great deal of what we have committed
needs additional funding to become a tangible realization.

Yet the very existence of these commitments—these promises to the American people, made by
this Congress and by the executive branch of the Government—are achievements in themselves, and
failure to carry through on our commitments would be a tragedy for this Nation.

This much is certain: No one man or group of men made these commitments alone. Congress and
the executive branch, with their checks and balances, reasoned together and finally wrote them into
the law of the land. They now have all the moral force that the American political system can summon when it acts as one.

They express America's common determination to achieve goals. They imply action.

In most cases, you have already begun that action—but it is not fully completed, of course.

Let me speak for a moment about these commitments. I am going to speak in the language which
the Congress itself spoke when it passed these measures. I am going to quote from your words.

In 1966, Congress declared that "improving the quality of urban life is the most critical domestic problem facing the United States." Two years later it affirmed the historic goal of "a decent home . . . for every American family." That is your language.

Now to meet these commitments, we must increase our support for the model cities program, where blueprints of change are already being prepared in more than 150 American cities.

To achieve the goals of the Housing Act of 1968 that you have already passed, we should begin this year more than 500,000 homes for needy families in the coming fiscal year. Funds are provided in the new budget to do just this. This is almost 10 times—10 times—the average rate of the past 10 years.

Our cities and our towns are being pressed for funds to meet the needs of their growing populations. So I believe an urban development bank should be created by the Congress. This bank could obtain resources through the issuance of taxable bonds and it could then lend these resources at reduced rates to the communities throughout the land for schools, hospitals, parks, and other public facilities.

Since we enacted the Social Security Act back in 1935, Congress has recognized the necessity to "make more adequate provision for aged persons . . . through maternal and child welfare . . . and public health." Those are the words of the Congress—"more adequate."

The time has come, I think, to make it more adequate. I believe we should increase social security benefits, and I am so recommending tonight.

I am suggesting that there should be an overall increase in benefits of at least 13 percent. Those who receive only the minimum of $55 should get $80 a month.

Our Nation, too, is rightfully proud of our medical advances. But we should remember that our country ranks 15th among the nations of the world in its infant mortality rate.

I think we should assure decent medical care for every expectant mother and for their children during the first year of their life in the United States of America.

I think we should protect our children and their families from the costs of catastrophic illness.

As we pass on from medicine, I think nothing is clearer to the Congress than the commitment that the Congress made to end poverty. Congress expressed it well, I think, in 1964, when they said: "It is the policy of the United States to eliminate the paradox of poverty in the midst of plenty in this nation."

This is the richest nation in the world. The antipoverty program has had many achievements. It also has some failures. But we must not cripple it after only 3 years of trying to solve the human problems that have been with us and have been building up among us for generations.

I believe the Congress this year will want to improve the administration of the poverty program by reorganizing portions of it and transferring them to other agencies. I believe, though, it will want to continue, until we have broken the back of poverty, the efforts we are now making throughout this land.

I believe, and I hope the next administration—I believe they believe—that the key to success in this effort is jobs. It is work for people who want to work.

In the budget for fiscal 1970, I shall recommend a total of $3.5 billion for our job training program, and that is five times as much as we spent in 1964 trying to prepare Americans where they can work to earn their own living.

The Nation's commitment in the field of civil rights began with the Declaration of Independence. They were extended by the 13th, 14th, and 15th amendments. They have been powerfully strengthened by the enactment of three far-reaching civil rights laws within the past 5 years, that this Congress, in its wisdom, passed.

On January 1 of this year, the Fair Housing Act of 1968 covered over 20 million American homes and apartments. The prohibition against racial discrimination in that act should be remembered and it should be vigorously enforced throughout this land.

I believe we should also extend the vital provisions of the Voting Rights Act for another 5 years.

In the Safe Streets Act of 1968, Congress determined "To assist state and local governments in reducing the incidence of crime."

This year I am proposing that the Congress provide the full $300 million that the Congress last year authorized to do just that.

I hope the Congress will put the money where the authorization is.

I believe this is an essential contribution to justice and to public order in the United States. I hope these grants can be made to the States and they can be used effectively to reduce the crime rate in this country.

But all of this is only a small part of the total effort that must be made—I think chiefly by the local governments throughout the Nation—if we expect to reduce the toll of crime that we all detest.

Frankly, as I leave the Office of the Presidency, one of my greatest disappointments is our failure to secure passage of a licensing and registration act for firearms. I think if we had passed that act, it would have reduced the incidence of crime. I believe that the Congress should adopt such a law, and I hope that it will at a not too distant date.

In order to meet our long-standing commitment to make government as efficient as possible, I believe that we should reorganize our postal system along the lines of the Kappel report.

I hope we can all agree that public service should never impose an unreasonable financial sacrifice on able men and women who want to serve their country.

I believe that the recommendations of the Commission on Executive, Legislative and Judicial Salaries are generally sound. Later this week, I shall submit a special message which I reviewed with the leadership this evening containing a proposal that has been reduced and has modified the Commission's recommendation to some extent on the congressional salaries.

For Members of Congress, I will recommend the basic compensation not of the $50,000 unanimously recommended by the Kappel Commission and the other distinguished Members, but I shall reduce that $50,000 to $42,500. I will suggest that Congress appropriate a very small additional allowance for official expenses, so that Members will not be required to use their salary increase for essential official business.

I would have submitted the Commission's recommendations, except the advice that I received from the leadership—and you usually are consulted about matters that affect the Congress—was that the Congress would not accept the $50,000 recommendation, and if I expected my recommendation to be seriously considered, I should make substantial reductions. That is the only reason I didn't go along with the Kappel report.

In 1967 I recommended to the Congress a fair and impartial random selection system for the draft. I submit it again tonight for your most respectful consideration.

I know that all of us recognize that most of the things we do to meet all of these commitments I talk about will cost money. If we maintain the strong rate of growth that we have had in this country for the past 8 years, I think we shall generate the resources that we need to meet these commitments.

We have already been able to increase our support for major social programs—although we have heard a lot about not being able to do anything on the home front because of Vietnam; but we have been able in the last 5 years to increase our commitments for such things as health and education from $30 billion in 1964 to $68 billion in the coming fiscal year. That is more than double. That is more than it has ever been increased in the 188 years of this Republic, notwithstanding Vietnam.

We must continue to budget our resources and budget them responsibly in a way that will preserve our prosperity and will strengthen our dollar.

Greater revenues and the reduced Federal spending required by Congress last year have changed the budgetary picture dramatically since last January when we made our estimates. At that time, you will remember that we estimated we would have a deficit of $8 billion. Well, I am glad to report to you tonight that the fiscal year ending June 30, 1969, this June, we are going to have not a deficit, but we are going to have a $2.4 billion surplus.

You will receive the budget tomorrow. The budget for the next fiscal year, that begins July 1—which you will want to examine very carefully in the days ahead—will provide a $3.4 billion surplus.

This budget anticipates the extension of the surtax that Congress enacted last year. I have communicated with the President-elect, Mr. Nixon, in connection with this policy of continuing the surtax for the time being.

I want to tell you that both of us want to see it removed just as soon as circumstances will permit, but the President-elect has told me that he has concluded that until his administration, and this Congress, can examine the appropriation bills, and each item in the budget, and can ascertain that the facts justify permitting the surtax to expire or to be reduced, he, Mr. Nixon, will support my recommendation that the surtax be continued.

Americans, I believe, are united in the hope that the Paris talks will bring an early peace to Vietnam. And if our hopes for an early settlement of the war are realized, then our military expenditures can be reduced and very substantial savings can be made to be used for other desirable purposes, as the Congress may determine.

In any event, I think it is imperative that we do all that we responsibly can to resist inflation while maintaining our prosperity. I think all Americans know that our prosperity is broad and it is deep, and it has brought record profits, the highest in our history, and record wages.

Our gross national product has grown more in the last 5 years than any other period in our Nation's history. Our wages have been the highest. Our profits have been the best. This prosperity has enabled millions to escape the poverty that they would have otherwise had the last few years.

I think also you will be very glad to hear that the Secretary of the Treasury informs me tonight that in 1968 in our balance of payments we have achieved a surplus. It appears that we have, in fact, done better this year than we have done in any year in this regard since the year 1957.

The quest for a durable peace, I think, has absorbed every administration since the end of World War II. It has required us to seek a limitation of arms races not only among the superpowers, but among the smaller nations as well. We have joined in the test ban treaty of 1963, the outer space treaty of 1967, and the treaty against the spread of nuclear weapons in 1968.

This latter agreement—the nonproliferation treaty—is now pending in the Senate and it has been pending there since last July. In my opinion, delay in ratifying it is not going to be helpful to the cause of peace. America took the lead in negotiating this treaty and America should now take steps to have it approved at the earliest possible date.

Until a way can be found to scale down the level of arms among the superpowers, mankind cannot view the future without fear and great apprehension. So, I believe that we should resume the talks with the Soviet Union about limiting offensive and defensive missile systems. I think they would already have been resumed except for Czechoslovakia and our election this year.

It was more than 20 years ago that we embarked on a program of trying to aid the developing nations. We knew then that we could not live in good conscience as a rich enclave on an earth that was seething in misery.

During these years there have been great advances made under our program, particularly against want and hunger, although we are disappointed at the appropriations last year. We thought they were woefully inadequate. This year I am asking for adequate funds for economic assistance in the hope that we can further peace throughout the world.

I think we must continue to support efforts in regional cooperation. Among those efforts, that of Western Europe has a very special place in America's concern.

The only course that is going to permit Europe to play the great world role that its resources permit is to go forward to unity. I think America remains ready to work with a united Europe, to work as a partner on the basis of equality.

For the future, the quest for peace, I believe, requires:

—that we maintain the liberal trade policies that have helped us become the leading nation in world trade,

—that we strengthen the international monetary system as an instrument of world prosperity, and

—that we seek areas of agreement with the Soviet Union where the interests of both nations and the interests of world peace are properly served.

The strained relationship between us and the world's leading Communist power has not ended—especially in the light of the brutal invasion of Czechoslovakia. But totalitarianism is no less odious to us because we are able to reach some accommodation that reduces the danger of world catastrophe.

What we do, we do in the interest of peace in the world. We earnestly hope that time will bring a Russia that is less afraid of diversity and individual freedom.

The quest for peace tonight continues in Vietnam, and in the Paris talks.

I regret more than any of you know that it has not been possible to restore peace to South Vietnam.

The prospects, I think, for peace are better today than at any time since North Vietnam began its invasion with its regular forces more than 4 years ago.

The free nations of Asia know what they were not sure of at that time: that America cares about their freedom, and it also cares about America's own vital interests in Asia and throughout the Pacific.

The North Vietnamese know that they cannot achieve their aggressive purposes by force. There may be hard fighting before a settlement is reached; but, I can assure you, it will yield no victory to the Communist cause.

I cannot speak to you tonight about Vietnam without paying a very personal tribute to the men who have carried the battle out there for all of us. I have been honored to be their Commander in Chief. The Nation owes them its unstinting support while the battle continues—and its enduring gratitude when their service is done.

Finally, the quest for stable peace in the Middle East goes on in many capitals tonight. America fully supports the unanimous resolution of the U.N. Security Council which points the way. There must be a settlement of the armed hostility that exists in that region of the world today. It is a threat not only to Israel and to all the Arab States, but it is a threat to every one of us and to the entire world as well.

Now, my friends in Congress, I want to conclude with a few very personal words to you.

I rejected and rejected and then finally accepted the congressional leadership's invitation to come here to speak this farewell to you in person tonight.

I did that for two reasons. One was philosophical. I wanted to give you my judgment, as I saw it, on some of the issues before our Nation, as I view them, before I leave.

The other was just pure sentimental. Most all of my life as a public official has been spent here in this building. For 38 years—since I worked on that gallery as a doorkeeper in the House of Representatives—I have known these halls, and I have known most of the men pretty well who walked them.

I know the questions that you face. I know the conflicts that you endure. I know the ideals that you seek to serve.

I left here first to become Vice President, and then to become, in a moment of tragedy, the President of the United States.

My term of office has been marked by a series of challenges, both at home and throughout the world.

In meeting some of these challenges, the Nation has found a new confidence. In meeting others, it knew turbulence and doubt, and fear and hate.

Throughout this time, I have been sustained by my faith in representative democracy—a faith that I had learned here in this Capitol Building as an employee and as a Congressman and as a Senator.

I believe deeply in the ultimate purposes of this Nation—described by the Constitution, tempered by history, embodied in progressive laws, and given life by men and women that have been elected to serve their fellow citizens.

Now for 5 most demanding years in the White House, I have been strengthened by the counsel and the cooperation of two great former Presidents, Harry S. Truman and Dwight David Eisenhower. I have been guided by the memory of my pleasant and close association with the beloved John F. Kennedy, and with our greatest modern legislator, Speaker Sam Rayburn.

I have been assisted by my friend every step of the way, Vice President Hubert Humphrey. I am so grateful that I have been supported daily by the loyalty of Speaker McCormack and Majority Leader Albert.

I have benefited from the wisdom of Senator Mike Mansfield, and I am sure that I have avoided many dangerous pitfalls by the good commonsense counsel of the President Pro Tem of the Senate, Senator Richard Brevard Russell.

I have received the most generous cooperation from the leaders of the Republican Party in the Congress of the United States, Senator Dirksen and Congressman Gerald Ford, the Minority Leader.

No President should ask for more, although I did upon occasions. But few Presidents have ever been blessed with so much.

President-elect Nixon, in the days ahead, is going to need your understanding, just as I did. And he is entitled to have it. I hope every Member will remember that the burdens he will bear as our President, will be borne for all of us. Each of us should try not to increase these burdens for the sake of narrow personal or partisan advantage.

Now, it is time to leave. I hope it may be said, a hundred years from now, that by working together we helped to make our country more just, more just for all of its people, as well as to insure and guarantee the blessings of liberty for all of our posterity.

That is what I hope. But I believe that at least it will be said that we tried.

3 0

Richard M. Nixon (1969–1974)

"I shall resign the Presidency effective at noon tomorrow." With that one sentence Richard Nixon made history. No previous U.S. president had resigned from office. The occasion made for a dark resignation speech, the likes of which had not been seen since Andrew Johnson's stormy exit. Up to that point in the nation's history, many presidents had seen articles of impeachment drawn up against them and introduced in the House of Representatives: Tyler, A. Johnson, Cleveland, Truman, Hoover. But in fact, only Johnson had been impeached. Just over a century later, Nixon very nearly became the second impeached president.

The threat of impeachment dramatically changes the tone and content of a farewell. Nixon used his final official address to achieve opposing, Janus-faced objectives: looking back, he tried to provide some plausible justification for his actions; looking forward, he began a campaign of personal vindication and rehabilitation. Nixon used the pronoun "I" fifty-six times in the fourteen-minute speech.

Nixon's presidency will forever be yoked to the burden of "Watergate." And he knew it. But rather than dodge the black mark on his presidency, he referred to Watergate twice in his resignation speech. Rhetorically it was a risky strategy, like a boxer leading with his chin. But the thirty-seventh president was experienced at using television to take his case directly to the American people when he was in political trouble. Early in his career, when he was fighting to be on Eisenhower's ticket as the vice presidential candidate, he had succeeded brilliantly in the famous "Checkers Speech."[1] His success at that make-or-break moment helps explain the similar approach twenty-two years later in the Resignation Speech. Nixon believed that he still enjoyed considerable support among the middle class. He wanted the "silent majority" to sympathize with his sense of duty and character. Thus, for example, he justified his decision to remain in office as long as he did in terms of duty—"I have felt it was my duty to persevere; to make every possible effort to complete the term of office to which you elected me." And he couched the decision in terms of character—"I have never been a quitter. To leave office before my term is completed is opposed to every instinct in my body." (Nixon had literally said, "I'm not a quitter" in his Checkers Speech, too.)

The problem, Nixon implied, was not lack of support from the people, but the erosion of his political base in the Congress. However, Nixon expressed his willingness to sacrifice himself for the people: "I would have preferred to carry through to the finish whatever the personal agony

433

it would have involved, and my family unanimously urged me to do so." But the political climate in Washington made it impossible to serve the people. "As I recall the high hopes for America with which we began this second term, I feel a great sadness that I will not be here in this office working *on your behalf* to achieve those hopes in the next two and a half years" [emphasis added].

Nixon's campaign to vindicate himself partially succeeded. He lived two decades more. By the time of his death in April 1994, he was regarded as an elder statesman and approached by leaders from both major parties who sought his counsel in foreign affairs—a domain in which he had shown great insight, creativity, and boldness.

Resignation Speech
(broadcast live by radio and television from the Oval Office)
August 8, 1974

Good evening. This is the 37th time I have spoken to you from this office, where so many decisions have been made that shape the history of this Nation. Each time I have done so to discuss with you some matters that I believe affected the national interest.

In all the decisions I have made in my public life, I have always tried to do what was best for the nation. Throughout the long and difficult period of Watergate, I have felt it was my duty to persevere, to make every possible effort to complete the term of office to which you elected me.

In the past few days, however, it has become evident to me that I no longer have a strong enough political base in the Congress to justify continuing that effort. As long as there was such a base, I felt strongly that it was necessary to see the constitutional process through to its conclusion, that to do otherwise would be unfaithful to the spirit of that deliberately difficult process and a dangerously destabilizing precedent for the future.

But with the disappearance of that base, I now believe that the constitutional purpose has been served, and there is no longer a need for the process to be prolonged.

I would have preferred to carry through to the finish, whatever the personal agony it would have involved, and my family unanimously urged me to do so. But the interests of the Nation must always come before any personal considerations.

From the discussions I have had with Congressional and other leaders, I have concluded that because of the Watergate matter I might not have the support of the Congress that I would consider necessary to back the very difficult decisions and carry out the duties of this office in the way the interests of the Nation will require.

I have never been a quitter. To leave office before my term is completed is abhorrent to every instinct in my body. But as President I must put the interests of America first. America needs a full-time President and a full-time Congress, particularly at this time with problems we face at home and abroad.

To continue to fight through the months ahead for my personal vindication would almost totally absorb the time and attention of both the President and the Congress in a period when our entire focus should be on the great issues of peace abroad and prosperity without inflation at home.

Therefore, I shall resign the Presidency effective at noon tomorrow. Vice President Ford will be sworn in as President at that hour in this office.

As I recall the high hopes for America with which we began this second term, I feel a great sadness that I will not be here in this office working on your behalf to achieve those hopes in the next two and a half years. But in turning over direction of the Government to Vice President Ford, I know, as I told the Nation when I nominated him for that office 10 months ago, that the leadership of America will be in good hands.

In passing this office to the Vice President, I also do so with the profound sense of the weight of responsibility that will fall on his shoulders tomorrow and, therefore, of the understanding, the patience, the cooperation he will need from all Americans.

As he assumes that responsibility, he will deserve the help and the support of all of us. As we look to the future, the first essential is to begin healing the wounds of this Nation, to put the bitterness and divisions of the recent past behind us, and to rediscover those shared ideals that lie at the heart of our strength and unity as a great and as a free people.

By taking this action, I hope that I will have hastened the start of that process of healing which is so desperately needed in America.

I regret deeply any injuries that may have been done in the course of the events that led to this decision. I would say only that if some of my judgments were wrong—and some were wrong—they were made in what I believed at the time to be the best interest of the Nation.

To those who have stood with me during these past difficult months—to my family, my friends, to many others who joined in supporting my cause because they believed it was right—I will be eternally grateful for your support.

And to those who have not felt able to give me your support, let me say I leave with no bitterness toward those who have opposed me, because all of us, in the final analysis, have been concerned with the good of the country, however our judgments might differ.

So let us all now join together in firming that common commitment and in helping our new President succeed for the benefit of all Americans.

I shall leave this office with regret at not completing my term, but with gratitude for the privilege of serving as your President for the past five and a half years. These years have been a momentous time in the history of our Nation and the world. They have been a time of achievement in which we can all be proud, achievements that represent the shared efforts of the Administration, the Congress, and the people.

But the challenges ahead are equally great. And they, too, will require the support and the efforts of the Congress and the people working in cooperation with the new Administration.

We have ended America's longest war. But in the work of securing a lasting peace in the world, the goals ahead are even more far-reaching and more difficult. We must complete a structure of peace so that it will be said of this generation—our generation of Americans by the people of all nations—not only that we ended one war but that we prevented future wars.

We have unlocked the doors that for a quarter of a century stood between the United States and the People's Republic of China. We must now insure that the one-quarter of the world's people who live in the People's Republic of China will be and remain, not our enemies, but our friends.

In the Middle East, 100 million people in the Arab countries, many of whom have considered us their enemy for nearly 20 years, now look on us as their friends. We must continue to build on that friendship so that peace can settle at last over the Middle East and so that the cradle of civilization will not become its grave.

Together with the Soviet Union, we have made the crucial breakthroughs that have begun the process of limiting nuclear arms. But we must set as our goal not just limiting, but reducing and finally destroying these terrible weapons so that they cannot destroy civilization and so that the threat of nuclear war will no longer hang over the world and the people. We have opened a new relation with the Soviet Union. We must continue to develop and expand that new relationship so that the two strongest nations of the world will live together in cooperation rather than confrontation.

Around the world—in Asia, in Africa, in Latin America, in the Middle East—there are millions of people who live in terrible poverty, even starvation. We must keep as our goal turning away from production for war and expanding production for peace so that people everywhere on this Earth can at last look forward, in their children's time if not in our own time, to having the necessities for a decent life.

Here in America we are fortunate that most of our people have not only the blessings of liberty but also the means to live full and good, and by the world's standards, even abundant lives. We must press on, however, toward a goal not only of more and better jobs but of full opportunity for every American, and of what we are striving so hard right now to achieve—prosperity without inflation.

For more than a quarter of a century in public life, I have shared in the turbulent history of this era. I have fought for what I believed in. I have tried, to the best of my ability, to discharge those duties and meet those responsibilities that were entrusted to me.

Sometimes I have succeeded and sometimes I have failed. But always I have taken heart from what Theodore Roosevelt said about the man in the arena, "whose face is marred by dust and sweat and blood, who strives valiantly, who errs and comes short again and again because there is not effort without error and shortcoming, but who does actually strive to do the deed, who knows the great enthusiasms, the great devotions, who spends himself in a worthy cause, who at the best knows in the end the triumphs of high achievements and who at the worst, if he fails, at least fails while daring greatly."

I pledge to you tonight that as long as I have a breath of life in my body, I shall continue in that spirit. I shall continue to work for the great causes to which I have been dedicated throughout my years as a Congressman, a Senator, Vice President, and President, the cause of peace—not just for America but among all nations—prosperity, justice, and opportunity for all of our people.

There is one cause above all to which I have been devoted and to which I shall always be devoted for as long as I live.

When I first took the oath of office as President five and a half years ago, I made this sacred commitment: to "consecrate my office, my energies, and all the wisdom I can summon to the cause of peace among nations."

I have done my very best in all the days since to be true to that pledge. As a result of these efforts, I am confident that the world is a safer place today, not only for the people of America but for the people of all nations, and that all of our children have a better chance than before of living in peace rather than dying in war.

This, more than anything, is what I hoped to achieve when I sought the Presidency. This, more than anything, is what I hope will be my legacy to you, to our country, as I leave the Presidency.

To have served in this office is to have felt a very personal sense of kinship with each and every American. In leaving it, I do so with this prayer: May God's grace be with you in all the days ahead.

The morning after Nixon delivered his Resignation Speech, he gave these apparently extemporaneous farewell remarks. The immediate audience was White House staff and friends. Since they were widely covered in the press, the larger audience was the court of public opinion in America and around the world. In both addresses, Nixon quoted Theodore Roosevelt, who knew suffering and grievous loss. The departing president also spoke poignantly of his mother and father, and he encouraged staff to tell their children that public service is a noble calling. He used the pronoun "I" fifty-seven times in the fifteen-minute speech.

Farewell Remarks to White House Staff
(broadcast live on nationwide radio and television
from the East Room at the White House)
August 9, 1974

Members of the Cabinet, members of the White House Staff, all of our friends here:

I think the record should show that this is one of those spontaneous things that we always arrange whenever the President comes in to speak, and it will be so reported in the press, and we don't mind, because they have to call it as they see it.

But on our part, believe me, it is spontaneous.

You are here to say goodbye to us, and we don't have a good word for it in English—the best is *au revoir*. We'll see you again.

I just met with the members of the White House staff, you know, those who serve here in the White House day in and day out, and I asked them to do what I ask all of you to do to the extent that you can and, of course, are requested to do so: to serve our next President as you have served me and previous Presidents—because many of you have been here for many years—with devotion and dedication, because this office, great as it is, can only be as great as the men and women who work for and with the President.

This house, for example—I was thinking of it as we walked down this hall, and I was comparing it to some of the great houses of the world that I have been in. This isn't the biggest house. Many, and most, in even smaller countries, are much bigger. This isn't the finest house. Many in Europe, particularly, and in China, Asia, have paintings of great, great value, things that we just don't have here and, probably, will never have until we are 1,000 years old or older.

But this is the best house. It is the best house, because it has something far more important than numbers of people who serve, far more important than numbers of rooms or how big it is, far more important than numbers of magnificent pieces of art.

This house has a great heart, and that heart comes from those who serve. I was rather sorry they didn't come down. We said goodbye to them upstairs. But they are really great. And I recall after so many times I have made speeches, and some of them pretty tough, yet, I always come back, or after a hard day—and my days usually have run rather long—I would always get a lift from them, because I might be a little down but they always smiled.

And so it is with you. I look around here, and I see so many on this staff that, you know, I should have been by your offices and shaken hands, and I would love to have talked to you and found out how to run the world—everybody wants to tell the President what to do, and boy, he needs to be told many times—but I just haven't had the time. But I want you to know that each and every one of you, I know, is indispensable to this Government.

I am proud of this Cabinet. I am proud of all the members who have served in our Cabinet. I am proud of our sub-Cabinet. I am proud of our White House Staff. As I pointed out last night, sure, we have done some things wrong in this Administration, and the top man always takes the responsibility, and I have never ducked it. But I want to say one thing: We can be proud of it—5½ years. No man or no woman came into this Administration and left it with more of this world's goods than when he came in. No man or no woman ever profited at the public expense or the public till. That tells something about you.

Mistakes, yes. But for personal gain, never. You did what you believed in. Sometimes right, sometimes wrong. And I only wish that I were a wealthy man—at the present time, I have got to find a way to pay my taxes—[*laughter*]—and if I were, I would like to recompense you for the sacrifices that all of you have made to serve in government.

But you are getting something in government—and I want you to tell this to your children, and I hope the Nation's children will hear it, too—something in government service that is far more important than money. It is a cause bigger than yourself. It is the cause of making this the greatest nation in the world, the leader of the world, because without our leadership, the world will know nothing but war, possibly starvation or worse, in the years ahead. With our leadership it will know peace, it will know plenty.

We have been generous, and we will be more generous in the future as we are able to. But most important, we must be strong here, strong in our hearts, strong in our souls, strong in our belief, and strong in our willingness to sacrifice, as you have been willing to sacrifice, in a pecuniary way, to serve in government.

There is something else I would like for you to tell your young people. You know, people often come in and say, "What will I tell my kids?" They look at government and say, sort of a rugged life, and they see the mistakes that are made. They get the impression that everybody is here for the purpose of feathering his nest. That is why I made this earlier point—not in this Administration, not one single man or woman.

And I say to them, there are many fine careers. This country needs good farmers, good businessmen, good plumbers, good carpenters.

I remember my old man. I think that they would have called him sort of a little man, common man. He didn't consider himself that way. You know what he was? He was a streetcar motorman first, and then he was a farmer, and then he had a lemon ranch. It was the poorest lemon ranch in California, I can assure you. He sold it before they found oil on it. [*Laughter*] And then he was a grocer. But he was a great man, because he did his job, and every job counts up to the hilt, regardless of what happens.

Nobody will ever write a book, probably, about my mother. Well, I guess all of you would say this about your mother—my mother was a saint. And I think of her, two boys dying of tuberculosis, nursing four others in order that she could take care of my older brother for 3 years in Arizona, and seeing each of them die, and when they died, it was like one of her own.

Yes, she will have no books written about her. But she was a saint.

Now, however, we look to the future. I had a little quote in the speech last night from T.R. As you know, I kind of like to read books. I am not educated, but I do read books—[*laughter*]—and the T.R. quote was a pretty good one.

Here is another one I found as I was reading, my last night in the White House, and this quote is about a young man. He was a young lawyer in New York. He had married a beautiful girl, and they had a lovely daughter, and then suddenly she died, and this is what he wrote. This was in his diary.

He said, "She was beautiful in face and form and lovelier still in spirit. As a flower she grew and as a fair young flower she died. Her life had been always in the sunshine. There had never come to her a single great sorrow. None ever knew her who did not love and revere her for her bright and sunny temper and her saintly unselfishness. Fair, pure and joyous as a maiden, loving, tender and happy as a young wife. When she had just become a mother, when her life seemed to be just begun and when the years seemed so bright before her, then by a strange and terrible fate death came to her. And when my heart's dearest died, the light went from my life forever."

That was T.R. in his twenties. He thought the light had gone from his life forever—but he went on. And he not only became President but, as an ex-President, he served his country, always in the arena, tempestuous, strong, sometimes wrong, sometimes right, but he was a man.

And as I leave, let me say, that is an example I think all of us should remember. We think sometimes when things happen that don't go the right way; we think that when you don't pass the bar exam the first time—I happened to, but I was just lucky; I mean, my writing was so poor the bar examiner said, "We have just got to let the guy through." We think that when someone dear to us dies, we think that when we lose an election, we think that when we suffer a defeat that all is ended. We think, as T.R. said, that the light had left his life forever.

Not true. It is only a beginning, always. The young must know it; the old must know it. It must always sustain us, because the greatness comes not when things go always good for you, but the greatness comes and you are really tested, when you take some knocks, some disappointments, when sadness comes, because only if you have been in the deepest valley can you ever know how magnificent it is to be on the highest mountain.

And so I say to you on this occasion, as we leave, we leave proud of the people who have stood by us and worked for us and served this country.

We want you to be proud of what you have done. We want you to continue to serve in government, if that is your wish. Always give your best, never get discouraged, never be petty; always remember, others may hate you, but those who hate you don't win unless you hate them, and then you destroy yourself.

And so, we leave with high hopes, in good spirit, and with deep humility, and with very much gratefulness in our hearts. I can only say to each and every one of you, we come from many faiths, we pray perhaps to different gods—but really the same God in a sense—but I want to say for each and every one of you, not only will we always remember you, not only will we always be grateful to you but always you will be in our hearts and you will be in our prayers.

Thank you very much.

Note

1. September 23, 1952. The Checkers Speech is rather lengthy at 4,674 words. The Resignation Speech is considerably shorter at 1,790 words.

3 1

Gerald R. Ford (1974–1977)

Gerald Ford was the first man to reach the White House without first going through the hurdle of a national election. Capping a long career in the U.S. House of Representatives, he became vice president in December 1973, after Nixon nominated him to fill the number two post upon Spiro Agnew's resignation and after a majority of the House and Senate confirmed the nomination. This marked the first time in American history that the vice president was chosen under the terms of the Twenty-fifth Amendment.[1] Ford became president just eight months later, in August 1974, upon Nixon's resignation. This marked the first time in U.S. history that a president resigned from office. These two firsts in American history prompted Ford to say, when he took the oath of office on August 9, 1974, "I assume the Presidency under extraordinary circumstances. . . . This is an hour of history that troubles our minds and hurts our hearts."

The mid-1970s were indeed a troublesome time in American history. True, the country celebrated its bicentennial in 1776. But the self-congratulations and cheering were subdued by doubts about what would become of America in the third century of its existence. Would it be the match for its challenges? The nation's confidence was shaken. After much public protest over the war in Southeast Asia, U.S. forces were being withdrawn from South Vietnam. The economy was being buffeted by the triple blows of inflation, energy shortages, and recession. Politically, Ford took the heat for pardoning former President Nixon. And he survived two assassination attempts.

Through it all, Ford tried to exert a healing, calming influence on the nation. Respected for his honesty and candor, the thirty-eighth president was a moderate when it came to domestic policy, a conservative when it came to fiscal policy, and a cautious interventionist when it came to foreign policy.

Ford delivered his final annual message in familiar territory and among colleagues he knew well. He addressed a joint session of Congress from the rostrum in the House, the chamber where he had spent a quarter of a century representing the state of Michigan and where, barely three years earlier, he had presided as House minority leader. While Ford was the consummate legislator, he did not hesitate to wield executive power. During his first fourteen months in office, he vetoed thirty-nine bills.

Of rhetorical note is the use of anaphora, or the parallel beginning, illustrated where Ford said three times in succession: "I am proud." In addition, there are memorable lines in the address, among them: "The Constitution is the bedrock of all our freedoms. Guard and cherish it, keep honor and order in your own house, and the Republic will endure."

Ford ended his address, as Eisenhower ended his farewell and as Nixon ended his Resignation Speech, with a simple prayer: "My fellow Americans, I once asked you for your prayers, and now I give you mine: May God guide this wonderful country, its people, and those they have chosen to lead them. May our third century be illuminated by liberty and blessed with brotherhood, so that we and all who come after us may be the humble servants of thy peace. Amen."

Third State of the Union Address
(speech before the Congress)
January 12, 1977

Mr. Speaker, Mr. Vice President, Members of the 95th Congress, and distinguished guests:

In accordance with the Constitution, I come before you once again to report on the state of the Union.

This report will be my last—maybe [*laughter*]—but for the Union it is only the first of such reports in our third century of independence, the close of which none of us will ever see. We can be confident, however, that 100 years from now a freely elected President will come before a freely elected Congress chosen to renew our great Republic's pledge to the Government of the people, by the people, and for the people.

For my part I pray the third century we are beginning will bring to all Americans, our children and their children's children, a greater measure of individual equality, opportunity, and justice, a greater abundance of spiritual and material blessings, and a higher quality of life, liberty, and the pursuit of happiness.

The state of the Union is a measurement of the many elements of which it is composed—a political union of diverse States, an economic union of varying interests, an intellectual union of common convictions, and a moral union of immutable ideals.

Taken in sum, I can report that the state of the Union is good. There is room for improvement, as always, but today we have a more perfect Union than when my stewardship began.

As a people we discovered that our Bicentennial was much more than a celebration of the past; it became a joyous reaffirmation of all that it means to be Americans, a confirmation before all the world of the vitality and durability of our free institutions. I am proud to have been privileged to preside over the affairs of our Federal Government during these eventful years when we proved, as I said in my first words upon assuming office, that "our Constitution works; our great Republic is a Government of laws and not of men. Here the people rule."

The people have spoken; they have chosen a new President and a new Congress to work their will. I congratulate you—particularly the new Members—as sincerely as I did President-elect Carter. In a few days it will be his duty to outline for you his priorities and legislative recommendations. Tonight I will not infringe on that responsibility, but rather wish him the very best in all that is good for our country.

During the period of my own service in this Capitol and in the White House, I can recall many orderly transitions of governmental responsibility—of problems as well as of position, of burdens as well as of power. The genius of the American system is that we do this so naturally and so normally. There are no soldiers marching in the street except in the Inaugural Parade; no public demonstrations except for some of the dancers at the Inaugural Ball; the opposition party doesn't go underground, but goes on functioning vigorously in the Congress and in the country; and our vigilant press goes right on probing and publishing our faults and our follies, confirming the wisdom of the framers of the first amendment.

Because of the transfer of authority in our form of government affects the state of the Union and of the world, I am happy to report to you that the current transition is proceeding very well. I was determined that it should; I wanted the new President to get off on an easier start than I had.

When I became President on August 9, 1974, our Nation was deeply divided and tormented. In rapid succession the Vice President and the President had resigned in disgrace. We were still struggling with the after-effects of a long, unpopular, and bloody war in Southeast Asia. The economy was unstable and racing toward the worst recession in 40 years. People were losing jobs. The cost of living was soaring. The Congress and the Chief Executive were at loggerheads. The integrity of our constitutional process and other institutions was being questioned. For more than 15 years domestic spending had soared as Federal programs multiplied, and the expense escalated annually. During the same period our national security needs were steadily shortchanged. In the grave situation which prevailed in August 1974, our will to maintain our international leadership was in doubt.

I asked for your prayers and went to work.

In January 1975 I reported to the Congress that the state of the Union was not good. I proposed urgent action to improve the economy and to achieve energy independence in 10 years. I reassured America's allies and sought to reduce the danger of confrontation with potential adversaries. I pledged a new direction for America. 1975 was a year of difficult decisions, but Americans responded with realism, common sense, and self-discipline.

By January 1976 we were headed in a new direction, which I hold to be the right direction for a free society. It was guided by the belief that successful problem-solving requires more than Federal action alone, that it involves a full partnership among all branches and all levels of government and public policies which nurture and promote the creative energies of private enterprises, institutions, and individual citizens.

A year ago I reported that the state of the Union was better—in many ways a lot better—but still not good enough. Common sense told me to stick to the steady course we were on, to continue to restrain the inflationary growth of government, to reduce taxes as well as spending, to return local decisions to local officials, to provide for long-range sufficiency in energy and national security needs. I resisted the immense pressures of an election year to open the floodgates of Federal money and the temptation to promise more than I could deliver. I told it as it was to the American people and demonstrated to the world that in our spirited political competition, as in this chamber, Americans can disagree without being disagreeable.

Now, after 30 months as your President, I can say that while we still have a way to go, I am proud of the long way we have come together.

I am proud of the part I have had in rebuilding confidence in the Presidency, confidence in our free system, and confidence in our future. Once again, Americans believe in themselves, in their leaders, and in the promise that tomorrow holds for their children.

I am proud that today America is at peace. None of our sons are fighting and dying in battle anywhere in the world. And the chance for peace among all nations is improved by our determination to honor our vital commitments in defense of peace and freedom.

I am proud that the United States has strong defenses, strong alliances, and a sound and courageous foreign policy.

Our alliances with major partners, the great industrial democracies of Western Europe, Japan, and Canada, have never been more solid. Consultations on mutual security, defense, and East-West relations have grown closer. Collaboration has branched out into new fields such as energy, economic policy, and relations with the Third World. We have used many avenues for cooperation, including summit meetings held among major allied countries. The friendship of the democracies is deeper, warmer, and more effective than at any time in 30 years.

We are maintaining stability in the strategic nuclear balance and pushing back the specter of nuclear war. A decisive step forward was taken in the Vladivostok Accord which I negotiated with General Secretary Brezhnev—joint recognition that an equal ceiling should be placed on the number of strategic weapons on each side. With resolve and wisdom on the part of both nations, a good agreement is well within reach this year.

The framework for peace in the Middle East has been built. Hopes for future progress in the Middle East were stirred by the historic agreements we reached and the trust and confidence that we formed. Thanks to American leadership, the prospects for peace in the Middle East are brighter than they have been in three decades. The Arab states and Israel continue to look to us to lead them from confrontation and war to a new era of accommodation and peace. We have no alternative but to persevere, and I am sure we will. The opportunities for a final settlement are great, and the price of failure is a return to the bloodshed and hatred that for too long have brought tragedy to all of the peoples of this area and repeatedly edged the world to the brink of war.

Our relationship with the People's Republic of China is proving its importance and its durability. We are finding more and more common ground between our two countries on basic questions of international affairs.

In my two trips to Asia as President, we have reaffirmed America's continuing vital interest in the peace and security of Asia and the Pacific Basin, established a new partnership with Japan, confirmed our dedication to the security of Korea, and reinforced our ties with the free nations of Southeast Asia.

An historic dialog has begun between industrial nations and developing nations. Most proposals on the table are the initiatives of the United States, including those on food, energy, technology, trade, investment, and commodities. We are well launched on this process of shaping positive and reliable economic relations between rich nations and poor nations over the long term.

We have made progress in trade negotiations and avoided protectionism during recession. We strengthened the international monetary system. During the past 2 years the free world's most important economic powers have already brought about important changes that serve both developed and developing economies. The momentum already achieved must be nurtured and strengthened, for the prosperity of the rich and poor depends upon it.

In Latin America, our relations have taken on a new maturity and a sense of common enterprise.

In Africa the quest for peace, racial justice, and economic progress is at a crucial point. The United States, in close cooperation with the United Kingdom, is actively engaged in this historic process. Will change come about by warfare and chaos and foreign intervention? Or will it come about by negotiated and fair solutions, ensuring majority rule, minority rights, and economic advance? America is committed to the side of peace and justice and to the principle that Africa should shape its own future, free of outside intervention.

American leadership has helped to stimulate new international efforts to stem the proliferation of nuclear weapons and to shape a comprehensive treaty governing the use of oceans.

I am gratified by these accomplishments. They constitute a record of broad success for America and for the peace and prosperity of all mankind. This administration leaves to its successor a world in better condition than we found. We leave, as well, a solid foundation for progress on a range of issues that are vital to the well-being of America.

What has been achieved in the field of foreign affairs and what can be accomplished by the new administration demonstrate the genius of Americans working together for the common good. It is this, our remarkable ability to work together, that has made us a unique nation. It is Congress, the President, and the people striving for a better world.

I know all patriotic Americans want this Nation's foreign policy to succeed. I urge members of my party in this Congress to give the new President loyal support in this area. I express the hope that this new Congress will reexamine its constitutional role in international affairs.

The exclusive right to declare war, the duty to advise and consent on the part of the Senate, the power of the purse on the part of the House are ample authority for the legislative branch and should be jealously guarded. But because we may have been too careless of these powers in the past does not justify congressional intrusion into, or obstruction of, the proper exercise of Presidential responsibilities now or in the future. There can be only one Commander in Chief. In these times crises cannot be managed and wars cannot be waged by committee, nor can peace be pursued solely by parliamentary debate. To the ears of the world, the President speaks for the Nation. While he is, of course, ultimately accountable to the Congress, the courts, and the people, he and his emissaries must not be handicapped in advance in their relations with foreign governments as has sometimes happened in the past.

At home I am encouraged by the Nation's recovery from the recession and our steady return to sound economic growth. It is now continuing after the recent period of uncertainty, which is part of the price we pay for free elections.

Our most pressing need today and the future is more jobs—productive, permanent jobs created by a thriving economy. We must revise our tax system both to ease the burden of heavy taxation and to encourage the investment necessary for the creation of productive jobs for all Americans who want to work.

Earlier this month I proposed a permanent income tax reduction of $10 billion below current levels, including raising the personal exemption from $750 to $1,000. I also recommended a series of measures to stimulate investment, such as accelerated depreciation for new plants and equipment in areas of high unemployment, a reduction in the corporate tax rate from 48 to 46 percent, and eliminating the present double taxation of dividends. I strongly urge the Congress to pass these measures to help create the productive, permanent jobs in the private economy that are so essential for our future.

All the basic trends are good; we are not on the brink of another recession or economic disaster. If we follow prudent policies that encourage productive investment and discourage destructive inflation, we will come out on top, and I am sure we will.

We have successfully cut inflation by more than half. When I took office, the Consumer Price Index was rising at 12.2 percent a year. During 1976 the rate of inflation was 5 percent.

We have created more jobs—over 4 million more jobs today than in the spring of 1975. Throughout this Nation today we have over 88 million people in useful, productive jobs—more than at any other time in our Nation's history. But there are still too many Americans unemployed. This is the greatest regret that I have as I leave office.

We brought about with the Congress, after much delay, the renewal of the general revenue sharing. We expanded community development and Federal manpower programs. We began a significant urban mass transit program. Federal programs today provide more funds for our States and local governments than ever before—$70 billion for the current fiscal year. Through these programs and others that provide aid directly to individuals, we have kept faith with our tradition of compassionate help for those who need it. As we begin our third century we can be proud of the progress that we have made in meeting human needs for all of our citizens.

We have cut the growth of crime by nearly 90 percent. Two years ago crime was increasing at the rate of 18 percent annually. In the first three quarters of 1976, that growth rate had been cut to 2 percent. But crime, and the fear of crime, remains one of the most serious problems facing our citizens.

We have had some successes, and there have been some disappointments. Bluntly, I must remind you that we have not made satisfactory progress toward achieving energy independence. Energy is absolutely vital to the defense of our country, to the strength of our economy, and to the quality of our lives.

Two years ago I proposed to the Congress the first comprehensive national energy program—a specific and coordinated set of measures that would end our vulnerability to embargo, blockade, or arbitrary price increases and would mobilize U.S. technology and resources to supply a significant share of the free world's energy after 1985. Of the major energy proposals I submitted 2 years ago, only half, belatedly, became law. In 1973 we were dependent upon foreign oil imports for 36 percent of our needs. Today, we are 40-percent dependent, and we'll pay out $34 billion for foreign oil this year. Such vulnerability at present or in the future is intolerable and must be ended.

The answer to where we stand on our national energy effort today reminds me of the old argument about whether the tank is half full or half empty. The pessimist will say we have half failed to achieve our 10-year energy goals; the optimist will say that we have half succeeded. I am always an optimist, but we must make up for lost time.

We have laid a solid foundation for completing the enormous task which confronts us. I have signed into law five major energy bills which contain significant measures for conservation, resource development, stockpiling, and standby authorities. We have moved forward to develop the naval petroleum reserves; to build a 500-million barrel strategic petroleum stockpile; to phase out unnecessary Government allocation and price controls; to develop a lasting relationship with other oil consuming nations; to improve the efficiency of energy use through conservation in automobiles, buildings, and industry; and to expand research on new technology and renewable resources such as wind power, geothermal and solar energy. All these actions, significant as they are for the long term, are only the beginning.

I recently submitted to the Congress my proposals to reorganize the Federal energy structure and the hard choices which remain if we are serious about reducing our dependence upon foreign energy. These include programs to reverse our declining production of natural gas and increase incentives for domestic crude oil production. I proposed to minimize environmental uncertainties affecting coal development, expand nuclear power generation, and create an energy independence authority to provide government financial assistance for vital energy programs where private capital is not available.

We must explore every reasonable prospect for meeting our energy needs when our current domestic reserves of oil and natural gas begin to dwindle in the next decade. I urgently ask Congress and the new administration to move quickly on these issues. This Nation has the resources and the capability to achieve our energy goals if its Government has the will to proceed, and I think we do.

I have been disappointed by inability to complete many of the meaningful organizational reforms which I contemplated for the Federal Government, although a start has been made. For example, the Federal judicial system has long served as a model for other courts. But today it is threatened by a shortage of qualified Federal judges and an explosion of litigation claiming Federal jurisdiction. I commend to the new administration and the Congress the recent report and recommendations of the Department of Justice, undertaken at my request, on "the needs of the Federal Courts." I especially endorse its proposals for a new commission on the judicial appointment process.

While the judicial branch of our Government may require reinforcement, the budgets and payrolls of the other branches remain staggering. I cannot help but observe that while the White House staff and the Executive Office of the President have been reduced and the total number of civilians in the executive branch contained during the 1970's, the legislative branch has increased substantially although the membership of the Congress remains at 535. Congress now costs the taxpayers more than a million dollars per Member; the whole legislative budget has passed the billion dollar mark.

I set out to reduce the growth in the size and spending of the Federal Government, but no President can accomplish this alone. The Congress sidetracked most of my requests for authority to consolidate overlapping programs and agencies, to return more decision-making and responsibility to State and local governments through block grants instead of rigid categorical programs, and to eliminate unnecessary red tape and outrageously complex regulations.

We have made some progress in cutting back the expansion of government and its intrusion into individual lives, but believe me, there is much more to be done—and you and I know it. It can only be done by tough and temporarily painful surgery by a Congress as prepared as the President to face up to this very real political problem. Again, I wish my successor, working with a substantial majority of his own party, the best of success in reforming the costly and cumbersome machinery of the Federal Government.

The task of self-government is never finished. The problems are great; the opportunities are greater.

America's first goal is and always will be peace with honor. America must remain first in keeping peace in the world. We can remain first in peace only if we are never second in defense.

In presenting the state of the Union to the Congress and to the American people, I have a special obligation as Commander in Chief to report on our national defense. Our survival as a free and independent people requires, above all, strong military forces that are well equipped and highly trained to perform their assigned mission.

I am particularly gratified to report that over the past $2\frac{1}{2}$ years, we have been able to reverse the dangerous decline of the previous decade in real resources this country was devoting to national defense. This was an immediate problem I faced in 1974. The evidence was unmistakable that the Soviet Union had been steadily increasing the resources it applied to building its military strength. During this same period the United States' real defense spending declined. In my three budgets we not only arrested that dangerous decline, but we have established the positive trend which is essential to our ability to contribute to peace and stability in the world.

The Vietnam war, both materially and psychologically, affected our overall defense posture. The dangerous anti-military sentiment discouraged defense spending and unfairly disparaged the men and women who serve in our Armed Forces.

The challenge that now confronts this country is whether we have the national will and determination to continue this essential defense effort over the long term, as it must be continued. We can no longer afford to oscillate from year to year in so vital a matter; indeed, we have a duty to look beyond the immediate question of budgets and to examine the nature of the problem we will face over the next generation.

I am the first recent President able to address long-term, basic issues without the burden of Vietnam. The war in Indochina consumed enormous resources at the very time that the overwhelming strategic superiority we once enjoyed was disappearing. In past years, as a result of decisions by the United States, our strategic forces leveled off, yet the Soviet Union continued a steady, constant buildup of its own forces, committing a high percentage of its national economic effort to defense.

The United States can never tolerate a shift in strategic balance against us or even a situation where the American people or our allies believe the balance is shifting against us. The United States would risk the most serious political consequences if the world came to believe that our adversaries have a decisive margin of superiority.

To maintain a strategic balance we must look ahead to the 1980's and beyond. The sophistication of modern weapons requires that we make decisions now if we are to ensure our security 10 years from now. Therefore, I have consistently advocated and strongly urged that we pursue three critical strategic programs: the Trident missile launching submarine; the B-1 bomber, with its superior capability to penetrate modern air defenses; and a more advanced intercontinental ballistic missile that will be better able to survive nuclear attack and deliver a devastating retaliatory strike.

In an era where the strategic nuclear forces are in rough equilibrium, the risks of conflict below the nuclear threshold may grow more perilous. A major, long-term objective, therefore, is to maintain capabilities to deal with, and thereby deter, conventional challenges and crises, particularly in Europe.

We cannot rely solely on strategic forces to guarantee our security or to deter all types of aggression. We must have superior naval and marine forces to maintain freedom of the seas, strong multipurpose tactical air forces, and mobile, modern ground forces. Accordingly, I have directed a long-term effort to improve our worldwide capabilities to deal with regional crises.

I have submitted a 5-year naval building program indispensable to the Nation's maritime strategy. Because the security of Europe and the integrity of NATO remain the cornerstone of American defense policy, I have initiated a special, long-term program to ensure the capacity of the Alliance to deter or defeat aggression in Europe.

As I leave office I can report that our national defense is effectively deterring conflict today. Our Armed Forces are capable of carrying out the variety of missions assigned to them. Programs are under way which will assure we can deter war in the years ahead. But I also must warn that it will require a sustained effort over a period of years to maintain these capabilities. We must have the wisdom, the stamina, and the courage to prepare today for the perils of tomorrow, and I believe we will.

As I look to the future—and I assure you I intend to go on doing that for a good many years—I can say with confidence that the state of the Union is good, but we must go on making it better and better.

This gathering symbolizes the constitutional foundation which makes continued progress possible, synchronizing the skills of three independent branches of Government, reserving fundamental sovereignty to the people of this great land. It is only as the temporary representatives and servants of the people that we meet here; we bring no hereditary status or gift of infallibility, and none follows us from this place.

Like President Washington, like the more fortunate of his successors, I look forward to the status of private citizen with gladness and gratitude. To me, being a citizen of the United States of America is the greatest honor and privilege in this world.

From the opportunities which fate and my fellow citizens have given me, as a Member of the House, as Vice President and President of the Senate, and as President of all the people, I have come to understand and place the highest value on the checks and balances which our founders imposed on government through the separation of powers among co-equal legislative, executive, and judicial branches. This often results in difficulty and delay, as I well know, but it also places supreme authority under God, beyond any one person, any one branch, any majority great or small, or any one party. The Constitution is the bedrock of all our freedoms. Guard and cherish it, keep honor and order in your own house, and the Republic will endure.

It is not easy to end these remarks. In this Chamber, along with some of you, I have experienced many, many of the highlights of my life. It was here that I stood 28 years ago with my freshman colleagues, as Speaker Sam Rayburn administered the oath. I see some of you now—Charlie Bennett, Dick Bolling, Carl Perkins, Pete Rodino, Harley Staggers, Tom Steed, Sid Yates, Clem Zablocki—and I remember those who have gone to their rest. It was here we waged many, many a lively battle—won some, lost some, but always remaining friends. It was here, surrounded by such friends, that the distinguished Chief Justice swore me in as Vice President on December 6, 1973. It was here I returned 8 months later as your President to ask not for a honeymoon, but for a good marriage.

I will always treasure those memories and your many, many kindnesses. I thank you for them all.

My fellow Americans, I once asked you for your prayers, and now I give you mine: May God guide this wonderful country, its people, and those they have chosen to lead them. May our third century be illuminated by liberty and blessed with brotherhood, so that we and all who come after us may be the humble servants of thy peace. Amen.

Good night. God bless you.

Note

1. Ratified only six years earlier, on February 10, 1967.

3 2

Jimmy Carter (1977–1981)

Jimmy Carter's farewell address dealt head on with the national "malaise" he had identified while in office. This malaise, he believed, was symptomatic of a dispirited America in the late 1970s. The causes were not historically distant. In the early 1970s, young Americans' idealism had been dashed by the Watergate scandal and by American involvement in Vietnam. The late 1970s brought their own share of challenges—increasing inflation, unemployment, energy shortages at home, and serious foreign policy challenges including the Soviet arms buildup, the invasion of Afghanistan, and the humiliating Iranian hostage crisis. The fact that Iran's audacious challenge to U.S. power lingered for so many months made America and the President look weak. It was not a happy time for the nation.

Carter asserted that there were intrinsic limitations in the nation's governing institutions—limitations that hampered the federal government's ability to deal with new challenges:

Today we are asking our political system to do things of which the founding fathers never dreamed. The government they designed for a few hundred thousand people now serves a nation of almost 230 million people. Their small coastal republic now spans beyond a continent, and we now have the responsibility to help lead much of the world through difficult times to a secure and prosperous future.

Today, as people have become ever more doubtful of the ability of the government to deal with our problems, we are increasingly drawn to single-issue groups and special interest organizations to ensure that whatever else happens our own personal views and our own private interests are protected.

This is a disturbing factor in American political life. It tends to distort our purposes because the national interest is not always the sum of all our single or special interests.

If from Carter's viewpoint the nation's governing institutions were stretched to the limit, her animating ideals were not. In this address, Carter meant to reawaken Americans to the noble vision of the Declaration of Independence—all were created equal and endowed by the creator with inalienable rights. He believed Americans could rediscover pride in their country by championing the human rights of all oppressed peoples of the world. In a memorable passage that touches on a common farewell theme—American exceptionalism—Carter said,

America did not invent human rights. In a very real sense, it is the other way round. Human rights invented America.

Ours was the first nation in the history of the world to be founded explicitly on such an idea. Our social and political progress has been based on one fundamental principle—the value and importance of the individual.

The fundamental force that unites us is not kinship or place of origin or religious preference. The love of liberty is a common blood that flows in our American veins.

Carter used the pronoun "I" twenty-eight times in the seventeen-minute speech.

Farewell Address
(televised live from the Oval Office)
January 14, 1981

Good evening. In a few days, I will lay down my official responsibilities in this office—to take up once more the only title in our democracy superior to that of president, the title of citizen.

Of Vice President Mondale, my Cabinet and the hundreds of others who have served with me during the last four years, I wish to say now publicly what I have said in private: I thank them for the dedication and competence they have brought to the service of our country. But I owe my deepest thanks to you, the American people, because you gave me this extraordinary opportunity to serve. We have faced great challenges together. We know that future problems will also be difficult, but I am now more convinced than ever that the United States, better than any other nation, can meet successfully whatever the future might bring.

These last four years have made me more certain than ever of the inner strength of our country, the unchanging value of our principles and ideals, the stability of our political system, the ingenuity and the decency of our people.

Tonight I would like first to say a few words about this most special office, the presidency of the United States. This is at once the most powerful office in the world and among the most severely constrained by law and custom. The president is given a broad responsibility to lead but cannot do so without the support and consent of the people, expressed formally through the Congress and informally in many ways through a whole range of public and private institutions. This is as it should be.

Within our system of government every American has a right and duty to help shape the future course of the United States. Thoughtful criticism and close scrutiny of all government officials by the press and the public are an important part of our democratic society. Now as in our past, only the understanding and involvement of the people through full and open debate can help to avoid serious mistakes and assure the continued dignity and safety of the Nation.

Today we are asking our political system to do things of which the Founding Fathers never dreamed. The government they designed for a few hundred thousand people now serves a nation of almost 230 million people. Their small coastal republic now spans beyond a continent, and we also now have the responsibility to help lead much of the world through difficult times to a secure and prosperous future.

Today, as people have become ever more doubtful of the ability of the government to deal with our problems, we are increasingly drawn to single-issue groups and special interest organizations to ensure that whatever else happens our own personal views and our own private interests are protected. This is a disturbing factor in American political life. It tends to distort our purposes because the national interest is not always the sum of all our single or special interests. We are all Americans together, and we must not forget that the common good is our common interest and our individual responsibility.

Because of the fragmented pressures of these special interests, it's very important that the office of the President be a strong one, and that its constitutional authority be preserved. The President is the only elected official charged with the primary responsibility of representing all the people. In the moments of decision, after the different and conflicting views have all been aired, it is the President who then must speak to the Nation and for the Nation.

I understand after four years in office, as few others can, how formidable is the task the new president-elect is about to undertake. To the very limits of conscience and conviction, I pledge to support him in that task. I wish him success, and Godspeed.

I know from experience that presidents have to face major issues that are controversial, broad in scope, and which do not arouse the natural support of a political majority. For a few minutes now, I want to lay aside my role as leader of one nation, and speak to you as a fellow citizen of the world about three issues, three difficult issues: The threat of nuclear destruction, our stewardship of the physical resources of our planet, and the pre-eminence of the basic rights of human beings.

It's now been 35 years since the first atomic bomb fell on Hiroshima. The great majority of the world's people cannot remember a time when the nuclear shadow did not hang over the Earth. Our minds have adjusted to it, as after a time our eyes adjust to the dark. Yet the risk of a nuclear conflagration has not lessened. It has not happened yet, thank God, but that can give us little comfort, for it only has to happen once.

The danger is becoming greater. As the arsenals of the superpowers grow in size and sophistication and as other governments . . . acquire these weapons, it may only be a matter of time before madness, desperation, greed, or miscalculation lets lose this terrible force.

In an all-out nuclear war, more destructive power than in all of World War II would be unleashed every second during the long afternoon it would take for all the missiles and bombs to fall. A World War II every second—more people killed in the first few hours than all the wars of history put together. The survivors, if any, would live in despair amid the poisoned ruins of a civilization that had committed suicide.

National weakness—real or perceived—can tempt aggression and thus cause war. That's why the United States can never neglect its military strength. We must and we will remain strong. But with equal determination, the United States and all countries must find ways to control and reduce the horrifying danger that is posed by the world's enormous stockpiles of nuclear arms.

This has been a concern of every American President since the moment we first saw what these weapons could do. Our leaders will require our understanding and our support as they grapple with this difficult but crucial challenge. There is no disagreement on the goals or the basic approach to controlling this enormous destructive force. The answer lies not just in the attitudes or the actions of world leaders but in the concern and demands of all of us as we continue our struggle to preserve the peace.

Nuclear weapons are an expression of one side of our human character. But there is another side. The same rocket technology that delivers nuclear warheads has also taken us peacefully into space. From that perspective, we see our Earth as it really is—a small and fragile and beautiful blue globe, the only home we have. We see no barriers of race or religion or country. We see the essential unity of our species and our planet. And with faith and common sense, that bright vision will ultimately prevail.

Another major challenge, therefore, is to protect the quality of this world within which we live. The shadows that fall across the future are cast not only by the kinds of weapons we have built, but by the kind of world we will either nourish or neglect. There are real and growing dangers to our simple and most precious possessions: the air we breathe, the water we drink, and the land which sustains us. The rapid depletion of irreplaceable minerals, the erosion of topsoil, the destruction of beauty, the blight of pollution, the demands of increasing billions of people, all combine to create problems which are easy to observe and predict, but difficult to resolve. If we do not act, the world of the year 2000 will be much less able to sustain life than it is now.

But there is no reason for despair. Acknowledging the physical realities of our planet does not mean a dismal future of endless sacrifice. In fact, acknowledging these realities is the first step in dealing with them. We can meet the resource problems of the world—water, food, minerals, farmlands, forests, overpopulation, pollution—if we tackle them with courage and foresight.

I've just been talking about forces of potential destruction that mankind has developed and how we might control them. It's equally important that we remember the beneficial forces that we have evolved over the ages and how to hold fast to them. One of those constructive forces is the enhancement of individual human freedoms through the strengthening of democracy and the fight against deprivation, torture, terrorism, and the persecution of people throughout the world. The struggle for human rights overrides all differences of color or nation or language. Those who hunger for freedom, who thirst for human dignity, and who suffer for the sake of justice, they are the patriots of this cause.

I believe with all my heart that America must always stand for these basic human rights at home and abroad. That is both our history and our destiny.

America did not invent human rights. In a very real sense, it is the other way around. Human rights invented America. Ours was the first nation in the history of the world to be founded explicitly on such an idea. Our social and political progress has been based on one fundamental principle: the value and importance of the individual. The fundamental force that unites us is not kinship or place of origin or religious preference. The love of liberty is a common blood that flows in our American veins.

The battle for human rights, at home and abroad, is far from over. We should never be surprised nor discouraged, because the impact of our efforts has had and will always have varied results. Rather, we should take pride that the ideals which gave birth to our Nation still inspire the hopes of oppressed people around the world. We have no cause for self-righteousness or complacency. But we have every reason to persevere, both within our own country and beyond our borders.

If we are to serve as a beacon for human rights, we must continue to perfect here at home the rights and values which we espouse around the world: a decent education for our children, adequate medical care for all Americans, an end to discrimination against minorities and women, a job for all those able to work, and freedom from injustice and religious intolerance.

We live in a time of transition, an uneasy era which is likely to endure for the rest of this century. It will be a period of tensions both within nations and between nations, of competition for scarce resources, of social, political, and economic stresses and strains. During this period we may be tempted to abandon some of the time-honored principles and commitments which have been proven during the difficult times of past generations. We must never yield to this temptation. Our American values are not luxuries, but necessities—not the salt in our bread, but the bread itself. Our common vision of a free and just society is our greatest source of cohesion at home and strength abroad, greater even than the bounty of our material blessings.

Remember these words: "We hold these truths to be self-evident, that all men are created equal; that they are endowed by their Creator with certain inalienable Rights; that among these are Life, Liberty, and the pursuit of Happiness."

This vision still grips the imagination of the world. But we know that democracy is always an unfinished creation. Each generation must renew its foundations. Each generation must rediscover the meaning of this hallowed vision in the light of its own modern challenges. For this generation, ours, life is nuclear survival; liberty is human rights; the pursuit of happiness is a planet whose resources are devoted to the physical and spiritual nourishment of its inhabitants.

During the next few days I will work hard to make sure that the transition from myself to the next President is a good one, that the American people are served well. And I will continue, as I have the last 14 months to work hard and to pray for the lives and the well-being of the American hostages held in Iran. I can't predict yet what will happen, but I hope you will join me in my constant prayer for their freedom.

As I return home to the South, where I was born and raised, I look forward to the opportunity to reflect and further to assess, I hope with accuracy, the circumstances of our times. I intend to give our new President my support, and I intend to work as a citizen, as I have worked here in this office as president, for the values this nation was founded to secure.

Again, from the bottom of my heart, I want to express to you the gratitude I feel. Thank you, fellow citizens, and farewell.

Two days following the farewell address, President Carter submitted his final state of the union message to the Congress. Like the messages of the nineteenth century, like Eisenhower's final state of the union, it was written, not spoken. It dealt with many of the details that Carter did not want to bog down his farewell address with. Interestingly, it offered a somewhat more optimistic picture of the state of the union than the address of two days earlier. It is by far the longest final annual message on record—33,667 words. Excerpts from the introduction and conclusion follow.

Fourth State of the Union Address
(written to the Congress)
January 16, 1981

To the Congress of the United States:

The State of the Union is sound. Our economy is recovering from a recession. A national energy plan is in place and our dependence on foreign oil is decreasing. We have been at peace for four uninterrupted years.

But, our Nation has serious problems. Inflation and unemployment are unacceptably high. The world oil market is increasingly tight. There are trouble spots throughout the world, and 52 American hostages are being held in Iran against international law and against every precept of human affairs.

However, I firmly believe that, as a result of the progress made in so many domestic and international areas over the past four years, our Nation is stronger, wealthier, more compassionate, and freer than it was four years ago. I am proud of that fact. And I believe the Congress should be proud as well, for so much of what has been accomplished over the past four years has been due to the hard work, insights, and cooperation of Congress. I applaud the Congress for its efforts and its achievements.

In this State of the Union Message I want to recount the achievements and progress of the last four years and to offer recommendations to the Congress for this year. While my term as President will end before the 97th Congress begins its work in earnest, I hope that my recommendations will serve as a guide for the direction this country should take so we build on the record of the past four years.

When I took office, our Nation faced a number of serious domestic and international problems: no national energy policy existed, and our dependence on foreign oil was rapidly increasing; public trust in the integrity and openness of the government was low; the Federal government was operating inefficiently in administering essential programs and policies; major social problems were being ignored or poorly addressed by the Federal government; our defense posture was declining as a result of a defense budget which was continuously shrinking in real terms; the strength of the NATO Alliance needed to be bolstered; tensions between Israel and Egypt threatened another Middle East war; and America's resolve to oppose human rights violations was under serious question.

Over the past 48 months, clear progress has been made in solving the challenges we found in January of 1977:

- almost all of our comprehensive energy program have been enacted, and the Department of Energy has been established to administer the program;
- confidence in the government's integrity has been restored, and respect for the government's openness and fairness has been renewed;
- the government has been made more effective and efficient: the Civil Service system was completely reformed for the first time this century;
- 14 reorganization initiatives have been proposed to the Congress, approved, and implemented;
- two new Cabinet departments have been created to consolidate and streamline the government's handling of energy and education problems;
- inspectors general have been placed in each Cabinet department to combat fraud, waste and other abuses;
- the regulatory process has been reformed through creation of the Regulatory Council, implementation of Executive Order 12044 and its requirement for cost-impact analyses, elimination of unnecessary regulation, and passage of the Regulatory Flexibility Act;
- procedures have been established to assure citizen participation in government;
- and the airline, trucking, rail, and communications industries are being deregulated;
- critical social problems, many long ignored by the Federal government, have been addressed directly;
- an urban policy was developed and implemented to reverse the decline in our urban areas;
- the Social Security System was refinanced to put it on a sound financial basis;
- the Humphrey-Hawkins Full Employment Act was enacted;
- Federal assistance for education was expanded by more than 75 percent;
- the minimum wage was increased to levels needed to ease the effects of inflation;
- affirmative action has been pursued aggressively: more blacks, Hispanics and women have been appointed to senior government positions and to judgeships than at any other time in our history;
- the ERA ratification deadline was extended to aid the ratification effort;
- and minority business procurement by the Federal government has more than doubled;
- the Nation's first sectoral policies were put in place, for the auto and steel industries, with my Administration demonstrating the value of cooperation between the government, business and labor;
- reversing previous trends, real defense spending has increased every year since 1977; the real increase in FY 1980 defense spending is well above 3 percent and I expect FY 1981 defense spending to be even higher; looking ahead, the defense program I am proposing is premised on a real increase in defense spending over the next five years of 20 percent or more;
- the NATO Alliance has proven its unity in responding to the situations in Eastern Europe and Southwest Asia and in agreeing on the issues to be addressed in the review of the Helsinki Final Act currently under way in Madrid;
- the peace process in the Middle East established at Camp David and by the Peace Treaty between Egypt and Israel is being buttressed on two fronts: steady progress in the normalization of Egyptian-Israeli relations in many fields, and the commitment of both Egypt and Israel, with United States' assistance, to see through to successful conclusion the autonomy negotiations for the West Bank and Gaza;

- the Panama Canal Treaties have been put into effect, which has helped to improve relations with Latin America;
- we have continued this Nation's strong commitment to the pursuit of human rights throughout the world, evenhandedly and objectively; our commitment to a worldwide human rights policy has remained firm; and many other countries have given high priority to it;
- our resolve to oppose aggression, such as the illegal invasion of the Soviet Union into Afghanistan, has been supported by tough action.

*   *   *

We have new support in the world for our purposes of national independence and individual human dignity. We have a new will at home to do what is required to keep us the strongest nation on earth.

We must move together into this decade with the strength which comes from realization of the dangers before us and from the confidence that together we can overcome them.

JIMMY CARTER
The White House
January 16, 1981.

3 3

Ronald Reagan (1981–1989)

Ronald Reagan is the president credited with catalyzing the renewal of America. The nation's economy, pride, and sense of purpose all rebounded during his eight years in office. A big part of his success was due to a powerful television persona. Trained as an actor, he parlayed well-honed Hollywood skills into electoral successes and earned the title of Great Communicator (duly noted in his farewell address).

Reagan wanted his speechwriter Peggy Noonan to help with the composition of the farewell address. In her book, *What I Saw at the Revolution*, Noonan describes what it was like to spend "five mellow winter afternoons" with the President, crafting a speech that Reagan ultimately made his own.[1]

The first part of the address illustrates why Reagan became known as the Great Communicator. The president set the stage by sharing with Americans what he thought about while looking out of a White House window. The personal touch reflected the former actor's skill at connecting with Americans via electronic media. The personal nature of Reagan's speech is also reflected in the fact that the pronoun "I" occurs seventy-two times—more times than in most other formal farewell addresses.

Note the fortieth president's masterful use of nautical images and figures of speech in the opening paragraphs. These serve imaginatively to unveil his theme and convey confidence in his leadership. He was not just an executive, but the captain of a great ship, entrusted with steering the "ship of state" through the stormy seas of the Cold War. "And at the end, we are reaching our destination." Reagan explained how "We meant to change a nation, and instead, we changed a world." It was no idle boast, considering the resurgence of American ideals around the world on the one hand and the demoralization and deterioration of the Soviet Union on the other.

Toward the end of his remarks, Reagan noted that "there is a great tradition of warnings" in farewell addresses. Rhetorically this serves as a "sit up and listen line," a technique speakers use to alert the audience that something especially important is to follow. Reagan used the setup to discuss the "culture war" that had been evident since the 1960s. He asked fellow citizens, "are we doing a good enough job teaching our children what America is and what she represents in the long history of the world? . . . We've got to do a better job of getting across that America is freedom—freedom of speech, freedom of religion, freedom of enterprise. And freedom is special and rare. It's fragile; it needs protection."

Farewell Address
(speech televised live from the Oval Office)
January 11, 1989

My fellow Americans

This is the 34th time I'll speak to you from the Oval Office and the last. We've been together 8 years now, and soon it'll be time for me to go. But before I do, I wanted to share some thoughts, some of which I've been saving for a long time.

It's been the honor of my life to be your President. So many of you have written the past few weeks to say thanks, but I could say as much to you. Nancy and I are grateful for the opportunity you gave us to serve.

One of the things about the Presidency is that you're always somewhat apart. You spend a lot of time going by too fast in a car someone else is driving, and seeing the people through tinted glass—the parents holding up a child, and the wave you saw too late and couldn't return. And so many times I wanted to stop and reach out from behind the glass, and connect. Well, maybe I can do a little of that tonight.

People ask how I feel about leaving. And the fact is, "parting is such sweet sorrow." The sweet part is California and the ranch and freedom. The sorrow—the goodbyes, of course, and leaving this beautiful place.

You know, down the hall and up the stairs from this office is the part of the White House where the President and his family live. There are a few favorite windows I have up there that I like to stand and look out of early in the morning. The view is over the grounds here to the Washington Monument, and then the Mall and the Jefferson Memorial. But on mornings when the humidity is low, you can see past the Jefferson to the river, the Potomac, and the Virginia shore. Someone said that's the view Lincoln had when he saw the smoke rising from the Battle of Bull Run. I see more prosaic things: the grass on the banks, the morning traffic as people make their way to work, now and then a sailboat on the river.

I've been thinking a bit at that window. I've been reflecting on what the past 8 years have meant and mean. And the image that comes to mind like a refrain is a nautical one—a small story about a big ship, and a refugee, and a sailor. It was back in the early 'eighties, at the height of the boat people. And the sailor was hard at work on the carrier *Midway*, which was patrolling the South China Sea. The sailor, like most American servicemen, was young, smart, and fiercely observant. The crew spied on the horizon a leaky little boat. And crammed inside were refugees from Indochina hoping to get to America. The *Midway* sent a small launch to bring them to the ship and safety. As the refugees made their way through the choppy seas, one spied the sailor on deck, and stood up, and called out to him. He yelled, "Hello, American sailor. Hello, freedom man."

A small moment with a big meaning, a moment the sailor, who wrote it in a letter, couldn't get out of his mind. And, when I saw it, neither could I. Because that's what it was to be an American in the 1980's. We stood, again, for freedom. I know we always have, but in the past few years the world again—and in a way, we ourselves—rediscovered it.

It's been quite a journey this decade, and we held together through some stormy seas. And at the end, together, we are reaching our destination.

The fact is, from Grenada to the Washington and Moscow summits, from the recession of '81 to '82, to the expansion that began in late '82 and continues to this day, we've made a difference. The way I see it, there were two great triumphs, two things that I'm proudest of. One is the economic recovery, in which the people of America created—and filled—19 million new jobs. The other is the recovery of our morale. America is respected again in the world and looked to for leadership.

Something that happened to me a few years ago reflects some of this. It was back in 1981, and I was attending my first big economic summit, which was held that year in Canada. The meeting place rotates among the member countries. The opening meeting was a formal dinner of the heads of government of the seven industrialized nations. Now, I sat there like the new kid in school and listened, and it was all François this and Helmut that. They dropped titles and spoke to one another on a first-name basis. Well, at one point I sort of leaned in and said, "My name's Ron." Well, in that same year, we began the actions we felt would ignite an economic comeback—cut taxes and regulation, started to cut spending. And soon the recovery began.

Two years later, another economic summit with pretty much the same cast. At the big opening meeting we all got together, and all of a sudden, just for a moment, I saw that everyone was just sitting there looking at me. And then one of them broke the silence. "Tell us about the American miracle," he said.

Well, back in 1980, when I was running for President, it was all so different. Some pundits said our programs would result in catastrophe. Our views on foreign affairs would cause war. Our plans for the economy would cause inflation to soar and bring about economic collapse. I even remember one highly respected economist saying, back in 1982, that "The engines of economic growth have shut down here, and they're likely to stay that way for years to come." Well, he and the other opinion leaders were wrong. The fact is what they call "radical" was really "right." What they called "dangerous" was just "desperately needed."

And in all of that time I won a nickname, "The Great Communicator." But I never thought it was my style or the words I used that made a difference: it was the content. I wasn't a great communicator, but I communicated great things, and they didn't spring full bloom from my brow, they came from the heart of a great nation—from our experience, our wisdom, and our belief in the principles that have guided us for two centuries. They called it the Reagan revolution. Well, I'll accept that, but for me it always seemed more like the great rediscovery, a rediscovery of our values and our common sense.

Common sense told us that when you put a big tax on something, the people will produce less of it. So, we cut the people's tax rates, and the people produced more than ever before. The economy bloomed like a plant that had been cut back and could now grow quicker and stronger. Our economic program brought about the longest peacetime expansion in our history: real family income up, the poverty rate down, entrepreneurship booming, and an explosion in research and new technology. We're exporting more than ever because American industry became more competitive and at the same time, we summoned the national will to knock down protectionist walls abroad instead of erecting them at home.

Common sense also told us that to preserve the peace, we'd have to become strong again after years of weakness and confusion. So, we rebuilt our defenses, and this New Year we toasted the new peacefulness around the globe. Not only have the superpowers actually begun to reduce their stockpiles of nuclear weapons—and hope for even more progress is bright—but the regional conflicts that rack the globe are also beginning to cease. The Persian Gulf is no longer a war zone. The Soviets are leaving Afghanistan. The Vietnamese are preparing to pull out of Cambodia, and an American-mediated accord will soon send 50,000 Cuban troops home from Angola.

The lesson of all this was, of course, that because we're a great nation, our challenges seem complex. It will always be this way. But as long as we remember our first principles and believe in ourselves, the future will always be ours. And something else we learned: Once you begin a great movement, there's no telling where it will end. We meant to change a nation, and instead, we changed a world.

Countries across the globe are turning to free markets and free speech and turning away from the ideologies of the past. For them, the great rediscovery of the 1980's has been that, lo and behold, the moral way of government is the practical way of government: Democracy, the profoundly good, is also the profoundly productive.

When you've got to the point when you can celebrate the anniversaries of your 39th birthday you can sit back sometimes, review your life, and see it flowing before you. For me there was a fork in the river, and it was right in the middle of my life. I never meant to go into politics. It wasn't my intention when I was young. But I was raised to believe you had to pay your way for the blessings bestowed on you. I was happy with my career in the entertainment world, but I ultimately went into politics because I wanted to protect something precious.

Ours was the first revolution in the history of mankind that truly reversed the course of government, and with three little words: "We the People." "We the People" tell the government what to do; it doesn't tell us. "We the People" are the driver; the government is the car. And we decide where it should go, and by what route, and how fast. Almost all the world's constitutions are documents in which governments tell the people what their privileges are. Our Constitution is a document in which "We the People" tell the government what it is allowed to do. "We the People" are free. This belief has been the underlying basis for everything I've tried to do these past 8 years.

But back in the 1960's, when I began, it seemed to me that we'd begun reversing the order of things—that through more and more rules and regulations and confiscatory taxes, the government was taking more of our money, more of our options, and more of our freedom. I went into politics in part to put up my hand and say, "Stop." I was a citizen politician, and it seemed the right thing for a citizen to do.

I think we have stopped a lot of what needed stopping. And I hope we have once again reminded people that man is not free unless government is limited. There's a clear cause and effect here that is as neat and predictable as a law of physics: As government expands, liberty contracts.

Nothing is less free than pure communism—and yet we have, the past few years, forged a satisfying new closeness with the Soviet Union. I've been asked if this isn't a gamble, and my answer is no because we're basing our actions not on words but deeds. The détente of the 1970's was based not on actions but promises. They'd promise to treat their own people and the people of the world better. But the *gulag* was still the *gulag*, and the state was still expansionist, and they still waged proxy wars in Africa, Asia, and Latin America.

Well, this time, so far, it's different. President Gorbachev has brought about some internal democratic reforms and begun the withdrawal from Afghanistan. He has also freed prisoners whose names I've given him every time we've met.

But life has a way of reminding you of big things through small incidents. Once, during the heady days of the Moscow summit, Nancy and I decided to break off from the entourage one afternoon to visit the shops on Arbat Street—that's a little street just off Moscow's main shopping area. Even though our visit was a surprise, every Russian there immediately recognized us and called out our names and reached for our hands. We were just about swept away by the warmth. You could almost feel the possibilities in all that joy. But within seconds, a KGB detail pushed their way toward us and began pushing and shoving the people in the crowd. It was an interesting moment. It reminded me that while the man on the street in the Soviet Union yearns for peace, the government is Communist. And those who run it are Communists, and that means we and they view such issues as freedom and human rights very differently.

We must keep up our guard, but we must also continue to work together to lessen and eliminate tension and mistrust. My view is that President Gorbachev is different from previous Soviet leaders. I think he knows some of the things wrong with his society and is trying to fix them. We wish him well. And we'll continue to work to make sure that the Soviet Union that eventually emerges from this process is a less threatening one. What it all boils down to is this: I want the new closeness to continue. And it will, as long as we make it clear that we will continue to act in a certain way as long as they continue to act in a helpful manner. If and when they don't, at first pull your punches. If they persist, pull the plug. It's still trust but verify. It's still play, but cut the cards. It's still watch closely. And don't be afraid to see what you see.

I've been asked if I have any regrets. Well, I do. The deficit is one. I've been talking a great deal about that lately, but tonight isn't for arguments, and I'm going to hold my tongue. But an observation: I've had my share of victories in the Congress, but what few people noticed is that I never won anything you didn't win for me. They never saw my troops, they never saw Reagan's regiments, the American people. You won every battle with every call you made and letter you wrote demanding action. Well, action is still needed. If we're to finish the job, Reagan's regiments will have to become the Bush brigades. Soon he'll be the chief, and he'll need you every bit as much as I did.

Finally, there is a great tradition of warnings in Presidential farewells, and I've got one that's been on my mind for some time. But oddly enough it starts with one of the things I'm proudest of in the past 8 years: the resurgence of national pride that I called the new patriotism. This national feeling is good, but it won't count for much, and it won't last unless it's grounded in thoughtfulness and knowledge.

An informed patriotism is what we want. And are we doing a good enough job teaching our children what America is and what she represents in the long history of the world? Those of us who are over 35 or so years of age grew up in a different America. We were taught, very directly, what it means to be an American. And we absorbed, almost in the air, a love of country and an appreciation of its institutions. If you didn't get these things from your family you got them from the neighborhood, from the father down the street who fought in Korea or the family who lost someone at Anzio. Or you could get a sense of patriotism from school. And if all else failed you could get a sense of patriotism from the popular culture. The movies celebrated democratic values and implicitly reinforced the idea that America was special. TV was like that, too, through the mid-sixties.

But now, we're about to enter the nineties, and some things have changed. Younger parents aren't sure that an unambivalent appreciation of America is the right thing to teach modern children. And as for those who create the popular culture, well-grounded patriotism is no longer the style. Our spirit is back, but we haven't reinstitutionalized it. We've got to do a better job of getting across that America is freedom—freedom of speech, freedom of religion, freedom of enterprise. And freedom is special and rare. It's fragile; it needs protection.

So, we've got to teach history based not on what's in fashion but what's important—why the Pilgrims came here, who Jimmy Doolittle was, and what those 30 seconds over Tokyo meant.

You know, 4 years ago on the 40th anniversary of D-day, I read a letter from a young woman writing to her late father, who'd fought on Omaha Beach. Her name was Lisa Zanatta Henn, and she said, "we will always remember, we will never forget what the boys of Normandy did." Well, let's help her keep her word. If we forget what we did, we won't know who we are. I'm warning of an eradication of the American memory that could result, ultimately, in an erosion of the American spirit. Let's start with some basics: more attention to American history and a greater emphasis on civic ritual.

And let me offer lesson number one about America: All great change in America begins at the dinner table. So, tomorrow night in the kitchen I hope the talking begins. And children, if your parents haven't been teaching you what it means to be an American, let 'em know and nail 'em on it. That would be a very American thing to do.

And that's about all I have to say tonight, except for one thing. The past few days when I've been at that window upstairs, I've thought a bit of the "shining city upon a hill." The phrase comes from John Winthrop, who wrote it to describe the America he imagined. What he imagined was important because he was an early Pilgrim, an early freedom man. He journeyed here on what today we'd call a little wooden boat; and like the other Pilgrims, he was looking for a home that would be free.

I've spoken of the shining city all my political life, but I don't know if I ever quite communicated what I saw when I said it. But in my mind it was a tall, proud city built on rocks stronger than oceans, windswept, God-blessed, and teeming with people of all kinds living in harmony and peace; a city with free ports that hummed with commerce and creativity. And if there had to be city walls, the walls had doors and the doors were open to anyone with the will and the heart to get here. That's how I saw it, and see it still.

And how stands the city on this winter night? More prosperous, more secure, and happier than it was 8 years ago. But more than that: After 200 years, two centuries, she still stands strong and true on the granite ridge, and her glow has held steady no matter what storm. And she's still a beacon, still a magnet for all who must have freedom, for all the pilgrims from all the lost places who are hurtling through the darkness, toward home.

We've done our part. And as I walk off into the city streets, a final word to the men and women of the Reagan revolution, the men and women across America who for 8 years did the work that brought America back. My friends: We did it. We weren't just marking time. We made a difference. We made the city stronger, we made the city freer, and we left her in good hands. All in all, not bad, not bad at all.

And so, goodbye, God bless you, and God bless the United States of America.

Note

1. Peggy Noonan, *What I Saw at the Revolution: A Political Life in the Reagan Era* (New York: Random House, 1990), 325–35.

3 4

George H. W. Bush (1989–1993)

Although George Herbert Walker Bush did not give a formal farewell address to the nation, a speech he delivered in his last month in office served the purpose. As if to tip off his audience that this was indeed a farewell, the "second George" to serve as U.S. president referenced the first George's 1796 Farewell Address. Actually Bush's speech sounded more like Truman's or Eisenhower's farewell, since it concentrated on the global reach and responsibility of American power.

Bush explained why the first president's advice did not fit well with the new reality:

> His [Washington's] was the right course for a new nation at that point in history. But what was "entangling" in Washington's day is now essential. This is why, at Texas A&M a few weeks ago, I spoke of the folly of isolationism and of the importance, morally, economically, and strategically, of the United States remaining involved in world affairs. We must engage ourselves if a new world order, one more compatible with our values and congenial to our interest, is to emerge. But even more, we must lead.

Bush did not want the United States to squander its new-found blessings and advantages. He and his predecessor Ronald Reagan had brought about one of the greatest achievements in American history: victory over the Soviet Union and an end to the Cold War. Drawing on extensive foreign policy experience and an excellent team of advisers, Bush expertly "managed" the fall of the Berlin Wall in 1989 and the collapse of the Soviet Empire in 1991. He was widely praised for not gloating or precipitating war. The United States came through these epochal events as the world's lone superpower. There was suddenly a "new world order" taking shape and Bush meant to define America's role in shaping and leading it.

America's global dominance was sealed by the successful repulsion of Iraqi forces from Kuwait, another important reference in this speech. The Persian Gulf War was the nation's first "stealth war," and its successful prosecution was made all the more possible by Bush's diplomatic skill in forging a historically unprecedented international alliance to wage war against the rogue Iraqi leader, Saddam Hussein.

Bush's West Point speech is 3,300 words—it took almost a half hour to deliver—and the tone reflects the genteel president's colloquial, easy-going style with audiences.

461

Remarks at the United States Military Academy
West Point, New York
January 5, 1993

Thank you all very much. Good luck. Please be seated. Thank you, General Graves, for that very kind introduction. Barbara and I are just delighted to be here and honored that we could be joined by our able Secretary of the Army, Mike Stone; of course, the man well-known here that heads our Army, General Sullivan, General Gordon Sullivan; and Gracie Graves, General Robert Foley, General Galloway; Shawn Daniel, well-known to everybody here, been our host, in a sense; and a West Point alum who has been at my side for 4 years, over here somewhere, General Scowcroft, graduate of this great institution who served his country with such distinction. May I salute the members of the Board of Visitors. I see another I have to single out, General Galvin, who served his country with such honor. And, of course, save the best for last, the Corps of Cadets, thank you for that welcome.

Let me begin with the hard part: It is difficult for a Navy person to come up to West Point after that game a month ago. Go ahead, rub it in. [Laughter] But I watched it. Amazing things can happen in sports. Look at the Oilers, my other team that took it on the chin the other day. [Laughter]

But I guess the moral of all of this is that losing is never easy. Trust me, I know something about that. [Laughter] But if you have to lose, that's the way to do it: Fight with all you have. Give it your best shot. And win or lose, learn from it, and get on with life.

I am about to get on with the rest of my life. But before I do, I want to share with you at this institution of leadership some of my thinking, both about the world you will soon be called upon to enter and the life that you have chosen.

Any President has several functions. He speaks for and to the Nation. He must faithfully execute the law. And he must lead. But no function, none of the President's hats, in my view, is more important than his role as Commander in Chief. For it is as Commander in Chief that the President confronts and makes decisions that one way or another affect the lives of everyone in this country as well as many others around the world.

I have had many occasions to don this most important of hats. Over the past 4 years, the men and women who proudly and bravely wear the uniforms of the U.S. armed services have been called upon to go in harm's way and have discharged their duty with honor and professionalism.

I wish I could say that such demands were a thing of the past, that with the end of the cold war the calls upon the United States would diminish. I cannot. Yes, the end of the cold war, we would all concede, is a blessing. It is a time of great promise. Democratic governments have never been so numerous. What happened 2 or 3 days ago in Moscow would not have been possible in the cold war days. Thanks to historic treaties such as that START II pact just reached with Russia, the likelihood of nuclear holocaust is vastly diminished.

But this does not mean that there is no specter of war, no threats to be reckoned with. And already, we see disturbing signs of what this new world could become if we are passive and aloof. We would risk the emergence of a world characterized by violence, characterized by chaos, one in which dictators and tyrants threaten their neighbors, build arsenals brimming with weapons of mass destruction, and ignore the welfare of their own men, women, and children. And we could see a horrible increase in international terrorism, with American citizens more at risk than ever before.

We cannot and we need not allow this to happen. Our objective must be to exploit the unparalleled opportunity presented by the cold war's end to work toward transforming this new world into a new world order, one of governments that are democratic, tolerant, and economically free at home and committed abroad to settling inevitable differences peacefully, without the threat or use of force. Unfortunately, not everyone subscribes to these principles. We continue to see leaders bent on denying fundamental human rights and seizing territory regardless of the human cost. No, an international society, one more attuned to the enduring principles that have made this country a beacon of hope for so many for so long, will not just emerge on its own. It's got to be built.

Two hundred years ago, another departing President warned of the dangers of what he described as "entangling alliances." His was the right course for a new nation at that point in history. But what was "entangling" in Washington's day is now essential. This is why, at Texas A&M a few weeks ago, I spoke of the folly of isolationism and of the importance, morally, economically, and strategically, of the United States remaining involved in world affairs. We must engage ourselves if a new world order, one more compatible with our values and congenial to our interest, is to emerge. But even more, we must lead.

Leadership, well, it takes many forms. It can be political or diplomatic. It can be economic or military. It can be moral or spiritual leadership. Leadership can take any one of these forms, or it can be a combination of them.

Leadership should not be confused with either unilateralism or universalism. We need not respond by ourselves to each and every outrage of violence. The fact that America can act does not mean that it must. A nation's sense of idealism need not be at odds with its interests, nor does principle displace prudence.

No, the United States should not seek to be the world's policeman. There is no support abroad or at home for us to play this role, nor should there be. We would exhaust ourselves in the process, wasting precious resources needed to address those problems at home and abroad that we cannot afford to ignore.

But in the wake of the cold war, in a world where we are the only remaining superpower, it is the role of the United States to marshal its moral and material resources to promote a democratic peace. It is our responsibility, it is our opportunity to lead. There is no one else.

Leadership cannot be simply asserted or demanded. It must be demonstrated. Leadership requires formulating worthy goals, persuading others of their virtue, and contributing one's share of the common effort and then some. Leadership takes time. It takes patience. It takes work.

Some of this work must take place here at home. Congress does have a constitutional role to play. Leadership therefore also involves working with the Congress and the American people to provide the essential domestic underpinning if U.S. military commitments are to be sustainable.

This is what our administration, the Bush administration, has tried to do. When Saddam Hussein invaded Kuwait, it was the United States that galvanized the U.N. Security Council to act and then mobilized the successful coalition on the battlefield. The pattern not exactly the same but similar in Somalia: First the United States underscored the importance of alleviating the growing tragedy, and then we organized humanitarian efforts designed to bring hope, food, and peace.

At times, real leadership requires a willingness to use military force. And force can be a useful backdrop to diplomacy, a complement to it, or, if need be, a temporary alternative.

As Commander in Chief, I have made the difficult choice to use military force. I determined we could not allow Saddam's forces to ravage Kuwait and hold this critical region at gunpoint. I thought then, and I think now, that using military force to implement the resolutions of the U.N. Security Council was in the interest of the United States and the world community. The need to use force arose as well in the wake of the Gulf war, when we came to the aid of the peoples of both northern and southern Iraq. And more recently, as I'm sure you know, I determined that only the use of force could stem this human tragedy of Somalia.

The United States should not stand by with so many lives at stake and when a limited deployment of U.S. forces, buttressed by the forces of other countries and acting under the full authority of the United Nations, could make an immediate and dramatic difference, and do so without excessive levels of risk and cost. Operations Provide Comfort and Southern Watch in Iraq and then Operation Restore Hope in Somalia all bear witness to the wisdom of selected use of force for selective purposes.

Sometimes the decision not to use force, to stay our hand, I can tell you, it's just as difficult as the decision to send our soldiers into battle. The former Yugoslavia, well, it's been such a situation. There are, we all know, important humanitarian and strategic interests at stake there. But up to now it's not been clear that the application of limited amounts of force by the United States and its traditional friends and allies would have had the desired effect, given the nature and complexity of that situation.

Our assessment of the situation in the former Yugoslavia could well change if and as the situation changes. The stakes could grow; the conflict could threaten to spread. Indeed, we are constantly reassessing our options and are actively consulting with others about steps that might be taken to contain the fighting, protect the humanitarian effort, and deny Serbia the fruits of aggression.

Military force is never a tool to be used lightly or universally. In some circumstances it may be essential, in others counterproductive. I know that many people would like to find some formula, some easy formula to apply, to tell us with precision when and where to intervene with force. Anyone looking for scientific certitude is in for a disappointment. In the complex new world we are entering, there can be no single or simple set of fixed rules for using force. Inevitably, the question of military intervention requires judgment. Each and every case is unique. To adopt rigid criteria would guarantee mistakes involving American interests and American lives. And it would give would-be troublemakers a blueprint for determining their own actions. It could signal U.S. friends and allies that our support was not to be counted on.

Similarly, we cannot always decide in advance which interests will require our using military force to protect them. The relative importance of an interest is not a guide: Military force may not be the best way of safeguarding something vital, while using force might be the best way to protect an interest that qualifies as important but less than vital.

But to warn against a futile quest for a set of hard-and-fast rules to govern the use of military force is not to say there cannot be some principles to inform our decisions. Such guidelines can prove useful in sizing and, indeed, shaping our forces and in helping us to think our way through this key question.

Using military force makes sense as a policy where the stakes warrant, where and when force can be effective, where no other policies are likely to prove effective, where its application can be limited in scope and time, and where the potential benefits justify the potential costs and sacrifice.

Once we are satisfied that force makes sense, we must act with the maximum possible support. The United States can and should lead, but we will want to act in concert, where possible involving the United Nations or other multinational grouping. The United States can and should contribute to the common undertaking in a manner commensurate with our wealth, with our strength. But others should also contribute militarily, be it by providing combat or support forces, access to facilities or bases, or overflight rights. And similarly, others should contribute economically. It is unreasonable to expect the United States to bear the full financial burden of intervention when other nations have a stake in the outcome.

A desire for international support must not become a prerequisite for acting, though. Sometimes a great power has to act alone. I made a tough decision—I might say, on advice of our outstanding military leaders who are so well known to everybody here—to use military force in Panama when American lives and the security of the Canal appeared to be threatened by outlaws who stole power in the face of free elections. And similarly, we moved swiftly to safeguard democracy in the Philippines.

But in every case involving the use of force, it will be essential to have a clear and achievable mission, a realistic plan for accomplishing the mission, and criteria no less realistic for withdrawing U.S. forces once the mission is complete. Only if we keep these principles in mind will the potential sacrifice be one that can be explained and justified. We must never forget that using force is not some political abstraction but a real commitment of our fathers and mothers and sons and daughters, brothers and sisters, friends and neighbors. You've got to look at it in human terms.

In order even to have the choice, we must have available adequate military forces tailored for a wide range of contingencies, including peacekeeping. Indeed, leading the effort toward a new world order will require a modern, capable military, in some areas necessitating more rather than less defense spending. As President, I have said that my ability to deploy force on behalf of U.S. interests abroad was made possible because past Presidents, and I would single out in particular my predecessor, Ronald Reagan, and past Secretaries of Defense sustained a strong military. Consistent with this sacred trust, I am proud to pass on to my successor, President-elect Clinton, a military second to none. We have the very best.

Yet, it is essential to recognize that as important as such factors are, any military is more than simply the sum of its weapons or the state of its technology. What makes any armed force truly effective is the quality of its leadership, the quality of its training, the quality of its people.

We have succeeded abroad in no small part because of our people in uniform. The men and women in our Armed Forces have demonstrated their ability to master the challenges of modern warfare. And at the same time, and whether on the battlefield of Iraq or in some tiny little village in Somalia, America's soldiers have always brought a quality of caring and kindness to their mission. Who will ever forget—I know I won't—those terrified Iraqi soldiers surrendering to American troops? And who will forget the way the American soldier held out his arms and said, "It's okay. You're all right now." Or in Somalia, the young marine, eyes filled with tears, holding the fragile arm of an emaciated child. There can be no doubt about it: The All Volunteer Force is one of the true success stories of modern day America.

It is instructive to look at just why this is so. At its heart, a voluntary military is based upon choice—you all know that—the decision freely taken by young men and women to join, the decision by more mature men and women to remain. And the institution of the Armed Forces has thrived on its commitment to developing and promoting excellence. It is meritocracy in action. Race, religion, wealth, background count not. Indeed, the military offers many examples for the rest of society, showing what can be done to eradicate the scourge of drugs, to break down the barriers of racial discrimination, to offer equal opportunity to women.

This is not just a result of self-selection. It also reflects the military's commitment to education and training. You know, people speak of defense conversion, the process by which the defense firms retool for civilian tasks. Well, defense conversion within the military has been going on for years. It is the constant process of training and retraining, which the military does so well, that allows individuals to keep up with the latest technology, take on more challenging assignments, and prepare for life on the outside.

Out of this culture of merit and competition have emerged hundreds of thousands of highly skilled men and women brimming with real self-confidence. What they possess is a special mix of discipline, a willingness to accept direction, and the confidence, a willingness to accept responsibility. Together, discipline and confidence provide the basis for winning, for getting the job done.

There is no higher calling, no more honorable choice than the one that you here today have made. To join the Armed Forces is to be prepared to make the ultimate sacrifice for your country and for your fellow man.

What you have done, what you are doing, sends an important message, one that I fear sometimes gets lost amidst today's often materialist, self-interested culture. It is important to remember, it is important to demonstrate that there is a higher purpose to life beyond one's self. Now, I speak of family, of community, of ideals. I speak of duty, honor, country.

There are many forms of contributing to this country, of public service. Yes, there is government. There is voluntarism. I love to talk about the thousand Points of Light, one American helping another. The daily tasks that require doing in our classrooms, in our hospitals, our cities, our farms, all can and do represent a form of service. In whatever form, service benefits our society, and it ennobles the giver. It is a cherished American concept, one we should continue to practice and pass on to our children.

This was what I wanted to share on this occasion. You are beginning your service to country, and I am nearing the end of mine. Exactly half a century ago, in June of 1942, as General Graves mentioned, we were at war, and I was graduating from school. The speaker that day at Andover was the then-Secretary of War, Henry Stimson. And his message was one of public service, but with a twist—on the importance of finishing one's schooling before going off to fight for one's country. I listened closely to what he had to say, but I didn't take his advice. And that day was my 18th birthday. And when the commencement ceremony ended, I went on into Boston and enlisted in the Navy as a seaman 2d class. And I never regretted it.

You, too, have signed up. You, too, will never regret it. And I salute you for it. Fortunately, because of the sacrifices made in years before and still being made, you should be able to complete this phase of your education.

A half century has passed since I left school to go into the service. A half century has passed since that day when Stimson spoke of the challenge of creating a new world. You will also be entering a new world, one far better than the one I came to know, a world with the potential to be far better yet. This is the challenge. This is the opportunity of your lifetimes. I envy you for it, and I wish you Godspeed. And while I'm at it, as your Commander in Chief, I hereby grant amnesty to the Corps of Cadets.

Thank you all very much. Thank you. Thank you very, very much. Good luck to all of you. Warm up here. Good luck to you guys. Thank you.